Census Substitutes & State Census Records

♦♦ 3rd Edition ♦♦

Volume 4
Southcentral & Four Corners States

by
William Dollarhide

Copyright © 2020
William W. Dollarhide and Leland K. Meitzler
All rights reserved.

No part of this book may be reproduced in any form without permission in writing from the author or publisher except in brief quotations in articles and reviews.

Published by Family Roots Publishing Co., LLC
PO Box 1682
Orting, WA 98360-1682
www.familyrootspublishing.com

Library of Congress Control Number: 2020934867

ISBN (Paperback): 978-1-62859-290-0
ISBN: (eBook): 978-1-62859-291-7

Recommended Citation:
Census Substitutes & State Census Records, 3rd Edition,
Volume Four – Southcentral & Four Corners States,
by William Dollarhide, publ. Family Roots Publishing Co., LLC, Orting, WA, 2020, 279 pages.

Printed in the United States of America

Contents – Vol. 4
Southcentral & Four Corners States

State Finder, Vols. 1 to 5 6
   Foreword 7
   Introduction 9
   Table 1: Non-State Census States 13
   Table 2: State Census States – AL -MI 14
   Table 2: State Census States – MN-WY 15
   Table 3: State Censuses in Common Years 16
   Table 4: Availability of Federal Censuses for each State 17

Vol. 4 States
   Missouri 19
   Kansas 41
   Arkansas 75
   Oklahoma 101
   Louisiana 123
   Texas 169
   New Mexico 191
   Arizona 213
   Colorado 239
   Utah 261

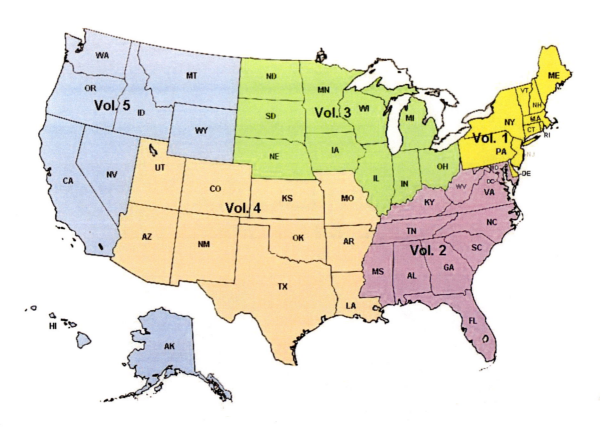

State Finder, Vols. 1-5

States	Vol.	Page
Alabama	2	233
Alaska	5	19
Arizona	4	213
Arkansas	4	75
California	5	57
Colorado	4	239
Connecticut	1	145
Delaware	1	223
District of Columbia	2	58
Florida	2	277
Georgia	2	193
Hawaii	5	37
Idaho	5	163
Illinois	3	119
Indiana	3	91
Iowa	3	179
Kansas	4	41
Kentucky	2	113
Louisiana	4	123
Maine	1	19
Maryland	2	19
Massachusetts	1	91

States	Vol.	Page
Michigan	3	43
Minnesota	3	225
Mississippi	2	259
Missouri	4	19
Montana	5	189
Nebraska	3	243
Nevada	5	107
New Hampshire	1	63
New Jersey	1	191
New Mexico	4	191
New York	1	173
North Carolina	2	145
North Dakota	3	273
Ohio	3	19
Oklahoma	4	101
Oregon	5	121
Pennsylvania	1	205
Rhode Island	1	133
South Carolina	2	177
South Dakota	3	261
Tennessee	2	161
Texas	4	169

States	Vol.	Page
Utah	4	261
Vermont	1	77
Virginia	2	79
Washington	5	141
West Virginia	2	97
Wisconsin	3	159
Wyoming	5	205

US Territories	Vol.	Page
Caribbean Region	1	245
Puerto Rico	1	246
US Virgin Islands	1	251
Panama Canal Zone	1	256
Pacific Region	1	259
Guam	1	260
No. Mariana Islands	1	262
American Samoa	1	264
The Philippines	1	268

US Nationwide	Vol.	Page
1790-1950 Maps / Descr.	5	217
US Census Substitutes	5	259

Foreword
by Leland K. Meitzler

In late 2003 Bill Dollarhide came by my office and asked if I had any ideas for *Genealogy Bulletin* articles. As it turned out, I had just finished organizing materials for a lecture on state and territorial census records and had a file folder full of data I had collected over the years on my desk. I suggested he put something together on that subject and gave him the file to review. After looking through my file, Bill decided that we needed to identify the many substitutes to censuses (statewide tax lists, voter registration lists, and such), as he quickly noted that a number of states didn't take any state or territorial censuses at all. Bill began compiling a bibliography of not only extant state and territorial censuses, but substitute lists as well.

Researched and compiled by region, he added timelines of historical references to show the jurisdictions in place at the time of each census. Compiling the material by region was a logical way to go, as we quickly realized that in most cases, it would have been very difficult to write about one state without writing about those surrounding it. So, if you start with Maine, for example, the adjoining state of New Hampshire would be the next chapter, then Vermont, Massachusetts, and so on.

Much of the data found in the two-volume First Edition (2008) was initially published in serial form in the old *Genealogy Bulletin (1983-2006)*. That said, the District of Columbia, for which there are many excellent sources, was never published. Also never published was The Oregon Country chapter. However, both chapters were included in the First Edition.

In the three-volume Second Edition (2016), numerous online sources were added, reflecting the ongoing efforts of both public and private companies to digitize relevant records.

In this new five-volume Third Edition (2020), the Northeastern States (Volume 1) adds seven (7) U.S. Territories for the first time. In addition, the *Western & Pacific States (V*olume 5) has an all-new *Maps, Descriptions, and Internet Access for the U.S. Federal Censuses, 1790-1950;* followed by an updated *U.S. Census Substitutes* chapter. Each of the 50 states & DC in this 3rd Edition has many more citations for newly added online databases and recently digitized microfilm collections – in just three years, the number went from 3,865 to 8,067 hyperlinks.

Bill also spent countless hours compiling tabulated charts that may be worth the cost of this book all by themselves. The first, found on page 13, is a chart for the non-state census states. There happens to be 13 of them (including the District of Columbia). This chart lists the states and the years covered by census substitutes. The second chart, found on pages 14-15, lists the 38 states that have extant colonial, pre-statehood, territorial, and state censuses, complete with the census year, and an indication if the census is available online as of the date of publication. The third chart, found on page 16, shows in graphic form the states that had censuses taken in common years – "on the fives." Census dates for some states are within a range. The fourth chart, on page 17, shows the availability of federal censuses for all states, 1790-1950.

Note that the title of this series of volumes is *Census Substitutes & State Census Records,* which reflects the fact that the volumes really contain a list of census substitutes, with state censuses turning out to be in the minority. Substitutes outnumber censuses by a factor of ten to one! However, the state censuses identified in this series are by far the most complete lists of

Colonial, Territorial, or State Censuses published to date.

State and Territorial Censuses have long fascinated me. Many were taken in order to get congress to allow statehood. Some territories would take censuses on a nearly annual basis, in the attempt to show that they had the population base necessary to justify statehood.

Other states, like New York, had authorization of non-federal censuses written into their state constitutions. New York was one of the most prolific when it came to state censuses, as it produced numerous schedules, most falling on the ubiquitous "fives." Today we have extant New York censuses for 1825, 1835, 1845, 1855, 1865, 1875, 1892, 1905, 1915, and 1925. Some of the early years are not complete, but what is available is certainly useful. The 1925 New York census was taken as well as any other, and the population returns are largely legible and complete. However, the census was wrought with scandal, leaving New Yorkers with a taste of bitterness for such things. To make a long story short, it seems that the New York Secretary of State, a former Dean of Home Economics at Syracuse University, Florence Elizabeth Smith Knapp, took nepotism to a whole new level. As the state official in charge of the 1925 census, she put family and friends on the payroll, and while this wasn't illegal, most of these folks did little or nothing to earn their salaries. Even her 74-year old mother, Ella Smith, enjoyed a non-working stint as an assistant supervisor. Florence's stepdaughter, Clara Blanche Knapp, a professor at Middlebury College in Vermont, was on the payroll for over $5,000 in income, while never leaving the state of Vermont. Moreover, checks written to both Ella and Blanche seemed to have been endorsed into Florence E.S. Knapp's bank account. Numerous other family members and friends were paid substantial sums for non-work. In 1928, Mrs. Knapp finally went on trial for her misdeeds, and found guilty of first-degree grand larceny for misappropriation of state funds. She served 30 days in the Albany Jail. She could have gotten 10 years. So ended the brief political career of the first woman ever to be elected to state-wide office in New York. So also ended the state censuses of New York State.

Iowa, Kansas, Rhode Island, Florida, North Dakota, and South Dakota also took censuses up through 1925. South Dakota and Florida even took censuses in 1935 and 1945! The real value of state censuses is found in the numerous schedules enumerated in the mid-nineteenth century. Thirty-eight states took non-federal censuses that are still extant today.

And then there are the substitutes. They are of prime importance, since 12 states, as well as the District of Columbia, took no state censuses at all. And even if your ancestors lived in a state where censuses were taken "on the fives," census substitutes are helpful, especially if the family was on the move.

Although Mr. Dollarhide has used all kinds of substitutes throughout this volume, more attention has been given to tax lists, voter registration rolls, vital records, directories, statewide probate indexes, land records, and even military censuses, than most others. These records are often easily accessible and using this guide, you will be able to quickly find them for your own use. You are in for a treat, so sit back and look up the states of your ancestors. You will find information on records you never knew existed. Then... go get the records, and happy hunting!

Leland K. Meitzler
Publisher

Introduction
Census Substitutes & State Census Records

Census Substitutes are those name lists derived from tax lists, directories, military lists, land ownership lists, voter registrations, and other compilations of names of residents for an entire state, or part of a state. A census substitute can be used to determine the names of residents in a given area when a federal or state census is missing. Moreover, a census substitute can be used as an alternative name list; confirming, contradicting, or adding to information found in a federal or state census.

This book identifies at least ten times the number of Census Substitute titles than any previous work ever published. All states are represented with significant alternative name lists – name lists that stop time for a certain year and place and name the residents of a certain place. Since all of these name lists are specific to a certain year, they are listed within each state category in chronological order. Incorporated into the lists are any State Census titles – a reference to a state census taken for a specific year.

Federal vs. State Censuses

Federal Censuses have their origins in the constitutional provision for apportionment of the U.S. House of Representatives. The first federal census was taken in 1790, and beginning about the same time, state censuses were conducted for the same reason, that is, apportionment of the various state legislatures.

Although the primary purpose of all censuses was to simply count the population, beginning with the first federal census of 1790, more information than a simple tally was added. This included the name and age of a person and progressively more details about a household for each subsequent census year. State censuses followed this same pattern.

State censuses usually add even more information than the federal censuses, and as a result, they are premier genealogical resources. Except in cases where a federal census is lost, state census records are not substitutes for the federal censuses – state censuses were almost always taken between federal census years, and usually add unique information and details about a household not found in a federal census. If a state census exists between federal census years, it may add marginally to the knowledge one gains about a family. But, more often, it will add critical information, such as more exact dates of birth, marriages, deaths; plus, additional children, different residences, other relatives living with a family; and more.

Non-State Census States

Thirteen (13) states (including DC) have never conducted a state-sponsored census. For these Non-State Census States, this review attempts to identify as many census substitutes as possible. In some cases, the census substitutes are for a single county within a state, and by listing multiple county name lists for about the same time period, regional coverage is achieved.

For an overview of the Non-State Census States, see Table 1 (page 13) showing the years for which census substitutes exist. More detail for each census substitute year indicated on the table is covered in the bibliographic sections.

State Census States

Thirty-eight (38) states have conducted censuses separate from the federal censuses. The number of censuses taken by each of the State Census States ranges from one (1) census year, e.g., the 1852 California; to twenty-four (24) census years, e.g., the 1792-1866 Mississippi territorial/state censuses. For this review, all of the state-sponsored censuses are identified, plus, to a lesser degree than the non-state census states, census substitutes available. See Table 2 (pages 14-15) for an overview of the State Census States, the year for each surviving census for a state; and an indication of which specific years are now available online as digitized databases.

Locating the Extant State Census Records

Generally, state censuses were conducted from the time of territorial status or early statehood up until about 1905, but a few continued until 1925, 1935, or 1945. The last state censuses taken by any of the states was in 1945 (Florida and South Dakota). Due to budget restraints, the Depression Era of the 1930s was a contributing factor to states ending their census-taking endeavors. Eventually, all states of the Union stopped using the population figures from state censuses and began using the federal census figures for apportionment of their state legislatures.

While the surviving federal census manuscripts are all located mostly in one repository (the National Archives), state census manuscripts are spread across the country in the various state archives or local repositories. The accessibility of state censuses may be just as good as federal censuses – but one needs to know where they are located first.

Beginning in 1941, the U.S. Bureau of the Census issued a bibliographic report attempting to identify all known state censuses, those undertaken by the various states separate from the federal censuses since 1790.[1] Prepared by Henry J. Dubester of the Library of Congress, the report was the first known attempt to research all of the state constitutions and subsequent laws related to state censuses for all of the states. The Dubester report sought, first, to identify what state censuses had ever been authorized by a state constitution or legislature; and second, to identify what census manuscripts still survive. The identification of extant state censuses was very incomplete, due to the war and under-funding of the project.

However, Dubester's review of each state's constitutional provisions for taking state censuses still stands as the best overview of what state censuses were ever authorized. The report cites the specific articles of the state constitutions or the actual state laws relating to censuses for all states.

Unfortunately, the fact that a state legislature authorized a state census does not mean one was actually taken. For example, the State Constitution of California of 1849 authorized a census in the years 1852 and 1855 and each ten years thereafter, all for the purpose of apportionment of its state legislature. Yet, only one was ever taken, that for 1852. Later, the California Constitution of 1879 provided that the decennial national census serve as the basis for legislative apportionment.[2]

This was fairly typical of all states. Even in those states for which several decades of state censuses now survive, they eventually got out of the census business, turning to the federal decennial censuses to determine apportionment. For example, New York took state censuses from 1825 and every ten years thereafter until 1925, yet, in 1938, New York decided to use the federal decennial censuses thereafter.[3]

Since the Dubester report, there have been several attempts to list all known state censuses, where they are located, and the contents of the census name lists. All of these attempts differ dramatically, because some of the lists rely on the Dubester report, which may have been accurate in identifying which state censuses were ever authorized but was not nearly complete in identifying the extant manuscripts of state census records. For example, Table 4-8 of *The Source*,[4] seems to use the census years cited in the Dubester report for "authorized state censuses" rather than those actually extant. There are lists of state censuses for each state in *The Red Book*,[5] but are only a slight improvement over those found in *The Source*. And, several Internet sites offer lists of state censuses, all of which seem to take data previously published in the *Source* or *The Red Book*, and similar publications.

Based on survey results from all states, the Family History Library prepared a two-volume publication, *U.S. State and Special Census Register: A Listing of Family History Library Microfilm Numbers,* compiled by G. Eileen Buckway and Fred Adams, a revised edition published by the FHL in 1992 (FHL book 973 X2 v. 1 & 2, and fiche #6104851 (vol. 1) and #6104852 (vol. 2). This is a very good guide to military censuses, school censuses, and special censuses of American Indian tribes. As a guide to state censuses, however, the list is incomplete. Since the results of the surveys from each of the states were only partially successful, there are many omissions.

Clearly, the best list of state censuses to date is Ann S. Lainhart, *State Census Records*, published by Genealogical Publishing Co., Inc., Baltimore, in 1992. The book identifies state censuses in 43 states, including 5 states without state censuses (but have major state-wide census substitutes available). For the 38 state census states, the lists generally do not include colonial or pre-territorial censuses. With a few exceptions, census substitutes such as those compiled from tax lists, voter registration lists, military lists, or other name sources, are also not included. Still, Lainhart's book stands as the most complete list ever done.

At the time when most of the previous state census lists were put together, there were some research tools unavailable to the authors. Today, the Internet as a resource for finding place-specific records is overwhelming. And, special tools such as the Periodical Source Index (PERSI)[6] which indexes articles in over 11,000 different genealogical periodicals (by subject, place, and surname) gives a big boost to the task of finding references to relevant articles using keywords such as "state census," "territorial census," or "tax list." In addition, the State Archives and/or State Libraries where obscure census originals and substitute name lists reside often have a website with an online searchable catalog.

For any genealogical research project, it helps to be close to the Family History Library (FHL) in Salt Lake City. But from any place where a researcher has access to the Internet, the FamilySearch™ online catalog as a genealogical research tool has no equal. Searching for published state censuses and census substitutes in the FHL catalog will not bring up every extant resource, but it is more complete than any other library in the world.

The Evolution of Regional Chapters to State Chapters

In the 2008 First Edition of this work, the two volumes had chapters for six (6) Eastern Regions and five (5) Western Regions of the United States.

For the 2016 Second Edition, the three volumes included an Eastern volume with five (5) regions; the Central Volume had three (3) regions; and the Western volume had four (4) regions; plus, an all-new Nationwide Chapter was added to the Western volume. A timeline for each region was prepared to put the area into a historical perspective from a genealogist's point of view.

This 2020 Third Edition was expanded to five volumes, each volume a region of the United States. Therefore, the content of each state's review now includes much of the content that was done at the regional level in the earlier editions, e.g., there is now a Timeline specific to each state.

The organization of the state bibliographic lists has changed as well. The Second Edition had six (6) listings for bibliographic entries, including State Resource Centers, Ancestry.com, USGenWeb.org, FamilySearch.org, and others. This Third Edition has just one (1) listing where all databases from any provider are presented in chronological order.

About PERSI

PERSI (PERiodical Source Index) is a digitized database project of the Allen County Public Library (ACPL), Fort Wayne, IN. Since 1986, the PERSI extractors have indexed article titles, places, and surnames from over 11,000 genealogical & historical periodicals. The PERSI database is currently available online through the FindMyPast.com subscription website.

A number of printed articles found in periodicals were included in the state bibliography listings that follow. The Fort Wayne library has an online order form for requesting a printed copy of any article indexed in the PERSI database, see http://genealogycenter.org/docs/default-source/resources/articlerequest.pdf?sfvrsn=2.

Federal Censuses

Since the Second Edition was published in 2016, the digital images of all federal censuses 1790-1940 became accessible to the public via the online FHL Catalog. It is now possible to view the digital images for any state's federal censuses separate from the various databases at FamilySearch.org, Ancestry.com, et al, and this meant adding the URL link for each state's digitized federal censuses in the state chapters.

The Nationwide Chapter (Vol. 5) was completely reorganized into Part 1: *Maps, Descriptions, and Internet Access for the U.S. Federal Censuses, 1790-1950;* and Part 2: *U.S. Census Substitutes.* To review the federal censuses in more detail, refer to *The Census Book*[7] for each census year. The new 2019 *Census Book* has a detailed review of published federal censuses online, 1790-1950.

The maps of the changing county boundaries for all of the states shown in *Map Guide to the U.S. Federal Census, 1790-1920*[8] should also be helpful for reviewing substitute or state census years between federal census years.

- bill$hide

Notes:

1. *State Censuses: An Annotated Bibliography of Censuses of Population Taken After the Year 1790 by States and Territories of the United States*, prepared by Henry J. Dubester, Chief, Census Library Project, Library of Congress, published Washington, DC, by United States Department of Commerce, Bureau of the Census, 1941, rev. 1948.

2. Dubester, *State Censuses*, p. 3.

3. Dubester, *State Censuses*, p. 50.

4. *The Source: A Guidebook of American Genealogy*, first edition, edited by Arlene Eakle and Johni Cerny, published by Ancestry, Inc., Salt Lake City, 1984.

5. *The Red Book: American State, County & Town Sources*, edited by Alice Eichholz, rev. ed., published by Ancestry, Inc., Salt Lake City, UT, 1992.

6. Allen County Public Library, *Periodical Source Index (PERSI)*, updated semi-annually. [database online at various contracted websites] Original data: Allen County Public Library. Periodical Source Index, Fort Wayne, IN: Allen County Public Library Foundation, 1985- .

7. *The Census Book: Facts, Schedules & Worksheets for the U.S Federal Censuses,* by William Dollarhide, publ. Family Roots Publishing Co., Orting, WA, 2019, 245 pages. See www.familyrootspublishing.com/store/product_view.php?id=3643

8. *Map Guide to the U.S. Federal Censuses, 1790-1920,* by William Thorndale and William Dollarhide, published by Genealogical Publishing Co., Inc., Baltimore, 1987-2016.

Table 1 – Non-State Census States. The following 13 states (including DC) have never conducted a state-sponsored census (or no state census survives). Census Substitutes for each state are shown for a range of years. Refer to the bibliographic listings for details about each.

State	Terr.	State	Years for which Census Substitutes are Available
Alaska	1912	1959	1870, 1873, 1878, 1885, 1887, 1890-1895, 1902-1912, 1905, 1908-1914, 1910- 1929, 1913-1916, 1917-1918, 1947, 1950, 1959-1986, and 1960-1985.
Delaware	—	1787	1609-1888, 1646-1679, 1680-1934, 1682-1759, 1684-1693, 1726, 1755, 1759, 1779, 1782, 1785, 1790, 1800, 1807, 1850-1860, and 1862-1872.
District* of Columbia	1801	1871*	1803, 1807, 1818, 1867, 1878, 1885, 1888, 1894, 1897, 1905-1909, 1912-1913, 1915, 1917, 1919, and 1925.
Idaho	1863	1890	1863, 1865-1874, 1871-1881, 1880, 1890, 1911-1937, 1911-1950, and 1930.
Kentucky	—	1792	1773-1780, 1774-1796, 1780-1909, 1781-1839, 1782-1787, 1782-1875, 1787, 1787-1811, 1787-1875, 1788-1875, 1789-1882, 1792-1830, 1792-1913, 1792-1796, 1793-1836, 1794-1805, 1794-1817, 1795, 1796-1808, 1797-1866, 1800, 1820-1900, 1851-1900, 1859-1860, 1860-1936, 1861-1865, 1862-1866, and 1895- 1896.
Montana	1864	1889	1860, 1856-1993, 1864-1872, 1868-1869, 1868-1929, 1870, 1880, 1870-1957, 1872- 1900, 1879-1880, 1881-1928, 1881-2000, 1891-1929, 1894, 1913, 1906- 1917, 1909- 1910, 1917-1918, 1921, and 1930-1975.
New Hampshire	—	1788	1648, 1709. 1723, 1736, 1740, 1763, 1767, 1775, 1776, 1779, 1789, 1795-1816, 1797, 1802, 1803, 1821, 1826, 1833, 1836, 1838, 1849, 1855 & 1865 MA, 1860, 1862-1866, 1903, and 1902-1921
Ohio	1787	1803	1787-1840, 1787-1871, 1788-1799, 1788-1820, 1790, 1800-1803, 1801-1814, 1801-1824, 1802, 1803-1827, 1804, 1807, 1810, 1812, 1816-1838, 1816-1838, 1825, 1827, 1832-1850, 1833-1994, 1835, 1846-1880, 1851-1900, 1851-1907, and 1907.
Pennsylvania	—	1787	1682-1950, 1759, 1680-1938, 1680s-1900s, 1760s-1790s, 1700s, 1780, 1798, 1740- 1900, 1887-1893, and 1870.
Texas	—	1845	1736-1838, 1700s-1800s, 1756-1830s, 1782-1836, 1809-1836, 1814-1909, 1821-1846, 1826, 1826-1835, 1820s-1846, 1820-1829, 1826-1836, 1829-1836, 1830-1839, 1835, 1835-1846, 1836, 1836-1935, 1837-1859, 1840-1849, 1840, 1846, 1837-1910, 1851-1900, 1858, 1861-1865, 1863, 1865-1866, 1867, 1874, 1882-1895, 1884, 1889-1894, 1890, 1914, 1917-1918, 1896-1948, and 1964-1968.
Vermont	—	1791	1770s-1780s, 1700s-1800s, 1654-1800, 1710-1753, 1721-1800, 1770-1832, 1771, 1782, 1788, 1793, 1796-1959, 1800s-1870, 1807, 1813, 1815, 1816, 1827-1833, 1828, 1832, 1843, 1852-1959, 1855-1860, 1861-1866, 1865, 1869, 1871-1908, 1874, 1880-1881, 1881-1882, 1882-1883, 1883-1884, 1884, 1887-1888, 1888, 1889, and 1895-1924.
Virginia	—	1788	1600s-1700s, 1600s, 1619-1930, 1623-1990, 1623-1800, 1632-1800, 1654-1800, 1704-1705, 1720, 1736-1820, 1740, 1744-1890, 1760, 1769-1800, 1779, 1779-1978, 1779-1860, 1782-1785, 1785, 1787, 1809-1848, 1810, 1815, 1828-1938, 1835, 1835-1941, 1840, 1861, 1861-1865, 1852, 1853-1896, and 1889-1890.
West Virginia	—	1863	1600s-1900s, 1777-1850, 1787, 1782-1907, 1782-1850, 1782-1860, 1782, 1783-1900, 1783-1850, 1785-1850, 1787,1850, 1789-1850, 1792-1850, 1797-1899, 1797-1851, 1799-1850, 1800, 1801-1850, 1810, 1811-1850, 1862-1866, 1863-1900, and 1899-1900.

From *Census Substitutes & State Census Records* by William Dollarhide, publ. Family Roots Publishing Co., Orting WA

Table 2 – State Census States – Alabama to Michigan

The following 38 states have state-sponsored censuses available:

State	Year a Terr.	Year a State	Years for which State Censuses are available (underlined year = an online database is available)	Notes
Alabama	1817	1819	**Colony:** 1706 1721 1764 1785 1786-1803 **AL Territory:** 1801* 1808* 1809* 1810* 1816* 1818 **State:** 1820** 1821 1823 1832 1838 1844 1850** 1855 1866.	* as part of MS Terr. ** separate from federal.
Arizona	1863	1912	**AZ Territory:** 1831 1864 1866 1867* 1869* 1874* 1876* 1882*	*1-2 counties only
Arkansas	1819	1836	**Colony:** 1686-1791 **AR Territory:** 1814* 1823 1827 1829 1833 1835 **State:** 1838 1854 1865	* as part of MO Terr.
California	—	1850	**Colony:** 1790 1790-1796 1822 1834 1836 1837 **State:** 1852 only	
Colorado	1861	1876	**CO Territory:** 1861 1866* **State:** 1885	* 2 counties only
Connecticut	--	1788	**Colony:** 1762 **State:** 1917*	* Military census, males over 16
Florida	1822	1845	**Colony:** 1759 1763-1779 1783-1814 **FL Territory:** 1825 1838 **State:** 1845** 1855 1864* 1867 1875 1885 1895 1935 1945	* Military census ** Statehood census
Georgia	—	1788	1800 federal* **State:** Partial lists only: 1827 1838 1845 1852 1859 1879 1890 federal** 1890 (statewide reconstruction).	* Oglethorpe Co only ** Washington Co only
Hawaii	1900	1959	**Kingdom of Hawaii:** 1840-1866 1878 1890 1896	
Illinois	1809	1818	**IL Territory:** 1810 **State:** 1818 1820* 1825 1830* 1835 1840* 1845 1855 1865.	* separate from federal
Indiana	1800	1816	**IN Territory:** 1807. **State:** A few townships only: 1857 1871 1877 1883 1889 1901 1913 1919 1931	
Iowa	1838	1846	As part of **WI Territory:** 1836 **IA Territory:** 1838 **State:** 1844 1845 1847 1849 1851 1852 1853 1854 1856 1859 1873 1875 1885 1888 1893 1895 1896 1897 1905 1915 1925	
Kansas	1854	1861	**KS Territory:** 1855 1856 1857 1858 1859 **State:** 1865 1875 1885 1895 1905 1915 1925	
Louisiana	1809	1812	**Orleans District:** 1804 **State:** 1833 1837 1890 federal*	*Ascension Parish only
Maine	—	1820	1837 only.	
Maryland	—	1788	1776 1778 1783*	* Tax list
Massachusetts	—	1788	1855 1865	
Michigan	1805	1837	**MI Territory:** 1827 1834 **State:** 1837 1845 1854 1864 1874 1884 1894	

From *Census Substitutes & State Census Records* by William Dollarhide, publ. Family Roots Publishing Co., Orting WA

Table 2 – State Census States – Minnesota to Wyoming

Continuation of states with state-sponsored censuses available:

State	Year a Terr.	Year a State	Years for which State Censuses are available (underlined year = an online database is available)	Notes
Minnesota	1849	1858	**MN Territory:** <u>1849</u> <u>1853</u> <u>1855</u> <u>1857</u>* **State:** <u>1865</u> <u>1875</u> <u>1885</u> <u>1895</u> <u>1905</u>	* special federal
Mississippi	1798	1817	**Colony:** <u>1792</u>** **MS Territory:** 1801 <u>1805</u> <u>1809</u> <u>1810</u> <u>1813</u> <u>1815</u> <u>1816</u> <u>1817</u> **State:** <u>1818</u> <u>1820</u>* <u>1822</u> <u>1823</u> <u>1824</u> <u>1825</u> <u>1830</u>* <u>1837</u> <u>1840</u>* <u>1841</u> <u>1845</u> <u>1850</u>* <u>1853</u> 1857 <u>1866</u>	* separate from federal ** Natchez District only
Missouri	1805	1821	**Colony:** <u>1752</u> <u>1791</u> <u>1797</u> **MO Territory:** <u>1817</u> <u>1818</u> <u>1819</u> **State:** <u>1844</u>* 1845* 1846* 1852* <u>1856</u>* 1864* <u>1868</u>* <u>1876</u>**	* 1-2 counties only ** 28 counties
Nebraska	1854	1867	**NE Territory:** <u>1854</u> <u>1855</u> <u>1856</u> <u>1865</u> **State:** Lancaster & Cass Co Only: <u>1874</u> <u>1875</u> <u>1876</u> <u>1877</u> <u>1878</u> <u>1881</u> <u>1882</u> <u>1883</u> <u>1884</u> <u>1885</u>	
Nevada	1861	1864	**NV Territory:** 1861 1862 <u>1863</u> **State:** 1864 <u>1875</u>	
New Jersey	—	1787	<u>1855</u> <u>1865</u> 1875* <u>1885</u> <u>1895</u> <u>1905</u> <u>1915</u>	* a few townships only
New Mexico	1850	1912	**Colony:** <u>1600</u> 1750 1790 **NM Territory:** <u>1885</u>	
New York	—	1788	1825 1835 1845 <u>1855</u> <u>1865</u> <u>1875</u> <u>1892</u> <u>1905</u> <u>1915</u> <u>1925</u>	
North Carolina	—	1789	**Pre-statehood:** 1784 -1787.	
North Dakota	1861*	1889	**Dakota Territory:** <u>1885</u> **State:** 1905 (statistics only) <u>1915</u> <u>1925</u>	* Dakota Territory
Oklahoma	1890	1907	**OK Territory:** <u>1890</u>* **State:** <u>1907</u> federal (Seminole Co. only)	* separate from federal
Oregon	1848	1859	**OR Provisional Territory:** <u>1842</u> 1843 <u>1845</u> <u>1846</u> **OR Territory:** <u>1849</u> <u>1853</u> 1854 <u>1855</u> <u>1856</u> <u>1857</u> 1858 1859 **State:** <u>1865</u>* <u>1875</u>* <u>1885</u>* <u>1895</u>* 1905	* indexes for a few counties only
Rhode Island	—	1790	<u>1865</u> <u>1875</u> <u>1885</u> <u>1905</u> <u>1915</u> <u>1925</u> <u>1935</u>	
South Carolina	—	1788	1829 1839 1869 1875	
South Dakota	1861*	1889	**Dakota Territory:** <u>1885</u> **State:** <u>1895</u> <u>1905</u> <u>1915</u> <u>1925</u> <u>1935</u> <u>1945</u>	* Dakota Territory
Tennessee	1790*	1796	**Southwest Territory:** 1790 (Reconstructed) **State:** 1891 (partial)	
Utah	1850	1896	**UT Territory:** <u>1856</u> only.	
Washington	1853	1889	**WA Territory:** <u>1851</u>* <u>1856</u> <u>1857</u> <u>1858</u> <u>1859</u> <u>1861</u> <u>1871</u> <u>1879</u> <u>1881</u> <u>1883</u> <u>1885</u> <u>1887</u> **State:** <u>1891</u> <u>1892</u> <u>1894</u> <u>1898</u>	* As part of Oregon Territory.
Wisconsin	1836	1848	**WI Territory:** <u>1836</u> <u>1838</u> 1842 <u>1846</u> <u>1847</u> **State:** <u>1855</u> <u>1865</u> <u>1875</u> <u>1885</u> <u>1895</u> <u>1905</u>	
Wyoming	1868	1890	**WY Territory:** 1869 1885*.	*1 county only

From *Census Substitutes & State Census Records* by William Dollarhide, publ. Family Roots Publishing Co., Orting, WA

Table 3 – State Censuses Taken in Common Years. As a means of comparing state censuses taken by the 38 state census states, this table shows the common years for which many states conducted a state census. Many were done in years ending in "5." Census dates for some states are within a range, e.g., within 3 years of 1825, are indicated in the 1825 column.

	1815	1825	1835	1845	1855	1865	1875	1885	1895	1905	1915	1925	1935	1945
Alabama	•	•	•	•	•	•								
Arizona						•								
Arkansas	•	•	•		•	•								
California					•									
Colorado							•		•					
Connecticut											•			
Florida		•			•			•	•	•		•	•	•
Georgia		•	•	•	•		•							
Hawaii					•		•	•		•				
Illinois			•	•	•	•								
Indiana					•			•	•		•			
Iowa				•	•	•		•	•	•	•	•		
Kansas					•		•	•	•	•	•	•	•	
Louisiana			•											
Maine			•											
Maryland														
Massachusetts					•	•								
Michigan		•	•	•	•	•	•	•	•					
Minnesota					•	•	•	•	•	•	•			
Mississippi	•	•	•	•	•	•								
Missouri					•	•	•	•						
Nebraska						•	•	•	•					
Nevada						•	•							
New Jersey					•	•	•	•	•	•	•			
New Mexico									•					
New York		•	•	•	•	•	•		•	•	•	•		
No. Carolina														
No. Dakota								•		•	•	•		
Oklahoma										•	•			
Oregon				•	•	•	•	•	•	•				
Rhode Island							•	•	•	•	•	•	•	
So. Carolina		•	•			•	•							
So. Dakota								•	•	•	•	•	•	•
Tennessee									•					
Utah					•									
Washington					•			•	•	•				
Wisconsin			•		•	•	•	•	•	•				
Wyoming						•								
No. of States:	3	8	12	11	21	20	17	16	16	11	9	7	3	2

From *Census Substitutes & State Census Records* by William Dollarhide, published by Family Roots Publishing Co., Orting WA

Table 4 - Availability of Federal Censuses for each State

State	Year a Terr	Year a State	1790	1800	1810	1820	1830	1840	1850	1860	1870	1880	1890	1900	1910	1920	1930	1940	1950
Alabama	1817	1819				lost	•	•	•	•	•	•	lost	•	•	•	•	•	•
Alaska (to US 1867)	1912	1959	No census taken, District of Alaska, 1870, 1880, or 1890 →								--	--	--	•	•	•	•	•	•
Arizona	1863	1912									•	•	lost	•	•	•	•	•	•
Arkansas	1819	1836				lost	•	•	•	•	•	•	lost	•	•	•	•	•	•
California (to US 1848)	—	1850							•	•	•	•	lost	•	•	•	•	•	•
Colorado	1861	1876									•	•	lost	•	•	•	•	•	•
Connecticut	—	1788	•	•	•	•	•	•	•	•	•	•	lost	•	•	•	•	•	•
Delaware	—	1787	•	•	•	•	•	•	•	•	•	•	lost	•	•	•	•	•	•
Distr. of Columbia	1801	—		•	•	•	•	•	•	•	•	•	lost	•	•	•	•	•	•
Florida	1822	1845							•	•	•	•	lost	•	•	•	•	•	•
Georgia	—	1788	lost	lost	lost	•	•	•	•	•	•	•	lost	•	•	•	•	•	•
Hawaii (to US 1898)	1900	1959												•	•	•	•	•	•
Idaho	1863	1890									•	•	lost	•	•	•	•	•	•
Illinois	1809	1818			part	•	•	•	•	•	•	•	lost	•	•	•	•	•	•
Indiana	1800	1816		lost	lost	•	•	•	•	•	•	•	lost	•	•	•	•	•	•
Iowa (* part of WI Terr.)	1838	1846						•*	•	•	•	•	lost	•	•	•	•	•	•
Kansas	1854	1861								•	•	•	lost	•	•	•	•	•	•
Kentucky (*Distr. of VA)	—	1791	lost*	lost	•	•	•	•	•	•	•	•	lost	•	•	•	•	•	•
Louisiana (*OrleansTer)	1809	1812			•*	•	•	•	•	•	•	•	lost	•	•	•	•	•	•
Maine (*Distr. of MA)	—	1820	•*	•*	•*	•	•	•	•	•	•	•	lost	•	•	•	•	•	•
Maryland	—	1788	•	•	•	•	•	•	•	•	•	•	lost	•	•	•	•	•	•
Massachusetts	—	1788	•	•	•	•	•	•	•	•	•	•	lost	•	•	•	•	•	•
Michigan	1805	1837				lost	•	•	•	•	•	•	lost	•	•	•	•	•	•
Minnesota	1849	1858	MN Terr. had a special federal census in 1857 →							•	•	•	lost	•	•	•	•	•	•
Mississippi	1798	1817		lost	lost	•	•	•	•	•	•	•	lost	•	•	•	•	•	•
Missouri	1805	1821			lost	lost	•	•	•	•	•	•	lost	•	•	•	•	•	•
Montana	1864	1889									•	•	lost	•	•	•	•	•	•
Nebraska	1854	1867								•	•	•	lost	•	•	•	•	•	•
Nevada	1861	1864									•	•	lost	•	•	•	•	•	•
New Hampshire	—	1788	•	•	•	•	•	•	•	•	•	•	lost	•	•	•	•	•	•
New Jersey	—	1787	lost	lost	lost	lost	•	•	•	•	•	•	lost	•	•	•	•	•	•
New Mexico	1850	1912							•	•	•	•	lost	•	•	•	•	•	•
New York	—	1788	•	•	•	•	•	•	•	•	•	•	lost	•	•	•	•	•	•
North Carolina	—	1789	•	•	•	•	•	•	•	•	•	•	lost	•	•	•	•	•	•
North Dakota*	1861	1889	*1860, 1870, 1880 as part of Dakota Territory →							•	•	•	lost	•	•	•	•	•	•
Ohio (*NW Terr.)	1787	1803		* lost	lost	•	•	•	•	•	•	•	lost	•	•	•	•	•	•
Oklahoma	1890	1907	1 month prior to statehood in 1907, Oklahoma Territory had a special federal census										lost	•	•	•	•	•	•
Oregon	1848	1859							•	•	•	•	lost	•	•	•	•	•	•
Pennsylvania	—	1787	•	•	•	•	•	•	•	•	•	•	lost	•	•	•	•	•	•
Rhode Island	—	1790	•	•	•	•	•	•	•	•	•	•	lost	•	•	•	•	•	•
South Carolina	—	1788	•	•	•	•	•	•	•	•	•	•	lost	•	•	•	•	•	•
South Dakota*	1861	1889	*1860, 1870, 1880 as part of Dakota Territory →							•	•	•	lost	•	•	•	•	•	•
Tennessee (*SW Terr)	1790	1796	* tally	lost	lost	part	•	•	•	•	•	•	lost	•	•	•	•	•	•
Texas (to US 1845)	—	1845							•	•	•	•	lost	•	•	•	•	•	•
Utah	1850	1896							•	•	•	•	lost	•	•	•	•	•	•
Vermont	—	1791	•	•	•	•	•	•	•	•	•	•	lost	•	•	•	•	•	•
Virginia	—	1788	lost	lost	•	•	•	•	•	•	•	•	lost	•	•	•	•	•	•
Washington	1853	1889									•	•	lost	•	•	•	•	•	•
West Virginia	—	1863	Part of Virginia, 1790-1860								•	•	lost	•	•	•	•	•	•
Wisconsin	1836	1848						•	•	•	•	•	lost	•	•	•	•	•	•
Wyoming	1868	1890									•	•	lost	•	•	•	•	•	•

From *Census Substitutes & State Census Records* by William Dollarhide, publ. Family Roots Publishing Co., Orting WA

18 • Census Substitutes & State Census Records

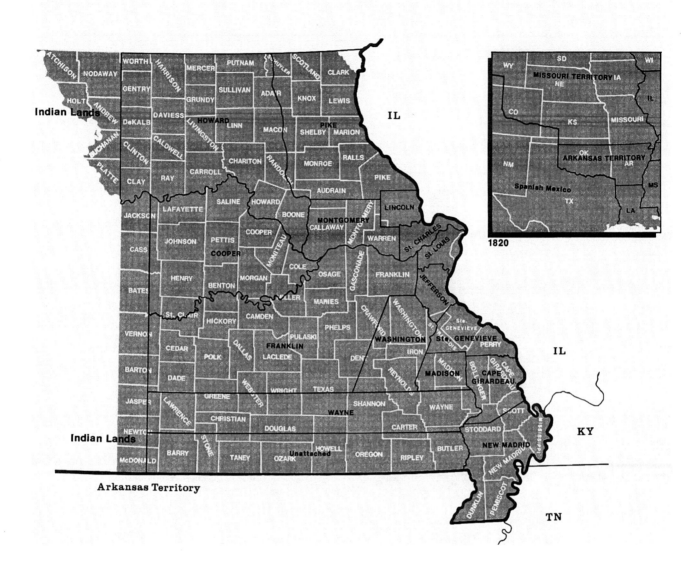

Missouri Territory • June 1820. The 16 counties of Missouri Territory at the time of the 1820 federal census are shown in black. Missouri's statehood: August 10, 1821. Missouri's 114 current counties (and the independent city of St. Louis) are shown in white. The inset map shows the expanse of 1820 Missouri Territory, which extended to the northern border of the U.S. The 1820 federal census taken for Missouri Territory was lost. See **http://usgwarchives.net/maps/cessions/ilcmap37.htm** for a detailed Indian Cessions Map (Royce Map, Missouri 1, Map 37). Several territorial censuses were taken for Missouri Territory, 1812-1819. The surviving name lists are for Arkansas County in 1814 (now at the AR State Archives), St. Charles County in 1817 and 1819, and Cape Girardeau and Ste. Genevieve in 1818; all at the MO State Archives. **Map Source:** Page 192, *Map Guide to the U.S. Federal Censuses, 1790-1920*, by William Thorndale and William Dollarhide.

Missouri
Censuses & Substitute Name Lists

Historical Timeline of Missouri, 1673-1965

1673. Mississippi River. French explorers Jacques Jolliet and Louis Marquette left their base at Ste. Sault Marie, and made their way to the Illinois River, which they descended to become the first Europeans to discover the Mississippi River. They floated down the Mississippi as far south as the mouth of the Arkansas River before returning to the Great Lakes area.

1682. Mississippi River. Following the same route as Jolliet and Marquette, René-Robert Cavelier (Sieur de LaSalle) floated down the Mississippi River, continuing all the way to its mouth at the Gulf of Mexico. He then claimed the entire Mississippi Basin for Louis XIV of France, for whom Louisiana was named.

1682-1720. Louisiana. During this period, the jurisdiction of Louisiana ran from the Gulf of Mexico to the junction of the Arkansas River with the Mississippi River. The French administered Arkansas Post, Natchez, Baton Rouge, New Orleans, Mobile, and Biloxi as part of Louisiana. Fort Louis de la Louisiane (now Mobile), was the capital of Louisiana, 1702-1720.

1720-1762. Upper and Lower Louisiana. By 1720, the Great Lakes / Illinois Country was separated from Quebéc and added to Louisiana. The original Louisiana area became known as Lower Louisiana. The capital of Lower Louisiana was at New Orleans, 1720-1762. Upper Louisiana extended from the Highlands (Terra Haute) on the Wabash River down the Ohio and Mississippi Valleys to the Arkansas River. The fur trading settlements of Upper Louisiana included Vincennes (now Indiana), Prairie du Chien (now Wisconsin); Cahokia, Kaskaskia, Chartres, Saint Philippe, and Prairie du Rocher (now Illinois); Ste. Genevieve (now Missouri), and Fort de Chavagnial on the Missouri River (now Kansas).

1763. Treaty of Paris. This was the end of the French and Indian war. (In Europe it was called the "Seven Years War.") At the 1763 treaty, the French surrendered all their claims in North America. Spain acquired the former French areas west of the Mississippi as *Spanish Louisiana*. Great Britain gained all of Québec, which they immediately renamed the *Province of Canada*. Britain also gained control of the rest of North America east of the Mississippi River. They named their entire area *British North America*.

1764. St. Louis was founded by French trader Pierre Laclede Liguest. Although part of Spanish Louisiana, St. Louis operated under French civilian control until it was occupied by Spanish soldiers in 1770.

1783. Treaty of Paris. As the official end of the Revolutionary War, the 1783 treaty recognized the United States as an independent republic, with borders from the Atlantic Ocean to the Mississippi River. The treaty also reaffirmed the claims of Britain to present-day Canada; and Spain's claim to lands west of the Mississippi River.

1800. Louisiana. Napoleon acquired title of Louisiana from Spain. At the Third Treaty of San Ildefonso, the Spanish acknowledged that it was too costly to explore the country and could not see the rewards being worth the investment. Spain retroceded Louisiana to France in exchange for the Grand Duchy of Tuscany (now part of Italy).

1803. Louisiana Purchase. The United States purchased Louisiana from France. Sent by President Jefferson to attempt the purchase of New Orleans, the American negotiators (James Madison and Robert Livingston) were surprised when Napoleon offered the entire tract to them. The Louisiana Purchase was officially described as the "drainage of the Mississippi and Missouri River basins." Adding the area doubled the size of the United States.

1804. On an expedition ordered by President Thomas Jefferson, Captains Meriwether Lewis and William Clark's Corps of Discovery left St. Louis in search of a passage to the Pacific Ocean. Based on bad information from his spies, the Spanish governor of New Mexico dispatched soldiers from Santa Fe to the Arkansas River to intercept the party and arrest them. But the Lewis and Clark party had taken a more northern route, following the Missouri River.

1804. Orleans Territory and **Louisiana District.** Congress divided the Louisiana Purchase into two jurisdictions. Orleans Territory had north and south bounds the same as the present state of Louisiana but did not include land east of the Mississippi River, and its northwestern corner extended on an indefinite line west into Spanish Texas. For a year, Louisiana District was attached to Indiana Territory for judicial administration.

1805. Louisiana Territory. Louisiana District became Louisiana Territory with its own Governor on July 4, 1805. First governor: James Wilkinson. First territorial capital: St. Louis.

1805. 1st Pike Expedition. Governor Wilkinson, still a U.S. Army General, picked Lieutenant Zebulon Pike to lead a small party of soldiers to investigate the Mississippi River above St. Louis. Pike was given specific orders to find the source of the Mississippi, and while doing so, to note "…any rivers, prairies, islands, mines, quarries, timber, and any Indian villages and settlements encountered."

1805. Louisiana Territory had five original subdivisions: St. Louis District, St. Charles District, Ste. Genevieve District, Cape Girardeau District and New Madrid District. The unpopulated area north of these original districts was referred to as Upper Louisiana and included all lands north to the U.S./British border and west to the Continental Divide.

1806-1807. 2nd Pike Expedition. Zebulon Pike, now a Captain, was again sent out, this time to explore and locate the source of the Red River in Lower Louisiana. From St. Louis, Pike's party followed the Missouri River to the mouth of the Kansas River, then connecting with the Arkansas River, which he followed to its source in the Rocky Mountains (now Colorado), Pike returned on a more southern route that took him into an area claimed by the Spanish as part of Nuevo Mexico. He and his men were arrested, taken to Santa Fe, but returned to the Arkansas River shortly thereafter. In 1810 Pike wrote a book describing his adventures in the Rocky Mountains that became a best seller in America and Europe. The book was the inspiration and guide for a good number of "mountain men" who were the only whites to venture into the Rocky Mountains for the next 35 years.

1812. Missouri Territory. Louisiana Territory was renamed Missouri Territory on June 4, 1812. This was to avoid any confusion after Orleans Territory became the State of Louisiana on April 30, 1812. The General Assembly of the Territory of Missouri met in St. Louis in October and converted the first five original districts into counties: Cape Girardeau, New Madrid, St. Charles, St. Louis, and Ste. Genevieve. A year later, the territorial legislature created Arkansas County from lands ceded by the Osage Indians.

1815-1819. Steamboats did not dominate river transportation until after the development of the classic flat-bottomed sternwheeler. By 1815, steamboats on the Ohio and Mississippi rivers had revolutionized river traffic. The first steamboats on the Missouri River began in 1819, but they could usually go no farther west than the mouth of the Kansas River, due to the periodic low water levels and heavy silt at that point.

1819. Arkansas Territory was created, reducing the size of Missouri Territory. The original area included all of present-day Arkansas and most of Oklahoma.

1820. The *Missouri Compromise* in Congress allowed Missouri to enter the Union as a slave state and Maine as a free state, thus keeping the balance of slave and free states equal in Congress. The Act dictated that the remaining area of Missouri Territory north of Latitude 36° 30' was to be free of slavery (that area included present Kansas, Nebraska, Iowa, Minnesota, North Dakota, South Dakota, Wyoming, and Montana).

1821. Aug 10th. Missouri was admitted to the Union as a state with St. Louis as the capital. After Missouri became a state, the remaining part of old Missouri Territory was officially described as *Unorganized Territory*.

1821. Sept. Santa Fe Trail. William Becknell, a Missouri trader, was the first American to follow the route that was to become known as the Santa Fe Trail, beginning at the Missouri River near present Independence, MO. His profitable success in trading with the newly independent Mexicans of Santa Fe was well publicized. Over the next few months, dozens of wagon trains were organized to transport and sell products to a new market.

1822. The Rocky Mountain Fur Company was formed by General William Ashley. He placed an ad in a St. Louis newspaper to recruit able-bodied men for his new fur-trading enterprise. There was no shortage of willing young men. Ashley did not build a chain of forts to manage his fur trading operation. Instead, he sent his men out alone with arrangements to meet them all at a central place a year later. When Ashley finally reached his men each year, it was cause for celebration – a wild party they called "the rendezvous." In 1826, William Ashley retired a wealthy man and sold the Rocky Mountain Fur Company to his employees.

1826. Missouri. The state capital was moved from St. Louis to Jefferson City.

1827. Independence, Missouri. The frontier town of Independence was founded in 1827, the farthest point westward on the Missouri River where steamboats could usually travel. (The nearby confluence of the Kansas River was part of the navigation problem, due to heavy silt and periodic shallow channels). Independence immediately became a supply point, staging area, and primary starting point for the growing number of trappers and traders using the Santa Fe Trail.

1829 Sublette's Trace/Oregon Trail. Before 1829, access to the Platte River Trail from Independence, Missouri, was via the Missouri River to the mouth of the Platte River in present Nebraska. But steamboat traffic usually ended at Independence and travel upriver at that time required human-powered keel boats. The overland route of the Santa Fe Trail now started at Independence as well, heading west several miles into present Kansas, then southwest towards Santa Fe. A few miles into the Santa Fe Trail in present Kansas, at a point later called the Oregon Trail Junction, fur trader William Sublette blazed a cut-off from the Santa Fe Trail, turning northwest and connecting with the Platte River in present Nebraska. The new route across present northeast Kansas was more direct than the river route, and later became the first leg of the Oregon Trail.

1832. After dredging projects near the mouth of the Kansas River, steamboat traffic continued up the Missouri River. In 1832, the steamboat *Yellowstone* began the first of its annual fur-trading voyages up the Missouri River, reaching Fort Union (present North Dakota/Montana line).

1841. The Western Emigration Society, a group of about 70 settlers bound for California and the Oregon Country set off on the Oregon Trail, beginning at Independence, Missouri. This was the first organized wagon train to head for California and Oregon. It is usually called the "Bartleson-Bidwell party" named for the two leaders. John Bartleson led about half of the group to Oregon's Willamette Valley. John Bidwell took the other half to California's Sacramento Valley.

1843. May. Oregon Trail. A wagon train with over 120 wagons, a large herd of livestock, and 1,000 pioneers left Elm Grove, MO and headed out on the Oregon Trail. The largest wagon train to date, it became the model for the thousands of wagon trains that followed. For an online list of the members of the 1843 Wagon Train, see the OR RootsWeb site:
http://freepages.history.rootsweb.ancestry.com/~mransom/pioneers.html

1849. California Gold Rush. With the discovery of gold in California, the Missouri towns of St. Louis, Independence, Westport, and St. Joseph became points of departure for emigrants bound for California, making Missouri the "Gateway to the West."

1860. Apr. Pony Express. The 1,900-mile Pony Express route ran from St. Joseph, Missouri, to Sacramento, California. In competition with the Butterfield Overland Stage company, which held the U.S. Mail contract until the start of the Civil War, the Pony Express riders made the northern journey from St. Joseph to Sacramento in 10 days' time. The Butterfield stages took a southern route from Memphis through Arkansas, Texas, New Mexico, and into Los Angeles, then to Sacramento in an average of 25 days' time.

1946. Missouri. Winston Churchill, former Prime Minister of Great Britain, delivered his famous "Iron Curtain" speech at Fulton's Westminster College.

1965 St. Louis, Missouri. The Gateway Arch (Jefferson National Expansion Memorial) designed by Eero Saarinen was completed. Located on the original settlement site of St. Louis, it symbolized the role of St. Louis in the development of the western frontier

Resources at the Missouri State Archives

The genealogy-friendly Missouri State Archives in Jefferson City features Missouri's history under French and Spanish colonial rule, as an American territory, and during early statehood. For a list of the record types available, see
www.sos.mo.gov/archives/resources/resources.
- Census Records 1752-1940
  - Territorial Censuses, 1752-1818; and Tax Lists, 1814-1821
  - State Censuses, 1840-1876; and Tax Lists (years vary by county)
  - Special Censuses, 1857-2004
  - Federal Censuses, 1830-1940
- County and Municipal Records
- Judicial Records
- Land Records
- Legislative records
- Manuscripts
- Military records of Missourians from the War of 1812 through World War I, including more than 9 million pages related to the Civil War
- Penitentiary Records
- Photographs and Digital Collections
- Resources for Family & Community History
- State agency records
- State government publications

Searchable Online Databases. Visit the Missouri State Archives website for access to each of following searchable databases. Some of these databases are also accessible at Ancestry.com or various websites. See
www.sos.mo.gov/archives/resources/resources.
- Archives' Online Catalog
- Birth & Death Records Database, pre-1910
- Civil War Provost Marshal Index Database
- Coroner's Inquest Database
- County and Municipal Records on Microfilm
- Digital Collections
- Finding Aids
- Land Records Database
- Local Records Inventory Database
- Missouri Death Certificates, 1910 – 1965
- Missouri Digital Heritage
- Missouri Judicial Records
- Missouri State Penitentiary Database
- Missouri Supreme Court Historical Database
- Naturalization Records Database
- Soldiers' Records: War of 1812 - World War I
- St. Louis Circuit Court Historical Records Project
- St. Louis Probate Court Digitization Project (now a part of Missouri Judicial Records)

Bibliography
Missouri Censuses & Substitutes

Missouri's Colonial, Territorial, State, and Federal Censuses can be associated with the historical jurisdictional eras of Missouri.

French Colonial Era, 1682-1763: The only settlement in the present Missouri area of French Louisiana was at Ste. Genevieve, established as a fur trading post in 1750. A few land records from the French era are located today at the Ste. Genevieve County Courthouse and a 1752 French tax list for Ste. Genevieve is at the MO State Archives.

Spanish Colonial Era, 1763-1800: At the 1763 Treaty of Paris ending the French and Indian War, France officially transferred title of Louisiana west of the Mississippi to Spain, and Louisiana east of the Mississippi to Britain. In 1764, French traders established the settlement at St. Louis. The existing French Louisiana settlements were occupied by the Spanish military between 1766 (New Orleans) and 1770 (St. Louis). For the next 30 years, the Spanish presence in Louisiana consisted of one governor at New Orleans, and about 30 soldiers, billeted at New Orleans, Baton Rouge, and St. Louis. Within the period 1770-1800, a few name lists of civilian residents exist for St. Louis, Ste. Genevieve, New Madrid, and Cape Girardeau, The Spanish government finally gave up on Louisiana in 1800, trading the tract to Napoleon for land in Europe. The civilian population (of European stock) in the area of Missouri at the end of the Spanish era was fewer than 2,500 persons.

American Jurisdictions: The United States purchased Louisiana from France in 1803. The following year, Congress created two jurisdictions in the area, Orleans Territory, which was nearly the same as the present-day state of Louisiana; and Louisiana District, the rest of the tract. In 1805, Louisiana District became Louisiana Territory, with the seat of government at St. Louis. When the state of Louisiana was admitted to the Union in 1812, the original Louisiana Territory was renamed Missouri Territory. The first General Assembly of the Territory of Missouri met in October 1812 and designated the first five districts as counties: Cape Girardeau, New Madrid, St. Charles, St. Louis, and Ste. Genevieve. In 1813, Arkansas County was created from lands ceded by the Osage Indians.

MO Territorial Censuses: Several censuses were taken for Missouri Territory, 1812-1819, and the surviving name lists are for Arkansas County in 1814 (now at the AR State Archives), St. Charles County in 1817 and 1819, and Cape Girardeau and Ste. Genevieve in 1818. The 1820 federal census taken for Missouri Territory was lost.

MO State Censuses: The state of Missouri took several state censuses, but few have survived. An inventory of county repositories at the Missouri State Archives reveals a few county copies of state censuses survive for 1844, 1845, 1846, 1852, 1856, 1864, 1868, and 1876. The most complete surviving census was for 1876, with 28 county name lists (out of 114 counties).

MO Censuses Online. The 1844-1881 MO State Census Collection at Ancestry.com includes some years which were tax lists, rather than censuses, all derived from the MO State Archives collection. The 1732-1933 MO Territorial and State Censuses database at FamilySearch.org starts with an Illinois census, not Missouri; but adds several county name lists not at the MO State Archives.

MO Census Substitutes: More common than censuses are the countywide tax lists from the 1820s to the 1890s, which exist for all 114 Missouri counties (and the independent city of St. Louis). Most of the county tax lists have been indexed in books, microfilm, or articles in periodicals. Unpublished extant tax lists can be found using the Missouri State Archives' Local Records Inventory Database. In addition to Missouri censuses, this bibliography identifies many extra name lists. Together, they include Territorial, State, and Federal Censuses, Court Records, Directories, County Indexes, State Military Lists, Tax Lists, Vital Records, and Voter Lists. The censuses and substitute name lists begin below in chronological order:

◆ ◆ ◆ ◆ ◆

1752-1933. *Missouri State and Territorial Census Records* **[Online Database],** digitized and indexed at the FamilySearch.org website. Source: MO State Archives (MSA) & FHL microfilm. The part of this collection from the MSA includes a copy of a French language census identified as "All Counties – 1732 Illinois Country," which has no Missouri locations. The earliest censuses for Missouri areas begin with a 1752 French census of Ste. Genevieve, followed by a 1791 Spanish census of St. Louis; and a 1797 Spanish census of New Madrid. American censuses begin with the 1818 MO Territorial census of Cape Girardeau and Ste. Genevieve. The MO State Archives set incorporates transferred county originals of territorial, state, or federal censuses, all from surviving county copies of the census records. Any of the county originals of federal census years should be compared with the federal copies on microfilm. This collection adds county tax lists and federal censuses from FHL county microfilm. From both MSA and FHL sources, the collection includes census images for the following **Counties,** Towns (years): **Adair,** Novinger (1906); **Atchison** (1876); **Barton,** Liberal (1908); **Benton** (1876); **Boone,** Centralia (1909); **Butler** (1876), **Callaway** (1850 federal, 1852, 1864, 1868, 1876); **Cape Girardeau** (1818, 1868), **Carroll** (1876); **Cass** (1876, 1880 federal); **Cass,** Belton (1911, 1927); **Christian** (1876); **Clinton,** Lathrop (1930 federal); **Daviess,** Gallatin (1915); **DeKalb,** Maysville (1931); **Franklin** (1868, 1876); **Gasconade** (1844); **Greene** (1844, 1852, 1876); **Greene,** Republic (1916); **Holt** (1876); **Howard** (1876); **Iron** (1876); **Jackson,** Grandview (1929); **Jackson,** Independence City (1887); **Jackson,** Sugar Creek (1922); **Jasper,** Carthage (1933); **Lincoln,** Elsberry (1906); **Madison** (1876); **McDonald** (1876); **Moniteau** (1876); **Montgomery** (1876); **New Madrid** (1797 Spanish, 1840 federal); **New Madrid,** Lilbourn (1930 federal); **Newton** (1840 federal); **Osage** (1876); **Perry** (1876, 1840 federal); **Pettis** (1840 federal); **Phelps** (1876); **Pike** (1840 federal); **Polk** (1840 federal); **Polk,** Humansville (1911); **Pulaski** (1840 federal); **Pulaski,** Richland (1920 federal); **Ralls** (1840 federal);

Randolph (1840 federal); **Randolph**, Higbee (1931); **Ray** (1840 federal); **Reynolds** (1876); **Ripley** (1876); **Rives** (1840 federal); **Saline** (1840 federal); **Scott** (1876); **Scott**, Illmo (1914); **Scott**, Oran (1931); **Shelby** (1840 federal); **St. Charles** (1868, 1876); **Ste. Genevieve** (1752 French, 1818, 1844); **St. Francois** (1876, 1840 federal); **St. Louis** (1791 Spanish); **Stoddard** (1840 federal); **Stone** (1876); **Taney** (1840 federal); **Van Buren** (1840 federal); **Warren** (1840 federal); **Washington** (1840 federal); **Wayne** (1840 federal); and **Webster** (1876). This database has 109,803 records. See
https://familysearch.org/search/collection/2075262.
- See also, *Illinois Country, Missouri Area, Census, 1732-1818* [Microfilm & Digital Capture], from the originals at the MO State Archives, digitized by FamilySearch International, 2012. Contents: 1732 Census of Illinois Country and recapitulation (no Missouri locations), 1752 Ste. Genevieve; 1752, 1791 Census of St. Louis and districts; 1797 New Madrid; 1800 Cape Girardeau; and 1818 St. Genevieve. To access the digital images, see the online FHL catalog: www.familysearch.org/search/catalog/2209208.

1754-1850. *Missouri, Compiled Marriages* [Online Database], indexed at Ancestry.com. Source: Jordan Dodd transcriptions from microfilm at the Family History Library in Salt Lake City, UT. This database of Missouri marriages to 1850 contains over 125,000 names. Each entry includes groom, bride, marriage date, county, and state, see
www.ancestry.com/search/collections/2094.

1763-1800. *Spanish Regime in Missouri: A Collection of Papers and Documents Relating to Upper Louisiana, Principally within the Present Limits of Missouri During the Dominion of Spain, From the Archives of the Indies at Seville, etc.* [Online Database], digitized and indexed at the Ancestry.com website. Source: Book, same title, publ. 1909. Included are censuses taken between 1770 and 1800 by the Spanish in Louisiana (including Cape Girardeau, St. Louis, Ste. Genevieve, and New Madrid). This database has 913 pages. See
http://search.ancestry.com/search/db.aspx?dbid=28134.

1765-1840. *Church of Ste. Genevieve Vital Records* [Online Database], indexed at the USGenWeb Archives site for Ste. Genevieve Co MO:
http://files.usgwarchives.net/mo/stegenevieve/vital/stegenvi.txt.

1766-1800. *Index to French and Spanish Land Grants, Recorded in Registers of Land Titles in Missouri: Books A, B, C, D, E* [Printed Book], copied from an index prepared by the staff at the Missouri State Archives by Betty Harvey Williams, Warrensburg, MO, 1977, 25 pages, FHL book 977.8 R22if.
- See also, *French and Spanish Archives, 1766-1816* [Microfilm & Digital Capture], from the original records at the St. Louis Archival Library, St. Louis, MO. Filmed on 3 rolls, beginning with FHL film #981650 (Documents No. 1-166, 1766-1775). To access the digital images, see the online FHL catalog: www.familysearch.org/search/catalog/219814.

1766-1839. *Missouri Genealogical Records & Abstracts* [Printed Book], by Sheridan K. Eddlemon; surname index by Marlene Towle, published by Heritage Books, Bowie, MD, 1990, 7 vols. Includes records from over 40 Missouri counties: marriage records, Spanish censuses, tax lists, estrays, cemetery listings, slave bills of sale, land records including French and Spanish land grants, military records, mortality schedules, court records, marriage records, etc. Contents: vol. 1: 1766-1839; vol. 2: 1752-1839; vol. 3: 1787-1839; vol. 4: 1741-1839; vol. 5: 1755-1839; vol. 6: 1621-1839; vol. 7: 1535-1839. FHL book 977.8 R4e, v.1-7.

1766-1850. *Missouri Marriages to 1850* [Online Database], indexed at the Ancestry.com website. Source: Jordan Dodd, compiler, from extractions of county marriage records on microfilm at the Family History Library, Salt Lake City, UT. Each record includes: Name, Spouse's name, Marriage date, and Marriage county. This database has 126,161 records:
http://search.ancestry.com/search/db.aspx?dbid=2094.

1766-1920. *Missouri Marriages* [Online Database], indexed at the FamilySearch.org website. FamilySearch extractions from records on microfilm at the Family History Library, Salt Lake City, UT. Each record includes: Name, Spouse's name, Marriage date, and Marriage place. This database has 473,531 records. See https://familysearch.org/search/collection/1680838.

1766-1983. *Missouri Marriages* [Online Database], indexed at the Ancestry.com website. Source: *Hunting for Bears* extractions from county records on microfilm at the Family History Library, Salt Lake City, UT. Each record includes: Name, Spouse's name,

Location, and State. This database has 116,795 records: http://search.ancestry.com/search/db.aspx?dbid=7843.

1766-1988. *Missouri, Wills and Probate Records* **[Online Database],** digitized and indexed at the Ancestry.com website. Source: Ancestry extractions from original records in Missouri county, district, and probate courts. The contents of a probate file can vary from case to case, but certain details are found in most probates, most importantly, the names and residences of beneficiaries and their relationship to the decedent. An inventory of the estate assets can reveal personal details about the deceased's occupation and lifestyle. There may also be references to debts, deeds, and other documents related to the settling of the estate. It is possible to browse the images in the database, organized by county, then Record Type, and Date Range. Most counties include index books to court records, probates, wills, etc. This database has 496,224 records. See
http://search.ancestry.com/search/db.aspx?dbid=9071.

1766-2010. *St. Louis, Missouri, Burial Index, Archdiocese of St. Louis,* **[Online Database],** indexed at the Ancestry.com website. Source: Archdiocese of Saint Louis: Cemeteries. This database is also accessible at the Archdiocese of St. Louis website. Each record includes: Name, Gender, Death date, Burial date, Burial place, Age, and Birth date. This database has 270,792 records. See
http://search.ancestry.com/search/db.aspx?dbid=70379.

1781-1797. *Anglo-Americans in Spanish Archives: Lists of Anglo-American Settlers in the Spanish Colonies of America; A Finding Aid* **[Printed Book],** by Lawrence H. Feldman, published by Genealogical Publishing Co., Inc., Baltimore, 1991, 349 pages. From source materials available in Spanish archives, the author has abstracted from original census documents genealogical data about individuals and families who settled in Spanish lands within the present-day states of Florida, Alabama, Mississippi, Louisiana, and Missouri in the US and parts of Central America. Includes bibliographical references and an index of personal names. FHL book 973 X2fe.

1790s-1803. *St. Louis Co, MO – Land Survey Decrees Before 1803* **[Online Database]**, indexed at the USGenWeb site for St. Louis Co MO. See
http://files.usgwarchives.net/mo/stlouis/land/1803land.txt.

1790s-1840. *Missouri Marriages Before 1840* **[Online Database],** digitized and indexed at the Ancestry.com website. Source: Book, same title, by Susan Ormesher, publ. 1998. See pages iii and iv for a list of counties included in this compilation of published marriages. This database has 321 pages. See
http://search.ancestry.com/search/db.aspx?dbid=48333.

1796 Census of New Madrid District **[Online Database],** a Spanish census taken for New Madrid, indexed at the RootsWeb, New Madrid Co MO. See
www.rootsweb.ancestry.com/~monewmad/sec2.html.

1800-1991. *Missouri, County Marriage, Naturalization, and Court Records* **[Online Database],** digitized and indexed at the FamilySearch.org website. Index and digital images of microfilmed marriage records from Missouri counties including recorded marriages, marriage applications, licenses, and certificates. This collection includes records from the microfilm collections of FamilySearch and of the Missouri State Archives in Jefferson City, Missouri. Each record includes: Name, Event type, Event date, Gender, Spouse's name, Spouse's gender, and page number. This database has 573,023 records and 2,513,517 images. See
https://familysearch.org/search/collection/2060668.
- See also, *Missouri, County Marriages, Naturalization, and Court Records, 1802-1969* **[Microfilm & Digital Capture],** this database has the digital images only. See the FHL catalog page for a complete list of counties, type of records, and inclusive dates, see
www.familysearch.org/search/catalog/2060668.

1800s-1900s Missouri Original Landowners **[Printed Books].** See the *Family Maps* series for Missouri counties, maps of all original land patents, compiled by Greg Boyd, publ. Arphax Publishing Co., Norman, OK. These privately produced computer-generated maps show the first property owners for an entire county, produced as a book of maps, each map laid out on the federal township grid, and includes indexes to help you locate a person, place-name, or cemetery. Additional maps are added for each county to show roads, waterways, railroads, selected city centers, and cemeteries within a county. At this writing, *Family Maps* books have been published for Audrain, Barry, Bates, Benton, Boone, Callaway, Camden, Carter, Cass, Clark, Clay, Clinton, Crawford, Dade, Dallas, Daviess, Dent, Douglas, Franklin, Gasconade,

Gentry, Harrison, Henry, Howell, Jackson, Jasper, Jefferson, Johnson, Knox, Linn, Macon, Madison, Miller, Monroe, Montgomery, Newton, Oregon, Ozark, Pettis, Phelps, Polk, Pulaski, Randolph, Scotland, Shelby, St. Clair, St. Francois, Ste. Genevieve, Sullivan, Taney, Texas, Washington, Wayne, and Wright County, Missouri. See www.arphax.com/.

1800s-1900s. *Missouri, Bible Records* **[Online Database]**, indexed at the Ancestry.com website. Source: Elizabeth Prather Ellsberry's *Bible Records of Missouri*, Vol. 1, publ. 1963. The database is the first volume in a series of Bible records that includes such information as births, marriages, probate information, and deaths of individuals who settled in Missouri. Some dates noted in the Bible records may precede Missouri settlement. This database has 8,699 records:
http://search.ancestry.com/search/db.aspx?dbid=5401.

1800s-1900s. Biography Index, St. Louis County, Missouri [Online Database], indexed at the GenealogyTrails.com website. See
http://genealogytrails.com/mo/stlouis/biographies.htm.

1800s-1998. *Missouri Probate Records* **[Online Database],** digitized at the FamilySearch.org website. Source: FHL microfilm. This image only database is a collection of probate records created by county courts including wills and records of estates. A starting date of 1750 is unlikely (for a probate document) - most of the records in this collection fall between 1840 and 1930, but the content and years of the court records varies by county. In a few instances, if the court heard other cases in addition to probate, such as civil disputes or even some criminal matters, the records are mixed in with the probate records. Browse through the images, organized by county, then vol. title (wills, probates, settlements, indexes, etc.), then by date range. This database includes all Missouri counties except Andrew and Cole, noted below. This database has 6,142,790 records. See
https://familysearch.org/search/collection/2399107.
- See also, *Missouri, Andrew, and Cole County Probate Records, 1826-1945* **[Online Database],** digitized at the FamilySearch.org website. Source: MO State Archives. The original probate records from these two counties were scanned by the MSA. This database has 160,690 records. See
https://familysearch.org/search/collection/2060218.
- NOTE: Browsing the records reveals that court records of Clinton County, Missouri are also included in this database. It appears that this Clinton set includes circuit court, probate court, and other records not included in the Clinton set digitized as part of the Missouri Probate Records database.

1800s-2000s. *Missouri GenWeb Archives* **[Online Database].** The MOGenWeb site offers free genealogical databases with searchable statewide name lists and for all Missouri counties. Databases may include Bibles, Biographies, Cemeteries, Censuses, Court Records, Deaths, Deeds, Directories, Histories, Marriages, Military, Newspapers, Obituaries, Photos, Schools, Tax Lists, Wills, and more. See
http://usgwarchives.net/mo/mofiles.htm.

1800s-2000s. *Linkpendium – Missouri: Family History & Genealogy, Census, Birth, Marriage, Death, Vital Records & More* **[Online Databases].** Linkpendium is a genealogical portal site with links to state, county, town, and local databases. Currently listed are selected sites for Missouri statewide resources (622), Renamed/Discontinued Counties (10), Adair County (315) Andrew County (457), Atchison County (252), Audrain County (395), Barry County (303), Barton County (372), Bates County (358) and 107 more Missouri counties. See
www.linkpendium.com/mo-genealogy.

1802-1900. *St. Louis Probate Court Digitization Project* **[Online Database],** digitized and indexed at the Missouri Digital Heritage website. This database has been incorporated into the Missouri Judicial Records section at the MO State Archives website. For the search screen, see
https://s1.sos.mo.gov/records/archives/archivesdb/JudicialRecords.

1804-1876. *St. Louis, Missouri Marriages* **[Online Database],** indexed at the Ancestry.com website. Source: St. Louis Marriage Index, 1804-1876, publ. 1999. Each record includes: Name, Spouse's name, Marriage date, and Vol./Page of the book. This database has 153,816 records. See
http://search.ancestry.com/search/db.aspx?dbid=5413.

1805-2002. *Missouri, Miscellaneous Records* **[Online Database],** digitized at the Ancestry.com website. Source: Various county records on microfilm at the MO State Archives. This is an image only database. Examples of types of miscellaneous records presented here include: Still birth records, School censuses, Board of Education minute books, Receipts, and Probate records. Browse through the records, organized by county. This database has 214,105 images. See
http://search.ancestry.com/search/db.aspx?dbid=1226.

1805-2002. *Missouri, Marriage Records* **[Online Database],** digitized and indexed at the Ancestry.com website. Source: MO State Archives. Each record may include: Groom's name, Groom's race, Groom's birth date or age, Groom's parents' names, Bride's name, Bride's race, Bride's birth date or age, Bride's parents' names, Marriage place, and Marriage date. More information may be available at the digitized document. This database has 6,334,653 records. See
http://search.ancestry.com/search/db.aspx?dbid=1171.

1807-1907. *Card Files (Index to Land Entry Files of General Land Offices, Eastern States)* **[Microfilm & Digital Capture],** from the original index cards at the Bureau of Land Management, Eastern States Office, Washington, DC. The card files serve as an index to the Tract Books, Plat Books, and Case Files relating to ten million public land sales in America. **Content:** Each card contains the following information: Certificate Number, District Land Office, Kind of entry (cash, credit, warrant, etc.), Name of Patentee (Buyer, Entryman, etc.), and county of origin, Land description, Number of acres, Date of patent, Volume, and Page where document can be located. Filmed by the Bureau of Land Management, Washington, DC, c1970, 160 rolls (including 7 rolls for Missouri GLOs), beginning with FHL film #1501676. To access the digital images, see the online FHL catalog page:
https://familysearch.org/search/catalog/511740.
- See also, **Bureau of Land Management – General Land Office Records [Online Database],** search for the name of any land purchaser of public land in the U.S. To access the search screen, see
https://glorecords.blm.gov/search/default.aspx.
- See also, **U.S. Indexed Early Land Ownership and Township Plats, 1785-1898 [Online Database],** indexed at the Ancestry.com website. This database has 165,796 records, with extracted names from the township plat maps from the Public Lands Survey in the United States initiated by the Land Ordinance Act of 1785. This collection includes maps of townships in all or parts of Alabama, Illinois, Indiana, Iowa, Kansas, Mississippi, Missouri, Ohio, Oklahoma, Oregon, Washington, and Wisconsin. The Public Lands Survey divided public lands west of the original colonies into a grid of townships and sections. A township was a square six miles to a side and contained 36 one-square-mile (or 640 acre) sections. These maps became the basis for property claims as public domain lands were transferred to private ownership. Search the entire collection by name, location, years; or browse the database by state, principal meridian, and range of Ranges/Townships.
http://search.ancestry.com/search/db.aspx?dbid=2179.

1807-1827 & 1842-1866. *Marriage Records, Ste. Genevieve County, Missouri* **[Online Database] [Online Database],** indexed at the Ancestry.com website. Source: Book, same title, by Howard W Woodruff, publ. 1970. Full text page images with an OCR index. This database has 80 pages. See
http://search.ancestry.com/Places/US/Missouri/Sainte-Genevieve/Default.aspx.

1808-1949. *Missouri Newspaper Archives* **[Online Database],** digitized and indexed newspapers at the GenealogyBank website for the following cities: Hannibal, Kansas City, Sedalia, St. Louis, and Washington, Missouri. See
www.genealogybank.com/explore/newspapers/all/usa/missouri.

1808-1853. *Divorces and Separations in Missouri* **[Printed Book & Digital Version],** compiled by Lois Stanley, George F. Wilson, and Maryhelen Wilson, publ. L. Stanley, St. Louis, MO, c1975, 35 pages, FHL book977.8 P2. To access the digital images, see the online FHL catalog:
www.familysearch.org/search/catalog/132574.

1810-1938. *Cape Girardeau and Adjoining Counties, Missouri, Cemetery Index* **[Online Database],** indexed at the Ancestry.com website. Source: Book, same title, by Elizabeth Prather Ellsberry, publ. 1965. The following cemeteries are included in the database: Akin or Kinder, Apple Creek, Baker, Bean, Bennett, Bethel, Bollinger, Born, Boss, Brent, Brinkman, Brown, Byrd, Clippard, Collins, Concord, Cracraft, Criddle, Davis, Davis, Day, Delph (Byrd), Dickman, Edinger, Eggimann, English, Erly, Ervin, Estes, Ferguson, Fleming, Foster, Fuerth, Fulbright, Fulenwider, Gladish, Grammer, Hager, Hahron, Hah's, Hampstead, Harris, Hartle, Hayden, Hays, Hilderbrand, Hines, Hitt (3), Hobbs, Hopewell, Horrell, Houck, Howard, Howard, Hoyer, Jackson, Johnson. Joyce, Juden, Kellar, Kirchoff, Klostermann, Koehler, Koker, Kurreville, Ladreiter, Laford, Lang, Lewis, Ludwig, Lueder, Lutheran, Martin, Mayfield, McKendree, Miller, Miller, Miller's, Minton, Minton, Mogler, Neely's, New Wells, Niswonger, Noland, Penrod, Pleasant Hill, Poage, Randol, Ringwald, Robertson, Rumfelt, Russell, Sachs, Schoults, Schwettman, Sheppard, Shiloh, Sides, Slagle, Smith, Snider, Statler, Stearns, Sudekum, Summers, Thompson, Tuschoff, Walker, Ware, Wilkerson, Willa, Wise, and Woodfin. Each index record includes: Name, Gender, Death age, Birth year, Death year, Burial

year, Burial place, Cemetery, Cemetery description, Spouse, and Comments. This database has 5,011 records. See
http://search.ancestry.com/search/db.aspx?dbid=5678.

1817-1819. *Enumeration of the County of St. Charles, Missouri Territory for the years 1817 and 1819: With Some Selected Marriage and Cemetery Records and a Full Surname Index* **[Printed Book]**, transcribed by Melvin B. Goe, Sr., publ. by McDowell Publications, Utica, KY, 1980, 63 pages. FHL book 977.839 X2g.

1817-1939. *Missouri Births* **[Online Database]**, an index to county birth records. Source: Missouri State Archives, Jefferson City, MO. A few church entries are included. This database has 135,466 records, see
www.familysearch.org/search/collection/2524491.

1818-1883 Missouri pioneers, New Madrid County **[Printed Book]**, compiled by Audrey L. Woodruff, published by Boyd Publications, Milledgeville, GA, 1995, 32 pages. From 1812 to 1830, New Madrid County covered an area of 23 modern Missouri counties. Includes abstracts of administrative [probate] records, Book A, 1832-1846, the 1860 mortality schedule for New Madrid County, an 1818 list of delinquent taxes for part of New Madrid County, and an 1883 list of military pensioners. Book A includes early wills and administrative bonds for intestate estates. Includes index of surnames. FHL book 977.8985 P2w.

1818-1944 Tax Lists, City of St. Louis, Missouri **[Microfilm & Digital Capture]**, of original records, as follows:
- 1818, 1820, 1822-1827, 1829, 1831-1835, 1837-1838 Tax Records, FHL film #980602.
- 1838, 1840, 1843, 1844 Tax records, FHL film #980603.
- 1844-1846 Tax records, FHL film #980604.
- 1846-1849 Tax records, FHL film #980605.
- 1849-1850 Tax records, FHL film #980606.
- 1850-1852 Tax records, FHL film #981624.
- 1852-1853, 1863, 1849 Tax records, FHL film #981625.
- 1828-1829, 1836-1837, 1843 Tax records, FHL film #981626.
- 1844, 1847-1848, 1850, 1898 Index to securities and contracts, 1900 Office plats; abstract of certified, special tax bills; and 1944 real estate tax book, FHL film #981627.
- 1824-1827, 1829, 1831 Tax records, FHL film #981628.
- 1859-1862 Collector's account; City revenue 1851-1870; and Record of real estate sales 1859, FHL film #981656.
- 1849-1851 Collector's account; Real estate assessments and collections 1860-1863; Personal property and poll tax 1862-1866, FHL film #981657.
- 1853 Account books of collection of taxes, real & personal property, Comptroller's Office, FHL film #981642.
- 1853-1904 Index card to special tax books, FHL #1001239, #1001238, and #1001240.
- 1864-1865 Individual Tax Bills Paid to St. Louis Assessor, FHL film #1005420.
- 1864-1866 Merchant, Real Estate, and Personal Tax Bills, Carondelet. FHL film # 981656.
- 1867-1869 Special Tax,; and 1863-1864 Delinquent tax claims, FHL film #981654.
- 1869-1881 St. Louis Comptroller's Office, 72 rolls, beginning with FHL film # 981637.
- 1861-1922 Special tax bills, FHL film #981653.

To access the digital images, see the online FHL catalog:
www.familysearch.org/search/catalog/219492.

1819-1826. *Missouri Taxpayers* **[Printed Book]**, compiled by Lois Stanley, George F. Wilson, and Maryhelen Wilson, published by the Southern Historical Press, Greenville, SC, 1990, 133 pages. Extracted from county tax lists in Missouri, the names are in alphabetical order by county. Includes about 14,000 names. FHL book 977.8 R4s.

1819-1900. *Ten Thousand Missouri Taxpayers* **[Printed Book]**, compiled by Sheridan K. Eddlemon, published by Heritage Books, Bowie, MD, 1996, 239 pages. FHL book 977.8 R48k.

1819-1931. *Missouri Ancestors* **[Printed Book]**, a compilation of various county records, published by Stan and Jackie Parks, Burkburnett, TX, 1980, 9 vols. Contents: vol. 1: Crawford County, index to probate records 1851-1920 and Pleasant Hill Baptist Cemetery records, compiled by Rosalea Hopper; vol. 2: Washington County deed book "A" 1821-1834 and Horine Cemetery, Richwoods, Missouri, Masonic Cemetery, Blackwell, Missouri; vol. 3: Jefferson County 1930 election poll book, DeSoto, Missouri, and Jefferson County cemeteries; vol. 4: General election poll book, DeSoto, Missouri 1928, and Jefferson County cemeteries; vol. 5: Potosi City Cemetery, Potosi, Missouri; vol. 6: Jefferson County original land entries; vol. 7: Wayne County cemeteries; vol. 8: Madison County deed books "A" & "B," 1819-1830;

and vol. 9: Jefferson County 1931 election poll book, DeSoto, Missouri, and Herculaneum Cemetery. FHL book 977.862 P22h.

1820-1874. *Missouri, Civil Marriages* **[Online Database]**, digitized and indexed at the FamilySearch.org website. Source: FamilySearch extractions from county records on microfilm at the Family History Library, Salt Lake City, UT. Currently, the index to selected marriage transcripts are from the counties of Greene, Jackson, Nodaway, and Pike counties, Missouri. Each record includes: Name, Event type, Event place, Gender, Spouse's name, and Spouse's gender. This database has 4,883 records. See https://familysearch.org/search/collection/2521615.

1820-1927. *Missouri, Cole County Circuit Court Case Files* **[Online Database]**, digitized at the FamilySearch.org website. Source: MO State Archives. This is an image only database of circuit court case files, primarily regarding disputed estates and divorces. Browse through the images, organized by case file number, then date range. This database has 185,934 records. See https://familysearch.org/search/collection/2076858.

1821-1835. *Baptisms, Church of the Immaculate Conception, New Madrid County, Missouri* [Online Database], The church was formerly St. Johns. Baptisms indexed at the RootsWeb site for New Madrid Co MO. See www.rootsweb.ancestry.com/~monewmad/nm-baptisms/nm-baptisms.htm.

1826-2014. *Jackson County, Missouri, Marriage Records* **[Online Database]**, indexed at the Ancestry.com website. This database is also accessible at the JacksonGov.org website. Each record includes: Name, Registration date, Marriage date, Marriage place, Spouse, and License number. This database has 1,408,681 records. See http://search.ancestry.com/search/db.aspx?dbid=60383.

1827-1860. *Jackson County, Missouri, Marriage Index* **[Online Database]**, indexed at the Ancestry.com website. Source: Elizabeth Prather Ellsberry's *Jackson County, Missouri Marriage Records, 1827-1860*, publ. 1965. Each record includes: Name, Gender, Marriage date, Marriage place, and Spouse. This database has 3,831 records: http://search.ancestry.com/search/db.aspx?dbid=5471.

1827-1935. *Missouri Births and Christenings* **[Online Database]**, indexed at the FamilySearch.org website. Source: FamilySearch extractions from records on microfilm at the Family History Library, Salt Lake City, UT. Each record includes: Name, Gender, Event type, Event date, Event place, Father's name, and Mother's name. This database has 66,660 records. See https://familysearch.org/search/collection/1680833.

1827-2004. *Missouri, Church Records* **[Online Database]**, Source: National Society of the Daughters of the Revolution & multiple religious organizations in Missouri. This collection contains Church records from various denominations in Missouri, 1827-2004. The record content and time period varies by denomination and locality. This database has 30,739 records, see www.familysearch.org/search/collection/2790252.

1830-1840. *Missouri, 1830 and 1840 Federal Census: Population* **[Microfilm & Digital Capture]**, filmed by the National Archives, 1950, 6 rolls, beginning with FHL film #14853 (1830: Lincoln, Marion, Chariton, Washington, Jefferson, Franklin, Gasconade, Crawford, Cole, Montgomery, Pike, St. Charles, St. Louis, Ste. Genevieve, Perry, St. Francois, and Cape Girardeau counties). To access the digital images, see the online FHL catalog: www.familysearch.org/search/catalog/745497.

1830-1870. *Missouri, Compiled Census and Census Substitutes Index* **[Online Database]**, indexed at the Ancestry.com website. Source: Accelerated Indexing Systems, Salt Lake City, UT. This collection contains the following indexes: 1830 Federal Census Index; 1830-39 Census Index; 1840 Federal Census Index; 1840 Pensioners List; 1850 Federal Census Index; 1850 Slave Schedules; 1860 Federal Census Index; 1860 Slave Schedules; 1870 Federal Census Index; Early Census Index. This database has 52,451 records: http://search.ancestry.com/search/db.aspx?dbid=3557.

1833-1843. *Greene County, Missouri Tax Assessors' List, 1833, 1834, 1835 & 1843* **[Printed Book]**, compiled by members of the Ozarks Genealogical Society, Springfield, MO, published by the society, 1988, 151 pages. During this period, Greene County comprised what is now all of the counties of: Barry, Barton, Christian, Dade, Greene, Jasper, Lawrence, McDonald, Newton, Stone and Webster, and portions of Cedar, Dallas, Douglas, Laclede, Polk, Taney, Vernon, and Wright. FHL book 977.878 R4g.

1833-1900. *Greene County Archives Material: Searchable* **[Online Database],** separate indexes to Greene County Divorces, Springfield MO Land Sales Records, Plat Records, and Naturalization Records, all at the home page of the RootsWeb site for Green Co MO. See
www.rootsweb.ancestry.com/~mogreene/test.html.

1834-1910. *Missouri, Death Records* **[Online Database],** digitized and indexed at the Ancestry.com website. Source: County death registers at the MO State Archives. Each record includes: Name, Death date, Birth date, County, Race/Ethnicity, Age, Mother's name, Father's name. The images may have more information. This database has 752,904 records:
http://search.ancestry.com/search/db.aspx?dbid=1172.

1836-1856. *Daviess County, Missouri, Marriage Index* **[Online Database],** indexed at the Ancestry.com website. Source: Book, same title, by Elizabeth Prather Ellsberry, publ. 1965. Each index records includes: Name, Gender, Marriage date, Marriage place, Spouse, and Officiant. This database has 1,322 records. See
http://search.ancestry.com/search/db.aspx?dbid=5483.

1836-1879. *Audrain County, Missouri, Marriage Records* **[Online Database],** indexed at the Ancestry.com website. Source: Book, same title, by E. P. Ellsberry, publ. 1960. A full text imaging with an OCR index. This database has 122 records. See
http://search.ancestry.com/search/db.aspx?dbid=29470.

1837-1879. *Audrain County, Missouri, Marriage Index* **[Online Database],** indexed at the Ancestry.com website. Source: Book, same title, by Elizabeth Prather Ellsberry, 1965. Each index record includes: Name, Gender, Marriage date, Marriage place, and Spouse. This database has 4,304 records:
http://search.ancestry.com/search/db.aspx?dbid=5972.

1840-1985. *Missouri, Jackson County Marriage Records* **[Online Database],** digitized and indexed at the Ancestry.com website. Source: Jackson Co Clerk's office, Kansas City, MO. Each record includes: Name, Gender, Marriage place, Record place, Spouse, Certificate number, and a link to an image of a marriage certificate. This database has 1,391,340 records. See
http://search.ancestry.com/search/db.aspx?dbid=8700.

1836 Tax List of St. Charles County, Missouri **[Printed Book],** photocopies of original records at the county courthouse in St. Charles, MO. Compiled by the St. Charles County Genealogical Society, published by the society, 1996, 40 pages. FHL book 977.839 R4e 1836.

1837 Tax List of St. Charles County, Missouri **[Printed Book],** photocopies of original records at the county courthouse in St. Charles, MO. Compiled by the St. Charles County Genealogical Society, published by the society, 1998, 50 pages. FHL book 977.839 R4s 1837.
- See also *Non-Resident Tax Lists, St. Charles Co., MO, 1836-1845*, FHL book 977.839 R4n.

1843. See *Residents of New Madrid City, 1843* **[Online Database],** indexed at the RootsWeb site for New Madrid Co MO. See
www.rootsweb.ancestry.com/~monewmad/nm-papers/nm-1845.htm.

1844 Missouri State Census, Callaway County, Missouri **[Microfilm & Digital Capture],** from the original records at the Callaway County courthouse, Fulton, MO. Filmed (with 1876 census) by the Genealogical Society of Utah, 1976, 2 rolls, FHL film #1006456. To access the digital images, see the online FHL catalog:
www.familysearch.org/search/catalog/206891.

1844-1881. *Missouri, State Census Collection* **[Online Database],** digitized and indexed at the Ancestry.com website. Source: MO State Archives. This database contains the images and index to the surviving state census records located at the MO State Archives. The following is a list of the counties and years covered in this database.
- **1844:** Callaway
- **1856:** Audrain
- **1857-1858:** St. Louis
- **1868-1869:** Cape Girardeau, Franklin
- **1873:** Cole (Jefferson City)
- **1876:** Atchison, Benton, Butler, Callaway, Cape Girardeau, Carroll, Cass, Christian, Daviess, Franklin, Gasconade, Greene, Holt, Howard, Madison, McDonald, Moniteau, Montgomery, Osage, Perry, Phelps, Reynolds, Ripley, St Francois, Stone, Texas, Webster, Worth
- **1880:** Cass (Big Creek, Pleasant Hill, City of Pleasant Hill). This is an 1880 federal census "short form."
- **1881:** Reynolds (these records are actually land list assessment records)

Information contained in this index includes: Name, Gender, County of enumeration, Marital status, Race, Age, Birth location (1857 only). Additional information about an individual may be found by viewing the corresponding image. The 1876 census recorded ages in categories according to race, gender, and age-span. Sections were also available to indicate whether a person was deaf and dumb, blind, or insane. In addition, information regarding people's livestock and agricultural products was recorded. This database has 315,589 records. See
http://search.ancestry.com/search/db.aspx?dbid=1024.

"1846 Missouri State Census, St. Joseph, Buchanan County" [Printed Article], name list in *Northwest Missouri Genealogical Society Journal,* Vol. 16, No. 1 (Apr 1996).

1847-1910. *Missouri, Birth Registers* **[Online Database],** digitized and indexed at the Ancestry.com website. Source: County birth registers at the MO State Archives. Each record includes: Name, Gender, Race/Ethnicity, Birth date, Birthplace, Father, and Mother. The images may have more information. This database has 1,986,085 records. See
http://search.ancestry.com/search/db.aspx?dbid=1170.

1848-1990. *Missouri, Western District Naturalization Index* **[Online Database],** indexed at the Ancestry.com website. Source: National Archives microfilm, records of U.S. District courts of Missouri, Kansas, and Oklahoma. This is a digitized card index to naturalization records. Each record may include: Given name and surname, Naturalization date, Birth date or age, Nationality, and reference to page/vol. no. This database has 127,004 records. See
http://search.ancestry.com/search/db.aspx?dbid=2494.

1850. *Missouri, 1850 Federal Census: Population Schedules* **[Microfilm & Digital Capture],** filmed by the National Archives, 1964, 36 rolls, beginning with FHL film #14871 (Adair, Andrew, Atchison, Audrain, and Barry counties). To access the digital images, see the online FHL catalog:
www.familysearch.org/search/catalog/744488.

1850-1902. *St. Louis City Death Records* **[Online Database],** indexed at the Ancestry.com website. Source: *Index to Death Records in the City of St. Louis, 1850-1902,* publ. 1999. This index covers all deaths recorded in the Death Registry Books for St. Louis during the period August 1850 through December 1902. There are some gaps in the records. This database has 368,300 records. See
http://search.ancestry.com/search/db.aspx?dbid=5696.

1850-1860. *Missouri, 1850 and 1860 Federal Census: Mortality Schedules Index* [Online Database]. Indexed at Ancestry.com. Original data: Ellsberry, Elizabeth Prather, comp. *Mortality Records of 1850 and Mortality Records of 1860,* Chillicothe, MO, USA: Elizabeth Prather Ellsberry, c1965. This database has 2,000 records, see
www.ancestry.com/search/collections/6052.

1850-1931. *Missouri, Death Records* **[Online Database],** digitized and indexed at Ancestry.com. Source: MO State Archives microfilm. Information contained in this database includes the following: Name of deceased, Gender, Race, Birth date or age at time of death, Death place, Death date, Father's name, Mother's name, Spouse's name, and Spouse's birth date or age. This database has 791,175 records, see
www.ancestry.com/search/collections/1172.

1851-1900. *Missouri Marriages* **[Online Database],** indexed at the Ancestry.com website. Source: Jordan Dodd, compiler, from extractions of county marriage records on microfilm at the Family History Library, Salt Lake City, UT. Each record includes: Name, Spouse's name, Marriage date, and Marriage county. This database has 116,919 records. See
http://search.ancestry.com/search/db.aspx?dbid=4474.

1856-1942. *Missouri, Federal Naturalization Records* **[Online Database],** indexed at the Ancestry.com website. Source: National Archives microfilm of Naturalization Indexes, Petitions, and Declarations from U.S. District Courts in Missouri Searchable fields include: Name, Birth Date, Birthplace, and Immigration Year. Additional information that may be provided in the original records includes: Place of Residence; Occupation; Date of Departure; Place of Departure; Place of Arrival; Spouse's Name, Birth Date, and Residence; Number of Children, Each child's Name, Birth Date, Birthplace, and Residence. This database has 72,971 records. See
http://search.ancestry.com/search/db.aspx?dbid=61203.

1852 Missouri State Census, St. Charles County, Missouri **[Printed Book],** extracted from originals at the St. Charles city clerk's office and the county clerk's office, by Mary Ethel Buschmeyer, Eunice Webbink, and Vera Haeussermann, published by Lineage Press, Bridgeton, MO, 1985, 63 pages. FHL book 977.839 X2st.

1856-1970. *Missouri, United Methodist Church Records* **[Online Database],** digitized and indexed at the Ancestry.com website. Source: MO United Methodist Commission on Archives and History, Fayette, MO. This collection contains indexed images of United Methodist Church registers from Missouri. The registers may contain baptisms, marriages, burials, memberships, and lists of clergy. Browse through the church registers, organized by the churches located at Armstrong, Berger, Bethel, Brighton, Conway, Crandall, Edgerton, Ferguson, Goodman, Miami, Missouri Valley, Moundville, Richwoods, Rocheport, Rockville, Salem, St. Joseph, St. Louis, Summersville, Swans Prairie, Vanduser, Vinta Park, and Woodlandville, Missouri. This database has 77,792 records. See
http://search.ancestry.com/search/db.aspx?dbid=60969.

1860. *Missouri, 1860 Federal Census: Population Schedules* **[Microfilm & Digital Capture],** filmed by the National Archives, 72 rolls, beginning with FHL film #803605 (2nd filming: Adair and Andrew counties). To access the digital images, see the online FHL catalog:
www.familysearch.org/search/catalog/705435.

1861-1865. *Missouri, Civil War Service Records of Union Soldiers* **[Online Database],** indexed at the FamilySearch.org website (with a link to the images at the Fold3 website). Source: National Archives microfilm series M405. The records include a jacket-envelope for each soldier, labeled with his name, his rank, and the unit in which he served. The jacket-envelope typically contains card abstracts of entries relating to the soldier as found in original muster rolls, returns, rosters, payrolls, appointment books, hospital registers, prison registers and rolls, parole rolls, inspection reports; and the originals of any papers relating solely to the particular soldier. This database has 2,099,748 records. See
https://familysearch.org/search/collection/1932408.

1861-1865. *Missouri, Civil War Service Records of Confederate Soldiers* **[Online Database],** indexed at the FamilySearch.org website (with a link to the images at the Fold3 website). Source: National Archives microfilm series M322. The records include a jacket-envelope for each soldier, labeled with his name, his rank, and the unit in which he served. The jacket-envelope typically contains card abstracts of entries relating to the soldier as found in original muster rolls, returns, rosters, payrolls, appointment books, hospital registers, Union prison registers and rolls, parole rolls, inspection reports; and the originals of any papers relating solely to the particular soldier. This database has 348,259 records. See
https://familysearch.org/search/collection/1932374.

1861. *Adjutant General's Report of Missouri State Militia for 1861* **[Online Database],** indexed at the Ancestry.com website. Source: Report, publ. 1962. This database has 16 pages. See
http://search.ancestry.com/search/db.aspx?dbid=29985.

1861-1865. *Missouri Confederate Death Records* **[Online Database],** indexed at the Ancestry.com website. Source: database, same title, compiled by Kenneth Weant, publ. 1999, from a list originally published in the *St. Louis Republic,* 1895. Each record includes: Soldier's name, County of residence, Location and/or cause of death, and Death Date. This database has 2,002 records. See
http://search.ancestry.com/search/db.aspx?dbid=3697.

1861-1865. *Missouri Confederate Volunteers* **[Online Database],** indexed at the Ancestry.com website. Source: database, same title, compiled by Debra Graden, publ. 1999, taken from *History of the First and Second Missouri Confederate Brigades, 1861-1865,* publ. 1879. Each record includes: Name, Unit, Residence, and Occupation. This database has 1,629 records. See
http://search.ancestry.com/search/db.aspx?dbid=3736.

1862-1866 Internal Revenue Assessment Lists for the State of Missouri **[Microfilm & Digital Capture],** from the originals at the National Archives, Washington, DC. Names are in alphabetical order by first letters of surnames only. Names are grouped by the divisions of each tax district. Typically, each roll of film contains several divisions. Filmed by the National Archives, series M0776, 1984, 22 rolls, District 1 (St. Louis), beginning with FHL film #1695299 (District 1, St. Louis Co, 1862). To access the digital images, see the online FHL catalog:
https://familysearch.org/search/catalog/479008.

1864 Missouri State Census, Gasconade County, Missouri **[Printed Book],** photocopies of original documents at the Gasconade County courthouse, Hermann, MO, reproduced and indexed by Robert E.

Parkin, published by Genealogical Research and Productions, 1980, 64 pages. FHL book 977.861 X2e and FHL film #6075652.

1865-1872. *Missouri, Freedmen's Bureau Field Office Records* **[Online Database],** digitized at the FamilySearch.org website. Source: National Archives microfilm series M1908. This is an image only database. The Bureau of Refugees, Freedmen, and Abandoned Lands (often called the Freedmen's Bureau) was created in 1865 at the end of the American Civil War to supervise relief efforts including education, health care, food and clothing, refugee camps, legalization of marriages, employment, labor contracts, and securing back pay, bounty payments and pensions. These records include letters and endorsements sent and received, account books, applications for rations, applications for relief, court records, labor contracts, registers of bounty claimants, registers of complaints, registers of contracts, registers of disbursements, registers of freedmen issued rations, registers of patients, reports, rosters of officers and employees, special and general orders and circulars received, special orders and circulars issued, records relating to claims, court trials, property restoration, and homesteads. Browse through the images, organized by 1) A descriptive pamphlet. 2) List of book records. And 3) Office of the disbursing officer (correspondence). This database has 24,504 records. See
https://familysearch.org/search/collection/2333775.

1867-1933. *Missouri, Quaker Records Index* **[Online Database],** indexed at the Ancestry.com website. Source: Missouri Monthly Meetings: Fairfield, Kansas City, Jackson County, and Jasper County, Missouri. This database contains records of Quaker Meetings for the late 19th and early 20th centuries. The data includes records of marriages, deaths, births, and other events for those living in the western portion of the state. This database has 2,604 records. See
http://search.ancestry.com/search/db.aspx?dbid=4998.

1867-1976. *Missouri Deaths and Burials* **[Online Database],** indexed at the FamilySearch.org website. Source: FamilySearch extractions from records on microfilm at the Family History Library, Salt Lake City, UT. Each record includes: Name, Gender, Death date, Death place, Age, Birth date, Birthplace, Occupation, Race, and Marital status. This database has 58,813 records. See
https://familysearch.org/search/collection/1680837.

1868 Missouri State Census, Cape Girardeau County, Missouri **[Microfilm & Digital Capture],** from the original records at the Cape Girardeau County courthouse, Jackson, Missouri. Filmed (with 1876 census) by the Genealogical Society of Utah, 1976, 1 roll, FHL film #1006668. To access the digital images, see the online FHL catalog:
www.familysearch.org/search/catalog/262333.

1868 Missouri State Census, St. Charles County, Missouri **[Printed Book],** transcribed from originals at the County Clerk of St. Charles County by Carrol Geerling, published by Lineage Press, Bridgeton, MO, 1988, 212 pages. FHL book 977.839 X2g.

1869 Census of Carondelet (now part of St. Louis, Missouri) **[Microfilm & Digital Capture],** from the originals by Carondelet city assessor, Filmed by the City of St. Louis, 1963, FHL film #981654. To access the digital images, see the online FHL catalog:
www.familysearch.org/search/catalog/219775.

1869-1964. **Daviess County, Missouri, Cemetery Index** **[Online Database],** indexed at the Ancestry.com website. Source: Book, same title, by Elizabeth Prather Ellsberry, 1965. Each index record includes: Name, Birth date, Death date, Burial place, Cemetery, and Description. This database has 2,976 records. See
http://search.ancestry.com/search/db.aspx?dbid=5707.

1870. *Missouri, 1870 Federal Census: Population Schedules* **[Microfilm & Digital Capture],** filmed by the National Archives, 97 rolls, beginning with FHL film #552254 (2nd filming: Adair and Andrew counties). To access the digital images, see the online FHL catalog:
www.familysearch.org/search/catalog/698906.

1870-1917. *Audrain County, Missouri Marriages* **[Online Database],** indexed at the Ancestry.com website. Source: Book same title, by Kenneth E. Weant, 2004. Each index record includes: Groom's name, Bride's name, Marriage date, and Volume & Page. This database has 8,715 records. See
http://search.ancestry.com/search/db.aspx?dbid=7586.

1873-1976. *Missouri, Deaths and Burials Index* **[Online Database],** indexed at the Ancestry.com website. Source: FamilySearch extractions from records on microfilm at the Family History Library, Salt Lake City, UT. Each record may include: Name,

Birth date, Birthplace, Age, Occupation, Race, Marital status, Gender, Residence, Street address, Date of death, Place of death, Date of burial, Place of burial, Cemetery, Father's name and birthplace, Mother's name and birthplace, Spouse's name, and FHL film number. This database has 36,148 records. See http://search.ancestry.com/search/db.aspx?dbid=2569.

1875-1887. See *Howell County, Missouri, Personal Property Tax Books, 1875 & 1885 and West Plains, Missouri, School Records, 1884-1887* **[Printed Book]**, compiled by Jacqueline Hogan Williams and Betty Harvey Williams, published by the authors, Warrensburg, MO, 1973, 61 pages. Includes index. FHL book 977.885 R4w.

1875-1920. *Missouri, Marriages* **[Online Database]**, This is a name index to marriage records from the state of Missouri. Microfilm copies of these records are available at the Family History Library. This database has 192,361 records and 3,971,477 names, see **www.familysearch.org/search/collection/1680838**.

1876 Missouri State Census, Benton County, Missouri **[Microfilm & Digital Capture]**, from the original records at the Benton County courthouse, Warsaw, MO. Filmed by the Genealogical Society of Utah, 1973, 1 roll, FHL film #945728. To access the digital images, see the online FHL catalog: **www.familysearch.org/search/catalog/53898**.
- See also, *1876 Benton County, Missouri State Census* **[Printed Index]**, compiled by Jacqueline Hogan Williams and Betty Harvey Williams, published by the authors, Warrensburg, MO, 1969, 119 pages, FHL book 977.849 X2p.

1876 Missouri State Census, Butler County, Missouri **[Printed Book]**, photocopies of original documents at the Butler County Courthouse, Poplar Bluff, MO, compiled by Thelma S. McManus and Robert E. Parkin, published by Genealogical Research & Publications, 1981, 80 pages. Includes index. FHL book 977.893 X2e. See also **"1876 Missouri State Census Index, Butler County"** **[Printed Article]**, in *Area Footprints*, Vol. 10, No. 3-4

1876 Missouri State Census, Callaway County, Missouri **[Microfilm & Digital Capture]**, from the original records at the Callaway County courthouse, Fulton, MO. Filmed (with 1844 census) by the Genealogical Society of Utah, 1976, 2 rolls, FHL film #1006456. To access the digital images, see the online FHL catalog: **www.familysearch.org/search/catalog/206891**.

1876 Missouri State Census, Cape Girardeau County, Missouri **[Microfilm & Digital Capture]**, from the originals at the Cape Girardeau County courthouse, Jackson, Missouri. Filmed with the 1868 census by the Genealogical Society of Utah, 1976, 2 rolls, FHL film #100666-1000667. To access the digital images, see the online FHL catalog: **www.familysearch.org/search/catalog/262333**.

1876 Missouri State Census, Christian County **[Microfilm & Digital Capture]**, from the original records at the Christian County courthouse, Ozark, MO. Filmed by the Genealogical Society of Utah, 1973, 1 roll, FHL film #931909. To access the digital images, see the online FHL catalog: **www.familysearch.org/search/catalog/314298**.

1876. *An Index to 1876 Census of Greene County, Missouri* **[Printed Book]**, compiled by the Greene County Archives and Records Center, Springfield, MO, 1992, 202 pages. FHL book 977.878 X22es.

1876 Missouri State Census, Holt County, Missouri **[Microfilm & Digital Capture]**, from the original records in the Holt County courthouse, Oregon, Missouri. Arranged by township and range numbers. Filmed by the Genealogical Society of Utah, 1976, 1 roll, FHL film #1005363. To access the digital images, see the online FHL catalog: **www.familysearch.org/search/catalog/236270**.

1876 Missouri State Census, Howard County, Missouri **[Microfilm & Digital Capture]**, from the originals at the County Clerk's office, Fayette, Missouri. Filmed by the Genealogical Society of Utah, 1974, 1 roll, FHL film #963407. To access the digital images, see the online FHL catalog: **www.familysearch.org/search/catalog/90921**.

1876 Census of the County of Iron, State of Missouri **[Printed Book]**, from originals at the Iron County Courthouse, Ironton, MO. Information transcribed by Millie and Edward Preissle, published by the authors, Houston, MO, c1985, 194 pages. Includes index. FHL book 977.8883 X2c and FHL film #1320670.

1876 Missouri State Census, McDonald County, Missouri **[Microfilm & Digital Capture],** from the original records at the Recorder of Deeds, McDonald County courthouse, Pineville, MO. Filmed by the Genealogical Society of Utah, 1984, 1 roll, FHL film #930080. Another filming, #1016634. To access the digital images, see the online FHL catalog: www.familysearch.org/search/catalog/390424.
- See also **"1876 Missouri State Census, McDonald County" [Printed Article],** in *Newton County Roots*, Vol. 4, No. 3 (Sep 1992).

1876 Missouri State Census, Moniteau County, Missouri, by Township **[Microfilm],** from the original manuscript at a private residence in California, Missouri. Filmed by the Missouri State Archives, 1983, 1 roll FHL film #1759291. To see if this microfilm was digitized yet, see the online FHL catalog: www.familysearch.org/search/catalog/457092.

1876 Census, Montgomery County, Missouri **[Printed Book],** extracted and published by Mid-Missouri Genealogical Society, Jefferson City, Missouri, 1996, 191 pages. Includes index. FHL book 977.8382 X2c.

1876. *County of Perry, State of Missouri, 1876* **[Printed Book],** compiled by Bill Bow for the Perry County Historical Society, Perryville, Missouri, 1989, 56 pages. Includes 1876 census; and some 1875-1876 articles from the Weekly Perryville Union. FHL book 977.8694 X2c.

1876 Missouri State Census, Phelps County, Missouri **[Printed Book],** from originals at the Phelps County Clerk's office, Rolla, MO. Copy transcribed by John E.C. Simmons, published by the author, St. John, MO, 1987, 3 pages, 238 columns. FHL book 977.8594 X2s.
- See also, **"1876 Missouri State Census, Phelps County" [Printed Article],** in *Phelps County Genealogical Society Quarterly*, Vol. 4, No. 2 (Apr 1988) through Vol. 5, No. 3 (Jul 1989).

1876 Missouri State Census, Reynolds County **[Microfilm & Digital Capture],** from originals at the County Clerk's office, Centerville, Missouri. Filmed by the Genealogical Society of Utah, 1977, as *Census Record, 1876*, FHL film #1016081. To access the digital images, see the online FHL catalog: www.familysearch.org/search/catalog/389088.

1876 Missouri State Census of St. Charles County, Missouri **[Printed Book],** transcribed and indexed by Carrol Geerling, published by Lineage Press, Bridgeton, MO, 1988, 333 pages.

1876 Missouri State Census, St. Francois County, Missouri **[Microfilm & Digital Capture],** from the original records at the St. Francois County Clerk's office, Farmington, Missouri. filmed by the Genealogical Society of Utah, 1976, 1 roll, FHL film #1006662. To access the digital images, see the online FHL catalog: www.familysearch.org/search/catalog/262293.

1876 Census, County of Texas, State of Missouri: Books One and Two **[Printed Book],** transcribed by Edward and Millie Preissle, published by Texas County Missouri Genealogical Society, Houston, MO, 1983, 180 pages. Includes surname index. Includes Boone, Carroll, Current, Date, Jackson, Lynch, Ozark, Ribidoux, Sherrill, and Upton townships. Parts of Clinton, Morris, Pierce, and Piney townships are also included. FHL book 977.884 X2c; FHL film #1597827; and microfiche # 6005969.

1876-1905. *Audrain County, Missouri Deaths* **[Online Database],** indexed at the Ancestry.com website. Source: Kenneth E. Weant's Selected Articles from the Mexico Weekly Ledger, 2001. Each index records includes: Name, Death date, and Issue date. This database has 21,670 records. See http://search.ancestry.com/search/db.aspx?dbid=7696.

1876-1906. *Index to Naturalization Records, U.S. District Court, Missouri Central Division* [Microfilm & Digital Capture], from the originals at the National Archives, Kansas City, MO. Filmed by the Genealogical Society of Utah, 1991, 1 roll, FHL film #1750543. To access the digital images, see the online FHL catalog: www.familysearch.org/search/catalog/437159.

1878. *Missouri Biographical Dictionary* **[Online Database],** digitized and indexed at the Ancestry.com website. Source: Book, same title, publ. 1878. This database has 1,103 pages. See http://search.ancestry.com/search/db.aspx?dbid=7980.

"1879-1880 Missouri Prisoners" [Printed Article & Digital Version], in *Genealogical Reference Builders Newsletter*, Vol. 10, No. 4 (1976). To access the digital version, see the online FHL catalog: www.familysearch.org/search/catalog/2526708.

1880. *Missouri, 1880 Federal Census: Soundex and Population Schedules* **[Microfilm & Digital Capture],** filmed by the National Archives, 185 rolls, beginning with FHL film #1254671 (Adair, Andrew, and Atchison counties). To access the digital images (Population Schedules), see the online FHL catalog: www.familysearch.org/search/catalog/676481.

1880-2009. *St. Louis, Missouri, St. Louis Post-Dispatch Obituary Index* **[Online Database],** indexed at the Ancestry.com website. This database is also accessible at the St. Louis Public Library website. Ancestry's index includes: Name, Death date, Publication date, Notes, and a link to the Obituary Search webpage of the St. Louis Public Library. This database has 516,250 records. See http://search.ancestry.com/search/db.aspx?dbid=70465.

1880-2011. *Missouri, St. Louis Public Library Obituary Index* **[Online Database],** indexed at the Ancestry.com website. This database is also accessible at the St. Louis Public Library website. Ancestry's index includes: Name, Death date, Publication date, Notes, and a link to the *Obituary Search* webpage of the St. Louis Public Library. This database has 1,083,256 records. See http://search.ancestry.com/search/db.aspx?dbid=9197.

1883-1927. *Missouri, County Naturalization Records* **[Online Database],** digitized at the FamilySearch.org website. Source: Clinton County Courthouse, Plattsburg, MO. This is an image only database, currently with Intentions, Petitions, and Naturalization records from Clinton Co MO only. Browse through the records, organized by county, then Record type, Year range, and Vol. No. This database has 898 records. See https://familysearch.org/search/collection/1880587.

1883-1930. *Missouri Deaths* **[Online Database],** digitized at the FamilySearch.org website. Source: MSA, Jefferson City. This is an image only database. Currently, the database has the images of county death registers for Andrew, Audrain, Buchanan, Cape Girardeau, Clinton, Cole, Howard, Jefferson, Macon, Marion, Monroe, Morgan, Scotland, Texas, and Warren County, Missouri. Browse through the images, organized by county, then Year range. This database has 13,734 images. See https://familysearch.org/search/collection/2448947.

1885-1903. *Audrain County, Missouri Obituaries* **[Online Database],** indexed at the Ancestry.com website. Source: Book, same title, edited by Kenneth Weant, 1999. Each index record includes: Last name, First name, Age or DOB, and Date of death. This database has 5,419 records. See http://search.ancestry.com/search/db.aspx?dbid=3927.

1887-1901. *Buchanan County, Missouri Taxpayers List* **[Printed Book],** compiled by Debra Graden, published by Grey Ink, Leavenworth, KS, 2001, 4 vols. Compiled from portions of the Hoye city directories. Contains names, townships, and post offices of taxpayers. Contents: Vol. 1: Taxpayers from St. Joseph, Missouri, 1887-1890; Vol. 2: Taxpayers from Buchanan County, Missouri (excluding St. Joseph, Missouri), 1902-1906; Vol. 3: Taxpayers from Buchanan County, Missouri (excluding St. Joseph, Missouri) 1891-1895 [and] 1896-1901, FHL book 977.8132 R4g, vol. 1-4.

1890 Census Substitute **[Online Database],** indexed at the Ancestry.com website. This is Ancestry's collection of city directories (and other name lists) from all over the U.S. for the time of the lost 1890 federal census. Included are city directories for Kansas City, St. Joseph, and St. Louis, Missouri. Go to *View All Collections Included in this Search* for a complete list of databases, alphabetically by place (county, city, state), and year. See http://search.ancestry.com/search/group/1890census.

1890 Real Estate Tax Book Index, St. Charles County, Missouri **[Printed Book],** compiled by Colleen Heitmann Schaeper, published by St. Charles County Genealogical Society, St. Charles, MO, 1999, 50 pages. FHL book 977.839 R42s 1890. See also *1890 School Tax Book Index, St. Charles County, Missouri* **[Printed Book],** compiled by Maryalee Roellig, published by St. Charles County Genealogical Society, St. Charles, Missouri, 1999, 73 pages, FHL book 977.839 R42r.

1897-1950. *Missouri, Confederate Pension Applications and Soldiers Home Applications* **[Online Database],** digitized at the FamilySearch.org website. Source: MO State Archives. These records are digital images of Confederate pension files and applications for admission to the Confederate soldiers' home. The pensions are for Confederate veterans who were living

in Missouri, although they may have enlisted from another state. The Confederate Soldiers' Home in Higginsville, Missouri, was open for infirm and dependent former Confederate soldiers and sailors, their wives, widows, and orphans. Browse through the images, organized by Pension Applications (Approved or Disapproved), then in alpha groups, A to Z; and by Soldiers Home Applications (Approved or Disapproved), A to Z. This database has 27,874 records. See
https://familysearch.org/search/collection/1865475.

1899. *Encyclopedia of the History of St. Louis: A Compendium of History and Biography for Ready Reference* **[Online Database],** digitized and indexed at the Ancestry.com website. Source: Book, same title, 4 vols., publ. New York, 1899. This database has 2,901 pages. See
http://search.ancestry.com/search/db.aspx?dbid=23727.

1900. *Missouri, 1900 Federal Census: Soundex and Population Schedules* **[Microfilm & Digital Capture],** filmed by the National Archives, 373 rolls, beginning with FHL film #1240836 (Adair, Andrew, and Atchison counties). To access the digital images, see the online FHL catalog:
www.familysearch.org/search/catalog/637143.

1900-1941. *Missouri, Pre-WWII Adjutant General Enlistment Contracts* **[Online Database],** digitized at the FamilySearch.org website. This collection includes records from the Missouri State Archives and from FamilySearch. This is an image only database, with digital images of enlistment papers and extracts from a soldier's service record for members of the Missouri National Guard. Includes records from all counties in Missouri. There are details about a person's birth, residence, physical exam results, and multiple pages of information concerning a person's enlistment. Browse through the images, organized in 450 alpha groups of about 1,300 names each, Aarant, Herald-Abbott, William to Zieba, Michael-Zytowski, Knighten T. This database has 607,070 records. See
https://familysearch.org/search/collection/2576872.

1901. *Missouri History Encyclopedia,* **[Online Database],** digitized and indexed at the Ancestry.com website. Source: Book, same title, 6 vols., publ. 1901. This database has 4,060 pages. See
http://search.ancestry.com/search/db.aspx?dbid=8553.

1904-1916. *Audrain County, Missouri Obituaries* **[Online Database],** indexed at the Ancestry.com website. Source: Book, same title, edited by Kenneth Weant, 1999. Each index record includes: Name, Age/Birth date, and death date. This database has 4,531 records. See
http://search.ancestry.com/search/db.aspx?dbid=4025.

1908. *A history of Missouri: From the Earliest Explorations and Settlements Until the Admission of the State into the Union* **[Online Database],** digitized and indexed at the Ancestry.com website. Source: Book, same title, publ. 1908. This database has 1,231 pages. See
http://search.ancestry.com/search/db.aspx?dbid=22578.

1910. *Missouri, 1910 Federal Census: Soundex and Population Schedules* **[Microfilm & Digital Capture],** filmed by the National Archives, c1970, 348 rolls, beginning with FHL film #1374779 (Adair, Andrew, and Atchison counties). To access the digital images, see the online FHL catalog:
www.familysearch.org/search/catalog/638147.

1910-1962. *Missouri, Death Certificates* **[Online Database],** indexed at the Ancestry.com website. This database is also accessible at the MO State Archives Digital Heritage website. Ancestry's index has a Name, Date of Death, Death place, and Certificate number only. At any record, go to the MO State Archives site to view the death certificate image for full details. This database has 2,413,021 records. See
http://search.ancestry.com/search/db.aspx?dbid=60382.

1916. See *Missouri National Guard, the Mexican Border, 1916* **[Online Database],** indexed at the Ancestry.com website. Source: Reports of the Adjutant General of Missouri, publ. 1915-1916. Each record includes: Name, Rank, Company, Regiment, Page No., and Place organized. This database has 6,274 records:
http://search.ancestry.com/search/db.aspx?dbid=4028.
- See also, *The Service of the Missouri National Guard on the Mexican Border, Under the President's order of June 18, 1916: With a Roster* **[Online Database],** digitized and indexed at the Ancestry.com website. Source: Report of the Adjutant General, publ. 1919. This database has 589 images. See
http://search.ancestry.com/search/db.aspx?dbid=25642.

1917-1929. *Audrain County, Missouri Obituaries* **[Online Database],** indexed at the Ancestry.com website. Source: Book, same title, edited by Kenneth Weant, 1999. Each index record includes: Given name, Surname, County/State of death, Death date, and Issue date. This database has 4,176 records. See
http://search.ancestry.com/search/db.aspx?dbid=3964.

1920. *Missouri, 1920 Federal Census: Soundex and Population Schedules* **[Microfilm & Digital Capture],** filmed by the National Archives, c1970, 334 rolls, beginning with FHL film #1820902 (Adair, Andrew, and Barton counties). To access the digital images (Population Schedules), see the online FHL catalog: www.familysearch.org/search/catalog/574799.

1921 History. See *Centennial History of Missouri (The Center State): One Hundred Years in the Union, 1820-1921* **[Printed Book & Digital Version],** by Walter Barlow Stevens, published by S.J. Clarke Pub. Co., St. Louis, 1921, 7 vols., FHL book 977.8 H2s. To access the digital version, see the online FHL catalog: www.familysearch.org/search/catalog/257209.
- See also, *Centennial History of Missouri, Deluxe Supplement* **[Printed Book & Digital Version],** by Stevens, publ. Clarke, St. Louis, 1921, 421 pages, filmed by W.C. Cox & Co., 1974, 1 roll, FHL 1000274. To access the digital images, see the online FHL catalog: www.familysearch.org/search/catalog/338781.
- See also, *Biographical Index to the Centennial History of Missouri: Vols 3 & 6,* compiled and published by Mrs. Leister E. Presley, Searcy, AR, 19??, 21 pages. FHL book 977.8 H2s index.
- See also *Biographical Index to the Centennial History of Missouri: Volumes III, IV, V, and VI,* by Elizabeth B. Langley, Billings, Missouri, 1968, 22 pages. FHL book 977.8 H2s index.

1921-1924. See *Report of the Adjutant General of Missouri, January 10, 1921 - December 31, 1924* **[Online Database],** digitized and indexed at the Ancestry.com website. Source: Report of the Adjutant General, publ. 1925. Index and images of rosters. This database has 171 pages. See
http://search.ancestry.com/search/db.aspx?dbid=27186.

1928-1956. *Missouri, Jackson County Voter Registration Records* **[Online Database],** digitized at the FamilySearch.org website. Source: Midwest Missouri Genealogy Center, Independence, MO. This image only database is a collection is digital images of voter registration books from Jackson County, Missouri. The information in the registers includes the voter's name, address, birthplace, race (color), term of residence, township and voting precinct. Browse through the images, organized by Blue Township, Brooking Township, Fort Osage Township, Sni-A-Bar Township, or Washington Township, then by Precinct Number, and Date Range. This database has 61,961 records. See
https://familysearch.org/search/collection/1992425.

1930. *Missouri, 1930 Federal Census: Population Schedules* **[Microfilm & Digital Capture],** filmed by the National Archives, c1970, 78 rolls, beginning with FHL film #2340909 (Adair and Andrew counties). To access the digital images, see the online FHL catalog: www.familysearch.org/search/catalog/1037435.

1930-1942. Audrain County, Missouri Obituaries [Online Database], indexed at the Ancestry.com website. Source: Book, same title, edited by Kenneth Weant, 1999. Each index record includes: Name, Age/Birth date, and Death date. This database has 4,860 records. See
http://search.ancestry.com/search/db.aspx?dbid=4100.

1940. *Missouri, 1940 Federal Census: Population Schedules* **[Digital Capture],** digitized images from the microfilm of original records held by the Bureau of the Census in the 1940s. After microfilming, Congress allowed the Census Bureau to destroy the originals to free up space for WWII-related files. Digitizing of the 1940 census schedules microfilm images was done for the National Archives and made public on April 2, 2012. To access the digital images, see the online FHL catalog page:
www.familysearch.org/search/catalog/2057776.

1940 Federal Census Finding Aids **[Online Database].** The National Archives prepared a special website online with a detailed description of the 1940 federal census. Included at the site are descriptions of location finding aids, such as Enumeration District maps, Geographic Descriptions of Census Enumeration Districts, and a list of 1940 City Directories available at the National Archives. The finding aids are all linked to other National Archives sites. The National Archives website also has a link to 1940 Search Engines using Stephen P. Morse's "One-Step" system for finding a 1940 E.D. or street address conversion. See
www.archives.gov/research/census/1940/general-info.html#questions.

1940-1945. *World War II Draft Registration Cards* **[Online Database],** Draft registration cards of men who registered during World War II, with the exception of the fourth registration. Images courtesy of Ancestry. The event place is the residence of the registrant. This database has 952,820 records, see www.familysearch.org/search/collection/2759143.

1941-1946. *Missouri, Reports of Separation Notices* **[Online Database],** indexed at the FamilySearch.org website. Index and images of World War II Reports of Separation, 1941-1946. The records are located at the Missouri State Archives in Jefferson City. This database has 316,539 records. See https://familysearch.org/search/collection/2392705.

1958-1963. *Missouri, Passenger Lists* **[Online Database],** digitized and indexed at the Ancestry.com website. Source: National Archives microfilm series A4194 (St. Louis) and A3511 (Kansas City), *Passenger & Crew Manifests of Airplanes Arriving at St. Louis and Kansas City, Missouri.* Each record includes: Name, Nationality, Age, Birth date, Birthplace, Arrival date, Arrival port, Airline, and Flight number. This database has 1,127 pages. See http://search.ancestry.com/search/db.aspx?dbid=9114.

1988-Current. *Missouri Recent Newspaper Obituaries* **[Online Database],** digitized and indexed newspaper obituaries at the GenealogyBank website, including newspapers for Ashland, Aurora, Belle-Fontaine-Neighbors, Belton, Bethany, Blue Springs, Boonville, Bowling Green, Brookfield, Byrnes Mill, California, Camdenton, Carthage, Chesterfield, Chillicothe, Farmington, Festus, Florissant-Blackjack, Fredericktown, Fulton, Grandview, Greenfield-Miller, Hannibal, Harrisonville, Hazelwood, Independence, Jefferson City, Joplin, Kansas City, Kirksville, Kirkwood, Lake Ozark, Laurie, Lebanon, Lee's Summit, Macon, Mansfield, Marshfield, Maryville, Mexico, Moberly, Monett, Neosho, Noel-Lanagan, O'Fallon, Oakville, Overland, Ozark, Park Hills, Raytown, Rolla, Sedalia, Seymour, St. Charles, St. James, St. Joseph, St. Louis, St. Peters, St. Robert, Stockton, Town and Country, Warrenton, Waynesville, Wentzville, and West Plains. See www.genealogybank.com/explore/obituaries/all/usa/missouri

2002-2010. *Jackson County, Missouri, Marriage Index* **[Online Database],** indexed at the Ancestry.com website. This database is also accessible at the JacksonGov.org website. Each record includes: Name, Spouse, Marriage date, and Marriage place. This database has 90,973 records. See http://search.ancestry.com/search/db.aspx?dbid=70488.

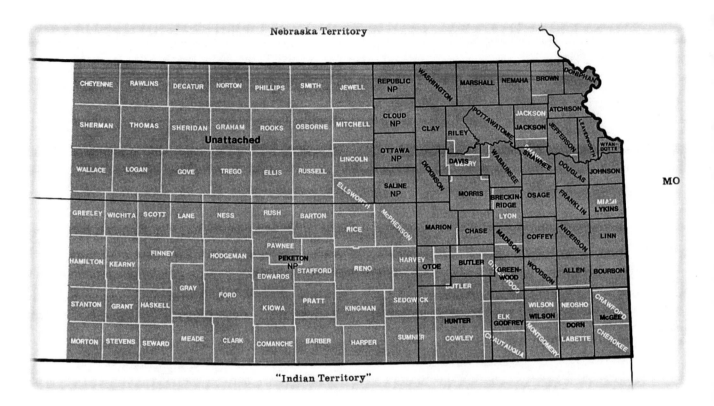

Kansas Territory • 1860. The map above shows the counties of Kansas Territory at the time of the June 1860 Federal Census. Shown in white are the 105 current counties of Kansas; shown in black are the 1860 county boundaries. Kansas Territory was created as part of the 1854 Kansas-Nebraska Act and became a state in 1861. For detailed maps of the Indian cessions in Kansas, see the Index to Maps (Map 26 and Map 27) at the **Indian Land Cessions** website. See **http://usgwarchives.net/maps/cessions.** From 1854 to 1861, both Kansas and Nebraska territories extended from the Missouri River to the Continental Divide (See the 1860 map on page 46). Colorado Territory was created in 1861, taken from parts of four territories: Utah, New Mexico, Nebraska, and Kansas territories. Not shown on the map is Arapahoe County, Kansas Territory, now a Colorado county. Five "paper counties" shown on the map were created in anticipation of people moving into them. They are marked "NP" for "No Population." Map Source: Page 118, *Map Guide to the U.S. Federal Censuses, 1790-1920,* by William Thorndale and William Dollarhide.

Kansas
Censuses & Substitute Name Lists

Historical Timeline for Kansas, 1540-1996

1540. Spaniard Francisco Vasquez de Coronado came searching for the Seven Cities of Cibola. Coronado never found the cities of gold, but he did find the Gulf of California, the Colorado River, the Grand Canyon, parts of present southern Utah and Colorado; and areas of southwest Kansas. He claimed the entire region as an addition to New Spain. The route Coronado followed in present Colorado and Kansas would later be called the Santa Fe Trail.

1609. Governor Pedro de Peralta founded Santa Fe as the new capital of the Spanish Province of Nuevo Mexico. In 1609, the Spanish map of New Spain encompassed lands visited by Coronado in 1540, including areas of present Colorado and Kansas along the Arkansas River Valley.

1673. Mississippi River. French explorers Jacques Jolliet and Louis Marquette left their base in Sault Ste. Marie and made their way to the Illinois River, which they descended to become the first Frenchmen to discover the Mississippi River. They floated down the Mississippi as far south as the mouth of the Arkansas River before returning to the Great Lakes area.

1682. Louisiana. Following the same route as Jolliet and Marquette, René-Robert Cavelier (Sieur de LaSalle) floated down the Mississippi River, continuing all the way to its mouth at the Gulf of Mexico. He then claimed the entire Mississippi Basin for Louis XIV of France, for whom Louisiana was named. The present Kansas watersheds of the Arkansas, Kansas, and Missouri Rivers were part of Louisiana.

1685-1720. La Louisiane Française extended from the Highlands (Terra Haute) on the Wabash River, down the Ohio and Mississippi Rivers to the Gulf of Mexico. Forts and settlements established by the French in the Mississippi Basin during this period included Prairie du Chien in 1685; Arkansas Post in 1686; Kaskaskia in 1703; Natchez, in 1716; New Orleans in 1718; Baton Rouge in 1719; and Fort de Charles in 1720. Of these settlements, just two of them included farming activities (Prairie du Chien and Arkansas Post), the others were mostly trading posts established to support the French Fur Trade.

1721. French and German colonists abandoned Arkansas Post, the largest settlement of all of French Louisiana. As a failed farming community, Arkansas Post was typical of the French efforts to colonize North America south of the Great Lakes. Arkansas Post continued as a trading post, and the French presence in the Mississippi Basin became one of mostly single French voyageurs paddling their canoes from one trading post to the next.

1722-1739. During this period of La Louisiane Française, a few more settlements and trading posts were established, including Fort du Rocher in 1722; Vincennes in 1732; Ste. Genevieve in 1735; and Fort Assumption in 1739.

1743. Using the trace of the Santa Fe Trail, French trappers and traders followed the Arkansas River in present Kansas to reach Santa Fe and began trade with the Spanish colonists of Nuevo Mexico.

1744. Fort de Cavagnial. The first Europeans to settle in present Kansas came when a French fort and trading post was established on the west side of the Missouri River, somewhere between present Leavenworth and Kansas City, Kansas.

1763. Treaty of Paris. The Seven Years War (in Europe and Canada), was called the French and Indian War in colonial America and ended with the Treaty of Paris. France ceded virtually all of its North American claims – Louisiana on the western side of the Mississippi was lost to Spain, the eastern side of the Mississippi and all of Quebec went to Britain.

1763-1770. Transition Period. Soon after the 1763 Treaty of Paris, a Spanish Louisiana governor was installed, headquartered at New Orleans.
- There was little military interference by anyone in former French La Louisiane for several years. By 1764, all French military personnel had left their North American posts. But the main French civilian settlements still existed in Lower Louisiana: New Orleans, Baton Rouge, Natchez, and Arkansas Post; and in Upper Louisiana: Prairie du Chien, Kaskaskia, and Vincennes.
- St. Louis was founded in 1764 by French Trader Pierre Laclede Liguest, after obtaining a trading license from the Spanish governor.
- Per terms of the Treaty of Paris of 1763, British forces began the imposed deportation of French Acadians from their homes in present Nova Scotia. The first shipload of Acadians arrived in Spanish Louisiana, just outside of New Orleans, in February 1765.
- The Louisiana Rebellion of 1768 was an unsuccessful attempt by Acadian, Creole, and German settlers around New Orleans to stop the handover of French La Louisiane to Spain.
- St. Louis operated under civilian French control until it was occupied by Spanish soldiers in 1770. About the same time, the British established a military presence within the former French settlements at Prairie du Chien, Kaskaskia and Vincennes.

1783. United States of America. The treaty of Paris of 1783 ended the Revolutionary War and first recognized the United States as an independent nation, with borders from the Atlantic Ocean to the Mississippi River, and from present Maine to Georgia. The treaty also reaffirmed the claims of Britain to present Canada; and Spain's claim to East Florida, West Florida, New Spain (including Nuevo Mexico & Tejas), and Louisiana west of the Mississippi River.

1800. Louisiana. Napoleon acquired title of Louisiana from Spain. At the Third Treaty of San Ildefonso, Spain retroceded Louisiana to France in exchange for the Grand Duchy of Tuscany (France got Louisiana – Spain got the Leaning Tower of Pisa).

1803. Louisiana Purchase. The United States purchased Louisiana from France. Sent by President Jefferson to attempt the purchase of New Orleans, the American negotiators (James Madison and Robert Livingston) were surprised when Napoleon offered the entire tract to them. The Louisiana Purchase was officially described as the "drainage of the Mississippi and Missouri River basins." Adding the area doubled the size of the United States.

1804. On an expedition ordered by President Thomas Jefferson, Captains Meriwether Lewis and William Clark's Corps of Discovery left St. Louis, then headed up the Missouri River in search of a passage to the Pacific Ocean. One of their early campsites was at Kaw Point, where the Kansas River enters the Missouri River (now Kansas City, Kansas). Captain William Clark wrote on June 27, 1804, that "the country about the mouth of this river is very fine." The expedition's journals also noted that the location would be appropriate for a fort, and that the area teemed with deer, elk, buffalo, and bear. On July 2, 1804, Lewis and Clark's journals noted the remains of old Fort Cavagnial, abandoned by the French in 1764. Soon after Lewis and Clark left St. Louis, Spanish soldiers were dispatched from Santa Fe into present Colorado and Kansas to intercept and arrest them. But the Lewis and Clark party was already well into present South Dakota by the time the Spanish troops finally gave up looking for them.

1804-1805. In 1804, Congress divided the Louisiana Purchase into two jurisdictions: **Louisiana District** and **Orleans Territory**. The latter had north and south bounds the same as the present state of Louisiana but did not include lands east of the Mississippi River, and its northwestern corner extended on an indefinite line west into Spanish Tejas. The first capital of Orleans Territory was New Orleans. For a year, Louisiana District was attached to Indiana Territory for judicial administration but became Louisiana Territory with its own Governor on July 4, 1805. St. Louis was the first capital of Louisiana Territory.

1805. 1st Pike Expedition. U.S. Army Lieutenant Zebulon Pike led a small party of soldiers to investigate the Mississippi River above St. Louis. He was given specific orders to find the source of the Mississippi, and while doing so, to note "…any rivers, prairies, islands, mines, quarries, timber, and any Indian villages and settlements encountered."

1805-1806. The Louisiana Territory in 1805 had five original subdivisions: St. Louis District, St. Charles District, Ste. Genevieve District, Cape Girardeau District and New Madrid District. In 1806, the territorial legislature created the District of Arkansas from lands ceded by the Osage Indians. The unpopulated area north of these original districts was known unofficially as "Upper Louisiana Territory," and included the area of present Kansas.

1806-1807. 2nd Pike Expedition. Zebulon Pike, now a Captain, was again sent out, this time to explore and find the source of the Red River in Lower Louisiana. Pike followed the route of the Santa Fe Trail starting near the mouth of the Kansas River (now Kansas City, Kansas). From there, he contacted the Arkansas River, which he followed through present southwest Kansas into Colorado. He then went on to the Rocky Mountains, where Pike's Peak was named for him. On his return, he skirted south in search of the headwaters of the Red River, putting him in an area claimed by the Spanish. Pike and his men were arrested by Spanish soldiers, taken to Santa Fe, Nuevo Mexico, but treated well and returned to the Arkansas River a few weeks later. Pike wrote a book about his travels in 1810 that was a best seller in both America and Europe. In addition to the first English language observations of the Spanish culture in North America, Pike's descriptions of the Rocky Mountains became the inspiration for a whole generation of "mountain men."

1812. June 4th. Louisiana Territory was renamed **Missouri Territory**. This was to avoid any confusion after Orleans Territory became the State of Louisiana on April 30, 1812. The General Assembly of the Territory of Missouri met in St. Louis in October and converted the first six original districts into counties: Arkansas, Cape Girardeau, New Madrid, St. Charles, St. Louis, and Ste. Genevieve. The area of present Kansas was without any white population, lying north of St. Charles County in the "Unattached" region of Missouri Territory.

1819. Arkansas Territory was created, taken from the southern area of Missouri Territory. The area included all of present-day Arkansas and most of Oklahoma.

1819. Adams-Onis Treaty. The treaty included the purchase of Florida, but also set the boundary between the U.S. and New Spain, from Louisiana to the Oregon Country. The treaty established the Sabine River and Red River borders with Spanish Tejas; formalized the Arkansas River as the border with Nuevo Mexico (from a point in southwest Kansas to its source in present Colorado); and established Latitude 42° North as the division between Spanish California and the Oregon Country. The treaty was named after John Quincy Adams, U.S. Secretary of State, and Luis de Onis, the Spanish Foreign Minister, the parties who signed the treaty at Washington on February 22, 1819. John Quincy Adams was given credit for a brilliant piece of diplomacy by adding the western boundary settlements with Spain to the Florida Purchase.

1820-1821. The 1820 "Missouri Compromise" in Congress allowed Missouri to enter the Union as a slave state and Maine as a free state, thus keeping the balance of slave and free states equal in Congress. Although Missouri was to become a slave state, the remainder of the old Missouri Territory areas north of Latitude 36° 30,' including present Kansas, were supposed to be forever free of slavery. After Missouri became a state in August 1821, the remaining part of old Missouri Territory was now described as "Unorganized Territory."

1821. Santa Fe Trail. A well-known Indian trail from the Kansas River to the Arkansas River and then into present Colorado and New Mexico, was a natural path that developed into a heavily traveled wagon road. As early as 1743, the trail had been used by French traders between Nuevo Mexico and La Louisiane Française. The first American trading venture to use the Santa Fe Trail was led by William Becknell of Franklin, Missouri. His timing was perfect. After the end of Spanish rule in September 1821, the new Republic of Mexico lifted the restrictions on trade with outsiders previously imposed by the Spanish government. In November 1821, Becknell organized a pack-team loaded with some $300.00 in goods for trade. After a month in Santa Fe, he returned with over $6,000 in gold coins. Becknell's next trip was in May 1822, and this time, he used horse-drawn wagons loaded with some $3,000 worth of goods and returned with a profit of around $90,000. His huge success was well publicized and soon dozens of wagon trains of traders converged on the Santa Fe Trail. Heavy commercial traffic on the trail continued until 1846, when the trail was used as the route for the American Army that invaded Mexico. After the Mexican Cession of 1848, the Santa Fe Trail was the primary access route used by Americans to settle areas of western Kansas, southern Colorado, New Mexico, and Arizona. By 1880, a railroad followed the same route and ended the need for the wagon road. In 1926, the same trace of the old Santa Fe Trail through Kansas was used as part of the newly constructed US Highway 50, which remains today.

1822. The Rocky Mountain Fur Company was formed by General William Ashley. He placed an ad in a St. Louis newspaper to recruit able-bodied men for his new fur-trading enterprise. There was no shortage of willing young men. Ashley did not build a chain of forts to manage his fur trading operation. Instead, he sent his men out alone with a promise to meet them all at a central place a year later. When Ashley finally reached his men each year, it was cause for celebration – a wild party they called "the rendezvous." In 1826, William Ashley retired a wealthy man and sold the Rocky Mountain Fur Company to his employees.

1827. Cantonment Leavenworth. The first U.S. Army installation in present Kansas was near the location of the 1744 French fort and trading post called Fort de Cavagnial, as well as the largest Indian village on the Missouri River (Kansa Indians). The main purpose of the U.S. Army garrison was to protect the Santa Fe Trail, now the most important wagon road west of the Mississippi River. Travelers on the trail had been stopped by Comanche Indians demanding payment for passage on the road. The U.S. Army began a campaign against the Comanche with numerous skirmishes, directed from their base at Cantonment Leavenworth, now Fort Leavenworth.

1827. Independence, Missouri. The frontier town of Independence was founded in 1827, the farthest point westward on the Missouri River where steamboats could travel. (The nearby confluence of the Kansas River was the navigation problem, due to heavy silt and shallow channels). Independence immediately became a supply point, staging area, and primary starting point for the growing number of trappers and traders using the Santa Fe Trail.

1829 Sublette's Trace. Before 1829, access to the Platte River Trail from Independence, Missouri, was via the Missouri River to the mouth of the Platte River in present Nebraska. But steamboat traffic ended at Independence and travel upriver from that point required human-powered keel boats. The overland route of the Santa Fe Trail now started at Independence as well, heading west about ten miles to present Kansas, then southwest towards Santa Fe. A few miles into the Santa Fe Trail in present Kansas, at a point later called the Oregon Trail Junction, fur trader William Sublette blazed a cut-off from the Santa Fe Trail, turning northwest and connecting with the Platte River in present Nebraska. The new route covered a distance of over 250 miles. Sublette's Trace across present northeast Kansas was more direct than the river route, and later became the first leg of the Oregon Trail.

1830. Jedediah Smith and William Sublette, now partners in the successor to William Ashley's fur trading company, led the first wagon train across the Rocky Mountains at South Pass and on to the Upper Wind River. The journey through Indian country proved that even heavily loaded wagons and livestock – the prerequisites for settlement – could travel overland to the Pacific.

1833. Bent's Fort was built by trading partners William Bent, Charles Bent and Ceran St. Vrain near the present city of La Junta, Colorado. From the present Kansas cities of Bend, Dodge, Garden, and Syracuse, the stretch of the Santa Fe Trail along the Arkansas River came to a junction at Bent's Fort, where the main trail crossed the river into Mexico, and headed south towards Santa Fe. From Bent's Fort, a road continued up the Arkansas River to present Pueblo, Canon City, and beyond, accessing the heaviest fur trapping areas of the Rocky Mountains. Bent's Fort became a mandatory stop on the Santa Fe Trail. Frequent visitors included Louis Vasquez, Kit Carson, Jim Baker, James Bridger, Thomas Fitzpatrick, and Jim Beckworth. Explorer John C. Fremont stopped there on two of his expeditions into the West. Virtually all of the Santa Fe Trail travelers to Bent's Fort began their trip near the junction of the Kansas River with the Missouri river.

1841. The Western Emigration Society, a group of about 70 settlers bound for California and the Oregon Country set off on the Oregon Trail, beginning at Independence, Missouri. This was the first organized wagon train to head for California and Oregon. It is usually called the "Bartleson-Bidwell party" named for the two leaders. John Bartleson led about half of the group to Oregon's Willamette Valley. John Bidwell took the other half to California's Sacramento Valley.

1843. Early treaties with the Plains Indians included Kansas areas, but the groups involved were all nomadic tribes following the buffalo herds, and with no permanent settlement home. In 1843, the first treaty settlement in present Kansas was established near Kaw Point, the present site of Kansas City, Kansas. The families were mostly Wyandotte Indians intermarried with whites, who had gone to Ohio some years earlier, and had been relocated to their native homeland in present Kansas by treaty. For more information on this group, see *Notes on the Wyandottes's from Ohio to Indian Territory,* by Toni Jollay Prevost, publ. by the author, Lake Mary, FL, 1992, 19 pages. See FHL book 970.1 P929n.

1843. A wagon train with over 120 wagons, a large herd of livestock, and nearly 1,000 pioneers left Independence, Missouri, and headed out on the Oregon Trail. The largest wagon train to date, it became the model for the hundreds of wagon trains that followed. For an online list of the members of the 1843 Wagon Train, see the OR RootsWeb site:
http://freepages.history.rootsweb.ancestry.com/~mransom/pioneers.html

1849-1853. After the discovery of gold in California, the Missouri River towns of Independence, Westport, and St. Joseph became staging areas and points of departure for emigrants bound for California. Over 30,000 travelers who joined the 1849 California gold rush came over the Oregon Trail to Fort Hall, and from there to the California Trail. The following year, it is estimated that as many as 55,000 made the trip. Heavy traffic continued on the trail for several more years. In the peak year of 1852, over 67,000 people traveled old Sublette's Trace across northeast Kansas and on to Oregon or California. By 1853, large areas of eastern Kansas had become ripe for settlement. Even before the 1854 Indian Land Cessions and government surveys were complete, a sizeable number of people saw the Kansas countryside as potential farmland, jumped off the wagon trains, and took up homesteads as squatters.

1854-1859. On May 30, 1854, the **Kansas-Nebraska Act** passed Congress and the territories of Kansas and Nebraska were established. As first specified in the "Compromise of 1850," the Kansas-Nebraska Act was the first to allow people in a new territory to decide for themselves whether or not to allow slavery within their borders. The Act provided that any proposed state constitution submitted to Congress should have a provision permitting or forbidding slavery. As such, the Act served to repeal the Missouri Compromise of 1820 which had prohibited slavery north of Latitude 36°30.´ Nebraska Territory was seen as a free-state shoo-in, with many of its first settlers coming from the existing free states of Iowa, Illinois, and Indiana. Kansas Territory, however, was just west of the slave state of Missouri, and was seen by many southerners as a potential slave state. When Kansas Territory was officially opened to settlement in 1854, pro-slavery settlers from neighboring Missouri rushed to the new territory. But, abolitionist Free-Staters from New England marshalled their forces and sent settlers to Kansas Territory as well. The area was to become the scene of violence and chaos in its early days as the Pro-Slave and Anti-Slave forces battled and became known as *Bleeding Kansas.* Annual censuses taken by Kansas Territory, 1855-1859, asked questions about a voter's preference on the slavery issue: whether for, against, or without an opinion. The censuses named the voters in a household; therefore, they served the same purpose as an election. The early census results were challenged for their accuracy since thousands of non-residents invaded the territory just to be included in a census tally. In the territory's first year, pro-slavery voters dominated the towns. During that time, there were three territorial capitals: Pawnee, Shawnee Mission, and Fort Leavenworth. From 1855 to 1861, the final territorial capital was the town of Lecompton.

- NOTE: Territorial Kansas Timeline, 1854-1861, is a webpage sponsored by the Kansas Historical Society. The Timeline gives a year-by-year look at the events and battles of *Bleeding Kansas*, when the fight for statehood was between Free-Staters and Pro-Slavery advocates. See
www.territorialkansasonline.org/~imlskto/cgi-bin/index.php?SCREEN=timeline.

1855. Arapahoe County was established to provide future county functions in the extreme western portion of Kansas Territory. Arapahoe was never organized, and the first white population did not arrive until 1858 with the founding of the gold rush town of Denver City. Arapahoe was one of several "paper counties" created by the Kansas territorial legislature in anticipation of people moving into them.

1857-1859. Under the provisions of the 1854 Kansas-Nebraska Act, Kansas Territory submitted four proposed state constitutions to Congress. The second, and most controversial constitution is referred to historically as the "Lecompton Constitution of 1857" and would have admitted Kansas as a slave state. The proposed state constitution was submitted to Congress for approval in 1858 and became part of the intense national debate on the slavery issue. The Lecompton Constitution was a main subject of the famous Abraham Lincoln vs Stephen Douglas debates held in Illinois in 1858. Congress rejected the Lecompton Constitution, and Kansas Territory did not become a state until a new territorial legislature was elected; and after the fourth (Wyandotte) state constitution was submitted to Congress in 1859.

1858. The discovery of placer gold deposits on the South Platte River, launched a gold rush and the birth of Colorado. In 1858, the first Colorado towns of Montana City, St. Charles, Auraria, and Denver City were founded. Pueblo was founded as Fountain City; Many of the "Pikes Peak or Bust" prospectors began their trip on the Santa Fe Trail to old Bent's Fort, then to Pueblo, Colorado Springs, and into the first gold fields located near Denver City. Other travelers came over the Oregon Trail through present Nebraska, then up the south branch of the Platte River to Denver City, old Arapahoe County, Kansas Territory.

1859. Arapahoe County, Kansas Territory was split into six counties: a much smaller Arapahoe, Broderick, El Paso, Fremont, Montana, and Oro counties. None of these six counties were ever organized. Many residents of the mining region felt disconnected from the territorial government, which was seated nearly 600 miles away, and they voted to form their own territory. In October, the **Provisional Territory of Jefferson** was organized to govern the first mining camps and towns of present Colorado. Officers were elected, several counties were established, and a territorial capital was established at Golden. Although the territorial government was never sanctioned by the U.S. Congress, Jefferson Territory operated with the consent of the local population.

1860. April. The **Pony Express** began operations. The 1,900-mile Pony Express ran from St. Joseph, Missouri, to Sacramento, California. The Pony Express riders followed the same general route as the Oregon-California Trail, beginning with the old Sublette's Trace in Kansas Territory. The central Pony Express route to California was 600 miles shorter than the southern **Butterfield Overland Mail Route**, the U.S. Post Office's contractor for handling all mail to California since 1857. The Butterfield stages took an average of 25 days to make the trip from St. Louis or Memphis to Sacramento; while the Pony Express riders took 10 days from St. Joseph to Sacramento. The onset of the Civil War in April 1861 saw the end of the Butterfield Mail contract, and the stage operation came under control of several Confederate states. In June 1861, the U.S. Post Office ignored the Pony Express, and adopted the **Central Overland California Route**, an upgraded stagecoach route used by Well Fargo and other express companies. The trans-continental telegraph line was completed in October 1861. Two days after the first telegraph message was transmitted from Washington, DC to Sacramento, CA, the Pony Express ceased operations.

1860. June. **Federal Census.** California's celebrated population increase went from less than 2,000 Americans in 1848 to over 380,000 by 1860. Much of California's gold-rush population passed through Kansas to get there. But there were obviously many who saw Kansas Territory as a destination as well. The population of Kansas Territory from its founding and opening of settlement in 1854 exploded to 107,206 people counted in the 1860 federal census. The map of 1860 Kansas Territory on page 40 shows that 40 counties had been organized in its first six years. For the 1860 federal census, the U.S. Census Office ignored Jefferson Territory, but included an enumeration of any inhabitants of present Colorado as part of four U.S. territories: New Mexico, Nebraska, Kansas, and Utah Territories. Most of the population of Arapahoe County, Kansas Territory was near Denver City.

1861. Jan 29th. **Kansas** entered the Union as the 34th state with the same boundaries as today. Between 1854 and 1861, Kansas Territory had seen several proposed state constitutions and several territorial censuses, as well as an official congressional investigation into voting frauds and the accuracy of the censuses. But Kansas entered the Union as a free state, and its voting representatives opposed to slavery now contributed to a majority in Congress.

1861. Feb 28th. **Colorado Territory** was established by the U.S. Congress with the same boundaries as the present state, ending the ephemeral reign of Jefferson Territory. The first Colorado Territorial Assembly met, created 17 counties, authorized a university, and selected Colorado City as the capital. Arapahoe County, first established as a Kansas Territory county in 1855, then a county of Jefferson Territory in 1859, became a much smaller county of Colorado Territory in 1861.

1861. Apr 12th. Confederate troops opened fire on Union-occupied Fort Sumter, South Carolina, the first shots of the American Civil War, 1861-1865.

1861. May 20th. The 1st Kansas Infantry Regiment was organized at Camp Lincoln, adjacent to Fort Leavenworth, Kansas. The 1st Kansas was to see action at the first major battle of the Civil War in the West, the Battle of Wilson's Creek, near Springfield, Missouri, on Aug 7, 1861. A member of F Company of the 1st Kansas Infantry was Jesse Dollarhide, a private, who was killed in the battle and buried in a mass grave at the battlefield site. Jesse was 18 years old when his family left West Union, Iowa and began a trip to California on the Oregon-California Trail, which they had approached via Council Bluffs, Iowa. At a point on the trail on the Platte River in present Nebraska, near the junction with Sublette's Trace, the Dollarhide wagons were stopped by Kansas Militia recruiters. They were asking for volunteers to fight for the Union in the War of the Rebellion. Jesse volunteered, followed the recruiters back to Kansas, and was mustered into the 1st Kansas Infantry on Jun 1, 1861. Jesse's parents and siblings continued on their way to California. They never saw Jesse again.
- NOTE: The sources for the above didactic item was the Family Bible of Rev. John Dollarhide (Jesse's father), and the online database, *Kansas Civil War Soldiers, 1861-1865*. (See page 58). -bill$hide.

1996. Republican Senator Bob Dole, from Russell, Kansas, ran for President of the United States. He lost.

Online Resources of the Kansas Historical Society

Kansas Memory. This digital archives preserves photographs, documents, and maps important to Kansas history. Use the Search Box to look for a keyword; or Browse by Kansas County (by clicking on a map); or use the Category Browser. A click on Douglas County on the map brought up 1,454 results, ranging from books, photographs, documents, or objects. An example from the list is an *Abstract of Census Returns*, documenting the 1859 election of delegates to the Wyandotte Constitutional Convention showing the number of votes cast by township for most Kansas counties. See **www.kansasmemory.org**.

Kansas Names Index. This index searches all of the combined biographical databases listed below. See **www.kshs.org/p/people/15899**.
- 1895 Kansas State Census
- Affidavits of Alien Enemies and Alien Females, 1917-1918
- Biographical sketches, obituaries, to the early 1900s
- License Application Files of Medical Doctors, 1901-2001
- A Day in My Community
- Fraternal Order Death Notices
- History of the State of Kansas by Andreas, 1883
- Index to Journal of the Kansas Medical Society
- Biographical clippings files
- Kansas Marriage Index, 1854-1861
- Kansas Physicians and Midwives
- Kansas State Soldiers' Home Admissions and Military History of Members
- Index to admissions to the Fort Dodge Soldier's Home from about 1890-1957
- Knights & Ladies of Security - Death Claims
- Pioneer Women (Lilla Day Monroe Collection)
- Taps index to death notices of the members of the United Spanish War Veterans group
- Topeka State Hospital Cemetery
- Who Was Who in America (People with Kansas Connections)
- Other Kansas research websites

Territorial Kansas Online, 1854-1861. This is a virtual repository for territorial Kansas history. **Topics:** Territorial Politics & Government; Border Warfare; Immigration & Early Settlement; Personalities; and National Debate About Kansas. **Resources:** Timeline, Annals of Kansas, Lesson Plans, Bibliography, Historic Sites, FAQs, and Related Links. See **www.territorialkansasonline.org/~imlskto/cgi-bin/index.php?SCREEN=location**.

Kansas Censuses, 1855-1940. Kansas territorial, state, and federal censuses are available at the Kansas Historical Society from 1855 through 1930 on microfilm. The 1940 federal census is available online only. Indexes for selected years are also available. The Kansas Territorial and State Census records are available online from Ancestry free to Kansans by verifying their driver's license. For the page at the Kansas Historical Society website, see **www.kshs.org/p/kansas-censuses-1855-1930/10961.**
This site has a description of each of the following:
- Guide to Kansas Census Indexes, 1855-1925
- Territorial censuses, 1855-1859
- 1860 Federal Census of Kansas Territory
- 1865 Kansas State Census
- 1870 Federal Census of Kansas
- 1875 Kansas State Census
- 1880 Federal Census of Kansas
- 1885 Kansas State Census
- 1890 Federal Census of Kansas
- 1895 Kansas State Census
- 1900 Federal Census of Kansas
- 1905 Kansas State Census
- 1910 Federal Census of Kansas
- 1915 Kansas State Census
- 1920 Federal Census of Kansas
- 1925 Kansas State Census
- 1930 Federal Census of Kansas
- 1940 Federal Census online

Each of the Kansas territorial and state census years are described in more detail in the chronological bibliography that follows. Federal censuses are described in more detail in the Nationwide Censuses & Name Lists chapter.

Kansas Military Index. This index searches all of the databases listed below. See **www.kshs.org/p/kansas-military-index/15797.**

Civil War
 - Kansas Adjutant General's Report, 1861-1865
 - Kansas Civil War Militia Index, 1861-1865
 - Civil War Veterans in Kansas
 - Kansas Members of the Grand Army of the Republic
 - Necrology (deaths) of Members of the Grand Army of the Republic
 - Sleeping Heroes: The Impact of Civil War Veterans on Kansas Communities

Spanish-American War
 - Kansas Adjutant General's Report, 1898-1899

World War I
 - World War I Bounty Claims Index
 - Kansas Soldiers of the Great War

World War II
 - World War II Selective Service Index
 - World War II Army Casualties
 - World War II Oral Histories
 - Burials/Memorials at World War II Military Cemeteries

Post-World War II Conflicts
 - Korean War Casualties
 - Vietnam War Casualties
 - Kansas Casualties in Iraq and Afghanistan

Links to Guides Not Included in The Military Index:
 - Civil War Research
 - Civil War on the Western Border - a digital project in partnership with Kansas City Public Library
 - Indian Wars. Index to Kansas 19th Cavalry Enlistments, 1868–1869
 - More information about finding KS military records
 - Kansas Military History Timeline

Kansas Newspapers on Microfilm. Search the Newspaper Database by the city of publication, word in newspaper title, county, state, and date range. The collection of Kansas Newspapers at the society is one of the largest and earliest, as the society's founders were newspaper editors. For the search screen, see **www.kshs.org/p/newspapers-in-kansas/11528.**

Kansas Digital Newspapers. The Kansas Historical Society's collection of historic Kansas newspapers are freely available on the websites of several digital partners:

- **Chronicling America.** Historic American Newspapers by the Library of Congress. For the links to Kansas newspapers, see
  http://chroniclingamerica.loc.gov/newspapers/?state=Kansas&ethnicity=&language=.
- **Newspapers.com.** Included with Ancestry.com databases, all historical Kansas newspapers are in the process of being digitized. Free to Kansas residents who can provide their driver's license. KS residents, see
  www.kshs.org/ancestry/drivers/dlverify.
- **Forsyth Library Digital Collection**, Fort Hays State University. Kansas Digital Newspapers. See
  http://contentcat.fhsu.edu/cdm/landingpage/collection/p15732coll8.

County Records on Microfilm. The Kansas Historical Society has thousands of reels of microfilm of Kansas county and city government records. Most of this film came to the society in cooperation with the Genealogical Society of Utah. Visit this site for a list of counties, and the types of records available for each. Some of the records are included in the bibliography under their Family History Library catalog description and call number. See
www.kshs.org/search/index/query:county%20records%20on%20microfilm.

Kansas Places Index. This index searches all of the databases listed below. See www.kshs.org/p/places-in-kansas/11306.

- **Post Offices.** Histories of Kansas post offices, including a database that can be searched by date, town, or county to find the location of every known Kansas post office with its dates of operation. These dates can indicate approximately when the town was established and, in some cases when it disappeared.
- **Little Known or Extinct Towns of Kansas ("Dead Towns").** Information about approximately 4,500 Kansas towns from the territorial period to ca. 1940.
- **Townships in Kansas.** In Kansas, townships are a government entity larger than a town or city but smaller than a county. Kansas state censuses for areas outside incorporated cities are grouped by the township divisions within the county. Over time, some of these government entities have changed their names and boundaries.
- **Counties.** Brief histories of current and former Kansas counties with a map showing their location and links to additional resources.
- **Cemeteries in Kansas, 1906.** A list of Kansas cemeteries, published in 1906, that gives the county and township or city where the cemetery is located, and the size of the cemetery in acres. Names of the people buried there are not included.

ATLAS – Associated Topeka Libraries Automated System. This is an online combined index to the catalog of holdings for the libraries listed below. See http://topekalibraries.info.
- Washburn University Mabee Library Catalog
- Washburn University Carnegie Education Library Catalog
- Washburn University School of Law Library Catalog
- State Library of Kansas Library Catalog
- Kansas Historical Society Catalog
- Kansas Supreme Court Law Library Catalog
- Search Other Library Catalogs:
  - Combined search: KU, K-State, and the Kansas Statewide Library Catalogs
  - Choose one or more library catalogs to search

Archives Catalog – Government Records, Manuscripts, Photos and Other Primary Sources. This is the main place to look for primary sources at the Kansas Historical Society. It includes government records, personal papers, records of organizations and businesses, and other unpublished materials. See www.kshs.org/p/archives-catalog/16432.

Bibliography
Kansas Censuses & Substitutes

KS Territorial Censuses. In 1855, Kansas Territory began taking annual censuses, mainly as a means of counting voters and to determine their political views on the slavery issue. In fact, some of these censuses were separated by voters who were "Free State," "Pro-Slavery," or "Doubtful," thus, the early Kansas territorial censuses served the same purpose as a local election. Censuses were taken in 1855, 1856, 1857, 1858, and 1859. Each were limited to the names of voters and heads of households. For genealogists searching for Kansas ancestors, the territorial censuses must be viewed with the historical background of a divided territory, in which thousands of non-residents invaded the area to vote. Over half of the voters were not registered in Kansas. One community census total was shown to have 20 registered voters out of the 600 who voted. But any census name list that survives is worthwhile because it identifies actual people by name, whether locals or invaders. And, comparing name lists from surrounding states for the same period may reveal which political side your ancestor favored.

KS State Censuses. As a means of apportioning the seats in the Kansas legislature, the first state census was taken in 1865, followed by 1875, 1885, 1895, 1905, 1915, and the last one in 1925. The Kansas legislature discontinued funding for state censuses in 1933, when the Great Depression was making state budgets sparse. Kansas then began using the population figures from the federal decennial censuses to apportion their state legislature.

All surviving territorial and state census originals are located today at the Kansas Historical Society in Topeka. They have all been microfilmed, and in cooperation with Ancestry.com and FamilySearch.org, digitized and indexed online. Both the microfilm and online publications are noted, and each of the census years are described in more detail in the bibliography that follows. Over the years, many periodicals published by genealogical societies in Kansas have printed extracts and indexes to censuses for one or more counties, and these articles are noted in the bibliography.

Adding the federal censuses to the Kansas territorial and state censuses totals 28 census years. This bibliography identifies the census name lists and adds many more census substitute name lists. Together, they include Territorial, State, and Federal Censuses, County Court Records, Directories, County Histories, State Military Lists, Tax Lists, Vital Records, and Voter Lists. The censuses and substitute name lists begin below in chronological order:

♦ ♦ ♦ ♦ ♦

1854-1856 Name Lists. See *Troubles in Kansas* **[Online Database],** an excellent review and name lists from the *Bleeding Kansas* era, with links to the following:
- A Brief History
- 1855 Kansas Census – Index of Voters
- Index of Testimony
- Emigrant Aid Society Settler List
- Further Reading
- Bibliography and Credits
- The KSGenWeb Page

See **www.ksgenweb.org/archives/troubles.html**.

1854-1856 Name Lists. See *The 1854-1856 Voters of the Territory of Kansas: Includes the Eighteen Original Districts and Voting Qualifications* **[Printed Book & Online Database],** compiled by Debra Graden, published 1999, publisher not noted, 630 pages. Lists voters alphabetically by surname. FHL book 978.1 N4g.
- This database of names was indexed online at the Ancestry.com website as *Kansas Voter Registration Lists, 1854-1856.* See **http://search.ancestry.com/search/db.aspx?dbid=3961**.

1854-1856 Name Lists. See *Report of the Special Committee Appointed to Investigate the Troubles in Kansas, With the Views of the Minority of Said Committee* **[Digitized Book],** original published Washington, DC, C. Wendell, Printer, 1856, 1,206 pages. Digitized by the Genealogical Society of Utah, 2013, from original copy at the Allen County Public Library, Ft. Wayne, IN. To view the digital images, see the online FHL catalog page for this title: **www.familysearch.org/search/catalog/2239035**.

1854-1856 Name Lists. See *An Index to the Report of the Special Committee Appointed to Investigate the Troubles in Kansas, 1856* **[Printed Book, Microfilm, & Online Database],** compiled by Robert A. Hodge, published by the author, Fredericksburg, Virginia, 1984, 2 vols. 396 pages. The Kansas-Nebraska Act of 1854 provided for the organization of the Kansas Territory in preparation for statehood. This act required the citizens of the territory to vote on the issue of slavery. Due to disagreement as to what constituted authorized voters, the House of Representatives of the U.S. Congress appointed a special committee to investigate the issue. The bulk of the report consisted of testimonies, lists of names from the census records, poll books and voting registers. This is an index to that report. Contents: Vol. 1: A-L. Vol. 2: M-Z. FHL book 978.1 X3h, v.1 & 2, also on 6 microfiche, FHL fiche #6111324.
- The 1854 and 1855 name lists were extracted from the report and indexed online at the Ancestry.com website with the title, *Kansas Election List, 1854,* see **http://search.ancestry.com/search/db.aspx?dbid=4099**.
- And, *Kansas Territorial Census, 1855,* see **https://search.ancestry.com/search/db.aspx?dbid=4056**.

1854-1856 Name Lists. See *Kansas Pioneers of 1855: That Came by Way of New England Emigrant Aid Company* **[Printed Book],** extracted by Debra F. Graden. In 1856 the U.S. House of Representatives ordered a special committee to investigate the pro-slave vs free-state troubles in Kansas. One purpose of the hearings was to determine whether the Massachusetts Emigrant Aid Society hired men to come to Kansas solely to manipulate the voting. This extract contains excerpts from testimony given by some of the settlers whose emigration to Kansas was sponsored by the New England Emigrant Aid Society. Also includes lists of all who emigrated to Kansas under the Emigrant Aid Society's sponsorship during early 1855. Published by the author, Leavenworth, KS, 1997, 72 pages, FHL book 978.1 W2g.

1854-1856 Name Lists. See *The Conquest of Kansas: by Missouri and her Allies; a History of the Troubles in Kansas, from the Passage of the Organic Act Until the Close of July 1856* **[Digitized book],** by William Phillips, published Boston, Phillips, Sampson, and Co., 1856, 414 pages. This is a history written during the era of *Bleeding Kansas* and is a rather one-sided view of the events taking place there. Written by a Boston editor, obviously on the Free-Stater side of things, he offers no apologies for his viewpoints. The book is listed here because many of the names of the players involved in the conflict are mentioned. See the FHL catalog page to access the digital images of this book. See **www.familysearch.org/search/catalog/2115851**.

1854-1856 Name Lists. See *List of Settlers, Miami County, Kansas, 1854* **[Online Database]**, indexed at the USGenWeb site for Miami Co KS. See www.ksgenweb.org/miami/library/1854Settlers.html.

1854-1861. *Death Notices from Kansas Territorial Newspapers* **[Printed Book]**, compiled by Alberta Pantle, originally published in the Kansas Historical Quarterly, reprinted by the Jefferson Co Genealogical Society, Oskaloosa, KS, ca1985, FHL book 978.1 V4p. For a digital version of this title, see the online FHL catalog page. See www.familysearch.org/search/catalog/360360.

1854-1873. *Kansas, Compiled Marriage Index from Select Counties* **[Online Database]**, indexed at the Ancestry.com website. Source: *Kansas Marriage Index, 1854-1873,* by Linda Carpenter. This database is a collection of marriage records for the state before and during these growth years. The names were extracted from LDS microfilms and local newspapers. Each entry shows the names of spouses, date of marriage, county in which the record is kept, and reference information about the source. See Ancestry's description page for the counties and number of marriages in each. This database has 21,805 records. See https://search.ancestry.com/search/db.aspx?dbid=3444.

1854-1879. *Kansas Settlers* **[Online Database]**, indexed at the Ancestry.com website. Original data: Gleed, Charles S., ed. *Kansas Memorial, A Report of the Old Settlers' Meeting Held at Bismark Grove, Kansas, September 15th and 16th, 1879.* This database is a collection of information gathered at that meeting regarding the settlement of the state. Taken from a register now in the Kansas State Historical Society, each record reveals the attendee's name, birthplace, and birth date. Additionally, each person's settlement location is provided along with the date of their arrival in the state, and current (1879) residence. This database has 3,263 records. See https://search.ancestry.com/search/db.aspx?dbid=4132.

1854-1880s. *Pioneers of the Bluestem Prairie, Full Name Index* **[Printed Book]**, compiled and published by the Riley County Genealogical Society, Manhattan, KS, 2005, 212 pages, FHL book 978.1 D3pi index.

1854-1900s. *Cemetery Records of Kansas* **[Printed Books]**, compiled by members of the Kansas Mission (LDS), published by the Family History Library, Salt Lake City, 1966 – , 18 vols., with the names of persons buried, name of cemetery, and name of county, as follows: Vol. 1: Cemeteries in Allen, Chase, Dickinson, Geary, Gove, Gray, Harvey, Montgomery, Pottawatomie, Reno, Riley, Sedgwick, and Sumner counties. Vol. 2: Hamilton, Harvey, Meade, Montgomery, Neosho, Rice, Riley, Saline, and Stafford counties. Vol. 3: Pottawatomie, and Sedgwick counties. Vol. 4: Butler, Finney, Grant, Kearney, Logan, Saline, Stanton, Pottawatomie, and Riley counties. Vol. 5: Allen, Dickinson, Geary, Harvey, Labette, Lyon, Montgomery, Neosho, and Sedgwick counties. Vol. 6: Butler, Harvey, Montgomery, Pottawatomie, Riley, Saline, and Sedgwick counties. Vol. 7: Butler, Clay, Montgomery, Marshal, Harvey, Seward, Sumner, Wabaunsee, Geary, Pottawatomie, and Riley counties. Vol. 8: Pottawatomie County. Vol. 9: Butler, Hamilton, Marshall, Montgomery, Pottawatomie, and Riley counties. Vol. 11: Clay, Cowley, Finney, Franklin, Grant, Greeley, Harvey, Haskell, Lincoln, Marshall, Montgomery, Morton, Pottawatomie, Saline, Sedgwick, Seward and Wichita counties. Vol. 11: Cowley, Edwards, Ford, Gray, Hodgeman, Edwards, Ford, Gray, and Hodgeman counties. Vol. 12: McPherson, Marshall, Montgomery, Reno, Sedgwick, Seward, Sumner, and Thomas counties. Vol. 13: Gove, Jewell, Montgomery, Ottawa, Saline, Scott, Sedgwick, Seward, Wallace, and Wichita counties. Vol. 14: Butler, Coffey, Greeley, Greenwood, Kingman, Republic, Sherman, Sumner, and Wallace counties. Vol. 15: Butler, Coffey, Greenwood, Kingman, Sedgwick, and Sumner counties. Vol. 16: Butler, Greenwood, Harvey, Jewell, Kingman, Ottawa, Sedgwick, and Sumner counties. Vol. 17: Cloud and Ottawa counties. Vol. 18: Butler, Crawford, Ellis, Jefferson, Jewell, Marion, Norton, Republic, Rooks, Russell, and Stafford counties. See FHL book 978.1 V22 v.1-18. Names of cemeteries/counties for all 18 volumes were indexed in *Cemetery Records of Kansas, Combined Table of Contents*, compiled by James Davis Moore, published by Genidex, Santa Margarita, CA, 1967, 10 pages, FHL book 978.1 V22 index.

1854-1917. See *Roll of Attorneys of the State of Kansas: Arranged (First) by Counties, and (Second) alphabetically regardless of Counties, Also a Register of the Supreme Court and Court Officers from 1854 to Date, etc.* **[Digitized Book]**, by D. A. Valentine, original published by the state printer, Topeka, KS, 1917, 65 pages. To view the digital images of the entire book, see the FHL catalog page for this title: www.familysearch.org/search/catalog/2013775.

1854-1936. *Kansas, Births and Christenings* **[Online Database],** indexed at the FamilySearch.org website. The starting year of 1818 is impossible. This is an index to births, baptisms, and christening records taken from FHL sources. This database has 49 records. See https://familysearch.org/search/collection/1674839.

1854-1935. *Kansas, Marriages* **[Online Database],** indexed at the FamilySearch.org website. The starting year of 1840 is impossible, since the first settlers came to Kansas Territory in 1854. This is an index to marriage records from Kansas records on microfilm at the FHL. This database has 286,775 records. See https://familysearch.org/search/collection/1674845.

1854-1984. *Kansas Newspaper Archives* **[Online Database],** digitized and indexed newspapers at the GenealogyBank website for the following cities: Atchison, Baxter Springs, Cedar Vale, Cherokee, Coffeyville, Emporia, Fort Riley, Fort Scott, Hutchinson, Kansas City, Lawrence, Leavenworth, Lincoln, Minneola, Nicodemus, Olathe, Oskaloosa, Parsons, Peru, Pittsburg, Salina, Sedan, Shawnee, Topeka, Valley Falls, Weir City, Wichita, and Winfield. See www.genealogybank.com/gbnk/newspapers/explore/USA/Kansas/.

1854-1911. *Kansas, Marriages* **[Online Database],** indexed at the FamilySearch.org website. Source: FamilySearch extractions from FHL microfilm. The starting year of 1811 is impossible. Each index record includes Name, Event type, Event date, Event place, Gender, Race, and Notes. This database has 103,966 records. See www.familysearch.org/search/collection/2381595.

1854-1981. *Kansas, Cemetery Records* **[Online Database],** digitized and indexed at the Ancestry.com website. Source: Kansas Historical Society, Topeka. The 1812 date is impossible for Kansas. This database is a compilation of cemetery records held at the Kansas State Historical Society that were scanned onsite. They include the following titles: Miscellaneous Cemetery Inscriptions, Jackson County Cemeteries, Miscellaneous Unbindable Cemetery Records, Index to Six Cemeteries of Southeast Kansas, Civil War Soldiers Buried in Kansas, Cherokee County Cemeteries Vol. 1, Cherokee County Cemeteries Vol. 2, Cherokee County Cemeteries Index, Big Springs Cemetery, Douglas County; Belle Springs Brethren Cemetery, Dickinson County; Church of God in Christ Cemetery Records, Montezuma; Vital Records, Graham County; McPherson City Cemetery Records Index; St. Patrick's Cemetery, Vine Creek; Wabaunsee County Cemetery; and Vital Records, Stafford County. Each index record includes: Name, Birth date, Age, Death date, Cemetery, and Description. This database has 31,123 records. See https://search.ancestry.com/search/db.aspx?dbid=5951.

1854-1987. *Kansas, Wills and Probate Records* **[Online Database],** digitized and indexed at the Ancestry.com website. Source: Kansas County, District, and Probate Courts. The date of 1803 may have been for a deceased's birth year, rather than a date of probate in Kansas. Probate records include Wills, Letters of Administration, Inventories, Distributions and Accounting, Bonds, and Guardianships. Each index record includes: Name, Probate date, Inferred death place, Case number, and Item description. A Table of Contents identifies the number of images by type of papers. The document image may have more information. This database has 160,938 records. See https://search.ancestry.com/search/db.aspx?dbid=9065.

1854-2000s. *Digital Library of the KSGenWeb* **[Online Databases].** The KSGenWeb is affiliated with the USGenWeb system. One of these webpages is the Digital Library of the KSGenWeb. Their Statewide Files & Projects include the following:
- Troubles in Kansas
- "A Standard History of Kansas and Kansans"
- 1917-1918 Civilian Draft Registration Cards
- Old Settlers' Tales
- Criminal X-Ray, October 1915
- The Kansas State Guard 1917-1919
- Alumni News Section of the Graduate Magazine of the University of Kansas
- Letters, Memoirs & Family Stories of our Kansas Ancestors
- 1912 Cyclopedia of Kansas
- The Fighting Twentieth
- 1883 List of Pensioners on the Roll
- Department of the Kansas G.A.R.
- World War II Honor List of Dead and Missing of the State of Kansas
- 1878 County Maps
- Kansas Migrations
- KSGenWeb Digital Library Military Events Page
- Kansas Decennial Census Forms and Agricultural Schedule 2's

This webpage also serves as the access to the Kansas County USGenWeb sites, where name lists are available for all Kansas counties. Typical county records include Bibles, Biographies, Cemeteries, Censuses, Court, Death, Deeds, Directories, Histories, Marriages, Military, Newspapers, Obituaries, Photos,

Schools, Tax Lists, Wills, and more. Visit the Digital Library of the KSGenWeb. See www.ksgenweb.org/archives.

1854-2001. *Kansas Biographical Index: Town, Community & Organization Histories: More Than 35,000 Citations From 258 Volumes of Kansas Town, Community and Organization Histories,* **[Printed Book & Digital Version]**, compiled by Patricia Douglass Smith and Stanley Clifford Smith, published by the authors, Garden City, KS, 2001, 1st Edition, 328 pages. 2nd Edition: "69,000 Citations From 183 Volumes." Index lists name of person, county or community name, and source, and page number in original source. FHL book 978.1 D32sp (1st ed.) and 978.1 D32sm (2nd ed.). To access the digital images, see the online FHL catalog: www.familysearch.org/search/catalog/701646.

1854-2000s. *Kansas, Cemetery Abstracts* **[Online Database]**, digitized and indexed at FamilySearch.org. Compiled by the Kansas Mission of the Church of Jesus Christ of Latter-day Saints. Includes records from Allen, Butler, Chase, Clay, Cloud, Coffey, Cowley, Crawford, Dickinson, Edwards, Ellis, Finney, Ford, Franklin, Geary, Gove, Grant, Gray, Greeley, Greenwood, Hamilton, Harvey, Haskell, Hodgeman, Jefferson, Jewell, Kearney, Kingman, Labette, Lincoln, Logan, Lyon, Marion, Marshall, McPherson, Meade, Montgomery, Morton, Neosho, Norton, Ottawa, Pottawatomie, Reno, Republic, Rice, Riley, Rooks, Russell, Saline, Scott, Sedgwick, Seward, Sherman, Stafford, Stanton, Sumner, Thomas, Wabaunsee, Wallace, and Wichita counties. See www.familysearch.org/search/collection/2568639.

1854-2000s. *Kansas Collection Catalog at MyHeritage.com* **[Online Database]**, Databases include censuses, directories, family histories, town histories, military rosters, college/school year books, and more. This is a subscription site, but all initial searches are free. A free search can be done for a name, place, year, or keyword. See www.myheritage.com/research/catalog?q=Kansas.

1854-2009. *Kansas, Vital Record Abstracts* **[Online Database]**, indexed at the Ancestry.com website. Source: KHS, Topeka. This collection contains various vital records from the state of Kansas, including births, baptisms, confirmations, marriages, deaths, and funerals. The content ranges from collated typed information to Bible records. These records are collected from other records and are not primary documents, with the exception of a few of the Bible records. Information in this database may include: Name, Age, Birth date and place, Marriage date and place, Death date and place, Spouse name, Spouse age and birthplace, and Parents' names. This database has 30,293 records. See https://search.ancestry.com/search/db.aspx?dbid=2551.

1855 Kansas Territorial Census [Microfilm], from the originals at the Kansas Historical Society, Topeka, KS. The 1855 census, called by the governor, lists the inhabitants of Kansas Territory by election districts. There is a map at the beginning of the microfilm showing the location of the election districts. KHS film #K-1 shows election districts, filmed in the following order: 1-4; 7-8; 5-6; 9-13; 15; 14; and 16-17. Reel KS-1 contains a name index to the entire state. Filmed by the society, 1951. FHL's copy is film #570188. To see if this microfilm was digitized yet, see the online FHL catalog: www.familysearch.org/search/catalog/188263.

1855. *The Census of the Territory of Kansas, February 1855: With Index and Map of Kansas Election Districts in 1854* **[Printed Book, Microfilm & Digital Version]**, edited by Willard C. Heiss, published by The Bookmark, Knightstown, IN, 1997, 38 pages. FHL book 978. X2p 1855 and FHL film #896835. To access the digital version, see the online FHL catalog: www.familysearch.org/search/catalog/173944.

"1855 Kansas Territorial Census" [Printed Article], name index serialized in *Kansas Records and Reviews*, beginning with Vol. 1, (Apr 1994); and in *Bluestem Root Diggers Genealogical Quarterly* (Fox Valley Genealogical Society, Eureka, KS), starting with Vol. 6, No. 3 (Jul 1996).

1855 and 1865 Kansas Censuses, Leavenworth County, Kansas [Printed Book], by the Leavenworth County Genealogical Society, Leavenworth, Kansas, 1996, 38 pages. Each section is arranged in alphabetical order by the person's surname. The 1855 census was compiled from voter records and gives name and birthplace. The 1865 census is divided into townships and gives name and page number. FHL book 978.138 X22sp.

1855-1865. *History of Bourbon County, Kansas to the Close of 1865* **[Online Database]**, digitized and indexed at the USGenWeb site for Bourbon Co KS. See www.ksgenweb.org/archives/bourbon/history/1894.

1855-1870s. *Index to The Early Settlements of Atchison County* **[Online Database]**, indexed at the USGenWeb site for Atchison Co KS. See www.ksgenweb.org/atchison/EarlySettlers.html.

1855-1870. *Kansas, Compiled Census Index* **[Online Database]**, indexed at the Ancestry.com website from census indexes obtained from Accelerated Indexing in 1999. Although the collection is supposed to include the 1850 federal census, no such census was taken in Kansas (which was first opened for white settlement in 1854). Also listed in the description is the 1890 Union Veterans Schedule for Kansas (which is not possible, since the Kansas veterans' schedules did not survive, and are not included in the National Archives set. Also, some of the KS territorial censuses are incorrectly labeled as "state census." That leaves the Kansas Territorial censuses of 1855, 1856, 1857, 1858, and 1859; the KS 1860 Federal Census Index; and the KS 1870 Federal Census Index. See http://search.ancestry.com/search/db.aspx?dbid=3548.

1855-1900s. *Naturalization Papers, Washington County, Kansas* **[Online Database]**, indexed at the USGenWeb site for Washington Co KS. See www.ksgenweb.org/washingt/naturali.htm.

1855-1911. *Kansas, County Marriages* **[Online Database]**, digitized and indexed at the FamilySearch.org website. The images are from marriage registers and records made by county clerks in Kansas. Includes the following counties: Allen, Anderson, Bourbon, Brown, Chase, Chautauqua, Cherokee, Clay, Coffey, Crawford, Doniphan, Douglas, Elk, Franklin, Geary, Greenwood, Harvey, Jackson, Jefferson, Johnson, Labette, Linn, Marshall, McPherson, Miami, Montgomery, Morris, Nemaha, Neosho, Osage, Pottawatomie, Riley, Saline, Sedgwick, Wabaunsee, Washington, Wilson, and Woodson. This database has 392,395 records. See https://familysearch.org/search/collection/1851040.
- See also, *Kansas, County Marriages, 1855-1911* **[Online Database]**, digitized at the Ancestry.com website. Ancestry's database is searchable using their *Browse this Collection* feature, which has a list of counties and year range of the records. This database has 154,156 records. See https://search.ancestry.com/search/db.aspx?dbid=60292.
- See also, *Kansas, County Marriage Records, 1811-1911* **[Online Database]**, digitized and indexed at the Ancestry.com website. (The 1811 date is impossible for Kansas). This database has 619,834 records. See https://search.ancestry.com/search/db.aspx?dbid=61371.

1855-1925. *Kansas State Census Collection* **[Online Database]**, digitized and indexed at the Ancestry.com website. This collection was acquired from the Kansas Historical Society (KHS) in Topeka, KS. The combined database has 8,238,557 records. The original microfilm was digitized and indexed by Ancestry from the following KHS microfilm titles:
- **1855** Kansas Territory Census. Microfilm reel K-1.
- **1856, 1857,** and **1858** Kansas Territory Censuses. Microfilm reel K-1.
- **1859** Kansas Territory Census. Microfilm reel K-1.
- **1865** Kansas State Census. Microfilm reels K-1 – K-8.
- **1875** Kansas State Census. Microfilm reels K-1 – K-20.
- **1885** Kansas State Census. Microfilm reels K-1-K-146.
- **1895** Kansas State Census. Microfilm reels K-1-K-169.
- **1905** Kansas State Census. Microfilm reels K-1-K-181.
- **1915** Kansas State Census. Microfilm reels K-1-K-271.
- **1925** Kansas State Census. Microfilm reels K-1-K-177.

Each index record includes: Name, Census date, Residence county, Residence state, Locality, Birthplace, Family number, Gender, Age, Birth year, Race, Other household members by name and age. See http://search.ancestry.com/search/db.aspx?dbid=1088.

✓ **NOTE: 1855-1925 Kansas State Census Collection.** This collection at the Ancestry.com website was acquired in 2009 and has a combined index to over 8.2 million records. By 2016, the FamilySearch.org website added all of the Kansas State Censuses as individual databases for each year (Listed herein by date). At first, one would expect the databases to be the same, because the images came from the same source. But there are minor differences between the two collections, mostly in the quality/readability of the image, as well as the quality/accuracy of the indexes. Checking several families in both collections revealed several minor differences, usually related to the spelling of names. The images are the same, but some of Ancestry's earlier images are not as clear or easy to read. Because of these differences, a researcher should check both collections for the same record.

1855-1926. *Vital Records, Woodson County, Kansas* **[Online Database]**, includes births and deaths, indexed in alpha groups at the USGenWeb site for Woodson Co KS. See www.ksgenweb.org/woodson/index.html.

1855-1956. *Postmasters of Franklin County* **[Online Database]**, listed at the Franklin CountyKansas.net website. See www.franklincountykansas.net/fcgs/v2n1/postmast.htm.

1855-1902. *Kansas, Fort Riley Hospital Muster Rolls* **[Online Database],** indexed at the Ancestry.com website. Source: Forts History Collection, KHS, Topeka. Established in 1853, A permanent hospital was first built there in 1855. The rolls may include the following details: Name, Rank, Unit, Date and length of enlistment, Date attached to the hospital and duties, and Date of the pay period and when last paid. This database has 7,421 records. See https://search.ancestry.com/search/db.aspx?dbid=2579.

1855-1940. See *Deed Records, 1857-1940; Indexes, 1855-1908, Leavenworth County, Kansas* **[Microfilm & Digital Capture],** from the original records at the Leavenworth courthouse. Filmed by the Genealogical Society of Utah, 1992, 92 rolls, beginning with FHL film #1853932 (Grantee and Grantor Indexes, 1855-1866). To access the digital images, see the online FHL catalog: **www.familysearch.org/search/catalog/584570**.

1855-2001 Probate Records, Coffee County, Kansas [Online Database], indexed alphabetically by surname groups, case no., party's last name, first name, date of filing, and type of case. Originally indexed at the KScourts.org site. For an archived database, see https://web.archive.org/web/20140506030454/www.kscourts.org/dstcts/4coprrec.htm.

1856, 1857, and 1858 Kansas Territorial Censuses **[Microfilm],** from the original records at the Kansas Historical Society in Topeka, KS. The 1856, 1857, and 1858 census name lists were filmed together on one roll (KHS reel no. K-1). Contents: **1856:** 4th district, Kansas Territory (includes part of Douglas, Johnson, and Franklin counties). District No. 4 was divided by "Free State," "Pro-Slavery," or "Doubtful." **1857:** Counties of Allen (part of 18th district), 4th district (copy of 1856 list), Anderson, Atchison (3rd district), Bourbon, Dorn, McGee, Brown, Calhoun, Davis, Doniphan, Douglas, Jefferson, Johnson, Leavenworth, Linn, Lykins, Marshall, Nemaha, Pottawatomie, and Riley. Also includes the census of Shawnees, native or adopted. **1858:** Johnson and Marshall counties only. These census records represent only a partial listing of voters. Filmed by the Kansas Historical Society, 1972, 1 roll, FHL film #1405337. To see if this microfilm was digitized yet, see the online FHL catalog: **www.familysearch.org/search/catalog/319728**.
- For descriptions of the 1855, 1856, 1857, 1858, and 1859 Kansas territorial censuses, visit the Kansas Historical Society webpage: **www.kshs.org/p/kansas-territorial-censuses-1855-1859/10960**.

"**1856 Kansas Territorial Census, Geary County**" **[Printed Article],** name list in *Kansas Kin* (Riley County Genealogical Society, Manhattan, KS), Vol. 18, No. 1 (Feb 1980).

"**1856 Kansas Territorial Census, Pottawatomie County**" **[Printed Article[,** name list in *Kansas Kin* (Riley County Genealogical Society, Manhattan, KS) Vol. 18, No. 1 (Feb 1980).

"**1856 Kansas Territorial Census, Riley County**" **[Printed Article],** name list in *Kansas Kin* (Riley County Genealogical Society, Manhattan, KS), Vol. 18, No. 1 (Feb 1980).

"**1857 Kansas Territorial Census, Bourbon County**" **[Printed Article],** name list in *Relatively Seeking* (Columbus, KS), Vol. 9, No. 1 (Spring 1988).

"**1857 Kansas Territorial Census, Calhoun County**" **[Printed Article],** name list in *Topeka Genealogical Society Quarterly*, Vol. 3, No. 1 (Jan 1973).

"**1857 Kansas Territorial Census, Davis County (now Geary County)**" **[Printed Article],** name list in *Kansas Kin* (Riley County Genealogical Society, Manhattan, KS), Vol. 17, No. 2 (May 1979).

"**1857 Kansas Territorial Census, Douglas County**" **[Printed Article],** name list in *Pioneer*, Vol. 6, No. 1 (Summer 1982).

"**1857 Kansas Territorial Census, Jefferson County**"**[Printed Article],** name list in *Yesteryears* (Wilson County Historical Society, Fredonia, KS) Vol. 5, No. 2 (Oct 1984).

"**1857 Kansas Territorial Census, Marshall County**" **[Printed Article],** name list in *Kansas Kin* (Riley County Genealogical Society, Manhattan, KS), Vol. 17, No. 2 (May 1979).

"**1857 Kansas Territorial Census, McGee County**" **[Printed Article],** name list in *Relatively Seeking* (Columbus, KS), Vol. 9, No. 1 (Spring 1988).

"**1857 Kansas Territorial Census, Nemaha County**" **[Printed Article],** name list in *Nemaha County Genealogical Society Newsletter* (Seneca, KS), Vol. 2, No. 3 (Feb 1995). An online version of this name list was indexed at the USGenWeb site for Nemaha Co KS: **http://files.usgwarchives.net/ks/nemaha/census/1857cens.txt**.

"**1857 Kansas Territorial Census, Neosho County**" **[Printed Article],** name list in *Relatively Seeking* (Columbus, KS), Vol. 9, No. 1 (Spring 1988).

"1857 Kansas Territorial Census, Pottawatomie County" [Printed Article], name list in *Kansas Kin* (Riley County Genealogical Society, Manhattan, KS), Vol. 17, No. 2 (May 1979).

"1858 Kansas Territorial Census, Marshall County" [Printed Article], name list in *Kansas Kin* (Riley County Genealogical Society, Manhattan, KS), Vol. 20, No. 3 (Aug 1982).

1858-1867. Old Settlers, Saline County, Kansas [Online Database], indexed at the USGenWeb site for Saline Co KS. See www.ksgenweb.org/saline/index.html.

1858-1928 Naturalizations, Franklin County, Kansas **[Online Database]**, originally indexed at the LouisReed.net site. For an archived database, see https://web.archive.org/web/20111006210339/www.louisreed.net/indexes/naturalizations.txt.

1859 Kansas Territorial Census **[Microfilm]**, from the original records at the Kansas Historical Society in Topeka, KS. The census lists voters by county, giving names of voters, dates of settlement, heads of families not voters, number of minors, number of colored persons, total, and remarks (often gives occupation). Filmed by the KSHS, 1972, reel No. K-1, FHL film #1654575. To see if this microfilm was digitized yet, see the online FHL catalog:
www.familysearch.org/search/catalog/553830.

1859 Census of Coffey County, Kansas **[Printed Book]**, compiled by Wanda Houck Christy, published by Coffey County Genealogical Society, Burlington, KS, 1985, FHL book 978.1 A1 no. 144.

1859 Woodson County, Kansas Census **[Printed Book]**, copied from original records by Wanda Christy, published by the Coffey County Genealogical Society, Burlington, KS, 1985, 8 pages. 978.1 A1 no. 54.

"1859 Kansas Territorial Census, Pottawatomie County" [Printed Article], name list in *Kansas Kin* (Riley County Genealogical Society, Manhattan, KS), Vol. 18, No. 4 (Nov 1980).

"1859 Kansas Territorial Census, Shawnee County" [Printed Article], name list in *Hedge Post*, Vol. 25, No. 3 (Dec 1999).

"1859 Kansas Territorial Census, Wabaunsee County" [Printed Article], in *Kansas Kin* (Riley County Genealogical Society, Manhattan, KS), Vol. 19, No. 2 (May 1981).

"1859 Kansas Territorial Census, Washington County" [Printed Article], name list in *Kansas Kin* (Riley County Genealogical Society, Manhattan, KS), Vol. 18, No. 3 (Aug 1980).

"1859 Kansas Territorial Census, Wyandot County" [Printed Article], see "Members of Wyandot families, 1859," in *Kansas State Historical Society Collections*, Vol. 15 (1919).

1859 Delinquent Tax List, Johnson County, Kansas **[Online Database]**, list by township at the USGenWeb site for Johnson Co KS:
www.ksgenweb.org/archives/johnson/land/taxes.txt.

1859-1935. *Kansas, Atchison, Topeka, and Santa Fe Railway Prior Service Records* **[Online Database]**, from a card index at the Kansas Historical Society in Topeka. The cards in this database serve as an index to "prior service" record files for employees of the Atchison, Topeka, and Santa Fe Railway. Prior service refers to employment with the railroad before 29 August 1935, when the Railroad Retirement Board took control of most railway employee pensions. Employees who retired before 29 August 1935 will not be included in the records unless they were rehired again sometime after 29 August 1935. This database has 95,958 records, see
www.ancestry.com/search/collections/2122.

1860. *Kansas Territory Federal Census (Federal Copy)* **[Microfilm & Digital Capture]**, from the original records at the National Archives, Washington, DC. Filmed twice by the National Archives, 1960, 1967, 9 rolls, beginning with FHL film #803346 (2nd filming, Allen, Anderson, Atchison, Bourbon, and Breckenridge counties). To access the digital images, see the online FHL catalog:
www.familysearch.org/search/catalog/704817.

1860 Kansas Territory Federal Census (Territory's Original Copy) and WPA Index **[Microfilm]**, from the original records at the Kansas Historical Society, Topeka, KS. This census manuscript is the original territorial set of the 1860 federal census, filmed separately from the federal copy. Filmed by the KHS, 4 reels, (no copies at FHL). In addition to the four reels of census schedules. a handwritten, eleven volume name index to the 1860 Kansas Territory Census was compiled by the WPA in the late 1930s and the index was microfilmed by the KHS on 33 reels. (No copy at FHL). For information, indexes, and the microfilm of the 1860 federal census schedules, see
www.kshs.org/genealogists/census/kansas/census1860ks.htm.

1860. *Kansas Territorial Settlers of 1860 who were born in Tennessee, Virginia, North Carolina, and South Carolina: A Compilation with Historical Annotations and Editorial Comment* **[Printed Book]**, by Clara Hamlett Robertson, published by Genealogical Publishing Co., Inc. Baltimore, 1976, 187 pages. Taken from the WPA index of the eleven-volume hand-written census books in the Kansas Historical Society archives together with maps of Kansas and eastern Colorado showing the area included in Kansas Territory, 1854-1860. FHL book 978.1 H2ro.

1860. *U.S. Census, Extracted From the 1860 U.S. Census of Arapahoe County, Kansas Territory* **[Printed Book]**, by Alan Granruth, published by the Foothills Genealogical Society, Lakewood, CO, 1995, 134 pages. For the areas of old Arapahoe County that included present Denver and Gilpin counties, Colorado, this is an alphabetized extract of the census households including dwelling, name, age, sex, color, occupation, personal property, & birthplace. FHL book 978.862 X28g. Also on microfilm, FHL film #2055223.

1860 Kansas Territorial Census Index, edited by Ronald Vern Jackson and Gary Ronald Teeples, published by Accelerated Indexing Systems, Bountiful, UT, 1978, 153 pages. Indexes names to pages from the federal copy and may not agree with indexed pages in the KS territorial set. FHL book 978.1 X22k 1860.

1860 Tax Roll, Chase County, Kansas **[Online Database]**, indexed at the USGenWeb site for Chase Co KS. See
www.ksgenweb.org/archives/chase/govt/taxroll.txt.

1860 Tax List, Miami County, Kansas **[Online Database]**, indexed for Richland and Wea Townships at the USGenWeb site for Miami Co KS. See
www.ksgenweb.org/miami/library/1860taxlist.html.

1860-1880. *Non-Population Census Schedules for Kansas, 1860-1880* **[Microfilm]**, from originals at the Kansas Historical Society, Topeka, KS; and National Archives, Washington, DC. Includes Industries-Manufacturers, Agriculture, Mortality, and Social Statistics Schedules. Filmed by the National Archives, 1988-1989, series A1130, 48 rolls, beginning with FHL film #1602429 (1860 Industries, Mortality & Social Statistics). To access the digital images, see the online FHL catalog:
www.familysearch.org/search/catalog/589474.

1860-1930. *Kansas Orphan Train Riders – These We Know* **[Printed Book]**, by Robert A. Hodge, first compiled in 1996 for the annual Kansas Orphan Train Reunion Group, Great Bend, Kansas. From 1860-1930, an estimated 5,000+ orphans and abandoned children were gathered from New York and brought to Kansas. This book contains three annual reports for the years 1996, 1997, and 1998, each with documented accounts of confirmed train arrivals arranged in geographical, then chronological order, and adds orphan train riders from sources other than the newspaper reports of their arrivals in Kansas. Published by the author, Emporia, KS, 1996-1998, 160+ pages, FHL book 978.1 J3h.

1860-1934 *City Directories, Leavenworth, Kansas* **[Microfilm]**, from originals by various publishers. Includes directories for 1860-1861, 1862-1863, 1863-1864, 1865-1866, 1866, 1868-1869, 1870-1871, 1872, 1873, 1874, 1875, 1877, 1878-1879, 1879-1880, 1880-1881, 1882, 1883, 1884, 1885, 1886, 1887, 1888, 1889, 1890, 1891-1892, 1892-1893, 1894-1895, 1896-1897, 1898-1899, 1900-1901, 1902-1903, 1903-1904, 1905-1906, 1907-1908, 1909, 1911-1912, 1913-1914, 1915-1916, 1917-1918, 1925, 1928, 1930, and 1934. Filmed by Research Publications, Woodbridge, CT, 1980-1984, 1992, 3 microfiche and 6 rolls, beginning with FHL fiche #60444042 (1860-1861 Leavenworth directory), and FHL film #1844155 (1863-1875 Leavenworth directories). For a complete list of roll numbers and contents of each roll, see the online FHL catalog page for this title:
www.familysearch.org/search/catalog/530189.

1860-1995 *Kansas Directories.* See *U.S. City Directories, 1822-1995* **[Online Database]**, digitized and indexed at the Ancestry.com website. See each directory title page image for the full title and publication information. This collection is one of the largest single databases on the Internet, with a total of 1.56 billion names, all indexed from scanned images of the city directory book pages. All states are represented except Alaska, and there are 143 cities of Kansas included, beginning with 1860 (Atkinson, Lawrence), 1862 (Leavenworth), 1868 (Topeka), and 1874 (Kansas City). For the complete list of Kansas cities/counties with directories, use Ancestry's *Browse this Collection* feature to choose a state, choose a city, and choose a directory year available for that city. See
https://search.ancestry.com/search/db.aspx?dbid=2469.

1861-1865. *Index to Compiled Service Records of Volunteer Union Soldiers Who Served in Organizations from the State of Kansas* **[Microfilm & Digital Capture]**, from the originals of the Adjutant General's Office, now at the National Archives, Washington, DC. Indexed by surname of soldier. Filmed by the National Archives, Washington, DC, 1964, FHL has 10 rolls,
- A-Br, FHL film #881837.

- Bu-C, FHL film #881838.
- D-F, FHL film #881839.
- G-Hom, FHL film #881840.
- Hon-Le, FHL film #881841.
- Lg-Mi, FHL film #881842.
- Mo-Ral, FHL film #881843.
- Ram-Sk, FHL film #881844.
- Sl-U, FHL film #881845.
- V-Z, FHL film #881846.

To access the digital images, see the online FHL catalog: **www.familysearch.org/search/catalog/313594**.

1861-1865. *United States Civil War Soldiers Index* **[Online Database]**, an index to soldiers who served in the Civil War, culled from 6.3 million soldier records in the General Index Cards to the Compiled Military Service Records in the National Archives. This index was a joint project of the U.S. National Park Service, the Federation of Genealogical Societies (FGS), and the Genealogical Society of Utah (GSU). Each record provides the full name of the soldier, state, regiment, whether Union or Confederate, the company, the soldier's rank, sometimes alternate names, the NARA publication and roll numbers. It is possible to search for Kansas regiments and see complete rosters of the soldiers. See **https://familysearch.org/search/collection/1910717**.

- See also, *Soldiers and Sailors Database, 1861-1865* **[Online Database]**, indexed at the National Park Service website. This is the original database containing information about the men who served in the Union and Confederate armies during the Civil War. Other information on the site includes histories of Union and Confederate regiments, links to descriptions of significant battles, and selected lists of prisoner-of-war records and cemetery records, which will be amended over time. This database has 6.3 million records. See **www.nps.gov/civilwar/soldiers-and-sailors-database.htm**.

1861-1865. *Kansas Civil War Soldiers* **[Online Database]**, indexed at the Ancestry.com website. Original data: Kansas Adjutant General Roll, Civil War Soldiers, 1861-1865. This database is a transcription of the Kansas Adjutant General's Roll of Civil War Soldiers. It provides the soldier's name, rank, residence, enlistment date, and muster date. It also has unit information and other helpful notes. This database has 20,644 records. See **https://search.ancestry.com/search/db.aspx?dbid=3916**.

1862-1866 Internal Revenue Lists for Kansas **[Microfilm & Digital Capture]**, from the originals at the National Archives, Central Plains Region, Kansas City, MO. Filmed by the National Archives, 1985, 3 rolls, as follows:
- Annual lists 1863-1864; Monthly lists Sept. 1862-Dec. 1864; and Special lists Aug.-Dec. 1864, FHL film #1578484.
- Annual lists 1865; Monthly lists 1865; Special lists 1865, FHL film #1578485.
- Annual lists 1866; Monthly lists 1866, FHL film #1578486.

To access the digital images, see the online FHL catalog: **www.familysearch.org/search/catalog/577948**.

1862-1868. *Kansas, Civil War Enlistment Papers, 1862, 1863, 1868* **[Online Database]**, indexed at the Ancestry.com website. Source: KHS, Topeka. This collection features enlistment papers of men who volunteered in Kansas to serve in the United States Army for up to three years during and just after the Civil War. The two-page forms include the recruit's name, birthplace, age, occupation, enlistment date, and unit. They also provide a short physical description. This database has 4,797 records. See **https://search.ancestry.com/search/db.aspx?dbid=1766**.

1862-1930. *Chase County, Kansas Registered Birth Index* **[Online Database]**, indexed at the Blue USGenWeb site for Chase Co KS. See **www.ksgenweb.org/chase/rodbirth.html**.

1862-2010. *Fort Scott, Kansas, Fort Scott National Cemetery* **[Online Database]**, digitized and indexed at the Ancestry.com website. This database contains digital images of all gravestones in Fort Scott National Cemetery, located in Fort Scott, Kansas. Fort Scott National Cemetery was established in 1862, and this collection includes burials through 2010 for more than 3,400 people. Cemetery section is provided for each image. Information on the markers varies. Some may contain only a number of initials; others may include facts such as name, birth date, death date, age, rank, and state of origin. This database has 6,426 records. See **https://search.ancestry.com/search/db.aspx?dbid=2300**.

1863-1899. *History of Chase County, Kansas: Professor D.A. Ellsworth's Abstracts* **(Online Database]**, indexed at the USGenWeb for Chase Co KS. See **www.ksgenweb.org/chase/ellsworth.html**.

1864-1972. *Kansas, Naturalization Abstracts* **[Online Database]**, indexed at the Ancestry.com website. KHS, Topeka, KS. This database includes one volume from Dickinson County (with a few entries from Marion, Logan, and possibly other counties). It lists only names with volumes and page numbers for record books listing declaration of intent, first papers, petition, and final papers. Some entries provide only a name, declaration or naturalization date, age, and native country, while others go into more detail and may include any of the following: Name, Birth date and place, Age, Country of origin, Naturalization or declaration date, Marital status, sometimes with date and place), Number of children, Date and port of entry to the U.S. Ship name or mode of travel, and Occupation. This database has 9,037 records. See https://search.ancestry.com/search/db.aspx?dbid=5175.

1865 Kansas State Census **[Microfilm & Digital Capture]**, from the originals at the Kansas Historical Society, Topeka, KS. The 1865 census lists all members of a household by name, including age, sex, race or color, and state or country of birth. Filmed by the KHS, 1951, 8 rolls, (FHL set has 9 rolls) as follows:
- Allen, Anderson, and Atchison Counties, KHS reel K-1, FHL film #570189.
- Bourbon, Brown, Butler, Chase, Clay, and Coffey Counties, KHS reel K-2; FHL film #570190.
- Davies, Dickinson, Doniphan, and Douglas Counties, KSHS reel K-3; FHL film #570191 (excludes Douglas).
- Douglas County, FHL film #570192.
- Franklin, Greenwood, Jackson, Jefferson, and Johnson Counties, KHS reel K-4; FHL film #570193.
- Linn, Lyon, Marion, Marshall, Miami, and Morris Counties, KHS reel K-6; FHL film #570195.
- Nemaha, Neosho, Osage, Ottawa, Pottawatomie, Riley, Saline, Shawnee, Wabaunsee, Woodson, and Wyandotte Counties, KHS reel K-7; FHL film #570196.

- To access the digital images, see the online FHL catalog: www.familysearch.org/search/catalog/188289.
- For indexes and microfilm of the KS 1865 state census schedules at the Kansas Historical Society, see www.kshs.org/genealogists/census/kansas/census1865ks.htm#microfilm.

1865 Kansas State Census **[Online Database]**, digitized and indexed at the FamilySearch.org website. Source: Kansas State Historical Society, Topeka. Each index record includes: Name, Event type, Event date, Event place, Gender, Age, Birth year, and Birthplace. A household listing shows all persons of the household as shown on the original record, plus much more information about the database, page no. FHL film number, etc. This database has 149,601 records. See www.familysearch.org/search/collection/1824715.

1865 Kansas State Census Index **[Microfilm]**, available at the Kansas Historical Society, Topeka, KS. (No copy at FHL). The KHS microfilm index circulates through interlibrary loan. Filmed by the KHS, 37 rolls, beginning with KS-1, No Name - Babcock, Eli). For indexes and microfilm of the KS 1865 state census schedules, see www.kshs.org/genealogists/census/kansas/census1865ks.htm#microfilm.

"1865 Kansas State Census, Bourbon County" [Printed Article], name list in *Four States Genealogist* (Galena, KS), Vol. 2, No. 2 (Jan 1970).

"1865 Kansas State Census, Butler County" [Printed Article], extract and index in *Midwest Genealogical Register* (Wichita, KS), Vol. 19, No. 3 (Oct 1984).

"1865 Kansas State Census, Franklin County" [Printed Article], surname index in *Franklin County Kansas Genealogical Society Quarterly* (Ottawa, KS), Vol. 3, No. 2 (Feb 1995).

1865 Kansas State Census (KHS) **[Printed Articles]**, countywide extracts and/or indexes, available at the Kansas Historical Society:
- **Leavenworth County** (call no. K 929.4 Pam vol. 1, no. 2).
- **Osage County** (call no. K 929.4 - Os1 1865).
- **Ottawa County** (call no. K 929.4 - Sa3c 1865).
- **Pottawatomie County** (call no. K 929.4 - P85 1865).
- **Riley County** (call no. 929.4 -R45 1855-1880).
- **Saline County** (call no. K 929.4 - Sa3c 1865).
- **Wabaunsee County** (call no. K 929.4 - W11 1865).

1865 Kansas State Census (FHL) **[Printed Articles]**, Countywide extracts and/or indexes, available at the Family History Library:
- **Atchison County**, FHL book 978.136 X2o 1865.
- **Dickinson County**, FHL book 978.1 A1 no. 67.
- **Greenwood County**, FHL book 978.1 A1 no. 202.
- **Leavenworth County**, FHL book 978.138 X22sp (includes 1855)
- **Ottawa County**, FHL book 978.1 A1 No. 186.
- **Pottawatomie County**, FHL book 978.132 X2p.
- **Riley County**, FHL book 978.1 A1 No. 151.
- **Saline County**, FHL book 978.1 A1 No. 186.
- **Wabaunsee County**, FHL book 978.1 A1 No. 109.

1865-1984. *Kansas, Federal Naturalization Records* **[Online Database]**, digitized and indexed at the Ancestry.com website. Source: National Archives records of District Courts of the U.S. The records include Petitions, Declarations, and Certificates. Each index record includes: Name, Gender, Record type, Birth date, Birthplace, Arrival date, Arrival place, and names of relatives. The document image has more information. This database has 31,597 records. See https://search.ancestry.com/search/db.aspx?dbid=61199.

1866-1931. *Kansas, Grand Army of the Republic Bound Post Records* **[Online Database],** indexed at the Ancestry.com website. Source: KHS, Topeka, KS. Records in this database come from GAR posts throughout the state of Kansas. Most are descriptive rolls or medical rolls. Details may include the following: Name, Age, Birthplace, Residence, Occupation, Service history, Unit(s), Rank, Discharge details, Engagements, Wounds, Date joined the GAR, Date, and place of death. This database has 29,019 records. See
https://search.ancestry.com/search/db.aspx?dbid=2580.

1866-1993. *Leavenworth County, Kansas Records at Ancestry.com* **[Online Database],** indexed at the Ancestry.com website. There are 42 databases with name lists from births, marriages, deaths, military, newspapers, tax lists, and histories, with over 600,000 records. See
https://search.ancestry.com/Places/US/Kansas/Leavenworth/Default.aspx.

1867 Miami County, Kansas Census **[Online Database],** this is unique county census for Miami County only, giving the names of persons 21 years or older and township of residence, indexed at the USGenWeb site for Miami Co KS.
- For surnames A-K, see
www.ksgenweb.org/miami/library/1867census1.html.
- For surnames L-Z, see
www.ksgenweb.org/miami/library/1867census2.html.

1867-1937. *Russell County, Kansas, Vitals and Newspaper Records* **[Online Database],** indexed at the Ancestry.com website. Original data: J. C. Ruppenthal, comp. Russell County Vitals and Probate Records 1800-1937. KHS, Topeka. Russel Co KS was established in 1867. This database contains index cards with birth, marriage, death, and other information extracted from the Russell County Record and other area newspapers. This database has 32,781 records:
https://search.ancestry.com/search/db.aspx?dbid=2201.

1868-1935 City Directories, Topeka, Kansas **[Microfilm]**, from originals of various publishers. Includes directories for 1868-1869, 1870-1871, 1871, 1872-1873, 1876-1877, 1878-1879, 1880, 1902, 1906, 1907, 1909, 1910, 1912, 1916, 1921, 1924, 1925, 1926, 1927-1928, 1929-1930, 1931, 1933, and 1935. Filmed by Research Publications, Woodbridge, CT, 1980-1984, 6 rolls, beginning with FHL film #1377556 (1868-1880 Topeka directories). For a complete list of roll numbers and contents of each roll, see the online FHL catalog page:
https://familysearch.org/eng/library/fhlcatalog/printing/titledetailsprint.asp?titleno=546282.

1870. *Kansas, 1870 Federal Census: Population Schedules* **[Microfilm & Digital Capture]**, from the originals at the National Archives. Filmed twice by the National Archives, 1962, 1968, 21 rolls, beginning with FHL film #545927 (Allen, Anderson, and Atchison Cos). To access the digital images, see the online FHL catalog: **www.familysearch.org/search/catalog/698897.**

1870 Kansas Census Index **[Printed Book]**, edited by Raeone Christensen Steuart, published by Heritage Quest, Bountiful, UT, 2000, 798 pages, FHL book 978.1 X22k 1870.

1870s-1890s. *Early Settlers, Smith County, Kansas* **[Online Database]**, indexed at the USGenWeb site for Smith Co KS. See
www.ksgenweb.org/archives/smith/local/settlers.txt.

1870-1906 Naturalizations, Sedgwick County, Kansas **[Online Database]**, indexed at the USGenWeb site for Sedgwick Co KS.
http://mhgswichita.org/Sedgnaturalizations.html.

1870-1892. See *Kansas, Swedish Church Records, 1861-1918* **[Digital Capture],** includes records of the First Lutheran Church, Mission Hills, Johnson Co KS, for the period 1870-1892. To access the digital images, see the online FHL catalog:
www.familysearch.org/search/catalog/3042282.

1870-1954 Coroner's Records Index Cards, Sedgwick County, Kansas **[Microfilm & Digital Capture]**, from originals at the Sedgwick County Clerk's office, Wichita, KS. Filmed by the Genealogical Society of Utah, 2004, 2 rolls, FHL film #1221012 (Index cards: Abel, Grace – Nussbaum, John), and FHL film #1221013 (Index cards: O'Brien, Ed – Williams, Jim). To access the digital images, see the online FHL catalog: www.familysearch.org/search/catalog/1219565.

1872 List of Barton County Residents **[Online Database]**, listed at the USGenWeb site for Barton Co KS. See **www.ksgenweb.org/barton/1872list.html.**

1872 Census of Ford County, Kansas **[Microfilm & Digital Capture]**, from a typescript copy, taken from "Early Ford County" by Ida Ellen Rath. Includes list from coroner's records of Ford County (1883-1938). Arranged alphabetically by surname. Filmed by the Genealogical Society of Utah, 1983, 1 roll, FHL film #1035609). To access the digital images, see the online FHL catalog:
www.familysearch.org/search/catalog/162561.

1873-1969. *Kansas, Fraternal Order Death Index* **[Online Database]**, indexed at the Ancestry.com website. This is a shared database, *Fraternal Order Death Notices*, with the Kansas Historical Society. Each record includes: Name, Residence place, Death date, Notes, and a link the KHS website, where there are good details about the fraternal orders involved. This database has 53,132 records. See
https://search.ancestry.com/search/db.aspx?dbid=70657.

1874. *Index and Business Directory from 1874 Atlas of Johnson County, Kansas* **[Online Database]**, indexed at the USGenWeb site for Johnson Co KS. See www.ksgenweb.org/archives/johnson/bkindex/atlas.txt.

1874-1875 City Directory, Topeka, Kansas **[Online Database]**, indexed at the USGenWeb site for Shawnee Co KS. See
www.ksgenweb.org/shawnee/library/topekdir.htm.

1875 Kansas State Census **[Microfilm]**, from originals at the Kansas Historical Society, Topeka, KS. The 1875 census lists all members of household by name, including age, sex, race or color, state, or country of birth, and where from to Kansas (state or country). Filmed by the KHS, 21 rolls, 1951, beginning with KHS reel 1875 K-1 (Allen, Anderson, Atchison, and Barber Counties). For the indexes and microfilm of the KS 1875 state census schedules, see
www.kshs.org/p/kansas-1875-state-census/10946.

- See also, *1875 Kansas State Census Index* **[Microfilm]**, available at the Kansas Historical Society, Topeka, KS. (No copy at FHL). The KSHS microfilm index circulates through interlibrary loan. List the year and reel number when placing an interlibrary loan request. Filmed by the KHS, 157 rolls, beginning with reel #KS-1 (Child – Alexander, E. M.), see www.kshs.org/p/kansas-1875-state-census/10946.

- See also, *State Census of 1875* **[Microfilm & Digital Capture]**, digitized at FamilySearch.org. The FHL set contains 23 rolls, beginning with FHL film #570198 (Allen – Barber counties). To access the digital images, see the online FHL catalog:
www.familysearch.org/search/catalog/188296.

- See also, *Kansas State Census, 1875* **[Online Database]**, digitized and indexed at the FamilySearch.org website. Source: Kansas State Historical Society, Topeka. Each index record includes: Name, Event type, Event date, Event place, and Page no. The format of the 1875 KS state census page was similar to the 1860 federal census. Every member of a household was listed, but no relationships given. In addition to the place of birth for each person was the question, "Where from to Kansas – naming State or Territory of U.S. or country, if a Foreigner." This database has 618,774 records. See
www.familysearch.org/search/collection/1825178.

"1875 Kansas State Census, Barton County" **[Printed Article]**, name list in *Barton County Genealogical Society Quarterly* (Great Bend, KS), beginning with Vol. 10, No. 2 (Spring 1990).

1875 Kansas State Census (KHS) **[Printed Articles]**, countywide extracts and/or indexes, available at the Kansas Historical Society:
- **Crawford County** (call no. K 929.4 -C85 1875)
- **Dickinson County** (call no. K 929.4 -D56 1875)
- **Harvey County** (call no. K 929.4 Pam vol. 1, no. 1)
- **Jefferson County** (call no. K 929.4 -J35 1875)
- **Montgomery County**, Cherry Township (call no. K 929.4 -M76 1870-1900)
- **Pawnee County** (call no. K 929.4 - P28 1875)
- **Phillips County** (call no. K 929.4 -P54 1875)
- **Riley County** (call no. K 929.4 – R45 1855-1880)
- **Saline County** (city of Salina only) (call no. K 929.4 -Sa3 Sa33 1875)
- **Sedgwick County** (call no. K 929.4 -Se2 1875)
- **Sumner County** (call no. K 929.4 - Su6 1875)
- **Wilson County** (call no. 929.4 - W69 1875)

1875 Kansas State Census (FHL) **[Printed Articles]**, countywide extracts and/or indexes, available at the Family History Library:
- **Atchison County**, see FHL book 978.136 X2o 1865
- **Douglas County**, see FHL book 978.165 X2d 1875
- **Jefferson County**, see FHL book 978.137 X22ei 1875
- **Riley County**, FHL book 978.128 X2d
- **Sedgwick County**, FHL book 978.186 X2c 1875
- **Wilson County**, FHL book 978.1925 X2i

1875 List of Destitute Persons, Miami County, Kansas **[Online Database]**, indexed at the USGenWeb site for Miami Co KS. See
www.ksgenweb.org/miami/library/1875destitute.html.

1876 Tax Roll for Phillips County, Kansas **[Online Database]**, indexed at the USGenWeb site for Phillips Co KS. See
www.ksgenweb.org/phillips/pl1876taxroll.html.

1877. *The History of Anderson County, Kansas from its First Settlement to the Fourth of July 1876* [Online database], indexed by chapters at the USGenWeb site for Anderson Co KS. See http://files.usgwarchives.net/ks/anderson/history/1877/anderson.

1878 City Directory, Wichita, Kansas [Online Database], indexed at the USGenWeb site for Sedgwick Co KS. See http://mhgswichita.org/1878dir.html.

1878 Atlas, List of Patrons, Miami County, Kansas [Online Database], indexed at the USGenWeb site for Miami Co KS. See www.ksgenweb.org/miami/library/1878Atlas.html.

1879-1890 Birth Announcements, Rawlins County, Kansas [Online Database], indexed at the USGenWeb site for Rawlins Co KS: www.ksgenweb.org/rawlins/births1890.html.

1879 Kansas Biographical Dictionary [Online Database], Original data: The United States Biographical Dictionary and Portrait Gallery of Eminent and Self-Made Men. Chicago and Kansas City, USA: S. Lewis, 1879. See www.ancestry.com/search/collections/7709.

1880. *Kansas, 1880 Federal Census: Soundex and Population Schedules* [Microfilm & Digital Capture], from the original records at the National Archives. Filmed by the National Archives, ca1970, 80 rolls, beginning with FHL film #446997 (Soundex, A000-A536), and FHL film #1254372 (Population schedules: Allen, Anderson, Arapahoe, and Atchison Co). To access the digital images, see the online FHL catalog: www.familysearch.org/search/catalog/673553.

1880 Kansas Federal Census (Short Form), Brown County, Kansas [Microfilm], from the original records at the Brown County Courthouse in Hiawatha, Kansas. This is the county's copy of the 1880 federal census, often called the "Short Form," retained at the courthouse. Kansas had 93 counties in 1880, and every one of them had a Short Form prepared. Only the Brown County list survives today. The name lists are divided by township and arranged within each township in alphabetical order by the first letter of a surname. The abbreviated list gives a name, color, sex, and age only. Filmed by the Genealogical Society of Utah, 1993, 1 roll, FHL film #1871055. To see if this microfilm was digitized yet, see the online FHL catalog: www.familysearch.org/search/catalog/673870.

1880 Kansas Post Offices: Originally Published in Edwin Green's Leavenworth City Directory [Digitized Book], extracted by Debra F. Graden, ca2000, 29 pages. To view a digital version of this book, visit the online FHL catalog page: https://dcms.lds.org/delivery/DeliveryManagerServlet?dps_pid=IE208979.

1880-1940. *Kansas Grand Army of the Republic Post Reports* [Online Database], indexed at the Ancestry.com website. Source: KHS, Topeka. This collection consists of quarterly muster rolls sent to the state department from 500 local posts. Each index record includes: Name, Age, Birthplace, Residence, Occupation, and Military service. This database has 563,516 records: https://search.ancestry.com/search/db.aspx?dbid=1700.

1880s-1890s. *Naturalization Records, District Court of Rawlins County, Kansas* [Online Database], index of final naturalization records, listed at the USGenWeb site for Rawlins Co KS. See www.ksgenweb.org/rawlins/final%20naturalization.html. For first Naturalization records, see www.ksgenweb.org/rawlins/first%20naturalization.html.

1881 Township Histories, Wilson County, Kansas [Online Database], township histories from the Historical Atlas of Wilson County, Kansas, published in 1881. Indexed at the USGenWeb site for Wilson Co KS. See www.ksgenweb.org/wilson/library/history/index.html.

1881-1886 Poor Farm Records, McPherson County, Kansas [Online Database], extracted at the USGenWeb site for McPherson Co KS. See www.ksgenweb.org/mcpherso/Mc%20Pherson%20Poor Farm%20Book1.htm.

1881-1896 Index to Naturalization Papers, Rooks County, Kansas [Online Database], indexed at the USGenWeb site for Rooks Co KS. See www.ksgenweb.org/archives/rooks/citizen/natural.txt.

1882 Historical Plat Book, Doniphan County, Kansas [Online Database], indexed at the RootsWeb site for Doniphan Co KS. See http://freepages.genealogy.rootsweb.ancestry.com/~pyle/DoniphanPlat1882.html.

1883 Andreas History. See *History of the State of Kansas: Containing a Full Account of its Growth from an Uninhabited Territory to a Wealthy and Important State, of its Early Settlement, A Supplementary History and Description of its Counties,*

Cities, Towns and Villages, Their Advantages, Industries and Commerce, to Which Are Added Biographical Sketches and Portraits of Prominent Men and Early Settlers **[Printed Book, Microfilm & Digital Version]**, by A. T. Andreas, original published Chicago, 1883, reprint published by Walsworth Pub. Co., Marceline, MO, 1976, 2 vols., Includes index. FHL book 978.1 H2hi 1976 and FHL film #982248. To access the digital version, see the online FHL catalog: www.familysearch.org/search/catalog/173714.

1883 Andreas History, Chautauqua County, Kansas **[Online Database]**, includes the extracted chapter for Chautauqua with an added index at the Kancoll.org website. See www.kancoll.org/books/cutler/chautauqua/chautauqua-co-p1.html.

1883 List of Farmers, Miami County, Kansas **[Online Database]**, indexed at the USGenWeb site for Miami Co KS. See www.ksgenweb.org/miami/library/1883Farmers.html.

1883. *Pensioners on the Roll, January 1, 1883* **[Online Database]**, a transcription of the 1883 list of all military pensioners for the state of Kansas. This was a statewide project of the KSGenWeb Digital Library. Most of the pensioners listed were Union veterans of the Civil War, but an occasional veteran of the War of 1812 shows up as well. For a county selection page, see www.ksgenweb.org/archives/pensions.htm.

1883 City Directory, Wichita, Kansas **[Online Database]**, indexed at the USGenWeb site for Sedgwick Co KS. See http://mhgswichita.org/1883dir.html.

1885 Kansas State Census **[Microfilm]**, from the originals at the Kansas Historical Society, Topeka, KS. The 1885 census lists all members of a household by name, including age, sex, race or color, and state or country of birth. Also listed: where from to Kansas (state or country) and military record (condition of discharge, state of enlistment, letter or name of company or command, number of regiment or other organization to which attached, arm of the service, and name of military prison if confined in one). Filmed by the society, 1969-1970, 146 rolls beginning with KHS reel K-1 (Allen Co. – Humboldt city and twp.; Iola Twp.). For indexes and microfilm of the KS 1885 state census schedules, see www.kshs.org/p/kansas-1885-state-census/10948#microfilm.

- See also, *1885 Kansas State Census Index (City of Topeka)* **[Microfilm]**, available at the Kansas Historical Society, Topeka, KS. (No copy at FHL). The KSHS microfilm index circulates through interlibrary loan. List the year and reel number when placing an interlibrary loan request. Filmed by the KSHS, 7 rolls, beginning with reel #KS-1 (Abarr, Mary - Collisi, Wm.). For the indexes and microfilm of the KS 1885 state census schedules, see www.kshs.org/p/kansas-1885-state-census/10948#microfilm.

- See also, *State Census of 1885* **[Microfilm & Digital Capture]**, digitized at FamilySearch.org. The FHL set contains 151 rolls, beginning with FHL film #975699 (Allen Co. - Humboldt city and twp.; Iola Twp.). To access the digital images, see the online FHL catalog: www.familysearch.org/search/catalog/292166.

- See also, *Kansas State Census, 1885* **[Online Database]**, digitized and indexed at the FamilySearch.org website, see www.familysearch.org/search/collection/1825188.

1885. See *Kansas Settlers of the Grand Army of the Republic, 1885: A Compiled List of Union Soldiers Listed in the State Census of 1885 from Dickinson, Ellsworth, Lincoln, McPherson, Ottawa and Saline Counties* **[Printed Book]**, compiled by Robert A. VanDyne, published by Smoky Valley Genealogical Society, Salina, KS, ca1985, 82 pages. Gives name, age, birthplace, regiment and company, and other notes. Includes index. FHL book 978.15 M2v.

"1885 Kansas State Census, Butler County" **[Printed Article]**, name list published serially in *Midwest Genealogical Register* (Wichita, KS), beginning with Vol. 18, No. 2 (Jul 1983).

"1885 Kansas State Census, Cherokee County" **[Printed Article]**, complete name index published in *Relatively Seeking* (Columbus, KS), Vol. 11, No. 1 (Spring 2000).

"1885 Kansas State Census, Franklin County" **[Printed Article]**, name lists by townships, in *Franklin County Kansas Genealogical Society Quarterly* (Ottawa, KS), beginning with Vol. 7, No. 1 (1999).

1885 Kansas State Census (KHS) **[Printed Articles]**, countywide extracts and/or indexes, available at the Kansas Historical Society:
- **Crawford County** (call no. K 929.4 - C85 1885)
- **Dickinson County** (call no. K 929.4 -D56 1885)
- **Jefferson County** (call no. K 929.4 -J35 1885)
- **Leavenworth County** (call no. K 929.4 -L48 1885)
- **Montgomery County**, Cherry Township (call no. K 929.4 -M76 1870-1900)
- **Montgomery County**, W. Cherry Township (call no. K 929.4 -M76 1880-1900)

- **Riley County** (call no. K 929.4 - R45 1885)
- **Wilson County** (call no. K 929.4 - W69 1885)

1885 Kansas State Census (FHL) [Printed Articles], countywide extracts and/or indexes, available at the Family History Library:
- **Leavenworth County**, FHL book 978.138 X22s
- **Riley County**, FHL book 978.128 X2dk
- **Wilson County**, FHL book 978.1925 X22i

1885 City Directory, Wichita, Kansas [Online Database], indexed at the USGenWeb site for Sedgwick Co KS. See
http://mhgswichita.org/1885dir.html.

1885-1911. Kansas County Birth Records [Online Database], indexed at the FamilySearch.org website. Index and images of birth records from a few county courthouses in Kansas. Counties include Butler, Cherokee, Clay, Elk, and Marion. Date ranges and record content vary by county. Images are not available for Elk and Marion counties. Each index record includes: Name, Event type, Event date, Event place, and Gender. This database has 21,152 records. See
www.familysearch.org/search/collection/2727732.
- See also, **Kansas, Births and Christenings Index, 1885-1911 [Online Database],** indexed at the Ancestry.com website. This database has 51,418 records. See
https://search.ancestry.com/search/db.aspx?dbid=2567.

1885-1930. Kansas, Deaths and Burials [Online Database], indexed at the FamilySearch.org website. This is a name index to deaths and burial records from the state of Kansas taken from FHL sources. Each index record includes: Name, Gender, Death date, Death place, Age, Birth date, Birthplace, Race, and Marital status. This set has 31,747 records. See
https://familysearch.org/search/collection/1674844.
- This same database is available at the Ancestry.com website, see
https://search.ancestry.com/search/db.aspx?dbid=2570.

1885-1999. Riley County, Kansas Records at Ancestry.com [Online Database], indexed at the Ancestry.com website. There are 9 databases from obituaries, funeral cards, state censuses and agricultural censuses. These databases have over 72,000 records:
https://search.ancestry.com/Places/US/Kansas/Riley/Default.aspx.

1886-1935 City Directories, Wichita, Kansas [Microfilm], from the originals by various publishers, Includes directories for 1886, 1887, 1888, 1892, 1894, 1898-1899, 1900, 1903-1904, 1904-1905, 1906, 1907, 1908, 1909, 1910, 1911, 1912, 1913, 1914, 1915, 1916, 1917, 1918, 1919, 1920, 1922, 1923, 1924, 1925, 1926, 1927, 1928, 1929, 1930, 1931, 1932, 1934, and 1935. Filmed by Research Publications, Woodbridge, CT, ca1995, 16 rolls, beginning with FHL film #2258174. For a complete list of roll numbers and contents of each roll, see the online FHL catalog for this title:
www.familysearch.org/search/catalog/1025593.

1887 City Directory, Wichita, Kansas [Online Database], indexed at the USGenWeb site for Sedgwick Co KS. See
http://mhgswichita.org/1887dir.html.

1887-1888 Directories, Reno County, Kansas [Online Database], city directories for Arlington, Haven, Partridge, Plevna, South Hutchinson, Sylvia and Turon. Indexed at the USGenWeb site for Reno Co KS. See
www.ksgenweb.org/reno/citydirectory.htm.

1887-1910. Index to Certificates of Death for Wichita, Kansas [Microfilm & Online Database], from a manuscript in the collections of the Midwest Historical and Genealogical Society in Wichita, KS. Filmed by the Genealogical Society of Utah, 2003, 1 roll, FHL film #2365654. To see if this microfilm was digitized yet, see the online FHL catalog:
www.familysearch.org/search/catalog/1161846.
- An online database of this index is available at the USGenWeb site for Sedgwick Co KS. See
www.ksgenweb.org/sedgwick/death.html.

1888 City Directory, Wichita, Kansas [Online Database], indexed at the USGenWeb site for Sedgwick Co KS. See
http://mhgswichita.org/1888dir.html.

1889 City Directory, Wichita, Kansas [Online Database], indexed at the USGenWeb site for Sedgwick Co KS. See
http://mhgswichita.org/1889STREETDIRECTORY.html.

1889. Kansas, Enrollment of Civil War Veterans [Online Database], indexed at the Ancestry.com website. Source: Records of the Adjutant General's Office. KSH, Topeka. This collection includes benefit enrollment records for Union army and navy veterans and their widows and orphans who were living in Kansas. The enrollments were taken in 1889, grouped by the state of enlistment, and compiled into volumes. The enrollment form asked for the following details: Name of soldier and widow, Rank at discharge, Company, Regiment, State, Unit, Whether a prisoner of war, Wounds or diseases contracted, If pensioner,

Amount of pension, Whether a member of the G.A.R. and what post, Present address, If deceased, date, and place of death, Whether indigent or dependent on other for support, Names of orphan children under age 16, and Remarks. This database has 50,977 records. See https://search.ancestry.com/search/db.aspx?dbid=2956.

1889 Roster of Ex-Union Soldiers and Soldiers' Widows in Lincoln County, Kansas [Online Database], extracted from a newspaper article, listed at the RootsWeb site for Lincoln Co KS. See http://freepages.genealogy.rootsweb.ancestry.com/~lincolncounty/index.html.

1889 List of the Old Soldiers, Rawlins County, Kansas [Online Database], indexed at the USGenWeb site for Rawlins Co KS. See www.ksgenweb.org/rawlins/soldiers.html.

1889 Business Directory, Seward County, Kansas [Online Database], indexed at the USGenWeb site for Seward Co KS. See http://files.usgwarchives.net/ks/seward/directories/business/1889/1889sout98ms.txt.

1890. Johnson County, Kansas, Personal Property Taxpayers – 1890 [Microfilm], from the originals published in the Olathe Mirror newspaper. Filmed by the Genealogical Society of Utah, 1990, 1 roll, FHL film #1597757.

1891 Voters List, Decatur County, Kansas [Online Database], indexed by name and PO address at the USGenWeb site for Decatur Co KS. See www.ksgenweb.org/decatur/index.html.

1891 City Directory, Wichita, Kansas [Online Database], indexed at the USGenWeb site for Sedgwick Co KS. See http://mhgswichita.org/1891dir.html.

1891-1899 Birth Announcements, Rawlins County, Kansas [Online Database], indexed at the USGenWeb site for Rawlins Co KS: www.ksgenweb.org/rawlins/births1891.html.

1894 GAR Posts, Clay County, Kansas [Online Database], indexed by post at USGenWeb site for Clay Co KS. See www.ksgenweb.org/clay/GAR.html.

1895 Kansas State Census [Microfilm], from the originals at the Kansas Historical Society, Topeka, KS. The 1895 census lists all members of household by name, including age, sex, race or color, and state or country of birth. Also listed: where from to Kansas (state or country) and military record (condition of discharge, state of enlistment, letter or name of company or command, number of regiment or other organization to which attached, arm of the service, and name of military prison if confined in one). Filmed by the society, 1953-1958, KHS set contains 169 rolls, beginning with #1895-K-1 (Allen County, townships, A-Z) For the Indexes and Microfilm of the KS 1895 state census schedules, see www.kshs.org/p/kansas-1895-state-census/10951.

- *See also, 1895 Kansas State Census Index* [Microfilm & Online Database], available at the Kansas Historical Society, Topeka, KS. Includes indexes for Clay and Ness counties and the cities of Topeka and Fort Scott, and Soldier and Topeka townships in Shawnee county. (No FHL film). This microfilm circulates through interlibrary loan from KSHS:
- 1895 Index - Clay & Ness Counties (KS-1-7).
- 1895 Index - City of Fort Scott (KS-8-11).
- 1895 Index - City of Topeka, Topeka Township & Soldier Township, all in Shawnee County

Online Index: A searchable index is now located at this site, representing the results of a volunteer project to index each of the 1895 Kansas counties. Search by Surname, Soundex, First name, City/township, and/or County. Visit the site for the list of counties included in the index. See www.kshs.org/p/kansas-1895-state-census/10951.

- See also, *State Census of 1895* [Microfilm & Digital Capture], digitized at FamilySearch.org. The FHL set contains 202 rolls, beginning with FHL film #570221 (Allen County, townships, C-S). To access the digital images, see the online FHL catalog: www.familysearch.org/search/catalog/188308.

- See also, *Kansas State Census, 1895* [Online Database], digitized and indexed at the FamilySearch.org website. Source: Kansas State Historical Society, Topeka. Each index record includes: Name, Event type, Event date, Event place, Gender, Age, Birth year, Birthplace, and Page number. This database has 1,364,060 records. See www.familysearch.org/search/collection/1825193.

1895 Kansas State Census (KHS) [Printed Articles], countywide extracts and/or indexes, available at the Kansas Historical Society:
- **Atchison County, City of Atchison** call no. K 929.4 -At2 1895)
- **Clay County** (call no. K 929.4 - C57 1895)
- **Crawford County, City of Pittsburg** (card index)
- **Montgomery County, Cherry Township** (call no. K 929.4 -M76 1870-1900)

- Montgomery County, West Cherry Township (call no. K 929.4 -M76 1880-1900)
- Phillips County, Prairie View Township (call no. 978.1 -P54 P884, pgs. 371-382)
- Reno County, City of Hutchinson (card index)
- Riley County (call no. K 929.4 - R45 1895)
- Thomas County (card index)
- Trego County (card index)
- Wilson County (call no. K 929.4 - W69 1895)

1895 Kansas State Census [Printed Articles], countywide extracts and/or indexes, available at the Family History Library:
- Jefferson County, FHL book 978.137 X22i 1895
- Clay County, FHL book 978.1275 X2b 1895
- Riley County, FHL book 978.128 X22k 1895
- Wilson County, FHL book 978.1925 X22i

"1895 Kansas State Census, Cherokee County" [Printed Article], name list in *Prospectors, Diggers, and Doers*, beginning with Vol. 5 (1983).

"1895 Kansas State Census, Barton County" [Printed Article], name list in *Barton County Genealogical Society Quarterly (Great Bend, KS)*, beginning with Vol. 2, No. 2 (1982).

"1895 Kansas State Census, Morton County" [Printed Article], in *Genealogical Council of Kansas Newsletter* (Topeka, KS), beginning with Vol. 21, No. 1 (Jul 1995).

"1895 Kansas State Census, Sedgwick County" [Printed Article], as "Residents age 21+ years, 1895," in *Midwest Genealogical Register* (Wichita, KS), Vol. 6, No. 1 (Jun 1971).

1895-1936. Leavenworth, Kansas, U.S. Penitentiary, Name Index to Inmate Case Files [Online Database], indexed at the Ancestry.com website. National Archives, Records of the Bureau of Prisons. This series consists of an index of 49,000 records from the Leavenworth, Kansas U.S. Penitentiary of individual inmate case files. While the contents of the files vary from inmate to inmate, nearly all include a Record Sheet that gives several details about the inmate's crime, court fines, sentence, etc. Most files also include a mug shot photograph of the inmate with front and profile views and could also include a rap sheet of prior and subsequent arrests, convictions, and incarcerations: https://search.ancestry.com/search/db.aspx?dbid=34594.

1895-1982. Kansas, Grant County, Census Records [Online Database], digitized and indexed at FamilySearch.org. Source: Grant County Clerk, Ulysses, KS. This database has 7,330 images, see www.familysearch.org/search/collection/3288444.

1898-1899. See *The Fighting Twentieth: 20th Kansas Volunteer Infantry: An Account of the Kansas Volunteers in the Spanish-American War, 1898-1899* [Online Database], includes rosters, indexed at The Digital Library of the KSGenWeb. See www.ksgenweb.org/archives/statewide/military/ks20.htm.
- See also, *Kansas Troops in the Volunteer Service of the United States in the Spanish and Philippine Wars, Mustered in Under the First and Second Calls of the President of the United States: May 9, 1898-October 28, 1899* [Digital Capture], the Adjutant General of the State of Kansas, digitized by FamilySearch International, 2011. To access the digital images, see the online FHL catalog: www.familysearch.org/search/catalog/666770.

1900. Kansas, 1900 Federal Census: Soundex and Population Schedules [Microfilm & Digital Capture], from the original records held by the Bureau of the Census in the 1940s. After microfilming, Congress allowed the Census Bureau to destroy the originals to free up space for WWII-related files. Filmed on 185 rolls, ca1970, beginning with FHL film #1243904 (Soundex: A000 thru A325), and FHL film #1240469 (Population schedules: Allen and Anderson Cos.). To access the digital images (Population Schedules), see the online FHL catalog: www.familysearch.org/search/catalog/652372.

1901 History of Labette County, Kansas [Online Database], indexed at the USGenWeb site for Labette Co KS. See www.ksgenweb.org/archives/labette/1901/index.html.

1901-1929 Naturalization Records, Decatur County, Kansas [Online Database], indexed at the USGenWeb site for Decatur Co KS: www.ksgenweb.org/decatur/Naturalization/naturalization_record_1901_1929.htm.

1902. Department of Kansas G.A.R. – to the 36th National Encampment, Washington, DC, Oct 1902 [Online Database], a reproduction of the originals, a state project of The Digital Library of the KSGenWeb. See www.ksgenweb.org/archives/gar2/1902/index.html.

1902-1928 City Directories, Lawrence, Kansas **[Microfilm]**, from the originals by various publishers. Includes directories for 1902-1903, 1905, 1907, 1909, 1911, 1913-1914, 1915, 1917, 1919, 1925-1926, and 1927-1928. Filmed by Research Publications, Woodbridge, CT, ca1995, 2 rolls, FHL film #2308854 (1902-1914 Lawrence directories) and FHL film #2308855 (1915-1928 Lawrence directories).

1902-1930. ***Kansas, Security Benefit Association, Death Index*** **[Online Database],** indexed at the Ancestry.com website. Original data: Knights and Ladies of Security/Security Benefit Association. Index to Death Claims. Kansas Historical Society. This is a shared database with the Kansas Historical Society website. Each index record includes: Name, Death date, Death place, and a link to the KHS website (with a good description of these records). This database has 10,209 records. See
https://search.ancestry.com/search/db.aspx?dbid=70658.

1902-1935 City Directories, Salina, Kansas **[Microfilm]**, from the originals by various publishers. Includes directories for 1902-1903, 1904-1905, 1907-1908, 1909, 1911, 1913, 1915, 1917, 1919, 1921, 1923, 1925, 1927, 1929, 1931, 1933, and 1935. Filmed by Research Publications, Woodbridge, CT, ca1995, 4 rolls, beginning with FHL film #2310452 (Salina & Saline Co Directory). For a complete list of roll numbers and the contents of each roll, see the online FHL catalog page for this title. See **www.familysearch.org/search/catalog/1051402**.

1903 Biographical History of Cloud County, Kansas **[Online Database]**, includes an Historical Index and a Biographical Index, at the USGenWeb site for Cloud Co KS. See
www.ksgenweb.org/archives/cloud/1903.

1904-1911 Birth Records, Scott County, Kansas **[Online Database],** indexed at the USGenWeb site for Scott Co KS. See
www.ksgenweb.org/scott/EarlyBirths.html.

1904-1935 City Directories, Hutchinson, Kansas **[Microfilm]**, from the originals by various publishers. Includes directories for 1904, 1906, 1907, 1909, 1910, 1912, 1913, 1915, 1917, 1919, 1923, 1924, 1933, and 1935. Filmed by Research Publications, Woodbridge, CT, ca1995. 4 rolls, beginning with FHL film #2308844 (1904 Hutchinson City Directory). For a complete list of roll numbers and the contents of each roll, see the online FHL catalog page for this title. See **www.familysearch.org/search/catalog/1050888**.

1905 Standard Atlas of Decatur County, Kansas **[Online Database]**, indexed by Landowners, Township Plats, Portraits, and Patron's Directory at the RootsWeb site for Decatur Co KS. See **www.rootsweb.ancestry.com/~ksdecatu/Plat/1905_standard_atlas_of_decatur.htm**.

1904 History of Cherokee County, Kansas **[Online Database]**, indexed at the USGenWeb site for Cherokee Co KS. See
www.ksgenweb.org/archives/cherokee/cherokee-1904ndx.html.

1904-1934 City Directories, Kansas City & Wyandotte County, Kansas **[Microfilm]**, from the originals by various publishers. Includes directories for 1904, 1909, 1912, 1924-1925, 1925, 1927, 1929, 1930, 1932, and 1934. Filmed by Research Publications, Woodbridge, CT, c1995, 4 rolls, beginning with FHL film #2308850 (1904, 1909, 1912 Kansas City, KS directories). For a complete list of roll numbers and the contents of each roll, see the online FHL catalog page for this title:
www.familysearch.org/search/catalog/1050979.

1905 Kansas State Census **[Microfilm]**, from the originals at the Kansas Historical Society, Topeka, KS. The 1905 census lists all members of household by name, including age, sex, race or color, and state or country of birth. Also listed: where from to Kansas (state or country) and military record (condition of discharge, state of enlistment, letter or name of company or command, number of regiment or other organization to which attached, arm of the service, and name of military prison if confined in one). Filmed by the society, 181 rolls, beginning with #1905-K-1 (Allen County cities of Bassett, Elsmore, Gas City, Humboldt & Iola, pt. 1). (The FHL does not have this series of microfilm). For the Indexes and microfilm of KS 1905 state census schedules, see **www.kshs.org/p/kansas-1905-state-census/10953**.
- See also, ***1905 Kansas State Census Index*** **[Microfilm]**, (For residents of selected cities), from the originals at the Kansas Historical Society, Topeka, KS. Arranged by city, then alphabetically by surname. Index lists full name, county of residence, and page on the census schedules where the person was shown. Index for the following cities:
- **Ft. Scott** (Bourbon Co.), KS-1-4.
- **Pittsburg** (Crawford Co.), KS-41-45.
- **Lawrence** (Douglas Co.), KS-29-33.
- **Ottawa** (Franklin Co.), KS-39-41.
- **Leavenworth** (Leavenworth Co.), KS-33-39.
- **Hutchinson** (Reno Co.), KS-4-7.

- **Salina** (Salina Co.), KS-45-47.
- **Topeka** (city), **Topeka Township**, and **Soldier Township** (Shawnee Co.), KS-48-60.
- **Wichita** (Sedgwick Co.), KS-60-69.
- **Kansas City**, **Argentine** and **Rosedale** (Wyandotte Co.), KS-7-29.

This microfilm circulates through interlibrary loan from KHS. (No FHL film). When ordering, list the year and reel number when placing an interlibrary loan request (e.g., "1905-KS-7"). For the Indexes and microfilm of KS 1905 state census schedules, see www.kshs.org/p/kansas-1905-state-census/10953.
- See also, *Kansas State Census (Index), 1905* [Digital Capture], digitized by FamilySearch International, 2016, an index to all Kansas counties of 1905. To access the digital images, see the online FHL catalog: www.familysearch.org/search/catalog/2659394.

"1905 Kansas State Census, Wilson County" [Printed Article], index of names in *Heritage Genealogical Society Quarterly*, Vol. 16, No. 2 (Sep 1986) through Vol. 17, No. 1 (Jul 1987).

1905 Kansas State Census [Printed Articles], countywide extracts and/or indexes, available at the KHS & FHL:
- **Riley County** (call no. K 929.4 - R45 1905)
- **Riley County**, FHL book 978.128.
- **Wilson County** (call no. K 929.4 - W69 1905)

1905 History of Crawford County, Kansas [Online Database], indexed at the USGenWeb site for Crawford Co KS. See www.ksgenweb.org/archives/crawford/history/1905/.

1906 Standard Atlas, Rawlins County, Kansas [Online Database], indexed at the USGenWeb site for Rawlins Co KS. See http://skyways.lib.ks.us/genweb/rawlins/1906%20Atlas/atlas_a_b.htm.

1907 Business Directory and History of Wabaunsee County, Kansas [Online Database], indexed at the USGenWeb site for Wabaunsee Co KS: www.ksgenweb.org/archives/wabaunse/1907/index.html.

1907 and 1928 Plat Map Index, Cheyenne County, Kansas-German Russian People [Online Database], indexed at the odessa3.org site. See www.odessa3.org/collections/land/kansas/link/cheyenn.txt.

1909-1950. Kansas, Grove County, Enumeration Books and List of Residents [Online Database], list organized by township. Source: Grove Co KS register of deeds. This database has 98.094 records, see www.familysearch.org/search/collection/2854369.

1910. *Kansas, 1910 Federal Census: Soundex and Population Schedules* [Microfilm & Digital Capture], from the original records held by the Bureau of the Census in the 1940s. After microfilming, Congress allowed the Census Bureau to destroy the originals to free up space for WWII-related files. Filmed on 176 rolls, ca1970, beginning with FHL film #1370301 (Soundex: A000-A346), and FHL film #1374444 (Population schedules: Allen, Anderson, and Atchison Cos.). To access the digital images (Population Schedules), see the online FHL catalog: www.familysearch.org/search/catalog/652668.

1910. *Kansas 1910 U.S. Federal Census Index* [CD-ROM], compiled and published by Heritage Quest, Bountiful, UT, 2001, FHL CD No. 1194.

1910-1911 Plat Book of Scott County, Kansas [Online Database], list of patrons indexed at the USGenWeb site for Scott Co KS. See www.ksgenweb.org/scott/Patrons1910.html.

1911 Sunflower, Yearbook of Kansas State Normal School, Emporia, Kansas [Online Database], indexed at USGenWeb site for Lyon Co KS. See http://files.usgwarchives.net/ks/lyon/schools/1911sunflower.txt.

1911 History of Wyandotte County, Kansas [Online Database], indexed at the USGenWeb site for Wyandotte Co KS. See www.ksgenweb.org/archives/wyandott/history/1911/volume1/index.html.

1911-1924. Chase County, Kansas Doctor's Birth Register Index [Online Database], indexed at the USGenWeb site for Chase Co KS. See www.ksgenweb.org/chase/DoctorBirths.html.

1912 Polk's Kansas State Gazetteer and Business Directory, Cherokee County, Kansas Sections [Online Database], indexed at the USGenWeb site for Cherokee Co KS. See www.ksgenweb.org/cherokee/library2/polk/index.html.

1912 Polk's Kansas State Gazetteer and Business Directory, Gove County, Kansas Sections [Online Database], indexed at the USGenWeb site for Gove Co KS. See www.ksgenweb.org/archives/1912/g/gove_county.html.

1912 Polk's Kansas State Gazetteer and Business Directory, Jewell County, Kansas Sections [Online Database], indexed at the USGenWeb site for Jewell Co KS. See www.ksgenweb.org/jewell/library/polk.html.

1912 Polk's Kansas State Gazetteer and Business Directory, Shawnee County, Kansas Sections [Online Database], indexed at the USGenWeb site for Shawnee Co KS. For Topeka, see www.ksgenweb.org/shawnee/library/polk1912.htm. For Auburn, Berryton, Dover, Oakland, Pauline, Rossville, Silver Lake, and Tecumseh, see www.ksgenweb.org/shawnee/library/polk1912b.htm.

1914-1919. *Kansas, Camp Funston Military Records* [Online Database], indexed at the Ancestry.com website. Source: Military History Collection, KHS, Topeka. Camp Funston was established at Fort Riley in Kansas as a World War I training center for recruits from Arizona, Colorado, Kansas, Missouri, Nebraska, New Mexico, and South Dakota. This collection includes personnel records from the 89th Division, 353rd Infantry, and the 314th Engineers. Personnel forms vary but may contain a variety of details, such as the following: Name, Enlistment date, Next of kin, Home address, Education level, Occupation, Rank and serial number, Posts held, Promotions, and Record of injuries. This database has 49,580 records. See https://search.ancestry.com/search/db.aspx?dbid=2396.

1915 Kansas State Census [Microfilm], from the originals at the Kansas Historical Society, Topeka, KS. (No FHL film). The 1915 census lists all members of household by name, including age, sex, race or color, and state or country of birth. Also listed: where from to Kansas (state or country) and military record (condition of discharge, state of enlistment, letter or name of company or command, number of regiment or other organization to which attached, arm of the service, and name of military prison if confined in one). Filmed by the society, 271 rolls, beginning with #1915-K-1 (Allen County cities of Bassett, Carlyle, Elsmore, Gas City, Geneva, Humboldt & Iola, pt. 1). For the indexes and microfilm of the KS 1915 state census schedules, see www.kshs.org/p/kansas-1915-state-census/10955.
- See also, *1915 Kansas State Census Index* [Microfilm], (For residents of selected cities), from the originals at the Kansas Historical Society, Topeka, KS. (No FHL film). This microfilm circulates through interlibrary loan from KHS. List the year and reel number when placing an interlibrary loan request.
  • **Fort Scott** (Bourbon County), 1915-KS-69, KS-1, and KS-2
  • **Pittsburg** (Crawford County), 1915-KS-36-40.
  • **Leavenworth** (Leavenworth County), 1915-KS-30-36.
  • **Topeka Township** (excludes city of Topeka), and **Soldier Township** (Shawnee County), 1915-KS-41- 42.
  • **Wichita** (Sedgwick County), 1915 - KS-42-57.
  • **Kansas City & Rosedale** (Wyandotte County), 1915-KS-3-30.

For the indexes and microfilm of the KS 1915 state census schedules, see www.kshs.org/p/kansas-1915-state-census/10955.
- See also, *Kansas State Census, 1915* [Digital Capture], digitized at FamilySearch.org. Includes all Kansas counties of 1915. To access the digital images, see the online FHL catalog: www.familysearch.org/search/catalog/2640442.
- See also, *Kansas State Census, 1915* [Online Database], digitized and indexed at FamilySearch.org, with 301,658 records. www.familysearch.org/search/collection/2640442.

1915 Kansas State Census (KHS) [Printed articles], countywide extracts and/or indexes, available at the Kansas Historical Society:
  • **Atchison**, **Lawrence**, & **Topeka** street address index.
  • **Benton City** (Butler County), call no. K 369.133 K133m Ser.2 v.164 p.1).
  • **Kiowa County** card index.
  • **Riley County** (call no. K 929.4 - R45 1915 vol. 1-4).

1915 Landowners Directory, Sedgwick County, Kansas [Online Database], indexed at the USGenWeb site for Sedgwick Co KS. www.ksgenweb.org/sedgwick/land/landowners1915.html.

1915 Kansas State Census Abstract, Riley County [Printed Book], compiled by Stella Frey, Golda Sitz, and Peggy Ward, editing assistance by Mary Cottom, published by the Riley County Genealogical, Society, Manhattan, KS, 1990, 459 pages. FHL book 978.128 X2f 1915.

1917 History of Marshall County, Kansas [Online Database], indexed at the USGenWeb site for Marshall Co KS. See http://files.usgwarchives.net/ks/marshall/bookindx/marshsur.txt.

1917-1918. *Kansas, World War I Selective Service System Draft Registration Cards, 1917-1918* [Microfilm & Digital Capture], from the originals at the National Archives, East Point, GA. The draft cards are arranged alphabetically by county or city, then by the surname of the registrants. Filmed by the National Archives, 1987-1988, 71 rolls, beginning with FHL film #1643420 (KS Allen Co A-Z, Anderson Co A-G). To access the digital images, see the online FHL catalog: www.familysearch.org/search/catalog/746978.

1917-1918. See *Kansas, 1917-1918 Civilian Draft Registration Cards* [Online Database], indexed by county, this index is a work in progress by the KSGenWeb. For the list of counties available, see www.ksgenweb.org/archives/regcards.htm.

1917-1918. See *Registration of Axis Aliens in Kansas: January 1918 through June 1918* [Printed Book], indexed and published by Kansas Statistical Publications Company, Overland Park, KS, 1992, 76 pages. All males not naturalized who were subjects of the German Empire, Alsace-Lorraine in France, and Schleswig-Holstein in Denmark were required to register with the Department of Justice. A number of their spouses were also listed. See FHL book 978.1 P4r. To access a digital version of this book, see the online FHL catalog for this title. See www.familysearch.org/search/catalog/640820.

1917-1918. *Kansas, Registration Affidavits of Alien Enemies* [Online Database], digitized and indexed at the Ancestry.com website. Source: National Archives microfilm M1997. When the United States declared war on Germany in 1917, President Wilson authorized the registration of aliens living in the United States. This included all non-naturalized German males aged 14 and older, who were classified as enemy aliens. A later proclamation in April 1918 required Austro-Hungarian nationals and women within the age and nationality requirements to register as well. This included American-born wives of non-naturalized Germans, who had to register as alien females. Each index record has an extensive array of questions, along with a list of household members by name and relation; and the document image provides even more information. This database has 21,741 records. See https://search.ancestry.com/search/db.aspx?dbid=2137.

1917-1919. *Kansas Casualties in the World War* [Digitized Book], originally published by the Kansas Adjutant General, 1921, 162 pages. To access the digital version, see the online FHL catalog page: www.familysearch.org/search/catalog/1989419.

1917-1919. *Kansas, World War I Veteran Collection* [Online Database], indexed at the Ancestry.com website. Source: KHS, Topeka. This is an image-only database, and includes newspaper clippings, photos, service records, letters from family and friends, biographical sketches, and other documents related to Kansas veterans who served in World War I. The collection came about in large part as the Kansas State Historical Society solicited and compiled items about Kansas veterans, asking specifically for "letters, especially from overseas; a photograph; and a brief biography containing date and place of birth, residence, parents' names, occupation, and names of spouse and children." Use the Browse this Collection feature to find materials, all filed by name and arranged alphabetically. See https://search.ancestry.com/search/db.aspx?dbid=2021.

1917-1919. *The Kansas State Guard* [Online Database], transcribed from *History and Roster of the Kansas State guard, August 6, 1817 to November 11, 1919.* The Roster and Reports of Activities section includes the names of every member, by company, battalion, and location. This was a statewide project of the Digital Library of the KSGenWeb. See www.ksgenweb.org/archives/military/ksguard.

1918 Registration Affidavits of Aliens, Kansas [Microfilm & Digital Capture], from the originals at the National Archives Branch in Kansas City, Missouri. Alphabetical name lists are by county. Filmed by the Genealogical Society of Utah, 1991, 20 rolls, beginning with FHL film #1769240 (Registration affidavits of alien enemy 1918, Allen County-Atchison County. To access the digital images, see the online FHL catalog: www.familysearch.org/search/catalog/663093.

1919-1961. *Kansas, City and County Census Records* [Online Database], digitized and indexed at the Ancestry.com website. Original data: *State Board of Agriculture. Population Schedules and Statistical Rolls: Cities (1919–1961)*. Kansas State Historical Society, Archives Division, Topeka, KS. Although less known than the Kansas state census database, this collection contains three times the number of entries. Included are various city and county census records and population schedules from all of Kansas. They include information about inhabitants of a town, enumeration of livestock, and agriculture. Prior to 1953 the population schedules list the address, name of the head of household, and the number of individuals living in the household. Beginning in 1953 the schedules list all the members of the household and their ages. The images of the original forms can provide details about crops, livestock, and other items. This database has 26,670,748 records. See https://search.ancestry.com/search/db.aspx?dbid=2270. - NOTE: As a comparison, a search in this database for the surname Dollarhide had 2,750 hits; while a search in Ancestry's *Kansas State Census Collection, 1855-1925* had 816 hits.

1920. *Kansas, 1920 Federal Census: Soundex and Population Schedules* **[Microfilm & Digital Capture]**, from the original records held by the Bureau of the Census in the 1940s. After microfilming, Congress allowed the Census Bureau to destroy the originals to free up space for WWII-related files. Filmed on 164 rolls, ca1970, beginning with FHL film #1820522 (Population schedules: Allen, Anderson, and Chautauqua Cos.). To access the digital images (Population Schedules), see the online FHL catalog: www.familysearch.org/search/catalog/570083.

1920 Medical Directory, Barber County, Kansas **[Online Database]**, indexed at the USGenWeb site for Barber Co KS. See
http://files.usgwarchives.net/ks/barber/directories/business/1920/barberco28nms.txt.

1920 Medical Directory, Bourbon County, Kansas **[Online Database]**, indexed at the USGenWeb site for Bourbon Co KS. See
http://files.usgwarchives.net/ks/bourbon/directories/business/1920/bourbonc30nms.txt.

1920 Medical Directory, Cherokee County, Kansas **[Online Database]**, indexed at the USGenWeb site for Cherokee Co KS. See
http://files.usgwarchives.net/ks/cherokee/directories/business/1920/cherokee35nms.txt.

1920 Medical Directory, Crawford County, Kansas **[Online Database]**, indexed at the USGenWeb site for Crawford Co KS. See
http://files.usgwarchives.net/ks/crawford/directories/business/1920/crawford43nms.txt.

1920 Medical Directory, Douglas County, Kansas **[Online Database]**, indexed at the USGenWeb site for Douglas Co KS. See
http://files.usgwarchives.net/ks/douglas/directories/business/1920/douglasc47nms.txt.

1920 Medical Directory, Ellsworth County, Kansas **[Online Database]**, indexed at the USGenWeb site for Ellsworth Co KS. See
http://files.usgwarchives.net/ks/ellsworth/directories/business/1920/ellswort51nms.txt.

1920 Medical Directory, Harvey County, Kansas **[Online Database]**, indexed at the USGenWeb site for Harvey Co KS. See
http://files.usgwarchives.net/ks/harvey/directories/business/1920/harveyco64nms.txt.

1920 Medical Directory, Labette County, Kansas **[Online Database]**, indexed at the USGenWeb site for Labette Co KS. See
http://files.usgwarchives.net/ks/labette/directories/business/1920/labettec74nms.txt.

1920 Medical Directory, Linn County, Kansas **[Online Database]**, indexed at the USGenWeb site for Linn Co KS. See
http://files.usgwarchives.net/ks/linn/directories/business/1920/linncoun78nms.txt.

1921 Standard Atlas of Decatur County, Kansas **[Online Database]**, indexed by Landowners, Township Plats, Portraits, and Patron's Directory at the RootsWeb site for Decatur Co KS. See
www.rootsweb.ancestry.com/~ksdecatu/1921/1921_standard_atlas_of_decatur_c.htm.

1921 Social Register, Wichita, Kansas **[Online Database]**, indexed at the USGenWeb site for Sedgwick Co KS. See
http://files.usgwarchives.net/ks/sedgwick/bios/kssocreg.txt.

1921. See *Wyandotte County, Kansas Farmers 1921: Extracted from Kansas Farmer & Mail & Breeze, Directory of Farmers & Breeders of Leavenworth, Wyandotte and Johnson Counties, 1921* **[Printed Book]**, extracted by Debra F. Graden, published by the author, Leavenworth, KS, 1999, 282 pages, FHL book 978.139 E4g.

1921. See *Johnson County, Kansas Farmers 1921: Extracted from Kansas Farmer & Mail & Breeze, Directory of Farmers & Breeders of Leavenworth, Wyandotte and Johnson Counties, 1921* **[Printed Book]**, extracted by Debra F. Graden, published by the author, Leavenworth, KS, 1999, 270 pages, FHL book 978.1675 E4g. For a digital version of this book, see the FHL catalog page for this title:
www.familysearch.org/search/catalog/1531091.

1925 Kansas State Census **[Microfilm]**, from the originals at the Kansas Historical Society, Topeka, KS. (No FHL film). The 1925 census lists all members of household by name, including age, sex, race or color, marital status, state or country of birth, and relationship to head of household. Also listed: where from to

Kansas (state or country), military record (condition of discharge, state of enlistment, letter or name of company or command, number of regiment or other organization to which attached, arm of the service, and name of military prison if confined in one), and citizenship (year of immigration to the U.S. and year of naturalization if naturalized). Filmed by the society, 177 rolls, beginning with KHS reel #1925-K-1 (Allen County: Bassett, Elsmore, Gas City, Humboldt, Iola, LaHarpe, Mildred, Moran, Carlyle & Cottage Grove Twp.). Locate film numbers for all 271 reels at the KSHS website. For the indexes and microfilm of the KS1925 state census schedules, see
www.kshs.org/p/kansas-1925-state-census/10957.
- See also, *1925 Kansas State Census Index, Shawnee County* [Microfilm], from the originals at the Kansas Historical Society, Topeka, KS. (No FHL film). This microfilm circulates through interlibrary loan from KSHS. List the year and reel number when placing an interlibrary loan request.
- **Topeka Township** (excluding city of Topeka) & **Soldier Township** (Shawnee County), 1925-K-57, K - 1, & K – 2.

For the indexes and microfilm of the KS 1925 state census schedules, see **www.kshs.org/p/kansas-1925-state-census/10957.**
- See also, *Kansas State Census, 1925* [Digital Capture], digitized by FamilySearch International, 2016. To access the digital images, see the online FHL catalog: **www.familysearch.org/search/catalog/2659395.**
- See also, *Kansas State Census, 1925* [Online Database], indexed at FamilySearch.org, includes all household members, see
www.familysearch.org/search/collection/2659395.

1928 Standard Atlas, Rawlins County, Kansas [Online Database], indexed at the USGenWeb site for Rawlins Co KS. See
www.ksgenweb.org/rawlins/1928%20Atlas/atlas_a_b.htm.

1930. *Kansas, 1930 Federal Census: Population Schedules* [Microfilm & Digital Capture], from the original records held by the Census Bureau in the 1940s. After microfilming, Congress allowed the Census Bureau to destroy the originals to free up space for WWII-related files. Filmed on 39 rolls, ca1970, beginning with FHL film #2340427 (Allen, Anderson, and Barber Cos.). To access the digital images (Population Schedules), see the online FHL catalog: **www.familysearch.org/search/catalog/1035341.**

1930. *Kansas, Enrollment of WWI Veterans* [Online Database], indexed at the Ancestry.com website. Source: *Enrollment of World War One Veterans or Their Widows and Orphans, 1930*, KHS, Topeka, KS. This database contains forms used to enroll eligible Kansans for World War I veterans' benefits. Forms were to be filled out by anyone who had served in any branch of service during World War I or by a widow or child under sixteen whose deceased husband or father had served. The forms asked for the following details: Name, Branch of service, Address, Widow's name (if applicable), Names and addresses of orphan children under 16, Rank at discharge, whether wounded, injured, or deceased, and American Legion post if a member. This database has 34,377 records. See
https://search.ancestry.com/search/db.aspx?dbid=2955.

1940. *Kansas, 1940 Federal Census: Population Schedules* [Digital Capture], digitized images taken from the microfilm of original records held by the Bureau of the Census in the 1940s. After microfilming, Congress allowed the Census Bureau to destroy the originals to free up space for WWII-related files. Digitizing of the 1940 census schedules microfilm images was done for the National Archives and made public in 2012. No microfilm copies were distributed. To access the digital images, see the online FHL catalog: **www.familysearch.org/search/catalog/2057756.**

1940 Federal Census Finding Aids [Online Database]. The National Archives prepared a special website online with a detailed description of the 1940 federal census. Included at the site are descriptions of location finding aids, such as Enumeration District maps, Geographic Descriptions of Census Enumeration Districts, and a list of 1940 City Directories available at the National Archives. The finding aids are all linked to other National Archives sites. See
www.archives.gov/research/census/1940/general-info.html#questions.

1940-1946. *Kansas, WWII Selective Service Index* [Online Database], indexed at the Ancestry.com website. Source: KHS, Topeka. Each index record includes: Name, Entry date, Entry place, Military branch, Service number, and a link to the KHS website. This database has 26,398 records. See
https://search.ancestry.com/search/db.aspx?dbid=70795.

1940-1947. *Kansas, World War II Draft Registration Cards* [Digital Capture], from the originals at the National Personnel Records Center, St. Louis, MO.

Digitized by FamilySearch International, 2017. To access the digital images, see the online FHL catalog: www.familysearch.org/search/catalog/2796751.

1941-1946. *State of Kansas World War II Army Casualties: Between May 27, 1941 and January 31, 1946, Indexed A-Z* **[Printed Book]**, compiled by Joy L. Snow, Published ca2000, 179 pages, FHL book 978.1 M2s.

1942. *Kansas, Military Records: World War II 4th Draft Registration Cards* **[Digital Capture],** from the original records at the National Personnel Records Center, St. Louis, MO. These cards represent older men, ages 45 to 65 in April 1942, that were registered for the draft. They had birth dates between 28 Apr 1877 and 16 Feb 1892. Includes name of individual, date and place of birth, address, age, telephone number, employer's name and address, name and address of person who would know where the individual can be located, signature, and physical description. Digitized by FamilySearch International, 2015. To access the digital images, see the online FHL catalog: www.familysearch.org/search/catalog/2624880.

1945-1970. *Kansas, United Spanish War Veterans Reports of Deaths* **[Online Database],** indexed at the Ancestry.com website. Source: KHS, Topeka, KS. These are death notices (called *Taps*) for members who belonged to United Spanish War Veterans camps in Kansas. These are veterans who did not die in the war, so the death dates can be decades later. Members were not necessarily born in or die in Kansas. Most of the records are on a standard form that can include: Name, Office/rank in USWV, Military rank, Ship or regiment, Marital , Status, Name and address of widow, Birth date, Birthplace, Death date, Place of death, Place of burial, and Cemetery (location). This database has 1,201 records. See https://search.ancestry.com/search/db.aspx?dbid=1680.

1984-Current. Kansas Recent Newspaper Obituaries [Online Database], digitized and indexed newspaper obituaries at the GenealogyBank website, including newspapers from these cities: Abilene, Augusta, Chanute, Columbus, Derby, Dodge City, El Dorado, Emporia, Garden City, Girard, Greensburg, Hays, Hutchinson, Johnson County, Junction City, Kansas City, Lansing, Lawrence, Leavenworth, Liberal, Manhattan, McPherson, Newton, Olathe, Ottawa, Parsons, Pittsburg, Pratt, Salina, St. John, Topeka, Wamego, Wellington, , and Wichita. See www.genealogybank.com/gbnk/obituaries/explore/USA/Kansas.

74 • *Census Substitutes & State Census Records*

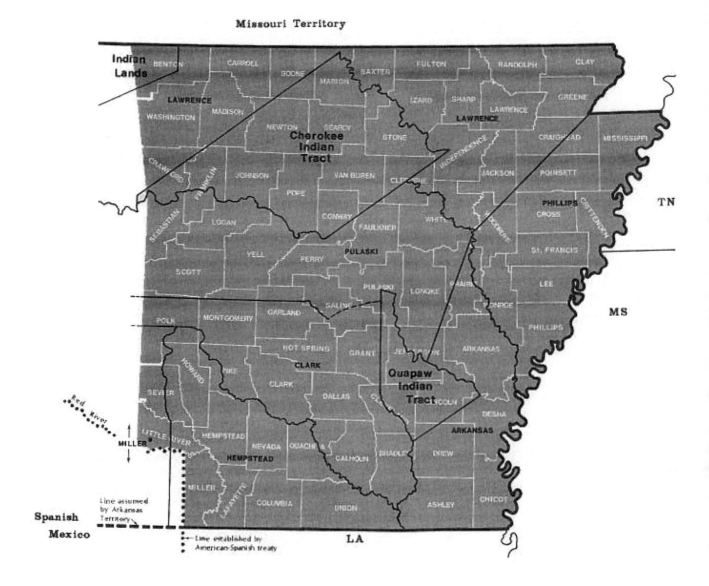

Arkansas Territory in 1820. This map shows the territory at the time of the August 1820 federal census. That census year was lost for the entire territory, but the map shows Arkansas's earliest political jurisdictions. The 75 modern counties of Arkansas are shown in white, while the 1820 jurisdictions are shown in black. When first created in July 1819, Arkansas Territory included most of the lands of present Oklahoma. Not shown on the map is the so-called "Indian Territory," separated from Arkansas Territory in 1828. For detailed maps of the Indian Land Cessions in Arkansas, see **http://usgwarchives.net/maps/cessions/ilcmap5.htm.** (Arkansas 1, Map 5 includes Quapaw Indian Tract); and **http://usgwarchives.net/maps/cessions/ilcmap6.htm.** (Arkansas 2, Map 6 includes Cherokee Indian Tract). * **Note:** The strange case of Miller County was the only time in history when an American county was created outside of the U.S. Old Miller was established in April 1820 by an Arkansas Territorial legislature that did not clearly understand the 1819 treaty boundary between the U.S. and Spain. Settlers in Miller County living south of the Red River were actually in Spanish Mexico (now Texas). **Map source:** page 33, *Map Guide to the U.S. Federal Censuses, 1790-1920,* by William Thorndale and William Dollarhide.

Arkansas
Censuses & Substitute Name Lists

Historical Timeline for Arkansas, 1539-1860

1539-1542. Spaniard Hernando DeSoto was a famous Conquistador, having spent time as a loyal captain under Francisco Pizarro in the conquest of Peru in 1532. He had returned to Spain a hero in 1534 where he was granted an enormous share of the treasure of the Inca conquest.

He requested from King Charles I the governorship of Guatemala, and to lead an expedition for the "discovery of the South Sea." But Charles gave him the Governorship of Cuba instead. On his own in 1539, DeSoto assembled and financed a party of some 620 men, 500 beef cattle, 250 horses and 200 pigs. He had a mandate from Charles I to find gold, find the Pacific Ocean, and find a direct passage to China.

He embarked from Havana with a total of nine ships and landed on present Florida's West Coast. The DeSoto party traveled on land past Tampa Bay and then further north to present-day Georgia. DeSoto and his party were the first Europeans to travel inland into present-day Georgia, South Carolina, North Carolina, Kentucky, Tennessee, Alabama, Mississippi, and Arkansas.

He seemed to like Arkansas, because he meandered within the land of the Osage and Quapaw for nearly a year. At one point, he had floated down the Mississippi as far south as the mouth of the Arkansas River. To gain dominance over the Quapaw Indians, DeSoto had tried to convince them that he was immortal, but when he died from fever in 1542, his men wrapped his body in blankets filled with sand and then tossed him unceremoniously into the Mississippi to prevent his discovery. Today, there are at least three towns along the Mississippi River that claim to be the burial site of Hernando DeSoto.

Hernando DeSoto's legacy in Arkansas lives on with the domestic pigs he intentionally released to run wild there. Their descendants are now called Razorbacks.

1673. Floating down river from the Great Lakes, French Jesuit Father Jacques Marquette and trader Louis Juliet reached the Quapaw villages of Arkansae and Kappa.

1682. French explorer René-Robert Cavelier (Sieur de la Salle) erected a cross near the confluence of the Mississippi River and the Gulf of Mexico, after floating down rivers from the Great Lakes area. He claimed the entire Mississippi Basin for Louis XIV of France, for whom Louisiana was named. All of the rivers and streams flowing into the Mississippi were part of the Mississippi Basin and included in the Louisiana claim.

1686. Arkansas Post. A son of an expatriated Italian, French soldier/trader/explorer Henri DeTonti founded Arkansas Post, a few miles up the Arkansas River from its mouth at the Mississippi. Arkansas Post was the first white settlement in the Lower Mississippi Valley. Only a few of the first settlers were French recruits, a larger group were Germans, recruited from the present Alsace-Loraine area.

1700. French Missionaries arrived in the Osage and Quapaw villages of present-day Arkansas to convert the natives to Catholicism.

1721-1762. French Louisiana. By 1721, several hundred French and German farming colonists abandoned Arkansas Post. Some returned to France, some relocated in the French Caribbean Islands, and some (mostly the Germans) moved further down the Mississippi closer to New Orleans. The trading fort at Arkansas Post remained and continued to be the focal point for trade with the Quapaw and Osage Indians in the region. As a failed farming community, Arkansas

Post was typical of the French efforts to colonize Louisiana. They were much more interested in trading for furs with the Indians.

For the next 40 years after the Arkansas Post experiment, the French presence in the Mississippi Basin consisted mainly of single French voyageurs paddling their canoes from one trading post to the next. The French established military forts at strategic locations, mainly as a means of protecting the trappers during their contacts with the Indians.

In comparison, the British colonies by 1762 had constructed over 2,500 miles of improved wagon roads on the Atlantic Coast between Boston and Charles Town. The British colonies had an economy based on town tradesmen surrounded by small farms, with the exchange of goods and produce up and down the coast. During this same period, the French had built one 12-mile-long road in all of Louisiana, and that was only to provide portage between rivers. In the Mississippi Basin, there were very few French farming communities, and there was very little exchanging of goods or produce, except for the trapping and trading of furs.

1762. The French secretly ceded Louisiana to Spain. The cession was formalized a year later at the end of the French and Indian War.

1763. The Seven Years War / French and Indian War ended with the 1763 Treaty of Paris. France lost virtually all of its North American claims: the western side of the Mississippi went to Spain (who gave Britain all of Florida in exchange); the eastern side of the Mississippi and all of Quebec went to Britain.

1783. United States of America. The treaty of Paris of 1783 first recognized the United States as an independent nation. Its borders were described generally from the Atlantic Ocean to the Mississippi River, and from Maine to Georgia.

1800. Louisiana. Napoleon acquired title of Louisiana from Spain. At the Third Treaty of San Ildefonso, the Spanish acknowledged that it was too costly to explore the country and could not see the rewards being worth the investment. Spain retroceded Louisiana to France in exchange for the Grand Duchy of Tuscany (now part of Italy).

1803. Louisiana Purchase. The United States purchased Louisiana from France. Sent by President Jefferson to attempt the purchase of New Orleans, the American negotiators (James Madison and Robert Livingston) were surprised when Napoleon offered the entire tract to them. The Louisiana Purchase was officially described as the "drainage of the Mississippi and Missouri River basins." Adding the area doubled the size of the United States.

1804 Louisiana District and Orleans Territory. Congress divided the Louisiana Purchase into two jurisdictions: Louisiana District and Orleans Territory. The latter had north and south bounds the same as the present state of Louisiana but did not include land east of the Mississippi River, and its northwestern corner extended on an indefinite line west into Spanish Texas. For a year, Louisiana District was attached to Indiana Territory for judicial administration but became Louisiana Territory with its own Governor in 1805.

1805. The early Arkansas settlements were part of Louisiana Territory, contained within the New Madrid and Arkansas districts.

1806-1807. The **Pike Expedition** was a military effort authorized by the U.S. government to explore the south and west of the recent Louisiana Purchase. In progress at the same time as the more famous Lewis & Clark expedition, the Pike Expedition was led by Captain Zebulon Pike, and managed by General James Wilkinson, the first Governor of Louisiana Territory (later called Missouri Territory).

From documents released by Mexico many years after the death of James Wilkinson, there are now many historians who believe Wilkinson really sent Pike out to spy on the Spanish along the southern boundary of the original Louisiana Purchase area, and that Wilkinson was a double agent, paid by the Spanish Governor in Nuevo Mexico, as well as the U.S. government.

As the official military administrator of the Lewis and Clark expedition, Wilkinson was known to contact the Governor of Nuevo Mexico in Santa Fe informing him of an American intrusion into territory claimed by Spain.

This was also the same James Wilkinson who was the accuser of treason of his former friend, Aaron Burr. Under the urging of Thomas Jefferson, Burr was brought to trial but found not guilty, due to the lack of evidence other than the word of James Wilkinson.

Spies or not spies, Capt. Zebulon Pike's party were the first Americans to follow the Arkansas River into the Rocky Mountains, documented the discovery of Pikes Peak, and spent time trying to find the headwaters of both the Red and Arkansas Rivers. Pike's expedition was also credited as the first Americans to follow the Santa Fe Trail.

Likely due to Wilkinson's collusion with the Nuevo Mexico Governor, Pike and his entire party were arrested by Spanish soldiers near the Arkansas River on the return trip. These were the same soldiers who had been sent north from Santa Fe to arrest the Lewis & Clark party, but were unable to find them. Pike and his party were taken to Santa Fe, Nuevo Mexico, where they were treated very well, and soon after were escorted back to U.S Territory.

In 1810, Captain Pike's published book of his expedition included the first English language description of the Spanish culture in North America, as well as the first maps of the Rocky Mountains region, and was a best seller in America and Europe. The book was also the inspiration for a whole generation of Mountain Men roaming the Rocky Mountains for the next 35 years.

1806. Louisiana–Spanish Mexico Line. The Louisiana Purchase caused a border dispute between the U.S. and Spain over the Louisiana-Mexico boundary. Spain claimed east to the Red River; the U.S. claimed west to the Sabine River. They made a compromise in 1806 with the so-called Neutral Ground, where neither exercised jurisdiction. From 1806 to 1819, the Neutral Ground became a haven for outlaws, fugitives and pirates. (The French pirate, Jean Lafitte, was a frequent visitor to the Neutral Ground, in and around the Lake Charles and Calcasieu regions). Yet, in the 1810 census for Orleans Territory, a few thousand American settlers were actually enumerated within the Neutral Ground, most of whom could be traced back to the Arkansas settlements of Louisiana Territory.

1810. The **1810 Federal Census** was the first census taken in Louisiana Territory and Orleans Territory, but only the manuscripts from Orleans survive.

1812. April. **Orleans Territory** became the state of **Louisiana.**

1812. June. **Louisiana Territory** was renamed **Missouri Territory.** As early as 1805 the area was often referred to as "Upper Louisiana," but with the statehood of Louisiana, the confusion between the two had to be resolved. For two months in 1812, the U.S. had a Territory of Louisiana and a State of Louisiana at the same time.

1817. Fort Smith was established on the Arkansas River (near the present Oklahoma state line). Fort Smith's most famous resident was Judge Isaac Parker, who served as US District Judge from 1875-1896. He was nicknamed the "Hanging Judge" because in his first term after assuming his post he tried eighteen people for murder, convicted fifteen of them, sentenced eight of those to die, and hanged six of them in one day.

1818. The **Quapaw Indians** ceded their lands between the Arkansas and Red Rivers, opening the area to white settlement.

1819. February. **The Adams-Onis Treaty** between the U.S. and Spain set part of the international boundary between the U.S. and Spanish Mexico as the line of the Sabine River north to a point of intersection with Latitude 32°, then due north to the Red River. This is the modern boundary between Louisiana, Arkansas, and Texas.

1819. July. **Arkansas Territory** was created by Congress, taken from Missouri Territory. The territorial capital was at Arkansas Post. The area included all of present-day Arkansas and most of Oklahoma. Arkansas Territory misinterpreted the recent boundary with Spanish Mexico, believing their southern line with Louisiana extended west on the same latitude. The confusion came from the language of the treaty with Spain, which described the lay of the Sabine River without maps, and the only maps available to the Arkansas territorial legislators had the Sabine River incorrectly located. A new survey of the area was not done until 1828, and during that time Arkansas Territory created counties that extended well into Spanish Mexico.

1820. April. **Old Miller County, Arkansas Territory** was created in an area partly outside of the legal jurisdiction of Arkansas Territory, due to a misunderstanding of the 1819 Treaty with Spain. Old Miller County straddled the Red River with its northern portion well into present-day Oklahoma, an area legally part of Arkansas Territory; and its southern portion well into present-day Texas, which was still part of Spanish Mexico. The 1820 map on page 74 describes the situation.

1820. June. The **1820 Federal Census** was taken in Arkansas Territory, but the original manuscripts were lost.

1821. The Arkansas territorial capital was moved from Arkansas Post to Little Rock.

1821. August. **Missouri Statehood.** The southeastern portion of old Missouri Territory became the State of

Missouri. The large remaining area of the original Louisiana/Missouri Territory was mostly uninhabited, and Congress labeled the area officially as *Unorganized Territory*.

1821. September. **Mexico** gained independence from Spain. The part of Old Miller County, Arkansas Territory, south of the Red River was now in the Republic of Mexico.

1824. The **Quapaw Indians** were forced to cede their remaining lands south of the Arkansas River, leaving them with just the reservation lands in the area of present-day Lincoln, Jefferson, and Cleveland counties, Arkansas.

1825-1828. Indian Reserve. In 1825, a small area north of the Red River was separated from Arkansas Territory. In 1828, a larger area of Arkansas Territory was set aside by Congress as an *Indian Reserve*. The present western boundary of Arkansas was drawn, and for the first time, the law described the area west of that line as the exclusive domain of Indian tribes. But its jurisdiction was still part of the larger area officially called Unorganized Territory, an area that extended from the Red River of the South (present Texas) to the Red River of the North (present North Dakota).

1828. May. The **Cherokee Indians** were forced to sign a treaty giving up their Arkansas lands for a new home in the Indian Reserve (now Oklahoma).

1828. About half of Old Miller County, Arkansas Territory lay north of the Red River, and was impacted dramatically by the creation of the Indian Reserve. The inhabitants of Miller County north of the Red River were forced to move, and it could be the only time in U.S. history that whites were forced to leave their homes to make room for the Indians. (It was usually the other way around). Meanwhile, people living in the part of old Miller County south of the Red River were about to learn that they were actually living in Mexico.

1830. June. The **1830 Federal Census** was taken in Arkansas Territory, and the manuscripts survive for all twenty-three counties. Included was old Miller County, now entirely outside of the U.S. in Mexico's Province of Coahuila y Texas. The 1830 population of Arkansas Territory was at 30,388 people.

1834. Indian Country. Congress officially defined *Indian Country* as any portion of the western United States that was not part of a state or territory, thus, Indian Country was the same as Unorganized Territory. The new law also regulated certain activities of non-Indians within the region and established judicial boundaries: the northern portion of the region (modern Kansas) was to be under the control of the federal courts of Missouri; the southern portion (modern Oklahoma), under the federal courts of Arkansas. Federal censuses in the Indian Country taken from 1820 through 1870 for non-Indians were under the jurisdiction of the Missouri and Arkansas federal marshals. (Indians were specifically excluded from the federal censuses, except those who lived off reservations and subject to taxes like non-Indians).

1836. March. The **Republic of Texas** gained its independence from Mexico. Old Miller County tried in vain to reassert its position as an Arkansas county. When Texas created its Red River County in 1836, old Miller County effectively ceased to exist. Named to honor Arkansas Territory's first Governor, James Miller, the current Miller County was created in 1874, with a county seat located at Texarkana, Arkansas.

1836. June 15th. **Arkansas** became the 25th state in the Union. Little Rock continued as the state capital.

1840. June. The **1840 Federal Census** was taken for the state of Arkansas. The 1840 population was at 97,574 people.

1850. June. The **1850 Federal Census** was taken for the state of Arkansas. The 1850 population was at 209,897 people.

1860. June. The **1860 Federal Census** was taken for the state of Arkansas. The 1860 population was at 435,450 people. Evidence of non-Indians living in the Indian Country can be seen in the 1860 federal census, where whites, blacks, adopted, or intermarried persons living on "Indian Lands West of Arkansas" were named and listed at the end of the Arkansas census schedules.

Online Resources at the Arkansas State Archives

The Arkansas State Archives, part of the AR History Commission, is a genealogist's one-stop resource center for all of Arkansas. For example, there have been more copies of county records transferred to this state archives than any other state. Research in county records on microfilm from all 75 Arkansas counties can be accomplished in one research room. The main facility is located in Little Rock near the state capitol building. Regional facilities are located at Powhatan (Northeast Arkansas Regional Archives) and Washington (Southeast Arkansas Regional Archives. **Online Resources** are identified by visiting these resource websites:

The Arkansas Digital Ark-ives. This is an online digital archive of documents, visuals, maps, broadsides, pamphlets, and three-dimensional objects significant to Arkansas history and culture, from the holdings of the Arkansas History Commission, Arkansas's state archives. For a Browse, Advanced Search, and more, see http://documenting.arkansas.com.

Search Our Records. This is an online searchable database of resources from all AHC facilities, See http://archives.arkansas.gov/research/search-records.aspx.

Browse Archival Collections. The Arkansas State Archives houses approximately 13,000 cubic feet of state records and manuscript collections pertaining to the history of Arkansas and its people. These materials have been described and inventoried for ease of access. These inventories, called finding aids, are keyword searchable. See
http://archives.arkansas.gov/research/browse-archival-collections.aspx.

Search the Online Catalog. The Arkansas State Archives uses an online catalog search system called *SirisiDynex e-library*. For the search screen, see http://arkstar.asl.lib.ar.us/uhtbin/cgisirsi. Library: Arkansas State Archives.

Research Services. The Arkansas State Archives offers limited research services to patrons who cannot make it to one of their three locations. They currently offer up to two hours of free research. To use these services, simply fill out their *Ask an Archivist* form, or email them, and include: A description of the information or record type for which you are looking. And, provide any names, dates, counties, etc. you have that will help us narrow the search. Email address: state.archives@arkansas.gov.

Subject Guides. The subject guides are not meant to be comprehensive guides, but to provide starting points for research. The following online Subject Guides are available:
 - African American Research Resources at the AHC
 - Arkansas Governors: A Resource Guide
 - Arkansas State Parks Resource Guide
 - Arkansas Women's History Resource Guide
 - Arkansas's Multicultural Heritage Resource Guide
 - Everything Old is New Again: The Arkansas Foodways Movement Guide
 - Guide to Civil War Manuscripts at the AHC
 - Guide to Immigration Research at the AHC
 - Guide to World War I Resources at the AHC
 - Boom or Bust: Commerce and Development in Northeast Arkansas
 - Cemetery Research Resources at the AHC

Bibliography
Arkansas Censuses & Substitutes

Arkansas's Colonial, Territorial, and Statewide Censuses and Substitute Name Lists can be associated with its historical eras:

1682-1762. French Era. Lists of inhabitants of Arkansas Post and other places in French Louisiana were identified in French censuses of 1686, 1723, and 1749.

1763-1802. Spanish Era. 1791 and 1802 name lists survive for Arkansas Post in Spanish Louisiana during this period.

1813-1819. Arkansas County, Missouri Territory Era. Arkansas County had a countywide tax list taken in 1814 and another in 1816, which were the first American census substitutes for the populated area that became Arkansas Territory in 1819.

1819-1835 Arkansas Territory Era. Several censuses were authorized by the territorial legislature, and a few surviving name lists exist for 1823, 1827, 1829, 1833, and 1835. The territorial legislative act required that the censuses be conducted by the sheriff of each county. As a result, many of these territorial censuses were referred to as "Sheriff's Censuses."

1836-Current. State of Arkansas Era. Upon statehood in 1836, the Arkansas Constitution provided for enumerations of the inhabitants of the state every four years commencing in 1838 for the purpose of legislative apportionment. The General Assembly directed that a census be taken on January 1, 1842, and every four years thereafter. As was done in the territorial censuses, the Sheriffs of the various counties were to be in charge of conducting the state censuses.

Although authorized, it cannot be confirmed if all of them were actually taken. Only the state censuses of 1838, 1854, and 1865 have any extant manuscripts that can be found.

The first federal census taken under the name Arkansas was in 1820, but that census was lost. Beginning with the 1830 federal census through 1940, all of the censuses taken for Arkansas are complete, with the exception of the 1890 federal census which was lost due to a fire in Washington, DC in 1921.

All of Arkansas's colonial, territorial, and statewide name lists are identified together in chronological order, as follows:

♦ ♦ ♦ ♦ ♦

1686-1804 Arkansas Colonials: A Collection of French and Spanish Records Listing Early Europeans in the Arkansas Area [Printed Book]. Includes a number of censuses, militia lists and other records, by Morris S. Arnold and Dorothy Jones Core. FHL book 976.7 H2a.

"1723 Colonial French Census of Louisiana, Arkansas Colonists" [Printed Article]. Names listed in *Louisiana Genealogical Register,* Vol. 8, No. 2 (Jun 1961).

"1749 Colonial French Census of Louisiana, Arkansas Colonists" [Printed Article]. Names listed in *White County Heritage,* Vol. 2, No. 3 (Jul 1964); and in *Genealogical and Historical Magazine of the South,* Vol. 3, No. 3 (Aug 1986).

1779-1850. *Arkansas, Compiled Marriages* **[Online Database],** indexed at the Ancestry.com website. Source: *Early American Marriages: Arkansas to 1850,* compiled by Jordan R Dodd. Each entry includes groom, bride, marriage date, county, and state. This database has 18,173 records. See https://search.ancestry.com/search/db.aspx?dbid=2082.

1779-1992. *Arkansas, Compiled Marriages from Select Counties* **[Online Database],** digitized and indexed from the Hunting for Bears database at the Ancestry.com website. Counties included in this database: Ashley, Calhoun, Crawford, Franklin, Garland, Hempstead, Hot Springs, Jefferson, Logan, Phillips, Polk, Pope, Randolph, Saline, Sebastian, Stone, Union, Washing, and Yell. See http://search.ancestry.com/search/db.aspx?dbid=7845.

"1791 Colonial Spanish Census, Inhabitants of Arkansas Post" [Printed Article], name list in *Genealogical and Historical Magazine of the South,* Vol. 3, No. 2 (May 1986).

1807-1835. *Arkansas Marriage Records* [Printed Book], by James Logan Morgan, published by Arkansas Research, Conway, AR, 1981, 1994, 90 pages, FHL book 976.7 V2mj.

1807-1907. *Card Files (Index to Land Entry Files of General Land Offices, Eastern States)* **[Microfilm & Digital Capture],** from the original index cards at the Bureau of Land Management, Eastern States Office, Washington, DC. The card files serve as an index to the Tract Books, Plat Books, and Case Files relating to ten million public land sales in America. **Content:** Each card contains the following information: Certificate Number, District Land Office, Kind of entry (cash, credit, warrant, etc.), Name of Patentee (Buyer, Entryman, etc.), and county of origin, Land description, Number of acres, Date of patent, Volume, and Page where document can be located. Filmed by the Bureau of Land Management, Washington, DC, c1970, 160 rolls (including 2 rolls for Arkansas GLOs), beginning with FHL film #15016721948-1959. To access the digital images, see the online FHL catalog page: **https://familysearch.org/search/catalog/511740.**

- See also, *Bureau of Land Management – General Land Office Records* **[Online Database],** search for the name of any land purchaser of public land in the U.S. To access the search screen, see **https://glorecords.blm.gov/search/default.aspx.**

1808-1812. *Probate Records (Louisiana Territory)* **[Microfilm],** from an original manuscript, author/publisher not noted. The probates identified in this record are for all of old Louisiana Territory. Included are probates from Arkansas District, one of the five districts created in Louisiana Territory, 1805-1806. In 1812, the districts all became counties, and Louisiana Territory was renamed Missouri Territory. Filmed by the Genealogical Society of Utah, 1975, 1 roll, FHL film #978542. To see if this microfilm was digitized yet, see the online FHL catalog: **www.familysearch.org/search/catalog/92361.**

1810. *A Partial Census of the Louisiana/Missouri Territory for 1810* **[Printed Index],** compiled by John D. Stemmons. Arranged in alphabetical order by surname. Since the 1810 Louisiana Territory federal census was lost (there are no original manuscripts for 1810 at the National Archives or anywhere else), and Louisiana Territory was renamed Missouri Territory in 1812, it is not clear where the names for this "partial census" came from. Published by Census Pub. LC, Sandy, UT, 2004, 554 pages, FHL book 973 X28s 1810.

1811-1900. *Index to Wills and Administrations of Arkansas From the Earliest to 1900* **[Printed Book & Digital Version],** compiled and edited by Mrs. James Harold Stevenson, Honorary State Regent, and Mrs. Edward Lynn Westbrooke, Honorary State Regent, Daughters of the American Revolution. (Copyrighted by Corinne Cox Stevenson and Gilberta Wood Westbrooke). The index is organized by county, and shows a name, date of activity, and book and page number of the case. Published by C. Stevenson and G. Westbrooke, Jonesboro, AR, 1986, 748 pages, FHL book 976.7 P22st. To access the digital images, see the online FHL catalog:
www.familysearch.org/search/catalog/448242.

1812-1965. *Arkansas Births and Christenings* **[Online Database],** indexed at the FamilySearch.org website. Source: FamilySearch extractions. This database is an index to birth, baptism and christening records from the state of Arkansas. Included are a few records of events outside of Arkansas, some predating the Louisiana Purchase and the creation of the Arkansas territory. Each index record includes: Name, Gender, Birth Date, Birthplace, Race, Father's Name, Father's Birthplace, Mother's Name, and Mother's Birthplace. This database has 10,634 records. See www.familysearch.org/search/collection/1674674.

1814 Missouri Territory, Arkansas County Tax List **[Online Database],** from originals at the Missouri State Archives. See an online extract of the name list:
http://files.usgwarchives.net/ar/state/history/terr/1814.txt.

1816 Missouri Territory, Arkansas County Tax List **[Online Database],** from originals at the Missouri State Archives. See an online extract of the name list:
http://files.usgwarchives.net/ar/state/history/terr/1816.txt.

1817-1979. *Arkansas Probate Records* **[Online Database],** digitized at the FamilySearch.org website. Source: FamilySearch extractions from AR County Courthouses. This is an image-only collection of probate records, including estate files and other documents created by the probate courts of Arkansas counties. Probates were generally recorded in the county of residence. Browse through the images, organized by County, Volume Title, and Year. This database has 939,415 images. See
www.familysearch.org/search/collection/2061549.

1818-1900. See *Arkansas Pensioners, 1818-1900: Records of some Arkansas Residents Who Applied to the Federal Government for Benefits Arising from Service in Federal Military Organizations (Revolutionary War, War of 1812, Indian and Mexican Wars)* **[Printed Extract],** by Dorothy Payne. Includes muster rolls for Arkansas companies, 1836-1847. Published by Southern Historical Press, Easley, SC, 1985, 220 pages, FHL book 976.7 M2pa.

1818-1998. *Arkansas, Wills and Probate Records* **[Online Database],** indexed at the Ancestry.com website. Original data: Arkansas County, District and Probate Courts. Types of records: Wills, Letters of Administration, Inventories, Distributions and Accounting, Bonds, and Guardianships. Each index record includes: Name, Probate Date, Probate Place, Inferred Death Year, Inferred Death Place, and Item Description. This database has 120,781 records. See https://search.ancestry.com/search/db.aspx?dbid=8638.

1819-1839 Arkansas Tax Lists **[Printed Book],** edited by Ronald Vern Jackson, et al. Contents: Vol. 1: 1819-1829, Vol. 2: 1830-1839. Arranged in alphabetical order by surname. Published by Accelerated Indexing Systems, Salt Lake City, UT, 1980, 2 vols., FHL book 976.7 R48j.

1819-1845 Arkansas Marriage Notices **[Printed Book],** by James Logan Morgan, published by Arkansas Research, Conway, AR, 1992, 82 pages, FHL book 976.7 V2m.

1819-1870. *Arkansas, Compiled Census and Census Substitutes Index* **[Online Database],** a collection of census indexes originally compiled by Ronald Jackson of Accelerated Indexing Systems. They are all treated as one searchable database at the Ancestry.com website. Included are the following censuses/tax lists:
- 1819-1829 Tax List
- 1820 Federal Census Index (reconstructed)
- 1823 Sheriff's Census Index
- 1829 Sheriff's Census Index
- 1830 Federal Census Index
- 1830-1839 Tax Lists Index
- 1840 Federal Census Index
- 1840 Pensioners Index
- 1850 Federal Census Index
- 1850 Slave Schedule
- 1860 Federal Census Index
- 1870 Federal Census Index

This database has 210,599 records. See
http://search.ancestry.com/search/db.aspx?dbid=3534.

1819-1879. *The Arkansas Gazette Obituaries Index* **[Printed Index],** by Stephen J. Chism. The newspaper is published in Little Rock, Pulaski County, Arkansas. From the Intro: "In this index, we have included 14,329 entries for the years 1819-1879, while the Arkansas Index for the same period lists 4,201 names under the heading 'deaths.' This can be attributed to our inclusive policy of listing every mention of death, whether it appears in an obituary column or in the text of an article on another subject." Published by Southern Historical Press, Greenville, SC, 1990, 109 pages, FHL book 976.773/L1 V42c.

1819-1881. *Arkansas Gazette Index: An Arkansas Index* **[Printed Index],** by Shannon J. Henderson, from the preface, "The Arkansas Gazette has long been considered the prime source for information on the social, cultural, and political affairs of the people of Arkansas." Contents: Vol. 1: 1819-1829; Vol. 2: 1830-1839; Vol. 3: 1840-1849; Vol. 4: 1850-1859; Vol. 5: 1860-1869; Vol. 6: 1870-1873; Vol. 7: 1874-1879; Vol. 8: 1880-1881. Published 1876, 8 vols., FHL book 976.7 B32.

1819-1907. *Arkansas, Homestead and Cash Entry Patents, Pre-1908* **[Online Database],** indexed at the Ancestry.com website. Original data: United States, Bureau of Land Management. Arkansas Pre-1908 Homestead and Cash Entry Patents. General Land Office Automated Records Project, 1993. A land patent is a document recording the passing of a land title from the government, or other proprietor, to the patentee/grantee. This is the first-title deed and the true beginning of private ownership of the land. The patent describes in legal terms the land to which the title is given. Information recorded in these records includes: Name, Land Office, Sequence, Document number, Total acres, Signature, canceled document, Issue date, Mineral rights reserved, Metes and bounds, Statutory reference, Multiple warrantee and patentee names, Act or treaty, Entry classification, and Land description. This database has 157,594 records. See https://search.ancestry.com/search/db.aspx?dbid=2070.
- See also, *Index to the Arkansas General Land Office, 1820-1907* **[Printed Book],** by Sherida K. Eddlemon. Organized by county. 7 Volumes, publ. Heritage Books, Bowie, MD, 1998-2002, 7 vols., FHL book 976.7 R22e v.1-7.

1819-1950. *Arkansas Biographical Card File Index* **[Microfilm & Digital Capture],** from the originals at the Arkansas History Commission, Little Rock, AR. Source listings include freedmen records, county histories, biographies, military records, newspapers, Bible records, land records, and church records. Filmed by the Genealogical Society of Utah, 1994, 53 rolls, beginning with FHL film #1926788 (unnamed-Alston, Mrs. Robert B.). To access the digital images, see the online FHL catalog: www.familysearch.org/search/catalog/239800.

1819-1999. *Arkansas Newspaper Archives* **[Online Database],** digitized and indexed at the GenealogyBank.com website. Includes newspapers from the following Arkansas cities are available: Camden, Denson, Forrest City, Fort Chaffee, Fort Smith, Heber Springs, Helena, Hot Springs, Jonesboro, Leachville, Little Rock, McGehee, Pine Bluff, and Van Buren. See www.genealogybank.com/gbnk/newspapers/explore/USA/Arkansas/.

1820 Census of the Territory of Arkansas (Reconstructed) **[Printed Book]** by James Logan Morgan, published by Arkansas Research, Conway, AR, 1992, 108 pages. FHL book 976.7 X2. The 1820 Arkansas Territory Federal Census was lost. A reconstruction was compiled from tax lists, voter lists, and other sources, first by Bobbie Jones McLane in 1965, and again in 1992 by James Logan Morgan.

1820. *Arkansas Territory 1820 Census Index* **[Printed Index],** Ronald Vern Jackson, editor, Accelerated Indexing, Salt Lake City, 1982, 57 pages. Since the 1820 AR Territory census was lost, and Mr. Jackson does not indicate where the names came from, it is assumed that he got the names from James Morgan's 1992 work. The Accelerated Indexing book is FHL book 976.7 X22a.

1820-1949. See *Arkansas, Compiled Marriages from Select Counties, 1820-1949* **[Online Database],** digitized and indexed from the *Hunting for Bears* database at the Ancestry.com website. Counties and years included in this database (number of records):
- Calhoun, 1851-1890 (1,400)
- Crawford, 1877-1887 (2,400)
- Garland, 1879-1949 (5,000)
- Hempstead, 1820-1881 (2,900)
- Hot Spring, 1825-1880 (1,000)
- Jefferson, 1830-1861 (950)
- Phillips, 1820-1879 (4,350)
- Pope, 1830-1859 (400)
- Saline, 1836-1875 (1,500)
- Stone, 1873-1890 (950)
- Union, 1830-1869 (2,350)
- Washington, 1870-1879 (2,000)
- Yell, 1841-1878 (400) See

http://search.ancestry.com/search/db.aspx?dbid=7841.

1821 Hempstead / Miller County Index **[Online Database]**, names of early Hempstead and Miller County (Arkansas Territory) settlers who signed an 1821 petition concerning the Choctaw treaty. These people were all caught in the area that was ceded to the Indians and were being told they had to move. Indexed at the TXGenWeb site. See http://txgenwebcounties.org/redriver/miller/Miller5.htm.

1821-1884. *Arkansas Tax Records* **[Microfilm & Digital Capture]**, from the originals at the Arkansas History Commission, Little Rock, AR. Filmed by the Genealogical Society of Utah, 1994, 2002, 72 rolls, beginning with FHL film #1954757 (List of available county tax records, Arkansas-Yell County); and FHL film #1955034 (List of Arkansas county tax records (Revised), Arkansas-Yell County). To access the digital images, see the online FHL catalog: www.familysearch.org/search/catalog/636459.

1823 Sheriff's Census, Arkansas County, Missouri Territory **[Printed Typescript]**, a typescript of the name list, 3 pages. See FHL book 976.786 X2p. This data base is also online at the USGenWeb site. See http://files.usgwarchives.net/ar/state/history/terr/sheriff1.txt.

1823-1829. See *Arkansas Sheriff's Censuses, 1823 & 1829* **[Printed Index]** by Ronald Vern Jackson, et al, Accelerated Indexing Systems, Salt Lake City, UT. FHL book 976.7 X2s 1823, 1829.

1824-1907 Land Patents–Arkansas **[Online Database]**, digitized and indexed at the MyHeritage website. The pre-1908 Arkansas Land Records documents the transfer of land ownership from the federal government to individuals. This data can help genealogists associate an individual with a specific location, date and time to authenticate the title transfer and find clues to their family line. Individuals described in this set would be patentees, assignees, warrantees, widows or heirs of the transfer. The legal land description location is given, along with the issue date of the title transfer. Source: United States, Bureau of Land Management, Pre-1908 Patents: Cash, Homestead, Choctaw Scrip, Hot Spring Townsite, Military Warrant & Public Land Donation; Cadastral Survey Plat Index 1824 to present. GLO Automated Records Project, Arkansas, 1998. See www.myheritage.com/research/collection-10074/land-patents-arkansas.

1825 Miller County Petition **[Online Database}**, names of petitioners to the President from Miller County, Arkansas Territory, people who were caught in the cession of lands to the Choctaw Indians. Extracted from Territorial Papers, Arkansas Territory. http://txgenwebcounties.org/redriver/miller/Miller1.htm.

"1827 Arkansas Territory Census, Phillips County" [Printed Article]. Name list published in *Tri-County Genealogy,* Vol. 9, No. 3 (Fall 1994).

1828 Miller County Petition **[Online Database]**, names of petitioners to the Governor of Arkansas Territory, those residing near Pecan Point, Miller County, Arkansas Territory (which was entirely outside of the legal bounds of the Territory, but they didn't know it), asking for the Indians to be removed from their land. See http://txgenwebcounties.org/redriver/miller/Miller3.htm.

1828-1829 Tax List, LaFayette County, Arkansas **[Online Database]**, indexed at the USGenWeb site for LaFayette Co AR. See http://files.usgwarchives.net/ar/lafayette/taxlists/laftax1.txt.

1829 Sheriff's Census, Clark County, Arkansas [Online Database], indexed at the peahs.org site. See www.pcahs.org/census/davidkelley/CEN29CLK.HTM.

1829 Lawrence County, Arkansas Sheriff's Census **[Printed Extract & Index]**, transcribed by Marion Stark Craig, 1994, 30 pages. Includes photocopy of original records along with transcription and full-name index. See FHL book 976.725 X2c.

1829 Sheriff Census, Johnson County, Arkansas **[Online Database]**, indexed at the Johnson County Genealogy website. See www.johnsoncountygenealogy.com/1829sheriffcensus.html.

1829 Tax Census, Lawrence County, Arkansas **[Online Database]**, indexed at the Arkansas Genealogy.com website. See www.arkansasgenealogy.com/lawrence/1829tax.htm.

1829-1838 Tax Records, Lawrence County, Arkansas **[Online Database]**, indexed at the USGenWeb site from Lawrence Co AR. See http://files.usgwarchives.net/ar/lawrence/history/pub/lawtx29.txt.

1830 and 1832 Tax Records, Miller County, Arkansas **[Online Database]**, names extracted from the original records located at the Texarkana Public Library in the Arkansas Section. See http://files.usgwarchives.net/ar/miller/taxlists/tax30.txt.

1830 and 1840 Arkansas Federal Census **[Microfilm & Digital Capture]**, from the originals at the National Archives, Washington, DC. The 1830 and 1840 censuses were filmed by the National Archives together as one set, 2 rolls, FHL film #2473 (AR 1830 census) and FHL film #2474 (AR 1840). To access the digital images, see the online FHL catalog: **www.familysearch.org/search/catalog/745481**.

1830. *An Index to Fifth Census of the United States, 1830, Population Schedules, Territory of Arkansas* **[Printed Index & Digital Version]**, compiled by Bobbie Jones McLane, published by McLane & Cline, 1965, Hot Springs National Park, AR, 45 pages. Arranged in alphabetical order. See FHL book 976.7 X2. Also microfilm, see FHL film #1036552. To access the digital images, see the online FHL catalog: **www.familysearch.org/search/catalog/66249**.

1832 Tax Records, Hot Spring County, Arkansas **[Online Database]**, indexed at the USGenWeb site for Hot Spring Co AR. See **http://files.usgwarchives.net/ar/hotspring/taxlists/tax1832.txt**.

1832-1890 Divorces of Jackson County, Arkansas **[Online Database]**, indexed at the RootsWeb site for Jackson Co AR. See **www.rootsweb.ancestry.com/~arjackso/divorces.htm**.

1833 Tax Records, Hot Spring County, Arkansas **[Online Database]**, indexed at the USGenWeb site for Hot Spring Co AR. See **http://files.usgwarchives.net/ar/hotspring/taxlists/tax1833.txt**.

1833 Reconstructed Census of Scott County, Arkansas **[Printed Book]**, researched and compiled by John Paul O'Nale, Scott County Historical & Genealogical Society, Waldron, AR, 19??, 20 pages, 2 maps. Census and land records were among the records used to reconstruct the census. Includes index. See FHL book 976.744 X2o 1833.

1834 Tax Records, Hot Spring County, Arkansas **[Online Database]**, indexed at the USGenWeb site for Hot Spring Co AR. See **http://files.usgwarchives.net/ar/hotspring/taxlists/tax1834.txt**.

1834-1852 Tax Lists, Carroll County, Arkansas **[Online Database]**, indexed at the RootsWeb site for Carroll Co AR. See **www.rootsweb.ancestry.com/~arcchs/Tax/1834_38_tax.html**.

1834-1853 Tax Records, Pike County, Arkansas **[Online Database]**, indexed at the Pike County Archives & History Society site. See **www.pcahs.org/pcaolr/tax.htm**.

1834-1840 Tax Records, Greene County, Arkansas **[Online Database]**, indexed at the USGenWeb site for Greene Co AR. See **www.argenweb.net/greene/COURTRECORDS/18341840.htm**.

1835 Poll Tax, Pope County, Arkansas **[Online Database]**, indexed at the USGenWeb site for Pope Co AR. See **www.argenweb.net/pope/poll.html**.

1835 Federal Pension Roll, Arkansas **[Online Database]**, indexed at the USGenWeb site for Arkansas. See **http://files.usgwarchives.net/ar/state/military/revolution/index35.txt**.

"1835 Arkansas Territory Census" [Printed Article]. Names listed in *Tracks and Traces*, Vol. 18, No. 2 (Nov 1996).

1835 Tax Records, Hot Spring County, Arkansas **[Online Database]**. indexed at the USGenWeb site for Hot Spring Co AR. See **http://files.usgwarchives.net/ar/hotspring/taxlists/tax1835.txt**.

1836 Tax Rolls, Saline County, Arkansas [Online Database], indexed at the USGenWeb site for Saline Co AR. See **www.argenweb.net/saline/newtxls.htm**.

1837-1839 Tax Records, Van Buren County, Arkansas **[Online Database]**, indexed at the RootsWeb site for Van Buren Co AR. See **www.rootsweb.ancestry.com/~arvanbur/cocourt/1833tax.htm**.

1837-1944. *Arkansas Marriages* **[Online Database]**, indexed at the FamilySearch website. Source: FamilySearch extractions from Arkansas county courthouses. An exact county citation is given at each indexed record. This is a name index to marriage records from the state of Arkansas. Each index record includes: Name, Birth Date, Age, Spouse's Name, Spouse's Birth Date, Spouse's Age, Event Date, and Event Place. This database has 945,778 records. See **www.familysearch.org/search/collection/1674711**.
- See also, *Arkansas County Marriages, 1837-1957* **[Online Database]**, digitized and indexed at the FamilySearch website. Source: FamilySearch extractions from Arkansas county courthouses. This

database includes index and images of marriages recorded in counties of Arkansas. There may be related records included with marriage records. Once an image of a marriage record is located, browse through preceding and following images to check for related records. This project was indexed in partnership with the Arkansas Genealogical Society. Each index record includes: Name, Event Type, Event Date, Event Place, Gender, Marital Status, Spouse's Name, and Spouse's Gender. This database has 1,869,736 records. See www.familysearch.org/search/collection/1417439.

-See also *Arkansas, County Marriages Index, 1837-1957* [Online Database], indexed at the Ancestry.com website. Source: FamilySearch. This database has 3,554,006 records. See https://search.ancestry.com/search/db.aspx?dbid=2548.

"1838 Arkansas State Census, Madison County" [Printed Article], name list published in *Madison County Musings,* Vol. 1, No. 2 (Summer 1982).

1838-1916. *Masonic Deaths in Arkansas* **[Printed Book],** abstracted and compiled by Arlene LaGrone. Extracted from the annual proceedings of Most Worshipful Grand Lodge of the State of Arkansas (F. & A. Masons). Includes supplements added by the society. Published by the Arkansas Genealogical Society, Hot Springs, AR, 1999, 183 pages, FHL book 976.7 C42L.

1840. See *An Index to 1840 United States Census of Arkansas* [Printed Index & Digital Version], compiled by Bobbie Jones McLane, published by McLane & Cline, 1967, Hot Springs National Park, AR, 127 pages. Arranged in alphabetical order. See FHL book 976.7 X22m 1840 index. To access the digital version, see the online FHL catalog: www.familysearch.org/search/catalog/178318.
- See also, *Arkansas Census, 1840.* [Online Database], same book, Indexed at Ancestry.com, see https://search.ancestry.com/search/db.aspx?dbid=3117.

1840 Tax List, Saline County, Arkansas [Online Database], indexed at the USGenWeb site for Saline Co AR. See www.argenweb.net/saline/saldel40.htm.

1841 Tax List, Saline County, Arkansas [Online Database], indexed at the USGenWeb site for Saline Co AR. See www.argenweb.net/saline/saltx41.html.

1841-1844 Tax Records, Van Buren County, Arkansas [Online Database], indexed at the RootsWeb site for Van Buren Co AR. See www.rootsweb.ancestry.com/~arvanbur/cocourt/1841tax.html.

1843 Tax List, Pope County, Arkansas [Online Database], indexed at the USGenWeb site for Pope Co AR. See http://files.usgwarchives.net/ar/pope/taxlists/1843pope-tax.txt.

1844 Tax List, Pope County, Arkansas [Online Database], indexed at the USGenWeb site for Pope Co AR. See http://files.usgwarchives.net/ar/pope/taxlists/1844pope-tax.txt.

1844 Tax List, Saline County, Arkansas [Online Database], indexed at the USGenWeb site for Saline Co AR. See www.argenweb.net/saline/saltx44.html.

1845 Tax List, Saline County, Arkansas [Online Database], indexed at the USGenWeb site for Saline Co AR. See www.argenweb.net/saline/saltx45.html.

1845-1941. *Arkansas, Washington County Marriage Records* [Online Database], digitized and indexed at the Ancestry.com website. Source: Washington County Archives, Fayetteville, AR. Each record includes the full names of the bride and groom, year, volume, page number, as well as an image of the original record. This database has 60,721 records. See https://search.ancestry.com/search/db.aspx?dbid=60627.

1845 & 1846 Polk County Tax Lists [Online Database], indexed at the USGenWeb site for Polk Co AR. See http://argenweb.net/polk/taxrec.htm.

1846 Tax List, Saline County, Arkansas [Online Database], indexed at the USGenWeb site for Saline Co AR. See www.argenweb.net/saline/saltx46.html.

1847 Tax List, Pope County, Arkansas [Online Database], indexed at the USGenWeb site for Pope Co AR. See http://files.usgwarchives.net/ar/pope/taxlists/1847pope-tax.txt.

1846-1847. *Arkansas Mexican War Soldiers* **[Printed Index],** compiled by Desmond Walls Allen. Contains a roster of 1,532 men who served in Arkansas units in the Mexican War, 1846-1847. The roster lists the soldier's name, rank, age, unit and company and remarks about death, discharge, prisoner status, enrollment date, desertion, transfer, and other comments found in the records. The roster is in alphabetical order. Published by Arkansas Research, Inc., 1988, 133 pages, FHL book 976.7 M22adwa.

1847 Tax List, Saline County, Arkansas **[Online Database],** indexed at the USGenWeb site for Saline Co AR. See **www.argenweb.net/saline/saltx47.html**.

1849-1852 Tax Records, Van Buren County, Arkansas **[Online Database],** indexed at the RootsWeb site for Van Buren Co AR. See **www.rootsweb.ancestry.com/~arvanbur/cocourt/1849.html**

1850. *Arkansas: 1850 Federal Census: Population Schedules* **[Microfilm & Digital Capture],** from the originals at the National Archives, Washington, DC. Filmed by the National Archives, 1964, 8 rolls, beginning with FHL film #2479 (Arkansas: Arkansas, Ashley, Benton, Bradley, Carroll, Chicot, Clark, Conway, Crawford, and Crittenden counties). To access the digital images, see the online FHL catalog: **www.familysearch.org/search/catalog/744470**.

1850. *Arkansas 1850 Census Every-Name Index* **[Printed Index],** by Bobbie Jones McLane and Desmond Walls Allen. Also includes index of those with different surnames than the heads of households with whom they reside. Published by Arkansas Research, Conway, AR, 1995, 456 pages, FHL book 976.7 X2m 1850 index.

1850. *Arkansas 1850 Census Index* **[Printed Index],** edited by Ronald Vern Jackson, et al, published by Accelerated Indexing Systems, Bountiful, UT, 1976, 98 pages, FHL book 976.7 X2.

1850. *Arkansas Census, 1850 Surname Index* **[Printed Index],** by Mrs. Leister E. Presley, published L. E. Presley, Searcy, AR, 1974, 318 pages, FHL book 976.7 X22. Also on microfiche, FHL fiche #6093735 (4 fiche).

1850. *Arkansas 1850 Mortality Schedule* **[Printed Index],** extracted from the original records on microfilm by Emily Tucker, published by Arkansas Research, 2005, Conway, AR, 49 pages, FHL book 976.7 X28.

1850 Mortality Schedules of Arkansas **[Printed Index],** by Bobbie Jones McLane and Capitola Hensley Glazner, published by Bobbie Jones McLane, 1968, Hot Springs National Park, AR, 64 pages, FHL book 976.7 X2.

1850. *Arkansas 1850 Slave Schedule Index* **[Printed Index],** compiled by Ronald Vern Jackson, et al, published by Accelerated Indexing Systems, Salt Lake City, UT, 1998, 210 pages, FHL book 976.7 X22.

1850-1880. *Arkansas Mortality Schedules, Production of Agriculture Schedules and Manufacturer's Schedule* **[Microfilm & Digital Capture],** from the original records at the National Archives, Washington, DC. Filmed by the National Archives, 5 rolls, beginning with FHL film #1549729 (AR Mortality schedule, 1860 Crittenden-Yell. To access the digital images, see the online FHL catalog: **www.familysearch.org/search/catalog/620295**.

1851-1900. *Arkansas, Compiled Marriages* **[Online Database],** digitized and indexed at the Ancestry.com website, these are extractions from certain Arkansas counties for which there exists FHL microfilm. The database was compiled by Jordan Dodd of Liahona Research. Includes records from Ashley, Baxter, Benton, Carroll, Clark, Clay, Cleveland, Conway, Craighead, Crawford, Cross, Dallas, Fulton, Garland, Grant, Hempstead, Hot Spring, Howard, Independence, Johnson, Lafayette, Lawrence, Logan, Lonoke, Marion, Montgomery, Nevada, Phillips, Pike, Polk, Prairie, Randolph, St. Francis, Scott, Sebastian, Sharp, Stone Yell, Union, Washington, and White Counties. This database has 142,055 records. See **http://search.ancestry.com/search/db.aspx?dbid=4383**.

1853 Tax List, Pope County, Arkansas **[Online Database],** indexed at the USGenWeb site for Pope Co AR. See **http://files.usgwarchives.net/ar/pope/taxlists/1853.txt**.

1854 Tax List, Martin Township, Pope County, Arkansas **[Online Database],** indexed at the USGenWeb site for Pope Co AR. See **http://files.usgwarchives.net/ar/pope/taxlists/1854pope-tax.txt**.

1854 Tax List, Allen & North Fork Townships, Pope County, Arkansas **[Online Database],** indexed at the USGenWeb site for Pope Co AR. See **http://files.usgwarchives.net/ar/pope/taxlists/1854.txt**.

"1854 Arkansas State Census, Madison County" [Printed Article]. Name list published in *Madison County Musings,* Vol. 2, No. 1 (Spring 1983).

1854-1855 Circuit Court Records, White County, Arkansas **[Online Database]**, indexed at the USGenWeb site for White Co AR. See http://files.usgwarchives.net/ar/white/court/whcircct.txt.

1855 Tax Records, Van Buren County, Arkansas **[Online Database]**, indexed at the RootsWeb site for Van Buren Co AR. See
www.rootsweb.ancestry.com/~arvanbur/cocourt/1855.html

1856 Tax List, Allen & North Fork Townships, Pope County, Arkansas **[Online Database]**, indexed at the USGenWeb site for Pope Co AR. See http://files.usgwarchives.net/ar/pope/taxlists/1856.txt.

1858-1861 Deaths Abstracted from the Earliest County Newspapers, Prairie County, Arkansas **[Online Database]**, indexed at the RootsWeb site for Prairie Co AR. See
www.rootsweb.ancestry.com/~arprairi/Newspapers/dacitizen.htm.

1860. *Arkansas, 1860 Federal Census: Population Schedules* **[Microfilm & Digital Capture]**, from the originals at the National Archives, Washington, DC. Filmed by the National Archives, 22 rolls, 1st filming, 1950; 2nd filming 1967. The 2nd filming is easier to read because the film has one page per frame, while the 1st filming has 2 pages per frame. In both filmings, the Indian Territory lands for the five civilized tribes were enumerated for non-Indians as the last roll in the series. The filming begins with the 2nd filming on FHL film #803037 (Arkansas, Ashley, and Benton counties). To access the digital images, see the online FHL catalog: www.familysearch.org/search/catalog/704521.

1860 Arkansas Federal Census – Indian lands **[Online Database]**, an index to the names of the non-Indians living in the Indian Territory in 1860, attached to the end of the Arkansas county lists. The names are organized by the five civilized tribes with whom the non-Indians were living: Cherokee, Chickasee, Choctaw, Creek, and Seminole. See
www.rootsweb.ancestry.com/~cenfiles/ar/indianlands/1860/

1860. *Arkansas 1860 Census Index* **[Printed Index]**, by Ronald Vern Jackson, et al, published by Accelerated Indexing Systems, Salt Lake City, UT, 1985, 56 pages, FHL book 976.7 X22.

1860 Mortality Schedules of Arkansas **(Printed Index]**, by Capitola Hensley Glazner, published by Glazner and McLane, Hot Sprints National Park, AR, 1974, 108 pages, FHL book 976.7 X2pm 1860.

1860-1876. *Arkansas Church Marriages* **[Online Database]**, indexed at the FamilySearch.org website. Source: FamilySearch extractions from various churches and Arkansas History Commission. Each index record includes: Name, Event Type, Event Date, Event Place, Gender, Spouse's Name, and Spouse's Gender. This database has 542 records. See www.familysearch.org/search/collection/2546158.

1861 Ouachita County Land Ownership Tax Rolls (For Areas Currently in Nevada County, Arkansas) **[Online Database]**, indexed at the USGenWeb site for Nevada Co AR:
www.argenweb.net/nevada/land1861.htm.

1861-1865. *Index to Compiled Service Records of Confederate Soldiers Who Served in Organizations from the State of Arkansas* **[Microfilm & Digital Capture]**, from the original records at the National Archives. Each index card contains the name of the soldier, his rank, and the unit in which he served. Filmed by the National Archives, 26 rolls, beginning with FHL film #821811 (Surnames starting with the letter A). To access the digital images, see the online FHL catalog:
www.familysearch.org/search/catalog/452498.

1861-1865. *Index to Arkansas Confederate Soldiers* **[Printed Book]**, compiled by Desmond Walls Allen, published by Arkansas Research, Inc., 1990, 3 vols., FHL book 976.7 M22adwe.

1861-1865. See *Arkansas Civil War Service Records of Confederate Soldiers* **[Online Database]**, digitized and indexed at the FamilySearch website, index courtesy of Fold3. The database includes Confederate service records of soldiers who served in organizations from Arkansas. The records include a jacket-envelope for each soldier, labeled with his name, his rank, and the unit in which he served. The jacket-envelope typically contains card abstracts of entries relating to the soldier as found in original muster rolls, returns, rosters, payrolls, appointment books, hospital registers, Union prison registers and rolls, parole rolls, inspection reports; and the originals of any papers relating solely to the particular soldier. For each military unit the service records are arranged alphabetically by the soldier's surname. This database has 532,541 records. See **www.familysearch.org/search/collection/1932365**.

1861-1865. *Index to Compiled Service Records of Volunteer Union Soldiers Who Served in Organizations from the State of Arkansas* **[Microfilm & Digital Capture],** from the original records at the National Archives. Each index card contains the name of the soldier, his rank, and the unit in which he served. Filmed by the National Archives, 4 rolls, beginning with FHL film #881488 (A-F). To access the digital images, see the online FHL catalog: **www.familysearch.org/search/catalog/314403**.

1861-1865. *Arkansas Civil War Service Records of Union Soldiers* **[Online Database],** digitized and indexed at the FamilySearch website, index courtesy of Fold3. The database includes Union service records of soldiers who served in organizations from Arkansas. The records include a jacket-envelope for each soldier, labeled with his name, his rank, and the unit in which he served. The jacket-envelope typically contains card abstracts of entries relating to the soldier as found in original muster rolls, returns, rosters, payrolls, appointment books, hospital registers, Union prison registers and rolls, parole rolls, inspection reports; and the originals of any papers relating solely to the particular soldier. For each military unit the service records are arranged alphabetically by the soldier's surname. This database has 158,093 records. See **www.familysearch.org/search/collection/1932392**.

1861-1865. *Arkansas' Damned Yankees: An Index to Union Soldiers in Arkansas Regiments* **[Printed Book],** by Desmond Walls Allen. Arranged in alphabetical order by surname. Published by Allen, Conway, AR, 1987, 220 pages, FHL book 976.M28.

1861-1865. *Arkansas Union Soldiers Pension Application Index* **[Printed Index],** compiled by Desmond Walls Allen. The index contains the veteran, company, unit, and type of application. Includes death dates and places of Arkansas Union veterans. Published by Rapid Rabbit Copy, 1987, 180 pages, FHL book 976.7 M22a.

1861-1865 Confederate Patriots, Prairie County, Arkansas **[Online Database],** index at the RootsWeb site for Prairie Co AR. See **www.rootsweb.ancestry.com/~arprairi/REBELS/rebels.htm**.

1861-1865 Civil War Veterans Buried in Stone County, Arkansas Cemeteries **[Online Database],** indexed at the RootsWeb site for Stone Co AR. See **www.rootsweb.ancestry.com/~arscgs/cwveterans.htm**.

1861-1970s White County Muster Rolls **[Online Database],** Index to soldiers from White County, Arkansas: Confederate Soldiers of the Civil War, Spanish American War, World War I, World War II, and the Vietnam War, at the USGenWeb site for White Co AR. See **http://files.usgwarchives.net/ar/white/military/civilwar/whmuster.txt**.

1863 Tax List, Drew County, Arkansas **[Online Database],** images scanned at the backwardbranch.com website. For an archived database, see **https://web.archive.org/web/20110915151624/http://backwardbranch.com/ardrew/DrewCountyArkansas1863TaxList.pdf**.

1864-1872. *Arkansas, Freedmen's Bureau Field Office Records* **[Online Database],** digitized at the FamilySearch.org website. Source: National Archives microfilm M1901. This is an image-only database from the Bureau of Refugees, Freedmen, and Abandoned Lands (often called the Freedmen's Bureau), created in 1865 at the end of the American Civil War to supervise relief efforts including education, health care, food and clothing, refugee camps, legalization of marriages, employment, labor contracts, and securing back pay, bounty payments and pensions. These records include letters and endorsements sent and received, account books, applications for rations, applications for relief, court records, labor contracts, registers of bounty claimants, registers of complaints, registers of contracts, registers of disbursements, registers of freedmen issued rations, registers of patients, reports, rosters of officers and employees, special and general orders and circulars received, special orders and circulars issued, records relating to claims, court trials, property restoration, and homesteads. This database has 223,972 images. See **www.familysearch.org/search/collection/2328125**.

1865 List of Persons Taking the Amnesty Oath, Drew County, Arkansas **[Online Database],** index and images at the backwardbranch.com website. For an archived database, see **https://web.archive.org/web/20120124034431/http://backwardbranch.com/ardrew/dcmil.html**.

1865 Arkansas State Census, Washington County **[Printed Extract & Index],** For the only AR county with extant records from the 1865 state census, see ***Washington County, Arkansas, Sheriff's Census for 1865*** by Nancy Maxwell, published by Heritage Books, Bowie, MD, 1993, 74 pages. Includes surname index. FHL book 976.714 X2m.

1865-1866. *Report of the Adjutant General of Arkansas, for the Period of the late Rebellion, and to November 1, 1866* [Online Database], digitized and OCR indexed at the Ancestry.com website. This database has 279 pages. See
https://search.ancestry.com/search/db.aspx?dbid=29991.

1865-1874. *Internal Revenue Assessment Lists for Arkansas: Annual, Monthly and Special Lists* [Microfilm & Digital Capture], from the originals at the National Archives, Washington, DC, series 755. Filmed by the National Archives, 1968, 4 rolls, beginning with FHL film #1578509 (1st District, 1865-1866). To access the digital images, see the online FHL catalog: www.familysearch.org/search/catalog/577963.

1866 List of Persons and Property Assessed for Taxation, Greene County, Arkansas [Online Database], indexed at the USGenWeb site for Greene Co AR. See
www.argenweb.net/greene/COURTRECORDS/1866ppt.htm.

1866-1869 Deaths Abstracted from the Earliest County Newspapers, Prairie County, Arkansas [Online Database], indexed at the RootsWeb site for Prairie Co AR. See
www.rootsweb.ancestry.com/~arprairi/Newspapers/dacitizen1.htm.

1866-1900. *Fort Smith, Arkansas, Criminal Case Files Index* [Online Database], indexed at the FamilySearch.org website. This database is an index to the criminal court cases of such famous outlaws as Wyatt Earp and "Cherokee Bill" Goldsby. Many of these 50,000 cases were heard by the famous "hanging" Judge Isaac C. Parker, appointed by President Grant to bring law and order to the territory of Arkansas. The descriptions provide the first and last name of the defendant, the type of crime, the year, the jacket number, and other information.
This database has 49,892 records. See
https://search.ancestry.com/search/db.aspx?dbid=3119.

1866-1900. See *Fort Smith, Arkansas, Criminal Case Files* [Online Database], indexed at the Ancestry.com website. This database consists of the defendant jacket files for court cases. Each index record includes: Name, Court Date, Jacket Number, and Record Type. View the document images for more possible information. This database has 45,858 records. See
https://search.ancestry.com/search/db.aspx?dbid=2117.

1866-1925 Probate Records, Mississippi County, Arkansas [Online Database], indexed at the USGenWeb site for Mississippi Co AR. See
http://files.usgwarchives.net/ar/mississippi/court/admins.txt.

1867 Tax List, Pope County, Arkansas [Online Database], indexed at the USGenWeb site for Pope Co AR. See
http://files.usgwarchives.net/ar/pope/taxlists/1867pope.txt.

1867-2010. See *Fort Smith, Arkansas, Fort Smith National Cemetery, 1867-2010* [Online Database], digitized and indexed at the Ancestry.com website. This database contains digital images of all gravestones in the cemetery with an index. This database has 13,007 records. See
https://search.ancestry.com/search/db.aspx?dbid=2301.

1867-2013. *Arkansas, Oakland and Fraternal Historic Cemetery Records* [Online Database], digitized and indexed at the FamilySearch.org website. Source: FamilySearch extractions from this Little Rock cemetery. This database includes burials, lot sales books, and 3 x 5 card index burial cards. This database has 84.121 records. See
www.familysearch.org/search/collection/2156084.

1868 Tax List, Little River County, Arkansas [Online Database], originally indexed at the backwardbranch.com site. Archived database:
https://web.archive.org/web/20101026161302/http://backwardbranch.com/lrcgs/lrctax.html.

1868 Voters List, Yell County, Arkansas [Online Database], indexed at the USGenWeb site for Yell Co AR. See
http://files.usgwarchives.net/ar/yell/history/yelvote2.txt.

1868 & 1872 Arkansas County Voter Lists [Microfilm & Digital Capture], from the originals microfilmed by the Genealogical Society of Utah, 1975. See FHL film #978533. To access the digital images, see the online FHL catalog:
www.familysearch.org/search/catalog/92369.

1868-1966. *Arkansas, Sevier County, Record of Voters* [Online Database], digitized and indexed at FamilySearch.org. This database has 3,368 images, see
www.familysearch.org/search/collection/2630413.

1870. *Arkansas, 1870 Federal Census: Population Schedules* [Microfilm & Digital Capture], from the originals at the National Archives, Washington, DC, filmed twice by the National Archives, 1962, 1968, 28 rolls total, beginning with FHL film #545546 (2nd filming Arkansas, Ashley, and Benton counties). To access the digital images, see the online FHL catalog: www.familysearch.org/search/catalog/698885.

1870. See *Arkansas 1870* **[Printed Index],** edited by Ronald Vern Jackson, arranged in alphabetical order by surname, published by Accelerated Indexing Systems, North Salt Lake, UT, 1987, 562 pages, FHL book 976.7 X2ja 1870.

1870. See *Arkansas 1870 Census Index* **[Printed Index],** compiled by Martha Vaughn, published by Arkansas Research, Conway, AR, 1999, 932 pages, FHL book 976.7 X22v.

1870. See *Arkansas 1870 Census Index: A – Z* **[Printed Index],** edited by Raeone Christensen Steuart, contains name, age, sex, race (or color), birthplace, county, locality, series, roll and page number. Published by Heritage Quest, Bountiful, UT, 2000, 867 pages, FHL book 976.7 X22ark.

1870-1874 Residents of Newport, Jackson County, Arkansas **[Online Database],** indexed at the RootsWeb site for Jackson Co AR. See www.rootsweb.ancestry.com/~arjackso/earlyres.htm.

1870-1879 Birth Records, Lafayette County, Arkansas **[Online Database],** extracted from the Social Security Death Index, at the USGenWeb site for Lafayette Co AR. See http://files.usgwarchives.net/ar/lafayette/vitals/births/births1870.txt.

1870s-1940s. *Greene County, Arkansas Court Records* **[Online Database],** index to various court records at the USGenWeb site for Greene Co AR. See www.argenweb.net/greene/COURTRECORDS/courtrecords.htm.

1870s-1950s. *Howard County, Arkansas Births* **[Online Database],** index compiled from county records and submittals from users at the genealogyshoppe.com website. For an archived database, see https://web.archive.org/web/20160313050839/www.genealogyshoppe.com/arhoward/birth.htm.

1871-1955. *Arkansas Donation Lands* **[Printed Book],** compiled by Desmond Walls Allen. These books contain indexes to Arkansas Donation Land applications. The records were taken from donation land ledger books in the Arkansas State Land Commissioner's Office. Contents: vol. 1: 1871-1875, vol. 2: 14 December 1876 - 30 April 1880, vol. 3: 1 May 1880 - 30 June 1882, vol. 4: 3 July 1882 - 6 December 1887, vol. 5: 6 December 1887 - 21 December 1893, vol. 6: 21 December 1893 - 29 March 1902, vol. 7: 1 April 1902 - 30 December 1926, vol. 8: 1 January 1927 - 28 September 1938, vol. 9: 28 September 1938 - 21 March 1955. Published by Arkansas Research, Conway, AR, 2001, 9 vols., maps, FHL book 976.7 R22al v.1-9.

1872 Tax List, North Folk Township, Pope County, Arkansas **[Online Database],** indexed at the USGenWeb site for Pope Co AR. See http://files.usgwarchives.net/ar/pope/taxlists/1872popetax.txt.

1872-1960s. See *Index to Boone County, Arkansas Will Books A, B, and C* **[Online Database],** index at the RootsWeb site for Boone Co AR. For an archived database, see https://web.archive.org/web/20150512163603/www.argenweb.net/boone/willindextab.html.

1873 Landowners, Faulkner County, Arkansas **[Online Database],** indexed at the backwardbranch.com website. For an archived database, see https://web.archive.org/web/20101120051304/http://backwardbranch.com/arfaulkner/fc1873.html.

1874-1880 Grammar School Rosters, Little Rock, Pulaski County, Arkansas **[Online Database],** indexed at the RootsWeb site for Pulaski Co AR. See http://freepages.genealogy.rootsweb.ancestry.com/~ouisersplace/rosters/Rosters.htm.

1875-1890. *20 Years in Miller County, Arkansas: Tax & Census Record Index* **[Printed Book],** by the Texarkana U.S.A. Genealogical Society, 200+ pages. Contains 1875 Miller County personal property tax assessment index, 1880 Miller County federal census index, 1885 Miller County personal property tax assessment index, 1890 Miller County personal property tax assessment index. See FHL book 976.756 R42.

1876 List of Persons and Personal Property, Greene County, Arkansas **[Online Database],** indexed at the USGenWeb site for Greene Co AR. See www.argenweb.net/greene/COURTRECORDS/1876assessedpersonnelprop.htm.

1877-1963. *Arkansas, Sebastian County Births and Deaths* **[Online Database]**, digitized and indexed at the FamilySearch.org website. Includes records of births and deaths from Sebastian County, Arkansas, 1877-1929. Also includes death records from Fort Smith, 1945-1963. This collection is part of a cooperative indexing project with the Central Arkansas Genealogical And Historical Society. This database has 32,250 records. See
www.familysearch.org/search/collection/1881199.

1877 Delinquent Tax List, Greene County, Arkansas **[Online Database]**, indexed at the USGenWeb site for Greene Co AR. See
www.argenweb.net/greene/COURTRECORDS/1877delinq1877.htm.

1877 Real Estate Tax List, Stone County, Arkansas **[Online Database]**, indexed at the RootsWeb site for Stone Co AR. Reach this website via the Census-Online service. See
www.census-online.com/links/AR/Stone.

1878 Personal Property Assessed, Greene County, Arkansas **[Online Database]**, indexed at the USGenWeb site for Greene Co AR. See
www.argenweb.net/greene/COURTRECORDS/1878persprassed.htm.

1879-1889 Tax Assessments, Saline County, Arkansas **[Online Database]**, indexed at the USGenWeb site for Saline Co AR. See
www.argenweb.net/saline/taxes.html.

1880 Personal Property Assessed, Greene County, Arkansas **[Online Database]**, indexed at the USGenWeb site for Greene Co AR. See
www.argenweb.net/greene/COURTRECORDS/1880personprop.htm.

1880. *Arkansas, 1880 Federal Census: Soundex and Population Schedules* **[Microfilm & Digital Capture]**, from the originals at the National Archives, Washington, DC (in 1970), now located at the Arkansas History Commission, Little Rock, AR. Filmed by the National Archives, 1970, 71 rolls, beginning with FHL film #1254038 (Population schedules: Benton, Boone, Bradley, Calhoun, and Carroll counties). To access the digital images, see the online FHL catalog:
www.familysearch.org/search/catalog/670365.

1880 Mortality Schedules of Arkansas **[Printed Index]**, by Capitola Hensley Glazner and Bobbie Lee Jones McLane, published by Glazner and McLane, Hot Springs National Park, AR, 1975, 261 pages, FHL book 976.7 X2pm 1880.

1882-1918 Index, Will Book A, Scott County, Arkansas **[Online Database]**, indexed at the USGenWeb site for Scott Co AR. See
www.argenweb.net/scott/will.htm.

1882-1963. See *Arkansas Deaths and Burials, 1882-1929; 1945-1963* **[Online Database]**, digitized and indexed at the FamilySearch website. Name index to death and burial records from the state of Arkansas. Microfilm copies of these records are available at the Family History Library and Family History Centers. This set contains 38,956 records.
www.familysearch.org/search/collection/1674710.

1883 Real Estate Tax Book, Pike County, **Arkansas [Online Database]**, indexed at the Pike County Archives & History Society site. See
www.pcahs.org/pcaolr/tax01/tax83pik.htm.

1884 Business Directory, Scott County, Arkansas **[Online Database]**, indexed at the USGenWeb site for Scott Co AR. See
www.argenweb.net/scott/citydir.htm.

1885 Tax List, Little River County, Arkansas **[Online Database]**, originally indexed at the BackwardBranch.com site. For an archived database:
https://web.archive.org/web/20101213055804/http://backwardbranch.com/lrcgs/1885LRC.html.

1887-1914 Index to Inventory Record A, Scott County, Arkansas **[Online Database]**, indexed at the USGenWeb site for Scott Co AR. See
www.argenweb.net/scott/scotti.htm.

1889 Personal Tax Book, Saline County, Arkansas **[Online Database]**, indexed at the USGenWeb site for Saline Co AR. See
www.argenweb.net/saline/tax1890.htm.

1890 Census of Clark County, Arkansas **[Printed Book]**, by William L. Newberry, Clark County Historical Association, Arkadelphia, Arkansas. The 1890 Federal census was completely destroyed for all of Arkansas. This book reconstructs the name lists from the Clark County Tax Receipt Book for 1890. FHL book 976.749 R48n.

1890 Reconstructed Census of Grant County, Arkansas **[Printed Book]**, compiled and published by Joan G. Threet, 72 pages. This reconstructed census was compiled by using personal property tax records, court minutes, marriage records & personal data from the compiler's husband's family. Also included: list of post offices; Pine Grove (at Grapevine, Ark.) & Dogwood school photos (3 altogether); data on Threet & Moore families (1 page). Includes full-name index. Also includes index to 1890 marriages. See FHL book 976.771 X2t 1890.

1890 Reconstructed Census of Greene County, Arkansas **[Printed Book]**, by the Greene County Historical and Genealogical Society, Paragould, AR, 1989, 50 pages. Includes surname index. Includes a 1930 map of school districts. This Greene County "census" was reconstructed through the use of tax records. See FHL book 976.7993 R4r.
- See also *Greene County, Arkansas, 1890 Reconstructed Census* **[Online Database]**. see www.argenweb.net/greene/CENSUS/1890censusdistricts.htm.

1890 Census of Howard County, Arkansas **[Printed Book]**, by Lucilee Westbrook. This "census" was compiled from tax assessment records. The names are in alphabetical order by school district. FHL book 976.7483 R4w.

1890 Tax List, Izard County, Arkansas **[Online Database]**, originally indexed at the CouchGen.com site. For an archived database, see https://web.archive.org/web/20100113093629/www.couchgenweb.com/arkansas/izard/Lunenburgtax.html.

1890 Property Tax List for Jackson County, Arkansas **[Online Database]**, indexed at the RootsWeb site for Jackson Co AR. See www.rootsweb.ancestry.com/~arjackso/taxlist.htm.

1890 Tax List, Lafayette County, Arkansas, Part One, A-L **[Online Database]**, indexed at the USGenWeb site for Lafayette Co AR. See http://files.usgwarchives.net/ar/lafayette/taxlists/1890tax.txt.

1890 Tax List, Lafayette County, Arkansas, Part Two, M-Z **[Online Database]**, indexed at the USGenWeb site for Lafayette Co AR. See http://files.usgwarchives.net/ar/lafayette/taxlists/1890tax2.txt.

1890 Personal Property Tax Records, Lincoln County, Arkansas **[Online Database]**, indexed at the RootsWeb site for Lincoln Co AR. See www.rootsweb.ancestry.com/~arlincol/1890taxroll.html.

1890 Tax List, Little River County, Arkansas **[Online Database]**, indexed at the backwardbranch.com website. For an archived database, see https://web.archive.org/web/20101213055741/http://backwardbranch.com/lrcgs/1890lrcTaxList.pdf.

1890 Tax Book (Reconstructed 1890 Census) Logan County, Arkansas **[Printed Book]**, compiled by Bill Hanks, Arkansas Ancestors, 1987, 118 pages. According to the transcriber, for the most part tax records are being used to reconstruct the 1890 census in Logan County, Arkansas. Names are listed in alphabetical order. See FHL book 976.737 X22h .

1890 Reconstructed Census of Mississippi County, Arkansas **[Printed Book]**, compiled and published by Joan G. Threet, 132 pages. This "census" was reconstructed from court records, marriage records, newspapers and family records. Names are in alphabetical order. See FHL book 976.795 X2t 1890.

1890 Census Reconstruction, Garland and Montgomery Counties, Arkansas **[Printed Book]**, reconstructed from 1890 tax receipt books, compiled by Inez Halsell Cline, Bobbie Jones McLane, Wendy Bradley Richter, Typescript, 132 pages, map. Arranged in alphabetical order by surname. See FHL book 976.74 X2c 1890.

1890 Phillips County, Arkansas "Census" From Real Estate Tax Records **[Printed Book]**, compiled by Carrie Davison and Rose Craig White of the Tri-County Genealogical Society, 1989, 84 pages, published by Ole English Press, Clarendon, AR. Includes surname index. See FHL book 976.788 X2.

1890 Census of Pike County, Arkansas **[Printed Book]**, by Russell Pierce Baker. This "census" is a reconstruction of the destroyed-by-fire federal census of 1890 from the 1893 Pike County tax receipt book. FHL book 976.7485 X2b 1890.

1890 Census, Polk County, Arkansas **[Printed Book]**, compiled by Wanda Tilley; typed and printed by Gypsie Cannon, Mena, AR, 198?, 21 pages. From preface: "Compiled from the 1888 real estate tax book; 1890 marriage records; and book of delinquent sales, 1878-1898, list of delinquent land sold on 10th day of June 1890." Arranged in alphabetical order by surname. See FHL book 976.745 X2.

1890 Partial Tax List, Pope County, Arkansas **[Online Database],** indexed at the USGenWeb site for Pope Co AR. See
http://files.usgwarchives.net/ar/pope/taxlists/1890.txt.

1890 Tax List, Allen Township, Pope County, Arkansas **[Online Database],** indexed at the USGenWeb site for Pope Co AR. See http://files.usgwarchives.net/ar/pope/taxlists/1890pope-tax.txt.

1890 Tax List, City of Russellville, Pope County, Arkansas **[Online Database],** indexed at the USGenWeb site for Pope Co AR. See http://files.usgwarchives.net/ar/pope/taxlists/russellville.txt.

1890. *Prairie County, Arkansas 1890 Census Reconstruction: A Sesquicentennial Project* **[Printed Book],** compiled by Margaret Harrison Hubbard, Hot Springs, AR, 1986, 105 pages, maps. This is a reconstruction made by using tax records and other records for that time period. Includes index. See FHL book 976.777 X2p 1890.

1890 Census of Randolph County, Arkansas as Constructed from the Personal Property Tax List **[Printed Book],** by Burton Ray Knotts. FHL book 976.724 R4k.

1890 Saline County, Arkansas Taxpayers: A Substitute for the Missing 1890 Census, with Full Name Index **[Printed Book],** compiled by Carolyn J. Billingsley, published by C. J. Billingsley, Alexander, AR, 1986, 103 pages. From preface: "This book was compiled from the 1889 Saline County tax book, the 1889 Saline County (paid) tax book, and the 1889 Saline County tax receipt book." Includes index. The names are arranged by school districts as they are on the tax books. See FHL book 976.772 R4b.

1890 Census (Reconstruction) of Sebastian County, Arkansas **[Printed Book],** compiled by members of the Frontier Researchers (Genealogical Society) of Fort Smith, AR, c1986, 223 pages. Includes indexed names from the following books: (1) Lower District Real Estate Tax Record Book; (2) Lower District Personal Property Tax Record Book; (3) Upper District Real Estate Tax Record Book; (4) Upper District Voter Registration for 1892; (5) Fort Smith City Directory; (6) Fort Smith Marriages for 1890; (7) Birnie Brothers Funeral Home Records for 1890, Fort Smith; (8) First Lutheran Church Records, Fort Smith. See FHL book 976.736 X22c 1890.

1890. *Sevier County, Arkansas, 1890 Census Reconstructed from Tax Records: Sesquicentennial Project of State History Commission* **[Printed Book],** compiled by Vinita Lovell Long, Martha Johnson, Mary McCrory, 1978, Arkansas, 83 pages. Includes index. See FHL 976.747 X28L 1890.

1890 Real Estate Tax List, Stone County, Arkansas **[Online Database],** indexed at the RootsWeb site for Stone Co AR. Use the Census-Online portal site to access this database. See
www.census-online.com/links/AR/Stone/.

1890 White County, Arkansas "Census," Reconstructed From the 1890 Personal Property Tax Book **[Printed Book],** compiled by Wensil Marsh Clark, Arkansas Genealogical Society, Hot Springs, AR, published by W. M. Clark, Little Rock, AR, 1986, 98 pages, map. Includes surname index. See FHL book 976.776 R48c.

1890 Surname List from the Tax Rolls, White County, Arkansas **[Online Database],** indexed at the USGenWeb site for White Co AR. See
www.argenweb.net/white/census/1890tax.html.

1890-1963. *Arkansas Confederate Soldier Home* **[Online Database],** digitized and indexed at FamilySearch.org. Images of files of veterans, widows and daughters who were inmates of the Arkansas Confederate Home in Little Rock. The files were acquired from the Arkansas State History Commission and are arranged alphabetically. This database has 1,531 records, see
www.familysearch.org/search/collection/2126715.

1891 Real Estate Tax Assessments, Marion County, Arkansas **[Online Database],** indexed at the USGenWeb site for Marion Co AR. See
www.argenweb.net/marion/transcribedrecords/index.html.

1891 Tax List, School District 95, Pope County, Arkansas **[Online Database],** indexed at the USGenWeb site for Pope Co AR. See http://files.usgwarchives.net/ar/pope/taxlists/1891pope-tax.txt.

1891-1935. *Arkansas, Confederate Pension Records* **[Online Database],** indexed at the Ancestry.com website. Source: Arkansas History Commission. Each index record includes: Name, Residence Location, State Served From, Division, Regiment, Vet Application year, and Comments. This database has 36,098 records. See https://search.ancestry.com/search/db.aspx?dbid=2281.

1891-1936. *Arkansas Confederate Veterans and Widows Pension Applications* **[Printed Index],** compiled by Frances T. Ingmire. Arranged in alphabetical order by surname of veteran. Published by F.T. Ingmire, St. Louis, MO, 1985, 442 pages, FHL book 976.7 M2B.

1891-1939. *Arkansas Ex-Confederate Pension Records* **[Online Database],** digitized and indexed at the FamilySearch.org website. This collection includes an index and images of pension records of former Confederate soldiers and widows who resided in the state of Arkansas. These records are the administrative records from the Arkansas State Auditor, which authorized and disbursed pension payments. Researchers should also check the pension application files (1901-1929) which are published on FamilySearch. This database has 172,347 records. See www.familysearch.org/search/collection/1921864.

1892 Nevada County Real Estate Tax List **[Online Database],** indexed at the USGenWeb site for Nevada Co AR. See www.argenweb.net/nevada/1892ne01.htm.

1892-1898 Voters Lists, Polk County, Arkansas **[Printed Book],** compiled, typed, and printed by Shirley "Gypsie" Cannon, Mena, AR, 198?, 65 pages. Arranged in alphabetical order by surname. See FHL book 976.745 N48.

1893 Voters List, Marion County, Arkansas **[Online database],** indexed at the USGenWeb site for Marion Co AR. See www.argenweb.net/marion/voterslist/index.html.

1893-1939. *Ex-Confederate Pension Records* **[Microfilm & Digital Capture],** from the original Digest of the Statutes of Arkansas, with lists of pension claims allowed. Filmed by the Genealogical Society of Utah, 2000, 11 rolls, beginning with FHL film #2209370 (list of pension claims allowed 1893-1939; 1891-1896 pension listings, Arkansas-Cleveland counties). To access the digital images, see the online FHL catalog: www.familysearch.org/search/catalog/722961.

1900. *Arkansas, 1900 Federal Census: Soundex and Population Schedules* **[Microfilm & Digital Capture],** from the original records at the National Archives, Washington, DC. Filmed by the National Archives, c1970, 167 rolls, beginning with FHL film #1242069 (Soundex: A100 thru A325); and FHL film #1240049 (Population schedules: Arkansas and Ashley Co.). To access the digital images, see the online FHL catalog: www.familysearch.org/search/catalog/647008.

1900 Newton County, Arkansas Census **[Online Database],** indexed at the Ancestry.com website. Source: book, same title, by Belinda Merritt, publ. 1999. Each index record includes race, sex, birth, age, marriage, and birthplace information. In addition, the number of children a mother gave birth to and the number still living are provided along with parent's birthplaces. This database has 11,143 records: https://search.ancestry.com/search/db.aspx?dbid=3806.

1901-1905. *Polk County, Arkansas, Marriage Index* **[Online Database],** indexed at the Ancestry.com website. Source: Book, same title, by Marilyn Brown, 1998. Each record of this database contains the name, age, and residence of the bride and groom and date of marriage. In addition, the name, age, and residence of the witness is also given. This database has 1,147 records. See https://search.ancestry.com/search/db.aspx?dbid=3434.

1901-1929. *Arkansas Confederate Pension Records* **[Microfilm & Digital Capture],** from the originals of the State Auditor of Arkansas, now at the Arkansas History Commission, Little Rock, AR. Files are generally in alphabetical order, with some disruptions. Filmed by the Arkansas History Commission, c1980, 121 rolls, beginning with FHL film #1722443 (Aaron – Adams, John). To access the digital images, see the online FHL catalog: www.familysearch.org/search/catalog/598195.
- See also, *Arkansas Confederate Pensions, 1901-1929* **[Online Database],** digitized and indexed at the FamilySearch website. Images of applications for pension (in alphabetical order) filed by Confederate veterans and widows living in the state of Arkansas.

This database has 159,626 images. See www.familysearch.org/search/collection/1837922.
- This database is also available at the Ancestry.com website. See https://search.ancestry.com/search/db.aspx?dbid=60237.

1893 Little Rock City Directory [Online Database], indexed at the RootsWeb site. See http://freepages.genealogy.rootsweb.ancestry.com/~ouisersplace/dirmast/dirmast.htm.

1899 Delinquent Tax List, Lincoln County, Arkansas [Online Database], indexed at the RootsWeb site for Lincoln Co AR. See www.rootsweb.ancestry.com/~arlincol/deltaxlst.html.

1906-1910. *Polk County, Arkansas, Marriage Index* [Online Database], indexed at the Ancestry.com website. Source: Book, same title, by Marilyn Brown, 1998. Each record of this database contains the name, age, and residence of the bride and groom and date of marriage. In addition, the name, age, and residence of the witness is also given. This database has 2,304 records. See https://search.ancestry.com/search/db.aspx?dbid=3439.

1907 Poll Tax Index, Saline County, Arkansas [Online Database], indexed at the USGenWeb site for Saline Co AR. See www.argenweb.net/saline/polltx07.html.

1907-1917 School Rosters, White County, Arkansas [Online Database], index at the USGenWeb site for White Co AR. See http://files.usgwarchives.net/ar/white/census/school/whschool.txt.

1907-1968. *Arkansas, Naturalization Records* [Online Database], indexed at the Ancestry.com website. Source: National Archives records of Naturalizations. Included are Petitions, Declarations, and Certificates. Each index record may include: Name, Age, Record Type, Date, Place, and Spouse. This database has 2,083 records. See https://search.ancestry.com/search/db.aspx?dbid=2506.

1908 Confederate Soldiers Reunion, Town of Leola, Grant County, Arkansas [Online Database]. Originally indexed at the USGenWeb site for Grant Co AR. For an archived database, see https://web.archive.org/web/20100105175030/http://argenweb.net/grant/texts/confederatereunion1908.txt.

1910. *Arkansas, 1910 Federal Census: Soundex and Population Schedules* [Microfilm], from the originals at the National Archives, Washington, DC. Filmed by the National Archives, c1970, 165 rolls, beginning with FHL film #1374056 (Population schedules: Arkansas, Ashley, Baxter, and Boone Co.). To access the digital images, see the online FHL catalog: www.familysearch.org/search/catalog/646941.

1910. *Arkansas 1910 Census Index* (Printed Index], compiled and published by Heritage Quest, Salt Lake City, UT, 2002, 4 vols: Vol. 1: A-Dyy; Vol. 2: E-Kin; Vol. 3: Kip-Rob; Vol.4: Roc-Z. FHL book 976.7 X22.

1910 Polk County Jurors – April Term [Online Database], indexed at the USGenWeb site for Polk Co AR. See http://argenweb.net/polk/jurors.htm.

1910 Directory, Randolph County, Arkansas [Online Database], indexed at the RootsWeb site for Randolph Co AR. See www.rootsweb.ancestry.com/~arrandol/books/directoryindex.htm.

1911 Census of Confederate Veterans [Printed Book], compiled by Bobbie Lee Jones McLane and Capitola Glazner. Complete for 44 counties. Includes the name of the veteran, address, date of birth, place of birth, where enlisted, names and birthplaces of the soldier's parents and grandparents, maiden name of wife, date and place of marriage, names of her parents, and names of children. Published by Arkansas Ancestors, Hot Springs, AR, 1981, 3 vols., FHL book 976.7 X2m v.1-3.
- Indexed separately by Bobbie Lee Jones McLane, as *An Index to the Three Volumes, Arkansas 1911 Census of Confederate Veterans,* FHL book 976.7 X2m index.

1911 Census of Confederate Veterans, Scott County, Arkansas [Online Database], indexed at the USGenWeb site for Scott Co AR. See www.argenweb.net/scott/1911index.htm.

1911 Poll Tax Index, Saline County, Arkansas [Online Database], indexed at the USGenWeb site for Saline Co AR. See www.argenweb.net/saline/polltx11.html.

1913-1970. *Headstones, Hot Springs, Arkansas Monument Company* [Printed Book], by Jimmie Lois Caton Jones. Contents: Vol. 1: 1913-1931, Vol. 2:

1934-1970. Includes names of purchasers, deceased, birth and death dates of deceased and the cemeteries where they are buried. Published by the author, 1990, 2 vols., FHL book 976.741/H1 U3J v.1-2.

1914-1923. *Arkansas, Sevier County, Death Records* **[Online Database],** digitized and indexed at FamilySearch.org, from the original records at the Sevier County Clerk's Office, DeQueen, AR. This database has 597 records, see
www.familysearch.org/search/collection/2630407.

1914-1948. *Arkansas Death Record Index* **[Printed Index],** prepared for publication by Desmond Walls Allen. Contains an index to the death records filed with the Arkansas State Department of Health. Includes full name, county and date of death for each deceased. Contents: Vol. 1: 1914-1923; Vol. 2: 1934-1940; Vol. 3: 1941-1948; Vol. 4: 1924 – 1933. Published by Ark. Research, Conway, AR, 1996-1999, FHL book 976.7 V22ad, v.1-4.

1914-1949 Arkansas Death Index, Prairie County, Arkansas **[Online Database],** abstracted from the state database at the RootsWeb site for Prairie Co AR. See www.rootsweb.ancestry.com/~arprairi/Death/deathltr.htm.

1914-1950. *Arkansas Death Index* **[Online Database],** digitized and indexed at the Ancestry.com website. Source: AR Div. of Vital Records, AR Dept of Health. Index by Ancestry.com. This database is an index to approximately 594,000 deaths that occurred in Arkansas between 1914 and 1950, from the Arkansas Department of Health microfiche by the Arkansas Genealogical Society, In addition to providing the name of the deceased, the index usually provides the date of death, county of death, gender, race, age at time of death, volume number, and certificate number. This database has 594,114 records. See
http://search.ancestry.com/search/db.aspx?dbid=8771.
- This database is also located at FamilySearch.org website. See
www.familysearch.org/search/collection/1940760.

1915-1929, 1960, 1990-2005. See *Index of Death Notices Appearing in the Arkansas Gazette* **[Printed Book],** by Oscar G. Russell. Published by the author, North Little Rock, AR, 1991-2006, FHL book 976.7 V42r pt. (year). See also FHL CD No. 3510.

1917 World War I Draft List, Saline County, Arkansas **[Online Database],** a list of young men from Saline County was published in The Benton Courier in July 1917. Indexed at the USGenWeb site for Saline Co AR. See www.argenweb.net/saline/wwidft.htm.

1917-1918 World War I Discharge Records, Scott County, Arkansas **[Online Database],** indexed at the USGenWeb site for Scott Co AR. See
http://files.usgwarchives.net/ar/scott/military/ww1/sctwwi.txt.

1917-1918. *Arkansas, World War I Selective Service System Draft Registration Cards* **[Microfilm & Digital Capture],** filmed by the National Archives, 1988, 71 rolls, beginning with FHL film #1522740 (Arkansas County, A-Z). The draft cards are arranged alphabetically by state, then alphabetically by county or city and then alphabetically by surname of the registrants. To access the digital images, see the online FHL catalog:
www.familysearch.org/search/catalog/746967.

1917-1919. *Arkansas, World War I American Expeditionary Forces, Deaths* **[Digital Capture],** digitized by FamilySearch International, 2018. To access the digital images, see the online FHL catalog: www.familysearch.org/search/catalog/3023914.

1920. *Arkansas, 1920 Federal Census: Soundex and Population Schedules* **[Microfilm],** from the originals at the National Archives in the early 1940s. Filmed by the U.S. Census Bureau, reproduced by the National Archives and others, 1941-1999, 165 rolls, beginning with FHL film #1823395 (Population schedules: Arkansas, Ashley, and Baxter counties). To access the digital images, see the online FHL catalog: www.familysearch.org/search/catalog/534277.

1920s-1990s. *Arkansas College Yearbooks, County Histories, Newspapers, Etc.* **[Online Database],** ranging from the early 1920s to the early 1990s, located at *Arkansas – Collection Catalog,* MyHeritage.com. For a complete list, see
www.myheritage.com/records/Arkansas/all-records.

1923-1939. *Arkansas Divorce Index* **[Online Database],** digitized and indexed at the Ancestry.com website. This database is an index to divorces that were filed in Arkansas from 1923-27 and 1934-39.

Information that may be found in this database includes plaintiff's name, defendant's name, date of divorce, county of divorce, and reference information for locating the divorce certificate, including a volume number, docket number, and certificate number (the certificate number will only be listed for the 1934-39 divorces). This database has 108,392 records. See http://search.ancestry.com/search/db.aspx?dbid=8770.
- This database is also located at the FamilySearch.org website. See www.familysearch.org/search/collection/1967739.

1926 Poll Tax Index, Saline County, Arkansas **[Online Database],** indexed at the USGenWeb site. See www.argenweb.net/saline/polltx26.html.

1926 Official List of Legal Voters of Howard County, Arkansas **[Printed Book],** published by Madigan's Books, Charleston, IL, 198?. See FHL book 976.7 A1 no. 137.

1929 Hope Phone Directory **[Online Database],** indexed at the RootsWeb site for Hempstead Co AR: http://freepages.genealogy.rootsweb.ancestry.com/~ousersplace/hope/hope.htm.

1930. *Arkansas, 1930 Federal Census: Population Schedules* **[Microfilm & Digital Capture],** from the original records filmed by the Census Bureau in the early 1940s, 136 rolls, beginning with FHL film #2338195 (Soundex: A000-A352); and FHL film #2339799 (Population schedules: Arkansas and Ashley counties). To access the digital images, see the online FHL catalog: www.familysearch.org/search/catalog/1037623.

1930-1931 Conway City Directory, Faulkner County, Arkansas **[Online Database],** originally indexed at the backwardsbranch.com website. For an archived database, see https://web.archive.org/web/20110929012309/http://backwardbranch.com/arfaulkner/1930city.pdf.

1933-1939. *Arkansas, Marriage Index* **[Online Database],** from the Arkansas Department of Health microfiche by the Arkansas Genealogical Society, digitized and indexed at the FamilySearch.org website. Information that may be found in this database for each entry includes groom's full name, bride's full name, their marriage date, license date, county of marriage, marriage certificate number, and the volume number in which the certificate is located. This database has 421,079 records. See www.familysearch.org/search/collection/1940215.
- This database is also available at the Ancestry.com website. See https://search.ancestry.com/search/db.aspx?dbid=8780.

1935-1937 Family Interviews, Prairie County, Arkansas **[Online Database],** from the book published by the WPA Federal Writer's Project. Indexed at the RootsWeb site for Prairie Co AR. See www.rootsweb.ancestry.com/~arprairi/WPA/WPAbk.htm

1935-1960. *Arkansas Death Certificate Index* **[CD-ROM],** compiled and published by the Arkansas Genealogical Society, Little Rock, AR, 2011, FHL CD No. 7269.

1938-1956 Burial Association, Boone County, Arkansas **[Online Database],** indexed at the RootsWeb site for Boone Co AR. See http://freepages.genealogy.rootsweb.ancestry.com/~jmwtlw/Boone_co_cem.htm.

1940. *Arkansas, 1940 Federal Census: Population Schedules* **[Digital Capture],** digitized images from the microfilm of original records held by the Bureau of the Census in the 1940s. After microfilming, Congress allowed the Census Bureau to destroy the originals to free up space for WWII-related files. Digitizing of the 1940 census schedules microfilm images was done for the National Archives and made public on April 2, 2012. To access the digital images, see the online FHL catalog: www.familysearch.org/search/catalog/2057742.

1940 Federal Census – Finding Aids **[Online Database].** The National Archives prepared a special website online with a detailed description of the 1940 federal census. Included at the site are descriptions of location finding aids, such as Enumeration District Maps, Geographic Descriptions of Census Enumeration Districts, and a list of 1940 City Directories available at the National Archives. The finding aids are all linked to other National Archives sites. The National Archives website also has a link to 1940 Search Engines using Stephen P. Morse's "One-Step" system for finding a 1940 E.D. or street address conversion. See www.archives.gov/research/census/1940/general-info.html#questions.

Sample, 1940-1945, Arkansas, First Draft Registration Cards.

1940-1945. *Arkansas, First Draft Registrations Cards* **[Digital Capture],** from the original records at the National Archives, Ft. Worth, TX. Digitized by FamilySearch International, 2009. Cards are arranged alphabetically by order of surname. To access the digital images, see the online FHL catalog: www.familysearch.org/search/catalog/1875142.

- See also, *Arkansas, First Draft Registration Cards. 1940-1945* **[Online Database],** digitized and indexed at the FamilySearch.org website. Source: National Archives microfilm. This is a name index and images of draft registration cards (SSS-1 forms) covering a special classification of individuals born between 1897 and 1928. This database has 359,665 records. See www.familysearch.org/search/collection/1875142.

1941-1990. *Masonic Death Records from the Grand Lodge of Arkansas* **[Printed Book],** compiled by Desmond Walls Allen. Contains a compilation of death records taken from annual volumes of the Proceedings M.W. Grand Lodge F&A Masons of Arkansas. There are 44,634 death records, listing the member's name, death date, Masonic lodge number, and volume year of the Proceedings from which it was taken. Published by Arkansas Research, Conway, AR, 1999, 301 pages, FHL book 976.7 V2a.

1942. *Arkansas Selective Service System Registration Cards. World War II: Fourth Registration* **[Microfilm & Digital Capture],** filmed by the Genealogical Society of Utah, 2002, 75 rolls, beginning with FHL film #2139687. Aarant, Walter – Burt, Aldy). This collection includes World War II draft registration cards only for men born on or between April 28, 1877 and February 16, 1897 who lived in Arkansas. These men were 45 to 64 years old when they registered on April 27, 1942. Men who had already enlisted in the Armed Forces and were serving on April 27, 1942 would not have registered. Cards are alphabetical by last name. Each card includes name of individual, date and place of birth, address, age, telephone number, employer's name and address, name and address of person who would know where the individual can be located, signature, and physical description. To access the digital images, see the online FHL catalog: www.familysearch.org/search/catalog/1057398.

1942 Arkansas, World War II 4th Draft Registration Cards **[2nd Digital Capture].** To access the digital images, see the online FHL catalog: www.familysearch.org/search/catalog/1390078.

1948-1959 Arkansas Second Registration Draft Cards **[Digital Capture],** digital images draft registration cards arranged numerically by local board number then alphabetically by surname of registrant. To access the digital images, see the online FHL catalog: www.familysearch.org/search/catalog/1914215.

1956 Record of Voters Poll Tax, Greene County, Arkansas **[Online Database],** indexed at the USGenWeb site for Greene Co AR. See www.argenweb.net/greene/COURTRECORDS/polltax56.htm.

1998-Current. *Arkansas Newspaper Obituaries* **[Online Database].** Digitized and indexed at the GenealogyBank.com website including obituaries from the following Arkansas newspapers: Arkadelphia, Batesville, Bella Vista, Benton, Bentonville, Booneville, Cabot, Camden, Carlisle, Charleston, Clinton, Conway, El Dorado, Farmington, Fayetteville, Fort Smith, Gravette, Greenwood, Harrison, Heber Springs, Helena, West Helena, Hope, Hot Springs, Jacksonville, Jasper, Jonesboro, Little Rock, Lonoke, Magnolia, Malvern, Maumelle, Newport, North Little Rock, Paragould, Paris, Pea Ridge, Pine Bluff, Prescott, Rogers, Russellville, Searcy, Sherwood, Siloam Springs, Springdale, Springdale/Rogers, Stuttgart, Van Buren, and White Hall. See www.genealogybank.com/gbnk/obituaries/explore/USA/Arkansas.

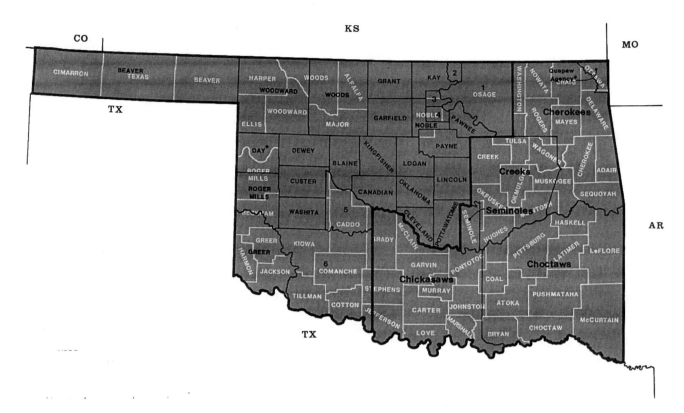

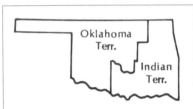

Oklahoma Territory & Indian Territory • June 1900. This map shows, in black, the counties and Indian jurisdictions of Oklahoma Territory and Indian Territory at the time of the 1900 Federal Census. The current 77 counties of the state of Oklahoma are shown in white. It is fitting to use 1900 as the sample for Oklahoma Territory and Indian Territory, since it is the only surviving federal census that included both territories prior to Oklahoma statehood in 1907. In 1900, Oklahoma Territory had the following Indian jurisdictions, shown on the map as: 1) Osage, 2) Kaw (alias Kansas), 3) Ponca, 4) Otoe and Missouri, 5) Wichita, and 6) Kiowa, Comanche, and Apache. The 1900 federal census is extant for all counties and Indian jurisdictions. The Poncas and Otoe/Missouri were also enumerated in Noble County, Oklahoma Territory. The Quapaw Agency in the Indian Territory contained reservations for the Quapaw, Peoria, Ottawa, Shawnee, Modoc, Wyandot, and Seneca. Day County in Oklahoma Territory was abolished by not being included in the 1907 constitution for the state of Oklahoma. The 1890 (census lost) and 1900 (census extant), were the first federal censuses in which American Indians were included. They were enumerated separately on "Indian Population" forms and added to the county lists for every applicable state. Indians did not appear in federal censuses again until 1930, after the 1924 Supreme Court ruling and Act of Congress that declared American Indians as U.S. Citizens. Between 1887 and 1907, the General Indian Allotment Acts divided tribal property and dissolved tribal agreements, essentially ending tribal land ownership in present-day Oklahoma. The allotments of land were divided among individual Indians. The bibliography that follows includes the Indian Censuses that were conducted related to the allotment process. **Map Source:** Page 278, *Map Guide to the U.S. Federal Censuses, 1790-1920*, by William Thorndale and William Dollarhide.

Oklahoma
Censuses & Substitute Name Lists

Jurisdictional History of the Indian Territory, Oklahoma Territory, and Oklahoma

The term *Indian Country* was used to describe the western areas encompassing several Indian tribes, whether nations, reservations, or those roaming free over the Great Plains. The evolution of the Indian Country into an official Indian Territory took place over the whole of the 19th Century. However, Indian Territory was never a territory in the official sense of the term. For the entire period of its existence, it never had a combined territorial government or a federally appointed territorial governor.

- Soon after the 1803 Louisiana Purchase, Thomas Jefferson urged the resettling of tribes of the eastern United States on lands west of the Mississippi. In 1804, Congress passed legislation authorizing the negotiation of removal treaties with the eastern tribes, and over the next twenty years, several tribes or portions of tribes moved west.

This first phase of removal was mostly voluntary, and often conflicted with white settlers moving west of the Mississippi at the same time. For example, when Arkansas Territory was established in 1819, it included most of the area of present-day Oklahoma. And in 1821, Missouri was admitted to the Union, further reducing the perceived range of land that was to be dedicated to the relocation of eastern Indian tribes.

- In 1828, the present western boundary of Arkansas was drawn, and for the first time, a law described the area west of that line as the exclusive domain of Indian tribes. But its jurisdiction was still part of the larger area officially called *Unorganized Territory*.

- Due to a misunderstanding of the Arkansas boundary, early white settlers north of the Red River (in present-day McCurtain County, Oklahoma) thought they were living in old Miller County, Arkansas Territory. In 1828, several hundred families were moved to areas south of the Red River to vacate the newly defined Indian domain. This was a rare case in American history where whites were relocated to make room for Indians – it was usually the other way around.

- In the 1830s, forced removal of eastern Indian tribes began, the most notorious being the Cherokee removal, which history remembers for the "trail of tears" they experienced.

- In 1834, legislation defined "Indian Country" as any portion of the western United States that was not part of a state or territory, thus, Indian Country was the same as Unorganized Territory. The new law also regulated certain activities of non-Indians within the region and established judicial boundaries: the northern portion of the region (modern Kansas) was to be under the control of the federal courts of Missouri; the southern portion (modern Oklahoma), under the federal courts of Arkansas. Federal censuses in the Indian Country taken from 1820 through 1870 for non-Indians were under the jurisdiction of the Missouri and Arkansas federal marshals. (Indians were specifically excluded from the federal censuses, except those who lived off reservations and subject to taxes like non-Indians).

- In the Indian Country, the most populous of the tribes were located in the southern portion, namely, the relocated Choctaw, Cherokee, Chickasaw, Creek, and Seminole Nations (the so-called Five Civilized Tribes). To the north in present-day Kansas were the reservations of numerous small Midwestern and Plains tribes.

A second removal and concentration of Indian populations took place in 1854, when twelve treaties were negotiated with tribes living in the northern part of the Unorganized Territory. Together, these agreements opened most of present-day Kansas for white settlement. That same year Congress created Kansas Territory, which encompassed the remaining

101

tribes and their diminished reservations. As a result, the Indian Country was reduced to the area of present-day Oklahoma (except for the Panhandle) with most of the land owned by the Five Civilized Tribes.

- Evidence of non-Indians living in the Indian Country can be seen in the 1860 federal census, where whites, blacks, adopted, or intermarried persons living on "Indian Lands West of Arkansas" were named and listed at the end of the Arkansas census schedules.

- In 1865, because the governments of the Five Civilized Tribes had supported the South during the Civil War, the federal government declared void its existing treaties with the five tribes. New treaties were negotiated the following year, in which the tribes either ceded the western portions of their lands to the federal government for the resettlement of more Indians, or, in the case of the Cherokees, provided for the sale of their western lands (the Cherokee Outlet).

A third wave of removals took place between 1866 and 1885, as the government started moving remaining tribes from Texas, Kansas, Nebraska, and elsewhere into the southern region. This is where the newly ceded western lands of the Five Civilized Tribes were now available for Indian settlement. During this time, the Cheyenne and Arapaho, the Comanche, Kiowa, and Apache, the Wichita and Caddo, the Potawatomi and Shawnee, the Kickapoo, the Iowa, the Sauk and Fox, the Pawnee, the Oto and Missouri, the Ponca, the Tonkawa, the Kaw, the Osage, the Peoria, the Wyandot, the Eastern Shawnee, the Modoc, and the Ottawa reservations were established in the Indian Country.

- In the Osage Reservation Act of 1872, the law stated that the reservation was located in *Indian Territory*, and all subsequent tribal agreements, executive orders, and other federal actions relative to the region now referred to the area officially as Indian Territory.

- In 1887, Congress passed the General Indian Allotment Act, which initiated the process of dividing tribal property and dissolving tribal agreements. Subsequent allotment acts by 1906 had essentially ended tribal land ownership in present-day Oklahoma, with allotments of land divided among individual Indians. Records of the allotments, including a final "census" of the families involved, provides the most complete list of inhabitants of the Indian Territory for that time period.

- In 1889, Congress established a separate federal court at Muskogee for Indian Territory, and for the first time it officially defined the area's boundaries: Indian Territory was the area bounded by the states of Kansas, Missouri, Arkansas, and Texas, and the Territory of New Mexico. On April 22, the Unassigned Lands were opened to settlement by non-Indians in the first of the famous land runs. Over fifty thousand homesteaders settled in the region on that day. (Try that today without computers).

- In May 1890 Indian Territory was divided into Oklahoma Territory and Indian Territory. Oklahoma Territory was defined as incorporating the Unassigned Lands and all reservations, with the exception of those of the Five Civilized Tribes and a few small reservations. While all of the reservations in the Cherokee Outlet were to be part of Oklahoma Territory, that portion of the Outlet still owned by the Cherokee Nation would remain as part of Indian Territory until purchased by the government. Almost immediately a special commission was organized to negotiate the allotment of the reservations in Oklahoma Territory and the sale of unallotted lands so that they could be opened for non-Indian settlement.

- Special censuses were taken periodically for Indians, and in the 1890 and 1900 federal censuses, Indian tribes were enumerated with Indian population schedules added to the regular schedules for each territory or state (1890 lost, 1900 extant).

- In 1893 the Cherokees sold their remaining portion of the Outlet, which was immediately incorporated into Oklahoma Territory and opened for settlement. Thus by 1893 Indian Territory had been reduced to just the reservations of the Five Civilized Tribes proper and the small reservations in the northeast.

- Later in 1893, the Dawes Commission was created by Congress to negotiate agreements with the Five Civilized Tribes to allot their lands, and in 1898 the allotment process began in what remained of Indian Territory.

- In a futile attempt to maintain some semblance of continued Indian separation, leaders of the Five Civilized Tribes organized a constitutional convention in 1905, drew up a constitution, and asked to be admitted to the Union as the state of Sequoyah. Congress rejected the plan and in 1907 approved a statute that joined Indian Territory with Oklahoma Territory to create the new state of Oklahoma.

Online Resources at the Oklahoma Historical Society

The OHS in Oklahoma City has many databases of interest to genealogists, whether for the Indian Country, Indian Territory, Oklahoma Territory, or the State of Oklahoma. Review their Genealogical Resources page. at **www.okhistory.org/research/genealogy**, leading to the following resources:

Online Catalog: includes many resources pertaining to genealogical research, including cemetery books, birth, death and marriage indexes, and county histories.

American Indian Ancestry: databases with online searching include the following:
- 1896 Applications for Enrollment.
- Dawes Final Rolls of the Five Civilized Tribes
- Hastain's Township Plats of the Creek Nation
- Moore's Seminole Roll and Land Guide
- Individual Indian Files
- Official Register of the United States Indian Agency Employees & Officials
- Finding Your American Indian Ancestors (PDF)

Oklahoma Genealogical Resources: Databases with online searching include the following:
- US Census Records. Search the 1933 Unemployment Relief database with more than 100,000 names listed. The complete 1890 OK Territorial Census is indexed here as well. Censuses on microfilm are identified here as the 1860 Lands West of Arkansas, 1890 Veterans & Widows; and 1900 Federal Census of Oklahoma Territory
- 1889 Oklahoma County Land Database & Map. This index includes names extracted from U.S. land patents homesteads: Oklahoma County, Oklahoma Territory Land Run of April 22, 1889
- 1901 El Reno Land Lottery - individuals whose names were drawn
- 1901 El Reno and Lawton land lottery tickets (partial listing)
- Biographical & Topical Vertical Files
- City Directories, Phone Books, Yearbooks
- Daughters of Union Veterans Application Index
- Divorce records from Oklahoma County
- Deaths found in OKC City Directories, 1918, 1920-23
- Family Histories
- Gateway to OK History - Newspapers and Photos Online
- Grant County, Mills Funeral Home
- Grant County, Wilson Funeral Home
- Indian Pioneer Histories (Available online through the University of Oklahoma)
- Marriage Records Collection Updated
- Newspaper Archives
- Official Register of the United States Indian Agency Employees & Officials
- Oklahoman Obituary Index
- Oklahoma City Death Register, 1908-1926
- Oklahoma Military Casualties Database Online Exhibit
- Oklahoma Military Hall of Fame Online Exhibit
- Oklahoma Military Deaths – WWI to Korea
- Oklahoma State Penitentiary Records, 1930s
- Probate Records from Oklahoma County, 1890-1928
- Teacher's Reports from the Dawes Commission Records
- Smith's First Directory of Oklahoma Territory
- United Daughters of the Confederacy Applications

Bibliography
Censuses & Substitutes for Indian Territory, Oklahoma Territory, and Oklahoma

Several censuses were taken by the Five Civilized Tribes separate from the federal censuses or those taken by Oklahoma Territory. They included censuses taken in 1880 and 1890 by the Cherokee government; an 1885 Choctaw census; and an 1890 census by the Chickasaw tribe. The Indian censuses identify both Indians and non-Indians living on their reservations.

- The 1890 federal census included population schedules for the newly formed Oklahoma Territory, and added the Indian tribes of Indian Territory on separate schedules. Unfortunately, most of the 1890 federal censuses were burned or destroyed after a fire in the Commerce Building in Washington, DC in 1921. But some relief to the 1890 disaster exists, since Oklahoma Territory took a special territorial census in 1890 for its original seven counties (Beaver, Canadian, Cleveland, Kingfisher, Logan, Oklahoma, and Payne), which all survive.

- The 1900 federal census for Oklahoma Territory included separate population schedules for Indians.

- Just prior to statehood in 1907, the federal government sponsored a census for Indian and Oklahoma territories. However, of the 75 counties enumerated, only the name list for Seminole County survives at the National Archives.

- There are more census substitutes than censuses and the combined list begins below in chronological order:

♦ ♦ ♦ ♦ ♦

1828-1900s. *Cherokee Nation* **[Microfilm & Digital Capture],** from the originals in the Oklahoma Historical Society, Indian Archives Division, Oklahoma City, OK. Includes correspondence, census records, enrollment records, laws and acts, journals, national council and senate records, court records, vital records, probate records, land and property records, school records, and other miscellaneous documents. Includes Register of Persons... Under Treaty of 1817, Cherokee (Tahlequah) Census; Includes Cherokee Nation East, Roll of 1835; Cherokees Census of Flint District, With a Complete List of Names of Emigrants, 1855; Includes Enrollments and Censuses, 1867-1920; Supplemental Roll of Those Left Off the Rolls of 1880, Cherokee (Tahlequah), Per Capita; and the Hester Roll

of Eastern Cherokees (those living east of the Mississippi River in 1884). Filmed by the Oklahoma Historical Society, 1976, 129 rolls, beginning with FHL film #1666294. To access the digital images, see the online FHL catalog:
https://familysearch.org/search/catalog/529945.

1828-1900s. *Choctaw Nation* **[Microfilm & Digital Capture],** from the originals at the Oklahoma Historical Society, Indian Archives Division, Oklahoma City, OK. Includes census, Choctaw Indians, government records, correspondence, occupations, vital statistics, probate records, land and property, court records, military records, schools, and other miscellaneous information. Filmed by the Oklahoma Historical Society, 90 rolls, beginning with FHL film #1666451 (Census and citizenship: Mississippi Choctaw census and citizenship 1830-1899). To access the digital images, see the online FHL catalog: **https://familysearch.org/search/catalog/544264**.

1828-1900s. *Sac and Fox, and Shawnee Nations* **[Microfilm] & Digital Capture,** from the originals in the Oklahoma Historical Society, Indian Archives Division, Oklahoma City, OK. Includes correspondence, census records, enrollment records, laws and acts, journals, national council and senate records, court records, vital records, probate records, land and property records, school records, and other miscellaneous documents. Filmed by the Oklahoma Historical Society, 1971, 64 rolls, beginning with FHL film #1671001. To access the digital images, see the online FHL catalog:
https://familysearch.org/search/catalog/544287.

1828-1900s. See *Indians and Intruders* **[Printed Book],** compiled by Sharron Standifer Ashton, published by Ashton Books, Norman, OK, 1996-2002, 5 vols., index included in each volume. Contents: **Vol. 1:** White intruders in the Old Creek Nation, 1831; intruders in the Choctaw Nation, 1882; 1860 Indian Territory slave schedules, Chickasaw District and Choctaw Nation; records of burials, baptisms, marriages and deaths at Fort Supply, Indian Territory; evidence of marriage in the Creek national records; Chickasaw traders in 1766; Cherokee Nation permits; intruders and non-citizens in the Creek Nation; **Vol. 2:** Cherokee voters in the Old Cherokee Nation, 1835; Creek nation licenses and permits, 1875-1895; Choctaw Nation divorce records, 1875-1905; records undated; Choctaw Nation marriages, 1889-1898; **Vol. 3:** Creek Indian light horseman; Cherokee Civil War claims index; Chickasaw Nation citizenship records; Our brother in red, Indian Territory news, January 1890-May 1891; early Choctaw Mission students, 1823; map of Pushmataha District, Choctaw Nation; Choctaw Nation Court records, Blue County, 1852-1858; Peter James Hudson; Indian captives in the Southwest, 1870-1872; **Vol. 4:** List of valuations of Cherokee improvements, 1835; roll of Pickens County, Chickasaw Nation, 1866; murder in the Choctaw Nation; Choctaw deaths, 1837-1854; Our brother in red, Indian Territory news, June 1891-August 1891; index to Chickasaw Nation record book, 1837-1855; abstracts from The Cherokee advocate, 1878; murders in the Cherokee and Choctaw Nations; register of Cherokee claims, 1842. Family History Library has bound v. 3-4 as one volume. FHL book 970.3 C424as, vols. 1-5, and FHL fiche #6002360-6002361.

1831-1832. See *Register of Choctaw Emigrants to the West, 1831 and 1832* **[Printed Book],** compiled by Betty C. Wiltshire, published by Pioneer Publ., Carrollton, MS, 199? 160 pages. FHL book 970.3 C451wb.

1831-1847. See *Choctaw and Chickasaw Early Census Records* **[Printed Book],** compiled by Betty Wiltshire, published by Pioneer Publ., Carrollton, MS, c1995, 173 pages. Includes index. Includes census of Choctaws, 1831 (Armstrong rolls) for the districts of Mushuluatubbee, Leflore and Natachache; muster rolls of Chickasaws, 1847; and rolls of Chickasaws, 1839. FHL book 970.1 W712c.

1832-1900s. *Creek Nation* **[Microfilm & Digital Capture],** from the originals at the Oklahoma Historical Society, Indian Archives Division, Oklahoma City, OK. Includes census, correspondence, Creek Indians, Shawnee Indians, court records, government records, military records, land and property, vital statistics, schools, and other miscellaneous records. Filmed by the Oklahoma Historical Society, 1971, 51 rolls, beginning with FHL film #1666121To access the digital images, see the online FHL catalog:
https://familysearch.org/search/catalog/544270.

1835-1908. *Cherokee National Records and Other Documents* **[Microfilm & Digital Capture],** filmed by the OK Hist. Soc., Indian Archives Div., Oklahoma City, OK, 3 rolls, beginning with FHL film #166294 (Cherokee census, letters, and documents 1880-1908). To access the digital images, see the online FHL catalog: **www.familysearch.org/search/catalog/778912**.

1837-1847 Chickasaw Indians Census Rolls, Indian Territory [Printed Book], abstracted and edited by Bennie Coffey Loftin and Johnny Cudd, published by the Pittsburg County Genealogical and Historical Society, McAlester, OK, c1995, 120 pages. FHL book 970.3 C432ci.

1837-1920s. Chickasaw Nation Records [Microfilm & Digital Capture], filmed by the OK Hist. Soc., Indian Archives Div., 1971, 31 rolls, beginning with FHL film #1666136. Includes census, citizenship, court records, laws and treaties, schools, land and property, taxation, probate records and other miscellaneous information. To access the digital images, see the online FHL catalog:
www.familysearch.org/search/catalog/544208.

1841-1927. Oklahoma and Indian Territory, Marriage, Citizenship and Census Records [Online Database], digitized and indexed at the Ancestry.com website. Source: Oklahoma Historical Society, Oklahoma City. Each index record includes; Name, Gender, Marriage age, Marriage date, Event date, Spouse, Spouse gender, Spouse age, and Marriage place. The document images may have more information. This database has 32,299 records. See http://search.ancestry.com/search/db.aspx?dbid=9026.

1845-1923. Oklahoma Newspaper Archives [Online Database], digitized and indexed at the GenealogyBank website. Search newspapers for Caddo, Doaksville, Eufaula, Fort Washita, Guthrie, Hobart, Langston, Miami, Oklahoma City, Perry, Tahlequah, and Tulsa, Oklahoma. See www.genealogybank.com/explore/newspapers/all/usa/oklahoma.

1851 Cherokee Old Settlers' Annuity Roll [Printed Book], transcribed by Marybelle W. Chase, published by the author, Tulsa, OK, 1993, 132 pages. Includes Index. FHL book 970.3 C424cha.

1851-1902. Oklahoma (Western) Cherokee Rolls/Censuses [Online Database], an essay on the types of censuses taken for the western Cherokees who first started moving into the area of present southern Missouri as early as the 1790s. Each of Cherokee Rolls/Censuses are identified by year and locations, 1851-1902. See
http://files.usgwarchives.net/ok/adair/census/cherokee/cherwest.txt.

1851-1959. Oklahoma and Indian Territory, Indian Censuses and Rolls [Online Database], digitized and indexed at the Ancestry.com website. Source: Selected Tribal Records, National Archives. This collection includes a variety of tribal rolls, censuses, and other records created by the Bureau of Indian Affairs. Records in the collection relate to the Arapaho, Cherokee, Eastern Cherokee, Cheyenne, Chickasaw, Choctaw, Creek, Delaware, Kickapoo, Miami, Muskogee, Osage, Potawatomi, Sac and Fox, Seminole, and Shawnee tribes. Each index record includes: Name, Gender, Birth date, Residence date, Age, and Native American tribe. This database has 640,670 records. See
http://search.ancestry.com/search/db.aspx?dbid=8810.

1852-1948. Oklahoma, Church Marriages [Online Database], indexed at FamilySearch.org. Records so far are from Trinity United Methodist Church, Purcell, OK, and unnamed church records at the OK Hist. Soc., Oklahoma City, OK. This database has 314 records, see www.familysearch.org/search/collection/2534474.

1854-1934. Kiowa Nation [Microfilm & Digital Capture], from the originals at the Oklahoma Historical Society, Indian Archives Division, Oklahoma City, OK. Includes census, enrollments, correspondence, court records, government relations, and other miscellaneous information. Filmed by the Oklahoma Historical Society, 1971, 116 rolls, beginning with FHL film #1666146 (Kiowa Agency census and enrollment...). To access the digital images, see the online FHL catalog:
https://familysearch.org/search/catalog/544279.

1855 Census of Choctaw Nation, Indian Territory (Oklahoma) [Printed Book], by Alma Mason, published by the author, McAlester, OK, c1995, 107 pages. Includes Apukshunnubbee District, which is Cedar, Boktucklo, Eagle, Nashoba, Red River, Towson and Wade counties; Moshulatubbee District, which is Gaines, San Bois, Skullyville, Sugar Loaf, and Tobucksy counties; and Pushmataha District which is Atoka, Blue, Jack's Fork, Kiamichi and Pushmataha counties. FHL book 976.6 X2m.

1856-1933. Oklahoma, Historical Indian Archives Index [Online Database], indexed at the Ancestry.com website. Source: OK Historical Society, Oklahoma City, OK. This database is an index to a collection of titles held by the Oklahoma Historical Society, whose staff created the index on cards over the years. They include censuses, missionaries, permits for doctors, Indians in specific tribes, elections, legislators, chiefs, teachers, businesses, trading posts, schools, and the Cherokee Nation. This database has 80,327 records:
http://search.ancestry.com/search/db.aspx?dbid=9205.

1860 Census of the Free Inhabitants of Indian Lands West of Arkansas **[Printed Book],** compiled by Carole Ellsworth and Sue Emler, publ. Oklahoma Roots Research, Gore, OK, 1984, 48 pages. Includes index. This census was taken of the free inhabitants of the following Indian Nations: Creek, Cherokee, Chickasaw, Choctaw, and Seminole. Enumeration includes whites, and those blacks who were considered free, living in the Indian Nation. Included are surnames when given, age and sex, occupation and country or state of birth. In the Creek Nation, the census taker noted those citizens who were married to natives (Indians), and whether they had been adopted by one of the tribes. See FHL book 976.6 X2e.
- See also, *1860 Index of Indian Lands West of Arkansas* **[Online Database],** list of names of whites, blacks, adopted, or intermarried persons living on Indian Country lands west of Arkansas. See **http://us-census.org/pub/usgenweb/census/ar/indianlands/1860**.

1860-1900. *Notes on the Wyandotte's From Ohio to Indian Territory* **[Printed Book],** by Toni Jollay Prevost, published by the author, Lake Mary, FL, 1992, 19 pages. Contains information about the Treaty of the 6th of April 1816 in Ohio concerning the Wyandottes; the Wyandotte land improvements in Ohio in 1843; Wyandotte children enrolled in the Shawnee Methodist Mission school in Kansas in 1851; Wyandottes who served in the Civil War from Wyandotte County, Kansas; Wyandottes on the 1860 and 1870 federal census of Wyandotte County, Kansas; abstracted index of the Wyandottes on the 1900 federal census in Indian Territory from Canada, Ohio, and Kansas; and biographical reference information on prominent Wyandotte families. FHL book 970.1 A1 No. 166 and FHL film #1697876. To see if this microfilm was digitized yet, see the online FHL catalog: **www.familysearch.org/search/catalog/548479**.

1861-1865. *Index to Applications for Pensions from the State of Oklahoma, Submitted by Confederate Soldiers, Sailors and Their Widows* **[Printed Book & Digital Version],** publ. 1955, Oklahoma Genealogical Society, as Special Publication No. 2. This is an index to 2,908 applications for a pension for service in the Confederate Army or Navy of any Confederate State, authorized by the Oklahoma legislature in 1915. The applicant had to be a current resident of Oklahoma for at least one year. Not all of the applicants were approved. To access the digital images, see the online FHL catalog:
www.familysearch.org/search/catalog/2281844.

1863-1886. See *Executive Department, Cherokee Nation G.W. Ross Sec'ty, October 24, 1865: Rebound Title Acts and Resolutions 1863-1886 Cherokee Nation* **[Microfilm & Digital Capture],** from the originals at the Oklahoma Historical Society, Indian Archives Division, Oklahoma City, OK. Some text written in the Cherokee language. From intro: "This group of records includes various census rolls from 1835 through 1868, Civil War rosters of Indian Home Guards, claims for Civil War service being made in 1899, list of potential claimants who were supposed to be living in Indian Territory and some marriages (in the Cherokee language) performed by Reverend George Swimmer from 1864 to 1895. Filmed by the Oklahoma Historical Society, 1976, 1 roll, FHL film #1666301. To access the digital images, see the FHL catalog: **www.familysearch.org/search/catalog/778919**.

1864-1909. See *Quapaw Nation* **[Microfilm & Digital Capture],** from the originals at the Oklahoma Historical Society, Indian Archives Division, Oklahoma City, OK. Includes census; vital statistics; correspondence; Chippewa, Munsee or Christian Indians; Citizen Potawatomi Indians; Delaware Indians; Kansas or Kaw Indians; Miami Indians; New York Indians; Nez Perce Indians; Oneida Indians; Modoc Indians; Ottawa Indians; Ponca Indians; Seneca Indians, Shawnee Indians; Tonkawa Indians: Peoria and Confederated tribes; Wyandot Indians; military history; court records; history; land and property; schools and other miscellaneous information. Filmed by the Oklahoma Historical Society, 25 rolls, beginning with FHL film #1671120 (Census and Enrollment). To access the digital images, see the online FHL catalog: **https://familysearch.org/search/catalog/544282**.

1869-1933. *Cheyenne and Arapaho Nations* **[Microfilm & Digital Capture],** from the originals at the Oklahoma Historical Society, Indian Archives Division, Oklahoma City, OK. Includes census, correspondence, Cheyenne Indians, Arapaho Indians, Concho Indians, and other miscellaneous information. Filmed by the Oklahoma Historical Society, 1971, 115 rolls, beginning with FHL film #1670886 (Census, Letters sent). To access the digital images, see the online FHL catalog:
https://familysearch.org/search/catalog/544274

1870-1930. *Oklahoma Marriages* **[Online Database],** indexed at the FamilySearch.org website. Source: FamilySearch extractions from marriage registers on microfilm at the Family History Library, Salt Lake

City, UT. Each index record includes: Name, Spouse's name, Event place, and Event date. This database has 9,655 records. See
https://familysearch.org/search/collection/1681007.

1870-1930. *Oklahoma, Select Marriages* **[Online Database],** indexed at the Ancestry.com website. Source: FamilySearch extractions from records on microfilm at the Family History Library, Salt Lake City, UT. Each index record includes: Name, Gender, Age, Birth date, Marriage date, Marriage place, Father, Mother, Spouse, and FHL film number. This database has 24,708 records. See
http://search.ancestry.com/search/db.aspx?dbid=60105.

1870-1930. *Pawnee Agency* **[Microfilm & Digital Capture],** from the originals at the Oklahoma Historical Society in Oklahoma City, OK. Includes Pawnee, Kaw, Ponca, Nez Perce, Oto, Missouri, and Tonkawa-Lipan Apache. Includes census, enrollments, council minutes, correspondence, court records, military records, history, cultural information, land and property, schools, and other miscellaneous information. Filmed by the Oklahoma Historical Society, 55 rolls, beginning with FHL film #1671065. To access the digital images, see the online FHL catalog:
https://familysearch.org/search/catalog/538241.

1873-1909. *Elections in the Cherokee Nation for all Districts* **[Microfilm & Digital Capture],** filmed by the OK Hist. Soc., Indian Archives Div., 2 rolls, FHL film #1666197-8. To access the digital images, see the online FHL catalog:
www.familysearch.org/search/catalog/787238.

"1874 Canadian District Per Capita Tax, Cherokee Nation" [Printed Article], in *The Cherokee Tracer* (Marybelle W. Chase, Tulsa, OK), Vol. 6, No. 3 (Summer 1996).

"1874 Cherokee Nation Receipt Roll" [Printed Article], in *The Cherokee Tracer* (Marybelle W. Chase, Tulsa, OK), Vol. 7, No. 1 (Winter 1997).

"1874 Tahlequah Receipt Roll, Cherokee Nation: [Printed Article], in *The Cherokee Tracer* (Marybelle W. Chase, Tulsa, OK),, Vol. 10, No. 1 (Winter 2000).

1874-1881. See *Expanded Index of the Peoria Census, Annuity Rolls and Administrations, 1874-1881: With Undated Material, Quapaw Agency, Indian Territory* **[Printed Book],** extracted from original records at the Oklahoma Historical Society, Indian Archives Division, Oklahoma City, OK, published by Gregath, Wyandotte, OK, c1995, 32 pages. FHL book 970.1 A1 No. 198.

1878 *Annuity Rolls and 1890 Census of Chickasaw Nation, Indian Territory* **[Printed Book],** compiled by Joyce A. Rex, published McClain County Historical Society, Purcell, Oklahoma, 1990, 3 vols. FHL book 970.3 C432rj v. 1-3. Also available on 11 microfiche, FHL film #6125933-6125935.

1878-1883. *Expanded Index of the Ottawa Census, Annuity Rolls and Administrations: 1878-1883, With Undated Material, Quapaw Agency, Indian Territory* **[Printed Book],** extracted from original records at the Oklahoma Historical Society, Indian Archives Division, Oklahoma City, OK, published by Gregath, Wyandotte, OK, 199?, 18 pages. FHL book 970.1 A1 No. 196.

1880 *Cherokee Nation Census, Indian Territory (Oklahoma)* **[Printed Book, CD-ROM, Microfilm & Digital Capture],** from microfilmed originals at the National Archives, Ft. Worth, TX, both a book and CD-ROM publication, transcribed by Barbara Benge, published by Heritage Books, Bowie, MD, 2000, 596 pages. Includes index. Contains transcriptions of the original 1880 census of the Cherokee Nation, which is also available on FHL film #989204. Transcribed publication: FHL CD-ROM No. 1682 and FHL book 970.3 C424vLb. To access the digital images, see the online FHL catalog:
www.familysearch.org/search/catalog/51409.

1880 and 1890 Census, Canadian District, Cherokee Nation, Indian Territory [Printed Book], transcribed by Sharron Standifer Ashton, published by Oklahoma Genealogical Society, Oklahoma City, 1978, 90 pages. The Canadian District of the Cherokee Nation covered the area that is now Muskogee and McIntosh Counties, Oklahoma. FHL book 970.3 C424ash.

"1880-1895 Tax Lists, Greer County, Texas (now Oklahoma)" [Printed Article], in *Oklahoma Genealogical Society Bulletin* (Oklahoma City, OK), Vol. 35, No. 4 (1990).

"1881-1886 Tax Records, Greer County, Texas (now Oklahoma)" [Printed Article], in *Western Trails Newsletter,* (Western Trails Genealogical Society, Altus, OK), Vol. 2, No. 4 (Oct 1989).

1884-1934. *Oklahoma and Indian Territory, Land Allotment Jackets for Five Civilized Tribes* **[Online Database],** digitized and indexed at the Ancestry.com website. Source: National Archives, Records of the Bureau of Indian Affairs. This collection includes the

allotment records for those who were listed on the final membership rolls. The files often include receipts for allotment certificates and certificates of eligibility for allotment. Applications for minor children generally include letters of guardianship or administration. Each index record includes: Name, Tribe, Allotment category, Roll number, and Card number. The document images have more information. This database has 204,413 records. See
http://search.ancestry.com/search/db.aspx?dbid=3999.

1885 Choctaw Census, Indian Territory **[Printed Book]**, transcribed by Monty Olsen, published by the Bryan County Heritage Association, 1996-2000, 4 vols. Index included in each volume. Contents: vol. 1: Blue County; vol. 2: Kiamitia County; vol. 3: Pushmataha District: Atoka County [and] Jacks Fork County; vol. 4: Apukshunnubbee District: Cedar County, Wayne County, Boktoklo County, Towson County, Nashoba County, Eagle County and Red River County. The FHL has bound together all of Apukshunnubbee District including Eagle, Boktoklo, Towson, Nashoba, Eagle, Red River, Wade and Cedar Counties as one volume, and has bound together Atoka and Jacks Fork Counties. FHL book 970.3 C451 v. 1-4.

- See also, *Index to the 1885 Choctaw Census* **[Microfilm & Digital Capture]**, from the original manuscript at the National Archives branch at Ft. Worth, TX. Filmed by the National Archives, c1985, series 75, 1 roll, FHL film #505975. To access the digital images, see the online FHL catalog:
www.familysearch.org/search/catalog/371687.

- See also, *The 1885 census of Atoka County, Choctaw Nation, Indian Territory* **[Printed Book]**, by James P. Cummings, published by the author, Mesquite, TX, 1976, 39 pages. FHL book 970.1 A1 No. 86.

1885-1940 Indian Census Rolls **[Microfilm & Online Database]**, from the original records of the Bureau of Indian Affairs, now located at the National Archives, Washington, DC, Series M-595, 692 rolls. Contains census lists that were usually submitted each year by agents or superintendents in charge of Indian reservations, as required by an act of 1884. Usually given are the English and/or Indian name of the person, roll number, age or date of birth, sex, and relationship to head of family. Beginning in 1930, the rolls also show the degree of Indian blood, marital status, ward status, place of residence, and sometimes other information. For certain years (including 1935, 1936, 1938, and 1939) only supplemental rolls of additions and deletions were compiled. Most of the 1940 rolls have been retained by the Bureau of Indian Affairs and are not included in this publication. The FHL has the entire collection but cataloged by the various Indian agencies or tribes that originally generated the census name lists. (Several tribe lists are included in this bibliography).

- A descriptive bulletin was published by the National Archives, FHL's copy titled, *Indian Census Rolls, 1885-1940: National Archives Microfilm Publications, Pamphlet Describing M595*, 34 pages. FHL book 973 J53m no. 595.

- See also, *U.S., Indian Census Rolls, 1885-1940* **[Online Database]**, digitized and indexed at the Ancestry.com website. Source: National Archives microfilm series M595, Records of the Bureau of Indian Affairs. This database has the full image census pages for every Indian census taken in the U.S., 1885 through 1940. Included on the rolls are the largest concentrated group of Indians in the U.S., those living in the jurisdictions of the Indian Territory, Oklahoma Territory, or within the state of Oklahoma. Each index record includes: Name, Date of birth, Age, Gender, Marital status, Relation to head of household, Tribe, Reservation, Agency, Last census number, Census date, and Neighbors (view others on page). The census page images include more information about place of enrollment, residence, degree of blood, etc. This database has 7,559,854 records. See
http://search.ancestry.com/search/db.aspx?dbid=1059.

1886-1927 Indian Census Rolls, Ponca Agency, **[Microfilm & Digital Capture]**, from the originals of the Bureau of Indian Affairs, now at the National Archives, Washington, DC., Includes the following: 1886: Ponca, Oto, Tonkawa 1887: Pawnee, Ponca, Tonkawa, Oto 1888: Ponca, Oto, Missouri, Tonkawa 1889-1890: Pawnee, Ponca, Oto, Tonkawa (not always in this order) 1891-1901: Ponca, Pawnee, Oto, Missouri, Tonkawa (not always in this order) 1902-1903: Tonkawa, Oto, Missouri, Ponca (not always in this order) 1904-1912: Ponca, Tonkawa (not always in this order) 1913: Ponca, Tonkawa, Kaw 1914: Ponca, Tonkawa 1915-1919: Ponca, Tonkawa, Kaw 1922-1924: Ponca, Tonkawa, Oto, Missouri (not always in this order) 1925-1927: Ponca, Oto, Tonkawa. Filmed by the National Archives, 1965, 6 rolls, beginning with FHL #580765 (Ponca 1886-1890). To access the digital images, see the online FHL catalog:
https://familysearch.org/search/catalog/746171.

"1887 Personal Property Tax Warrants, Garfield County, Oklahoma" [Printed Article], in *Four States Genealogist* (Tulsa, OK), Vol. 2, No. 2 (Jan 1970).

1887-1939 Indian Census rolls, Cheyenne, and Arapaho **[Microfilm & Digital Capture]**, from the originals at the National Archives, Washington, DC. (part of series M595). Includes the following: 1887: Cheyenne, enlisted scouts, Arapaho 1888: Arapaho,

Cheyenne, Fort Reno scouts, Cheyenne (other areas) 1889-1890: Missing 1891-1927: Arapaho, Cheyenne (not always in this order) 1928-1934: Alphabetical 1931: Supplemental rolls for births, deaths, adjustments 1932: Supplemental rolls for births, additions, deaths, adjustments 1933: Supplemental rolls for additions, deductions, adjustments, deaths 1934: Supplemental rolls for adjustments, additions, deductions, births, deaths, stillbirths 1935: Supplemental rolls only for adjustments 1936: Supplemental rolls only for adjustments, marriages 1937: Census rolls with supplemental rolls for births, deaths 1938: Supplemental rolls only for births, deaths, deductions, additions 1939: Supplemental rolls only for births, stillbirths, deaths, deduction, and adjustments. Filmed by the National Archives, 1965, 6 rolls, beginning with FHL film #574191. To access the digital images, see the online FHL catalog:
www.familysearch.org/search/catalog/361040.
- See also, *Cheyenne Indian Census Rolls, Indian Territory, 1895-1900* **[Printed Book],** compiled by Valorie Millican, publisher not noted, 2003, 226 pages. FHL book 970.3 C429mv.

1887-2008. *Oklahoma Probate Records* **[Online Database],** indexed at the FamilySearch.org website. Source: FamilySearch extractions from Oklahoma county courthouses. This image only database includes Wills, Letters of Administration, Inventories, Distribution and Accounting, Bonds, and Guardianships. The contents of a probate file can vary from case to case, but certain details are found in most probates. Most importantly, the names and residences of beneficiaries and their relationship to the decedent may be found in the file. An inventory of the estate assets can reveal personal details about the deceased's occupation and lifestyle. There may also be references to debts, deeds, and other documents related to the settling of the estate. Browse through the images, organized by county, then Volume Title, and Year. This database has 6,044,798 records. See
https://familysearch.org/search/collection/2063710.

1889-1926. *Oklahoma, Land Run, and other Land Records* **[Online Database],** digitized and indexed at the Ancestry.com website. Source: Federal Tract Books of Oklahoma Territory, microfilm at the Oklahoma Historical Society, Oklahoma City. This is an image only database containing the images to the federal tract books in which Oklahoma land grants were recorded. The various openings and land runs relate to specific dates in the tract book entries. Individual land ownership in Oklahoma began in 1902 with the allotment of lands by the Dawes Commission. Prior to that time, land in the Indian Territory belonged to the respective Indian Nation in which the individual lived. In Oklahoma Territory, with the exception of Indian allotments, ownership began in 1889. Land ownership in the Panhandle was possible after the first official survey for the area was completed in the 1890s. There were eight land openings total: five were done by land runs, two by land lotteries, and one by sealed bid. Browse through the images, organized by Roll number and Vol. number (in chronological sequence). See http://search.ancestry.com/search/db.aspx?dbid=9244.

1889-1951. *Oklahoma County, Oklahoma, Marriage Index* **[Online Database],** indexed at the Ancestry.com website. This database is also accessible at the Oklahoma Historical Society website. Each index record includes: Name, Spouse's name, Marriage date, Marriage place, and Notes. This database has 205,434 records. See
http://search.ancestry.com/search/db.aspx?dbid=9233.

1889-1991. *Oklahoma, Naturalization Records* **[Online Database],** digitized and indexed at the Ancestry.com website. Source: National Archives, Records of District Courts (Declarations & Petitions). Each record index includes: Name, Gender, Petition age, Record type, Birth date, Birthplace, Petition date, Petition place, Petition number, and Court district. The document image has much more information. This database has 34,261 records. See
http://search.ancestry.com/search/db.aspx?dbid=2508.

1890. *An Index to the 1890 United States Census of Union Veterans and their Widows in Oklahoma and Indian Territories: including old Greer County and Soldiers Stationed at Military Installations in the Territories (section I) Also an Index to Records from the Oklahoma Union Soldiers' Home Including Civil War Veterans and their Dependents* **[Printed Book & Digital Version],** compiled by the OK Gen. Soc., Special Publication No. 3, 1970, 53 pages, FHL book 976.6 M2. To access the digital version, see the online FHL catalog:
www.familysearch.org/search/catalog/144576.

1890-1893. *U.S., Wallace Roll of Cherokee Freedmen* **[Online Database],** indexed at the Ancestry.com website. In accordance with an 1866 treaty, in 1888 the Congress of the United States appropriated $75,000 to be shared between the Cherokee, Shawnee and Delaware Indian tribes. This database is a transcription of the Wallace Roll of Cherokee Freedmen intended to identify those Cherokee entitled to a share of this money. Compiled by Special Agent John Wallace, it includes authenticated freedmen, admitted freedmen, those who died between 1883 and 1890, and "Free Negroes" associated with the tribe. Researchers will find information on over 3,800 Cherokee including age, sex, and residence. The Wallace roll was set aside as "fraudulent" by a decree of 8 May 1895 of the United States Court of Indian Affairs. Each record includes: Last name, Office #, Wallace #, First name, Age, Sex, Residence, and Record type. This database has 3,806 records. See http://search.ancestry.com/search/db.aspx?dbid=3912.

1890 Oklahoma Territorial Census **[Online Database],** indexed at the Oklahoma Historical Society website. The 1890 Oklahoma Territorial Census lists individuals residing in the seven counties, often listed only by number on the census. The counties and their accompanying numbers are: County No. 1: Logan County; No. 2: Oklahoma County; No. 3: Cleveland County; No. 4: Canadian County; No. 5: Kingfisher County; No. 6: Payne County; and No. 7: Beaver County. The 1890 Oklahoma Territorial Census recorded the individual's name, age at nearest birthday, relationship to the head of the family, birthplace, sex, color, number of years in the United States, length of residence in the territory, if they were a soldier, if they had been naturalized, and if they were able to read or write. The county and town were also listed. See **www.okhistory.org/research/1890.php.**

1890. See *First Territorial Census of Oklahoma, 1890* **[Microfilm & Digital Capture],** from the original schedules at the Oklahoma Historical Society, Oklahoma City, OK. Contains population schedules for the seven original counties of Logan, Oklahoma, Cleveland, Canadian, Kingfisher, Payne, and Beaver. Filmed by the Historical Society of Oklahoma, 1961, 1 roll, FHL film #227282. To access the digital images, see the online FHL catalog: **www.familysearch.org/search/catalog/126946.**

1890 Census of Chickasaw Nation, Indian Territory: And Other Records **[Printed Book],** by Joyce A. Rex, published by McClain County Historical & Genealogical Society, Purcell, OK, 1993, 3 vols., full-name index included in each volume. Contents: vol. 1: Pontotoc County (now McClain County and portions of Grady, Garvin, Murray, Pontotoc, Johnston and Coal Counties); vol. 2: Pickens County (now Carter, Love and Marshall Counties and portions of Garvin, Grady, Stephens, Jefferson, Murray and Johnston Counties); vol. 3: Tishomingo and Panola Counties (now Bryan County and portions of Pontotoc and Murray Counties). FHL book 970.3 C432 v.1-3.

1890 Census of the Cherokee Nation, Tahlequah District **[Microfilm & Digital Capture],** from the originals at the Oklahoma Historical Society, Indian Archives Division, Oklahoma City, OK. Some text written in the Cherokee language. Includes Tahlequah District census, schedule 1 in 7 volumes. In each volume abbreviations in columns 2 and 3 are "C" for Cherokee, "N" for native, "A" for adopted, "W" for white, "Col." for Colored, "D" for Delaware, "S" for Shawnee and "NC" for Native Cherokee. Filmed by the Oklahoma Historical Society, 1976, 2 rolls, as follows:
- **Tahlequah District Census,** schedule 1 1890 book 1 A-C, FHL film #1666299.
- **Tahlequah District Census,** schedule 1, 1890, book 2, C-F; book 3 F-H; book 4, H-M; book 5, N-R; book 6, R-T; book 7, T-Y; FHL film #1666300.

To access the digital images, see the online FHL catalog: **www.familysearch.org/search/catalog/779071.**

1890 Census of the Cherokee Nation, Flint District **[Microfilm & Digital Capture],** from the originals at the Oklahoma Historical Society, Indian Archives Division, Oklahoma City, OK. Some text written in the Cherokee language. Filmed by the Oklahoma Historical Society, 1976, 1 roll, FHL film #1666298. To access the digital images, see the online FHL catalog: **www.familysearch.org/search/catalog/779065.**

1890 Census of the Cherokee Nation, Going Snake District **[Microfilm & Digital Capture],** from the originals at the Oklahoma Historical Society, Indian Archives Division, Oklahoma City, OK. Some text written in the Cherokee language. Filmed by the Oklahoma Historical Society, 1976, 1 roll, FHL film #1666298. To access the digital images, see the online FHL catalog: **www.familysearch.org/search/catalog/779067.**

1890 Census of the Cherokee Nation, Illinois District **[Microfilm & Digital Capture],** from the originals at the Oklahoma Historical Society, Indian Archives Division, Oklahoma City, OK. Some text written in the Cherokee language. Filmed by the Oklahoma Historical Society, 1976, 1 roll, FHL film #1666299. To access the digital images, see the online FHL catalog: **www.familysearch.org/search/catalog/779066.**

1890 Census of the Cherokee Nation, Sequoyah District **[Microfilm & Digital Capture],** from the originals at the Oklahoma Historical Society, Indian Archives Division, Oklahoma City, OK. Some text written in the Cherokee language. Includes Sequoyah

District census. Schedule 1 is in 2 volumes. In each volume abbreviations in columns 2 and 3 are "C" for Cherokee, "N" for native, "A" for adopted, "W" for white, "Col." for colored, "D" for Delaware, "S" for Shawnee, and "NC" for native Cherokee. Filmed by the Oklahoma Historical Society, 1976, 1 roll, FHL film #1666299. To access the digital images, see the online FHL catalog:
www.familysearch.org/search/catalog/779069.

1890 Census of the Cherokee Nation, Saline District **[Microfilm & Digital Capture]**, from the originals at the Oklahoma Historical Society, Indian Archives Division, Oklahoma City, OK. Some text written in the Cherokee language. Includes Saline District census, schedule 1 is in 2 volumes. In each volume abbreviation in columns 2 and 3 are "C" for Cherokee, "N" for native, "A" for adopted, "W" for white, "Col" for colored "D" for Delaware and "S" for Shawnee, "NC" for Native Cherokee. Filmed by the Oklahoma Historical Society, 1976, 1 roll, FHL film #1666299. To access the digital images, see the online FHL catalog: **www.familysearch.org/search/catalog/779068**.

1890 Census of the Cherokee Nation, Canadian District **[Microfilm]**, from the originals at the Oklahoma Historical Society, Indian Archives Division, Oklahoma City, OK. Some text written in the Cherokee language. Includes Canadian District census, schedule 1 is in 4 volumes. In each volume, abbreviations in columns 2 and 3 are "C" for Cherokee, "N" for native, "A" for adopted, "W" for white, "Col." for colored, "D" for Delaware and "S" for Shawnee, "NC" for Native Cherokee. Filmed by the Oklahoma Historical Society, 1976, 1 roll, FHL film #1666296. To access the digital images, see the online FHL catalog: **www.familysearch.org/search/catalog/779062**.
- See also, *Oklahoma, County Marriages, 1880 and 1890 Census, Canadian District, Cherokee Nation, Indian Territory* **[Printed Book]**, transcribed by Sharron Standifer Ashton, published by Oklahoma Genealogical Society, Oklahoma City, 1978, 90 pages. The Canadian District of the Cherokee Nation covered the area that is now Muskogee and McIntosh Counties, Oklahoma. FHL book 970.3 C424ash.

1890 & 1907. *Oklahoma, Territorial Census, 1890 and 1907* **[Online Database]**, digitized and indexed at the Ancestry.com website. Source: National Archives microfilm series M1811 (1890) and M1814 (1907). In June 1890, a territorial census of Oklahoma was taken. It enumerated the following seven counties: Beaver, Canadian, Cleveland, Kingfisher, Logan, Oklahoma, and Payne Co OK Territory. In 1907 a census of Indian and Oklahoma territories, comprising the proposed state of Oklahoma, was also taken. However, only the schedules for Seminole County exist. Information available in this database includes: Enumeration place (town, county, state), Name of individual, Relationship to the head of household, Race, Gender, Age, Place of birth (1890 only), Number of years in the U.S. (1890 only). Additional information about an individual may be listed on the original record. This information can be obtained by viewing the census image. This database has 65,696 records. See
http://search.ancestry.com/search/db.aspx?dbid=8925.

1890-1995 Oklahoma, County Marriages **[Online Database]**, digitized and indexed at the FamilySearch.org website. Source: FamilySearch extractions from original county records on microfilm at the Family History Library, Salt Lake City, UT. The images are from the record copy of an Application for Marriage License, Marriage License, and Certificate of Marriage. Each index record includes: Name, Event type (Marriage), Event date, Event place, Gender, Age, Birth year (estimated), Spouse's name, Spouse's gender, Spouse's age, Spouse's birth year (estimated), Spouse's father's name, and Page number. This database has 1,469,882 records. See
https://familysearch.org/search/collection/1709399.

1890s-2008. *Oklahoma, Wills and Probate Records* **[Online Database]**, indexed at the Ancestry.com website. Source: Ancestry. extractions from Oklahoma county, district, and probate courts. The 1801 title starting date comes from an uncorrected record dated 1891. This database includes Wills, Letters of Administration, Inventories, Distribution and Accounting, Bonds, and Guardianships. The names and residences of beneficiaries and their relationship to the decedent may be found. An inventory of the estate assets can reveal personal details about the deceased's occupation and lifestyle. It is possible to browse through the images, organized by county, then type of record. Each index record includes: Name, Probate date, Probate place, Inferred death year, Inferred death place, Case number, and Item Description (type of record). This database has 250,454 records. See
http://search.ancestry.com/search/db.aspx?dbid=9077.

1890s-1900s Oklahoma Original Landowners. See the *Family Maps* series for Oklahoma counties, maps of all original land patents, compiled by Greg Boyd, publ. Arphax Publishing Co., Norman, OK. These privately produced computer-generated maps show the first property owners for an entire county, produced as a book of maps, each map laid out on the federal township grid, and includes indexes to help you locate a person, place-name, or cemetery. Family Maps books have been published for Canadian County, Cleveland County, Harper County, and Tillman County, Oklahoma. See **www.arphax.com**.

1890s-1900s. *Oklahoma US GenWeb Archives* **[Online Databases],** name lists are available for all counties. Typical county records include Bibles, Biographies, Cemeteries, Censuses, Court, Death, Deeds, Directories, Histories, Marriages, Military, Newspapers, Obituaries, Photos, Schools, Tax Lists, Wills, and more. Links to all Oklahoma counties and projects are located at the USGenWeb website for Oklahoma. See **http://usgwarchives.net/ok/okfiles.htm**.

1890s-1900s. *Linkpendium – Oklahoma: Family History & Genealogy, Census, Birth, Marriage, Death, Vital Records & More* **[Online Databases].** Linkpendium is a genealogical portal site with links to state, county, town, and local databases. Currently listed are selected sites for Oklahoma statewide resources (539), Renamed/Discontinued Counties (19), Adair County (132) and 76 more Oklahoma counties. See **www.linkpendium.com/ok-genealogy**.

1891 Census Roll of Citizen Band of Potawatomi Indians Residing in Oklahoma, Indian Territory, Kansas, and Elsewhere **[Microfilm],** from the handwritten records made by Samuel L. Patrick, U.S. Indian Agent, filmed by the Genealogical Society of Utah, 1979, 1 roll, FHL film #1036363. To see if this microfilm was digitized yet, see the online FHL catalog: **www.familysearch.org/search/catalog/625342**.

1891 History. See *Leaders and Leading Men of the Indian Territory: With Interesting Biographical Sketches…Profusely Illustrated with Over Two Hundred Portraits and Full-Page Engravings* **[Printed Book & Digital Version],** by H.F. O'Beirne, publ. 1891, Chicago: American Publishers' Assoc., digitized by FamilySearch International, 2017. To access the digital version, see the online FHL catalog: **www.familysearch.org/search/catalog/281941**.

1891-1895 Tax rolls, Cleveland County, Oklahoma **[Microfilm & Digital Capture],** from the original manuscripts at the Cleveland County Genealogical Society, Norman, OK. Lists are arranged by township and then alphabetically by surname. Filmed by the Genealogical Society of Utah, 1999, 2 rolls, FHL film #2168965 (vol. 1, 1891; vol. 2, 1892; vol. 3, 1893; and vol. 4, 1894) and FHL film #2168966 (vol. 5, 1895; and vol. 6, 1895). To access the digital images, see the online FHL catalog: **www.familysearch.org/search/catalog/967971**.

- See also *Cleveland County, Oklahoma Census of Taxpayers, 1891* **[Microfilm],** compiled by the Cleveland County Genealogical Society, manuscript microfilmed by the Genealogical Society of Utah, 1977. Part one contains an alphabetical list of taxpayers which gives name, page number in original tax rolls, town, or township where the property was located and a brief legal description of the property. Part two contains the same information transcribed in the order it appeared in the tax rolls. See FHL film #2168969. To access the digital images, see the online FHL catalog: **www.familysearch.org/search/catalog/1045597**.

1893-1966 Kay County. See *Old Census Records, Petition to Incorporate, 1893-1966* **[Microfilm & Digital Capture],** from the originals at Kay County Clerk's Office, Newkirk, OK. Filmed by the Genealogical Society of Utah, 1996, 2 rolls: FHL film #2048208 (old census records, Town of Blackwell, 1893; Town of Braman, 1898; Town of Cross 1893; Town of Dilworth, 1917; Town of Kardy, 1906; Town of Kildare, 1902; Town of Nardin, 1898; Town of Kildare Census, 1894; Town of Newkirk, 1893; Town of Parker, 1893) and FHL film #2048209 (Town of Peckham, 1902; Town of Ponca city, 1893; Town of Tonkawa, 1894; Town of Washunga, 1923; Town of Uncas, 1966). To access the digital images, see the online FHL catalog: **www.familysearch.org/search/catalog/777391**.

1894-1907 Election Returns, Greer County, Texas (to 1896); Greer County, Oklahoma (after 1896) **[Microfilm],** from the originals at the Greer County courthouse, Mangum, OK. Filmed by the Genealogical Society of Utah, 1994, 1 roll, FHL film #1954679. To see if this microfilm was digitized yet, see the online FHL catalog: **www.familysearch.org/search/catalog/456166**.

1894-1922 Tax Records, Kay County, Oklahoma, **[Microfilm & Digital Capture],** from the originals at the Kay County Courthouse, Newkirk, OK. Filmed by the Genealogical Society of Utah, 1996, 8 rolls, beginning with FHL film #2048694 (Personal Tax Rolls, 1894-1922). To access the digital images, see the online FHL catalog: **www.familysearch.org/search/catalog/781604**.

"**1895 Tax Receipts, Beaver County, Oklahoma**" **[Printed Article]**, in *Beaver County Heritage News*, Vol. 4, No. 4 (Oct 1996); and Vol. 5, No. 1 (Jan 1997).

1895-1899. Caddo *Indian Census at Kiowa Agency, Oklahoma Territory* **[Microfilm & Digital Capture]**, filmed by the National Archives, 1965, 6 rolls, beginning with FHL film #576900. To access the digital images, see the online FHL catalog: www.familysearch.org/search/catalog/723541.

1895-1914. *U.S., Native American Citizens and Freedmen of Five Civilized Tribes* **[Online Database]**, indexed at the Ancestry.com website. Source: National Archives microfilm series T529-Final Rolls of Citizens. This database contains the federal government's official tribal rolls (the "**Dawes Rolls**") for the Five Civilized tribes. The rolls provide details on Indians who could claim tribal membership by blood or marriage. They are organized by tribe and can be further broken down by claims by blood, marriage, minor children, newborns, and freedmen, which were former slaves held by Indians. They may list Name, Age, Gender, and Census card number. Rolls include both approved and disapproved names. This database has 104,657 records. See http://search.ancestry.com/search/db.aspx?dbid=2976.

1895-1936. *Oklahoma, School Records* **[Online Database]**, digitized and indexed at the FamilySearch.org website. FamilySearch indexing project, with cooperation from the Northwest OK Gen. Soc. for Woodward Co OK records. Each index record includes: Name, Event type, Event date, Event place, Gender, Birth date, and Parent name. The document images have more information. This database has 19,912,431 records, see https://familysearch.org/search/collection/1926701.

1895-1940 Indian Census Rolls **[Microfilm & Digital Capture]**, from the originals of the Bureau of Indian Affairs, now located at the National Archives, Washington, DC. Filmed by the National Archives, 1965, series M0595, 692 rolls. Includes census rolls for the entire U.S.
- Census rolls are available for the following Oklahoma Territory tribes:
  - **1897-1898** Kechai Indian Census at Anadarko Agency, Oklahoma Territory, FHL film #5765900.
  - **1897-1898** Wacoe Indian Census at Anadarko Agency, Oklahoma Territory, FHL film # 576900.
  - **1897-1898** Tawakoni Indian Census at Anadarko Agency, Oklahoma Territory, FHL film #576900.
  - **1897-1898** Delaware Indian Census at Kiowa Agency, Oklahoma Territory, FHL film # 576900.
  - **1895-1934** Kiowa Indian Census at Kiowa Agency, Oklahoma Territory, 7 rolls, beginning with FHL film #576900 (census of 1895).
  - **1895-1915** Comanche Indian Census at Anadarko Agency, Oklahoma Territory, 6 rolls, beginning with FHL film #576900 (census of 1895). Selected census years extracted and published as Comanche Indian Census Rolls, Indian Territory, 1900-1903, compiled by Valorie Millican, publisher not noted, 2003, 117 pages. Includes a transcription of the census arranged alphabetically by name of individual, followed by a transcription arranged by household for each census year. FHL book 970.3 C73m.
  - **1896-1930** Apache Indian Census at Kiowa Agency, Oklahoma Territory, 8 rolls, beginning with FHL film #576900 (census of 1896).
  - **1895-1899** Caddo Indian Census at Kiowa Agency, Oklahoma Territory, 6 rolls, beginning with FHL film #576900 (census of 1895).
  - **1895-1924** Wichita Indian Census at Anadarko, Oklahoma Territory, 6 rolls, beginning with FHL film #576900 (census of 1895).

To access the digital images, see the online FHL catalog: www.familysearch.org/search/catalog/297519.

"**1896 Tax List, Greer County, Oklahoma**" **[Printed Article]**, published serially in *Western Trails Newsletter,* (Western Trails Genealogical Society, Altus, OK), Vol. 10, No. 1 (Jan 1998) through Vol. 11, No. 3 (Jul 1998).

1896. *Index to Payment Roll for Old Settlers Cherokee* **[Printed Book]**, transcribed by Marybelle W. Chase, published by the author, Tulsa, OK, c1985, 41 pages. Living persons were indexed separately from those who were dead at the date of payment. The payment roll of 1896 was prepared in accordance with an 1846 treaty which provided for payment of shares from funds established by the treaty to Cherokee Old Settlers in Indian Territory as original beneficiaries or as their legal heirs. The Old Settlers were Cherokees who began voluntary migration to land in what is now Arkansas after an 1817 treaty between the Cherokee Tribe and the United States. FHL book 970.3 C424cmwin. Also available on microfiche, filmed by the Genealogical Society of Utah, 1993, 2 microfiche, #6101765.

1896 Tobucksy County, Choctaw Nation, Indian Territory **[Printed Book]**, copied by Alma Burke Mason; typed by Bennie Lou Coffey Loftin, published by Pittsburg County Genealogical Society, McAlester, OK, 1988, 28 pages. FHL book 970.3 C451ma.

1896 Census of Citizens of Tahlequah District, Cherokee Nation [Microfilm & Digital Capture], from the original records in Tahlequah, OK. Alphabetically arranged by first letter of surname. Most of Tahlequah District, Cherokee Nation is now Cherokee County, Oklahoma. Filmed by the Genealogical Society of Utah, 1976, 1 roll, FHL film #989203. To access the digital images, see the online FHL catalog:
www.familysearch.org/search/catalog/276495.

1896. U.S., *Native American Applications for Enrollment in Five Civilized Tribes (Overturned)* **[Online Database],** digitized and indexed at the Ancestry.com website. Source: National Archives microfilm series M1650, Records of the Bureau of Indian Affairs. The index record includes: Name, Tribe, Application number, Roll number, and Roll description. The corresponding image record is a typescript index with the same information. It appears that this database is an index to Roll 1 only (Master Index). The microfilm series M1650 has 54 rolls, with many different types of documents related to the application process, all part of the enrollments by the Dawes Commission, but the textual portion is not evident here. Also, since there is no explanation of the meaning of "Overturned," it is assumed that all of the applications in this database were denied. This database has 13,848 records. See
http://search.ancestry.com/search/db.aspx?dbid=1238.
- For another version of this database, see
http://search.ancestry.com/search/db.aspx?dbid=3075.

1896-1897. *U.S., Citizenship Case Files in Indian Territory* **[Online Database],** digitized and indexed at the Ancestry.com website. Source: National Archives microfilm series P2293. This database contains court case files from the U.S. Court in Indian Territory regarding applicants seeking enrollment in the Cherokee and Creek tribes. Each index record includes: Name, Case name, and Case number. The digitized images may have more information. This database has 9,494 records. See
http://search.ancestry.com/search/db.aspx?dbid=2136.

1896-1909 Dawes Rolls. *Applications for Enrollment of the Five Civilized Tribes, Dawes Commission* **[Microfilm & Digital Capture],** from the original Bureau of Indian Affairs records now at the National Archives, Washington, DC. From introduction: "An act of Congress approved March 3, 1893 authorized the establishment of the Commission to negotiate agreements with the Cherokee, Choctaw, Chickasaw, Creek, and Seminole tribes providing for the dissolution of the tribal governments and the allotment of land to each tribal member. Senator Henry L. Dawes of Massachusetts was appointed Chairman of this Commission on November 1, 1893, after which it has commonly been referred to as the Dawes Commission. The Commission was authorized by an act of Congress approved June 28, 1898 to prepare citizenship (tribal membership) rolls for each tribe. These final rolls were the basis for allotment. Under this act, subsequent acts, and resulting agreements negotiated with each tribe, the Commission received applications for membership covering more than 250,000 people and enrolled more than 101,000. The Commission enrolled individuals as "citizens" of a tribe under the following categories: citizens by blood, citizens by marriage, newborn citizens by blood, minor citizens by blood, freedmen (former black slaves of Indians, later freed and admitted to tribal citizenship), newborn freedmen, and minor freedmen. Delaware Indians adopted by the Cherokee tribe were enrolled as a separate group within the Cherokee. All decisions of the Commission were sent to the Secretary of the Interior for final approval. Filmed by the National Archives, 1983, series M1301, 468 rolls, beginning with FHL film #1439798 (Choctaws by blood 1-148). To access the digital images, see the online FHL catalog:
https://familysearch.org/search/catalog/361915.

1896-1916 Tax Rolls, Greer County, Oklahoma **[Microfilm & Digital Capture],** from the originals at the office of the County Clerk, Lawton, OK. Filmed by Southwest Oklahoma Genealogical Society, c1985, 20 rolls, beginning with FHL film #1324619 (1896To access the digital images, see the online FHL catalog:
https://familysearch.org/search/catalog/78235.

1896-1930. *Apache Indian Census at Kiowa Agency, Oklahoma Territory* **[Microfilm & Digital Capture],** filmed by the National Archives, 1965, 8 rolls, beginning with FHL film #576900. To access the digital images, see the online FHL catalog:
www.familysearch.org/search/catalog/723542.

1896-1950 Seminole County, Konawa Area. See *They Came From Everywhere* **[Printed Book],** by Arthur Ward Kennedy, published by Rapid Rabbit Copy, Conway, AR, 1993, 3 vols. Contents: vol. 1: The people: census of Konawa and Avoca townships, 1896-1920; vol. 2: Part one of history, introduction, background and story of the Konawa area through 1930; vol. 3: Part two of history, the Konawa area during two decades of crises 1930-1950. FHL book 976.671 X2k, vol. 1-3.

1897-1984. *Oklahoma, Church Records* [Online Database]. This collection contains Church records from various denominations in Oklahoma, 1897-1984. The record content and time period varies by denomination and locality. This database has 934 records, see
www.familysearch.org/search/collection/2790264.

"1897 Tax List, Washington County, Oklahoma" [Printed Article], in *Bartlesville Genealogical Society Newsletter*, July 1999 issue.

"1897 Tax Roll, Greer County, Oklahoma" [Printed Article], in *Tree Tracers*, (Southwest Oklahoma Genealogical Society, Lawton, OK), Vol. 5, No. 2 (Winter 1980).

"1897 Occupation Tax, Osage County, Oklahoma" [Printed Article], in *Bartlesville Genealogical Society Newsletter*, July 1999 issue.

1897-1914 Tribal Census for Annuity Rolls, Pawnee Agency [Microfilm], from the originals at the Regional National Archives, Ft. Worth, TX. Filmed by the National Archives, 1978, 1 roll, FHL film #1028501. To see if this microfilm was digitized yet, see the online FHL catalog:
www.familysearch.org/search/catalog/402199.

1898. See *Complete Delaware Roll 1898* [Printed Book], by Dorothy Tincup Mauldin and Jeff Bowen, published by Native American Genealogical Research & Publishing, Hixson, Tennessee, 2001, 100 pages. Includes every name index. In 1867, Delaware tribal members who wished to preserve tribal membership when they were removed from Kansas to Indian Territory purchased 157,000 acres from the Cherokee in Indian Territory. This tract of land was large enough to provide 160 acres for each of the 985 members on the roll taken in Kansas. This 1898 roll was a list of the 1867 enrollees who were still living or their heirs and a list of their holdings. FHL book 970.3 D376m.

"1898 Assessment Roll, Greer County, Oklahoma" [Printed Article], in *Oklahoma Genealogical Society Bulletin*, (Oklahoma City, OK), Vol. 16, No. 2 (Jun 1971).

"1898 Tax Assessment Roll, Jackson County, Oklahoma" [Printed Article], in *Oklahoma Genealogical Society Bulletin*, (Oklahoma City, OK), Vol. 15, No. 1 (Mar 1970) through Vol. 16, No. 1 (Jan 1971).

1898-1914. *Oklahoma and Indian Territory, Dawes Census Cards for Five Civilized Tribes* [Online Database], digitized and indexed at the Ancestry.com website. Source: National Archives microfilm series M1186. This database contains the citizenship enrollment cards, sometimes referred to as census cards, which were prepared by the Dawes Commission. Individuals were enrolled as citizens of tribes according to the following categories: By blood, By marriage; Newborns, by blood; Minors, by blood; Freedmen (former black slaves of Indians); Newborn freedmen; Minor freedmen; and Delaware Indians adopted into the Cherokee tribe. Each index record includes: Name, Gender, Age, Father name, Mother name, Census card number, Tribe, and Enrollment category. This database has 197,656 records. See
http://search.ancestry.com/search/db.aspx?dbid=60543.

- See also, *Oklahoma Applications for Enrollment to the Five Civilized Tribes, 1898-1914* [Online Database], indexed at the FamilySearch.org website. Source: National Archives microfilm series M1301. These records list the individuals who were accepted as eligible for tribal membership in the Five Civilized Tribes: Cherokees, Creeks, Choctaws, Chickasaws, and Seminoles. This record set is also known as the *Final Rolls of Citizens and Freedmen of the Five Civilized Tribes: Applications for Enrollment of the Commission to the Five Civilized Tribes, 1898-1914*. The records include 101,000 names from 1898-1914 (primarily from 1899-1906) and provide the enrollee's name, sex, blood degree, and census card number. This database has 882,272 records. See
https://familysearch.org/search/collection/1852353.

- See also, *U.S., Native American Applications for Enrollment in Five Civilized Tribes, 1898-1914* [Online Database], digitized and indexed at the Ancestry.com website. See
http://search.ancestry.com/search/db.aspx?dbid=2397.

- See also, *U.S., Native American Enrollment Cards for the Five Civilized Tribes, 1898-1914* [Online Database], digitized and indexed at the Ancestry.com website. Source: National Archives microfilm series M1186, Records of the Bureau of Indian Affairs. This database contains the citizenship enrollment cards, sometimes referred to as census cards, which were prepared by the Dawes Commission. Individuals were enrolled as citizens of tribes according to the following categories: By blood, by marriage; Newborns, by blood; Minors, by blood; Freedmen (former black slaves of Indians); Newborn freedmen; Minor freedmen; and Delaware Indians adopted into the

Cherokee tribe. Each index record includes: Name, Gender, Age at census enrollment, Enrollment date, Tribal affiliation, Census card number, and Dawes Roll number. This database has 101,523 records. See http://search.ancestry.com/search/db.aspx?dbid=1241.

1898-1914. *Indian Records, Choctaw by Blood: Choctaw Nation, Indian Territory, Final Rolls* **[Printed Book],** transcribed, indexed, and published by Arlene LeMaster, Family Heritage Resources, Poteau, OK, 1990, 3 vols. This is an extraction of the Choctaw applications for enrollment from the **Dawes Rolls**. FHL book 970.3 C451 v. 1-3.

1898-1914. See *Campbell's Abstract of Seminole Indian Census Cards and Index* **[Printed Book],** compiled by John Bert Campbell, published by Oklahoma Print, Muskogee, OK, 1925, 120 pages. Appears to be an extract of Seminole census cards from the "Index to the Final Rolls." FHL book 970.3 Se52c. Also on microfiche, filmed by the Genealogical Society of Utah, 1995, 2 microfiche, FHL film #6111030.

1899-1907. *Oklahoma Applications for Allotment, Five Civilized Tribes* **[Online Database],** indexed at the FamilySearch.org website. Source: National Archives, Records of the Bureau of Indian Affairs. This is an image only database with digital images of land allotment records for the Five Civilized Tribes in Indian Territory. Under the terms of the 1887 Dawes Act, Indian reservations were surveyed, and lands held in common by the tribes were allotted in smaller parcels to individual members of the tribe. These records describe the parcels of land and name the tribal member to whom each parcel was allotted. Records are arranged by name of tribe (Cherokee, Choctaw, Chickasaw, Creek and Seminole), by membership designation (member by blood, by intermarriage or freedmen), application number and according to age group – newborn and minor children are listed separately. Browse through the images, organized by Tribe membership designation (Cherokee by blood, Choctaw by marriage, etc.), then chronologically by Application number. An index for this database is in progress and will be published when completed. This database has 1,406,867 records. See
https://familysearch.org/search/collection/1390101.

1900. *Oklahoma Territory, 1900 Federal Census: Soundex and Population Schedules* **[Microfilm & Digital Capture],** filmed by the National Archives, c1970, 52 rolls, beginning with FHL film #1241335 (Population schedules: Beaver, Blaine, and Canadian counties); and FHL film #1241344 (Population schedules, Oklahoma Territory Indian Nations in the following order: Cherokee, Chickasaw, Choctaw, Creek, Peoria, Quapaw, Seneca, Wyandotte, Seminole, Modoc, Ottawa, and Shawnee Nations). To access the digital images, see the online FHL catalog: www.familysearch.org/search/catalog/641563.

- NOTE: Indians in the U.S. Federal Censuses. Native Americans did not receive citizenship in the U.S. until a Supreme Court ruling and an Act of Congress in 1924. Thus, American Indians did not appear as a regular part of the U.S. population until the 1930 federal census. Before that, Indians were specifically excluded from the federal censuses, as they had no part of the count to apportion the seats in the U.S. House of Representatives. But beginning in 1890, the U.S. Census Office created a special Indian Population Schedule, similar to the regular schedule, and canvassed all Indian tribes for their members. All regular schedules and Indian population schedules of the 1890 federal census were lost in a fire in Washington, DC in 1921. However, the Census Office repeated the added Indian Population Schedule for the 1900 federal census, which survives. The 1900 was the last federal census naming Indians in this manner.

1900 Creek Nation Census **[Printed Book],** compiled by Carole Ellsworth and Sue Emler, published by Oklahoma Roots Research, 1984, FHL book 970.3 C861e and FHL film #6101319.

1900 Personal Property Tax, Canadian County, Oklahoma" [Printed Article], in *Oklahoma Genealogical Society Bulletin,* (Oklahoma City, OK), Vol. 17, No. 1 (Jan 1972); and Vol. 17, No. 2 (Jun 1972).

"1900-1906 Tax Rolls, Logan County, Oklahoma" [Printed Article], in *Logan County Genealogical Society News,* (Guthrie, OK), Vol. 5, No. 2 (Jan 1986) and Vol. 5, No. 4 (Jul 1986).

1901-1907 Native American Census: Seneca, Eastern Shawnee, Miami, Modoc, Ottawa, Peoria, Quapaw, and Wyandotte Indians (under Seneca School, Indian Territory) **[Printed Book],** compiled by Jeff Bowen, published Mountain Press, Signal Mountain, TN, 199?, 223 pages. Includes index. These censuses were taken at the Seneca School in Indian Territory. Wyandotte (or Wyandot) Indians are included with the Huron Indian materials. FHL book 970.1 B675ba.

1901-1920 Kay County. *Treasurer's Tax rolls* **[Microfilm & Digital Capture],** from the original records at the Kay County Courthouse in Newkirk, OK. Includes some Kaw Indians, also known as the Kansa

Indians, who lived on a reserve in the eastern portion of what is now Kay County. Filmed by the Genealogical Society of Utah, 1996, 37 rolls, beginning with FHL film #2056845 (Treasurer's tax rolls Ponca City, Parker, Waltham, Weston, 1901 Blackwell, Cross Cities; and railroads). To access the digital images, see the online FHL catalog:
https://familysearch.org/search/catalog/679511.

"1902-1903 Tax Rolls, Kiowa County, Oklahoma" [Printed Article], published serially in *Kiowa County Genealogical Society Newsletter,* (Hobart, OK), beginning with Vol. 7, No. 1 (Feb 2000).

"1903 Tax List, Garfield County, Oklahoma" [Printed Article], published serially by township in *Garfield County Roots and Branches,* (Geary, OK), beginning with Vol. 9 No. 4 (Fall 1986).

1904-1915, Kiowa Indian Census [Microfilm & Digital Capture], from the original records at the Anadarko Philamanthic Museum, Anadarko, OK. Also contains records for Wichita, Caddo, Apache, and Comanche tribes that were under the Kiowa Agency. Filmed by the Genealogical Society of Utah, 1996, 1 roll, FHL film #2031240. To access the digital images, see the online FHL catalog:
www.familysearch.org/search/catalog/780909.

1905. See *Census of the Comanche Tribe of Indians, Kiowa Indian Agency, O. T., June 30, 1905* [Printed Book], extracted from FHL film #576902, by Faye Riddles Washburn, published by Southwest Oklahoma Genealogical Society, 1990, 57 pages. FHL book 970.1 A1 no. 192.

1905 History. See *Makers of Oklahoma: Biographies and Photographs of Men Who Have Played an Important Part in the History of Oklahoma, Together with a Brief History of the Territory* [Printed Book & Digital Version], by John H. N. Tindall, publ. Guthrie, OK, State Capital Co., 1905, 116 pages, includes index. Digitized by FamilySearch International, 2008. To access the digital images, see the online FHL catalog:
www.familysearch.org/search/catalog/1540844.

1905-1906 Oklahoma City Directory [Printed Book & Digital Version], R. L. Polk and Co., Dallas, TX. FHL book 976.638 E4p (book includes directories for 1916, 1941, 1960, 1969, 1975, and 1986, by various publishers. See also, FHL film #928379 (1905-1906 directory only). To access the digital version, see the online FHL catalog:
www.familysearch.org/search/catalog/806371.

"1905-1914 Tax Lists, Wagoner County, Oklahoma" [Printed Article], published serially in *Wagoner Genealogist,* (Wagoner, OK), beginning with Vol. 7, No. 2 (Jun 1987).

1905-1917. *Garfield County, Oklahoma Taxpayers* [Printed Book], compiled by Garfield County Genealogists, Inc., Enid, OK, 2000, 2 vols. Contains indexes to county tax records for 1905-1907 and an alphabetical list of taxpayers and their post office addresses copied from the R.L. Polk City directory of Enid, Oklahoma, 1917. FHL book 976.628 R4g v. 1-2.

"1906 Tax List, Okmulgee County, Oklahoma" [Printed Article], in *Okmulgee County Genealogical Society Newsletter,* (Okmulgee, OK), (Vol. 9, No. 2 (May 1994).

1907 Dawes Commission, Published Report. See *The Final Rolls of Citizens and Freedmen of the Five Civilized Tribes in Indian Territory, prepared by the Dawes Commission and Commissioner to the Five Civilized Tribes, 1907* [Printed Book], Government Printing Office, 2 vols., 1,267 pages. Reprinted by Genealogical Publishing Co., Inc., Baltimore, 2003, 2 vols., 633 & 635 pages. Includes Creek, Seminole, Cherokee, Choctaw, and Chickasaw Indian Rolls, vol. 1 is a combined index, "Index to the Final Rolls." FHL has the original book, FHL book 970.1 Un3c v. 1-2 and FHL film #962366 (vol. 1); FHL film #908371 (vol. 2). The index can be used as a finding aid to the Dawes Commission Allotments, 1896-1909, which includes a complete census listing of all Indian families involved in the allotments (over 250,000 applications and over 101,000 individuals enrolled).
- To find the census cards see the "**Dawes Rolls**," (*Applications for Enrollment of the Five Civilized Tribes, Dawes Commission, 1896-1909).*
- See also, *The Index of Citizens and Freedmen of the Choctaw and Chickasaw Tribes in Indian Territory* [Printed Book & Digital Version], prepared by the Commissioner to the Five Civilized Tribes, publ. 1907, 647 pages, see FHL book 970.1 Un3. Although the title only refers to the Choctaw and Chickasaw, this is an Index to *The Final Rolls of Citizens and Freedmen of the Five Civilized Tribes in Indian Territory.* To access the digital version, see the online FHL catalog:
www.familysearch.org/search/catalog/822882.

1907 Tax List, Garfield County, Oklahoma" [Printed Article], in *Garfield County Roots and Branches,* (Geary, OK), (1990 issue).

"1907 Tax List, Stephens County, Oklahoma" **[Printed Article]**, published serially in *FootSteps*, (Stephens Co Genealogical Society, Duncan, OK), beginning with Vol. 1, No. 1 (Jan1986).

1908 Tax Roll, Muskogee County, Oklahoma **[Microfilm]**, from the originals at the Muskogee County courthouse, Muskogee, OK. Filmed by the Genealogical Society of Utah, 1993, 1 roll, FHL film #1902077.

1908 Craig County, Oklahoma, First Tax List After Statehood: Beginning with 1908, roll books I, II, III, IV. **[Printed Book]**, copied & indexed by Alta Mae Bowman and Mary Nell Bowman, published by the Craig County Genealogical Society, 1995, 96 pages. This index covers four volumes of Craig County tax records now in the Archives of the Vinita Public Library. FHL book 976.698 R42b.

1908 Indian Tax Rolls, McCurtain County, Oklahoma **[Printed Book]**, compiled and published by the McCurtain County Genealogical Society, Idabel, OK, 1987, 10 pages. Includes history of the county and a list of cemeteries in the county. This is an index to taxation of Choctaw Indians in McCurtain County, Oklahoma, in 1908. FHL book 970.1 A1 no. 135.

"1908 Tax List, Bryan County, Oklahoma" **[Printed Article]**, in *Bryan County Heritage Quarterly*, (Calera, OK), Vol. 1, No. 3 (Feb 1985); May, August, and November issues, 1994; and Feb 1997 – Feb 2000).

"1908 Taxpayers, Coal County, Oklahoma" **[Printed Article]**, in *Oklahoma Genealogical Society Bulletin*, (Oklahoma City, OK), Vol. 28, No. 2 (1983).

"1908 Assessment Roll, Logan County, Oklahoma" **[Printed Article]**, in *Logan County Genealogical Society News*, (Guthrie, OK), Vol. 20, No. 2 (Spring 2001).

"1908 Personal Property Tax List, Pontotoc County, Oklahoma" **[Printed Article]**, published serially in *Pontotoc County Quarterly*, (Ada,. OK), beginning with Vol. 4, No. 2 (Feb 1973).

1908-1910. *U.S. Records Related to Enrollment of Eastern Cherokee by Guion Miller* **[Online Database]**, indexed at the Ancestry.com website. Source: National Archives microfilm series M685. In 1906, the U.S. Court of Claims appointed Guion Miller from the Interior Department to determine who was eligible for funds under the treaties of 1835-1836 and 1845 between the United States and the Eastern Cherokee. Applications typically include the applicant's name, Indian name, residence, date and place of birth, marriage status, and name of spouse. Also included are the names of siblings, parents, aunts and uncles, grandparents, and great-grandparents, further establishing family relationships vital to affirming tribal connections. This database has 79,496 records. See http://search.ancestry.com/search/db.aspx?dbid=60555.

1908-1927. *Oklahoma, Indian Land Allotment Sales* **[Online Database]**, digitized and indexed at the Ancestry.com website. Source: National Archives, Records of the Bureau of Indian Affairs. Land distributed to Native Americans through government allotment (such as via the Dawes Commission) came with many restrictions governing its sale or lease. An act passed in May 1908 removed many of these restrictions. In particular, this allowed Indians to sell or lease, and incoming settlers to obtain allotment lands. Records include the applicant's name, enrollment number, tribe, degree of Indian blood, address, legal description of the land to be sold, date petition was filed, date approved, and date of sale. Each index record includes: Name, Residence year, Residence place, Filed date, Tribe, Enrollment number, and Application number. This database has 26,700 records. See http://search.ancestry.com/search/db.aspx?dbid=60544.

1910. *Oklahoma, 1910 Federal Census: Soundex and Population Schedules* **[Microfilm & Digital Capture]**, filmed by the National Archives, c1970, 179 rolls, beginning with FHL film #1375155 (Population: Adair, Alfalfa, Atoka, and Beaver counties). To access the digital images, see the online FHL catalog: www.familysearch.org/search/catalog/639623.

1910. See *McAlister, Pittsburg County, Oklahoma, an Extraction of Records From the Oklahoma State Prison in 1910: Copied From the Census Records of 1910, Indexed by Volume* **[Printed Book]**, extracted by John D. Woods, published by the author, Pleasant View, UT, 1993, 6 vols. FHL book 976.675 X28W 1910, vol. 1-6 and FHL film #1750784.

1911 Index to Tax Lists of Comanche County, Oklahoma, and Tax Information Extracted from R. L. Polk & Co.'s Lawton City Directory, 1911 **[Printed Book]**, compiled by Jewell (Rone) Tankersley, published by the author, Lawton, OK, 1984, 111 pages. FHL book 976.648 R4t.

1912-1921. *Oklahoma, Creek Equalization Records* **[Online Database]**, indexed at the Ancestry.com website. Source: National Archives microfilm, Bureau of Indian Affairs. This collection contains applications to prove heirship by descent among members of the

Creek nation. Many of the files include Proof of Heirship forms which contain the name of the deceased allottee, date and place of death, name of spouse, and the names of the allottee's children and the heirs of deceased children. There are numerous gaps. Forms may include other details as well, including age, tribal affiliation, whether spouse is alive or deceased, names of other spouses, number of children, post office, and names of informants. This database has 3,634 records: http://search.ancestry.com/search/db.aspx?dbid=60542.

1912-1926 School Censuses, Woodward County, Oklahoma **[Microfilm & Digital Capture],** from the original records at the Woodward County Courthouse, Woodward, OK. Most volumes individually indexed. Filmed by the Genealogical Society of Utah, 1989, 11 rolls, beginning with FHL film #1639863 (1912-1913 enumerations). To access the digital images, see the online FHL catalog:
https://familysearch.org/search/catalog/521441.

1912-1934 Scholastic Enumeration Records, Major County, Oklahoma **[Microfilm & Digital Capture],** from the originals at the Major County courthouse in Fairview, OK. Some books and years missing. Filmed by the Genealogical Society of Utah, 1991, 12 rolls, beginning with FHL film #1787502 (Enumeration records, 1912). To access the digital images, see the online FHL catalog:
https://familysearch.org/search/catalog/519319.

1912-1936 Dewey County, Oklahoma. See *Scholastic Census, 1912-1936; and Pupil's High School Credit Records, 1901-1952* **[Microfilm & Digital Capture],** from the original records of the Dewey County Superintendent of Schools, Taloga, OK. Most names arranged alphabetically within districts. Filmed by the Genealogical Society of Utah, 1989-1990, 25 rolls, beginning with FHL film #1664668 (1912). To access the digital images, see the online FHL catalog:
www.familysearch.org/search/catalog/517713.

1912-1936 School District Enumeration Reports, Ellis County, Oklahoma **[Microfilm & Digital Capture],** from the originals of the Office of the County Superintendent at the Ellis County courthouse in Arnett, Oklahoma. Ellis County was organized in 1907 from Woodward County and half of Day County (formerly known as "E" County in Oklahoma Territory). Filmed by the Genealogical Society of Utah, 1990, 12 rolls, beginning with FHL film #1065158 (1912-1914). To access the digital images, see the online FHL catalog:
https://familysearch.org/search/catalog/367110.

1915-1955. *Oklahoma, Confederate Pension Index* **[Online Database],** indexed at the Ancestry.com website. This database is also accessible at the OK Dept of Library's Digital Prairie website. Each index record includes: Name, Residence, Spouse, and a link to the OK Dept of Libraries site. This database has 8,029 records. See
http://search.ancestry.com/search/db.aspx?dbid=9236.

1916 County Register of Electors, Latimer County, Oklahoma **[Microfilm & Digital Capture],** from the original records at the Latimer County Courthouse, Wilburton, OK. Contains an alphabetical list of registered voters including name, school district number, date of registration, age, residence, occupation, race, political affiliation, and registration certificate number. Filmed by the Genealogical Society of Utah, 1998, 1 roll, FHL film #2129955. To access the digital images, see the online FHL catalog:
www.familysearch.org/search/catalog/822165.

1916-1920. *Census Records, Pawnee Agency* **[Microfilm & Digital Capture],** filmed by the National Archives, 1965, 1 rolls, FHL film #1249780. To access the digital images, see the online FHL catalog: www.familysearch.org/search/catalog/402696.

1916-1920 County Register of Electors, Cotton County, Oklahoma **[Microfilm & Digital Capture],** from the original records at the Cotton County Courthouse in Walters, OK. Names are listed under the first letter of the last name. Information includes name of voter; school district; date of registration; age, address, and occupation of voter; occupation, race, color and political affiliation of voter and registration certificate number. Filmed by the Genealogical Society of Utah, 1998, 1 roll, FHL film #2109807. To access the digital images, see the online FHL catalog:
www.familysearch.org/search/catalog/1044302.

1916-1922 Precinct Voting Registers, McClain County, Oklahoma **[Microfilm & Digital Capture],** from the original records at the McClain County Clerk's office in Purcell, OK. Filmed by the Genealogical Society of Utah, 1997, 1 roll, FHL #2108408. To access the digital images, see the online FHL catalog:
www.familysearch.org/search/catalog/1057974.

1916-1920 Census Records, Pawnee Agency **[Microfilm & Digital Capture],** from the originals at the Regional National Archives, Ft. Worth, TX. Filmed by the National Archives, 1978, 1 roll, FHL film

#1249780. To access the digital images, see the online FHL catalog:
www.familysearch.org/search/catalog/402696.

1916-1933 Voter Registration Records, Canadian County, Oklahoma [Microfilm & Digital Capture], from the original records at the Canadian County Courthouse in El Reno, OK. Volume 2 is indexed. Index is at beginning of volume. Filmed by Genealogical Society of Utah, 2001, 1 roll, FHL film #2257892. To access the digital images, see the online FHL catalog:
www.familysearch.org/search/catalog/1171051.

1916-1946 Precinct Registers, Alfalfa County, Oklahoma [Microfilm & Digital Capture], from the originals at Alfalfa County Museum, Cherokee, OK. Names in the register are listed alphabetically under each town. Information for each person listed in the register includes name, school district, date of registration, age, residence, occupation, race, color, and political party. Precinct registers are not numbered. Filmed by the Genealogical Society of Utah, 1999, 1 roll, FHL film #2134766. To access the digital images, see the online FHL catalog:
www.familysearch.org/search/catalog/955834.

1916-1948. See *Precinct Registers, 1916-1948; Register of Electors, 1916-1918, Greer County, Oklahoma* [Microfilm], of originals in the Greer County courthouse in Mangum, OK. Most volumes individually indexed (formatted in the "ABC self-indexing format"). Some of the registers give birth dates as early as 1856. Filmed by the Genealogical Society of Utah, 1994, 1 roll, FHL film #1954680. To see if this microfilm was digitized yet, see the online FHL catalog:
www.familysearch.org/search/catalog/677757.

1917 Comanche Indian Census, Kiowa Indian Agency, Anadarko, Caddo County, Oklahoma [Printed Book], compiled by Polly Lewis Murphy, et al, published by the authors, Anadarko, OK, 1990, 71 pages. FHL book 970.3 C73c.

1917-1918. *Oklahoma, World War I Selective Service System Draft Registration Cards* [Microfilm & Digital Capture], filmed by the National Archives, 1988, 76 rolls, beginning with FHL film #1851604 (Adair County, A-Z; and Alfalfa County, A-R). To access the digital images, see the online FHL catalog:
www.familysearch.org/search/catalog/746995.

1917-1919. *Oklahoma, World War I American Expeditionary Forces, Deaths* [Digital Capture], digitized by FamilySearch International. To access the digital images, see the online FHL catalog:
www.familysearch.org/search/catalog/3023946.

1917-1982. *Oklahoma, Oklahoma City, Rose Hill Burial Park, Interment Cards* [Online Database], digitized and indexed at FamilySearch.org. This database has 1,985 records, see
www.familysearch.org/search/collection/2790264.

1920. *Oklahoma, 1920 Federal Census: Soundex and Population Schedules* [Microfilm & Digital Capture], filmed by the National Archives, c1970, 195 rolls, beginning with FHL film #1821451 (Population: Adair and Beckham counties). To access the digital images, see the online FHL catalog:
www.familysearch.org/search/catalog/555224.

1921. *Oklahoma Osage Tribe Roll* [Online Database], indexed at the Ancestry.com website. Original data: Electronic reproduction of a report submitted by the Osage Indian Agency in Pawhuska, Oklahoma to the Secretary of the Interior in Washington, D.C. in 1921. By an Act of Congress in 1906, the lands of the Osage Nation in what is now Osage County, Oklahoma were divided among the 2,229 members of the tribe. Each member received an allotment of 657 acres of surface rights. This database is a census of the tribe conducted in 1908 and certified by the Osage Indian Agency in 1921. In addition to providing the tribe member's name, each record also includes birth information, sex, and relationship to the head of the household. Affidavit numbers are provided for those who applied for proof of Indian blood and to what degree. This database has 2,348 records. See
http://search.ancestry.com/search/db.aspx?dbid=4663.

1923-1942. *Oklahoma County, Oklahoma, Divorce Index* [Online Database], indexed at the Ancestry.com website. This database is also accessible at the Oklahoma Historical Society website. Each index record includes: Name, Spouse name, Divorce date, Divorce place, and Notes (record type, source). This database has 44,010 records. See
http://search.ancestry.com/search/db.aspx?dbid=9234.

1924-1929. *U.S., Cherokee Baker Roll and Records* [Online Database], digitized and indexed at the Ancestry.com website. Source: National Archives microfilm series M2104, Records of the Bureau of Indian Affairs. The Baker Roll was the final roll compiled for determining membership in the Eastern Band of Cherokees. Documents include applications for tribal membership, correspondence regarding applications and other matters, transcripts of testimony, copies of decisions and findings by the Enrolling Commission, and indexes created for the collections. This database has 20,005 records. See http://search.ancestry.com/search/db.aspx?dbid=2398.

1930. *Oklahoma, 1930 Federal Census: Population Schedules* **[Microfilm & Digital Capture],** filmed by the Bureau of the Census, c1942, 47 rolls, beginning with FHL film #3241626 (Adair, Beaver, Alfalfa and Atoka counties). To access the digital images, see the online FHL catalog: www.familysearch.org/search/catalog/1037508.

1937. *Oklahoma and Indian Territory, Indian and Pioneer Historical Collection* **[Online Database],** digitized and indexed at the Ancestry.com website. Source: Indian Pioneer History Collection, edited by Grant Foreman, Indian Archives Division, Oklahoma Historical Society, Oklahoma City. This collection contains transcripts of oral histories about pioneer life in Oklahoma in the early twentieth century. The project was funded by the WPA in 1937. The original collection was made up of some 80,000 entries and contains 116 volumes. The information may include names, residence, birth date and place, interview date, death date, age at death, burial place. Interviews may also mention names of neighbors, family members, doctors, teachers, missionaries, and others. This database has 46,724 records. See http://search.ancestry.com/search/db.aspx?dbid=9025.

1940. *Oklahoma, 1940 Federal Census: Population Schedules* **[Digital Capture],** digitized images taken from the microfilm of original records held by the Bureau of the Census in the 1940s. After microfilming, Congress allowed the Census Bureau to destroy the originals to free up space for WWII-related files. Digitizing of the 1940 census schedules was done by the National Archives and made public in 2012. Roll numbers (digital filming numbers) begin with #5454569 (Adair and Alfalfa counties). To access the digital images, see the online FHL catalog: www.familysearch.org/search/catalog/2057781.

1940 Federal Census Finding Aids **[Online Database].** The National Archives prepared a special website online with a detailed description of the 1940 federal census. Included at the site are descriptions of location finding aids, such as Enumeration District maps, Geographic Descriptions of Census Enumeration Districts, and a list of 1940 City Directories available at the National Archives. The finding aids are all linked to other National Archives sites. See www.archives.gov/research/census/1940/general-info.html#questions.

1940-1945. *Oklahoma, World War II Draft Registration Cards* **[Digital Capture],** digitized by FamilySearch International. includes draft registration cards of men who registered during World War II, with the exception of the fourth registration. Images courtesy of Ancestry. The event place is the residence of the registrant.
www.familysearch.org/search/catalog/2710650.

1972-2012. *Oklahoma, Oklahoman Obituary Index* **[Online Database],** indexed at the Ancestry.com website. This database is also accessible at the Oklahoma Historical Society website. Each index record includes: Name, Death year, Death country (USA), Publication date (of the obituary), and Publication place. This database has 241,026 records: http://search.ancestry.com/search/db.aspx?dbid=9235.

1981-Current. *Oklahoma Recent Newspaper Obituaries* **[Online Database],** digitized and indexed at the GenealogyBank.com website. Search Oklahoma newspaper obituaries for Ada, Altus, Alva, Antlers, Ardmore, Bartlesville, Bethany, Broken Arrow, Chickasha, Claremore, Coweta, Duncan, Durant, Edmond, Enid, Fairland, Frederick, Grove, Guymon, Lawton, McAlester, Miami, Midwest City, Moore, Muskogee, Norman, Nowata, Oklahoma City, Owasso, Pauls Valley, Pawhuska, Perry, Poteau, Pryor, Sand Springs, Shawnee, Skiatook, Stillwater, Tahlequah, Tulsa, Tuttle, Vinita, Wagoner, Waurika, Weatherford, and Woodward, Oklahoma. See www.genealogybank.com/explore/obituaries/all/usa/oklahoma.

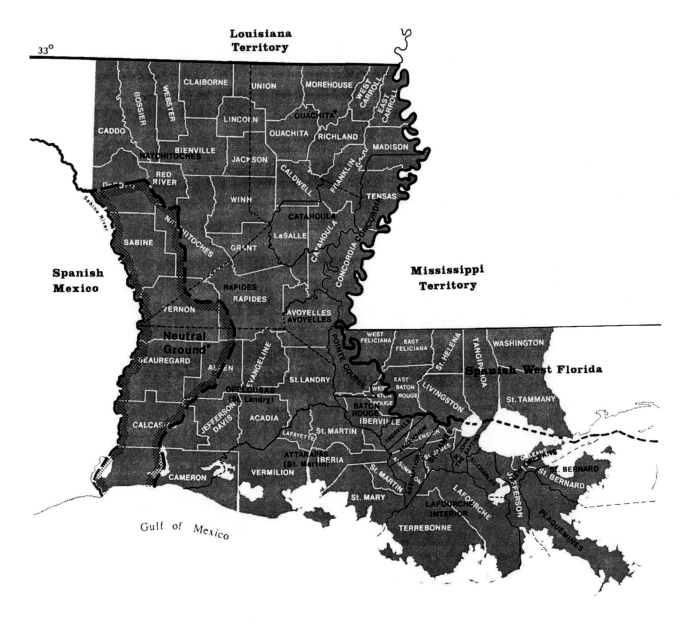

Louisiana (as Orleans Territory) • **1810.** The 20 parishes of Orleans Territory at the time of the August 1810 Federal Census are shown in black. The current 64 parishes of Louisiana are shown in white. Parish boundaries shown as dashed lines are uncertain due to poorly defined ecclesiastical jurisdictions and imprecise surveys. *Map Notes: The 1803 Louisiana Purchase caused a dispute with Spain over the resulting international boundary. Spain claimed east to the Red River; the U.S. claimed west to the Sabine River. In 1806, they made a temporary compromise with the so-called *Neutral Ground*, where neither exercised jurisdiction. The remaining disputed area northwest of the Neutral Ground reflected the view the U.S. held regarding the limits of the Louisiana Purchase. In October 1810, by means of a proclamation by President James Madison, the U.S. arbitrarily annexed Spain's West Florida from the Mississippi River to the Perdido River. The area included Baton Rouge, Biloxi, and Mobile. Spain did not recognize the annexation, and continued their claim to West Florida in dispute with the U.S. In 1812 Congress added to Orleans Territory the portion of the West Florida annexation from the Pearl River to the Mississippi River including present Baton Rouge. That area of present Louisiana east of the Mississippi is often referred to as "The Florida Parishes." **Map Source:** Page 133, *Map Guide to the U.S. Federal Censuses, 1790-1920,* by William Thorndale and William Dollarhide.

Louisiana
Censuses & Substitute Name Lists

Historical Timeline for Louisiana, 1673-1865

1673. Mississippi River. French explorers Jacques Jolliet and Louis Marquette left their base in Ste. Sault Marie, Quebéc, and made their way to the Illinois River, which they descended to become the first Frenchmen to discover the Mississippi River. They floated down the Mississippi as far south as the mouth of the Arkansas River before returning to the Great Lakes area.

1682. Louisiana. Following the same route as Jolliet and Marquette, René-Robert Cavelier (Sieur de LaSalle) floated down the Mississippi River, continuing all the way to its mouth at the Gulf of Mexico. He then claimed the entire Mississippi Basin for Louis XIV of France, for whom Louisiana was named. The French later established *La Louisiane Française* as a district of New France.

1685-1716. The French claims in North America now included all of the present Maritime Provinces, the St. Lawrence River Valley, the Great Lakes area, and the entire Mississippi Basin. French Forts and settlements established in the region during this period included Prairie du Chien (1685), Arkansas Post (1686), Kaskaskia (1703), and Fort Rosalie/Natchez (1716).

1713. Queen Anne's War. At the Treaty of Utrecht ending the war, France ceded to Britain its claims to the Hudson's Bay region, Newfoundland, and peninsular French Acadia (which the British renamed Nova Scotia). The remaining French claims in North America were contained within two jurisdictions: *Quebéc,* including the St. Lawrence River Valley and Great Lakes region; and *La Louisiane Française*.

1718. La Nouvelle-Orleans (New Orleans) was founded by Jean-Baptiste Le Moyne (Sieur de Bienville). It was named for Philippe II, Duke of Orleans, the Regent of France. That year saw hundreds of French colonists arriving in Louisiana.

1719. Baton Rouge was established by the French as a military post.

1721. The German Coast. French/German colonists abandoned Arkansas Post, the largest settlement of all of French Louisiana. As a failed farming community, Arkansas Post was typical of the French efforts to colonize North America south of the Great Lakes. Arkansas Post continued as a trading post, and the French presence in the Mississippi Basin now became one of mostly single French voyageurs, fur trappers, and traders, paddling their canoes from one trading post to the next.
- A group of German immigrants who had first settled at Arkansas Post, acquired farmland on the east side of the Mississippi River north of New Orleans. Many were German-speaking Alsace-Lorraine natives of France. They easily adapted themselves to the French culture of Louisiana, and later intermarried with the French Acadians coming into the same area. Their main settlements were at Karlstein, Hoffen, Mariental, and Augsburg, all part of the *German Coast*.
- For a transcript of a lecture on the first Germans to settle the lower Mississippi (in German), see **www.familysearch.org/search/catalog/474083**.

1722-1739. During this period of La Louisiane Française, a few more settlements and trading posts were established, including Prairie du Rocher (Illinois) in 1722; Vincennes (Indiana) in 1732; Ste. Genevieve (Missouri) in 1735; and Fort Assumption (Memphis) in 1739.

1755-1758. Expulsion of the Acadians. When the British took over part of the area known as Acadia in 1713, they asked the French Acadians to swear allegiance to Britain or leave. Many of the Acadians left the Acadia Peninsula (now Nova Scotia), crossing the Bay of Fundy to areas of Acadia still under control of the French (now New Brunswick and Maine). They had a fairly peaceful coexistence with the British until 1755, when the British completed their conquest of Acadia. By then, Britain had become extremely anti-Catholic politically, and they began forcibly removing the Acadians, deporting them to the Atlantic British colonies or transporting Acadians back to their original homelands in France. Some of the Acadians left voluntarily, making their way to other areas of North America held by the French.

1763. Treaty of Paris. The French and Indian War in colonial America ended. In Europe and Canada, it was called the Seven Years War. As the big loser in the war, France formally ceded all of its North American claims – Louisiana on the western side of the Mississippi was lost to Spain, the eastern side of the Mississippi and all of French Quebéc/Canada went to Britain. Soon after the treaty, all French military personnel left their North American posts. But French civilian settlements continued in Lower Louisiana, such as those at New Orleans, Baton Rouge, Arkansas Post, and Natchez; and in Upper Louisiana, such as Prairie du Chien, Kaskaskia, and Vincennes. Spain did not take military control of Spanish Louisiana until 1766 (at New Orleans) and 1770 (at St. Louis).

1764-1765. Acadian Coast. In 1764, British troops began the forced deportation of French Acadians from their homes in present Nova Scotia, New Brunswick, and Maine. The remaining Acadians were all herded onto ships. The destinations were not always clear, and the displaced Acadians were sometimes unloaded in Boston, New York, Baltimore, Charleston, Savannah, or Mobile. After a few initial families made their way to New Orleans via Mobile in early 1764, several shiploads of Acadians arrived in New Orleans in early 1765. Their first settlements were on the west side of the Mississippi River, near the present areas of St. James and Ascension Parishes. That first area became known as the *Acadian Coast*. Today there are 22 parishes of Louisiana considered part of *Acadiana*, a modern description of the region of southern Louisiana west of the Mississippi River first settled by French Acadians. For more details on the first Acadians in Louisiana, visit the Acadian-Cajun Genealogy & History website. See www.acadian-cajun.com/hiscaj2b.htm.

1766. Antonio de Ulloa **was** the first Spanish governor of Louisiana, headquartered at New Orleans. He was a brilliant scientist (discoverer of the element Platinum), highly regarded by Spanish Royalty, but rose to his highest level of incompetence as a military leader.

1768. The Louisiana Rebellion of 1768 was an attempt by a combined armed force of French Acadians, French Creoles and German Coast settlers around New Orleans to stop the handover of French La Louisiane to Spain. The rebels forced Spanish Governor de Ulloa to leave New Orleans and return to Spain, but his replacement Alejandro O'Reilly was able to crush the rebellion. O'Reilly, an Irishman turned Cuban, was responsible for establishing military rule in Spanish Louisiana.

1777-1778. During the Revolutionary War, a number of French-speaking Acadians from Louisiana joined their counterparts from the leftover French settlements of Kaskaskia and Vincennes. They were added to the Virginia Militia force commanded by General George Rogers Clark. General Clark later noted that the fiercely anti-British fighters he gained from the French communities contributed greatly to his monumental victories against the British in the conquest of the Old Northwest.

1783. United States of America. The treaty of Paris of 1783 first recognized the United States as an independent nation, with borders from the Atlantic Ocean to the Mississippi River, and from present Maine to Georgia. The treaty also reaffirmed the claims of Britain to present Canada; and Spain's claim to East Florida, West Florida, New Spain (including Nuevo Mexico & Tejas), and Louisiana west of the Mississippi River.

1800-1802. Louisiana. In Europe, Napoleon regained title to Louisiana from Spain, after trading them a duchy in Italy. However, Napoleon found that his troops in the Caribbean were under siege and unable to provide much help in establishing a French government in Louisiana. Several months later, when American emissaries showed up in Paris trying to buy New Orleans from him, Napoleon decided to unload the entire tract – legally described as "the drainage of the Mississippi and Missouri Rivers."

1803. Louisiana Purchase. President Thomas Jefferson urged Congress to vote in favor, and the U.S. purchased the huge area from France, doubling the size

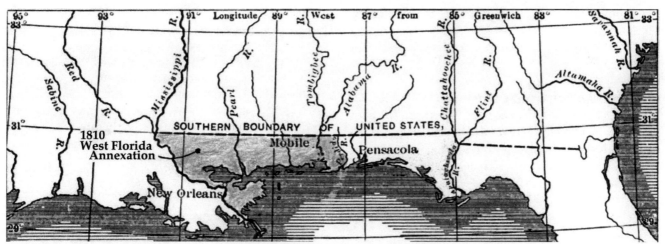

1810 West Florida Annexation

of the United States. But, disputed claims to areas of Lower Louisiana now existed between Spain and the U.S., in particular, the area between the Red River and Sabine River in present Louisiana; and the area of West Florida, east of the Mississippi River.

1804-1805. In 1804, Congress divided the Louisiana Purchase into two jurisdictions: **Louisiana District** and **Orleans Territory**. The latter had north and south bounds the same as the present state of Louisiana, but did not include its present Florida Parishes, and its northwest corner extended on an indefinite line west into Spanish Tejas. The first capital of Orleans Territory was New Orleans. For a year, Louisiana District was attached to Indiana Territory for judicial administration but became Louisiana Territory with its own Governor on July 4, 1805. St. Louis was the first capital of Louisiana Territory.

1806. The dispute between the U.S. and Spain over the Louisiana-Spanish Mexico boundary was informally addressed by the two parties. Spain claimed east to the Red River; the U.S. claimed west to the Sabine River. In 1806, they made a temporary compromise with the so-called Neutral Ground, where neither exercised jurisdiction, creating a haven for fugitives. That lack of jurisdiction inspired the French Pirate, Jean Laffite, to use bayous within the Neutral Ground as a base of operations. The boundary issue was not resolved until the Adams-Onis Treaty, ratified in 1821. See the 1810 Orleans Territory map on page 122 showing the area of the Neutral Ground.

1810. August. The **1810 Federal Census** was taken in Orleans Territory. Although outside U.S. jurisdiction, the Neutral Ground was included in the enumeration. The population of Orleans Territory in 1810 was 76,556 people.

1810. September. A small group of Americans overcame the Spanish garrison at Baton Rouge and unfurled the new flag of the Republic of West Florida.

1810. October. **West Florida Annexation.** In a proclamation by President James Madison, the U.S. arbitrarily annexed Spain's West Florida from the Mississippi River to the Perdido River, an area that the U.S. believed should have been part of the Louisiana Purchase. The area included the existing towns of Baton Rouge, Biloxi, and Mobile. Spain disagreed that the area was ever part of Louisiana, refused to recognize the annexation, and continued their claim to West Florida in dispute with the U.S. for another ten years.

1811. The side-wheeler *New Orleans* was the first Mississippi River steamboat. Launched in Pittsburgh, it was first used between Natchez and New Orleans. The port of New Orleans and other ports along the Mississippi River were to see dramatic increases in docking, warehousing, and manufacturing related to the huge increase in river traffic after the introduction of steamboats.

1812. January. Congress added to Mississippi Territory the portion of the West Florida annexation from the Perdido River to the Pearl River, an area which included Mobile and Biloxi; and the portion from the Pearl River to the Mississippi River was added to Orleans Territory (an area that included Baton Rouge).

1812. April 30th. The area of Orleans Territory became **Louisiana,** the 18th state in the Union. New Orleans was the first state capital.

1812. June 4th. Louisiana Territory was renamed **Missouri Territory**. For a few weeks in 1812, a Louisiana Territory and a State of Louisiana existed at the same time.

1815. January. **Battle of New Orleans.** Major General Andrew Jackson commanded an American force of about 3,100 men that prevented an invading British Army with about 7,500 men from seizing New Orleans. Word of the December 1814 Treaty of Ghent officially ending the war had not reached New Orleans yet, and upon the retreat of the British Army, the Battle of New Orleans became the final American victory in the War of 1812.

1820. Federal Census. Louisiana had a population of 153,407 people.

1821. Adams-Onis Treaty. The treaty included the purchase of Florida, but also set the boundary between the U.S. and New Spain, from Louisiana to the Oregon Country. The treaty established the Sabine River and Red River borders with Spanish Tejas; ending any further claim by the U.S. to Texas as part of the Louisiana Purchase. The treaty also formalized the Arkansas River as the border with Nuevo Mexico; and established Latitude 42º North as the division between California and the Oregon Country. The treaty was named after John Quincy Adams, U.S. Secretary of State, and Luis de Onis, the Spanish Foreign Minister, the parties who signed the treaty at Washington in 1819. It was ratified by the U.S. Senate in 1821. John Quincy Adams was given credit for a brilliant piece of diplomacy by adding the western boundary settlements with Spain to the Florida Purchase.

1830. Federal Census. Louisiana had a population of 215,739 people.

1840. Federal Census. Louisiana had a population of 352,411 people.

1849. The Louisiana state capital was moved from New Orleans to Baton Rouge.

1850. Federal Census. Louisiana had a population of 517,762 people.

1860. Federal Census. Louisiana had a diverse population of 708,002 people. The slave population of 331,726 was about 47% of the total, the largest percentage of any state. In 1860, the Acadians, German Coast settlers, and Creoles (descendants of colonial French, Spanish, or African settlers) outnumbered the Anglo-Americans, who were less than 20% of the population, the smallest number of any state.

1861-1865. Louisiana seceded from the Union in January 1861 and joined the Confederate States of America soon after. New Orleans was the largest city in the Confederacy and was an early target by Union forces to control and maintain the flow of cotton on the Mississippi River to northern textile manufacturers. The city was captured in April 1862 and ruled by a Union Army General for the duration of the war.

Online Databases at the Louisiana State Archives

The Louisiana State Archives in Baton Rouge is administered by the Secretary of State of Louisiana. Online searchable databases include the Vital Records Index, Passenger Manifests, and the Confederate Pension Application Database.

Vital Records Index. Original vital records at the state archives are only available for births over 100 years old, and deaths and marriages over 50 years old. The archives will issue a birth, marriage, or death certificate for certain records for a small fee. Access the Vital Records Index at
www.sos.la.gov/HistoricalResources/ResearchHistoricalRecords/Pages/OnlinePublicVitalRecordsIndex.aspx.

New Orleans Ship Passenger List Online Index – January to July 1851. This is an online index to a portion of the New Orleans ship passenger lists available on microfilm in the Research Library at the Louisiana State Archives. This index covers the roughly six-month period from January 1 to July 7, 1851. This online index is an attempt to fill in the previously unindexed two-year period of 1851 and 1852. Information provided in this database includes passenger name, date of arrival, name of ship and port of departure. See
www.sos.la.gov/HistoricalResources/ResearchHistoricalRecords/LocateHistoricalRecords/Pages/default.aspx.

Confederate Pension Application Index. This index contains over 49,000 names that were included in the applications submitted to the Board of Pension Commissioners. The collection consists of alphabetically arranged pension applications for pensions that were granted to veterans and widows beginning in 1898 and are recorded on 152 reels of microfilm. The records were later transferred to the Archives after the last pension was paid in the 1950s. More than 18,000 applications were microfilmed and are available to researchers at the Archives Research Library. The pension applications may include service information, occupation, place of residence, and number of children. Other materials that may have been included with applications are letters, notes, copies of checks, newspaper clippings, court papers of various types, obituaries, and other miscellaneous papers. See www.sos.la.gov/HistoricalResources/ResearchHistoricalRecords/LocateHistoricalRecords/Pages/ConfederatePensionDatabase.aspx.

Louisiana State Vital Records Registry

Birth records less than 100 years old and Death and Marriages less than 50 years old are located at the Vital Records Registry, State Registrar & Vital Records, Baton Rouge. For information, see www.sos.la.gov/HistoricalResources/ResearchHistoricalRecords/Pages/OnlinePublicVitalRecordsIndex.aspx.

Louisiana Historical Center

The Louisiana State Museum and Historical Center is located in the French Quarter of New Orleans (the old U.S. Mint) and is another valuable archives for the preservation of Louisiana history. As the holder of various original manuscripts of significance to genealogists interested in early Louisiana, the Historical Center is referenced often in the bibliography that follows .For more information, see www.crt.state.la.us/louisiana-state-museum/collections/historical-center/index.

New Orleans Public Library's Louisiana Division, City Archives, & Special Collections

The Louisiana Division collects resources relating to the study of Louisiana and its citizens. Included are books by or about Louisianans; city, regional, and state documents; manuscripts, maps, newspapers, periodicals, microfilms, photographs, slides, motion pictures, sound recordings, video tapes, postcards, and ephemera of every sort. The Genealogy Collection contains books, periodicals, microfilms, and CD-ROMs with emphasis on the Southeast United States, Nova Scotia, France, and Spain. **The City Archives** is the official repository of the records of New Orleans municipal government, and the **Special Collections** maintained by the Division are the Rare Vertical File, the Carnival Collection, the Louisiana and New Orleans Photograph Collection, the Map Collection, the Menu Collection, the Postcard Collection, the Manuscript Collection, and the Rare Book Collection. For the home webpage of the Louisiana Division/City Archives/Special Collections, see http://nutrias.org/spec/speclist.htm.

Searchable Online Databases, New Orleans Public Library Website

The New Orleans Public Library is the main provider of online databases for anyone interested in genealogical research in Louisiana. The library has a strong Internet presence, using its own *Nutrias.org* domain for preserving resources online. The various online genealogy indexes available are identified briefly here and described in more detail in the bibliography, organized in chronological order, and where the online indexes are cited first by their inclusive dates.

The Louisiana Biography/Obituary Index references obituaries and death notices published in New Orleans newspapers from 1804-1972 and biographical information published in older Louisiana collective biographies. The original card index is housed in the Louisiana Division. An online index is available. See the **1804-1972** citation.

Index to the Justices of the Peace Marriage Records, 1846-1880. From 1846, the Justices of the Peace were the exclusive source for civil marriage licenses in Orleans Parish, which was divided into six districts, each of which was to elect a justice. Justices continued to function until 1880, when the judges of the newly established City Court assumed responsibility for issuance of civil marriage licenses. An online index to the Grooms and Brides is available. See the **1846-1880** citation.

New Orleans Newspaper Marriage Index, 1837-1857 – Daily Picayune. Indexed online by the first letter of a surname.

NOVA Transcriptions of City Archives Records. The New Orleans Volunteer Association (NOVA) is a loosely organized group of genealogists transcribing records from Orleans Parish. Transcriptions now online as searchable databases include the following (Bibliography locations added):

Records Relating to Insanity:
- Registers of Patients Transported to the State Insane Asylum, see **1882-1917**
- New Orleans City Insane Asylum Record of Patients, see **1882-1884; 1888**, 1 vol.
- New Orleans City Insane Asylum Record of Next of Kin, see **1875-1877**, 1 vol.

Records Relating to Death:
- Orleans Parish Coroner's Office Reports of Deaths, see **1862-1863**
- Records of Interments in the Non-Municipal Cemeteries of New Orleans, see **1841-1846**, vol. 1 Protestant (Girod Street) Cemetery, July – December 1841

Records Relating to Marriage:
- New Orleans Justices of the Peace, Index to Marriage Records, see **1846-1880**
- Louisiana 2nd District (Orleans Parish), Marriages, see May 12, **1879** to April 12, **1880**

Records Relating to Orphans:
- New Orleans Office of the Mayor – Records of the Disposition of Destitute Orphans, see **1852-1893**

Records Relating to Voter Registration:
- Orleans Parish Registrar of Voters - Index to Registr. of Foreign-Born Persons, see **1880-1916**

Records Relating to Relief:
- New Orleans Second Municipal Council – List of Fire Victims and their Losses, see **1844**

Each of the databases are described in more detail in the bibliography that follows. For a link to each of the NOVA transcriptions, see
http://nutrias.org/~nopl/spec/novainnutrias.htm.

Online Research Guides

Online informational guides available at the FamilySearch.org website, Ancestry.com website and the NOPL's Nutrias.org website are noted here with a link to a webpage for more information.

Guide to Depositories of Manuscript Collections in Louisiana. This book was prepared by the Louisiana Historical Records Survey, Works Progress Administration, 1941, a copy located at the LA State Archives, digitized by the Genealogical Society of Utah, 2014. To access a digital version, see the online FHL catalog page:
www.familysearch.org/search/catalog/2357204.

An Atlas of Louisiana Surnames of French and Spanish Origin. A book by Robert C. West, publ. 1986, LSU, Baton Rouge, LA, 217 pages. From Preface: "This study deals with the historical geography of 100 surnames of French or Spanish origin in Louisiana and adjacent states. Presented in atlas form, the study consists of maps, each depicting the present-day distribution of a given surname within the area designated… each map is followed by a short historical interpretation of the distribution with emphasis on the time and place of initial settlement by families carrying that surname, and the subsequent spread of the family." Includes index. See FHL book 976.3 D4w. To access a digital version of this atlas, visit the online FHL catalog page. See
www.familysearch.org/search/catalog/468302.

Florida y Luisiana. A series of 271 maps and plans obtained by the Family History Library from the Archivo General de Indias (Sevilla), Sección de Mapas y Planos. Some of the maps cover the period of colonial Spanish Louisiana, 1767-1800. For access to digital versions of the 271 maps, visit the online FHL catalog page. See
www.familysearch.org/search/catalog/315172.

Directory of Louisiana Cities, Towns and Villages: 1976 Bicentennial Edition, compiled by the Department of Public Works, Baton Rouge, LA, 1975, 167 pages, FHL book 976.3 E4d. For access to a digital version of this book, visit the online FHL catalog page. See
https://familysearch.org/search/catalog/2223351.

Louisiana City Parish Index. An online version of Darlene Bechel Schnatz's *Louisiana City Parish Index*, at the Ancestry.com website. The information was collected from new and old maps, census records, city directories, and family histories. Each parish is linked from Ancestry.com to other internet pages which provide more detailed information regarding that particular parish. With 1,615 towns listed, it is a comprehensive town index for the entire state. See
https://search.ancestry.com/search/db.aspx?dbid=3666.

Guide to Genealogical Materials in the New Orleans Public Library's Louisiana Division & City Archives. The published version of *Genealogical Materials* is currently out of print but is being updated here in the online version. See
http://nutrias.org/~nopl/guides/genguide/gguide4.htm.

Information on New Orleans City Directories. The first three volumes were business directories for 1805, 1807, and 1809. New Orleans directories of businesses and residents was irregular for several years and include 1811, 1822-1824, 1827, 1830-1838, 1841-1859, 1860-

1866, 1933-1938, 1940-1949, 1952-1958, 1960-1969, 1971-1983, 1985-1988, 1990-2007, and 2009-present. Most of the directories are on microfilm. More information about the city directories is available. See http://nutrias.org/~nopl/info/louinfo/citydir.htm.

Information about the Louisiana Division's service to search through "Records of the Day" newspaper columns. The columns carried reports of births supplied by the New Orleans Board of Health, see http://nutrias.org/~nopl/info/louinfo/births.htm.

Information on Records of Passenger Arrivals at the Port of New Orleans. This webpage identifies the National Archives passenger lists and indexes on microfilm, plus local indexing projects, and other local finding aids: http://nutrias.org/~nopl/info/louinfo/louinfo3.htm.

Information on Naturalization Records in New Orleans. The Louisiana Division has the original naturalization records from the Civil Courts of New Orleans, 1827-1906. Included are certificates of naturalization, declarations of intention to become a citizen (also known as "first papers"), and oaths of applicants and witnesses. The records are included in ninety-seven volumes, most of which contain indexes. Includes records from the criminal courts of New Orleans (1853-1906) and the U.S. District Court of the Eastern District of Louisiana (1813-1929). For details, see http://nutrias.org/~nopl/info/louinfo/louinfo4.htm.

Bibliography
Louisiana Censuses & Substitutes

This bibliography identifies the available censuses and substitutes for Louisiana, beginning with those from the colonial periods:

French and Spanish Colonial Eras: Surviving original manuscripts of colonial French censuses and substitute name lists taken in North America reside in the Archives Nationales in Paris. For the Louisiana area, the earliest are for 1679, and all are available on microfilm. Most have been extracted and published, as noted in the bibliography.
- Original colonial Spanish censuses and name lists are located at the archives in Seville beginning with 1770, also available on microfilm. A number of colonial census compilations have been published for Louisiana areas from a variety of sources, the most impressive being the *Mississippi Valley Mélange, 1723-1791*, compiled by Winston DeVille.
- The Louisiana State Archives in Baton Rouge has name lists from various regions from 1759 to 1812.

Orleans Territory: In its first legislative session of 1806, Orleans Territory authorized a census for that year. Although statistical returns were transmitted to the federal government, there appears to be no name list associated with the census report.

State Censuses: For the purpose of apportioning the state legislature, the constitution of 1812 provided for state censuses to be taken every four years commencing in 1813. It is not known if the law was followed consistently, e.g., if actually conducted in every possible census year, there could have been over 1,200 county name lists generated. Yet, only one (1) has ever been found: the 1833 state census for St. Tammany Parish.
- In 1898, Louisiana adopted the Federal decennial censuses as the means of apportionment of its state legislative districts.

Federal Censuses: The U.S. Federal Census name lists open to the public begin with the 1810 Orleans Territory, followed by Louisiana 1820-1940 (except 1890, like all other states, was lost in a fire in Washington, DC in 1921.
- A complete 1890 census name list for Ascension Parish, Louisiana is one of only two parishes/counties in the U.S. for which a copy was made and survived in the local courthouse.

Census Substitutes: In addition to the local and federal censuses, there are many census substitute name lists that fill out the bibliography. Name lists may include Local Census Records, Parish Court Records, Directories, Parish Histories, State Militia Lists, Tax Lists, Vital Records, and Voter Lists. They begin below in chronological order:

◆ ◆ ◆ ◆ ◆

1679-1803. *Records of the French Superior Court* **[Microfilm & Digital Capture],** from the originals at the Louisiana Historical Center, New Orleans. Filmed by the Genealogical Society of Utah, 1980, 82 rolls, beginning with FHL film #1295659. For a complete list of roll numbers, roll contents, and the digital images for each roll, see the online FHL catalog page for this title: www.familysearch.org/search/catalog/301227.

1679-1804. See *Name Card Index to Records of the French Superior Council, 1679-1803; & Judicial Records of the Spanish Cabildo, 1769-1804* **[Microfilm & Digital Capture],** from the originals at the Louisiana Historical Center, New Orleans. Filmed by the Genealogical Society of Utah, 1981, 9 rolls, beginning with FHL film #1276244 (Abad, Juan – Azurto, Pablo). To access the digital images, see the online FHL catalog:
https://familysearch.org/search/catalog/251081.

1696-1781. *Recensements et Correspondence Général* **[Microfilm],** from the French language originals of the Governor-Generals of La Louisiane Française located at les Archives Nationales, Paris. Includes correspondence, passenger lists, censuses, and land grants during the French administration of Louisiana. Filmed by the Genealogical Society of Utah, 1974, 2 rolls, FHL film #1080001 (1696-1781) & FHL film #1080002 (1706-1732). To see if this microfilm was digitized yet, see the online FHL catalog:
www.familysearch.org/search/catalog/505489.

1699-1732. *The Census Tables for the French Colony of Louisiana from 1699 through 1732* **[Printed Book & Digital Version],** compiled by Charles R. Maduell, first published 1916, reprinted by Genealogical Publishing Co., Inc., Baltimore, 1965, 190 pages. FHL book 976.3. To access the digital version, see the online FHL catalog:
http://search.ancestry.com/search/db.aspx?dbid=48009.

1699-1769. *France's Forgotten Legion, a CD-ROM Publication: Service Records of French Military and Administrative Personnel Stationed in the Mississippi Valley and Gulf Coast Region* **[CD-ROM],** by Carl A. Brasseaux, publ. LSU Press, Baton Rouge, 2000. See FHL CD No. 1400.

1699-1803. *The First Families of Louisiana: An Index to Glenn R. Conrad's 2-Volume Series of 1970* **[Printed Index & Digital Capture],** compiled by Donna Rachal Mills, publ. by Mills Historical Press, 1992, 89 pages, FHL book 976.3 D2c. For access to a digital version of this title, see the FHL catalog page:
https://familysearch.org/search/catalog568/996.

1699-1820. *Early Louisiana Settlers* **[CD-ROM].** This is CD No. 525 produced for the Family Tree Maker (Broderbund) archives in collaboration with Genealogical Publishing Co., Inc., Baltimore, 2000. Contents: *The Canary Islands Migration to Louisiana, 1778-1783: the History and Passenger Lists of the Islenos Volunteer Recruits and their Families,* compiled and written by Sidney Louis Villeré; *The Settlement of the German Coast of Louisiana and the Creoles of German Descent,* by J. Hanno Deiler; *The Census Tables for the French Colony of Louisiana from 1699 through 1732,* compiled and translated by Charles R. Maduell; *Louisiana Census Records, 1810 & 1820;* compiled by Robert Bruce L. Ardoin (vols. I-II); *Gulf Coast Colonials: A Compendium of French Families in early Eighteenth Century Louisiana,* by Winston De Ville: *The New Orleans French, 1720-1733: A Collection of Marriage Records Relating to the First Colonists of the Louisiana Province,* by Winston De Ville; *Old Families of Louisiana,* by Stanley Clisby Arthur, editor and compiler, George Campbell Huchet de Kernion, collaborator and historian; *Louisiana Troops, 1720-1770,* by Winston De Ville; *Louisiana Colonials: Soldiers and Vagabonds,* translated and compiled by Winston De Ville; and *Louisiana Soldiers in the War of 1812;* by Marion John Bennett Pierson. See FHL CD No. 9, part 525.

1699-1820. *Old Louisiana Plantation Homes and Family Trees* **[Online Database],** digitized and OCR indexed at the Ancestry.com website. Source: Seebold, Herman de Bachellé, *Old Louisiana Plantation Homes and Family Trees,* c1941. Use the "Browse this Collection" feature to see the table of contents for chapters, locations, and family names. This database has 972 pages. See
https://search.ancestry.com/search/db.aspx?dbid=24424.

1699-1860. *Databases for the Study of Afro-Louisiana History and Genealogy* **[CD-ROM],** compiled by Gwendolyn Midlo Hall, published by Louisiana State University, Baton Rouge, LA, 2000. Contains computerized information from original manuscript sources, including Louisiana slave database 1719-1820, Louisiana free database 1720-1820, Louisiana censuses 1699-1860, and censuses 1784-1850 for New Orleans, Louisiana; Pensacola, Florida; and Mobile, Alabama. See FHL CD No. 1380.

1700s-2000s. *Louisiana GenWeb Archives* **[Online Databases],** name lists are available for all 64 Louisiana parishes. Typical local records include Bibles, Biographies, Cemeteries, Censuses, Court, Death, Deeds, Directories, Histories, Marriages, Military, Newspapers, Obituaries, Photos, Schools, Tax Lists, Wills, and more. Access each parish site at the LAGenWeb website. See
http://sites.rootsweb.com/~lagenweb.

1700s–2000s. *Louisiana Collection Catalog at MyHeritage.com* **[Online Database],** 15 collections with 605,385 records. Databases include censuses, directories, family histories, town histories, military rosters, college/school year books, and more. This is a subscription site, but all initial searches are free. A free search can be done for a name, place, year, or keyword: www.myheritage.com/records/Louisiana/all-records.

1700s-2000s. *Linkpendium – Louisiana: Family History & Genealogy, Census, Birth, Marriage, Death Vital Records & More* **[Online Database].** Linkpendium is a portal to genealogical resources on the Internet. The Louisiana databases are organized by Statewide Resources (531 databases), Independent Cities, Renamed Counties, Discontinued Counties (8), Acadia Parish (265), Allen Parish (123), Ascension Parish (252), Assumption Parish (230), Avoyelles Parish (271), Beauregard Parish (123), Bienville Parish (308), Bossier Parish (241), Caddo Parish (751), Calcasieu Parish (421), Caldwell Parish (199), Cameron Parish (111), Catahoula Parish (216), Claiborne Parish (380), Concordia Parish (175), De Soto Parish (341), East Baton Rouge Parish (598), East Carroll Parish (170), East Feliciana Parish (306), Evangeline Parish (125), Franklin Parish (181), Grant Parish (242), Iberia Parish (302), Iberville Parish (253), Jackson Parish (201), Jefferson Davis Parish (114), Jefferson Parish (215), La Salle Parish (144), Lafayette Parish (359), Lafourche Parish (281), Lincoln Parish (196), Livingston Parish (196), Madison Parish (150), Morehouse Parish (191), Natchitoches Parish (473), Orleans Parish (3,121), Ouachita Parish (301), Plaquemines Parish (208), Pointe Coupee Parish (217), Rapides Parish (584), Red River Parish (159), Richland Parish (179), Sabine Parish (282), Saint Bernard Parish (146), Saint Charles Parish (160), Saint Helena Parish (181), Saint James Parish (222), Saint John the Baptist Parish (188), Saint Landry Parish (549), Saint Martin Parish (347), Saint Mary Parish (339), Saint Tammany Parish (205), Tangipahoa Parish (232), Tensas Parish (162), Terrebonne Parish (207), Union Parish (291), Vermilion Parish (252), Vernon Parish (204), Washington Parish (188), Webster Parish (213), West Baton Rouge Parish (194), West Carroll Parish (160), West Feliciana Parish (210), and Winn Parish (560). See www.linkpendium.com/la-genealogy.

1706-1741. See **"Early Census Tables, 1706-1741, Notes in French" [Printed Article],** in *Louisiana Historical Society Publications* (Louisiana Historical Society, New Orleans, LA), Vol. 5 (1911).

1714-1800. *English Language Summaries of the Records of the French Superior Council and the Judicial Records of the Spanish Cabildo* **[Microfilm & Digital Capture],** from the originals at the Louisiana Historical Center, New Orleans. This was a WPA project to provide translations into English of the French and Spanish records. Filmed by the Genealogical Society of Utah, 1981, 7 rolls, beginning with FHL film #1292541 (Summaries, 1714-1730). To access the digital images, see the online FHL catalog: www.familysearch.org/search/catalog/3625.

1718-1724. *Louisiane Passages* **[Microfilm & Digital Capture],** from the originals at the Louisiana Historical Center, Louisiana State Museum, New Orleans. Includes lists of passengers arriving in Louisiana. Text in French. Filmed by the Genealogical Society of Utah, 1981, 1 roll, FHL film #1305374. To access the digital images, see the online FHL catalog: www.familysearch.org/search/catalog/283283.
- See also, *Passage Index, Louisiana, 1718-1724* **[Microfilm & Digital Capture],** from the originals at the Louisiana State Museum in New Orleans. Text in French. Index to arrivals by ship in Louisiana. Filmed by the museum, 1980, 2 rolls, FHL film # 1292185 (Index, A-L) & FHL film #1292296 (Index, L-Z). To access the digital images, see the online FHL catalog: www.familysearch.org/search/catalog/740126.

1718-1900. *Marriage Records Index and Contracts, Louisiana* **[Microfilm & Digital Capture],** from the originals at the State Museum of New Orleans, a card file index of marriages records and contracts in various newspapers in Louisiana. Filmed by the museum, 1980, 1 roll, FHL film #1292185. To access the digital images, see the online FHL catalog: www.familysearch.org/search/catalog/740124.

1718-1925. *Louisiana, Marriages* **[Online Database],** indexed at the Ancestry.com website. From the original database by Hunting For Bears, this database is an index to over 560,000 individuals who were married in Louisiana. See http://search.ancestry.com/search/db.aspx?dbid=7837.

1719-1720. *Louisiana Colonials: Soldiers and Vagabonds* **[Printed Book],** by Winston De Ville. Descriptive list for 1719-1720, from originals in the Archives des Colonies, Paris. Publ. Mobile, AL, 1963, FHL book 976.3 M23d.

1719-1820. *Louisiana, Slave Records* **[Online Database],** indexed at the Ancestry.com website. Original data: Hall, Gwendolyn Midlo, compiler, *Afro-Louisiana History and Genealogy, 1719-1820.* This database is a compilation of information on over 100,000 slaves who came to Louisiana between 1719 and 1820. These descriptions of slaves were extracted from documents and records located in various places throughout Louisiana, as well as from some archives located in Texas, France, and Spain. Information in this database includes name of individual, name of master,

gender, race, birthplace, age, family relationships including mate and children, selling information such as name of seller, name of buyer, selling currency, and selling value, as well as retrieval information for the original document in which this information was found. Other interesting information relating to the individual's skill or trade, personality, and involvement in running away or conspiracies against slavery, if owner from a free person of African descent, and other interesting, comments may be provided. This database has 100,666 records. See
http://search.ancestry.com/search/db.aspx?dbid=7383.

1719-1820. *Louisiana Freed Slave Records* **[Online Database],** indexed at the Ancestry.com website. Original data: Hall, Gwendolyn Midlo, compiler, *Afro-Louisiana History and Genealogy, 1719-1820.* This database is a compilation of information on over four thousand slaves from Louisiana who were involved in manumission (the formal emancipation from slavery) between 1719 and 1820. The information provided in this database regards the manumissions of these slaves and was extracted from documents and records located in various places throughout Louisiana, as well as from some archives located in Texas, France, and Spain. Information contained in this database includes the means of manumission, the relationship of the freer to the freed when a third party bought the slave in order to free him, the name of the third party freer, reasons for manumission, whether a payment was made in order to free the slave and if so, how much it was, the conditions imposed in order to free the slave, and an indication as to whether the slave was likely actually freed. It also provides information on family relationships among the freed slaves, racial categories, ages, genders, birthplaces of mothers of slaves involved in manumission, and indications if an individual was possibly freed by a white father. This database has 4,064 records. See
http://search.ancestry.com/search/db.aspx?dbid=7382.

1720-1733. *The New Orleans French* **[Online Database],** digitized and OCR indexed at the Ancestry.com website. From the book, *The New Orleans French: A Collection of Marriage Records Relating to the First Colonists of the Louisiana Province,* by Winston De Ville. See
http://search.ancestry.com/search/db.aspx?dbid=48051.

1720-1763. *Marriage Contracts of French Colonial Louisiana* **[Online Database],** from the book, same title, by Henry Plauché Dart, New Orleans, 1934. Digitized and OCR indexed at the Ancestry.com website. This database has 17 pages:
https://search.ancestry.com/search/db.aspx?dbid=29706.

1720-1770. *Louisiana Troops* **[Online Database],** digitized and OCR indexed at the Ancestry.com website. From Winston De Ville's book, same title, listing French soldiers of 18th-century Louisiana, compiled from original documents in the Library of Congress. This database has 114 pages. See
http://search.ancestry.com/search/db.aspx?dbid=48043.

1721. "Census, 1721, Workers in Labor Force" **[Printed Article],** in *Louisiana Genealogical Register* (Louisiana Genealogical & Historical Society), Vol. 27, No. 2 (Jun 1980).

1722. *An Early Area Census in Louisiana, West Feliciana Parish, Louisiana, May 13, 1722* **[Online Database],** indexed at the USGenWeb site for West Feliciana Parish LA. See
http://files.usgwarchives.net/la/pointecoupee/census/1722cens.txt.

1722-1803 *Natchitoches Colonials: Censuses, Military Rolls, and Tax Lists* **[Printed Book],** Vol. 5 of Cane River Creole Series, by Elizabeth Shown Mills, published by Adams Press, Chicago, 1981, 161 pages. This is a very good listing of colonial name lists for the areas of Louisiana north and west of New Orleans. See FHL book 976.365 X2.

1722-1803. *German Ancestors and Patriots of Louisiana* **[Printed Book],** by Leroy E. Willie. Includes 1724 census & other name lists. FHL book 976.3 D2w.

1723-1791. *Mississippi Valley Mélange: a Collection of Notes and Documents for the Genealogy and History of the Province of Louisiana and the Territory of Orleans* **[Printed Book],** compiled by Winston De Ville, 3 vols., publ. Ville Platte & Baton Rouge, LA, 1996-2009. Includes indexes. **Vol. 1 includes:** *Illinois church records, 1723-1724; the French fort in the Tombigbee, 1729; on the founding of Pointe Coupée Post, 1729-1732; French troops of Illinois in 1752; Fuselier de la Claire and the lands of Attakapas and Opelousas in 1770; the census of Opelousas Post, 1774; Joachin de Ortega on the Texas Frontier--the Galvez correspondence of 1779; building Fort Miró in the Ouachita Valley of Spanish Louisiana, 1790-1791; slave owners of Pointe Coupée & False River in 1795; Metairie, Louisiana census of 1796; Bayou Sarah*

settlers in 1797; a Rapides Post petition of 1797 with 38 transcribed signatures; Southwest Louisiana ranchers, a ca. 1810 tax list. **Vol. 2 includes:** knighthood in colonial Louisiana; Juchereau de St. Denys and the Order of St. Louis; Louisiana officers in 1740—the Bienville recommendations; French troops in New Orleans, 1745; land owners below New Orleans in 1751; Acadians in Philadelphia; a prospective first militia of Attakapas Post—the roll of 1773; the D'Hauterive land grant of 1775—aristocratic perquisite in southwest Louisiana; Galvez rosters of 1779—soldier selection at the German and Acadian coasts during the American Revolution; southwest Louisiana militiamen during the American Revolution—the rosters of Attakapas and Opelousas posts in 1780; Louisiana loyalists in 1781; of clavinette and violin in colonial Louisiana—questions on Acadian music in 1785; Attakapas Post petitioners of 1791—an Acadian and Creole defense of a commandant; the greening of New Orleans in 1792—Governor Carondelet as environmentalist; lost in the Latin South—a petition of some Anglo-Americans, ca. 1792; turmoil in Spanish Louisiana—a public notice of 1793. **Vol. 3 includes:** *The Bermudez Manuscript of 1612; Louisiana officers in 1714; Military deserters of Louisiana in 1716; Constructing a future cathedral, 1724; A Natchitoches narrative of 1732; Four letters of 1734; on the family Fontenette; Anglo-Americans in British West Florida; The loyalist military in colonial Mississippi, 1779; Terre aux Boeufs militia men in 1779; Anglo-Americans in early Mobile, 1780; Public balls of New Orleans in 1792; the Ursuline convent in 1795;* and *Militia officers of Orleans Territory in 1808.* **Vol. 4 includes:** Bienville's cadets - The Order of St. Louis - Indians and Louisiana forts in 1732 - French troops in the province of Louisiana, 1758 - Naval officers of the Company of the Indies, 1769 - On obtaining French military service records - Opelousas District papers, 1777-1800 - Oaths of allegiance at Natchez, 1787 - St. Landry Catholic church of Opelousas, building materials for the 1827-1828 construction - Some petitions for Spanish land grants at Rapides Post 1800-1801. **Vol. 5 includes:** Colonial naval infantry ranks - French Colonial administration to 1763 - Louisiana officers & workers, 1715-1716 - The soldiers of Plantin's Company (1723-1730) - The 1759 log of personnel transfers - Observations on translations. **Vol. 6 includes:** Duplessis' Report on Conditions in Louisiana: 1758; Louisiana Officers in 1759; Denis Braud: Louisiana's First Publisher; Louisiana's Half-Pay Officers in 1769; De Mezière's Misery – evidence that he did not die from falling off a horse; General Inventory of the Property Belonging to the King…at Natchitoches; a very rare ship-list from Philadelphia to New Orleans in 1788, with many well-known American family members named, and their ages; a 1792 letter from General James Wilkinson to Governor Gayoso de Lemos; the 1792 origin of Juschereau de St. Denys' "painted leg"; a long letter of 1796 from "the ladies of Illinois" complaining of new immigrants; Babé, Free Negress vs Widow Lebleu: A Struggle for Freedom in Colonial Louisiana; Independence and Bastille Days in Territorial Louisiana; Jean Laffite's Crew in 1813.
See FHL book 976.3 D2de, vol. 1-5.

1724. "**1724 German Coast Census**" **[Printed Article & Digital Version],** in *Bean Stalk* (Southern Bean Association, Norman, OK), Vol. 35, Nos. 1 & 2 (Mar – June 2006). For access to a digital version of this article, see the online FHL catalog page: https://familysearch.org/search/catalog/1842321.

1724-1837. ***Guide to the Louisiana Miscellany Collection*** **[Printed Book],** compiled, translated, and edited by Judy Riffel, published Comité des Archives de la Louisiane, Baton Rouge, LA, 2006, 248 pages. From intro: "Abstracts of documents containing genealogical information found in the Louisiana section of Records of the states of the United States (four reels of microfilm) and Louisiana miscellany 1724-1837 (five reels of microfilm). Includes "Baton Rouge district land concessions, 1785-1798, in one volume, and regulations concerning general police, June 1795, also in one volume. Other materials include Jean-Baptiste Bénard de la Harpe's journal historique, 1724; documents on French and Spanish management of Louisiana, 1731-1799; manuscripts of 1780 on Louisiana and Florida; surveyors' records, including correspondence of François Gonsolin, Louis LeBlanc, Carlos Laveau Trudeau, on the Attakapas district; a record book of Spanish land grants, 1785-1799, of 186 pages; a surveyor's notebook, 1795-1797; thirty-six manuscript plats for land grants located mostly in the Baton Rouge district; vital statistics from a Bible and other sources; and a few papers each for Bernardo de Gálvez, 1776-1786, and Manuel Gayoso de Lemos, 1794-1797; correspondence of American and French officials relating to the purchase of Louisiana, 1803-1804 … " See FHL book 976.3 A3rj.

1726. "**Residents, 1726, Natchitoches Post**" **[Printed Article],** in *Louisiana Genealogical Register* (Louisiana Genealogical & Historical Society, Baton Rouge, LA), Vol. 8, No. 3 (Sep 1961).

1728. "**Directory of New Orleans Inhabitants, 1728**" **[Printed Article],** in *Louisiana Genealogical Register* (Louisiana Genealogical & Historical Society, Baton Rouge, LA), Vol. 6, No. 4 (Aug 1959).

1728-1850. *Louisiana, Compiled Marriages* [Online Database], indexed at the Ancestry.com website. Source: Jordan R. Dodd, Early American Marriages: Louisiana to 1850, publ. Precision Indexing, Bountiful, UT, 1997. Each index record includes the Name, Spouse, Marriage date, and Marriage County/Parish. This database has 29,692 records. See
https://search.ancestry.com/search/db.aspx?dbid=2090.

1731 Ursuline Orphanage, New Orleans, Louisiana [Online Database], indexed at the USGenWeb site for Orleans Parish LA. See
http://files.usgwarchives.net/la/orleans/history/schools/orphans.txt.

1734-1850. *Louisiana Marriages to 1850* [Online Database], indexed at the Ancestry.com website. Originally compiled by Jordan Dodd, Liahona Research, acquired by Ancestry.com in 1997. Each entry includes a groom, bride, marriage date, and parish. The original database cited no sources, and this index should be used to find a name and parish to search the original records for verification. This database has 29,692 names. See
http://search.ancestry.com/search/db.aspx?dbid=2090.

1734-1925. *Louisiana, Marriages* [Online Database], indexed at the Ancestry.com website. Data was originally compiled for the Hunting For Bears database, acquired by Ancestry in 2004. In spite of the title date, inclusive dates begin with 1734 for Orleans Parish. Not all Louisiana parishes are represented - see the Ancestry site for a list of parishes included, and inclusive dates of marriages. See
http://search.ancestry.com/search/db.aspx?dbid=7837.

1745. *French Troops in the Mississippi Valley and on the Gulf Coast, 1745* [Printed Book], by Winston De Ville, publ. Ville Platte, LA, 1986, 42 pages, FHL book 976.3 M2dvw.

1745. *Pointe Coupee 1745 Census* [Online Database], indexed at the LouisianaLineage.com site:
http://louisianalineage.com/pc1745cen.htm.

1749. See "German Coast of LA, 1749: Reconstructed Families" [Printed Article] in *Louisiana Genealogical Register* (Louisiana Genealogical and Historical Society, Baton Rouge, LA), Vol. 29, No. 4 (Dec 1982).

1755-1800. *The Cajuns: From Acadia to Louisiana* [Printed Book], by William Faulkner Ruston, publ. Farrar, Straus and Giroux, New York, 1979, 342 pages, FHL book 976.3 F2ru.

1756-1984. *Louisiana, Wills and Probate Records* [Online Database], digitized and indexed at the Ancestry.com website. Source: Ancestry extractions from LA County; District and Probate Courts. Probate records include Wills, Letters of Administration, Inventories, Distributions and Accounting, Bonds, and Guardianships. Each index record includes: Name, Probate date, Probate place, Inferred death year, Inferred death place, Case number, and Item description. Cases with multiple pages have a Table of Contents showing the categories and numbers of papers. This database has 222,489 records. See
https://search.ancestry.com/search/db.aspx?dbid=9067.

1758-1796. *Some Late Eighteenth Century Louisianans* [Printed Book & Digital Version], by Jacqueline K. Voorhies, publ. Lafayette, LA, 1973, 613 pages, see FHL book 976.3 X2vjk. The book has three main sections: part I, census records of the inhabitants of the colony; part II, militias; part III, Acadians. To access the digital version, see the online FHL catalog:
www.familysearch.org/search/catalog/2623091.

1759-1813. *Natchez Trace Collection, Provincial and Territorial Records* [Microfilm], from the originals at the Center for American History, University of Texas at Austin. From the description on the first roll: "The Provincial and Territorial Records of the Natchez Trace Collection are mainly civil records of the various jurisdictions of colonial Louisiana, Mississippi, and adjacent areas from the middle of the eighteenth century through 1812, the year that Louisiana officially entered the Union as the eighteenth state. During that period Louisiana and part of Mississippi were governed as a colonial province or territory of France, Spain, and finally the westward-expanding United States. As the United States took control of these jurisdictions, both France and Spain removed their administrative records but left most of the civil records pertaining to property and personal matters of the region's inhabitants." Within the original papers are the following name lists: 1759-1812 Pointe Coupe, 1764, 1791, 1796, 1798 Natchitoches, 1767-1794 New Orleans, 1768 German Coast (Allemant), 1772 Natchez, 1772-1810; Iberville, 1784-1787 Missouri, 1793-1796 Rapides, 1793-1812

Feliciana &West Feliciana, 1794-1812 New Orleans, 1777-1811 Opelousas, 1777 Attakapas, 1783-1812 Natchez, 1783-1806 Avoyelles, 1798-1812 Baton Rouge & East Baton Rouge, 1803-1812 Concordia, 1804-1812 St. Helena, 1807, 1811 West Florida, 1810 Lafourche, and 1812 Acadia. Filmed by the Univ. of TX, 1997, 10 rolls, beginning with the FHL film #2261388 (Louisiana jurisdictions). To see if this microfilm was digitized yet, see the FHL catalog: https://familysearch.org/search/catalog/1141305.

- See also, *Calendar of the Natchez Trace Collection, Provincial & Territorial Documents, 1759-1813* [Printed Book], compiled by Judy Riffel, a description of the Natchez Trace Collection. From the intro: "...the documents are primarily from the colonial and territorial period of Louisiana and Mississippi and include civil records such as marriage contracts, conveyances, probates, and land surveys. Other types of documents such as receipts, letters, and journals were also found. The order of the entries in this calendar corresponds to the order in which the documents appear on the microfilm, which includes a full-name index. Publ. Comité des Archives de la Louisiane, Baton Rouge, LA, 1999, 217 pages, FHL book 976.R2.

- See also, *Inside the Natchez Trace Collection: New Sources for Southern History* [Printed Book], by Katherine J. Adams and Lewis L. Gould, University of Texas at Austin, Center for American History. Publ. LSU Press, Baton Rouge, LA, 1999, 207 pages, FHL book 976.3 H29ak.

1765-1803. *The Founding of New Acadia: The Beginnings of Acadian Life in Louisiana* [Printed Book], by Carl A. Brasseaux, publ. LSU Press, Baton Rouge, LA, 1987, 229 pages, FHL book 976.3 F2b.

1765-1803. *French, Cajun, Creole, Houma: A Primer on Francophone Louisiana* [Printed Book], by Carl A. Brasseaux, publ. LSU Press, Baton Rouge, LA, 2005, 159 pages, FHL book 976.3 H2bcr.

1766. "1766 Spanish Census, Pointe Coupee Parish, Louisiana" [Printed Article], in *Louisiana Genealogical Register* (Louisiana Genealogical & Historical Society, Baton Rouge, LA), Vol. 7, No. 3 (Sep 1960); and Vol. 7, No. 4 (Dec 1960).

1766, 1769, 1777. *Louisiana's Acadian Coast Census Index: With Annotations* [CD-ROM], by Phoebe Chauvin Morrison. CD-ROM Publication, published Houma, LA, 2001.

Index indicates both husbands and wives by family numbers, with annotated census records citing the sources of location: Fam. No., Name, Born, Married, Spouse, Parents, & Notes. See FHL CD-ROM no. 684.

1767. "Acadian Records, St. Gabriel, 1767" [Printed Article], in *New Orleans Genesis* (Genealogical Research Society of New Orleans), Vol. 10, No. 39 (Jun 1971).

1767-1892. *Bound Records of the General Land Office Relating to Private Land Claims in Louisiana* [Microfilm & Digital Capture], from the originals at the National Archives, Washington, DC. Text in English, French and Spanish. See beginning of film for a complete detailed explanation of information contain herein. These records relate to claims in Louisiana. Some of them pertain to land outside the present State of Louisiana, including land in Alabama, Mississippi, and Missouri. Private land claims are those based on grants, purchases, or settlements that took place before the United States acquired sovereignty over the land. Those in Louisiana are based on land transactions made by the French and Spanish governments before 1803. Filmed by the National Archives, series M1382, 8 rolls, beginning with FHL film #1605564. For a complete list of roll numbers, roll contents, and the digital images of each roll, see the online FHL catalog page for this title: www.familysearch.org/search/catalog/362788.

1768-1899. *Ascension Parish, Louisiana: Computer Indexed Marriage Records* [Printed Book], by Nicolas Russell Murray, publ. Hunting For Bears, Hammond, LA, 1975, 132 pages, FHL book 976.319 V22m.

1769-1785. *The Cabildo Records of New Orleans: An Index to Abstracts in the Louisiana Historical Quarterly* [Printed Book], by Verda Jenkins Ruff, publ. Provincial Press, Ville Platte, LA, 1987, 79 pages, FHL book 976.335 P22r.

1769-1800. *Rapides Post on Red River: Census and Military Documents for Central Louisiana* [Printed Book], by Winston DeVille, publ. Ville Platte, LA, 1985, 47 pages, FHL book 976.369 X2d.

1769-1804. See *Judicial Records, Louisiana Province, Cabildo* [Microfilm & Digital Capture], from the originals at the Louisiana Historical Center, New Orleans. Text in Spanish, English & French. Includes all manner of court records, especially land transactions and settlements of debts. Cabildo was the

Spanish governmental organization for the province of Louisiana established in 1769 and superseding the French Superior Council. Filmed by the Genealogical Society of Utah, 1979-1980, 239 rolls, beginning with FHL film #103128. For a complete list of roll numbers, roll contents, and the digital images of each roll, see the online FHL Catalog page for this title:
www.familysearch.org/search/catalog/207994.

1770-1957. *Louisiana, Ascension Parish, Index of Conveyances* **[Online Database],** indexed at FamilySearch.org. Conveyances document the transfer of land from one party to another. This database has 178,953 records, see
www.familysearch.org/search/collection/3019665.

1770. "Militia Lists, Acadian Coast, 1770" **[Printed Article],** in *Louisiana Genealogical Register* (Louisiana Genealogical & Historical Society, Baton Rouge, LA), Vol. 9, No. 2 (Jun 1962).

1770. *Opelousas Militia Muster Roll, St. Landry Parish, Louisiana* **[Online Database],** indexed at the USGenWeb site for St. Landry Parish LA. See
http://files.usgwarchives.net/la/stlandry/military/1770must.txt.

1770-1789. *Louisiana Census and Militia Lists, Volume I : German Coast, New Orleans, Below New Orleans and Lafourche* **[Printed Book & Microfiche],** from the book compiled, translated and edited by Albert J. Robichaux, Jr., original published: Harvey, LA, 1973, 170 pages. Census records acquired from the Papeles Procedentes de Cuba deposited in the General Archives de Indies in Seville, Spain. Includes: 1770 militia lists of New Orleans; 1777 general census of the city of New Orleans; 1770 militia of the German Coast; 1784 general census of the second German Coast; 1785 militia list of St. Charles Parish; 1770 general census below New Orleans; 1789 general census of Lafourche. Includes index. See FHL book 976.3 X2pr. Filmed by the Genealogical Society of Utah, 1991, FHL microfiche #6088510.

1770-1798. *Colonial Settlers Along Bayou Lafourche: Louisiana Census Records* **[Printed Book],** compiled, translated and edited by Albert J. Robichaux, taken from the Papeles Procedentes de Cuba deposited in the General Archives de Indies in Seville, Spain. Includes index. Contents: 1770 Census of the Acadian inhabitants of the Parish of Ascension; 1777 Census of the Parish of Ascension of Lafourche des Chetimachas; 1788 Census of the inhabitants established in Lafourche; 1795 Census of habitants of the Bayou of Valenzuela; 1797 General census of the habitants of Valenzuela in Lafourche; 1798 General census of the inhabitants of Lafourche; and 1791 Census of Lafourche des Chetimachas. publ. Harvey, LA, 1974, 219 pages, FHL book 976.3 X2pra. See also microfilm, FHL film #1597854; and microfiche, FHL fiche #6088511.

1770-1804. *Marriage Contracts, Wills and Testaments of the Spanish Colonial Period in New Orleans* **[Printed Book],** compiled and indexed by Charles R. Maduell, Jr., publ. New Orleans, 1969, FHL book 976.335/N1 V25mc.

1773-1785. *The Acadian Exiles in Chatellerault* **[Printed Book],** by Albert J. Robichaux, Publ. Herbert Pub., Eunice, LA, 190 pages, FHL book 944.63/C1 D2r.

1773-1963. *Louisiana, Ascension Parish, Index of Marriages* **[Online Database],** indexed at FamilySearch.org. This database has 39,839 records, see www.familysearch.org/search/collection/3021712.

1776. *Opelousas Militia Muster Roll, St. Landry Parish, Louisiana* **[Online Database],** indexed at the USGenWeb site for St. Landry Parish LA. See
http://files.usgwarchives.net/la/stlandry/military/1776must.txt.

1777. "New Orleans Census" **[Printed Article],** in *New Orleans Genesis* (Genealogical Research Society of New Orleans), Vol. 21, No. 81 (Jan 1982).

1777. *Point Coupee Militia, Pointe Coupee Parish, Louisiana* **[Online Database],** indexed at the USGenWeb site for Pointe Coupee Parish LA, See
http://files.usgwarchives.net/la/pointecoupee/military/1777arm.txt.

1778-1783. *The Canary Islands Migration to Louisiana* **[Online Database],** digitized and OCR indexed at the Ancestry.com website. From the book, *The History and Passenger Lists of the Islenos Volunteer Recruits and Their Families,* by Sidney L. Villeré. This database has 105 pages. See
http://search.ancestry.com/search/db.aspx?dbid=48007.

1778-1783. *The Canary Islanders of Louisiana* **[Printed Book],** by Gilbert C. Din, publ. LSU Press, Baton Rouge, LA, 256 pages, FHL book 976.3 F2d.

1779. *The Acadian Coast in 1779: Settlers of Cabanocey and La Fourche in the Spanish Province of Louisiana During the American Revolution* **[Printed Book],** by Winston De Ville, pub. 1993, Ville Platte, LA. Includes index. FHL book 976.3 X29d.

1781-1797. *Anglo-Americans in Spanish Archives: Lists of Anglo-American Settlers in the Spanish Colonies of America; A Finding Aid* **[Printed Book],** by Lawrence H. Feldman. Published by Genealogical Publishing Co., Inc., 1991, 349 pages. Abstracted from original census documents, includes genealogical data about individuals and families who settled in the French territories of Louisiana and the Floridas after they came under Spanish rule in 1766. Includes an index of personal names. FHL book 973 X2fe.

1785 List of Acadians Arriving in Louisiana

The first British-imposed deportations of French Acadians began in 1755, many of them transported back to France. But the Acadians had lived in North America for generations, intermarried with the natives, and had lost many of their family ties in France. Soon after the arrival of the first Acadians near New Orleans in early 1765, a communication began between the two groups, with an encouragement to the deposed Acadians back in France to come to Louisiana. Three bibliographic references to the list of 1,600 Acadians who arrived in New Orleans in 1785 are shown below.

1784-1785. *Acadian Emigrants to Louisiana* **[Microfilm & Digital Capture],** from the originals at the Louisiana Historical Center, New Orleans. Text in French. Filmed by the Genealogical Society of Utah, 1981, 1 roll, FHL film #1305383. For access to a digital version of this title, see the online FHL catalog page: **https://familysearch.org/search/catalog/248803.** (Source of illustration above).

1785. See *De Nantes à la Louisiane: en 1785, 1600 Acadiens quittent le vieux continent, à destination de la Nouvelle-Orléans: l'histoire de l'Acadie, l'odyssée d'un peuple exilé* **[Printed Book]**, by Gérard-Marc Braud. Covers the history of Acadia and those who took refuge in France after the English deported them in 1755 from what is now eastern Canada. It focuses on the 1,600 Acadians who left Nantes, France for New Orleans in 1785 and settled in various areas of Louisiana. Publ. Quest Editions, Nantes, France, 1994, 156 pages, FHL book 976.3 W2b.

1785. See *The Crew and Passenger Registration Lists of the Seven Acadian Expeditions of 1785: A Listing by Family Groups of the Refugee Acadians Who Migrated From France to Spanish Louisiana in 1785* **[Printed Book]**, compiled and edited by Milton P. Rieder, Jr. and Norma Gaudet Rieder, Publ. Metairie, LA, 1965, 103 pages, FHL book 976.3 W3r.

1781. "Census and Tax List for Church at Attakapas, 1781" [Printed Article], in *Attakapas Gazette* (Attakapas Historical Association, Lafayette, LA), Vol. 20, No. 1 (Spring 1985).

"1782 Census, Baton Rouge" [Printed Article], in *Louisiana Genealogical Register* (Louisiana Genealogical & Historical Society), Vol. 8, No. 4 (Dec 1961).

1782, 1786 & 1793. *Baton Rouge & New Feliciana: Census Reports for Louisiana's Florida Parishes* [Printed Book], by Albert J. Tate and Winston De Ville, publ. by Provincial Press, Lafayette, LA, 2000, 90 pages. Louisiana's "Florida Parishes" include the following parishes of today: East Baton Rouge, West Feliciana, East Feliciana, St. Helena, Livingston, Tangipahoa, Washington and St. Tammany. See FHL book 976.3 X2t.

1782-1816. *Spanish West Florida, Archives of the Spanish Government* [Online Database], digitized and indexed at the Ancestry.com website. Source: National Archives microfilm T1116. This collection consists of transcribed and translated records of the Spanish Empire related to the Spanish province of West Florida. Today, this region encompasses the panhandle of the state of Florida, the southernmost parts of the states of Mississippi and Alabama, and the Florida Parishes of the state of Louisiana (the area east of the Mississippi River and north of Lakes Pontchartrain and Maurepas). Included are records related to property sales, mortgages, inventories and assessments, money lending and debt settlements, wills and probates, inquests, and records related to slavery in Spanish West Florida. This database has 9,202 records. See https://search.ancestry.com/search/db.aspx?dbid=2454.

1784. *Valenzuela in the Province of Louisiana: A Census of 1784* [Printed Book], by Winston De Ville, publ. 1987, LA. The settlers were natives of the Canary Islands who arrived between 1778 and 1783. Includes surname index. FHL book 976.3 A1 no. 56.

1785 Census of Avoyelles Post, Avoyelles Parish, Louisiana [Online Database], indexed at the USGenWeb site for Avoyelles Parish LA. See http://files.usgwarchives.net/la/avoyelles/census/avoy1785.txt.

1785. *Spanish Baton Rouge Census of 1786* [Online Database], indexed at the USGenWeb site for East Baton Rouge Parish LA. See http://files.usgwarchives.net/la/eastbatonrouge/census/span1786.txt.

1785. See *Opelousas Militia 1785 Muster Roll, St. Landry Parish, Louisiana* [Online Database], indexed at the USGenWeb site for St. Landry Parish LA. See http://files.usgwarchives.net/la/stlandry/military/1785must.txt.

1788 Militia List, Post of Rapide, Rapides Parish, Louisiana [Online Database], indexed at the USGenWeb site for Rapides Parish LA. See http://files.usgwarchives.net/la/rapides/military/rapi1788.txt.

1789-1841. See *Index of New Orleans Confirmations, 1789-1841* [Printed Book], by Donald J Hebert, publ. Claitor's, Baton Rouge, LA, 1984, 119 pages, FHL book 976.3 K2f.

1790 Census Index, Miscellaneous Sources [Printed Book], a census substitute compiled from tax lists, "Vol. 13, Bicentennial Edition" is an attempt to replace the lost 1790 censuses with tax records from CA, FL, IL, LA, MS, OH, & NJ, edited by Ronald Vern Jackson, publ. Accelerated Indexing Systems, North Salt Lake, UT, 1990, FHL book 973 X22j. **Note:** Name lists for the time of the 1790 federal census were undoubtabley used here, but of the seven states mentioned, only New Jersey had a "lost" 1790 census, the other states never had a 1790 census taken. Various name lists from Louisiana places were presumably included in the list.

1790. See "Census of the Post of Ouachita, 1790" [Printed Article], in *New Orleans Genesis* (Genealogical Research Society of New Orleans), Vol. 20, No. 77 (Jan 1981).

1790-1791. *The Natchez Ledgers, 1790-1791: A Finding-Aid for Anglo-Americans in Pre-Territorial Mississippi* [Printed Book], compiled by Winston De Ville, publ. Ville Platte, LA, 1994, 89 pages. FHL book 976.2 R49d.

1790-1804. See *Lawsuits, Court of Louisiana, 1790-1804; Book No. 4078* [Microfilm & Digital Capture], from originals at the New Orleans Public Library. Text in French and Spanish with synopsis in English. Filmed by the Genealogical Society of Utah, 1972, 1 roll, FHL film #906355. To access the digital images, see the online FHL catalog: www.familysearch.org/search/catalog/299920.

1790-1904 Birth Indexes, Orleans Parish, Louisiana [Online Database], extracted from the State Archives Birth Index. Indexed at the USGenWeb site for Orleans Parish LA. See www.usgwarchives.net/la/orleans/birth-index.htm.

1790-1915. *New Orleans, Louisiana, Birth Records Index* **[Online Database],** indexed at the Ancestry.com website. Source: LA State Archives, Vital Records Indices. Each index record includes: Name, Birth date, Birthplace, Father, and Mother. This database has 1,082,267 records. See
https://search.ancestry.com/search/db.aspx?dbid=6587.

1791 Colonial Spanish Census of New Orleans **[Printed Book],** An English translation, made by the City Archives Department, is filed under call number AA840, New Orleans Public Library. The census is indexed in *New Orleans Genesis,* vol. 1; the original index to the census is housed at the Louisiana State Museum. This census, dated November 6, 1791, is arranged by street of residence of the enumerated individuals, apparently the heads of households. In addition to the named individuals, each entry also records the numbers of other members of the household by category as follows: white men, white women, free men of mixed blood, free women of mixed blood, free negro men, free negro women, male slaves of mixed blood, female slaves of mixed blood, negro male slaves, and negro female slaves. See the NOPL webpage for this item:
http://nutrias.org/~nopl/inv/neh/nehother.htm#az3.

1791-1890. *Louisiana, Compiled Census and Census Substitute Index* **[Online Database],** indexed at the Ancestry.com website. Data obtained in 1999 from Accelerated Indexing Systems, containing the following indexes:
- 1791 Census of New Orleans
- 1810 Federal Census Index
- 1820 Federal Census Index
- 1830 Federal Census Index
- 1840 Federal Census Index
- 1840 Pensioners List
- 1850 Federal Census Index
- 1850 Slave Schedule
- 1850-1860 Sugar Census Index
- 1860 Federal Census Index
- 1870 Federal Census Index
- 1890 Veterans Schedules
- Early Census Index

This database has 188,900 records. See
http://search.ancestry.com/search/db.aspx?dbid=3550.

1793. *New Feliciana in the Province of Louisiana: A Guide to the Census of 1793* **[Printed Book],** by Winston De Ville, publ. 1987, 32 pages. Includes index. See FHL book 976.3 A1 No. 57.

1793. "1793 Tax List, Natchitoches Parish, Louisiana" **[Printed Article],** in *Louisiana Genealogical Register* (Louisiana Genealogical & Historical Society, Baton Rouge, LA), Vol. 18, No. 1 (Mar 1971), and Vol. 27, No. 3 (Sep 1980).

1793 Tax List, Natchitoches Parish, Louisiana **[Online Database],** extracted at the USGenWeb site for Natchitoches Parish LA. See
http://files.usgwarchives.net/la/natchitoches/taxlists/tax1793.txt.

1795 Chimney Tax of New Orleans: A Guide to the Census of Proprietors and Residents of the Vieux Carré **[Printed Book],** compiled by Winston De Ville, publ. Ville Platte, LA, 1995, 31 pages, FHL book 976.335/N1 R4d.

1795. "Tax on Slave Owners, 1795," **[Printed Article],** in *La Raconteur* (La Comité des Archives de la Louisiane, Baton Rouge, LA), Vol. 13, No. 1 (Apr 1993) and Vol. 2, No. 12 (Aug 1992) and Vol. 3-4 (Dec 1992).

1794 Militia List, Post of Rapide, Rapides Parish, Louisiana **[Online Database],** indexed at the USGenWeb site for Rapides Parish LA. See
http://files.usgwarchives.net/la/rapides/military/rapi1794.txt.

1795-1799. *Militia List, Post of Rapide, Rapides Parish, Louisiana* **[Online Database**], indexed at the USGenWeb site for Rapides Parish LA:
http://files.usgwarchives.net/la/rapides/military/rapi1790.txt.

1795-1808. See *Lawsuits in New Orleans* **[Microfilm & Digital Capture],** from the originals at the New Orleans Public Library. Filmed by the Genealogical Society of Utah, 1972, 1 roll, FHL film #906356. To access the digital images, see the online FHL catalog: www.familysearch.org/search/catalog/299891.

1796. "Persons Residing Along Ouachita River, 1796" **[Printed Article],** in *New Orleans Genesis* (Genealogical Research Society of New Orleans), Vol. 16, No. 63 (Jun 1977).

1796-1947 Index of Land Records, Rapides Parish, Louisiana **[Online Database],** indexed at the USGenWeb site for Rapides Parish LA. See
http://files.usgwarchives.net/la/rapides/deeds/land-ind.txt.

1799. *Rapides Post: A Brief Study in Genealogy and Local History* **[Printed Book],** by Winston DeVille, publ. Genealogical Publishing Co, Baltimore, 1968, FHL book 976.369 X2d.

1800-1857. *Proofs of Citizenship Used to Apply for Seamen's Protection Certificates for the Port of New Orleans, Louisiana, 1800, 1802, 1804-1807, 1809-1812, 1814-1816, 1818-1819, 1821, 1850-1851, 1855, 1857: NARA RG 36 Publication M1826* **[Microfilm & Digital Capture],** from the originals at the National Archives, Washington, DC. From intro: "On May 28, 1796, an act for the relief and protection of American seamen, which includes instructions for the issuance of certificates of citizenship to seamen, was signed into law. These documents later became commonly known as seamen's protection certificates. These certificates were issued by the Collector of Customs at individual ports of entry to merchant seamen and masters of merchant vessels engaged in foreign trade. The object was to prevent the detention and impressment of American seamen lawfully engaged in the service of a U.S. merchant vessel. Certificates were issued only after the seaman produced proof of citizenship." Proofs or declarations of citizenship include a number, assigned by the Collector of Customs, name of the witness, name, age, place of birth and residence of the seaman at the time the declaration was signed. Also includes the seaman's height, hair color, eye color, and complexion. Filmed by the National Archives, 2001, 12 rolls, beginning with the FHL film #2311056 (Proofs of citizenship, 1800-1805). To access the digital images, see the online FHL catalog:
https://familysearch.org/search/catalog/1124840.

1800-1870. *Index of Ouachita Parish, Louisiana, Probate Records* **[Digitized Book],** compiled by Margery Wright, digitized by the Genealogical Society of Utah, 2014, 18 pages. For access to the digital version, see the online FHL catalog page for this title. See https://familysearch.org/search/catalog/2367034.

1800-1890. *Index to Ouachita Parish, Louisiana Marriages* **[Microfilm & Digital Capture],** from original typescript compiled by Ben Achee and Margery McGraw, filmed by the Genealogical Society of Utah, 1971, 1 roll, FHL film #855262. To access the digital images, see the online FHL catalog:
https://familysearch.org/search/catalog/341712.

1803. "Appraisement of Property, 1803, Ouachita Parish, Louisiana" **[Printed Article],** in *Northeast Louisiana Genealogical Society Quarterly* (NLGS, Monroe, LA), Vol. 2, No. 3 (Jul 1976).

1803-1877. *Acadian to Cajun: Transformation of a People* **[Printed Book],** by Carl A. Brasseaux, publ. University Press of Mississippi, Jackson, MS, 1992, 252 pages, FHL book 976.3 F2bc.

1803-2017. *Louisiana Newspaper Archives* **[Online Database],** digitized and indexed newspapers at the GenealogyBank website for the following cities: Alexandria, Baton Rouge, Covington, Franklin, Natchitoches, New Iberia, New Orleans, St. Francisville, St. Martinville, and Vidalia. Search by first name, last name. See
www.genealogybank.com/gbnk/newspapers/explore/USA/Louisiana.

1804. *Mayor's Office, Census of the City of New Orleans* **[Microfilm & Digital Capture],** from the originals at the New Orleans Public Library, filed under call number TK840 1804. Contains a record in English and French, giving names of male residents and their wives or other adult women living in the household, the profession and employment of the male, the age of males and females, the number of boys and girls living in the household, and, usually, their ages. The number of male and female adult and juvenile slaves in each household is also tallied; no names are recorded for slaves. A final column, labeled "Observations," indicates the head of household's military status, listing the company in which he served. FHL film #1309932. To access the digital images of this roll, see the online FHL catalog page:
www.familysearch.org/search/catalog/250907.

1804-1820. *New Orleans Marriage Contracts: Abstracted from the Notarial Archives of New Orleans* **[Printed Book],** by Charles R. Maduell, Jr., publ. Polyanthos, New Orleans, 1977, 137 pages, FHL book 976.335/N1 V25md.

1804-1820. *Land Claims, Concordia Parish, Louisiana* **[Online Database],** indexed at the USGenWeb site for Concordia Parish LA. See http://files.usgwarchives.net/la/concordia/deeds/land01.txt.

1804-1846. *Louisiana, Orleans Parish Estate Files* **[Online Database],** digitized and indexed at the FamilySearch.org website. Includes a name index and images of estate files. Each estate file consists of multiple images derived from New Orleans City Archives. The event date noted in the index is date of probate. This database has 7,080 records. See https://familysearch.org/search/collection/1388197.
- This database is also available at the Ancestry.com website, see
https://search.ancestry.com/search/db.aspx?dbid=60297.

1804-1895 Death Indexes, Orleans Parish, Louisiana [Online Database], extracted from the State Archives Death Index. Indexed at the USGenWeb site for Orleans Parish LA. See www.usgwarchives.net/la/orleans/death-alpha.htm.

1804-1899. *Newspaper Marriage Index, New Orleans, Louisiana* [Microfilm & Digital Capture], from the originals at the New Orleans Public Library. Filmed by the Genealogical Society of Utah, 2005-2006, 4 rolls, beginning with FHL film #2397871 (Abbatt, Robert – Byrnes, Wm. J.). For a complete list of roll numbers, roll contents, and the digital images of each roll, see the online FHL catalog page for this title. See https://familysearch.org/search/catalog/1333348.

1804-1949. *New Orleans, Louisiana, Death Records Index* [Online Database], indexed at the Ancestry.com website. Source: LA State Archives, Vital Records Indices. Each index record includes: Name, Gender, Age, Birth year, and Death date. This database has 686,801 records. See https://search.ancestry.com/search/db.aspx?dbid=6606.

1804-1972. *Louisiana Biography/Obituary Index* [Online Database], indexed at the New Orleans Public Library's Louisiana Division website. This database references obituaries and death notices published in New Orleans newspapers from 1804-1972 and biographical information published in older Louisiana collective biographies. The original index, housed in the Louisiana Division of New Orleans Public Library, is an alphabetical card file of more than 650,000 names: http://nopl.minisisinc.com/NOPL/SCRIPTS/MWIMAIN.DLL/144/obit_public?directsearch.
- See also, *Louisiana Biography and Obituary Index, 1804-1972: A Card Index to Biographies and New Orleans Newspapers* [Microfilm & Digital Capture], digitized at FamilySearch.org. To access the digital images, see the online FHL catalog: www.familysearch.org/search/catalog/1130042.

1805. *New Orleans in 1805: A Directory and a Census Together with Resolutions Authorizing Same, Now Printed for the First Time from the Original Manuscript; Facsimile* [Digitized Book], by Charles Louis Thompson, Mathew Flannery, and Dolley Madison Heartman, publ. Pelican Gallery, New Orleans, 1936, 107 pages. For access to a digital version of the book, see the online FHL catalog page: https://familysearch.org/search/catalog/2204410.

1805 New Orleans City Directory [Online Database], extracted and indexed at the USGenWeb site for Orleans Parish LA. See http://files.usgwarchives.net/la/orleans/history/directory/1805nocd.txt.

1805. *Residents on the Rio Hondo in 1805, Sabine Parish, Louisiana* [Online Database], indexed at the USGenWeb site for Sabine Parish LA. http://files.usgwarchives.net/la/sabine/deeds/reoho.txt.

1805-1890. *Early Settlers of St. Landry Parish, Louisiana* [Online Database], extracted and indexed at the USGenWeb site for St. Landry Parish LA. See http://files.usgwarchives.net/la/stlandry/history/settlers.txt.

1805-1920. *Louisiana, Orleans Parish Will Books* [Online Database], digitized at the FamilySearch.org website. This image-only database includes the Will Books for Orleans Parish courts with copies of all wills filed in Orleans Parish, 1805-1920. The will books comprise 39 bound volumes. Each volume is individually indexed at the front of each book. The will books were created in several courts including the Court of Probates (1805-1846), Second District Court (1846-1880) and Civil District Court (1880-1920). Volume 31, No. 11 is missing. This database has 25,285 images. See https://familysearch.org/search/collection/2019728.

1805-1940. *New Orleans (Louisiana) City Directories* [Microfilm], from the originals of various publishers, filmed by Research Publications, Woodbridge, CT, 1980-1984, 158 microfiche, 389 microfilm rolls. FHL has the following years: 1805, 1807, 1809, 1811, 1822-1824, 1832, 1834, 1838, 1841-1843, 1846, 1851-1852, 1854-1855, 1857-1859, 1860-1861, 1866-1933, 1935, and 1940. FHL fiche #60442250 (1805-). For a complete list of fiche and roll numbers, see the online FHL catalog for this title: https://familysearch.org/search/catalog/543152.

1805-1971 City Directories, New Orleans, Louisiana [Online Database], includes separate indexes for 1805, 1811, 1822-1824, 1832, 1834, 1838, 1841, 1842-1843, 1846, 1849, 1859, 1861, 1866, 1867, 1868-1915, 1931-1935, 1938-1940, 1942, and 1971. Indexed at the USGenWeb site for Orleans Parish LA. See www.usgwarchives.net/la/orleans/directry.htm.

"1806 Tax Roll, Iberville Parish, Louisiana" [Printed Article], in *Baton Rouge Newsletter* (Baton Rouge Genealogical & Historical Society, Baton Rouge, LA), Vol. 5, No. 3 (Aug 1985).

1807. *Southwest Louisiana in 1807: The Land and Slave Tax of St. Landry Parish in the Territory of Orleans* **[Printed Book],** by Winston De Ville, publ. Ville Platte, LA, 1993, 51 pages. FHL book 976.346 R4d.

1807 Settlers of Lake Charles, Louisiana **[Online Database],** indexed at the USGenWeb site for Calcasieu Parish LA. See http://files.usgwarchives.net/la/calcasieu/history/pioneers/settlers.txt.

1807-1810. See *First Landowners and 1810 Annotated Census of Lafourche Interior Parish, Louisiana: Lafourche & Terrebonne* **[Printed Book],** by Audrey B. Westerman, publ. Terrebonne Genealogy, Thibodaux, LA, 1995, FHL book 976.339 X2w.

1807-1860. *New Orleans, Louisiana, Slave Manifests* **[Online Database],** digitized and indexed at the Ancestry.com website. From Slave Manifests of Coastwise Vessels Filed at New Orleans, Louisiana, 1807–1860, National Archives publication M1895. Though an 1807 law banned the trans-Atlantic slave trade to the United States slaves could still be bought and sold (and transported) within the country. Masters of vessels carrying slaves in coastal waters were required to provide a manifest detailing their slave cargo when leaving or entering a port. This collection can now be searched by ship name, port and date of departure, date of arrival, name, estimated birth year, gender, and color. The records may contain the following additional information: Slave's age and height, Date of manifest, Slave owners'/shippers' name(s) and residence, Port of destination, Captain's name, and Dates of certification by the collector of customs. The manifests can also be browsed by date of departure or arrival and ship. This database has 104,117 records. See
http://search.ancestry.com/search/db.aspx?dbid=1562.

1807-1889. *Biographical and Historical Memoirs of Northwest Louisiana: Comprising a Large Fund of Biography of Actual Residents, and an Interesting Historical Sketch of Thirteen Parishes* **[Digitized Book],** from the original published by the Southern Publishing Co, Nashville, 1890, 703 pages. Historical sketches for Avoyelles, Bienville, Bossier, Caddo, Claiborne, DeSoto, Grant, Natchitoches, Rapides, Red River, Sabine, Webster, and Winn Parishes. Digitized by the Genealogical Society of Utah, 2009. For a digital version, see the online FHL catalog page:
https://familysearch.org/search/catalog/1556609.

1807-1899. *Deaths, Obits & Cemeteries Terrebonne & Lafourche Parishes, LA: Annotated* **[CD-ROM],** compiled by Phoebe Chauvin Morrison, publ. P.C. Morrison, 2001, FHL CD No. 4824.

1807-1930. *Rapides Parish Louisiana: A History* **[Digitized Book],** from the original by G.P. Whittington, first printed in the Louisiana Historical Quarterly, 1932-1935. Digitized by the Genealogical Society of Utah, 2014. For access to the digital version, see the FHL catalog page:
https://familysearch.org/search/catalog/2367035.

"1808 Taxpayers, Ouachita Parish, Louisiana" [Printed Article], in *Louisiana Genealogical Register* (Louisiana Genealogical & Historical Society, Baton Rouge, LA), Vol. 9, No. 4 (Dec 1962).

"1808 Militia Officers" [Printed Article], in *New Orleans Genesis* (Genealogical Research Society of New Orleans), Vol. 1, No. 3 (Jun 1962).

1808, 1814-1828. *Miscellaneous Louisiana Militia Records* **[Microfilm],** from the originals at the Jackson Barracks Military Library, New Orleans, LA. Filmed by the Genealogical Society of Utah, 1990, 1 roll, FHL film #1704156. To see if this microfilm was digitized yet, see the online FHL catalog:
www.familysearch.org/search/catalog/192705.

1808-1839. *First Settlers of Catahoula Parish, Louisiana* **[Online Database],** full text and index at the USGenWeb site for Catahoula Parish LA. See www.usgwarchives.net/la/catahoula/titlepg.htm.

1808-1845. *Computer Indexed Marriage Records: Lafourche Parish Louisiana* **[Digitized Book],** digital images of original published Hammond, LA, Hunting For Bears, 122 pages. For access to a digital version, see the online FHL catalog page for this title. See
https://familysearch.org/search/catalog/1784156.

1808-1900. *Probate Records, East Baton Rouge Parish, Louisiana* **[Microfilm & Digital Capture],** from the original records at the LA District Court, Baton Rouge, LA. Filmed by the Genealogical Society of Utah, 1963, 120 rolls, beginning with FHL film #330098 (Index to probate records, 1808-1924). To access the digital images, see the online FHL catalog:
www.familysearch.org/search/catalog/307217.

1809-1984. *Louisiana Military Obituaries, 1809-1984* **[Microfilm & Digital Capture],** from the originals at the Louisiana National Guard, Jackson Barracks, New Orleans. Filmed by the Genealogical Society of Utah, 1990, 1 roll, FHL film #1704157. To access the digital images of this roll, see the online FHL catalog page: www.familysearch.org/search/catalog/587355.

1810. *Population Schedules of the Third Census of the United States, 1810, Louisiana (Orleans Territory)* **[Microfilm],** from the originals at the National Archives, Washington, DC. Filmed by the National Archives, 1958, 1 roll, FHL film #1017433.
- See also, *Federal Census of 1810, Territory of Orleans, Excluding the Parish of Orleans* **[Printed Book & Digital Version],** publ. 1961, Louisiana Genealogical and Historical Society, Baton Rouge, LA. To access the digital version, see the online FHL catalog: www.familysearch.org/search/catalog/3016117.

1810. *Louisiana [Orleans Territory] 1810 Census* **[Printed Index],** edited by Ronald Vern Jackson, publ. by Accelerated Indexing Systems, Bountiful, UT, 1973, 151 pages, FHL book 976.3 X2st.

1810. "1810 Delinquent Taxpayers, Attakapas Parish, Louisiana" **[Printed Article],** in *Attakapas Gazette* (Attakapas Historical Association, Lafayette, LA), Vol. 10, No. 4 (Winter 1975).

1810. "1810 Landowners and Slave Owners, Attakapas Parish, Louisiana" **[Printed Article],** in *Attakapas Gazette* (Attakapas Historical Association, Lafayette, LA), Vol. 11, No. 2 (Summer 1976).

1810-1820. *Louisiana Census Records. Volume I: Avoyelles and St. Landry Parishes* **[Online Database],** from the 1970 book by Robert Ardoin, digitized and OCR indexed at the Ancestry.com website. See http://search.ancestry.com/search/db.aspx?dbid=48583.

1810- 1820. *Louisiana Census Records. Volume II: Iberville, Natchitoches, Pointe Coupee, and Rapides Parishes, 1810 and 1820* **[Online Database],** from the 1972 book by Robert Ardoin, digitized and OCR indexed at the Ancestry.com website. See http://search.ancestry.com/search/db.aspx?dbid=48584.

1810-1820. *Louisiana's Households of Free People of Color: Residing Outside of Orleans Parish & the City of New Orleans in 1810 & 1820* **[Printed Book & Digital Version],** compiled by Vincent M. Roux and Kenneth d. Roux, publ. 1995, San Francisco, CA: V.M. Roux, 7 2 pages, FHL nook 976.3 X28. To access the digital version, see the online FHL catalog: www.familysearch.org/search/catalog/747065.

1810-1840. See *Louisiana, 1810 thru 1840 Federal Census: Population Schedules* **[Microfilm & Digital Capture],** from the originals at the National Archives, Washington, DC. Filmed as one series by the National Archives, 1938-1961, 11 rolls, beginning with FHL film #181355 (1810: Ascension-St. John the Baptist parishes). For a complete list of roll numbers, roll contents, and the digital images of each roll, see the online FHL catalog page for this title. See https://familysearch.org/search/catalog/745491.

1811 New Orleans City Directory **[Online Database],** indexed at the USGenWeb site for Orleans Parish LA: http://files.usgwarchives.net/la/orleans/history/directory/1811nocd.txt.

"**1811-1812 Tax List, St. Tammany Parish, Louisiana,**" **[Printed Article]** in *Louisiana Genealogical Register* (Louisiana Genealogical & Historical Society, Baton Rouge, LA), Vol. 14, No. 4 (Dec 1967).

1811-1875. *East Baton Rouge Pariah, Louisiana: Computer Indexed Marriage Records* **[Printed Book],** by Nicholas Russell Murray, publ. Hunting for Bears, Hammond, LA, 1997, 116 pages, FHL book 976.318 V22m.

1811-1893. *Death Notices From Louisiana Newspapers* **[Printed Book],** compiled by Brenda Lagroue Mayers and Gloria Lambert Kerns. Contents: Vol. 1: Indexes obituaries from Ascension, East Feliciana, Livingston, St. Helena, Tangipahoa, and West Feliciana parishes, 1811- 1819; Vol. 2: Indexes obituaries from Ascension, East Baton Rouge, and Pointe Coupee parishes, 1822-1914; Vol. 3: Indexes obituaries from Ascension, East Baton Rouge, Iberville, and Washington parishes, 1833-1917; Vol. 4: Indexes obituaries from East Baton Rouge, St. Charles, St. John the Baptist, St. Tammany, 1847-1893; Vol. 5: Indexes obituaries from Assumption, East Baton Rouge, Iberia, Lafourche, Orleans, St. John the Baptist, St. Martin, and St. Mary parishes, 1824-1887; and Vol. 6: Indexes obituaries from Acadia, Iberia, Rapides, St. Landry, St. Mary parishes, 1836-1887. Publ. Folk Finders, Baker, LA, 1984, 6 vols., FHL book 976.31 V4m.

1811-1934. See *Louisiana, Births and Christenings, 1811-1830; 1854-1934* [Online Database], indexed at the FamilySearch.org website. Includes a name index to births, baptisms, and christenings from the state of Louisiana, based on data collected by the Genealogical Society of Utah. This database has 29,548 records. See https://familysearch.org/search/collection/1674847.

1812 Tax List, St. Tammany Parish, Louisiana [Online Database], indexed at the USGenWeb site for St. Tammany Parish LA. See
http://files.usgwarchives.net/la/sttammany/taxlists/1812tax.txt.

1812-1815. *Index to Compiled Service Records of Volunteer Soldiers Who Served During the War of 1812 in Organizations from the State of Louisiana* [Microfilm & Digital Capture], from the originals at the National Archives, Washington, DC. Filmed by the National Archives, 1955, series M0229, 3 rolls, beginning with FHL film #880010. For a complete list of roll numbers, roll contents, and the digital images of each roll, see the online FHL catalog page for this title: www.familysearch.org/search/catalog/313063.

1812-1815. See *Louisiana, Soldiers in the War of 1812* [Printed Book & Online Database], compiled by Marion John Bennett Pierson, publ. Louisiana Genealogical & Historical Society, Baton Rouge, LA, 1963, 124 pages, FHL book 976.3 M23p. A digitized version of this book is available at the Ancestry.com website. For a fully indexed database, see
https://search.ancestry.com/search/db.aspx?dbid=3339.

1812-1815 & 1873-1879 See *Louisiana, War of 1812 Pension Lists* [Online Database], digitized at the FamilySearch.org website. This is an image-only database with images of pension lists for those with military service 1812-1815, recorded between 1873 and 1879. Some lists are arranged in alphabetical order by surname. Includes lists of veterans and lists of claimants. This database has 149 images. See
https://familysearch.org/search/collection/1527724.
- This image-only database is also available at the Ancestry.com website. See
https://search.ancestry.com/search/db.aspx?dbid=60300.

1812-1900. *Terrebonne Parish, Louisiana Computer Indexed Marriage Records* [Digitized Book], compiled for Hunting For Bears, Hammond, LA, 83 pages. For access to a digital version, see the online FHL catalog page for this title. See
https://familysearch.org/search/catalog/30903.

1812-1900. *Records of St. Tammany Parish, Louisiana: Index to the Marriages* [Printed Book & Digital Capture], by Bertha Neff, 1969, 171 pages, FHL book 976.312 V25n. To access a digital version of this book, see the online FHL catalog page: www.familysearch.org/search/catalog/149970.

1812-1970. *Louisiana Tombstone Inscriptions* [Online Database], digitized and indexed at FamilySearch.org. Includes tombstone inscriptions gathered by members of the Daughters of the American Revolution in New Orleans, Louisiana. This database has 76,308 records, see
www.familysearch.org/search/collection/3041284.

1813. See "Census of 1813 - Territory of Louis Carriere" [Printed Article], in *Louisiana Genealogical Register* (Louisiana Genealogical & Historical Society, Baton Rouge, LA), Vol. IIV, No. 2 (Jun 1967).

1813. See "1813 Tax List, St. Mary Parish, Louisiana" [Printed Article], in *Attakapas Gazette* (Attakapas Historical Association, Lafayette, LA), Vol. 12, No. 4 (Winter 1977).

1813-1824 Holders of Valid Land Titles, West Feliciana Parish, Louisiana [Online Database], indexed at the USGenWeb site for West Feliciana Parish LA. See
http://files.usgwarchives.net/la/westfeliciana/deeds/wfpland.txt.

1813-1846. *Case Papers, Orleans Parish: first Judicial District Court* [Microfilm & Digital Capture], from the originals at the New Orleans Public Library's City Archives. Includes interdictions, divorces, authorizations, separations of bed and board, successions, emancipations, separations of property, and tutorships. Filmed by the Genealogical Society of Utah, 1990, 42 rolls, beginning with FHL film #1710492 (case papers, 1813). For a complete list of roll numbers, roll contents, and the digital images of each roll, see the online FHL catalog page.
https://familysearch.org/search/catalog/424157.

1813-1963. *New Orleans, Passenger Lists* [Online Database], digitized and indexed at the Ancestry.com website. Images derived from five National Archives publications: 1) New Orleans Passenger Lists, 1813-1945; 2) Passenger Lists, 1820-1945; 3) Passenger departing New Orleans, 1867-1871; 4) Crew lists of

arriving vessels, 1910-1945; and 5) WPA transcripts of passengers arriving, 1813-1849. This database has 4,288,331 records. See
http://search.ancestry.com/search/db.aspx?dbid=7484.

1813-1851. *Orleans Parish Court Cases* **[Microfilm & Digital Capture],** from the originals at the New Orleans Public Library. Selected cases, including interdictions, divorces, authorizations, separations of bed and board, successions, emancipations, separations of property and tutorships. Filmed by the Genealogical Society of Utah, 1991-1992, 222 rolls, beginning with FHL film #1822283 (Parish Court Cases, 1813). For a complete list of roll numbers, roll contents, and the digital images of each roll, see the online FHL catalog page for this title. See
https://familysearch.org/search/catalog/520814.

1815-1977. *New Orleans, Louisiana, Deaths Index* **[Online Database],** indexed at the Ancestry.com website. Compiled by Gladys Stovall Armstrong, 1998. Taken from small local newspapers, many of these newspapers, like the New Orleans Parish, are obscure and contained printed obituaries for persons larger newspapers may not have printed. Information provided includes date of death and, in some cases, relatives still living. This database has 1,098 records:
https://search.ancestry.com/search/db.aspx?dbid=3528.

1816-1906. *Louisiana, Marriages* **[Online Database],** digitized and indexed at the FamilySearch.org website. This is a name index to marriage records from the state of Louisiana, based on data collected by the Genealogical Society of Utah. This database has 133,813 records. See
https://familysearch.org/search/collection/1674881.

1817-1818. See *Land Holders of Southwest Louisiana: Tax Lists for St. Landry Parish, 1817 and 1818* **[Printed Book],** compiled by Ramona A. Smith, publ. Ville Platte, LA, 1990, 70 pages. FHL book 976.346 R2s.

1817-1866. *Registres des émigrés* **[Microfilm],** also known as *Alsace Emigration Index*. from the original records of the Ministère de l'Intérieurm, Paris. Includes records of those traveling through Colmar and Strasbourg, France and emigrating throughout the world including other European countries, the U.S., Algeria, and New Caledonia. Also includes a card index to emigration records of Europeans traveling through the Alsace region of France. Filmed by the Genealogical Society of Utah, 6 rolls, beginning with FHL film #11250002 (Index, A-C). To see if this microfilm was digitized yet, see the online FHL catalog:
https://familysearch.org/search/catalog/372046.

1818-1820 Slave Manifests, Port of New Orleans **[Online Database],** transcriptions indexed at the Afrigeneas.com site. See
http://afrigeneas.com/slavedata/Roll.1.1818-1820.html.

1818-1860 Slave Manifests, Port of New Orleans **[Online Database],** transcriptions indexed at the Afrigeneas.com site. See
www.afrigeneas.com/slavedata/manifests.html.

1819 Grand Jury List, Catahoula Parish, Louisiana **[Online Database],** indexed at the USGenWeb site for Catahoula Parish LA. See
http://files.usgwarchives.net/la/catahoula/court/1819jury.txt.

1819-1906. *Louisiana, Orleans Parish, Birth Records* **[Online Database],** indexed at FamilySearch.org, from the original records at the LA State Archives. Each index record may include Name, Event type, Event date, Event place, Gender, Race, Parent name, Parent 2 name, and Certificate number. This database has 260,356 records, see

1819-1964. *Louisiana, Statewide Death Index* **[Online Database],** indexed at the Ancestry.com website. Source: LA State Archives, Vital Record Indices. Each index record includes: Name, Age, Birth year, Death date, and Death place.
This database has 2,081,698 records. See
https://search.ancestry.com/search/db.aspx?dbid=6697.

1820 Louisiana Federal Census Index **[Printed Book],** edited by Ronald Vern Jackson, publ. Accelerated Indexing Systems, Bountiful, UT, 1981, 91 pages, FHL book 976.3 X22j.

1820-1830. *Marriages and Family Relationships of New Orleans* **[Printed Book & Digital Version],** by Charles R. Maduell, publ. New Orleans, 1969, 153 pages, FHL book 976.335/N1 V2m2
https://familysearch.org/search/catalog/149846.

1820-1852. *The "Foreign French:" Nineteenth Century French Immigration into Louisiana* **[Printed Book],** by Carl A. Brasseaux, published by the Center for Louisiana Studies, University of Southwestern

Louisiana, Lafayette, LA , 1990-1993. Contents: Vol. 1: 1820-1839; Vol. 2: 1840-1848; Vol. 3: 1849-1852. 3 vols, FHL book 976.3 W3b v. 1-3.

1820-1875. *New Orleans, Passenger List Quarterly Abstracts5* **[Online Database],** digitized and indexed at the Ancestry.com website. This database contains abstracts created from passenger lists of foreign vessels arriving at New Orleans. The abstracts were copies of the main passenger lists, required to be sent to Washington, DC on a quarterly basis. This database has 408,999 records. See
http://search.ancestry.com/search/db.aspx?dbid=2860.

1820-1945. *Louisiana, New Orleans Passenger Lists* **[Online Database],** digitized and indexed at the FamilySearch.org website. This collection corresponds to two National Archives publications: M259: Passenger Lists of Vessels Arriving at New Orleans, Louisiana, 1820-1902 and T905: Passenger Lists of Vessels Arriving at New Orleans, Louisiana, 1903-1945. Some arrival dates are not represented in the data. This database has 1,214,574 records. See
https://familysearch.org/search/collection/1916009.

1821 Slave Manifests, Port of New Orleans **[Online Database],** transcriptions indexed at the Afrigeneas site. See
http://afrigeneas.com/slavedata/Roll.2.1821.html.

1821-1907. *Louisiana, Homestead and Cash Entry Patents, Pre-1908* **[Online Database],** digitized and indexed at the Ancestry.com website. The Louisiana land entries were part of the 13-state collection, *U.S. General Land Office Records, 1796-1907.* Information recorded in land patents includes name of patentee, issue date, state of patent, acres of land, legal land description, authority under which the land was acquired, and other details relating to the land given. With a land description, one can access land ownership maps showing the exact location of property and relationship to other landowners in an area. This database has 78,869 records. See
http://search.ancestry.com/search/db.aspx?dbid=2074.

1822 Slave Manifests, Port of New Orleans **[Online Database],** transcriptions indexed at the Afrigeneas site. See
http://afrigeneas.com/slavedata/Roll.3.1822.html.

1822 New Orleans City Directory **[Online Database],** indexed at the USGenWeb site for Orleans Parish LA: http://files.usgwarchives.net/la/orleans/history/directory/1822nocd.txt.

1822-1846. *Louisiana, 1st Judicial District Court Records* **[Microfilm & Digital Capture],** filmed by the Genealogical Society of Utah, 1985, 3 rolls, beginning with FHL film #1420516 (Index to the 1st Judicial District Court, 1822-1840). To access the digital images, see the online FHL catalog:
www.familysearch.org/search/catalog/489415.

1822-1880. *Louisiana, Orleans Court Records* **[Online Database],** digitized at the FamilySearch.org website. This image-only database includes dockets and indexes for the Parish Court, 1822-1840; Commercial Court, 1839-1846, First Judicial District Court, 1839-1842; Second, Third, Fourth and Fifth Judicial Court, 1846-1880 and the Sixth and Seventh Judicial District Courts, 1854-1880. This database has 48,176 images. See
https://familysearch.org/search/collection/2030501.
- See also, *Index to Defendant and Plaintiff Dockets, 1846-1880* **[Microfilm & Digital Capture],** filmed by the Genealogical Society of Utah, 1985, 4 rolls, beginning with FHL film #1420521. To access the digital images, see the online FHL catalog:
www.familysearch.org/search/catalog/489590.

1822-1985. *History of Livingston Parish, Louisiana* **[Printed Book],** compiled and edited by History Book Committee of Edward Livingston Historical Association, publ. Curtis media, Dallas, TX, 1986, 630 pages, FHL book 976.314 H2h.

1823-1971. See *Marriage Licenses, Records, 1823-1916; Marriage Index, 1823-1971* **[Microfilm & Digital Capture],** from the original records at the Lafayette Parish Courthouse, Lafayette, LA. Filmed by the Genealogical Society of Utah, 1971, 20 rolls, beginning with FHL film #871178 (Brides Index A-Z 182301967). To access the digital images, see the online FHL catalog:
www.familysearch.org/search/catalog/293279.

1823-1887. *District and Parish Court Minutes, LaFayette Parish, Louisiana* **[Microfilm & Digital Capture],** from originals at the Lafayette Parish Courthouse, LaFayette, LA. Filmed by the Genealogical Society of Utah, 1971, 2 rolls, FHL film

871200 (Parish/District Court Minutes, 1823-1877) & FHL film # 871199 (District Court Minutes, 1841-1866). To access the digital images, see the online FHL catalog: www.familysearch.org/search/catalog/297436.

1823-1830. *LaFayette Parish Marriage Records: Marriage Book I, Part 1, with Genealogical Notes* **[Printed Book],** compiled and edited by Harold Prejean. Includes marriage records, divorce records and other vital records of genealogical value. publ. Baton Rouge, LA 1984, 146 pages, FHL book 976.347 V2p.

1823-1958. *The Attakapas Country, A History of LaFayette Parish, Louisiana* **[Printed Book],** by Harry Lewis Griffin. Includes index. Publ. Pelican Pub, New Orleans, 1959, 263 pages, FHL book 976.347 H2g.

1823-1971. *Successions, LaFayette Parish, Louisiana, 1848-1868; Index to Successions, 1823-1971* **[Microfilm & Digital Capture],** from the original (probate-inheritance) records at the LaFayette Parish Courthouse, Lafayette, LA. Filmed by the Genealogical Society of Utah, 1971, 4 rolls, beginning with FHL film #871173 (Index, 1823-1971). To access the digital images, see the online FHL catalog: https://familysearch.org/search/catalog/293374.
- NOTE: The legal term *succession* refers to the process of transferring property/assets to the legal heirs when there is no valid will in a probate case. The term is more commonly used in Louisiana probate courts than in other states, where the term *intestate* is more common.

1824 New Orleans City Directory **[Online Database],** indexed at the USGenWeb site for Orleans Parish LA. http://files.usgwarchives.net/la/orleans/history/directory/1824nocd.txt.

"1825 Voter Registration, Iberville Parish, Louisiana" [Printed Article], in Le *Raconteur* (Le Comité des Archives de la Louisiana, Baton Rouge, LA), Vol. 14, No. 1 (Apr 1994).

1825-1840. *Abstracts of Some East Feliciana Probate Records* **[Online Database],** extracted at the USGenWeb site for East Feliciana Parish LA. See http://files.usgwarchives.net/la/eastfeliciana/wills/efprob.txt.

1827-1899. *Succession and Probate Records of Jefferson Parish* **[Microfilm & Digital Capture],** from the originals at the Jefferson Parish Courthouse, Gretna, LA. Filmed by the Genealogical Society of Utah, 1965, 73 rolls, beginning with FHL film #402561 (General Index to Probate Matters, 1825-1951). To access the digital images, see the online FHL catalog: www.familysearch.org/search/catalog/245353.

1830 Louisiana Federal Census Index **[Printed Index],** edited by Ronald Vern Jackson, publ. Accelerated Indexing Systems, Bountiful, UT, 1981, 95 pages, FHL book 976.3 X22j.

1830-1840. *Marriages and Family Relationships of New Orleans* **[Printed Book],** by Charles R. Maduell, Jr. Publ. Hebert Publications, 1980, 255 pages, FHL book 976.335/N1 V2mm.

1830-1860. *North Louisiana Census Reports* **[Printed Book],** edited by Marleta Childs, published Polyanthos, New Orleans, 1975-1999, 5 vols. Surname index included in each volume. Contents: vol. 1: 1830 and 1840 schedules of Catahoula, Concordia, Ouachita, Caldwell, Carrol, Madison, and Union Parishes; vol. 2: 1830 and 1840 schedules of Caddo, Claiborne, and Natchitoches Parishes; vol. 3: 1850 and 1860 schedules of Union Parish ; vol. 4. 1850 schedule of Natchitoches Parish; vol. 5: The 1850 slave schedule of Natchitoches Parish, Louisiana. See FHL book 976.38 X2p v. 1-5.

1831-1906. Louisiana, Naturalization Records [Online Database], digitized at the FamilySearch.org website. These naturalization records are from the National Archives - Southwest Region and includes the National Archives' *Louisiana Index to Certificates 1831-1906*. Additional records will be added as they are completed. This database has 20,710 records. See https://familysearch.org/search/collection/1459894.

1831-1964. *New Orleans, Louisiana, Marriage Records Index* **[Online Database],** indexed at the Ancestry.com website. The database was obtained from the Louisiana State Archives in 2002. In addition to providing the names of the people who were married, the index provides their ages, sex, marriage date, and a reference to the original record.
This database has 834,468 records. See http://search.ancestry.com/search/db.aspx?dbid=6500.

1832 New Orleans City Directory **[Online Database],** indexed at the USGenWeb site for Orleans Parish LA: http://files.usgwarchives.net/la/orleans/history/directory/1832nocd.txt.

1832-1860. *Early Settlers, Sabine parish, Louisiana* **[Online Database].** Includes some text re the "Neutral Strip and Pioneers" from *History of Sabine Parish Louisiana,* by John F. Belisle, 1913; with a list of

settlers who obtained government land between 1832 and 1860. Indexed at the USGenWeb site for Sabine Parish LA:
http://files.usgwarchives.net/la/sabine/deeds/nspio.txt.

1833 State Census, St. Tammany Parish, Louisiana [Online Database], the only known surviving state census name list for all of Louisiana, indexed at the USGenWeb site for St. Tammany Parish LA. See http://files.usgwarchives.net/la/sttammany/census/cens1833.txt.

1833 Voter List, St. Tammany Parish, Louisiana [Online Database], indexed at the USGenWeb site for St. Tammany Parish LA. See
http://files.usgwarchives.net/la/sttammany/court/vote1833.txt.

1833 Grand Jury List, Catahoula Parish, Louisiana [Online Database], indexed at the USGenWeb site for Catahoula Parish, LA. See http://files.usgwarchives.net/la/catahoula/court/1833jury.txt.

1833-1849. Early Settlers, Terrebonne Parish, Louisiana [Online Database], indexed at the RootsWeb site for Terrebonne Parish LA. See www.rootsweb.ancestry.com/~laterreb/caillou.htm.

1833-1912. Marriages, Jefferson Parish, Louisiana [Printed Book], compiled by Bartley A. Bowers, publ. Gretna, LA, 1991, 413 pages, FHL book 976.338 V2b.

1833-1998. Military Records of East Baton Rouge Parish, Louisiana, 1833 (Rev. War Pension)-1898 (Vietnam MIAs) [Online Database], indexed at the USGenWeb site for East Baton Rouge Parish LA: www.usgwarchives.net/la/eastbatonrouge/ebtr-military.htm.

1835 Tax List and 1840 Census, St. Helena Parish, Louisiana [Printed Book], compiled by Donald W. Johnson and Inez B. Tate. Includes 1835 tax information in a case of miscellaneous papers in the office of the clerk of court, St. Helena Parish, Louisiana, published by the St. Helena Historical Association, Greensburg, Louisiana, 2000, 22 pages. FHL Book 976.315 R4j.

1835-1880. Case Papers, Orleans Parish: Third Judicial District Court [Microfilm & Digital Capture], from the originals at the New Orleans Public Library's City Archives. Includes interdictions, divorces, authorizations, separations of bed and board, successions, emancipations, separations of property, and tutorships. Filmed by the Genealogical Society of Utah, 1990, 31 rolls, beginning with FHL film #1064600 (case papers, 1846-1853). To access the digital images, see the online FHL catalog:
https://familysearch.org/search/catalog/430509.

1836. Index to Compiled Service Records of Volunteer Soldiers Who Served During the Florida War in Organizations from the State of Louisiana [Microfilm & Digital Capture], from the originals at the National Archives, Kansas City, MO. For service in a conflict referred to as *The Florida War* (aka Seminole War), the index cards give the name of the soldier, his rank, and the unit in which he served. There are cross-reference cards for soldiers' names that appeared in the records under more than one spelling. Filmed by the National Archives, series M0239, 1 roll, FHL film #880843. To access the digital images of this roll, see the online FHL catalog page:
www.familysearch.org/search/catalog/312962.
- See also, *Index to Compiled Service Records of Volunteer Soldiers Who Served During the War of 1837-1838 in Organizations from the State of Louisiana* [Microfilm & Digital Capture], from the originals at the National Archives, Washington DC. This is an alphabetical card index to the compiled service records of volunteer soldiers belonging to units from the state of Louisiana who served in Florida in a campaign referred to as the *War of 1837-38* (aka 2nd Seminole War). The cards give the name of the soldier, his rank, and the unit in which he served. Filmed by the National Archives, series M0241, 1 roll, FHL film #880844. To access the digital images of this roll, see the online FHL catalog page for this title:
www.familysearch.org/search/catalog/312983.

1836-1938. Louisiana Church Records [Online Database], digitized and indexed at FamilySearch.org, church records from different denominations located in several counties in Louisiana. This database has 3,727 records, see
www.familysearch.org/search/collection/2790251.

1836-1972. Louisiana, New Orleans, Interment Registers [Online Database], indexed at FamilySearch.org, from an index at the New Orleans Public Library. Each index record contains: Name, Event type, Event date, Event place, Age, Race, Birth year, Birthplace, and Death date. This database has 326,032 records, see
www.familysearch.org/search/collection/3288441.

1836-1998. *Louisiana, Naturalization Records* **[Online Database],** digitized and indexed at the Ancestry.com website. The Louisiana records were extracted from two National Archives publications relating to the U.S. District Courts for all states: 1) Repatriation Oaths of Allegiance; and 2) Declarations of Intention for Citizenship, compiled 1919-1929. This database has 121,859 records. See
http://search.ancestry.com/search/db.aspx?dbid=2507.

1837. *Assessment of Property and Census of Slaves and their Owners (Orleans Parish, LA)* **[Microfilm & Digital Capture].** Originals at Orleans Parish Courthouse, filmed by the Genealogical Society of Utah, 1972, FHL film #906708. To access the digital images, see the online FHL catalog:
www.familysearch.org/search/catalog/187101.

"1837 Voters, St. Tammany Parish, Louisiana" [Printed Article], in *New Orleans Genesis* (Genealogical Research Society of New Orleans), Vol. 25, No. 103 (Jul 1987).
- This same database was indexed online at the USGenWeb site for St. Tammany Parish LA. See
http://files.usgwarchives.net/la/sttammany/court/vote1837.txt.

"1837 Census of Voters, Ascension Parish, Louisiana" [Printed Article], in *Le Raconteur* (Le Comité des Archives de la Louisiana, Baton Rouge, LA), Vol. 22, No. 3-4 (Dec 2002).

1837-1839 Slave Manifests, Port of New Orleans **[Online Database],** transcriptions indexed at the Afrigeneas.com site. See
http://afrigeneas.com/slavedata/Roll.12.1837-1839.html.

1837-1857. New Orleans Newspaper Marriage Index – Daily Picayune **[Online Database],** indexed online at the New Orleans Public Library's Louisiana Division website:
http://nutrias.org/~nopl/info/louinfo/newsmarr/newsmarr.htm.

1837-1857. *Louisiana, Parish Marriages* **[Online Database],** digitized and indexed at the FamilySearch.org website. Marriages recorded in Louisiana Parish courthouses. This database has 1,329,791 records. See
https://familysearch.org/search/collection/1807364.

1838 Jury List, St. Tammany Parish, Louisiana **[Online Database],** indexed a the USGenWeb site for St. Tammany LA. See
http://files.usgwarchives.net/la/sttammany/court/jury1838.txt.

1838-1861. *Louisiana, Eastern District Naturalization Petitions* **[Online Database],** indexed at the FamilySearch.org website. Includes naturalization petitions filed in the U.S. District Court for the Eastern District of Louisiana, which was located in New Orleans. The set includes papers filed in naturalization proceedings including petitions for naturalization and oaths of the petitioner and two witnesses. Occasionally declarations of intention filed in other courts are included. The information given for each petition includes the name and residence of the petitioner, country of birth, city and date of arrival, and the names of two witnesses. NARA publication P2233: US District Court at New Orleans, Naturalization Petitions, 1838-1861. Index provided by Fold3. This database has 1,450 records. See
https://familysearch.org/search/collection/1854308.

1838-1890. *Early Landowners in Bienville Parish, Louisiana* **[Online Database],** indexed at the USGenWeb site for Bienville Parish LA, See
http://files.usgwarchives.net/la/bienville/land/earland.txt.

1838-1900. *Caddo Parish, Louisiana Marriage Records* **[Microfilm & Digital Capture],** from the originals at the Caddo Parish Courthouse, Shreveport, LA. Filmed by the Genealogical Society of Utah, 1960, 18 rolls, beginning with FHL film #266250 (Marriage index 1838-1910). For a complete list of roll numbers, roll contents, and the digital images of each roll, see the online FHL catalog page for this title. See
https://familysearch.org/search/catalog/70665.

1839 Grand Jury List, Catahoula Parish, Louisiana **[Online Database],** indexed at the USGenWeb site for Catahoula Parish LA. See
http://files.usgwarchives.net/la/catahoula/court/1839jury.txt.

1840 Louisiana Federal Census Index **[Printed Index],** edited by Ronald Vern Jackson, publ. Accelerated Indexing Systems, North Salt Lake, UT, 1976, 142 pages, FHL book 976.3 X22L.

1840-1900. *Marriage Licenses, East Baton Rouge Parish, Louisiana* **[Microfilm & Digital Capture],** from the records at the Clerk of the District Court, Baton Rouge, LA. Filmed by the Genealogical Society of Utah, 1963, 29 rolls, beginning with FHL film #327734 (Index, 1840-1910). For a complete list of roll numbers, roll contents, and the digital images of each roll, see the online FHL catalog page:
www.familysearch.org/search/catalog/128716.

1840-1906. *Southwest Louisiana, Deaths Index* **[Online Database],** indexed at the Ancestry.com website. From a publication by FamilySearch, Salt Lake City, 2009, an index to death records in seven Louisiana parishes: Calcasieu, Iberia, Lafayette, St. Landry, St. Martin, St. Mary, and Vermillion. The majority of the records are for the years 1861–1865, 1873–1876, and 1879–1882. Each entry includes a name, birth, death, burial, and possibly other information. This database has 6,016 records. See http://search.ancestry.com/search/db.aspx?dbid=2553.

1840-1971. *Index to Successions, Calcasieu Parish, Louisiana* **[Microfilm & Digital Capture],** from the (probate-inheritance) originals at the Calcasieu Parish Courthouse, Lake Charles, LA. Filmed by the Genealogical Society of Utah, 1971, 1 roll, FHL film #871910. To access the digital images of this roll, see the online FHL catalog page: www.familysearch.org/search/catalog/287086.

1840-1986. *Pioneers of Calcasieu Parish* **[Printed Book],** by Nola Mae Wittler Ross, publ. Knight Mfg., Lake Charles, LA, 1987. Contents: vol. 1: Memories of early Calcasieu and information concerning the Moss, Hebert, Thomson, Ball, Armistead, White, Caldwell, Ousley, and Bartlett families; Vol. 2: Pioneers of Calcasieu Parish; Vol. 3: Pioneers of Calcasieu and Cameron Parish. Each volume indexed. See FHL book 976.354. H2r v.1-3.

1840-1910. *Imperial Calcasieu Successions Index* **[Online Database],** indexed at the USGenWeb site for Calcasieu Parish LA. See http://files.usgwarchives.net/la/calcasieu/court/successions/sucindx.txt.

"1841 Voters, West Baton Rouge Parish, Louisiana" [Printed Article], in *West Baton Rouge Genealogical Society Newsletter* (Port Allen, LA), Vol. 10, No. 1 (Jan 1995).

1841-1846. *Records of Interments in the Non-Municipal Cemeteries of New Orleans, 1841-1846, vol. 1 Protestant (Girod Street) Cemetery, July – December 1841* **[Online Database],** a compiled list of names, age, sex, birth, death, residence, marital status, and remarks. Online at the New Orleans Public Library's Louisiana Division website. See http://nutrias.org/~nopl/inv/prot1841.htm.

1842 *New Orleans City Directory* **[Online Database],** indexed at the USGenWeb site for Orleans Parish. 1842 is included in the extensive list of directory years available. See http://files.usgwarchives.net/la/orleans/history/directory.

1842. *Sugar Planters & Manufactures in 1842: Ascension Parish, Louisiana* **[Online Database],** indexed at the USGenWeb site for Ascension Parish: http://files.usgwarchives.net/la/ascension/history/sugar.txt.

1842. *Sugar Planters & Manufacturers in 1842: Jefferson Parish, Louisiana* **[Online Database],** indexed at the USGenWeb site for Jefferson Parish LA: http://files.usgwarchives.net/la/jefferson/history/sugar.txt.

1842. *Sugar Planters & Manufacturers in 1842: St. Charles Parish, Louisiana* **[Online Database],** indexed at the USGenWeb site for St. Charles Parish LA. See http://files.usgwarchives.net/la/stcharles/history/sugar.txt.

1842. *Sugar Planters & Manufacturers in 1842: St. James Parish, Louisiana* **[Online Database],** indexed at the USGenWeb site for St. James Parish LA: http://files.usgwarchives.net/la/stjames/history/business/sugar.txt.

1842. *Sugar Planters & Manufacturers in 1842: St. John the Baptist Parish, Louisiana* **[Online Database],** indexed at the USGenWeb site for St. John the Baptist Parish LA. See http://files.usgwarchives.net/la/stjohnthebaptist/history/industry/sugar.txt.

1842. *Sugar Planters & Manufacturers in 1842: St. Mary & St. Martin Parishes, Louisiana* **[Online Database],** indexed at the USGenWeb site for St. Martin Parish LA. See http://files.usgwarchives.net/la/stmartin/history/business/sugar.txt.

1842. *Sugar Planters & Manufacturers in 1842: Orleans Parish, Louisiana* **[Online Database],** indexed at the USGenWeb site for Orleans Parish LA; http://files.usgwarchives.net/la/orleans/history/business/sugar.txt.

1842-1854. *Case Papers, Orleans Parish, First District Court* **[Microfilm & Digital Capture],** from the originals at the New Orleans Public Library's City

Archives. Includes interdictions, divorces, authorizations, separations of bed and board, successions, emancipations, separations of property, and tutorships. Filmed by the Genealogical Society of Utah, 1991-1992, 106 rolls, beginning with FHL film #1787350 (Case papers No. 1-101, 1843-1854). To access the digital images, see the online FHL catalog: www.familysearch.org/search/catalog/518279.

1843-1871. *Marriage and Death Notices, Caddo Parish, Louisiana and Environs* **[Printed Book & Digital Capture],** compiled by Juanita Davis Cawthon, publ. J.D. Cawthon, Shreveport, LA, 1992, 115 pages, FHL book 976.399 V4c. For access to a digital version of this book, see the FHL online catalog page: https://familysearch.org/search/catalog/636835.

1843-1900. *Bossier Parish, Louisiana Marriage Records* **[Printed Book],** compiled by John C. Head, publ. J & W Enterprises, 1989, 137 pages, FHL book 976.397 V2h.

1843-1909. See *Index of Succession Records, DeSoto Parish, Louisiana, Book D thru K 1843-1909* **[Online Database],** indexed at the USGenWeb site for DeSoto Parish LA. See www.countygenweb.com/DeSotoParishLA/succession_index.htm.

1843-1966. "Parish (Church) History, De Soto Parish, Louisiana" **[Printed Article],** in *DeSoto Plume*, DeSoto Historical Society, Mansfield, LA, Vol.1 (Feb 1966).

1843-1993. *Bossier Parish History: The First 150 Years* **[Printed Book],** by Clifton D. Cardin, publ. ImagePress, Shreveport, LA, 1993, Includes Indian legends, early settlers, early towns, court records, religious history, transportation, military history and records. Includes partial index.
FHL book 976.397 H29c.

1844. *New Orleans Second Municipal Council – List of Fire Victims and their Losses* **[Online Database].** The records of the Second Municipality Council include a volume of the minutes of the 1844 "distribution committee," appointed to apportion a $1,000.00 appropriation for the relief of the victims of an October fire in the Fourth Ward. Also included among the Council's records is a separate volume, listing the names of the fire victims, along with a brief description of their families and losses, with the committee's appropriation toward their relief also recorded. See
http://nutrias.org/~nopl/inv/firevictims1844.htm.

1844-1846 *Census of Licensed Merchants, City of Lafayette. Commissary of Police* **[Microfilm].** The City of Lafayette, covering the area now known as the Garden District and the Irish Channel, was incorporated as part of Jefferson Parish in 1833. In 1852, it was annexed to the City of New Orleans as the Fourth Municipal District. Its original boundaries were the River, Toledano Street, St. Charles Avenue, and Felicity Street. This census, arranged by type of business (e.g., coffee houses or taverns; dry goods merchants), gives the name and location of businesses, the date the license was issued, the term of the license, and its expiration date. Original records at the New Orleans Public Library, filed under call number II LM430 1841-1849.

1844-1880. *Land Claim Case Files of the U.S. District Court for the Eastern District of Louisiana, 1844-1880* **[Microfilm & Digital Capture],** from the originals at the National Archives, Washington, DC. Filmed by the National Archives, series M1115, 16 rolls, beginning with FHL film #1549535 (Minutes, dockets, and judgements 1844-1880). To access the digital images, see the online FHL catalog: www.familysearch.org/search/catalog/589386.

1845 Pointe Coupee Census **[Online Database],** an. extract of names archived at
http://web.archive.org/web/20080830063634/http://www.geocities.com/Heartland/Acres/5571/pc1745cen.htm.

1845. "1845 List of Voters, Lafourche Parish, Louisiana" **[Printed Article],** in *Terrebonne Life Lines* (Terrebonne Genealogical Society, Houma, LA), Vol. 27, No. 3 (Fall 2008).

1846-1859. *Marriage Licenses, Jefferson Parish, Louisiana* **[Microfilm & Digital Capture],** from the originals at the Jefferson Parish Courthouse, Gretna, LA. Filmed by the Genealogical Society of Utah, 1972, 2 rolls, FHL film #900164 (Licenses 1846-1859) & FHL film #900165 (Licenses 1847-1853). To access the digital images, see the online FHL catalog: www.familysearch.org/search/catalog/185578.

1846-1880. *Case Papers, Orleans Parish, Fifth District Court* **[Microfilm & Digital Capture],** from the originals at the New Orleans Public Library's City Archives. The records include interdictions, divorce authorizations, separations of bed and board, successions, emancipations, separations of property, and tutorships. Filmed by the Genealogical Society of Utah, 1990-1992, 72 rolls, beginning with FHL film #1753120 (Case papers No. 3-141, 1846-1848). To access the digital images, see the online FHL catalog: www.familysearch.org/search/catalog/440077.

1846-1880. *Index to Defendant and Plaintiff Dockets* **[Microfilm & Digital Capture],** from the originals of the Louisiana District Court, Fifth District, New Orleans, now at the New Orleans Public Library. Filmed by the Genealogical Society of Utah, 1985, 4 rolls, beginning with FHL film #1420521 (Index). To access the digital images, see the online FHL catalog: www.familysearch.org/search/catalog/489590.

1846-1880. *Index to the Justices of the Peace Marriage Records* **[Online Database],** indexed online at the Louisiana Division website, New Orleans Public Library. From 1846 to 1870, the Justices of the Peace were the exclusive source for civil marriage licenses in Orleans Parish, which was divided into six districts, each of which was to elect a justice. Justices continued to function until 1880, when the judges of the newly established City Court assumed responsibility for issuance of civil marriage licenses. Indexed by alpha groups for Grooms and Brides. See
http://nutrias.org/~nopl/inv/jpmarrindex/jpmarrindex.htm.

1846-1880. *Louisiana, Orleans Parish Second District Judicial Court Case Files* **[Online Database],** digitized at the FamilySearch.org website, an image-only database from original records at the New Orleans City Archives. The collection is being published as images become available. This database has 287,610 records. See
https://familysearch.org/search/collection/1879925.

1846-1889 Ships and Passenger Lists, Orleans Parish, Louisiana **[Online Database],** indexed at the USGenWeb site for Orleans Parish LA. See
www.usgwarchives.net/la/orleans/ships.htm.

1846-1918 Military Records, Orleans Parish, Louisiana **[Online Database],** indexed at the USGenWeb site for Orleans Parish LA. See
www.usgwarchives.net/la/orleans/military.htm.

1846-1924 Naturalizations, East Carroll Parish, Louisiana **[Online Database],** indexed at the USGenWeb site for East Carroll Parish LA. See
http://files.usgwarchives.net/la/eastcarroll/court/naturalizations.

1849-1899. See *Naturalization Records, 2nd District Court, Orleans Parish* **[Microfilm & Digital Capture],** from originals at the New Orleans Public Library. Each volume indexed. Filmed by the Genealogical Society of Utah, 1981, 20 rolls, beginning with FHL film #1306172 (Declarations of Intention, 1849-1853). To access the digital images, see the online FHL catalog:
https://familysearch.org/search/catalog/282887.

1850. *Louisiana, 1850 Federal Census: Population Schedules* **[Microfilm & Digital Capture],** from the originals at the National Archives, Washington, DC. Filmed by the National Archives, 1964, 19 rolls, beginning with FHL film #9696 (Ascension, Assumption, Avoyelles, East Baton Rouge, and West Baton Rouge Parishes). To access the digital images, see the online FHL catalog:
https://familysearch.org/search/catalog/744481.

1850 Louisiana Census Index **[Printed Index],** edited by Ronald Vern Jackson, publ. Accelerated Indexing Systems, Bountiful, UT, 1976, 266 pages, FHL book 976.3 X2p.

1850-1890. *Zur Geschichte der Deutschen Kirchengemeinden im Staate Louisiana* **[Microfilm & Digital Capture],** from a book by J. Hanho Deiler, publ. New Orleans, 1894: *The History of the German Church in Louisiana.* Includes a history of the Germans of the lower Mississippi with a census of New Orleans German schools and foreign inhabitants, 1850-1890. Includes index. Filmed by the Genealogical Society of Utah, 1981, 1 roll, FHL film #1305374. To access the digital images of this roll, see the online FHL catalog page for this title:
www.familysearch.org/search/catalog/237334.

1850-1956. See *Louisiana Deaths, 1850-1875, 1894-1960* **[Online Database],** indexed at the FamilySearch.org website. The statewide records for all parishes cover 1911-1959. Coverage outside these dates for individual Parishes varies. This collection does not include records for deaths from 1875-1893 and has only a few entries for 1894-1904. Death records for 1850-1875 are for Jefferson Parish only. The records derive from the Louisiana State Board of Health, Bureau of Vital Statistics. This database has 776,611 records. See
https://familysearch.org/search/collection/1609793.

1851. *New Orleans Ship Passenger List Online Index — January to July 1851* **[Online Database],** indexed at the Louisiana State Archives Historical Resources webpage. This is an online index to a portion of the New Orleans ship passenger lists available on microfilm in the Research Library at the Louisiana State Archives. Information provided in this database includes passenger name, date of arrival, name of ship and port of departure. With the date of arrival and name of ship, researchers can then locate on microfilm the ship manifest listing all passengers on that particular ship. Information available on these lists includes age, sex, occupation, country to which the passengers belong, country to which they intend to become inhabitants and the number that died on the passage: www.sos.la.gov/HistoricalResources/ResearchHistoricalRecords/Pages/PassengerManifests.aspx.

1850-1851 *Census of Sugar Cane Planters and Productions, Rapides Parish, Louisiana* [Online Database], indexed at the USGenWeb site for Rapides Parish LA. See
http://files.usgwarchives.net/la/rapides/census/sugar.txt.

1851-1855 *Probate Records Index, Claiborne Parish, Louisiana* [Online Database], indexed at the USGenWeb site for Claiborne Parish LA. See http://files.usgwarchives.net/la/claiborne/court/1851-55.txt.

1851-1900. *Louisiana Marriage Records* [Online Database], indexed at the Ancestry.com website. Originally compiled by Jordan Dodd, Liahona Research, acquired by Ancestry.com in 2000. This update adds the records for Bienville, Caldwell, Jackson, and Ouachita parishes to those of Bossier, Lincoln, and Sabine for the years 1851 through 1900. Each entry lists, at a minimum, spouses' names and the date of the marriage. This database has 43,140 records: http://search.ancestry.com/search/db.aspx?dbid=5228.

1852-1893. *New Orleans Office of the Mayor – Records of the Disposition of Destitute Orphans* [Online Database], transcriptions by year at the Louisiana Division website, New Orleans Public Library. See
http://nutrias.org/~nopl/inv/orphanstranscriptions.htm.

1854 History. See *History of Louisiana* **[Online Database],** digitized and OCR indexed at the Ancestry.com website. Original data: Gayarré, Charles, *History of Louisiana,* New York: W.J. Widdleton, c1854. This database has 2,274 pages. See
https://search.ancestry.com/search/db.aspx?dbid=28137.
- A later edition of the 2-vol printed set and a digital version is accessible at the online FHL library catalog page: www.familysearch.org/search/catalog/2357292.

1853-1868. *Will Book, Jefferson Parish, Louisiana* [Microfilm & Digital Capture], from the originals at the Jefferson Parish Courthouse, Gretna, LA. Filmed by the Genealogical Society of Utah, 1965, 1 roll, FHL film #402549. To access the digital images, see the online FHL catalog:
www.familysearch.org/search/catalog/245320.

1853-1880. *Case Papers, Orleans Parish, Sixth District Court* [Microfilm & Digital Capture], from the originals at the New Orleans Public Library's City Archives. Includes interdictions, divorces, authorizations, separations of bed and board, successions, emancipations, separations of property, and tutorships. Filmed by the Genealogical Society of Utah, 1991, 43 rolls, beginning with FHL film #1769585 (District Court Cases No. 5226-5266 1853-1856). To access the digital images, see the online FHL catalog:www.familysearch.org/search/catalog/520820.

1853-1952. *Louisiana, New Orleans, Index to Passenger Lists (Arrivals)* [Online Database], indexed at FamilySearch.org, from the original records at the National Archives, microfilm series T527. The index cards may include full name, age, gender, marital status, nationality, last permanent residence, birthplace, and final destination. This database has 439,344 records, see
www.familysearch.org/search/collection/2443949.

1854-1857 *Census, City of Carrollton* [Microfilm], from original records at the New Orleans Public Library. The City of Carrollton was incorporated in 1845 as part of Jefferson Parish and, in 1874, was annexed to the City of New Orleans. The boundaries of Carrollton were the River, the present Jefferson Parish line, the shore of Lake Pontchartrain, and Lowerline Street (and its projected extension to the Lake). This census gives the name and occupation of householders in the City of Carrollton and tallies the number of males and females in each household, and the number of children in general age groups. The names are grouped alphabetically by first letter of the name only. Original records at the New Orleans Public Library, Volume 1 (1854-1855) is not filmed. Volume 2 is filed under call number IV TK840 1854-1857.

1854-1858 Baptismal Register, St. Mary Magdaleine Church, Vermilion Parish, Louisiana [Online Database], indexed at the USGenWeb site for Vermilion Parish LA. See http://files.usgwarchives.net/la/vermilion/churches/stmavol1.txt.

1855 Jury List, Washington Parish, Louisiana [Online Database], indexed at the USGenWeb site for Washington Parish LA. See http://files.usgwarchives.net/la/washington/court/jury1855.txt.

1855-1856 New Orleans Census of Merchants and Persons Following Professions Requiring Licenses, [Original Bound Volumes], 3 vols., original records at the New Orleans Public Library, filed under call number LC840. These volumes give name, residence or place of business, callings or professions, number of license, amount paid, and remarks; individuals are listed together by square of property occupied; related forms are also included at the front of each volume. Volume one (1855) is for the Second Ward; volume two (1855) covers the Third Ward; and volume three (1856) is for the Third Municipal District. Indexed.

1855-1856. New Orleans Deaths and Marriages [Digitized Book], from the original publ. Houston, TX, 1976, 53 pages. For access to the digital version, see the online FHL catalog page: https://familysearch.org/search/catalog/2364608.

1856. St. James Parish, Louisiana, Sugar Planters [Online Database], indexed at the USGenWeb site for St. James Parish LA. See www.stjamesparish.jwebre.com/sugar_planters_1856.htm.

"1858 Insolvent Tax List" [Printed Article], in *Friends of Genealogy Journal* (Shreveport, LA), Vol. 3, No. 3 (1991).

"1859 Voters, Union Parish, Louisiana" [Printed Article], in *Genie* (Ark-La-Tex Genealogical Association, Shreveport, LA), Vol. 28, No. 2 (1994). - For a digital version of this database, see the USGenWeb site for Union Parish LA. See http://files.usgwarchives.net/la/union/court/voter1859.txt.

1860. Louisiana, 1860 Federal Census: Population Schedules [Microfilm & Digital Capture], from the originals at the National Archives, Washington, DC. Filmed twice by the National Archives, 1950, 1967, 29 rolls, beginning with FHL film #803407 (2nd filming: Ascension, Assumption, and Avoyelles Parishes). To access the digital images, see the online FHL catalog: https://familysearch.org/search/catalog/704922.

1860 Louisiana Census Index [Printed Index], edited by Ronald Vern Jackson, publ. Accelerated Indexing Systems, Bountiful, UT, 1985, 507 pages, FHL book 976.3 X22j.

1860 Slave Owners, Plaquemine Parish [Online Database], indexed at the USGenWeb African American Archives site. See http://files.usgwarchives.net/la/state/history/afriamer/slaves/plaq1.txt.

1860-1930. Louisiana United States National Cemeteries Burials [Microfilm & Digital Capture], from the original records at the Louisiana National Guard, Jackson Barracks, LA. Filmed by the Genealogical Society of Utah, 1990, 13 rolls, beginning with FHL Film #1704335. For a complete list of roll numbers, roll contents, and the digital images of certain rolls, see the online FHL catalog page for this title: www.familysearch.org/search/catalog/556828.

1861 Tax List, Slave Owners, DeSoto Parish, Louisiana [Online Database], indexed at the USGenWeb site for DeSoto Parish LA. See http://files.usgwarchives.net/la/desoto/taxlists/slaves.txt.

1861-1865. The Civil War Tax in Plaquemine Parish, Louisiana [Online Database], indexed at the USGenWeb site for Plaquemine Parish LA. See http://files.usgwarchives.net/la/plaquemines/history/civiltax.txt.

1861-1865. Index to Compiled Service Records of Confederate Soldiers Who Served in organizations from the State of Louisiana [Microfilm & Digital Capture], from the originals at the National Archives, Washington, DC. Filmed by the National Archives, series M378, 1962, 31 rolls, beginning with FHL film #881457 (Index, A). For a complete list of roll numbers, roll contents, and the digital images of each roll; and access to the U.S. Civil War Soldiers Index available online, view the online FHL catalog page: https://familysearch.org/search/catalog/316173.

1861-1865. Louisiana, Civil War Service Records of Confederate Soldiers [Online Database], digitized and indexed at the FamilySearch.org website. The records include a jacket-envelope for each soldier, labeled with his name, his rank, and the unit in which he served. The jacket-envelope typically contains card abstracts of entries relating to the soldier as found in the original muster rolls, returns, rosters, payrolls,

appointment books, hospital registers, Union prison registers and rolls, parole rolls, inspection reports; and the originals of any papers relating solely to the particular soldier. For each military unit the service records are arranged alphabetically by the soldier's surname. The images came from the National Archives microfilm, series M321. Index courtesy of Fold3.com. This database has 778,925 records. See
https://familysearch.org/search/collection/1932372.

1861-1865. *Louisiana, Confederate Soldiers Index* **[Online Database],** indexed at the Ancestry.com website. From Andrew B. Booth's *Records of Louisiana Confederate Soldiers & Confederate Commands.* Vol. I-III. New Orleans, LA, 1920. This database constitutes 3 volumes of records of Louisiana Confederate soldiers and commands. This alphabetized roll contains over 120,000 records of individuals. It also provides a brief history of Louisiana's 982 companies in the Confederate army:
http://search.ancestry.com/search/db.aspx?dbid=3199.

1861-1865. *Index to Compiled Service Records of Volunteer Union Soldiers Who Served in Organizations from the State of Louisiana* **[Microfilm & Digital Capture],** from the originals at the National Archives, Washington, DC. Filmed by the National Archives, series M387, 4 rolls, beginning with FHL film #821926 (Index A-E). To access the digital images, see the online FHL catalog:
https://familysearch.org/search/catalog/319046.

1861-1865. *Louisiana, Civil War Service Records of Union Soldiers* **[Online Database],** digitized and indexed at the FamilySearch.org website. The records include a jacket-envelope for each soldier, labeled with his name, his rank, and the unit in which he served. The jacket-envelope typically contains card abstracts of entries relating to the soldier as found in original muster rolls, returns, rosters, payrolls, appointment books, hospital registers, prison registers and rolls, parole rolls, inspection reports; and the originals of any papers relating solely to the particular soldier. For each military unit the service records are arranged alphabetically by the soldier's surname. The images came from the National Archives microfilm, series M396. Index courtesy of Fold3.com. This database has 119,515 records. See
https://familysearch.org/search/collection/1932399.

1861-1865. *Index to Prisoners of War Compiled from Various Union Prisons* **[Microfilm & Digital Capture],** from the originals located at the Jackson Barracks Military Library, New Orleans, LA. Filmed by the Genealogical Society of Utah, 1990, 1 roll, FHL film #1685402. To access the digital images, see the online FHL catalog:
www.familysearch.org/search/catalog/596985.

1861-1865. See *Confederate Veterans Buried in Beauregard and Vernon Parishes, Louisiana* **[Online Database],** indexed at the US GenWeb site for Beauregard Parish LA. See
http://files.usgwarchives.net/la/beauregard/military/veteran.txt.

1861-1928. *Marriage Records, Rapides Parish, Louisiana* **[Microfilm & Digital Capture],** from the originals at the Rapides Parish Courthouse, Alexandria, LA. All volumes indexed. Filmed by the Genealogical Society of Utah, 1982, 59 rolls, beginning with FHL film #1316122 (Direct and Indirect index A-D). For a complete list of roll numbers, roll contents, and the digital images of each roll, see the online FHL catalog page for this title. See
https://familysearch.org/search/catalog/272420.

1861-1960 Louisiana Directories, as part of *U.S. City Directories, 1822-1995* **[Online Database],** digitized and OCR indexed at the Ancestry.com website. See each directory title page image for the full title and publication information. This collection is one of the largest single databases on the Internet. All states are represented (except Alaska) with a total of 1.56 billion names, all indexed from scanned images of the city directory book pages. Louisiana directories are listed here for a **LA City** (No. of years), and Date-Range: **Alexandria** (18) 1912-1950, **Baton Rouge** (39) 1905-1960, **Lafayette** (9) 1939-1959, **Lake Charles** (31) 1911-1960, **Monroe** (7) 1912-1959, **New Iberia** (4) 1940-1960, **New Orleans** (82) 1861-1960, **Opelousas** (3) 1956-1960, and **Shreveport** (44) 1875-1960. Use Ancestry's *Browse this Collection* feature to choose a state, choose a city, and choose a directory year available for that city. This U.S. database has 1,560,284,702 records. See
https://search.ancestry.com/search/db.aspx?dbid=2469.

1861-1998. *Military Records of Livingston Parish, Louisiana* **[Online Database],** indexed at the USGenWeb site for Livingston Parish LA. See
www.usgwarchives.net/la/livingston/liv-mil.htm.

1862 Slave Holders, Natchitoches Parish, Louisiana **[Online Database],** includes some slaves held in Winn Parish as well. Indexed at the USGenWeb site for Winn Parish LA. See
http://files.usgwarchives.net/la/winn/history/slav1862.txt.

1862-1863. *Orleans Parish Coroner's Office Reports of Deaths* **[Online Database],** extracted at the New Orleans Public Library's Louisiana Division website. Some, but not all, of the deaths also appear in the official record of Inquests and Views. These deaths are of special interest since they occurred during the period of Union occupation of New Orleans following the city's fall in April 1862. The data in the notebook were transcribed by members of NOVA (the New Orleans Volunteer Association) and made available to New Orleans Public Library for inclusion on its web site. Several of the reports are accompanied by links to newspaper accounts of the deaths. See
http://nutrias.org/~nopl/inv/coroner/th1862to1863.htm.

1862-1926. See *Miscellaneous Death Reports and Indexes, 1862-1863, 1926* **[Microfilm & Digital Capture],** from originals at a location not noted, but probably New Orleans Public Library (based on year of filming). Filmed by the Genealogical Society of Utah, 1972, 1 rolls, FHL film #906706. To access the digital images, see the online FHL catalog:
www.familysearch.org/search/catalog/97188.

1862-1865. *Deaths and Burials of Confederate Soldiers in New Orleans, Louisiana* **[Microfilm & Digital Capture],** from the originals at the Jackson Barracks Military Library, New Orleans. Includes register of Confederate soldiers who died in Camp Douglas, 1862-65 and lie buried in Oakwoods Cemetery, Chicago, IL, 1892, newspaper articles, register of the Confederate dead buried on Johnson's Island, correspondence, and manuscript listings of confederate deaths. Filmed by the Genealogical Society of Utah, 1990, 1 roll, FHL film #1710607. To access the digital images, see the online FHL catalog:
www.familysearch.org/search/catalog/583230.

1863-1866 Internal Revenue Assessment Lists for Louisiana, Bureau of Internal Revenue **[Microfilm & Digital Capture],** from the originals at the National Archives, Central Plains Region, series M769. **District 1:** Ascension, Jefferson, Lafourche, Livingston, Orleans, Plaquemines, St. Bernard, St. Charles, St. Helena, St. James, St. John the Baptist, St. Tammany, Terrebonne, & Washington parishes. **District 2:** Assumption, Avoyelles, Calcasieu, East Baton Rouge, East Feliciana, Iberville, Lafayette, Natchitoches, Pointe Coupee, Rapides, Sabine, St. Landry, St. Martin, St. Mary, Vermilion, West Baton Rouge, & West Feliciana parishes. **District 3:** Bienville, Bossier, Caddo, Caldwell, Carroll, Catahoula, Claiborne, Concordia, De Soto, Franklin, Jackson, Madison, Morehouse, Ouachita, Tensas, Union, & Winn parishes. Filmed by the National Archives, 1985, beginning with FHL film #1578469 (District 1: 1863-1864). To access the digital images, see the online FHL catalog:
https://familysearch.org/search/catalog/577907.

1862. *Natchitoches Parish Slave Holders in 1862* **[Online Database],** extracted at the USGenWeb site for Natchitoches Parish LA. See
http://files.usgwarchives.net/la/natchitoches/history/slav1862.txt.

1863-1921. *Marriage Records, Jefferson Parish, Louisiana* **[Microfilm & Digital Capture],** from originals at the Jefferson Parish Courthouse, Gretna, LA. Filmed by the Genealogical Society of Utah, 1965, 9 rolls, beginning with FHL film #402550 (Marriage Index books A-H 1863-1913To access the digital images, see the online FHL catalog:
https://familysearch.org/search/catalog/245323.

"**1864 Direct tax, Ascension Parish, Louisiana**" **[Printed Article],** in *Ascension Roots* (East Ascension Genealogical & Historical Society), Vol. 10, No. 1 (Mar 1990).

"**1864 Taxpayers List, Bossier Parish & Caddo Parish, Louisiana**" **[Printed Article],** in *Genie* (Ark-La-Tex Genealogical Association, Shreveport, LA), Vol. 23, No. 3 (1989).

1864. *Bossier Parish Taxpayers Listed in 1864* **[Online Database],** indexed in the USGenWeb site for Bossier Parish LA. See
http://files.usgwarchives.net/la/bossier/court/1864tax.txt.

1864 Civil War Tax, St. Tammany Parish, Louisiana **[Online Database],** indexed at the USGenWeb site for St. Tammany Parish LA. See
http://files.usgwarchives.net/la/sttammany/taxlists/1864cwtx.txt.

1864 Tax List, Winn Parish, Louisiana **[Online Database],** indexed at the USGenWeb site for Winn Parish LA. See
http://files.usgwarchives.net/la/winn/taxlists/tax1864.txt.

1864-1940. *Name Index to Some Probate Dockets of Rapides Parish, Louisiana* **[Printed Book],** compiled by Norma Rose, publ. J & W Enterprises, Shreveport, LA, 1999, 61 pages, FHL book 976.369 P22r.

1864-2003. *Chalmette, Louisiana, Chalmette National Cemetery* **[Online Database],** digitized and indexed at the Ancestry.com website. Cemetery section is provided for each image. Information on the markers varies. Some may contain only a number of initials; others may include facts such as name, birth date, death date, age, rank, and state of origin. This database has 8,525 records. See
https://search.ancestry.com/search/db.aspx?dbid=2293.

1865. *The Civil War Tax in Louisiana, 1865: Based on Direct Tax Assessments of Louisianans,* original printed 1892 with the title, *List of Names of Citizens of Louisiana From Whom the United States Direct Tax was Collected in 1865, Together with the Amounts Paid by Each* **[Printed Book].** Reprinted 1975 by Polyanthos, Inc., New Orleans, 363 pages. See FHL book 976.3 R4c. For access to a digital version of this title, see the online FHL catalog page:
https://familysearch.org/search/catalog/153997.

1865 Tax List, Caddo Parish, Louisiana **[Online Database],** indexed at the USGenWeb site for Caddo Parish LA. See
http://files.usgwarchives.net/la/caddo/taxlists/1865tax.txt.

1865 Tax Roll, Calcasieu Parish, Louisiana **[Online Database],** indexed at the USGenWeb site for Calcasieu Parish LA. See
http://files.usgwarchives.net/la/calcasieu/taxlists/taxroll.txt.

1865 U.S. Direct Tax, Caldwell Parish, Louisiana **[Online Database],** indexed at the USGenWeb site for Caldwell Parish LA. See
http://files.usgwarchives.net/la/caldwell/taxlists/1865tx.txt.

1865 U.S. Direct Tax, Grant Parish, Louisiana **[Online Database],** indexed at the USGenWeb site for Grant Parish LA. See
http://files.usgwarchives.net/la/grant/taxlists/tax1865.txt.

1865. "Civil War Tax Roll, Plaquemines Parish, Louisiana" **[Printed Article],** in *Deep Delta,* (Plaquemines Deep Delta Genealogical Society, Buras, LA), Vol. 1, No. 2 (May 1983).

1865. *U.S. Direct Tax, St. James Parish, Louisiana* **[Online Database],** indexed at the USGenWeb site for St. James Parish LA. See
www.stjamesparish.jwebre.com/1865_tax_records.htm.

1865. *U.S. Direct Tax, Winn Parish, Louisiana* **[Online Database],** indexed at the USGenWeb site for Winn Parish LA. See
http://files.usgwarchives.net/la/winn/taxlists/tax1865.txt.

1865. "1865 Delinquent Taxpayers, Lafourche Parish, Louisiana" **[Printed Article],** in *Acadian Genealogy Exchange* (Mrs. Janet B. John, Covington, KY), Vol. 10, No. 1 (Jan 1981).

"1865-1870 Tax Roll, Lafayette Parish, Louisiana" **[Printed Article],** in *Louisiana Genealogical Register* (Louisiana Genealogical & Historical Society, Baton Rouge, LA), Vol. 26, No. 2 (Jun 1979).

"1865-1870 Tax Roll, Non-Residents, Lafayette Parish, Louisiana" **[Printed Article],** in *Louisiana Genealogical Register* (Louisiana Genealogical & Historical Society, Baton Rouge, LA), Vol. 26, No. 2 (Jun 1979).

1865-1872. *Louisiana, Freedmen's Bureau Field Office Records* **[Online Database],** digitized at the FamilySearch.org website. This is an image-only database, with records from the Bureau of Refugees, Freedmen, and Abandoned Lands (often called the Freedmen's Bureau), created in 1865 at the end of the American Civil War to supervise relief efforts including education, health care, food and clothing, refugee camps, legalization of marriages, employment, labor contracts, and securing back pay, bounty payments and pensions. These records include letters and endorsements sent and received, account books, applications for rations, applications for relief, court records, labor contracts, registers of bounty claimants, registers of complaints, registers of contracts, registers of disbursements, registers of freedmen issued rations, registers of patients, reports, rosters of officers and employees, special and general orders and circulars received, special orders and circulars issued, records relating to claims, court trials, property restoration, and homesteads. This database has 97,119 images. See
www.familysearch.org/search/collection/2333781.

1865-1912. *Weekly Thibodaux Sentinel: Microfilm Index; 8-5-1865 thru 12-7-1912; Deaths, Weddings, Births* **[Printed Book],** compiled by Phillip Chauvin, publ. Terrebonne Genealogy Society, Houma, LA, 216 pages, FHL book 976.339 V42c.

"1866 Assessment Roll, Bienville Parish, Louisiana" **[Printed Article],** in *Claiborne Parish Trails* (J & W Enterprises, Shreveport, LA), Vol. 11, No. 2 (May 1996).

1866-1872. *District Court Cases, Louisiana, Orleans Parish, Seventh District* **[Microfilm & Digital Capture],** from the originals at the New Orleans Public Library. Selected suits were microfilmed, including interdictions, divorces, authorizations, separations of bed and board, successions, emancipations, separations of property and tutorships. Filmed by the Genealogical Society of Utah, 1991, 2 rolls, FHL film #1822282 (1870-1871) & FHL film #1822283 (1866-1872). To access the digital images, see the online FHL catalog: www.familysearch.org/search/catalog/521209.

1866-1963. *Louisiana, State Penitentiary Records* **[Online Database],** digitized at the FamilySearch.org website. This is an image-only database with images of indexes and registers of convicts admitted to the prison. This database has 21,796 images. Browse through the images, organized by Record Type, Volume, and Year Range. See
https://familysearch.org/search/collection/1931391.
- This image-only database is also available at the Ancestry.com website. See
https://search.ancestry.com/search/db.aspx?dbid=60299.

"1867 Voter Registration Roll, St. John the Baptist Parish, Louisiana" [Printed Article], in *Les Voyageurs* (German-Acadian Coast historical & Genealogical Society, Destrehan, LA), Vol. 33, No. 3 (Sep 2012).

"1867 Assessment Roll, Terrebonne Parish, Louisiana" [Printed Article], in *Terrebonne Life Lines* (Terrebonne Genealogical Society, Houma, LA), Vol. 2, No. 1 (Spring 1983); Vol. 2, No. 2 (Summer 1983); and Vol. 2, No. 3 (Fall 1983).

1867 Voter Registration, Union Parish, Louisiana **[Online Database],** indexed at the USGenWeb site for Union Parish LA. See
http://files.usgwarchives.net/la/union/court/voter1867.txt.

"1867-1868 Voter Registration Rolls, St. Tammany Parish, Louisiana" [Printed Article], in *Florida Parishes Genealogical Newsletter* (Baton Rouge, LA), Vol. 9, No. 4 (Jul 1987).

1867-1905. *Louisiana, Orleans and St. Tammany Parish, Voter Registration Records* **[Online Database],** digitized and indexed at FamilySearch.org, from original records at the New Orleans Public Library and St. Tammany Parish Courthouse, Covington, LA. Each index record may include Name, Event type, Event date, Event place, Race, Birth date, and Birthplace. This database has 132,854 records, see
www.familysearch.org/search/collection/3326775.

1867-1940. *Voting Registers, St. Tammany Parish, Louisiana0* **[Microfilm & Online Database],** from the originals at the St. Tammany Parish Courthouse, Covington, LA. Lists date of registry, name, place of residence, precinct, time resident in state, parish, precinct, native, how & when naturalized, and remarks. Filmed by the Genealogical Society of Utah, 1987, 17 rolls, beginning with FHL film #1509704 (Voter Registration, 1867-1868). To access the digital images, see the online FHL catalog:
https://familysearch.org/search/catalog/536867.
- The 1868-1870 part of this database was indexed online at the USGenWeb site for St. Tammany Parish LA. See
http://files.usgwarchives.net/la/sttammany/court/voters.txt.

1867-1871. *Louisiana, New Orleans Passenger Departures* **[Online Database],** digitized and index at FamilySearch.org, from original records at the National Archives, microfilm series M2115. Each index record includes Name, Event type, Event date, Event place, Gender, Age, Birth year, and Birthplace. This database has 5,123 records, see
www.familysearch.org/search/collection/3326858.

1868 Tax List, Winn Parish, Louisiana **[Online Database],** indexed at the USGenWeb site for Winn Parish LA. See
http://files.usgwarchives.net/la/winn/taxlists/tax1868.txt.

1868-1873. *District Court Cases, Louisiana, Orleans Parish, Seventh District* **[Microfilm & Digital Capture],** from the originals at the New Orleans Public Library. Selected cases have been microfilmed, including interdictions, divorces, authorizations, separations of bed and board, successions, emancipations, separations of property and tutorships. Filmed by the Genealogical Society of Utah, 1991, 8 rolls, beginning with FHL film #1498094 (Cases No. 1-451 1868-1869). To access the digital images, see the online FHL catalog:
www.familysearch.org/search/catalog/521028.

1869 Tax List, Winn Parish, Louisiana **[Online Database],** indexed at the USGenWeb site for Winn Parish LA. See
http://files.usgwarchives.net/la/winn/taxlists/tax1869.txt.

1869-1870 Orleans Parish Poll Tax Rolls **[Printed Book],** compiled by Judy Riffel, et al., publ. Baton Rouge, LA, 1996, 258 pages. This is an index to the original tax records for the city of New Orleans, Louisiana. The original microfilm reels are located at the Louisiana State Archives (accession numbers: P1978-170 for 1869; P1978-172 for 1870). Index book only at FHL, book 976.335/N1 R42r.

1869-1900. *Early Tangipahoa Parish: Including the 1870 (1st) Census, Confederate Soldiers, Towns, Old Families, Voters, Pensioners, Parish Officials, Excerpts from Old Newspapers, the First Schools* **[Printed Book],** by Elias Wesley & Mary E. Sandel, Includes index. Publ. 1984, 359 pages, FHL book 976.313 X2sa.

1870. *Louisiana, 1870 Federal Census: Population Schedules* **[Microfilm & Digital Capture],** from the original records at the National Archives, Washington, DC. Filmed twice by the National Archives, 1962, 1968, 41 rolls, beginning with FHL film #552004 (2nd filming: Ascension and Assumption Parishes). To access the digital images, see the online FHL catalog: https://familysearch.org/search/catalog/698899.

1870 Louisiana Census Index **[Printed Index],** edited by Raeone Christensen Steuart, publ. Heritage Quest, Bountiful, UT, 2000, Vol. 1: A-K; Vol. 2: L-Z, FHL book 976.3 X22L.

1871 Tax List, Winn Parish, Louisiana **[Online Database],** indexed at the USGenWeb site for Winn Parish LA. See
http://files.usgwarchives.net/la/winn/taxlists/tax1871.txt.

1870-1871. *U.S. District Court, Eastern District of Louisiana, New Orleans Criminal Cases* **[Online Database],** an image-only database, digitized at the Ancestry.com website. Part of the larger *U.S. Circuit Court Criminal Case Files, 1790-1871*. Go to "Browse this collection" to select the Louisiana case files. This database has 20,061 images. See
http://search.ancestry.com/search/db.aspx?dbid=1248.

1872 Tax List, Winn Parish, Louisiana **[Online Database],** indexed at the USGenWeb site for Winn Parish LA. See
http://files.usgwarchives.net/la/winn/taxlists/tax1872.txt.

1872-1905. *Marriage Records, Tangipahoa Parish, Louisiana* **[Microfilm & Digital Capture],** from the originals at the Tangipahoa Parish Courthouse, Amite, LA. Filmed by the Genealogical Society of Utah, 1964, 5 rolls, beginning with FHL film #364081 (Marriage Records 1872-1886). To access the digital images, see the online FHL catalog:
https://familysearch.org/search/catalog/292944.

1873-1922. *Successions, Cameron Parish, Louisiana* **[Online Database],** indexed at the USGenWeb site for Cameron Parish LA. See
http://files.usgwarchives.net/la/cameron/court/succabc.txt.

1874. "Registered Voters List, 31 Oct 1874, Tangipahoa Parish, Louisiana" **[Printed Article],** in *Louisiana Genealogical Register* (Louisiana Genealogical & Historical Society, Baton Rouge, LA), Vol. 36, No. 4 (Dec 1969).
- For an online digital version of this database, see the USGenWeb site for Tangipahoa Parish LA. See
http://files.usgwarchives.net/la/tangipahoa/misc/vote1874.txt.

1875. "Assessment Roll Name List, Bienville Parish, Louisiana" **[Printed Article],** in *Genie* (Ark-La-Tex Genealogical Association, Shreveport, LA), Vol. 39, No. 3 (2005).

1875-1877. *New Orleans City Insane Asylum Record of Next of Kin, 1875-1877, 1 vol.* **[Online Database],** extracted at the Louisiana Division website, New Orleans Public Library. Includes the patient's name and the name and address of the person to be referred to--i.e., the next of kin. The volume is in very poor condition, with many pages either cut or torn out. Most of the entries are overwritten with "died," "removed," "released," etc. See
http://nutrias.org/~nopl/inv/next%20of%20kin.htm.

1875-1933. *Probate Indexes, Livingston Parish, Louisiana* **[Printed Book],** compiled by Gloria L. Kerns, publ. Baker, LA, 15 pages, FHL book 976.3 A1 No. 46.

1877-1902. *Succession Records, Settlements of Estates, Tangipahoa Parish, Louisiana* **[Microfilm & Digital Capture],** originals at the Tangipahoa Parish Courthouse, Amite, LA. Filmed by the Genealogical Society of Utah, 1964, 2 rolls, FHL film #364087 (Vol. 2-3, 1877-1888) & FHL film #354088 (Vol. 4, 1887-1902). To access the digital images for these rolls, see the online FHL catalog page:
www.familysearch.org/search/catalog/266855.

"1879 Delinquent Tax List, Lafayette Parish, Louisiana" **[Printed Article],** in *Louisiana Genealogical Register* (Louisiana Genealogical & Historical Society, Baton Rouge, LA), Vol. 21, No. 3 (Sep 1974).

1879 Tax List, Winn Parish, Louisiana **[Online Database],** indexed at the USGenWeb site for Winn Parish LA. See
http://files.usgwarchives.net/la/winn/taxlists/tax1879.txt.

1879-1880. See *Louisiana 2nd District (Orleans Parish), Marriages, May 12, 1879 to April 12, 1880* **[Online Database],** transcribed online at the Louisiana Division website, New Orleans Public Library. Judges

in Louisiana have been authorized to celebrate marriages since 1820; only one volume of marriage records has survived from the Second District Court in New Orleans. See
http://nutrias.org/~nopl/inv/2dcmarriages.htm.

1879, 1881, 1885, 1890 Louisiana Tax Rolls, Madison Parish **[Printed Book & Online Database],** compiled by Richard P. Sevier, published Midland, TX, 1998, 2 vols. Names are in alphabetical order. For each person/year: name; ward; plantation or property name and/or location; property description; number of acres; assessed value of land; line number. See FHL book 976.381 R4m v.1 (1879 & 1881) & 976.381 R4 v.2.(1885 & 1890). The Vol. 1 database (1879 & 1881) was indexed online at the RootsWeb site for Madison Parish LA. For an archived database
https://web.archive.org/web/20160404201842/http://www.rootsweb.ancestry.com/~lamadiso/mptr7981index.htm.

1879-1920. *Livingston Parish, Louisiana: Computer Indexed Marriage Records* **[Printed Book],** compiled and published by Nicholas Russell Murray, Hunting for Bears, Hammond, LA, 1985, 54 pages, FHL book 976.314 V22m.

1880. *Louisiana, 1880 Federal Census: Soundex and Population Schedules* **[Microfilm & Digital Capture],** from the originals at the National Archives, Washington, DC (ca 1985). After filming, the original 1880 population schedules for Louisiana were transferred to Louisiana State University, Baton Rouge. Filmed on 83 rolls, beginning with FHL film #447123 (1880 Soundex: A000 thru A450); and FHL film #1254447 (1880 Population schedules: Ascension and Assumption Parishes). To access the digital images, see the online FHL catalog:
https://familysearch.org/search/catalog/673559.

1880 Census of New Orleans **[Printed Book],** compiled by Patricia Ann Fenerty and Patricia White Fernandez, each volume indexed. Publ. Padraigeen, New Orleans, 1991-2003, 8 vols., FHL book 976.335 X2f.

1880 Tax List, Winn Parish, Louisiana **[Online Database],** indexed at the USGenWeb site for Winn Parish LA. See
http://files.usgwarchives.net/la/winn/taxlists/tax1880.txt.

"1880-1882 Voter Registration Book, St. Martin Parish, Louisiana" [Printed Article], in *Le Raconteur* (Le Comité des Archives de la Louisiana, Baton Rouge, LA), Vol. 26, No. 3 (Sep 2006).

1880-1916. *Orleans Parish Registrar of Voters - Index to Registrations of Foreign-Born Persons* **[Online Database],** the index records for each registrant his name, address, ward, precinct, country of birth, age, place and date of naturalization, and date of registration. Each volume is divided into alphabetical sections with data entered in order more or less by ward and precinct. See
http://nutrias.org/~nopl/inv/vx/vx100.htm.

1880-1925. *Civil Suits, Caddo Parish, Louisiana, 1880-1925* **[Microfilm & Digital Capture],** from the originals at the Caddo Parish Courthouse, Shreveport, LA. Includes indexes. Civil suits arranged according to Successions, Emancipations, and Interdictions. Filmed by the Genealogical Society of Utah, 1961, 169 rolls, beginning with FHL film #265690 (Direct index, plaintiffs, 1880-1925). To access the digital images, see the online FHL catalog:
https://familysearch.org/search/catalog/397925.

1880-1929. *Case Papers, Louisiana, Civil District Court, Orleans Parish* {**Microfilm & Digital Capture],** from the originals now at the New Orleans Public Library. Selected suits were microfilmed, including interdictions, divorces, authorizations, separations of bed and board, successions, emancipations, separations of property, and, tutorships. Includes index organized alphabetically within years. Filmed by the Genealogical Society of Utah, 1986-1992, 1,310 rolls, beginning with FHL film #483919. To access the digital images, see the online FHL catalog:
www.familysearch.org/search/catalog/42396.

1881 Tax List, Winn Parish, Louisiana **[Online Database],** indexed at the USGenWeb site for Winn Parish LA. See
http://files.usgwarchives.net/la/winn/taxlists/tax1881.txt.

1882 Tax List, Winn Parish, Louisiana **[Online Database],** indexed at the USGenWeb site for Winn Parish LA. See
http://files.usgwarchives.net/la/winn/taxlists/tax1882.txt.

1882-1917. *Registers of Patients Transported to the State Insane Asylum* **[Online Database],** indexed at the Louisiana Division website, New Orleans Public Library. The Civil Sheriff was responsible for transporting to the State Insane Asylum at Jackson persons judged by the Civil District Court to be insane. In three volumes the Sheriff recorded the number of the suit record ordering the patient to be sent to Jackson;

the date that he took the patient into custody; the patient's name, age, sex, color, address, nativity, occupation, marital status, disease, duration and cause of insanity; and remarks. See http://nutrias.org/~nopl/inv/civilsheriff/vf350.htm.

1882-1888. *See New Orleans City Insane Asylum Record of Patients, 1882-1884; 1888* **[Online Database],** indexed at the Louisiana Division website, New Orleans Public Library. This volume contains information on insane patients visited by the City Physician and recommended to the State Asylum. For each patient, the record includes name, race, sex, age, place of birth (in general terms), type of insanity and sometimes a description of the patient's behavior. An index is included at the end of the volume. Transcription are by page numbers. See http://nutrias.org/~nopl/inv/cityinsaneasylum.htm.

1883 Tax List, Winn Parish, Louisiana **[Online Database],** indexed at the USGenWeb site for Winn Parish LA. See http://files.usgwarchives.net/la/winn/taxlists/tax1883.txt.

"1883 Tax Collector Sales, Assumption Parish, Louisiana" [Printed Article], in *Terrebonne Lifelines* (Terrebonne Genealogical Society, Houma, LA), Vol. 24, No. 1 (Spring 2005) & Vol. 24, No. 2 (Summer 2005).

1884 Tax List, Winn Parish, Louisiana **[Online Database],** indexed at the USGenWeb site for Winn Parish LA. See http://files.usgwarchives.net/la/winn/taxlists/tax1884.txt.

1884-1944. *Register Books, [Soldiers' Home of Louisiana-New Orleans; Index* **[Microfilm & Digital Capture],** from the originals at the Jackson Barracks Military Library, New Orleans. The Soldiers' Home was also known as Camp Nichols. Filmed by the Genealogical Society of Utah, 1990, 5 rolls, beginning with FHL film #1685399 (Index to registers, 1905-1944To access the digital images, see the online FHL catalog: https://familysearch.org/search/catalog/581318.

1885 Delinquent Tax Notice, Rapides Parish, Louisiana **[Online Database],** indexed at the USGenWeb site for Rapides Parish LA. See http://files.usgwarchives.net/la/rapides/taxlists/tax1885.txt.

"1887 Tax roll, Winn Parish, Louisiana," in *Legacies & Legends of Winn Parish*, (Winn Parish Genealogical & Historical Association), Vol. 1, No. 1 (Apr 1997) thru Vol. 4, No. 3 (Oct 2000).

"1888 State Tax Sale, St. Bernard Parish, Louisiana" [Printed Article], in *L'Heritage* (St. Bernard Genealogical Society, Chalmette, LA), Vol. 7, No. 27 (Jun 1984).

1890. *Ascension Parish, Louisiana, 1890 U. S. Census* **[Printed Book],** compiled and edited by Rita Babin Butler, published by Oracle Press, Baton Rouge, LA, 1983, 256 pages. This is an extract and index to an original "Short Form" copy of the 1890 federal census at the Ascension Parish Courthouse in Donaldsonville, LA – one of only two counties/parishes in the U.S. for which a copy of the 1890 name lists exist. (The other was Washington County, Georgia). From the intro: "In 1890, Ascension parish consisted of eight wards, with Wards 1, 2, 3, and 4 on the west side of the Mississippi River and Wards 5, 6, 7, and 8 on the east side. Apparently, Modeste, Hohen Solms, Port Barrow, and part of Smoke Bend were 1; Smoke Bend, for the most part, was in Ward 2; Ward 3 was the center of Donaldsonville; the outskirts of Donaldsonville and Point Houmas, Lemanville, and Abend were in Ward 4; Darrow and Burnside were in Ward 5; Geismar and Belle Helene were in Ward 6; Gonzales was in Ward 7; and Galvez, Hope Villa, Oak Grove, Prairieville, and Duplessis were in Ward 8." See FHL book 976.319 X2b.
- A microfilm copy of the book is held by the Louisiana State Archives in Baton Rouge.

1890 Louisiana Census Index: Special Schedule of the Eleventh Census (1890) Enumerating Union Veterans and Widows of Union veterans of the Civil War, Ronald Vern Jackson, editor, Accelerated Indexing, Salt Lake City, 198?, 126 pages. FHL book 976.3 X22L.

1890 Louisiana Census Index of Civil War Veterans or their Widows, Bryan Lee Dilts, editor, publ. 1984, Salt Lake City, 68 pages. FHL book 976.3 X2d.

"1890 Tax Roll, Livingston Parish, Louisiana" [Printed Article], in *Florida Parishes Genealogical Newsletter* (Baton Rouge, LA), Vol. 1, No. 1 (Jan 1979).

1890. See **"Delinquent Taxes, March 1890, Terrebonne Parish, Louisiana" [Printed Article],** in *Terrebonne LifeLines* (Terrebonne Genealogical Society, Houma, LA), Vol. 3, No. 1 (Spring 1984).

1890 Assessment Rolls, West Carroll Parish, Louisiana **[Online Database],** indexed at the USGenWeb site for Carroll Parish LA. See http://files.usgwarchives.net/la/westcarroll/taxlists/wc1890.txt.

1891-1952. *Voter Registration Records, Orleans Parish, Louisiana* **[Microfilm & Digital Capture],** from the original records at the New Orleans Public Library. Filmed by the New Orleans Public Library, 393 rolls, beginning with FHL film #1002225 (Voter Registration cards, Aa – Adams). To access the digital images, see the online FHL catalog: www.familysearch.org/search/catalog/46406.

1892 History. See *Louisiana, Biographical and Historical Memoirs* **[Online Database & Digital Version],** digitized and OCR indexed at the Ancestry.com website. This database contains Goodspeed's *Biographical and Historical Memoirs of Louisiana*. The work is comprised of a brief history of the state and a number of biographical sketches of distinguished and prominent citizens from the area. This database has 1,041 pages. See https://search.ancestry.com/search/db.aspx?dbid=7664. - The 2-vol. book is available at the Family History Library in Salt Lake City. To access the digital version, see the online FHL catalog: www.familysearch.org/search/catalog/294001.

1892-1899. See *Rosters and Applications (United Confederate Veterans), 1892-1896; and Rosters, 1895-1899* **[Microfilm & Digital Capture],** from the originals at the Jackson Barracks Military Library, New Orleans, LA. The United Confederate Veterans (UCV) organization began in 1889 in New Orleans, where the national headquarters was located until the UCV disbanded in the early 1950s. One of the early Commanders-in-Chief of the UCV was also the Adjutant General of the State of Louisiana, a former Confederate officer, and keeper of the records for the national organization. These records of the rosters of the various UCV Camps from all over the country, and the original applications for membership ended up in the Jackson Barrack Military Library, the site of the National Guard of Louisiana. Filmed by the Genealogical Society of Utah, 1990, 8 rolls, beginning with FHL film #1685778. To access the digital images, see the online FHL catalog: www.familysearch.org/search/catalog/582952.

1892-1898. *Register of Direct Taxpayers* **[Microfilm & Digital Capture],** from the original records located at the LA State Archives, Baton Rouge. Covers all Louisiana Parishes except Acadia, Calcasieu, Cameron, Grant, Iberia, Lincoln, Red River, Richland, Tangipahoa, Union, Vermilion, Vernon, and Webster parishes. Filmed by the Genealogical Society of Utah, 1985. 5 rolls, beginning with FHL film #1412744. To access the digital images, see the online FHL catalog: www.familysearch.org/search/catalog/306257.

1895. "Public Road Right-of-Way Name List, Calcasieu Parish, Louisiana, 1895" **[Printed Article],** in *Kinfolks* (Southwest Louisiana Genealogical Society, Lake Charles, LA), Vol. 28, No. 4 (Dec 2004).

"1898 Voter Register Book, Terrebonne Parish, Louisiana" [Printed Article], in *L'Heritage* (St. Bernard Genealogical Society, Chalmette, LA), Vol. 2, No. 5 (Jan 1979) thru Vol. 4, No. 15 (Jun 1981).

1898 Voter's Registration, Washington Parish, Louisiana **[Online Database],** indexed at the USGenWeb site for Washington Parish LA. See http://files.usgwarchives.net/la/washington/court/vote1898.txt.

1898 Voter List, Winn Parish, Louisiana **[Online Database],** indexed at the USGenWeb site for Winn Parish LA. See http://files.usgwarchives.net/la/winn/taxlists/voters/vote1898.txt.

1898. *Louisiana Volunteers in the War of 1898* **[Printed Book],** compiled by Nancy Lowrie Wright and Cathy Dantin Shannon, publ. Wright Shannon Publications, Houma, LA, 1989, 94 pages, FHL book 976.3 M2w.

1898. *Index to Compiled Service Records of Volunteer Soldiers Who Served During the War With Spain in Organizations from the State of Louisiana* **[Microfilm & Digital Capture],** from originals at the National Archives, Washington, DC. From intro: "This microfilm publication reproduces an alphabetical card index to the compiled service records of volunteer soldiers of the War with Spain belonging to units from the state of Louisiana. The cards give the name of the soldier, his rank, and the unit in which he served." Filmed by the archives, series M240, 1957, 1 roll, FHL film #880013. To access the digital images, see the online FHL catalog: www.familysearch.org/search/catalog/313086.

1898-1950. *Louisiana, Confederate Pensions* **[Online Database],** digitized at the FamilySearch.org website. This is an image-only database with the images of application forms for a pension and associated documents, such as affidavits, correspondence, etc. The records are organized by the name of the applicant (soldier or widow) in alpha order. This database has 199,883 images. See https://familysearch.org/search/collection/1838535. - This database is also available at the Ancestry.com website. See https://search.ancestry.com/search/db.aspx?dbid=60295.

1899 Property Tax Rolls, Tensas Parish, Louisiana [Online Database], indexed at the USGenWeb site for Tensas Parish LA. See http://files.usgwarchives.net/la/tensas/court/prop0002.txt.

1899 Census of Vernon Parish, Louisiana, Children Between the ages of 6 and 18 years [Printed Book], compiled by Karl R. & Doris H. Mayo, publ. Leesville, LA, 1990, 70 pages. Includes children's ages, sex, and race in alphabetical order by ward. See FHL book 976.361.

1900. *Louisiana, 1900 Federal Census: Soundex and Population Schedules* [Microfilm & Digital Capture], from the original records held by the Bureau of the Census in the 1940s. After microfilming, Congress allowed the Census Bureau to destroy the originals to free up space for WWII-related files. Filmed on 177 rolls, beginning with FHL film #1244251 (1900 Soundex: A000 Hamilton thru A325 Laura).; and FHL film #1240556 (1900 population schedules: Acadia Parish) To access the digital images, see the online FHL catalog:
https://familysearch.org/search/catalog/655664.

1900-1949. *Louisiana, Statewide Death Index* [Online Database], indexed at the Ancestry.com website. Data obtained in 2002 from the Louisiana State Archives. The index includes the deceased's Name, Age, Date of death, Parish of death, and a Reference to the actual record (a volume number, a certificate number, and the year in which the certificate was issued). For the years 1930-1949 the gender and race will also be given. The keeping of vital records did not become a statewide mandate in Louisiana until 1914. This database has 582,379 records. See http://search.ancestry.com/search/db.aspx?dbid=6697.

1900-1964. *Louisiana, Orleans Parish Vital Records* [Online Database], digitized and index at FamilySearch.org, from the original records at the LA State Archives. Each index record may include Name, Event type, Event date, Event place, Gender, Age, Birth date, Father's name, Mother's name, and Spouse's name. This database has 180,915 records, see www.familysearch.org/search/collection/1929995.

1904 History. See *Louisiana History, 1904* [Online Database], digitized and indexed at the Ancestry.com website. Original data: Fortier, Alcée. *A History of Louisiana.* Vol. I: 1512-1768; Vol. II: 1769-1803; Vol. III: 1803-1861; Vol. IV: 1861-1903. Publ. Manzi, Joyant and Co., New York, 1904. Topics covered in this history include exploration and explorers, early settlements, development, colonization, Indians, wars, etc. This database has 2,274 pages. See http://search.ancestry.com/search/db.aspx?dbid=7741.

1905-1910. *Italian Passengers to Louisiana* [Online Database], digitized and indexed at the Ancestry.com website. Italian immigrants were extracted from a Louisiana State Archives database, *Citizens and Alien Manifests of Ships to the Port of New Orleans.* Included in the lists are names, ages, occupations, native countries or towns, and destinations for more than 7,000 Italian immigrants. This database contains records of sixteen Italian passenger vessels arriving in New Orleans on various dates between May 1905 and February 1910. This database has 10,276 records. See http://search.ancestry.com/search/db.aspx?dbid=4742.

1905-1963. See *Louisiana, Orleans Parish Vital Records, 1905-1913, 1955-1963* [Online Database], digitized and indexed at the FamilySearch.org website. This collection includes birth records and index for 1905-1913. It also includes marriages from 1960 and death records from 1955-1963 acquired from the Louisiana State Archives. This database has 131,971 records. See
www.familysearch.org/search/collection/1929995.

1906-1909 Coroner's Inquest Book, St. Landry Parish, Louisiana [Online Database], indexed at the USGenWeb site for St. Landry Parish LA. See http://files.usgwarchives.net/la/stlandry/vitals/deaths/coroner.txt.

1908-1909. *Bouchereau's Revised Directory of the Sugar and Syrup Manufacturers and Cane Growers of Louisiana (Arranged Alphabetically)* [Printed Book & Digital Capture], by A. Bouchereau, publ. New Orleans, 1909, FHL book 976.3 U24b. Also on microfiche, see FHL fiche #6005738. To access a digital version of this book, see the online FHL catalog page for this title:
www.familysearch.org/search/catalog/836217.

1910. *Louisiana, 1910 Federal Census: Soundex and Population Schedules* [Microfilm & Digital Capture], from the original records held by the Bureau of the Census in the 1940s. After microfilming, Congress allowed the Census Bureau to destroy the originals to free up space for WWII-related files. Filmed on 161 rolls, beginning with FHL film #1370640 (1910 Soundex: A000 thru A416 J).; and FHL film #1374520 (1910 population schedules: Acadia and Ascension Parishes) To access the digital images, see the online FHL catalog:
https://familysearch.org/search/catalog/636630.

1910-1920. *Crew Lists of Vessels Arriving at New Orleans, Louisiana* **[Microfilm & Digital Capture],** from the originals at the National Archives, Washington, DC. Filmed by the National Archives, series T0939, 48 rolls, beginning with FHL film #1490956 (Crew lists, Jan 1910-Jun 1910). To access the digital images, see the online FHL catalog: www.familysearch.org/search/catalog/573400.

1910-1929. *Marriage Records, Calcasieu Parish, Louisiana* **[Microfilm & Digital Capture],** from the original records at the Calcasieu Parish Courthouse, Lake Charles, LA. Filmed by the Genealogical Society of Utah, 1984, 16 rolls, beginning with FHL film #1405689 (Index to Marriages, v. A – Laz 1910-1963). To access the digital images, see the online FHL catalog: www.familysearch.org/search/catalog/294204.

1910-1960. See *Louisiana, Orleans Parish Vital Records, 1910, 1960* **[Online Database],** digitized and indexed at the FamilySearch.org website. This collection includes birth records and index for 1910. It also includes marriage and death records and indexes for 1960. The records were provided by the Louisiana State Archives from their archive of birth records over 100 years old, and death and marriage records over 50 years old. This collection is being published as images become available. See https://familysearch.org/search/collection/1929995.

1910-1971. See *Marriages, Calcasieu Parish Louisiana, 1910-1917; Marriage Index, 1910-1971* **[Microfilm & Digital Capture],** from the originals at the Calcasieu Parish Courthouse, Lake Charles, LA. Filmed by the Genealogical Society of Utah, 8 rolls, beginning with FHL film #871804 (Index, A-K, 1910-1963). To access the digital images, see the online FHL catalog: https://familysearch.org/search/catalog/287078.

1911. *Enumeration of Ex-Confederate Soldiers and Widows of Deceased Soldiers of Louisiana* **[Microfilm & Digital Capture],** from the original records located at the Louisiana State Archives, Baton Rouge, LA. Filmed by the Genealogical Society of Utah, 1985, 1 roll, FHL film #1412742. To access the digital images, see the online FHL catalog: www.familysearch.org/search/catalog/201807.

1911. *An Index to the Census of 1911 of Confederate Veterans or their Widows, Pursuant to Act 71 of 1908* **[Printed Index],** by Houston C. Jenks, Index lists, alphabetically, names of soldiers or their widows, and includes their parish, age, state where he enlisted for service, his regiment and company in which he served, an assessment and a valuation of property, any infirmities the soldier or widow might have, the date of their marriage, and the reel number where the data was found at the Louisiana State Archives. Publ. H.C. Jenks, Baton Rouge, LA, 1989, 115 pages, FHL book 976.3 M22j.

1911-1912 Successions, Calcasieu Parish, Louisiana **[Online Database],** indexed at the USGenWeb site for Calcasieu Parish LA. See http://files.usgwarchives.net/la/calcasieu/court/successions/success.txt.

1911-1935 *Livingston Parish, Louisiana Family Census* **[Microfilm],** from the originals at the Livingston Parish Courthouse, Livingston, LA. (Family Census = School Census). Filmed by the Genealogical Society of Utah, 1992, 2 rolls, FHL film #1854259 (Family Census ages 6-18 (1911-1919) age 1-18 (1935) & FHL film # 1854260 (Family Census ages 1-18 cont. (1935). To see if this microfilm was digitized yet, see the online FHL catalog: www.familysearch.org/search/catalog/580240.

1912-1936. *Louisiana Confederate Veterans Pensions* **[Microfilm],** from the originals at the Jackson Barracks Military Library, New Orleans, LA. Filmed by the Genealogical Society of Utah, 1990, 1 roll, FHL film #1704156. To see if this microfilm was digitized yet, see the online FHL catalog: www.familysearch.org/search/catalog/194794.

"1913 Poll Tax List, Natchitoches Parish, Louisiana" [Printed Article], in *Natchitoches Genealogist* (Natchitoches Genealogical & Historical Association, Natchitoches, LA), Vol. 32, No. 1 (Apr 2007).

1913 Voter Registration List, Caldwell Parish, Louisiana **[Online Database],** indexed at the USGenWeb site for Caldwell Parish LA. See http://files.usgwarchives.net/la/caldwell/court/voterreg/vote1913.txt.

1917-1918. See *Louisiana, World War I Selective Service System Draft Registrations Cards* **[Microfilm & Digital Capture],** from the originals at the National Archives. The draft cards are arranged alphabetically by state, then alphabetically by county or city, and then alphabetically by surname of registrants. Cards are in rough alphabetical order. Filmed by the National Archives, 1987-1988, 70 rolls, beginning with FHL film #1653576 (Acadia Parish, A-M). To access the digital images, see the online FHL catalog: www.familysearch.org/search/catalog/747006.

1917-1920. *Louisiana World War I Service Records* **[Online Database],** digitized and indexed at the FamilySearch.org website. Source: LA State Archives. This database is an Index and images of enlistment or induction records from World War I. The collection is arranged alphabetically by parish name. This database has 74,174 records. See
www.familysearch.org/search/collection/2489920.

1917-1925. *Shreveport City Directory* **[Printed Book & Digital Capture],** by various publishers. FHL has directories for 1917, 1921, 1923, 1924, and 1925: To access the digital images, see the online FHL catalog: https://familysearch.org/search/catalog/1922034.

1920. *Louisiana, 1920 Federal Census: Soundex and Population Schedules* **[Microfilm & Digital Capture],** from the original records held by the Bureau of the Census in the 1940s. After microfilming, Congress allowed the Census Bureau to destroy the originals to free up space for WWII-related files. Filmed on 169 rolls, beginning with FHL film #1825520 (1920 Soundex: A000 thru A126); and FHL film #1820603 (1920 population schedules: Acadia Parish). To access the digital images, see the online FHL catalog:
https://familysearch.org/search/catalog/571304.

1920-1940 New Orleans Voter Registration Cards, New Orleans Registrar of Voters **[Microfilm & Digital Capture],** from the original records located at the New Orleans Public Library's Louisiana Division. Contains names, birthplace, age, date of birth, sex, race, and political persuasion. Filmed by the New Orleans Public Library, Louisiana Division, 1983, 11 rolls.
- Also available at the FHL as *Voter Registration Cards, 1920-1940, Second Series*, FHL film #1412334-1412343, and 1689670. To access the digital images, see the online FHL catalog:
www.familysearch.org/search/catalog/396782.

1924 & 1933. *Civil War Pensions in Louisiana: Veterans & Widows* **[Printed Book],** by Winston De Ville, publ. Provincial Press, Lafayette, LA, 2000, 140 pages, FHL book 976.3 M2dw.

1927 Directory, East Baton Rouge Parish, Louisiana **[Online Database],** indexed by groups of page numbers at the East Baton Rouge Parish USGenWeb site. See
http://files.usgwarchives.net/la/eastbatonrouge/history/directories/1927.

1930. *Louisiana, 1930 Federal Census: Soundex and Population Schedules* **[Microfilm & Digital Capture],** from the original records held by the Bureau of the Census in the 1940s. After microfilming, Congress allowed the Census Bureau to destroy the originals to free up space for WWII-related files. Filmed on 191 rolls, beginning with FHL film #2338670 (1930 Soundex: A000 thru A235.; and FHL film #2340517 (1930 population schedules: Acadia & Allen Parish). To access the digital images, see the online FHL catalog:
https://familysearch.org/search/catalog/1036354.

1936-1959. *Houma Courier Microfilm Index Deaths* **[Printed Book],** compiled by Phillip C. Chauvin for the Terrebonne Genealogical Society, Houma, LA. Includes index. Contents: Vol. 1. 1936-1950; Vol. 2. 1950-1959. See FHL book 976.341 V42ch.

1937 List of Pensioners of the State of Louisiana, West Carroll Parish, Louisiana **[Online Database],** indexed at the USGenWeb site for West Carroll Parish LA. See
http://files.usgwarchives.net/la/westcarroll/military/civilwar/pension.txt.

1938-1939 Voter Registrations, Natchitoches Parish, Louisiana **[Online Database],** includes links to the images of each voter's registration page, indexed at the USGenWeb site for Natchitoches Parish LA. See www.usgwarchives.net/la/natchitoches/voters.htm.

1940. See *Louisiana, 1840 Federal Census: Population Schedules* **[Digital Capture],** from the original records held by the Bureau of the Census in the 1940s. After microfilming, Congress allowed the Census Bureau to destroy the originals to free up space for WWII-related files. Filmed on 92 rolls, beginning with FHL film #5454613 (Acadia Parish). The Family History Library (FHL) has the microfilm archived at their Granite Mountain Record Vault. To access the digital images, see the online FHL catalog:
https://familysearch.org/search/catalog/2057758.

1940 Federal Census Finding Aids **[Online Database].** The National Archives prepared a special website online with a detailed description of the 1940 federal census. Included at the site are descriptions of location finding aids, such as Enumeration District maps, Geographic Descriptions of Census Enumeration Districts, and a list of 1940 City Directories available at the National Archives. The finding aids are all linked to other National Archives sites. The National Archives website also has a link to 1940 Search Engines using Stephen P. Morse's "One-Step" system for finding a 1940 E.D. or street address conversion. See **www.archives.gov/research/census/1940/general-info.html#questions.**

1940-1945. *Louisiana First Registration Draft Cards* **[Online Database],** digitized and indexed at the FamilySearch.org website. Draft registration cards of the Selective Service System, covering a special classification of individuals born between February 17, 1897 to 1928. The cards are arranged alphabetically by surname. The collection was acquired from the National Archives Southwest Region in Fort Worth, Texas. This database has 394,546 records. See **https://familysearch.org/search/collection/1916286.**

1941 *WPA Historical Records Survey: Inventories of Municipal Archives, Church Archives, and Parish Archives of Louisiana* **[Online Databases].** The following Louisiana titles are available at the Ancestry.com website:
• *Inventory of the Municipal Archives of Louisiana (Thibodaux).* See
https://search.ancestry.com/search/db.aspx?dbid=24402.
• *Inventory of the Church and Synagogue Archives of Louisiana.* See
https://search.ancestry.com/search/db.aspx?dbid=29776.
• *Inventory of the Parish Archives of Louisiana: Allen Parish.* See
https://search.ancestry.com/search/db.aspx?dbid=24411.
• *Inventory of the Parish Archives of Louisiana: Assumption Parish.* See
https://search.ancestry.com/search/db.aspx?dbid=24415.
• *Inventory of the Parish Archives of Louisiana: Beauregard Parish.* See
https://search.ancestry.com/search/db.aspx?dbid=24414.
• *Inventory of the Parish Archives of Louisiana: Bossier Parish.* See
https://search.ancestry.com/search/db.aspx?dbid=24423.
• *Inventory of the Parish Archives of Louisiana: Calcasieu Parish.* See
https://search.ancestry.com/search/db.aspx?dbid=24413.
• *Inventory of the Parish Archives of Louisiana: Grant Parish.* See
https://search.ancestry.com/search/db.aspx?dbid=24412.
• *Inventory of the Parish Archives of Louisiana: Lafayette Parish.* See
https://search.ancestry.com/search/db.aspx?dbid=24401.
• *Inventory of the Parish Archives of Louisiana: Lafourche Parish.* See
https://search.ancestry.com/search/db.aspx?dbid=24410.
• *Inventory of the Parish Archives of Louisiana: Morehouse Parish.* See
https://search.ancestry.com/search/db.aspx?dbid=24406.
• *Inventory of the Parish Archives of Louisiana: Ouachita Parish.* See
https://search.ancestry.com/search/db.aspx?dbid=24403.
• *Inventory of the Parish Archives of Louisiana: Plaquemines Parish.* See
https://search.ancestry.com/search/db.aspx?dbid=24434.
• *Inventory of the Parish Archives of Louisiana: Natchitoches Parish.* See
https://search.ancestry.com/search/db.aspx?dbid=24435.
• *Inventory of the Parish Archives of Louisiana: Preliminary Inventory of Notarial Records in Orleans Parish.* See
https://search.ancestry.com/search/db.aspx?dbid=24436.
• *Inventory of the Parish Archives of Louisiana: Terrebonne Parish.* See
https://search.ancestry.com/search/db.aspx?dbid=24407.
• *Inventory of the Parish Archives of Louisiana: Saint Bernard Parish.* See
https://search.ancestry.com/search/db.aspx?dbid=24408.
• *Inventory of the Parish Archives of Louisiana: Saint Charles Parish.* See
https://search.ancestry.com/search/db.aspx?dbid=24409.
• *Inventory of the Parish Archives of Louisiana: Sabine Parish.* See
https://search.ancestry.com/search/db.aspx?dbid=24405.
• *Inventory of the Parish Archives of Louisiana: Webster Parish.* See
https://search.ancestry.com/search/db.aspx?dbid=24404.

1941-1945. *Index to The Fighting Men of Louisiana* **[Printed Index],** compiled by Judy Riffel. This is an index to the book T*he Fighting Men of Louisiana and a History of World War II,* prepared by the Louisiana Historical Institute, Shreveport, Louisiana, 1946. This book is divided into two parts - biographical and historical. Publ. Baton Rouge, LA, 1981, 18 pages, FHL book 976.3 M2f.

1942. *Louisiana, Military Records: World War II 4th Draft Registration Cards* **[Microfilm & Digital Capture],** digitized from the National Archives microfilm by the Genealogical Society of Utah, 2002-

2003, 215 rolls, beginning with FHL film 4434480To access the digital images, see the online FHL catalog: www.familysearch.org/search/catalog/1459325.

1946-1951. *Louisiana Statewide Marriage Index by Groom* **[Microfilm & Digital Capture],** from the originals at the LA State Archives, Baton Rouge. Digitized by the Genealogical Society of Utah, from 6 rolls of film, beginning with FHL film #4151761 (1946). For a complete list of roll numbers, roll content, and the digital images of each roll, see the online FHL catalog page for this title:
www.familysearch.org/search/catalog/1388227.

1948-1959. *Louisiana, Second Registration Draft Cards* **[Digital Capture],** from the original records at the National Archives, Fort Worth, TX. Includes name of individual, date and place of birth, address, age, employer's name and address, name and address of person who would know where the individual can be located, signature, and physical description. Draft registration cards arranged numerically by local board number then alphabetically by surname of registrant. Digitized by FamilySearch International, 2011. To access the digital images, see the online FHL catalog:
www.familysearch.org/search/catalog/1921443.

1950-1953. *Louisiana, Military Records, Korean War Bonuses* **[Digital Capture],** digitized from 134 rolls of film by the Genealogical Society of Utah, 2017. Source: LA State Archives, Baton Rouge. To access the digital images, see the online FHL catalog page for this title: www.familysearch.org/search/catalog/2821873.

1950-2001. *Sabine Parish Funeral Records* **[Online Database],** a surname index with over 4,000 entries and links to a detailed funeral record for each deceased person. Indexed and extracted at the USGenWeb site for Sabine Parish LA. See
www.usgwarchives.net/la/sabine/funeral/funa.htm.

1953-1958. *Family History, Sunday Sun and The Sun, Hammond, LA* **[Printed Book & Digital Capture),** the Family History column of the newspaper from 1953 to 1958, paste ups in 2 vols. See FHL book 976.313/H1 D2s v. 1-2. For digital versions of Part 1 and Part 2, see the online FHL catalog page.
https://familysearch.org/search/catalog/154255.

1986-Current. *Louisiana Recent Newspaper Obituaries* **[Online Database]**, digitized and indexed newspaper obituaries at the GenealogyBank website, including newspapers from these cities: Abbeville, Amite, Arabi, Basile, Bastrop, Baton Rouge, Belle Chasse, Bogalusa, Bossier City, Church Point, Clinton, Columbia, Covington, Crowley, De Ridder, Denham Springs, Ponchatoula, Donaldsonville, Eunice, Fort Polk, Franklin, Gonzales, Greensburg, Gretna, Gueydan, Hammond, Houma, Kaplan, Kentwood, Kinder, La Place, Lafayette, Lake Arthur, Lake Charles, Leesville, Marksville, Metairie, Minden, Morgan City, New Iberia, New Orleans, Oak Grove, Oakdale, Pierre Part, Plaquemine, Rayne, Rayville, St. Francisville, St. Martinville, St. Tammany, Sulphur, Tallulah, Thibodaux, Ville Platte, and Zachary. See www.genealogybank.com/gbnk/obituaries/explore/USA/Louisiana.

168 • **Census Substitutes & State Census Records**

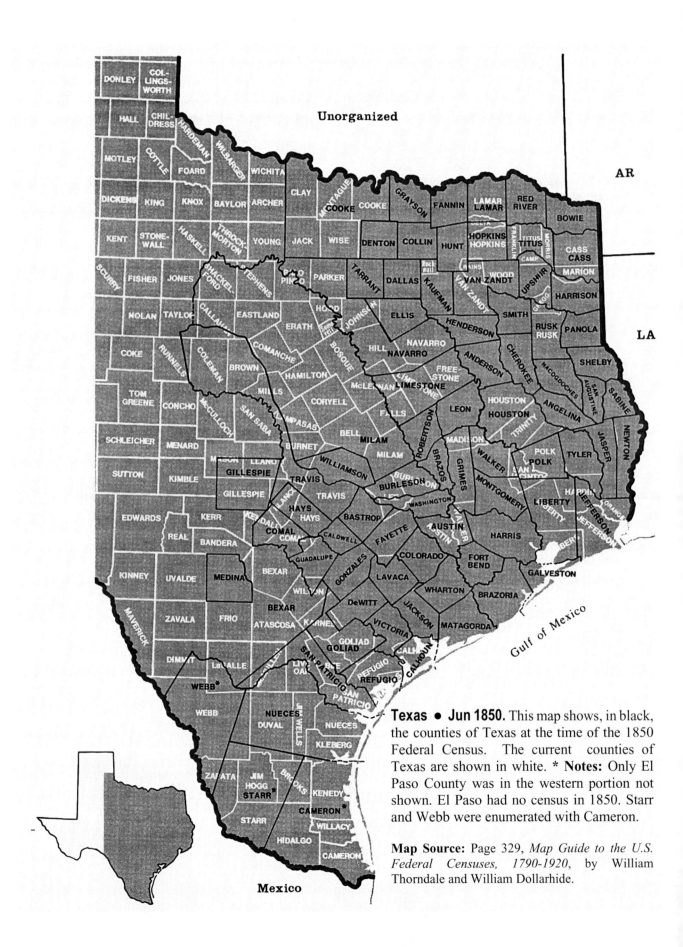

Texas • Jun 1850. This map shows, in black, the counties of Texas at the time of the 1850 Federal Census. The current counties of Texas are shown in white. * **Notes:** Only El Paso County was in the western portion not shown. El Paso had no census in 1850. Starr and Webb were enumerated with Cameron.

Map Source: Page 329, *Map Guide to the U.S. Federal Censuses, 1790-1920*, by William Thorndale and William Dollarhide.

Texas
Censuses & Substitute Name Lists

Texas Jurisdictions, 1691-1896

Texas was closely linked with Coahuila Province during all of the years of the Spanish era of Mexico, 1691-1820. The earliest populations in the region began when troops from Coahuila established Nacogdoches in 1716, San Antonio de Bexar in 1718, and La Bahia del Espiritu Santo in 1722, the last-mentioned post being moved in 1749 to what is now Goliad. The Medina River just west of San Antonio became the western boundary of the "Texas" command, while the lower Nueces River marked the boundary with New Santander province.

- Texas became a separate province about 1726, with San Antonio as its capital from 1773. The Spanish government in Madrid in 1805 formally defined the west boundary (a northwestern trace from the Medina River to the southeastern corner of present-day New Mexico, and from that point to the Red River, at the southwestern corner of present-day Oklahoma). West of that line was the colonial Spanish province of Santa Fe de Nuevo Mexico.

- At the end of the Spanish era in 1820, Texas was a moribund province, its few thousand Hispanics living mainly in San Antonio, LaBahia (Goliad), and Nacogdoches. The ruins of destroyed and abandoned settlements and missions dotted this Indian besieged province barely maintaining its population in the years 1790-1820. To the east, American frontier families were beginning to cross the Sabine, while in the extreme northeast the Americans along the Red River were a de facto part of old Miller County, Arkansas Territory. Towards the west in 1820, the Rio Grande valley contained a few towns such as Laredo, Presidio del Rio Grande, and Paso del Norte, but the valley was not part of Texas until 1848.

- The Louisiana Purchase of 1803 by the United States forced a formal clarification of the eastern boundary of Texas. Spain claimed east to the Red River; the U.S., west to the Sabine. They compromised in 1806 with the so-called Neutral Ground, a buffer zone where neither would exercise jurisdiction in what was to be a no-man's land. But actually, it became a haven for pirates, outlaws, fugitives, and others enjoying freedom from government. The Neutral Ground was bounded west by the Sabine and east by Louisiana's Calcasieu River and Bayou Pierre. Finally, the Spanish-American treaty of 1819 (ratified by the parties in 1821 and by Mexico in 1828) set the east Texas border to run up the Sabine to the 32nd parallel and then due north to the Red River. This is the modern Texas line with Louisiana and Arkansas, but it took nearly two decades to clarify just where that due-north line met the Red River. This uncertainty made it possible for Arkansas Territory in April 1820 to create Miller County partly in what is now northeast Texas.

- Mexico became independent in 1821. It renamed New Santander province as the State of Tamaulipas and in 1824 joined Texas to Coahuila as the State of Coahuila y Texas.

- Mexico in the 1820s tried to build a barrier against on-coming Americans by encouraging "fit" Anglo settlers to take up land. This began in earnest with an 1823 contract with Stephen Austin to bring in 300 families, giving Austin authority to grant these families land. In 1824 a similar contract was made with Green DeWitt for 400 families. Further such empresario grants were made until by 1830 most of present-day Texas was covered by such grants, although some grants along the Red River and in the Texas panhandle never functioned.

- Politically, Texas in 1830 was the department of Bexar within the state of Coahuila and Texas. The western boundary remained unchanged from 1805, though common usage and contemporary maps increasingly marked the whole Nueces River as the boundary. Within the department of Bexar were four jurisdictions called municipalities. These were headquartered at San Antonio, LaBahia (Goliad), San

Felipe de Austin (Austin's colony), and Nacogdoches.
- As American population rapidly increased in east Texas and in the empresario colonies south and southeast of San Antonio, more municipalities were created and some of these were subdivided into districts. By 1828, Austin's colony had seven such districts.
- The Mexican congress by act of 6 April 1830 barred further American immigration into Texas. Mexican troops were stationed around east Texas to enforce the ban, though Austin and DeWitt were allowed to bring in a few families in fulfillment of their contracts. Significant legal immigration from the U.S. resumed only in 1834. The last two years of Mexican government in Texas saw a typical American scramble for land.
- By 1834, new departments of Brazos and Nacogdoches were carved from Bexar and four new municipalities were created: Bastrop, Matagorda, San Augustine, and San Patricio. By the end of the Mexican era in 1835, the entity called Texas was composed of three departments, each with representation in the state legislature of Coahuila and Texas. These departments were subdivided into municipalities and some further into districts. Add the empresario grants, new towns, and clusters of farms informally called "settlements" and Texas was a mosaic of jurisdictions, with a population of about 24,000 Americans and 6,000 Hispanics. Maps in William Pool's *Historical Atlas of Texas* (Encino Press, Austin, TX, 1975) may be the best source for locating places in Texas at the time of independence.
- The Texas war for independence began in October 1835 at Gonzales and climaxed on 21 April 1836 with the battle of San Jacinto, where the Mexican president-dictator Gen. Antonio Lopez de Santa Ana was captured. He agreed (at least while a prisoner) to Texas independence and to the withdrawal of Mexican forces across the Rio Grande.
- The Texas provisional government in December 1835 proceeded to claim the Rio Grande for a western boundary, even up in New Mexico, but the Republic of Texas could never assert its authority west of the Nueces. The Mexican congress refused to confirm the Santa Ana agreement, never recognized the Texas republic, and treated it as a province in rebellion. Mexican forces in 1841 crossed the Nueces and briefly occupied San Antonio, thereby pushing Texas another step toward eventual annexation by the United States in 1845.
- With the annexation of Texas came the claim to the Rio Grande and in 1846 U.S. troops crossed the Nueces, bringing war with Mexico and the American capture of the Rio Grande Valley in 1847-1848.

- Having given credence to the Texas claim, the U.S. now bought out that claim to New Mexico, paying ten million dollars to Texas by act of 9 September 1850, ratified by Texas 25 November 1850. This act established the present Texas boundaries.
- A later claim by Texas in 1860 for the northern branch of the Red River as its boundary, allowed Greer County to be created and settled by Texans – but the U.S. government forced Texas to transfer old Greer County to Oklahoma Territory in 1896.
- NOTE: The essay above was first published in *Map Guide to the Texas Censuses, 1820-1920,* by William Thorndale and William Dollarhide, publ. Dollarhide Systems, Blaine, WA, 1985).

Online Resources at the Texas State Library & Archives Commission
www.tsl.texas.gov

Republic Claims. This series is now available in digital form as well as microfilm. It includes claims for payment, reimbursement, or restitution submitted by citizens to the Republic of Texas government from 1835 through 1846. It also includes records relating to Republic pensions and claims against the Republic submitted as public debt claims after 1846.

Republic of Texas Passports. The collection of 55 documents has been digitized and a complete listing of names is available. Added to the lists are 287 names as part of the Sutherland Passport.

County Records Available on Microfilm is available online, along with instructions for borrowing rolls through Interlibrary loan. County records include vital records, court records, and tax rolls. Most of the microfilm is housed in depository libraries throughout Texas. Select a county and see a list of records and years available, e.g., Bowie County Records (Available from Texas A&M University-Commerce), includes Death records, Deeds, Marriages, Medical register, Probates, Civil court cases, Divorces, Naturalizations, School censuses, and more.

Texas Adjutant General Service Records, 1836-1935. The Service Records Series combines both official service record files from the Adjutant General's Office and alphabetical files created by other agencies which contain records related to an individual's service in a military unit.

Confederate Indigent Families Lists, 1863-1865. View the names of families that received aid through the 1863 *Act to Support the Families and Dependents of Texas Soldiers.*

Confederate Pension Applications provide the names, county of residence, and pension number for some 54,634 approved, rejected, and home pensions issued by the Texas government between 1899 and 1975.

Frequently Asked Questions About Texas Vital Statistics Indexes. Includes information about what records are available, births, marriages, divorces, deaths, and copies of certificates.

Texas County Tax Rolls. Microfilmed copies of the Texas county tax rolls are available for on-site use in the Genealogy Collection of the Texas State Library. This online inventory identifies each county and the tax rolls available for all 254 Texas counties.

Texas City Directories from the past are available for on-site use. This online list identifies the cities and years.

Newspapers Available on Microfilm. The microfilm is available for on-site viewing or to be borrowed through interlibrary loan. An alpha list of newspapers is here for locating one of interest.

1867 Voters' Registration. The U.S. Congress passed legislation that called for a registration of qualified voters in each of the former Confederate states. These lists would be used to determine all who would be eligible to vote for any proposed Constitutional Convention in the state. This is an information page and list of microfilm available. **Note**: TX 1867-1869 Voter Registration database was digitized and indexed at the Ancestry.com website.

Texas Convict Record Ledgers and Indexes. The record ledgers are excellent sources of individual convict descriptions and information regarding their incarceration. Although the original records are too fragile to be used, they have been microfilmed and may be viewed on-site or borrowed through the interlibrary loan program. This site has a table with the volume number, years of coverage, and roll number.

Bibliography
Texas Censuses & Substitutes

This chronological listing of censuses and substitutes is related to the historical eras of Texas:

Spanish Era, 1716-1821. The elaborate Spanish bureaucracy required detailed reports from its frontier posts. This included population data, especially after a royal order of 1776 from Madrid commanded periodic censuses from its American colonies. A good many Texas censuses survive for towns, missions, and their environs, and some have been published, such as for Nacogdoches 1792 and Salcedo 1805. Others can be found in the microfilmed archives for San Antonio de Bexar, Nacogdoches, and Laredo, now located at the State Archives in Austin.

Mexican Era, 1821-1836. There are lists of American settlers, such as the Austin and DeWitt colony lists of 1826-1828 and the published lists for what seems to be the department of Nacogdoches. An inventory of extant Spanish and Mexican censuses for Texas does not at present exist – the bibliography identifies those that are known and have been published.

Republic of Texas, 1836-1845. The Republic took no known national census. Publications purporting to be such "censuses" are usually the tax lists required yearly from January 1837 as compiled by the county assessors. Such ad valorem tax lists (containing real, personal, and poll/head tax information) were made in two copies, one sent to the Texas capital. Thousands of State's tax lists have been microfilmed, digitized, and made available online, in particular, those from 1837 through the late 1970s.

State Censuses. Texas was annexed to the U.S. as the 26th state in the Union in 1845. References were found to possible state censuses in 1847-1848, 1851, 1858, and 1887. It seems likely the county assessors doing the enumeration were required only to tally the population by several age/sex/race categories and send the counts to Austin. The state and university libraries and archives in Austin could produce no actual name lists for any of the state censuses, except one county list for 1858 Austin County.

Federal Censuses. The first U.S. federal census in Texas were those for Miller County, Arkansas Territory. The 1820 Miller census (lost) included the parts of present-day Oklahoma, Texas, and Arkansas where those states now corner. In 1828, the Indian boundary was established at the present Oklahoma-Arkansas line and Arkansas Territory adjusted its counties so that the Miller 1830 census (extant) was totally south of the Red River in what is now Texas.
- The U.S. federal censuses, 1850-1940 are complete for all Texas counties, except for the 1890, lost for all states. The orderly way large areas of north and northwest Texas were sectioned into counties with little or no population does mean that the 1860 and 1870 censuses had many unorganized counties without population.

Census Substitutes. In addition to the local and federal censuses, there are many census substitute name lists that fill out the bibliography. Name lists may include Local Census Records, County Court Records, Directories, County Histories, State Militia Lists, Tax Lists, Vital Records, and Voter Lists. They begin below in chronological order:

♦ ♦ ♦ ♦ ♦

1716-2008. See *Texas, Land Title Abstracts, 1700-2008* **[Online Database],** indexed at the Ancestry.com website. This database contains abstracts of original titles located in the archives of the Texas General Land Office in Austin, Texas. The records provide information about lands granted and transferred within the present state of Texas including some Spanish land grants as early as 1716. Fields of information include the district name (a three-letter code) the county, page in original document, grantee, patentee, date, volume, description/location, acreage, class, file, and any additional data found in the record. This database has 442,615 records. See
http://search.ancestry.com/search/db.aspx?dbid=5112.

1736-1838. *Bexar County Spanish Archives (San Antonio, Texas)* **[Microfilm & Digital Capture],** from the original records at the Bexar County courthouse. Includes index compiled by Richard G. Santos. Filmed by the Genealogical Society of Utah, 1977, 13 rolls, beginning with FHL film #1019360 (Index to Bexar County Spanish archives, 1736-1838; wills and estates No. 1-9, 1736-1838). To access the digital images, see the online FHL catalog:
https://familysearch.org/search/catalog/414789.

1749-1872. *Indexes to the Laredo Archives* **[Printed Book],** compiled by Robert D. Wood, published by Burke Pub., 1993, 138 pages. Includes a chronological, topical/subject, person name (surname) and place name index. Index to records referred to as the Laredo Archives that document early government in the town of Laredo, Texas. Those records in the archives of interest to genealogists consist mainly of court records, with some references to probate and tax matters. FHL book 976.4462/L1 N22w.

1756-1830s. *Lost Spanish Towns: Atascosito and Trinidad de Salcedo* **[Printed Book],** by Jean L. Epperson, published by Dogwood Press, Woodville, TX, 1996, 118 pages. This book covers a part of the history of Southeast Texas from 1756 to the 1830s. From introduction: "Atascosito, located near the lower Trinity River was a recognized geographical place in 1756, a small rancho in 1766, a temporary Indian mission in 1785, and a Spanish military post from 1805 through 1812. "The villa and military post of Santisima Trinidad de Salcedo was founded in January 1806 on the east side of the Trinity River... The Spanish Royalist Army destroyed Salcedo in September 1813." FHL book 976.4 H2ej.

1767-1835. *Index to Spanish and Mexican Land Grants in Texas* **[Printed Book],** by Virginia H. Taylor, published by Lone Star Press, Austin, TX, 1995, 258 pages. FHL book 976.4 R22t.

1782-1836. *Residents of Texas* **[Printed Book],** compiled by the Institute of Texan Cultures, University of Texas, published by the Institute, San Antonio, TX, 1984, 3 vols. Each volume includes an index. Consists chiefly of names of residents and information concerning their wives and children. Vol. 3 contains transcriptions of proceedings involving land and property and other matters. Vol. 1 has period dates 1782-1806. FHL book 976.4 D2rte vol. 1-3.

1782-1880. *Texas Censuses* **[Online Database],** indexed at the USGenWeb site for Texas. Includes separate databases for 1782, 1790, 1792, 1810, 1831, 1832, 1833, 1834, 1835, 1850, and 1880. See
http://files.usgwarchives.net/tx/census.

1800-1900. *Texas, Index Card Collections* **[Online Database],** digitized and indexed at the Ancestry.com website. Source: TX State Archives. This collection contains a card catalog pertaining to people and organizations influential to Texas history, organized by the following: The **Biographical index Cards** are arranged alphabetically by subject. Individual people are listed on the cards, as well as schools, business, and other non-human entities. Each card contains the name of the person or organization, as well as a reference to a book in the biographical collection (not included in this collection). Cards may also contain a date, or location reference. The **Ships at Texas Ports** collection is arranged chronologically and lists the date the ship arrived or departed from a Texas port. These cards include the years 1836 – 1843. These cards do not refer to a specific person and are not searchable by any names. **Colonial Ship Lists and Customs House Ship Lists** may contain the name of the person on the card, the name of the colony and ship, date they arrived or departed, age, occupation, and point of origin. This database has 102,875 records. See
http://search.ancestry.com/search/db.aspx?dbid=2265.

1800s-1900s. *Texas, Gonzalez de la Garza Genealogy Collection* **[Online Database],** indexed at the FamilySearch.org website. digitized at the FamilySearch.org website. This is an image only database of a genealogical card file containing some 270,000 cards, compiled by Rudolfo Gonzalez de la Garza. The card file indexes thousands of families of Southern Texas and Northern Mexico. The original card file is at the Laredo Public Library. Browse the images of the cards, organized in alpha order. This database has 270,253 records. See https://familysearch.org/search/collection/1918470.

1800-1990. *Texas Probate Records* **[Online Database],** digitized at the FamilySearch.org website. Source: FamilySearch extraction from county records on microfilm at the Family History Library, Salt Lake City, UT. This is an image only database. Browse through the records, organized by County, then Volume Title and Year. Many county records include index books to probates, or wills. This database has 1,164,427 records. See
https://familysearch.org/search/collection/2016287.

1800-2012. *Tarrant County, Texas, Probate Index* **[Online Database],** indexed at the Ancestry.com website. Source: Tarrant County Clerk Office, Fort Worth, TX. Each index record includes: Name, Address, File date, Party type, Case type description, Case number, Case status, and Style (notes). This database has 408,124 records. See
http://search.ancestry.com/search/db.aspx?dbid=7004.

1809-1836. *Citizens & Foreigners of the Nacogdoches District* **[Printed Book],** by Carolyn Reeves Ericson, published by the author, Nacogdoches, TX, 1981, 2 vols., FHL book 976.4 H2e, v.1-2.

1813-1900s. *Linkpendium – Texas: Family History & Genealogy, Census, Birth, Marriage, Death, Vital Records & More* **[Online Databases].** Linkpendium is a genealogical portal site with links to state, county, town, and local databases. Currently listed are selected sites for Texas statewide resources (1,012), Renamed/Discontinued Counties (15), Anderson County (309) Andrews County (109), Angelina County (270), Aransas County (129), Archer County (143), Armstrong County (187), Atascosa County (195) and 247 more Texas counties. See
www.linkpendium.com/tx-genealogy.

1813-1900s Texas Original Landowners. See the *Family Maps* series for Arkansas counties, maps of all original land patents, compiled by Greg Boyd, publ. Arphax Publishing Co., Norman, OK. These privately produced computer-generated maps show the first property owners for an entire county, produced as a book of maps, each map laid out on the federal township grid, and includes indexes to help you locate a person, place-name, or cemetery. Additional maps are added for each county to show roads, waterways, railroads, selected city centers, and cemeteries within a county. At this writing, *Family Maps* books have been published for the following Texas counties: Angelina, Austin, Bastrop, Bell, Bosque, Bowie, Burnet, Caldwell, Cameron, Collin, Colorado, Comal, Cooke, Dallas, Denton, Duval, Ellis, Fannin, Foard, Grayson, Gregg, Grimes, Hall, Hardin, Harrison, Henderson, Hopkins, Hunt, Lamar, Lavaca, Leon, Mason, McLennan, Medina, Montague, Montgomery, Nacogdoches, Navarro, Red River, Roberts, Rusk, Smith, Stephens, Tarrant, Taylor, Tom Green, Upshur, Uvalde, Washington, Wise, Wood, and Young County, Texas. Visit the publisher's information and ordering website for more details and updated county coverage. See **www.arphax.com.** Arphax's entire *Family Maps* series is also available as a subscription service online. See **www.historygeo.com.**

1813-1993. *Texas Newspaper Archives* **[Online Databases],** digitized and indexed newspapers at the GenealogyBank website, for Austin, Beaumont, Beeville, Brazoria, Brownsville, Clarksville, Cleburne, Corpus Christi, Corsicana, Dallas, Denison, Edinburg, El Paso, Fort Worth, Galveston, Henderson, Houston, Huntsville, Kingsville, Laredo, Marshall, Nacogdoches, Palestine, Paris, Pittsburg, Richardson, Rusk, San Antonio, San Augustine, San Luis, Taft, Victoria, Waco, and West Columbia, Texas. See
www.genealogybank.com/explore/newspapers/all/usa/texas.

1829-1965. *Texas, County Marriage Records* **[Online Database],** indexed at Ancestry.com. Includes marriages in Crane, Crosby, Culberson, Gonzales, Hudspeth, Jeff Davis, Not Stated, and Ward counties, TX. The earliest year from any of the counties was indicated as 1829 (Gonzales Co), but there may be a marriage record incorrectly dated as 1817 (the title year of this database). Source: TX State Archives, Austin, TX. This database has 3,185,816 records, see
www.ancestry.com/search/collections/61383.

1820-1829. *Texas, Index of County Tax Lists* **[Printed Book],** edited by Ronald Vern Jackson, et al, published by Accelerated Indexing Systems, North Salt Lake, UT, 1981, 55 pages. FHL book 976.4 X2j 1820-1829.

1820-1846. *Red River County Deed Abstracts* **[Printed Book],** by Joyce Martin Murray, published by the author, Dallas, TX, 1986, 2 vols. Includes index of names, index of places, and index of slave names. Contents: Vol. 1: Republic of Texas and state of Coahuila and Texas (Mexico); Abstracts of deed record books A-B, A-B-C, D, F, to 19 Feb. 1846, annexation to United States; Vol. 2: Red River County, Texas, abstracts of deed record books F, G, H, I, J, and part of K. FHL book 976.4212 R28m.

1820-1890. *Texas, Compiled Census and Census Substitutes Index* **[Online Database],** indexed at the Ancestry.com website. Source: Accelerated Indexing Systems, Salt Lake City, UT, 1999. This collection contains the following indexes: 1850 Federal Census Index; 1850 Slave Schedule; 1860 Federal Census Index; 1860 Slave Schedule; 1870 Federal Census Index; 1880 Federal Census Index; 1890 Veterans Schedule; Tax List Indexes 1820-1829; Tax List Indexes 1830-1839; Tax List Indexes 1840-1849. Each index record includes: Name, State (TX), County, year, and Database (census, tax list, etc.). This database has 79,060 records. See
http://search.ancestry.com/search/db.aspx?dbid=3575.

1821-1846. *Coahuila y Texas: Desde la Consumación de la Independencia Hasta el Tratado de Paz de Guadalupe Hidalgo, (An historical unfolding of Coahuila and Texas from Independence to the Treaty of Guadalupe Hidalgo)* **[Printed Book],** by Vito Alessio Robles, published in Mexico, D.F., Editorial Porrea, 2 vols., 1,082 pages. Includes indexes and bibliographical references. FHL book 972.14 H2r.

1821-1846. *Apellidos de Tamaulipas, Nuevo León, Coahuila y Texas, (Surnames of Tamaulipas, Nuevo León, Coahuila, and Texas)* **[Printed Book],** by Rudolfo Gonzales de la Garza, published by Nuevo Laredo, Mexico, 1980, 351 pages. FHL book 972 D4g.

1823-1824. *The Old Three Hundred: Austin's Original Colony* **[Printed Article & Digital Version],** from an article in *Quarterly of the South Texas Genealogical & Historical Society,* Vol. 1-2 (1966-1968). The three hundred families were all, or nearly all, in Texas before the end of 1824. The lands chosen by the settlers were the rich bottoms of the Brazos, the Colorado, and the Bernard, each grant having about 4,428 acres. Names of the settlers, where they settled, and the date the Grant was issued are listed. To access the digital images, see the online FHL catalog:
www.familysearch.org/search/catalog/2567849.

- See also, *Stephen F. Austin's Register of Families, 1823-1835* **[Printed Book],** edited by Villamae Williams from the originals in the General Land Office, Austin, Texas. Originally published: St. Louis, MO. Reprint by Genealogical Publishing Co., Inc., Baltimore, MD, 1989. Includes index. See FHL book 976.4 W2au 1989.

- See also, *Stephen F. Austin's Register of Families* **[Online Database],** digitized version of Villamae Williams' book at Ancestry.com, with an OCR index. This database has 196 pages, see
www.ancestry.com/search/collections/48403.

- See Also, *Index to Land Applications, Austin, Texas* **[Printed Book & Digital Version],** compiled by George W. Glass, c1965, Lists of names with notes and commentary, handwritten copy, taken from "Austin's application book or Registro de Familias" and "Memorandum: Book of application[s] for land, Austin's Colony vol. 2", digitized by FamilySearch International, 2018, To access the digital images, see the online FHL catalog:
www.familysearch.org/search/catalog/3033094.

1823-1861. *Early Texas Settlers, 1700s-1800s* **[CD-ROM],** originally published by Broderbund, Family Tree Maker's Family Archives, Genealogical Records No. 514, published 2000, in collaboration with Genealogical Publishing Co., Inc., Baltimore. Contents: *Austin Colony Pioneers: Including History of Bastrop, Fayette, Grimes, Montgomery and Washington Counties, Texas and Their Earliest Settlers,* by Worth S. Ray; *Ancestor Lineages of Members Texas Society, National Society Colonial Dames Seventeenth Century,* compiled by Jeanne Mitchell Jordan Tabb; *Stephen F. Austin's Register of Families,* edited by Villamae Williams from the originals in the General Land Office, Austin, Texas; *Character Certificates in the General Land Office of Texas,* edited by Gifford White from the files of the General Land Office, Austin, Texas; *Kentucky Colonization in Texas: A History of the Peters Colony,* by Seymour V. Connor; *Republic of Texas: Poll Lists for 1846,* by Marion Day Mullins; *A New Land Beckoned: German Immigration to Texas, 1844-1847,* compiled and edited by Chester W. and Ethel H. Geue; and *New Homes in a New land: German Immigration to Texas, 1847-1861,* by Ethel Hander Geue.

1824-1881. *Marriage Records of Nacogdoches County, Texas* **[Online Database],** digitized and indexed at the Ancestry.com website. Source: Book, same title, by Pauline Shirley Murrie, publ. 1968. The book text was scanned, with an OCR index. This database has 172 pages. See http://search.ancestry.com/search/db.aspx?dbid=29465.

1824-2014. *Texas, Marriage Index* **[Online Database],** indexed at Ancestry.com. This is an index to the names of the brides and grooms involved in 8.5 million marriages in Texas over span of nearly two hundred years. The collection of marriages comes from both FHL extractions and the TX Vital Statistics office. Each index record includes a Name, Gender, Birth year, Age, Marriage date, Marriage place, Name of spouse, Gender of spouse, and Age of spouse. There is one record for the Groom and another record for the Bride. This database has 17,135,048 records, see www.ancestry.com/search/collections/8795.

1825- 1827. See *Register of the Families Introduced by Green De Witt Empresario of De Witt's Colony: Under the Colonization Law of the State of Coahuila and Texas – dated the 24th of March 1825* **[Printed Article & Digital Version],** from the *Quarterly of the South Texas Genealogical & Historical Society,* Vol. 1-2 (1966-1968). This handwritten register consisting of only five pages (unnumbered) appears in a small volume of records made up mainly of early registered brands. It is stored in a locked drawer in the office of the County Clerk in Gonzales, Texas. It contains dates in 1826 and 1827. To access the digital images, see the online FHL catalog: www.familysearch.org/search/catalog/2567824.

1825-1835. *Character Certificates in the General Land Office of Texas* **[Online Database],** digitized and indexed at the FamilySearch.org website. Source: Book, same title, by Clifford White, publ. 1989. An immigrant into Mexican Texas between 1825 and 1835 had to meet specific requirements before becoming eligible to receive land. He was required to apply to the officials of the municipality or to the Commissioner where he proposed to settle and to prove his good character by binging credentials from his place of origin, or by two creditable witnesses. This book identifies the immigrants and details about each. The complete book text was digitized with an OCR index. There is an index to names included in the book as well. This database has 265 pages. See http://search.ancestry.com/search/db.aspx?dbid=48419.

1826. *The Atascosito Census of 1826* **[Photostat & Digitized Manuscript],** digitized from a photostatic copy of an original document in the Library of Congress. From introduction: "The Atascosito District is bounded as follows viz. On the west by the Colony of San Felipe de Austin on the north by the District of Nacogdoches, on the east by the reserved lands on the Sabine, on the south by the Gulf of Mexico including all Islands and Bays within three leagues of the Sea Shore." FHL book 976.4 A1 no. 149; also on microfiche, FHL film #6089073. To access the digital images, see the online FHL catalog: www.familysearch.org/search/catalog/335942.

1826-1835 *Colonial Deeds, San Felipe de Austin (Texas)* **[Microfilm & Digital Capture],** from a copy of photocopied loose deeds at the Austin County courthouse, Bellville, Texas. Filmed by the Genealogical Society of Utah, 1977, 3 rolls, as follows:
- Index to Colonial Deeds, 1826-1860; Vol.1, A1-C35; Vol. 2, C36-G34, FHL film #1019280.
- Vol. 3, G35 – L12, Vol. 4, L13- P83, FHL film #1019281.
- Vol. 5, P84-T34; Vol. 6, T35-Y7, FHL film #101982.

To access the digital images, see the online FHL catalog: www.familysearch.org/search/catalog/158294.

1826-1836 *Index of Documents, Department of Nacogdoches* **[Printed Book & Digital Version],** compiled and published by Carolyn Ericson, Nacogdoches, TX, 39 pages, FHL book 976.4182 P22i. To access a digital version of this book, see the online FHL catalog: https://familysearch.org/search/catalog/611776.

1829-1845. See *The First Census of Texas, 1829-1836: To Which Are Added Texas Citizenship Lists, 1821-1845 And Other Early Records of the Republic of Texas* **[Microfilm & Digital Version],** by Marion Day Mullins, from a reprint of the Special Publication of the National Genealogical Society, No. 22, 1962, 61 pages. Includes census, 1820-1836; citizenship lists, 1821-1845; certificates of entrance into Texas in 1835; election in San Augustine in November 1834. Filmed by the Genealogical Society of Utah, 1971, 1 roll, FHL film #844966. Another filming, FHL film #1000607. To access a digital version of this book, see the online FHL catalog: https://familysearch.org/search/catalog/738730.

- See also, *The First Census of Texas, 1829-1836, to Which are Added Texas Citizenship Lists, 1821-1845, and Other Early Records of The Republic of Texas* **[Online Database],** available at a RootsWeb site, see www.rootsweb.ancestry.com/~txjacks2/Index_First_Census.htm.

1830 Citizens of Texas: A Census of 6,500 Pre-Revolutionary Texas **[Printed Book]**, by Gifford White, published by Eakin Press, Austin, TX, 1983, 282 pages. Includes index and list of registered voters of 1867. FHL book 976.4 X2wh.

1830-1839. *Texas, Index of County Tax Lists* **[Printed Book]**, edited by Ronald Vern Jackson, et al, published by Accelerated Indexing Systems, North Salt Lake, UT, 1982, 39 pages. FHL book 976.4 X2j 1830-1839.

1830-1900. *Texas Ranger Service Records* **[Microfilm & Digital Capture]**, from the originals at the Texas State Archives, Austin, TX. Filmed by the TX State Archives, 1971, 2 rolls, as follows:
- Texas Ranger Service records, ca. 1830-1846 - Texas Ranger Service records, Minute men, (primarily), 1841 Acklin, John - Villareal, Juan, FHL film #2282494
- Texas Ranger Service records, Minute men, (primarily), 1841 Waddock, Bryan - York, H. - Texas Ranger Service records, (et al) 1847-1900, companies: Frontier Battalion companies, Minute men companies, Misc. Units companies. Companies are listed alphabetically within each of these groups - Minute men, commanding officers; Counties, Frontier battalions, commanding officers. These groups are listed alphabetically within county order - Ranger index, ca. 1847-1900 Abercrombie, J.W. - Zurcher, L., FHL film #2282495

To access the digital images, see the online FHL catalog: **www.familysearch.org/search/catalog/1044059**.

1833-1974. *Texas, Wills and Probate Records* **[Online Database]**, digitized and indexed at the Ancestry.com website. Source: Ancestry extractions from TX county, district, and probate courts. Probate records may include Wills, Letters of Administration, Distribution and Accounting Records, Bonds, and Guardianships. The contents of a probate file can vary from case to case, but usually, the names and residences of beneficiaries and their relationship to the decedent may be found in the file. An inventory of the estate assets can reveal personal details about the deceased's occupation and lifestyle. There may also be references to debts, deeds, and other documents related to the settling of the estate. This database has 110,887 records. See
http://search.ancestry.com/search/db.aspx?dbid=2115.

1835. **Index of Texas Statewide Census [Online Database]**, indexed at the USGenWeb site for Texas. See **http://files.usgwarchives.net/tx/census/1835**.

1835 Entrance Certificates, Nacogdoches District **[Printed Book]**, compiled by Betty Fagan Burr, published by Frances Terry Ingmire, St. Louis, MO, 1982, 40 pages. From bibliography: "From the R.B. Blake translation of the original Spanish certificates." Includes index. FHL book 976.4 P4n.

1835 Sabine District, Texas, Census **[Printed Book]**, compiled by Mrs. Helen Gomer Schluter, published by Ericson Books, Nacogdoches, TX, 1983, 56 pages. From Introduction: "This 1835 Sabine District, Texas, census was copied from the original Nacogdoches Archives, Austin, Texas, by Mr. R. B. Blake." Includes additions to the original census records and a comprehensive index by Mrs. Helen Gomer Schluter. FHL book 976.4177 X2sh.

1836. *A Brief Account of the Origin, Progress and Present State of the Colonial Settlements of Texas: Together With an Exposition of the Causes Which Have Induced the Existing War With Mexico* **[Printed Book]**, by William H. Wharton, extracted from a work entitled *A Geographical, Statistical and Historical Account of Texas*, originally publ. by S. Nye, Nashville, TN, 1836, 16 pages. Reprint published by Pemberton Press, Austin, TX, 1964. Filmed by the Genealogical Society of Utah, 1972, FHL film #874251. To see if this microfilm was digitized yet, see the online FHL catalog:
www.familysearch.org/search/catalog/25114.
NOTE: Wharton's *Historical Account of Texas* booklet had a huge response in Tennessee. Written in 1836 while the Texas Revolution was in progress, the booklet created intense curiosity about Texas. In fact, when Davey Crockett had campaigned for reelection to his Tennessee seat in the U.S. House of Representatives with the campaign promise, "If reelected, I will serve you faithfully, but if not, you might all go to h---, and I would go to Texas." Upon his arrival in Texas, Crockett said, "I was beaten, gentlemen, and here I am."

1836-1935. *Guide and Index to the Texas Adjutant General Service Records* **[Printed Book]**, by Anthony Black and the Texas State Archives; edited by Robert de Berardinis, Contents: Vol. 1: Cumulative Index; Vol. 2: Separate Indexes, publ. Heritage Books, Westminster, MD, 2009, 2 vols., FHL book 976.4 M22ba v. 1-2.

1837-1910. *Texas County Tax Rolls* **[Microfilm & Digital Capture]**, from the originals at the Texas State Archives, Austin, TX. filmed by the TX State Archives, 424 rolls, 1974-1975. A complete set is also located at the Family History Library in Salt Lake City.

Texas may not have state censuses, but there are thousands of name lists available from the tax rolls for all 254 Texas counties. The tax rolls are a boon for finding the name of an ancestor living in Texas, because the name of every taxpayer is shown, including real or personal property holders. Therefore, the tax rolls provide a good list of the adult (mostly male) residents of a county, often more so than any head of household census list. The 424 FHL rolls begin with FHL film #2282072 (Anderson Co, 1846-1881, A-C). To access the digital images, see the online FHL catalog: **https://familysearch.org/search/catalog/986276**.
- NOTE: The TX State Archives microfilm collection is identified at their "Texas County Tax Rolls" information page, where lists of the Series and Range of Years is given. There is also good advice on using these tax rolls and possible problems to look out for. See **www.tsl.texas.gov/arc/taxrolls.html**.

1837-1900s. *Texas US GenWeb Archives* **[Online Databases],** name lists are available for all counties. Typical county records include Bibles, Biographies, Cemeteries, Censuses, Court, Death, Deeds, Directories, Histories, Marriages, Military, Newspapers, Obituaries, Photos, Schools, Tax Lists, Wills, and more. Links to all Texas counties and projects are located at the USGenWeb home page for Texas. See **www.txgenweb.org**.

1837-1910. *Texas, County Tax Rolls* **[Online Database],** digitized and indexed at the FamilySearch.org website. Source: Microfilm at the TX State Archives. The State Archives microfilm collection is identified with the contents of 424 rolls at their information page. Texas may not have state censuses, but there are thousands of name lists available from the tax rolls for 231 of the 254 Texas counties. The tax rolls are a boon for finding the name of an ancestor living in Texas, because the name of every taxpayer is shown, including real or personal property holders. Therefore, the tax rolls provide a good list of the adult residents of a county, often more so than a head of household census list. Each index record includes: Name, Event type, Event year, and County. The images of the registers add much more information. This database has 4,575,333 records. See **https://familysearch.org/search/collection/1827575**.

1837-1965. *Texas, County Marriage Records* **[Online Database],** digitized and indexed at the FamilySearch.org website. Source: Records of various county clerks at the TX State Archives. This database consists of various types of marriage records (registers, licenses, intentions to marry, etc.) from 183 of the 254 counties in Texas. Each index record includes: Name, Event type, Event date, Event place, Gender, Spouse's name, and Spouse's gender. The original document has more information. This database has 1,724,715 records. See **https://familysearch.org/search/collection/1803985**.
- See also, *Texas Marriages, 1837-1973* **[Online Database],** indexed at the FamilySearch.org website. Source: FamilySearch extractions from records on microfilm at the Family History Library, Salt Lake City, UT. Each index record includes: Name, Spouse's name, and Event place. This database has 1,695,783 records. See **https://familysearch.org/search/collection/1681052**.

1837-1965. *Texas, Select County Marriage Index* **[Online Database],** indexed at the Ancestry.com website. Source: FamilySearch extractions from records on microfilm at the Family History Library, Salt Lake City, UT. This database is an index to a variety of marriage records (registers, licenses, intentions to marry, etc.) from select counties in Texas - from 183 of the 254 counties in Texas. Each index record includes: Name, Gender, Marriage date, Marriage place, Spouse, and FHL film number. This database has 3,185,816 records. See **http://search.ancestry.com/search/db.aspx?dbid=60183**.
- See also, *Texas, County Marriage Index, 1837-1977* **[Online Database],** indexed at the FamilySearch.org website. Source: FamilySearch extractions from county records on microfilm at the Family History Library, Salt Lake City, UT. Each index record includes: Name, Event type, Event date, Event place, and Spouse's name. This database has 1,575,573 records. See **https://familysearch.org/search/collection/1803987**.
- NOTE: These two databases are probably one database, an example of how Ancestry.com and FamilySearch.org often work together. In some cases, Ancestry does the digitizing and FamilySearch does the indexes. In other cases, they reverse those roles. But apparently, Ancestry counts both the Bride and the Groom in the number of records; while FamilySearch counts the couple as one record.

1837-Current. *Surname Index - Texas General Land Office.* **[Online Database],** an important resource for genealogists. Established in 1837, the TX General Land Office Archives holds the original land grant records and maps dating to the 16th century that detail the passage of Texas public lands to private ownership. The Texas General Land Office Archives Surname Index contains alphabetical listings of grantees and patentees that were issued land grants by the Republic and State of Texas. The index also lists grantees for Spanish and Mexican land grants filed in the Spanish Collection. See **www.glo.texas.gov/history/archives/surname-index**.

1837-Current. *Briscoe Center for American History, Texas Newspaper Collection at the University of Texas at Austin* **[Online Database].** The Briscoe Center's Newspaper Collections contain more than 4,500 Texas, Southern, U.S., and non-U.S. titles and is the largest collection of its kind in Texas. For more information about a specific geographic focus at the Briscoe Center home page. See
www.cah.utexas.edu/research/newspapers.php.

1838-1900. *Texas, Muster Roll Index Cards* **[Online Database],** indexed at the Ancestry.com website. Source: TX State Archives. This database includes records of enlistments to Texas militia units of the Texas State Rangers, Confederate Army, and Union Army. Each index record includes: Name, Age, Estimated birth year, Enlistment date, Enlistment place, and Record type. The image of a card may have more information, depending on the type of record. This database has 116,060 records. See
http://search.ancestry.com/search/db.aspx?dbid=2059.

1840 Census of the Republic of Texas **[Printed Book],** edited by Gifford White, published by Pemberton Press, Austin, TX, 1966, 236 pages. In spite of the title – there was no census in Texas in 1840 – the names apparently were taken from the *First Settlers* book below. FHL book 976.4 X2w 1840.

1840. *First Settlers of the Republic of Texas: Headright Land Grants Which Were Reported as Genuine and Legal by the Traveling Commissioners, January, 1840* **[Printed Book],** 2 vols., originally published by Cruger & Wing, Austin, Texas, 1841; reproduced and indexed by Carolyn Reeves Ericson and Frances T. Ingmire, Nacogdoches, TX, 1982. Contents: Vol. 1: Counties of Austin, Bastrop, Bexar, Brazoria, Colorado, Fannin, Fayette, Fort Bend, Galveston, Goliad, Gonzales, Harris, Harrison, Houston, Jackson, and Jasper; Vol. 2: Counties of Jefferson, Liberty, Matagorda, Milam, Montgomery, Nacogdoches, Red River, Refugio, Robertson, Sabine, San Augustine, Shelby, Victoria, and Washington. FHL book 976.4 R2er v. 1&2.

1840s. *Early Settlers and Indian Fighters of Southwest Texas: Facts Gathered from Survivors of Frontier Days* **[Printed Book],** by A. J. Sowell, originally published by B. C. Jones, printers, 1900; facsimile reproduction, including new index, published by State House Press, Austin, TX, 1986, 861 pages. FHL book 976.4 H2saj 1986.

1840-1849. *Texas, Index of County Tax Lists* **[Printed Book],** edited by Ronald Vern Jackson, et al, published by Accelerated Indexing Systems, North Salt Lake, UT, 1982, 69 pages. FHL book 976.4 X2j 1840-1849.

1840-1981. *Texas Births and Christenings* **[Online Database],** indexed at the FamilySearch.org website. Source: FamilySearch extractions from records on microfilm at the Family History Library, Salt Lake City, UT. Each index record includes: Name, Gender, Birth date, Birthplace, Race, Father's name, and Mother's name. This database has 515,974 records. See
https://familysearch.org/search/collection/1681015.

1841-1843. "Kentucky Colonization in Texas: A History of the Peters Colony" **[Printed Article & Digital Version],** from the *Kentucky Register,* Vol. 52, No. 180 (July 1954). Lists name, age, occupation, marital status, county, and other information of colonists. The William Smalling Peters empresario grant was issued by the Republic of Texas in Aug 1841. The northeast corner of the original area was a point on the Red River in modern Grayson County, Texas. The extensive area of Peters Colony included today's Dallas-Fort Worth Metroplex, as well as all or portions of 26 modern northeast Texas counties: Denton, Collin, Cooke, Grayson, Dallas, Tarrant, Wise, Palo Pinto, Ellis, Johnson, Montague, Parker, Hood, Clay, Jack, Erath, Wichita. Archer, Young, Stephens, Eastland, Wilbarger, Baylor, Throckmorton, Shackelford, and Callahan counties. To access the digital version, see the online FHL catalog:
www.familysearch.org/search/catalog/2617381.
- See also, *Kentucky Colonization in Texas* **[Online Database],** digitized version of the *Kentucky Register* article at the Ancestry.com website, with an OCR index, see
www.ancestry.com/search/collections/48418.

1841-1985. *Texas, Mills County Clerk Records* **[Online Database],** digitized at the FamilySearch.org website. Source: Mills Co Clerk's Office, Goldthwaite, TX. This is an image only database, with Mills Co TX births, marriages, deaths, court records, deed records, divorce records, naturalization records, probate records, and indexes for each of the record types. Browse through the images, organized by Record Category, then Record Description. This database has 153,275 images. See
https://familysearch.org/search/collection/1837923.

1844-1847. *A New Land Beckoned: German Immigration to Texas* **[Online Database],** indexed at the Ancestry.com website. Source: Book, same title, by Chester W. Geue, publ. 1982. Includes an indexed list of 4,200 German immigrants. This database has 192 pages. See
http://search.ancestry.com/search/db.aspx?dbid=48470.
- See also, *A New Land Beckoned: German Immigration to Texas, 1847-1861* **[Online Database],** indexed at the Ancestry.com website. Source: Book, same title, by Chester W. Geue, publ. 1982. Includes an indexed list of German immigrants. This database has 173 pages. See
http://search.ancestry.com/search/db.aspx?dbid=48471.
- See also, *List of Names of the German Emigrants Emigrated to Texas Under the German Emigration Co. in 1845 and 1846 by Shiploads* **[Printed Book & Digital Version],** by Groos and Taylor, New Braunfels, TX, digitized by FamilySearch International, 2015, To access the digital images, see the online FHL catalog:
www.familysearch.org/search/catalog/2478261.

1846. *Republic of Texas Poll Lists for 1846* **[Online Database],** indexed at the Ancestry.com website. Source: Book, same title, by Marion Day Mullins, publ. 1974, 1982. The title "Republic of Texas" may come from the Poll Tax collection at the TX State Archives, from where this database was extracted, but this 1846 list was prepared after Texas was annexed to the U.S. as a state in 1845. This is an image only database, but the entire book is an index to the names of taxpayers, listed in alphabetical order. This list of names is the closest thing to a census for the first years of Texas statehood. Browse the collection, organized by Title Page, Forward, and Surname groups A-B through Y-Z. This database has 193 pages. See
http://search.ancestry.com/search/db.aspx?dbid=48427.
- See also, *Republic of Texas: Poll Lists For 1846* **[Printed Book],** by Marion Day Mullins, published by Genealogical Publishing Co., Inc., Baltimore, 1974, 189 pages. FHL book 976.4 R4m.

1846. *Taxpayers of the Republic of Texas: Covering 30 counties and the District of Panola* **[Printed Book],** compiled by Beth and Emily Dorman. Published by the authors, 1988, Grand Prairie, TX, 275 pages. Includes index. FHL book 976.4 R4d. Also on microfiche, FHL film #6007392.

1846-1848. *Compiled Service Records of Volunteer Soldiers Who Served During the Mexican War in Organizations from the State of Texas* **[Microfilm & Digital Capture],** from the originals at the National Archives, Washington, DC. Filmed by the National Archives, 1959, 19 rolls, beginning with FHL film #471519 (First Texas Mounted Rifles A-S). To access the digital images, see the online FHL catalog:
https://familysearch.org/search/catalog/316485.

1846-1910. *Texas, County Tax Rolls* **[Online Database],** indexed at the Ancestry.com website. Source: TX State Archives. Information in the tax records may include: Name of owner, Assessment number, Original grantee, Number of acres of land, Value, Town plot description, Name of city or town, Kind, number, and value of livestock, Kind, quantity, and value of farm commodities, Amount of state taxes, and Amount of county taxes. This database has 3,852,784 records. See
http://search.ancestry.com/search/db.aspx?dbid=60184.

1849-1982. *Texas, Cooke County, Probate Records* **[Online Database],** digitized and indexed at FamilySearch.org. Source: County Clerk, Cooke County, Texas. This database has 4,834 records, see
www.familysearch.org/search/collection/2804902.

1850. *Texas, 1850 Federal Census: Population Schedules* **[Microfilm & Digital Capture],** filmed by the National Archives, 1964, 11 rolls, beginning with FHL film #24887 (Anderson, Angelina, Austin, Bastrop, Bexar, Bowie, Brazoria, Brazos, and Burleson counties). To access the digital images, see the online FHL catalog:
www.familysearch.org/search/catalog/744500.
- See also *The State of Texas Federal Population Schedules, Seventh Census of the United States, 1850* **[Printed Book & Digital Version],** transcribed by Mrs. V. K. Carpenter, publ. Century Enterprises, Huntsville, AL, 1969, 5 vols. FHL book 976.4 X2. To access the digital images, see the online FHL catalog:
www.familysearch.org/search/catalog/190137.

1850-1880. *Mortality Schedules of Texas (1850, 1860, 1870, 1880); Mortality Schedules of Utah (1870)* **[Microfilm & Digital Capture],** filmed by the Texas State Library, 1950, 8 rolls, beginning with FHL film #1421044 (TX 1850: 1860, Anderson Co – Titus Co). To access the digital images, see the online FHL catalog: www.familysearch.org/search/catalog/343874.

1850-2005. *Texas, Select Headstone Photos* **[Online Database],** digitized and indexed at Ancestry.com. From a collection of photos provided by Allen Wheatley, teafor2.com. This database has photos of over 74,000 headstones with 94,225 inscribed names visible. There are headstones from a few different states, but the majority are from Texas cemeteries. See www.ancestry.com/search/collections/8792.

1851-Current. *Texas State Cemetery* **[Online Database],** indexed at the Cemetery.state.tx website. See www.cemetery.state.tx.us.

1852-1991. *Texas, Naturalization Records* **[Online Database],** digitized and indexed at Ancestry.com. This collection includes a variety of naturalization records from over 20 district courts in Texas. *Browse this Collection* by Court City for the titles and descriptions of the records from each court district. This database has 536,839 records, see www.ancestry.com/search/collections/2509.

1852-1994. *Texas, Church Records* **[Online Database],** includes records from St. Mathew's Episcopal Cathedral, Dallas; and First Presbyterian Church, Fort Worth. This database has 6,107 records, see www.familysearch.org/search/collection/2790180.

1858 State Census of Austin County, Texas, Copied Under the Supervision of the Littlefield Fund and Assisted by Project No. 43 of the Bureau of Research in the Social Sciences at the University of Texas From Original Manuscripts Located in the Courthouse at Bellville, Texas **[Microfilm & Digital Capture],** from the originals at the Austin County courthouse in Bellville, Texas. Filmed by the Genealogical Society of Utah, 1992, 1 roll, FHL film #1838537. To access the digital images, see the online FHL catalog: www.familysearch.org/search/catalog/615189.

1858-1955. *Texas, Comanche County Records* **[Online Database],** digitized and indexed at FamilySearch.org. Records include births, marriages, divorces, court records, probate records, and school records. This database has 48,522 records, see www.familysearch.org/search/collection/1831470.

1860. *Texas, 1860 Federal Census: Population Schedules* **[Microfilm & Digital Capture],** filmed by the National Archives, 1967, 32 rolls, beginning with FHL film #805287 (TX, 2nd filming: Anderson, Angelina, Atascosa, Austin, and Bandera counties). To access the digital images, see the online FHL catalog: www.familysearch.org/search/catalog/707058.

1860-1933. *Texas, Harrison County Delayed Birth Records* **[Online Database],** digitized and indexed at FamilySearch.org. Each index record includes Name, Event type, Event date, Event place, Gender, Father's name, Father's birthplace, Father's age, Mother's name, Mother's birthplace, Mother's age/birthyear and Certificate number. This database has 6,301 records, see www.familysearch.org/search/collection/3460988.

1861-1865. *Texas, Civil War Service Records of Confederate Soldiers* **[Online Database],** indexed at the FamilySearch.org website. Source: National Archives microfilm series M323. The records include a jacket-envelope for each soldier, labeled with his name, rank, and unit; and card abstracts of entries relating to the soldier as found in original muster rolls, returns, rosters, payrolls, appointment books, hospital registers, Union prison registers and rolls, parole rolls, or inspection reports. This database has 956,501 records. See https://familysearch.org/search/collection/1932381.

1861-1865. *Texas, Civil War Service Records of Union Soldiers* **[Online Database],** indexed at the FamilySearch.org website. Source: National Archives microfilm series M402. The records include a jacket-envelope for each soldier, labeled with his name, rank, and unit; and card abstracts of entries relating to the soldier as found in original muster rolls, returns, rosters, payrolls, appointment books, hospital registers, prison registers and rolls, parole rolls, or inspection reports. This database has 33,955 records. See https://familysearch.org/search/collection/1932425.

1861-1865. *Texas Confederate Index: Confederate Soldiers of the State of Texas* **[Microfilm & Digital Capture],** source not noted. Includes name, rank, commission, enlistment date and place, discharge date and place, company, description (age, residence, etc.). Filmed by Microfilm Service and Sales, Dallas, TX, 1961, 14 rolls, beginning with FHL film #227483 (Confederate Index, A-Bradford). To access the digital images, see the online FHL catalog: https://familysearch.org/search/catalog/424572.

1861-1865. *Index to Compiled Service Records of Confederate Soldiers Who Served in Organizations From the State of Texas* **[Microfilm & Digital Capture],** from the original records at the National Archives, Washington, DC, an alphabetical card index to the compiled service records of Confederate soldiers belonging to units from the State of Texas, series M323, 41 rolls, beginning with FHL film #880014 (Surnames A – As). To access the digital images (of certain rolls), see the online FHL catalog: https://familysearch.org/search/catalog/98127.

1861-1865. *Index to Compiled Service Records of Union Soldiers Who Served in Organizations From the State of Texas* **[Microfilm]**, from the original records at the National Archives, Central Plains Region, Kansas City, MO, series M402, 2 rolls, FHL film #881592 (Index, A-Ma, 1861-1865), and #881593 (Index, Mc-Z, 1861-1865). To see if this microfilm was digitized yet, see the online FHL catalog: www.familysearch.org/search/catalog/314346.

1861-1938. *Texas, Prison Employee Ledgers* **[Online Database]**, digitized and indexed at the Ancestry.com website. Source: TX State Archives. This collection is comprised primarily of payrolls for employees who worked in the Texas State Penitentiary System, including guards, physicians, sergeants, and others. You will also find some guard ledgers, with details on guards' service, and discharge records. Payroll records typically provide a name, date, pay, and occupation. Ledgers include name, prison assigned, date of assignment, and discharge, resignation, or suspension. Reasons for the discharge or suspension are often noted. This database has 207,611 records. See http://search.ancestry.com/search/db.aspx?dbid=1991.

1863-1970. *Texas, Gonzales County, Death Records* **[Online Database]**, digitized and indexed at FamilySearch.org. This database has 36,321 records, see www.familysearch.org/search/collection/2761118.

1865-1866 *Internal Revenue Assessment Lists for Texas* **[Microfilm & Digital Capture]**, from the original records at the National Archives in Washington, DC. Contents: District 2: Atascosas, Austin, Bee, Calhoun, Cameron, Colorado, De Witt, Duval, Encinal (no longer exists), Fayette, Fort Bend, Frio, Goliad, Gonzales, Hidalgo, Jackson, Karnes, La Salle, Lavaca, Live Oak, McMullin, Matagorda, Maverick, Nueces, Refugio, San Patricio, Starr, Victoria, Washington, Webb, Wharton, Zapata, and Zavala counties. District 3: Archer, Bandera, Bastrop, Baylor, Bill, Bexar, Blanco, Bosque, Brown, Buchanan (no longer exists), Burleson, Burnet, Caldwell, Clay, Colahan (Callahan), Comal, Comanche, Concho, Cooke, Coryell, Dawson, Denton, Eastland, Edwards, El Paso, Erath, Falls, Gillespie, Guadalupe, Hamilton, Hardeman, Haskell, Hays, Hill, Jack, Johnson, Jones, Kemble (Kimble), Kerr, Kinney, Knox, Lampasas, Llano, McCulloch, Mason, Medina, Menard, Milam, Montague, Palo Pinto, Parker, Presidio, Runnels, San Saba, Shackelford, Tarrant, Taylor, Throckmorton, Travis, Uvalde, Wichita, Wilbargar (Wilbarger), Williamson, Wise, and Young counties. District 4 pt. 1: Anderson, Bowie, Cass, Cherokee, Collin, Dallas, Ellis, Fannin, Freestone, Grayson, Harrison, Henderson, Hopkins, Hunt, Kaufman, Lamar, Limestone, Marion, Navarro, Panola, Red River, Rusk, Smith, Titus, Upshur, Van Zandt, and Wood counties. District 4 pt. 2: Ellis, Freestone, Limestone, and Navarro counties. Names are arranged by collection district and thereunder by division. Filmed by the archives, 1987, 2 rolls, FHL film #1578479 (District 2) and film #1578480 (Districts 3-4). To access the digital images, see the online FHL catalog: www.familysearch.org/search/catalog/577920.

1865-1870. *Texas, Freedmen's Bureau Field Office Records* **[Online Database]**, indexed at the FamilySearch.org website. digitized at the FamilySearch.org website. Source: National Archives microfilm series M1912. The Bureau of Refugees, Freedmen, and Abandoned Lands (often called the Freedmen's Bureau) was created in 1865 at the end of the American Civil War to supervise relief efforts including education, health care, food and clothing, refugee camps, legalization of marriages, employment, labor contracts, and securing back pay, bounty payments and pensions. These records include letters and endorsements sent and received, account books, applications for rations, applications for relief, court records, labor contracts, registers of bounty claimants, registers of complaints, registers of contracts, registers of disbursements, registers of freedmen issued rations, registers of patients, reports, rosters of officers and employees, special and general orders and circulars received, special orders and circulars issued, court trials, property restoration, and homesteads. This database has 29,370 records. See https://familysearch.org/search/collection/1989155.

1867. See *Texas 1867 Special Voters' Registration* **[Microfilm & Digital Capture]**, from the originals at the Texas State Library & Archives Commission, Austin, Texas. Available through Interlibrary loan from the TX archives. The Reconstruction Act of March 13, 1867 required the commanding officer in each military district to have, before September 1, a registration of all qualified voters in each county. These lists would be used to determine all who would be eligible to vote for any proposed Constitutional Convention in the state. Forms include the following information: date of registration; county and precinct of residence; years resided in state; years resided in county; years resided in precinct; native of what state or county; how, when, and where naturalized; signature; general remarks. Not all forms are completely filled out. Filmed by the Texas

State Library, 1984, FHL has 7 rolls, as follows:
- Anderson - Caldwell counties, 1867, FHL film #1929135.
- Calhoun - Falls counties, 1869, FHL film #1929136.
- Erath - Hamilton counties, FHL film #1929137.
- Hardin - Kinney counties, FHL film #1929138.
- Lamar - Orange counties, FHL film #1929139.
- Navarro - Tyler counties, FHL film #1929140.
- Tarrant - Zapata counties, FHL film #1929141.

To access the digital images, see the online FHL catalog: www.familysearch.org/search/catalog/676251.

- See also, *An index to the 1867 Voters Registration of Texas* [CD-ROM], compiled by Donaly E. Brice & John C. Barron, published by Heritage Books, Bowie, MD, 2000. Lists voters arranged by county including name, date of registration, voting precinct, years of residence, state, or country of birth. This includes the first statewide listing of freed slaves in Texas. See FHL CD-ROM No. 898.

- See also, *Texas, Voter Registration Lists, 1867-1869* [Online Database], digitized and indexed at the Ancestry.com website. Source: TX State Archives, Austin, TX. The Reconstruction Acts of 1867 required Southern states to ratify the 14th Amendment, draft new state constitutions, and register voters, both black and white, to vote in state constitutional conventions. In order to vote, men had to swear an oath of allegiance to the United States, and some were disqualified because of their participation in Confederate government posts. These records list the names of more than 139,000 men age 21 and over who registered to vote in Texas between 1867 and 1869. Each index record includes: Name, Birthplace, Registry date, County, and database IDs. The digitized images have more information about a person. This database has 140,267 records. See http://search.ancestry.com/search/db.aspx?dbid=2274.

- See also, *Texas, Special Voter Registration, 1867-1869* [Online Database], digitized and indexed at FamilySearch.org, this database has 121,271 records, see www.familysearch.org/search/collection/3163398.

1868-1949. *Eastland County, Texas, County Records* [Online Database], digitized and indexed at Ancestry.com. This collection was extracted from FHL microfilm by FamilySearch and shared with Ancestry.com. The records include District Court and Naturalizations from Eastland County, Texas. This database has 364,267 records, see https://www.ancestry.com/search/collections/60185.

1870. *Texas, 1870 Federal Census: Population Schedules* [Microfilm & Digital Capture], filmed by the National Archives, 1968, 48 rolls, beginning with FHL film #553072 (TX, 2nd filming: Anderson, Angelina, Atascosa, and Frio counties). To access the digital images, see the online FHL catalog: www.familysearch.org/search/catalog/698921.

1870-1930. *Confederate Pensions (Texas): Applications Approved and Rejected* [Microfilm & Digital Capture], from the originals at the TX Comptroller's Office, Austin, TX. Filmed by the Genealogical Society of Utah, 1974, 700 rolls, beginning with FHL film #960279 (Index to Applications Approved, Rejected, and Inmates of the Confederate Home). To access the digital images, see the online FHL catalog: https://familysearch.org/search/catalog/70567.

- See also *Confederate Pension Index for Texas, 1870-1930* [Microfilm & Digital Capture], from the original records at the TX State Archives, Austin, TX. Filmed by the Genealogical Society of Utah, 1996, 1 roll, FHL film #2031526. To access the digital images, see the online FHL catalog: www.familysearch.org/search/catalog/777370.

1870-2012. *Texas, County Marriage Records* [Online Database], indexed at the Ancestry.com website. Source: Bexar and Brazoria County, TX, from records at the Co Clerk's office, both counties. Each index record includes: Name, Gender, Marriage date, Recording date, Spouse, and Document number. This database has 3,829,639 records. See http://search.ancestry.com/search/db.aspx?dbid=9168.

1873-1876. *Texas, Cooke County, Birth Records* [Online Database], digitized and indexed at FamilySearch.org. Records from the Cooke County Clerk, Gainesville, TX. This database has 162 records, see www.familysearch.org/search/collection/2691683.

1874 History. See *A Texas Scrapbook: Made up of the History, Biography, and Miscellany of Texas and its People* [Printed Book], compiled by D. W. C. Baker, original published by A.S. Barnes and Co., New York, 1874, 657 pages. Filmed by W. C. Cox, Tucson, AZ, 1974, FHL film #1000596.

- See also, *Index to D. W. C. Baker's A Texas Scrapbook* [Printed Book], by Richard Morrison, published by the author, Austin, Texas, 1984, 153 pages. Includes name index, and index to sources and authors. FHL book 976.4 H2mr index.

1875-1945. *Texas, Convict and Conduct Registers* [Online Database], digitized and indexed at the Ancestry.com website. Source: TX State Archives. Each index record includes: Name, Birth year, Birthplace, Record date, Place of residence, Prison location, Age, and Convict number. The document images have more information about a prisoner. This database has 263,765 records. See http://search.ancestry.com/search/db.aspx?dbid=2143.

1877-1922. *Sanborn Fire Insurance Maps* – **Texas [Online Database]**, images at the Perry-Castañeda Library Map Collection – University of Texas, Austin, TX. See www.lib.utexas.edu/maps/sanborn/texas.html.

1878-1945. *Texas, Gonzales County, Birth Records* **[Online Database]**, digitized and indexed at FamilySearc.org. Records from the Gonzales County Court. This database has 53,451 records, see www.familysearch.org/search/collection/3023822.

1879-2012. *Texas, Swisher County Records* **[Online Database]**, digitized and indexed at FamilySearch.org, from records of the Swisher County and District Clerk. Records include vital records, military discharges, probate records, deed records, marks and brands, court records and civil case files from the county and district courts. This database has 11,109 records, see www.familysearch.org/search/collection/2103490.

1880. *Texas, 1880 Federal Census: Soundex and Population Schedules* **[Microfilm & Digital Capture]**, filmed by the National Archives, c1970, 124 rolls, beginning with FHL film #1255288 (Population: Anderson, Angelina, Aransas, Archer, Atascosa, Austin, Armstrong, Briscoe, Randall, and Swisher counties). To access the digital images, see the FHL catalog: www.familysearch.org/search/catalog/676524.

1880-1896. *Index to Some Texas Biographies* **[Digitized Book]**, digited by FamilySearch International, 2018. This was a 1969 project of the DAR Waco Chapter to index eleven biographical books located at the Library of the Masonic Grand Lodge, Waco, Texas. Page 1 has a list of the books by title and author, plus an indication of an FHL call number if available. The books are related to several counties of Texas: McLennan, Falls, Bell, and Coryell counties (publ. 1893); Tarrant and Parker counties (publ. 1895); Dallas County (publ. 1892); Miles, Williamson, Bastrop, Travis, Lee and Burleson counties (publ. 1893); Ellis County (1892); Houston and Galveston (publ. 1895); and Texas Statewide (publ. 1880), and Central Texas (publ. 1896). To access the digital version, see the online FHL catalog: www.familysearch.org/search/catalog/3031432.

1882-1888. *Texas, Capitol Building Payroll* **[Online Database]**, indexed at the Ancestry.com website. Source: TX State Archives. This database contains a collection of cards listing people on the payroll of the Texas State Capitol during the 1880s. Each card shows the person's name, occupation, and year of employment. Cards are arranged alphabetically by surname. This database has 6,906 records. See http://search.ancestry.com/search/db.aspx?dbid=2176.

1884 History. See *Rangers and Pioneers of Texas: With a Concise Account of the Early Settlements, Hardships, Massacres, Battles, and Wars, by Which Texas Was Rescued From the Rule of the Savage and Consecrated to the Empire of Civilization* **[Microfilm]**, from the book by A.J. Sowell, originally published by Shepard Bros. & Co., San Antonio, TX, 1884, 411 pages. Filmed for the FHL by the Library of Congress, 1991, 1 roll, FHL film #1730711.

1884-1958. *Alabama, Texas and Virginia, Confederate Pensions* **[Online Database]**, digitized and indexed at the Ancestry.com website. Source: AL, TX, and VA State Archives. Each index record includes: Name, Application place, Birthplace, Age, and Application type. The document images and the information on them vary from state to state. This database has 219,155 records. See http://search.ancestry.com/search/db.aspx?dbid=1677.

1890 Census Substitute **[Online Database]**, indexed at the Ancestry.com website. This is Ancestry's collection of city directories (and other name lists) from all over the U.S. for the time of the lost 1890 federal census. Included are city directories for **Austin**, 1887-1992; **Dallas**, 1889-1894; **Galveston**, 1888-1891; **Houston**, 1882-1895; **San Antonio**, 1891-1894; and **Waco**, 1890. Go to *View All Collections Included in this Search* for a complete list of databases, alphabetically by place (county, city, state, etc.), and year. See http://search.ancestry.com/search/group/1890census#databases.

1890 Reconstructed Census for Selected Texas Counties **[Printed Books]**, name lists compiled from local tax and other records, by Mary C. Moody and others, published for the following Texas counties:
- **Bexar County**, (tax rolls of 1890), FHL book 976.435 R4a.
- **Caldwell County**, FHL book 976.433 X2m.
- **Limestone County**, FHL book 976.4285 X2m.
- **Montgomery County**, FHL book 976.4153 X2m.
- **Nacogdoches County** (index to 1890 tax list), FHL book 976.4182 R42e.
- **Smith County** (index to 1890 tax book), FHL book 976.4225 R48e.
- **Travis County**, FHL book 976.431 X2m, pt. 1 & pt 2 (index).
- **Walker County**, FHL book 976.4169 X2m.

- **Cass County**, FHL book 976.4195 X28m.
- **Hamilton County**, FHL book 976.4549 X2m.
- **Kerr County**, FHL book 976.4884 X2d.
- **Leon County**, FHL book 976.4233 X28m.

1890-1976. *Texas Deaths* [Online Database], digitized and indexed at the FamilySearch.org website. Source: Vital Statistics Bureau, TX Dept of Health. This database includes images of death certificates and an index. Each index record includes Name, Event type, Event date, Gender, Marital status, Birth date, Father's name, Mother's name, and Certificate number. The certificate image has more information. This database has 4,543,234 records. See
https://familysearch.org/search/collection/1983324.

1892-1947. *Texas, Court of Criminal Appeal Indexes* [Online Database], digitized and indexed at the Ancestry.com website. Source: TX State Archives. This database contains a list of appellants and appellees involved in criminal court cases in the state of Texas (1892–1947). These records are an index to case records and so typically contain only the names of the appellant and appellee (which may be the state) and county. They may also indicate how a case was disposed of, who offered the opinion, and (beginning in 1909) docket number. This database has 42,793 records. See
http://search.ancestry.com/search/db.aspx?dbid=2147.

1892-2010. *Texas, Daughters of the Republic of Texas, Membership Applications* [Online Database], digitized at the FamilySearch.org website. Source: Daughters of the Republic of Texas, Austin, TX. This is an image only database with documents from the lineage society dedicated to preserving the memory of Texas pioneer families. Membership is limited to descendants of those who "rendered loyal service for Texas" prior to Feb 1846. These records consist of 1,525 booklets containing membership applications and their attendant documentation. Browse through images, organized by Vol. and Application No. Range. This database has 386,880 records. See
https://familysearch.org/search/collection/1918480.

1893-1963. *Texas Passenger Lists* [Online Database], digitized and indexed at the Ancestry.com website. Source: National Archives microfilm, Selected Passenger and Crew Lists and Manifests. These passenger and crew lists from both ships and aircraft were recorded a variety of forms, and usually include the name of the vessel and arrival date, ports of departure and arrival (as well as future destinations on a ship's itinerary), dates of departure and arrival, shipmaster, full name, age, gender, physical description, military rank (if any), occupation, birthplace, citizen of what country, and residence. This database has 1,027,708 records. See
http://search.ancestry.com/search/db.aspx?dbid=8722.

1893-2007. *Texas, Bexar County, San Antonio Cemetery Records* [Online Database], digitized and indexed at FamilySearch.org. Source: San Antonio Parks & Recreation Dept., with records from Odd Fellows Cemetery, Old City Cemetery, and San Jose Burial Park. This database has 59,760 records, see
https://familysearch.org/search/collection/1828544.

1895-1924. *Texas, Cooke County, Deeds* [Online Database], digitized and indexed at FamilySearch.org. Source: Cooke County Clerk, Gainesville, TX. This database has 32,703 records, see
www.familysearch.org/search/collection/2804974.

1895-1964. *Border Crossings: From Mexico to U.S.* [Online Database], digitized and indexed at the Ancestry.com website. Source: National Archives microfilm, publications from CA, AZ, NM, and TX ports of entry. This database includes records of border crossing in the Texas ports of entry at Brownsville, Del Rio, Eagle Pass, El Paso, Fabens, Fort Hancock, Hidalgo, Laredo, Presidio, Rio Grande City, San Antonio, Yseleta, and Zapata. Each index record includes: Name, Gender, Arrival age, Birth date, Arrival date, Arrival place, Record has photo (y/n), and Record type. The image of the records may have more information about a person. This database has 5,878,615 records. See
http://search.ancestry.com/search/db.aspx?dbid=1082.

1895-2008. *Texas, Houston, Historic Hollywood Cemetery Records* [Online Database], digitized at the FamilySearch.org website. Source: Historic Hollywood Cemetery, Houston, TX. This is an image only database with burial applications, obituaries, lot books, interment documents, mausoleum records, and plot maps from the Historic Hollywood Cemetery, near downtown Houston. This database has 41,543 images. See https://familysearch.org/search/collection/2040173.

1900. *Texas, 1900 Federal Census: Soundex and Population Schedules* [Microfilm & Digital Capture], filmed by the National Archives, c1970, 361 rolls, beginning with FHL film #1241607 (Population schedules: Anderson, Ector, Andrews, Angelina, and Aransas counties). To access the digital images, see the online FHL catalog:
www.familysearch.org/search/catalog/651136.

1901-1905. *Houston Chronicle Obituaries* **[Online Database],** indexed at the Ancestry.com website. Source: *Index to Obituary Notices in the Houston Chronicle,* compiled by Linda Bennett. This index not only provides the name of the deceased, but also the date of death, age at time of death, obituary date, and section and page number the obituary is found on. Dates are given in the month/day/year format. This database has 4,023 records. See
http://search.ancestry.com/search/db.aspx?dbid=7291.

1903-1910. *Texas and Arizona Arrivals* **[Online Database],** digitized and indexed at the FamilySearch.org website. Source: National Archives microfilm series A3365. This collection contains Lists of Aliens Arriving at Brownsville, Del Rio, Eagle Pass, El Paso, Laredo, Presidio, Rio Grande City and Roma, Texas, May 1903-June 1909, and at Aros Ranch, Douglas, Lochiel, Naco and Nogales, Arizona, July 1906-December. The records are arranged in order by the port city, then by date and usually contain the date of arrival, full name, age, gender, marital status, occupation, ability to read and write, nationality, race, town and country of last residence, birthplace, and final destination. Other forms might also include a physical description of the person. This database has 54,357 records. See
https://familysearch.org/search/collection/2423050.

1903-1929. *Texas, Laredo Index of Arrivals* **[Online Database],** digitized and indexed at the FamilySearch.org website. Source: National Archives microfilm series A3379 (Index). Each index record includes: Name, Event type, Event date, Event place, Gender, Age, Birth year (estimated), and Birth country. The index card image may have more information. This database has 616,001 records. See
https://familysearch.org/search/collection/2304686.

1903-1932. *Texas Birth Certificates* **[Online Database],** indexed at the Ancestry.com website. Source: Vital Statistics Bureau, TX Dept of health. Each index record includes: Name, Birth date, Gender, Birthplace, Father, Father birthplace, Mother, Mother birthplace, and Mother residence. The certificate image has more information. This database has 2,285,123 records. See
http://search.ancestry.com/search/db.aspx?dbid=2275.
- See also, *Texas Birth Certificates, 1903-1935* **[Online Database],** digitized and indexed at the FamilySearch.org website. Source: Vital Statistics Bureau, TX Dept of Health. Each index record includes: Name, Event type, Event date, Event place, Gender, Father's name, and Mother's name. The certificate images have more information about a person. This database has 2,278,910 records. See
https://familysearch.org/search/collection/1803956.
- See also, *Texas Index to Birth Records, 1903-1976* **[Microfilm & Digital Capture],** filmed by the Texas State Archives, 2001, 52 rolls, beginning with FHL film #2282010 (Index to births 1903-1909, vol. 1, Aaron, Bala – Cobb, J.T.). To access the digital images, see the online FHL catalog:
www.familysearch.org/search/catalog/986273.

1903-1945. *An Index to Death Records, Texas* **[Microfilm & Digital Capture],** filmed by the Texas State Library, 1988, 15 rolls, beginning with FHL film 1380775 (1903-1940: Vol. 1-4). To access the digital images, see the online FHL catalog:
www.familysearch.org/search/catalog/1013322.

1903-1955. *Texas, Laredo Arrival Manifests* **[Online Database],** digitized and indexed at the FamilySearch.org website. Source: National Archives microfilm series A3437. Each index record includes: Name, Event type, Event date, Event place, Gender, Age, Birth year (estimated), and Birth country. The original image has much more information about a person. This database has 533,162 records. See
https://familysearch.org/search/collection/2038112.

1903-1973. *Texas Deaths and Burials* **[Online Database],** indexed at the FamilySearch.org website. Source: FamilySearch extractions from records on microfilm at the Family History Library, Salt Lake City, UT. This database has 271,140 records. See
https://familysearch.org/search/collection/1681049.

1903-1982. *Texas Death Certificates* **[Online Database],** digitized and indexed at the Ancestry.com website. Source: Vital Statistics Bureau, TX Dept of Health. Each index record includes: Name, Birth date, Birthplace, Gender, Race, Residence, Father, Age at death, Death date, and Death place. The document image has more information. This database has 4,814,886 records. See
http://search.ancestry.com/search/db.aspx?dbid=2272.

1903-1997. *Texas Birth Index* **[Online Database],** indexed at the FamilySearch.org website. Source: Vital Statistics Bureau, TX Dept of Health. Each index record includes: Name, Event type, Event date, Event place, and Certificate number. This database has 17,102,196 records. See
https://familysearch.org/search/collection/1949342.

- See also, *Texas Birth Index, 1903-1997* [Online Database], digitized and indexed at the Ancestry.com website, see
http://search.ancestry.com/search/db.aspx?dbid=8781.

1903-2000. *Texas Death Index* [Online Database], indexed at the FamilySearch.org website. Source: Vital Statistics Bureau, TX Dept of Health. Each index record includes: Name, Event type, Event date, Event place, Gender, and Marital status. This database has 7,255,830 records. See
https://familysearch.org/search/collection/1949337.
- See also, *Texas Death Index, 1903-2000* [Online Database], indexed at the Ancestry.com website. See
http://search.ancestry.com/search/db.aspx?dbid=4876.

1905-1927. *Texas, El Paso Manifests of Arrivals at the Port of El Paso* [Online Database], digitized and indexed at the FamilySearch.org website. Source: National Archives microfilm series A3406. Includes manifests and index cards of alien arrivals. Each index record includes: Name, Event type, Event date, Event place, Gender, Age, Birth year (estimated), and Birthplace. The image of the card has more information. This database 294,100 records. See
https://familysearch.org/search/collection/2120714.

1905-1954. *Texas, Eagle Pass Arrival Manifests and Indexes* [Online Database], digitized and indexed at the FamilySearch.org website. Source: National Archives microfilm series M1755 and M2040. This collection contains arrival manifests and an index to a portion of the arrivals. The index only covers 1929-1954, while the manifests cover from 1905 to 1954. Each index record includes: Name, Event type, Event date, Event place, Age, Birthplace, and Birth year (estimated). The images of the documents have much more information about a person. This database has 122,918 records. See
https://familysearch.org/search/collection/1916041.

1906-1953. *Texas, Indexes and Manifests of Arrivals at the Port of Del Rio* [Online Database], digitized and indexed at the FamilySearch.org website. Source: National Archives microfilm series A3395. Each index record includes: Name, Event type, Event date, Event place, Gender, Age, and Birth year (estimated). The card image may have more information. This database has 104,679 records. See
https://familysearch.org/search/collection/2141027.

1906-1989. *Texas Naturalization Records* [Online Database], digitized and indexed at the FamilySearch.org website. Source: National Archives microfilm. Includes Records of Distr. Courts, Indexes, Declarations, and other Naturalization papers. Each index record includes: Name, Event type, Event date, Event place, Birth date, and Source reference. The images of the index cards have more information. This database has 88,140 records. See
https://familysearch.org/search/collection/1389983.
- See also, *Texas, Naturalization Records, 1906-1989* [Online Database], digitized and indexed at the Ancestry.com website. This database has 91,013 records. See
http://search.ancestry.com/search/db.aspx?dbid=60189.

1909-1924. *Texas, El Paso Alien Arrivals* [Online Database], digitized and indexed at FamilySearch.org, from National Archives microfilm series A3412. Each index record includes Name, Event type (Immigration), Event date, Event place (El Paso), Gender, Age, and Birth year (estimated). The original image may contain more information. This database has 200,166 records, see www.familysearch.org/search/collection/2306316.

1910. *Texas, 1910 Federal Census: Soundex and Population Schedules* [Microfilm & Digital Capture], filmed by the National Archives, c1970, 337 rolls, beginning with FHL film #1375540 (Population schedules: Anderson, Andrews, Angelina, and Armstrong counties). To access the digital images, see the online FHL catalog:
www.familysearch.org/search/catalog/646863.

1910-1970. *Texas, Gonzales County, School Records* [Online Database], digitized and indexed at FamilySearch.org, from records at the Gonzales County District Court. Each index records includes the Name, Event type (School Enrollment), Gender, and Age. The linked image shows the name of the parent of the child. This database has 839,140 records, see www.familysearch.org/search/collection/3019663.

1911-1958. *Texas, Gonzales County, Divorce Records* [Online Database[, digitized and indexed at FamilySearch.org. This database has 1,934 records, see www.familysearch.org/search/collection/3029257.

1914 History. See *History of the Cattlemen of Texas: A Brief Résumé of the Livestock Industry of the Southwest and a Biographical Sketch of Many of the Important Characters Whose Lives are Interwoven Therein* [Printed Book], with an introduction by Harwood P. Hinton; series editor, David Farmer, originally published by Johnston Printing & Advertising Co., 1914, 350 pages. Reprint by Texas State Historical Association in cooperation with the Center for Studies in Texas History at the University of

Texas at Austin. Includes index and bibliographical references. FHL book 976.4 U2h.
- See also *The Trail Drivers of Texas: Interesting Sketches of Early Cowboys and Their Experiences on the Range and on the Trail During the Days That Tried Men's Souls, True Narratives Related by Real Cow-punchers and Men Who Fathered the Cattle Industry in Texas* [Printed Book], originally compiled and edited by J. Marvin Hunter; introduction by B. Byron Price, published by the University of Texas Press, Austin, TX, 1985, 1,085 pages. Includes index. FHL book 976.4 H2hj.

1917. *Houston, Texas City Directory* [Online Database], indexed at the Ancestry.com website. Source: R. L. Polk's Houston City Directory, 1917. Each index record includes: Name, Trade, Business (name), Residence address, and Comments.
This database has 77,8881 records. See
http://search.ancestry.com/search/db.aspx?dbid=4398.

1917-1918. *Texas, World War I Selective Service System Draft Registration Cards* [Microfilm & Digital Capture], from the original records at the National Archives in East Point, Georgia. The draft cards are arranged alphabetically by state, then alphabetically by county or city, and then alphabetically by surname of registrants. Cards are arranged in a rough alphabetical order by surname. Filmed by the National Archives, 1987-1988, 183 rolls, beginning with FHL film #1927189 (Texas, Anderson County, A-I). To access the digital images, see the online FHL catalog:
https://familysearch.org/search/catalog/747002.

1917-1920. *Texas, World War I Records* [Online Database], digitized and indexed at the FamilySearch.org website. Source: Texas Military Forces Museum, Austin, TX. Each index record includes: Name, Event type, Event date, and Event place. The original document image has more information. This database has 209,675 records. See
https://familysearch.org/search/collection/2202707.

1920. *Texas, 1920 Federal Census: Soundex and Population Schedules* [Microfilm & Digital Capture], filmed by the National Archives, c1970, 462 rolls, beginning with FHL film #1821772 (Population schedules: Anderson Co. and Austin Co). To access the digital images, see the online FHL catalog:
www.familysearch.org/search/catalog/558325.

1923-1946. *Texas, Matagorda County, School Census Records* [Online Database], digitized and indexed at the FamilySearch.org website. Source: Matagorda Co Judge's office, Bay City, TX. Each index record includes Name, Event type, Event date, Event place, Residence, Gender, Age, Birth date, and Parent name. The images of the original records have much more information. This database has 372,298 records. See
https://familysearch.org/search/collection/1390096.

1924-1952. *Texas, El Paso Alien Arrivals* [Online Database], digitized and indexed at the FamilySearch.org website. Source: National Archives microfilm series A3396 (Index). Each index record includes: Name, Event type, Event date, Event place, Gender, Age, Birth year (estimated), and Birth country. The card image has more information about a person. This database has 200,315 records. See
https://familysearch.org/search/collection/2141040.

1924-1954. *Texas, Manifests of Aliens Granted Temporary Admission at El Paso* [Online Database], digitized and indexed at the FamilySearch.org website. Source: National Archives microfilm series M1757. Each index record includes: Name, Event type, Event date, Event place, Gender, Age, Nationality, and Birth year (estimated). The images of the record has more information. This database has 117,170 records. See
https://familysearch.org/search/collection/2299398.

1930. *Texas, 1930 Federal Census: Population Schedules* [Microfilm & Digital Capture], filmed by the National Archives, c1995), 127 rolls, beginning with FHL film #2342021 (Anderson, Andrews, and Austin counties). To access the digital images, see the online FHL catalog:
www.familysearch.org/search/catalog/1037517.

1933-1985. *Texas, Bexar County, San Antonio, Naturalization Index* [Digital Capture], digitized by FamilySearch International, 2006. To access the digital images, see the online FHL catalog:
www.familysearch.org/search/catalog/1459896.

1939-1945. *World War II Honor List of Dead and Missing: State of Texas* [Printed Book & Digital Version], from the Adjutant General's Office, Washington, DC, publ. 1946, 85 pages, digitized by FamilySearch International, 2015. To access the digital images, see the online FHL catalog:
www.familysearch.org/search/catalog/2481615,

1940. *Texas, 1940 Federal Census: Population Schedules* [Digital Capture], digitized by the National Archives, 2012, from microfilm of the original records held by the Bureau of the Census in the 1940s. After microfilming, Congress allowed the Census Bureau to destroy the originals to free up space for WWII-related files. Digitized beginning with FHL Digital File Folder #5456897 (Anderson County). To access the digital images, see the online FHL catalog:

1940 Federal Census Finding Aids **[Online Database].** The National Archives prepared a special website online with a detailed description of the 1940 federal census. Included at the site are descriptions of location finding aids, such as Enumeration District maps, Geographic Descriptions of Census Enumeration Districts, and a list of 1940 City Directories available at the National Archives. The finding aids are all linked to other National Archives sites. The National Archives website also has a link to 1940 Search Engines using Stephen P. Morse's "One-Step" system for finding a 1940 E.D. or street address conversion. See www.archives.gov/research/census/1940/general-info.html#questions.

1940-1947. *Texas, World War II Draft Registration Cards* **[Digital Capture],** digitized by Ancestry.com. To access the digital images, see the online FHL catalog:www.familysearch.org/search/catalog/2729394.

1941-1973. *Texas Index to Death Records* **[Microfilm & Digital Capture],** filmed by the Texas State Archives, 2001, 11 rolls, beginning with FHL film #22082061 (Index to deaths, 1941-1945). To access the digital images, see the online FHL catalog: www.familysearch.org/search/catalog/986275.

1942. *Texas Draft Registration Cards, 1942* **[Digital Capture],** digitized by FamilySearch International, 2006. These cards represent older men, ages 45 to 65 in April 1942, that were registered for the draft. They had birth dates between 28 Apr 1877 and 16 Feb 1892. Includes name of individual, date and place of birth, address, age, telephone number, employer's name and address, name and address of person who would know where the individual can be located, signature, and physical description. To access the digital images, see the online FHL catalog:
www.familysearch.org/search/catalog/1390012.

1943-1964. *Texas, Brownsville Passenger and Crew List of Airplanes* **[Online Database],** digitized and indexed at the FamilySearch.org website. Source: National Archives microfilm series A3423. Each index record includes: Name, Event type, Event date, Event place, Gender, Age, Birth year (estimated), and Birth country. The images of the registers have more information. This database has 190,879 records. See https://familysearch.org/search/collection/2141045.

1944-1952. *Texas, San Antonio, Alien Arrivals* **[Online Database],** digitized and indexed at the FamilySearch.org website. Source: National Archives microfilm series M1973. Each index record includes: Name, Event type, Even date, Event place, Gender, and Birth country. The image card has more information. This database has 4,445 records. See https://familysearch.org/search/collection/2299368.

1945-1952. *Texas El Paso, Applications for Non-Resident Aliens Border Crossing Identification Cards* **[Online Database],** digitized and indexed at FamilySearch.org, from National Archives microfilm series M1756. The card manifests (INS Form I-190) are mainly alphabetically by surname, then first name and include such information as the alien's name, address, date and place of birth, sex, marital status, occupation, nationality. Some cards may have a fingerprint and a photograph. This database has 141,366 records, see www.familysearch.org/search/collection/3155856.

1946-1954. *Texas, Houston Arrival Manifests of Airplanes* **[Online Database],** digitized at the FamilySearch.org website. Source: National Archives microfilm series A4025. This image only database contains arrival manifests which usually include full name, age, gender, marital status, citizenship, last permanent residence, birthplace, and final destination. Browse through the images, organized by date of arrival. This database has 4,360 images. See https://familysearch.org/search/collection/2443353.

1948-1959. *Texas, Passenger and Crew Lists of Vessels Arriving at Corpus Christi, Texas, and Vicinity* **[Online Database],** from the National Archives microfilm series A3458. The records usually include the name of the vessel, ports and dates of departure and arrival, and the following information about each crew member: full name, position in ship's company, age, gender, race, nationality. This database has 78,443 records, see
www.familysearch.org/search/collection/3160706.

1956-2009. *El Paso County, Texas, Death Index* **[Online Database],** indexed at the Ancestry.com website. This database is also accessible at the El Paso County Clerk's website. Each index record includes: Name, Death date, Death location, and a link to the El Paso County Clerk's website. This database has 125,547 records. See
http://search.ancestry.com/search/db.aspx?dbid=70089.

1964-1998. *Texas Death Index* **[Online Database],** indexed at the FamilySearch.org website. Source: Vital Statistic Bureau, TX Dept of Health. Each index record includes: Name, Gender, Event date, County, and Event place. This database has 4,113,934 records. See https://familysearch.org/search/collection/1375599.

1966-2010. *Texas Marriages* **[Online Database],** indexed at the FamilySearch.org website. Source: Vital Statistics Bureau, TX Dept of Health. Each index record includes: Name, Name suffix, Event type, Event date, Event place, Age, Birth year (estimated), Spouse's name, Spouse's age, Spouse's birth year (estimated), Certificate number, and Affiliate county code. This database has 7,606,159 records. See https://familysearch.org/search/collection/2031191.

1968-2010. *Texas Divorce Index* **[Online Database],** indexed at the FamilySearch.org website. Source: Vital Statistics Bureau, TX Dept of Health. Each index record includes: Name, Name suffix, Event type, Event date, Event place, Age, Marriage date, Birth year (estimated), Spouse's name, Spouse's birth year (estimated), Number of children under age 18, File number, and Affiliate county code.
This database has 3,599,300 records. See https://familysearch.org/search/collection/2038378.
- See also, *Texas, Divorce Index, 1968-2014* **[Online Database],** indexed at the Ancestry.com website. Source: Vital Statistics Bureau, TX Dept of Health. This database has 7,684,461 records, see http://search.ancestry.com/search/db.aspx?dbid=8794.

1977-1986. *Texas Deaths* **[Online Database],** digitized and indexed at the FamilySearch.org website. Source: Vital Statistics Bureau, TX Dept of Health. This database includes images of death certificates and an index. Each index record includes: Name, Event type, Event date, Event place, Gender, Age, Birth year (estimated), Father's name, Mother's name, and Certificate number. The certificate image has more information. This database has 108,598 records. See https://familysearch.org/search/collection/1930157.

1981-1992. *Texas, Naturalization Records* **[Online Database],** digitized and indexed at the Ancestry.com website. Source: National Archives, Records of District Courts. Includes Declarations of Intentions and Oaths of Allegiance/Naturalization Records. Each index record includes: Name, Gender, Age, Birth date, Birthplace, Record date, Court district, Court place, Record type, and Petition number. The document images give more information. This database has 219,151 records. See http://search.ancestry.com/search/db.aspx?dbid=2509.

1984-Current. *Texas Recent Newspaper Obituaries* **[Online Database],** digitized and indexed at the GenealogyBank.com website. Search Texas newspaper obituaries for Abilene, Alice, Allen, Alvarado, Amarillo, Angleton, Arlington, Athens, Atlanta, Austin, Bay City, Baytown, Beaumont, Bellaire, Big Sandy, Big Spring, Blanco, Bonham, Borger, Breckenridge, Brownsboro, Brownsville, Brownwood, Bryan-College Station, Buda, Bullard, Burleson, Burnet, Carrollton, Carthage, Celina, Cleburne, Cleveland, Clifton, Clute, Commerce, Conroe, Coppell, Corpus Christi, Corsicana, Cuero, Cypress, Daingerfield, Dallas, Dayton, Deer Park, Del Rio, Denton, Edinburg, Edna, El Paso, Ennis, Fairfield, Flower Mound, Fort Worth, Fredericksburg, Freer, Friendswood, Frisco, Gainesville, Galveston, Gladewater, Glen Rose, Graham, Grand Saline, Greenville, Gun Barrel City, Hallsville, Harlingen, Hearne, Hempstead, Highland Park-University Park, Houston, Humble, Huntsville, Ingleside, Irving, Jacksboro, Jacksonville, Jasper, Katy, Keller, Kerrville, Kilgore, Laredo, Lewisville, Lexington, Lindale, Linden, Little Elm, Llano, Longview, Lubbock, Lufkin, Lumberton, Magnolia, Mansfield, Marble Falls, Marlin, Marshall, McAllen, McKinney, Meridian, Mesquite, Mexia, Midland, Midlothian, Mineola, Mineral Wells, Mount Pleasant, Nacogdoches, New Boston, New Braunfels, Odessa, Olney, Orange, Overton, Palestine, Paris, Pasadena, Pearland, Pittsburg, Plainview, Plano, Port Arthur, Quitman, Red Oak, Robstown, Rowlett, Royse City, San Angelo, San Antonio, San Marcos, Seguin, Sherman, Southlake, Stephenville, Sugar Land, Sweetwater, Texarkana, Texas City, The Woodlands, Tomball, Travis County, Van Alstyne, Victoria, Waco, Waxahachie, Weatherford, Webster, West University Place, Whitehouse, Wichita Falls, and Yorktown, Texas. See
www.genealogybank.com/explore/obituaries/all/usa/texas.

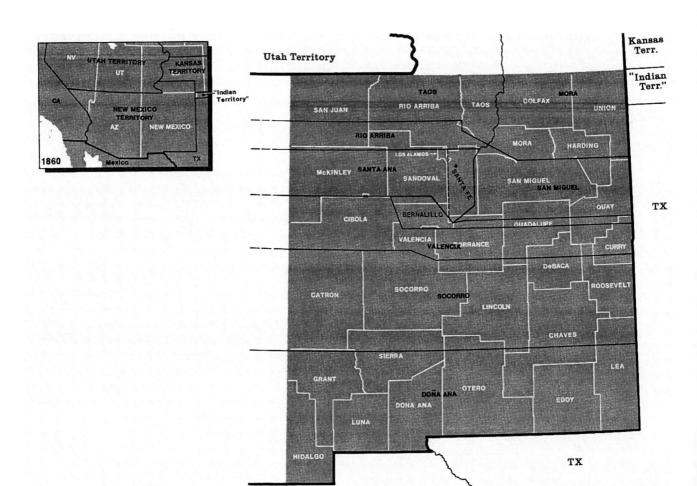

New Mexico Territory • June 1860. This map shows, in black, the 10 counties of New Mexico Territory at the time of the 1860 Federal Census. The current 33 counties of New Mexico are shown in white. New Mexico Territory's 1860 population of 93,516 people was enumerated in areas of present southern Colorado, and all of present Arizona and New Mexico. The inset map shows the area that became Arizona Territory in 1864; and the northern line of New Mexico Territory extending to the California border; and a portion of present southern Nevada (all of present Clark Co NV and the present city of Las Vegas). *** Note:** Santa Fe County's western boundary is approximate. **Map Source:** Page 228, *Map Guide to the U.S. Federal Censuses, 1790-1920*, by William Thorndale and William Dollarhide.

New Mexico
Censuses & Substitute Name Lists

Historical Timeline for New Mexico, 1536-1912

1536. Spanish explorer Cabeza de Vaca entered present New Mexico via the Rio Grande valley. He was supposedly the first Spaniard to relate the story of the Seven Cities of Cibola (or Seven Cities of Gold) he had learned about from the Indians. The local Indians perpetuated the rumor, by telling the Spaniards that the cities of gold were just a little further away. This ploy worked for 60 years, keeping the Spanish soldiers from staying long in one place.

1539. Franciscan friar Marcos de Niza and companion Esteban explored present New Mexico and Arizona looking for the Seven Cities of Cibola. They reached the Zuni village of Hawikuh where Esteban was killed.

1540. Francisco Vasquez de Coronado of Spain came searching for the Seven Cities of Cibola. Coronado never found the cities of gold, but did find the Gulf of California, Colorado River, Grand Canyon, and areas into present New Mexico, Colorado and Kansas. He claimed the entire region as part of New Spain.

1590. The first attempt to colonize Nuevo Mexico was made by Spaniard Gaspar de Sosa.

1598. Juan de Oñate founded the first permanent Spanish colony at San Juan de los Caballeros (near present-day Espanola, New Mexico). San Juan became the capital of the Province of Nuevo Mexico.

1600. San Gabriel was founded at the confluence of the Rio Grande and Chama Rivers. San Gabriel became the new capital of Nuevo Mexico.

1609. Governor Pedro de Peralta founded Santa Fe as the final capital and renamed the entire Spanish province as *Santa Fe de Nuevo Mexico*.

1680. The Pueblo Indians revolted and drove the Spanish out of northern Nuevo Mexico, who fled to El Paso del Norte.

1693. Diego de Vargas conquered Nuevo Mexico (again) for Spain.

1743. French Louisiana traders from Arkansas Post reached Santa Fe and initiated trade with the Spanish colonists.

1776. A route from Santa Fe to Los Angeles was explored, which later became known as the Spanish Trail.

1800. The Spanish colonial population of Santa Fe de Nuevo Mexico had reached about 20,000 people.

1804. Hearing of a supposed intrusion of Americans into their territory, Spanish troops were dispatched from Santa Fe to intercept the Lewis and Clark Expedition, but failed to find them.

1821. Mexico gained independence from Spain and exerted military control of the provinces of Santa Fe de Nuevo Mexico and Coahuila y Texas. That same year, traders from the United States come into the area via a route that became known as the Santa Fe Trail.

1829. The first commercial caravan along The Old Spanish Trail from Santa Fe to Los Angeles was led by Mexican trader Antonio Armijo. He is best known for naming an artesian spring in the desert (Las Vegas).

1836-1841. Texas Claim. As a province of Mexico, the southwestern border of Coahuila y Texas was along the Nueces River; a northwestern line to the SE corner of

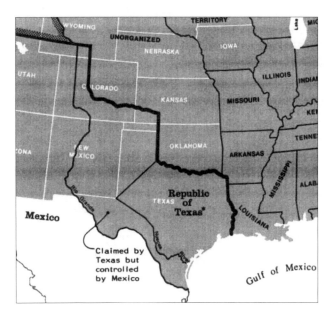

Republic of Texas and the
Texas Claim to the Rio Grande.

present New Mexico; then a northeastern line to the present SW corner of Oklahoma. In 1836, the border was arbitrarily extended by the new Republic of Texas from the Nueces to the Rio Grande, thus adding eastern New Mexico and areas of present Colorado. In 1841, Texas troops invaded Nuevo Mexico areas along the Rio Grande, attempting to possess their claim to the area, but the Texas troops were held at bay by Mexican forces.

1845. Texas was annexed to the United States as the 28th state. The U.S. wanted to also annex the area of the Texas Claim to the Rio Grande, but Mexico warned that a war would result from such an action.

1846. February. The U.S. made an offer to Mexico to purchase the area of the Texas Claim. Mexico rejected the offer.

1846. April. **Mexican-American War.** U.S. Forces quickly took control of the Rio Grande Valley. The captured area from the old Texas line to the Rio Grande was immediately annexed to the United States, based on the acquired Texas Claim.

1846. September. The **Provisional New Mexico Territory** was organized by General Stephen Kearny. Although Texas believed the area belonged to them, the local population remembered the Texas invasion of 1841 and strongly resisted their attempts to organize Eastern New Mexico as Santa Fe County, Texas.

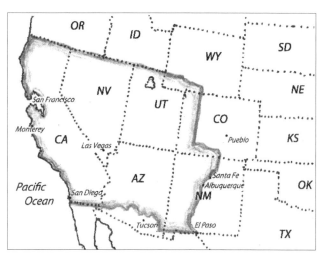

1848. May. **Mexican Cession.** As part of the Treaty of Guadalupe Hidalgo ending the war with Mexico, the United States gained ownership to the remainder of New Mexico west of the Rio Grande and adding most of present Arizona; a portion of western Colorado; part of southwestern Wyoming; and all of present Utah, Nevada, and California.
- In October, the Provisional New Mexico Territorial Legislature first met and immediately petitioned for official U.S. Territorial status. They also declared their opposition to slavery.

1850. June 1st. **Federal Census.** The provisional Territory of New Mexico was included in the 1850 census, with the original seven counties of Bernalillo, Rio Arriba, Santa Ana, Santa Fe, San Miguel, Taos, and Valencia counties.

1850. September 9th. California was admitted to the Union as the 31st state.
- On the same day, Congress established both Utah Territory and New Mexico Territory.
- Also on the same day, the U.S. bought out the Texas claim to New Mexico for ten million dollars. The act established the present Texas boundaries; including their border with New Mexico at its present position.

1852. Doña Ana County was established, stretching across the southern portion of New Mexico Territory, well into the area that later became Arizona.

1853. Gadsden Purchase. Seeking access for a southern railroad route, the U.S. paid Mexico a sum of 10 million dollars to purchase a 45,000 square mile tract of land south of the Gila River. The area was added to New Mexico Territory, which immediately expanded Doña Ana County to include the entire area.

1859. New Mexico Territory created Arizona County from Doña Ana, the Gadsden Purchase area of present Arizona south of the Gila River.

1860. April. **Proposed Territory of Arizona.** The Territory of New Mexico had concerns about being able to govern the southern part of its territory, given the difficult desert separating the northern and southern areas. In 1858, New Mexico's territorial legislature adopted a resolution in favor of the creation of Arizona Territory, splitting New Mexico in half on an East-West line. The resolution went to the U.S. Congress, but in 1860, after two years of no action, New Mexico delegates met in Tucson and drafted a constitution for a U.S. Territory of Arizona, with a capital at Tucson. The impending Civil War caused Congress to table the proposal.

1860. June. **Federal Census.** New Mexico's population of 93,516 people was enumerated within present Arizona, New Mexico, and southern Colorado.

1861. February. **Colorado Territory** was created by the U.S. Congress. New Mexico Territory lost the northern-most parts of Taos and Mora counties to the new territory.

1861. February. Confederate troops from Texas occupied New Mexico Territory, mostly the settlements along the Rio Grande Valley just north of El Paso, but also areas in the Gadsden Purchase region, including Tucson.

1861. March. The **Confederate Territory of Arizona** was declared with a capital at La Mesilla. The area of this "Horizontal Arizona" was the same as proposed by New Mexico Territory in 1860: the southern half of New Mexico Territory, stretching from Texas to California.

1862. April. The Civil War battle of Glorietta Pass in Northern New Mexico Territory was fought to a stalemate. But U.S. troops had burned the Confederate supply trains, and killed or drove off their horses and mules, forcing their eventual retreat from New Mexico.
- A few Confederate troops held on in the Tucson area, but after a force of some 2,000 Union troops from California marched on Tucson, the last of the Confederate troops retreated back to Texas in May 1862. Upon the U.S. capture of Tucson, the Confederate Territory of Arizona was returned to New Mexico Territory.

1863. Arizona Territory was created by the U.S. Congress, with Prescott as the first capital. The area of New Mexico Territory was reduced to its present size. Arizona Territory was created during the Civil War, and in response to the East-West Confederate Territory of Arizona, the new U.S. territory was drawn on a North-South axis. When Congress divided New Mexico Territory on the same meridian as Colorado's western line, the resulting map created the "Four Corners" of Colorado, Utah, Arizona, and New Mexico, the only point in the U.S. where four states meet at a quadripoint.

1870. Federal Census. New Mexico Territory's population was at 91,874.

1880-1881. In March 1880, The Southern Pacific railroad reached Tucson, Arizona Territory, and was now starting the connection through New Mexico Territory to Texas. In December 1881, with the completion of the leg to Sierra Blanca, Texas, the SP became the second transcontinental railroad.

1880. June. **Federal Census.** New Mexico Territory's population was at 119,565.

1885. June. A New Mexico territorial census was taken with federal assistance, the only territorial or state census in New Mexico.

1912. Jan 6. New Mexico became the 47th state, with Santa Fe as the state capital.

Bibliography
New Mexico Censuses & Substitutes

The chronological listing of censuses and substitutes is related to the historical eras of New Mexico:

Spanish Era, 1598-1821:
- Lists of settlers living in Santa Fe de Nuevo Mexico exist for as early as 1600.
- A 1750 census exists for Albuquerque, Belen, Santa Fe, and Valencia.
- A 1790 census for Santa Fe and Taos also survives.

Mexican Era, 1821-1848:
- An 1830 census for Santo Domingo is extant.
- An 1839 Valencia census also exists.

1846-1912 New Mexico Territory Era:
- Established in 1846 during the Mexican-American War, the Provisional Territory of New Mexico was included in the June 1850 federal census.
- Federal censuses for all New Mexico Territory counties are complete for 1850, 1860, 1870, 1880,

1900, and 1910. The 1890 was lost (as for all states).
- The only territorial or state census taken in New Mexico was the 1885 Territorial Census, enumerated with federal assistance.

1912 – Current. The State of New Mexico Era: After statehood in 1912, federal censuses for New Mexico are complete for all counties, 1920-1940. The 1950 census opens to the public on April 1, 2022.

Census Substitutes. In addition to the local and federal censuses, there are many census substitute name lists that fill out the bibliography. Name lists may include Local Census Records, County Court Records, Directories, County Histories, State Militia Lists, Tax Lists, Church & Vital Records, and Voter Lists. They begin below in chronological order:

◆ ◆ ◆ ◆ ◆

1600. See *Partial List of People Who Came to New Mexico in 1600* **[Online Database],** list of names at the USGenWeb site for Bernalillo Co NM. For each of the names listed, there are notes regarding the person's status in the colony, marriages, servants, and more. See http://bernalillo.nmgenweb.us/nm1600.htm.

1680 Census and Muster - Doña Ana County, Spanish Archives of New Mexico **[Online Database],** includes a list of refugees who fled to southern New Mexico after the onset of the Pueblo Revolt. This list is incomplete. The estimated number of refugees established by Antonio de Otermin was about 2,500 persons. See
http://files.usgwarchives.net/nm/donaana/census/1680/lasalineta.txt.

1681-1846 Vigil's Index **[Microfilm & Digital Capture],** from the original records at the U.S. Bureau of Land Management, Santa Fe, NM. General index of all the land documents from the time of the Spanish and Mexican governments until the year 1846. Text in Spanish. Filmed by the University of New Mexico Library, Albuquerque, NM, 1955-1957. FHL has 1 roll, FHL film #1016949. To access the digital images, see the online FHL catalog:
www.familysearch.org/search/catalog/430000.

1692-1846. *New Mexico, Land Records of New Spain (in Spanish)* **[Online Database],** indexed at the Ancestry.com website. This is an image only database, with several types of records related to land grants in Spanish/Mexican Nuevo Mexico. The documents are in Spanish only. Browse the images, organized by titles of documents, including names of pueblos, Indians, Land grants, and more. This database has 2,230 records. See
http://search.ancestry.com/search/db.aspx?dbid=60892.

1693. See *Census of Colonists Assembled at El Paso del Norte for the Second Entry into Santa Fe for the Re-conquest of New Mexico, September 1, 1693* **[Online Database].** Names listed at the USGenWeb website for New Mexico. In 1680, the Pueblo Indians revolted and drove the Spanish colonists out of northern Nuevo Mexico. Some of colonists fled to El Paso del Norte. In 1693, a Spanish force led by Diego de Vargas conquered Nuevo Mexico (again) for Spain. This is a list of names of colonists mustered at El Paso del Norte ready to return to their original settlements in the Mid-Rio Grande area.
http://files.usgwarchives.net/nm/santafe/census/1693/reconquest.txt.

1697-1821. *Guide to the Microfilm of the Spanish Archives of New Mexico* **[Microfilm & Digital Capture],** a manuscript filmed by the New Mexico State Records Center and Archives, Santa Fe, NM, 4 rolls, beginning with FHL film #468381 (Civil Records, Court Records). To access the digital images, see the online FHL catalog:
www.familysearch.org/search/catalog/339704.

1700s-2000s. *New Mexico GenWeb Archives* **[Online Database].** The NMGenWeb site offers free genealogical databases with searchable statewide name lists and for all New Mexico counties. Databases may include Bibles, Biographies, Cemeteries, Censuses, Court Records, Deaths, Deeds, Directories, Histories, Marriages, Military, Newspapers, Obituaries, Photos, Schools, Tax Lists, Wills, and more. See
http://usgwarchives.net/nm/nmfiles.htm.

1700s-2000s. *Linkpendium – New Mexico: Family History & Genealogy, Census, Birth, Marriage, Death, Vital Records & More* **[Online Databases].** Linkpendium is a genealogical portal site with links to state, county, town, and local databases. Currently listed are selected sites for New Mexico statewide resources (334), Bernalillo County (285), Catron County (113), Chaves County (170), Cibola County (115), Colfax County (207), Curry County (125), De Baca County (101), Dona Ana County (198), Eddy County (167), Grant County (184), Guadalupe County (103), Harding County (95), Hidalgo County (104), Lea County (132), Lincoln County (225), Los Alamos

County (59), Luna County (130), McKinley County (126), Mora County (119), Otero County (127), Quay County (124), Rio Arriba County (136), Roosevelt County (226), San Juan County (152), San Miguel County (174), Sandoval County (119), Santa Fe County (234), Sierra County (188), Socorro County (166), Taos County (181), Torrance County (113), Union County (114), and Valencia County (135). See www.linkpendium.com/nm-genealogy.

1701-1956. *Records, Our Lady of Guadalupe Catholic Church, Taos, New Mexico* **[Microfilm & Digital Capture],** from the original records at the Our Lady of Guadalupe Church, Taos, New Mexico. Text partly in English and partly in Spanish. Includes indexes. Filmed by Golightly, El Paso, TX, 1957, 14 rolls, as follows:
- Baptisms, 1701-1837, FHL film #17020.
- Baptisms, 1837-1850, FHL film 17021.
- Baptisms, 1850-1879, FHL film #17010.
- Baptisms, 1866-1871,1880-1887, FHL film #17011.
- Baptisms, 1887-1915, FHL film #17012.
- Baptisms, 1915-1925, FHL film #17013.
- Baptisms, 1925-1933, FHL film #17014.
- Baptisms, 1933-1956, FHL film #17015.
- Confirmations, 1894-1955, FHL film #17016.
- Marriages, 1777-1856, FHL film #17022.
- Marriages, 1856-1895, FHL film #17017.
- Marriages, 1895-1956, FHL film #17018.
- Deaths, 1827-1850, FHL film #17023.
- Deaths, 1850-1956, FHL film #17019.

To access the digital images, see the online FHL catalog: www.familysearch.org/search/catalog/414536.

"1705 Santa Fe Presidial Soldiers and Citizens" **[Printed Article],** in *Herencia*, (Hispanic Genealogical Research Center, Albuquerque, NM), Vol. 6, No. 3 (Jul 1998).

1710-1860. *Santa Cruz de la Cañada, Baptisms* **[Printed Book].** Baptism database held by the Archdiocese of Santa Fe and the State Archives of New Mexico, database entry by Thomas D. Martinez, Benito Estevan Montoya and Rosina LaSalle (nee Vigil), published San Jose, CA, 1993, 498 pages. Includes name, date of baptism, name of parents and godparents if recorded. Arranged in alphabetical order by surname. FHL book 978.956 K2ms.

1726-1918. *New Mexico Births and Christenings* **[Online Database],** indexed at the FamilySearch.org website. FamilySearch extractions from records on microfilm at the Family History Library, Salt Lake City, UT. Each index record includes: Name, Gender, Christening date, Birth date, Birthplace, Father's name, and Mother's name. This database has 229,946 records. See **https://familysearch.org/search/collection/1680839**.

1726-1956. *San Juan Pueblo, Catholic Church Records* **[Microfilm & Digital Capture],** from the original records at the San Juan de los Caballeros Church, San Juan, New Mexico. Text in Spanish and English. Includes indexes. Church may also be known as St. John the Baptist. The church directory lists this as the head church of Chamita parish. Retakes are located at the end of the film roll. Filmed by Golightly, El Paso, TX, 1956, 7 rolls, as follows:
- Baptisms 1726-1837, FHL film #16981.
- Baptisms 1849-1898, FHL film #16976.
- Baptisms 1899-1956, FHL film #16977.
- Marriages 1726-1776,1830-1836,1850-1855 (marriages 1777-1829 are not available); Deaths, 1726-1857, FHL film #16982.
- Confirmations, 1887-1954, FHL film #16978.
- Marriages, 1857-1956, FHL film #16979.
- Deaths, 1857-1956, FHL film #16980.

To access the digital images, see the online FHL catalog: **www.familysearch.org/search/catalog/399083**.

1727-1900. *New Mexico, Marriages* **[Online Database],** indexed at the Ancestry.com website. Source: Liahona Research extractions from records on microfilm at the Family History Library, Salt Lake City, UT, 2005. Each index record includes: Name, Gender, Spouse name, Marriage date, County, and Source (incl. FHL film No.). This database has 17,032 records. See **http://search.ancestry.com/search/db.aspx?dbid=7872**.

1728-1857 New *Mexico Marriages, Santa Fe, St. Francis Parish and Military Chapel of Our Lady of Light (La Castrense)* **[Printed Book]** extracted by Marie J. Roybal and Lila Armijo Pfeufer; compiled by Margaret Leonard Windham and Evelyn Lujan Baca, published by the New Mexico Genealogical Society, Albuquerque, NM, 1997, 417 pages. Includes several indexes. FHL book 978.956 K28r.

1736-1873. *New Mexico Baptisms, San Buenaventura de Cochiti Church* **[Printed Book],** extracted by Donald Dreesen and Evelyn Lujan Baca; compiled by Margaret Leonard Windham and Evelyn Lujan Baca, published by the New Mexico Genealogical Society, Albuquerque, NM, 2000, 409 pages. FHL book 978.957 K2d.

1747-1763; 1753-1770 Births or Christenings, San Francisco de Assisi (Cathedral), Santa Fe, Santa Fe, New Mexico **[Microfilm & Digital Capture],** from a computer printout; births or christenings, compiled by the Genealogical Department, The Church of Jesus

Christ of Latter-day Saints. Filmed by the Genealogical Society of Utah, 1977, 2 rolls, FHL film #1205005 (1747-1763), and FHL film #12005472 (1753-1770). To access the digital images, see the online FHL catalog: www.familysearch.org/search/catalog/285412.

1747-1851. *New Mexico Baptisms of Santa Fe: Parroquia de San Francisco de Assisi (Parish of Saint Francis of Assisi)* **[Printed Book],** compiled by Margaret Leonard Windham and Evelyn Lujan Baca, published by the New Mexico Genealogical Society, Albuquerque, NM, 2002, 4 vols. Includes bibliographic references. Includes indexes for baptisms, parents, godparents, grandparents and others. Contents: **Vol. 1:** 5 September 1747 to 17 July 1791; **Vol. 2:** 15 August 1796 to 30 December 1822; **Vol. 3:** 1 January 1823 to 26 June 1833; Castrense register, 9 June 1798 to 26 June 1833; **Vol. 4:** 18 February 1839 to 17 July 1851. FHL book 978.956/S1 K2w v. 1-4.

1747-1851 *Santa Fe Baptisms, Database of Archives Held by the Archdiocese of Santa Fe and the State Archive of New Mexico* **[Printed Book],** database entry by Thomas D. Martinez, Benito Estevan Montoya, Rosina LaSalle (nee Vigil), published San Jose, CA, 1993, 606 pages. FHL book 978.956 K2m.

1750-1830 Spanish and Mexican Censuses of New Mexico **[Printed Book],** compiled by Virginia Langham Olmsted, published by the New Mexico Genealogical Society, Albuquerque, NM, 1981, 305 pages. All items except names are in English. Includes index. FHL book 978.9 X2ov.

1750. *Index to the Spanish Census of 1750 for Albuquerque, New Mexico* **[Online Database],** indexed at the USGenWeb site, Bernalillo Co NM: http://files.usgwarchives.net/nm/bernalillo/census/1750.

1750. *Index to the Spanish Census of 1750 for Belen, New Mexico* **[Online Database],** indexed at the USGenWeb site for Valencia Co NM. See www.genealogybranches.com/valencia/belencensus.html.

1750. See *Index to the Spanish Census of 1750 for Santa Fe and Alamo, New Mexico* **[Online Database],** indexed at the USGenWeb site for Santa Fe Co NM. See http://files.usgwarchives.net/nm/santafe/census/1750.

1750. See *Index to the Spanish Census of 1750 for Valencia, New Mexico* **[Online Database],** indexed at the USGenWeb site for Valencia Co NM. See http://files.usgwarchives.net/nm/valencia/census/1750.

1751-1918. *New Mexico Marriages* **[Online Database],** indexed at the FamilySearch.org website. Source: FamilySearch extractions from records on microfilm at the Family History Library. Each index record includes: Name, Spouse's name, Spouse's birthplace, Event date, Event place, Father's name, Spouse's father's name, and Spouse's mother's name. This database has 93,308 records. See https://familysearch.org/search/collection/1680844.

"1764 & 1765 Census, San Gabriel" [Printed Article], in *Herencia,* (Hispanic Genealogical Research Center, Albuquerque, NM), in Vol. 5, No. 2 (Apr 1997).

1770-1860 Index to Taos Marriage **[Printed Book],** extracted by David Salazar, indexed by Bill Trujillo. Published by the Genealogical Society of Hispanic America, Southern California Branch, Santa Fe Springs, CA, 1994, 152 pages. Arranged in alphabetical order by surname. May include name, relationship, page number, and date of marriage. FHL book 978.953 VC22s.

1788-1955. See *New Mexico Deaths and Burials, 1788-1798; 1838-1955* **[Online Database],** indexed at the FamilySearch.org website. Source: FamilySearch extractions from records on microfilm at the Family History Library, Salt Lake City, UT. Each index record includes: Name, Gender, Burial date, Burial place, Death date, Birth date, Marital status, Spouse's name, Father's name, and Mother's name. This database has 1,633 records. See https://familysearch.org/search/collection/1680843.

1790. *New Mexico, Resident Index* **[Online Database],** indexed at the Ancestry.com website. Source: Lyman Platt's *New Mexico, Resident Index, 1790,* publ. 2000. New Mexico was a part of New Spain in 1790. This database is a collection of Hispanic family history records for area residents in that year. Each entry provides the individual's name and sex. Many entries include birth date and birthplace information. This database has 3,097 records. See http://search.ancestry.com/search/db.aspx?dbid=4652.

"1790 Census of the Presidio of Santa Fe" [Printed Article], in *Nuestras Raices,* (Genealogical Society of Hispanic America, Denver, CO), Vol. 8, No. 3 (Fall 1996).

"1790 Spanish Census of Taos" [Printed Article], in *New Mexico Genealogist,* (New Mexico Genealogical Society, Albuquerque, NM), Vol. 21, No. 3 (Sep 1982). See also **"1790 Taos Census,"** in *Herencia,* Vol. 5, No. 3 (Jul 1997).

1790-1841 Censuses. See *Early Taos Censuses and Historical Sources* **[Microfiche]**, from the original book compiled by Julián Josué Vigil, publ. J. J. Vigil, 1983, 172 pages. Includes index. Contains: 1790 census for Taos (incomplete); "Spaniards from the jurisdiction of Taos" Militia muster rolls, 1806 for Taos (incomplete); 1841 census for Taos; Ranchos de Taos Appendices: Taos genealogical materials in the archives of the Archdiocese of Santa Fe, microfilm edition; Taos materials in Fr. Angélico Chávez, "Archives of the Archdiocese of Santa Fe" (1957). Taos priests to 1850. (starts in 1701); Taos materials in Twitchell's "Spanish archives of New Mexico," vol. 1-2. Above documents in "Calendar of microfilm edition of the Spanish archives of New Mexico, 1621-1821"; Additional Taos materials in above "Calendar" (no Twitchell numbers). Early Taos materials in the Ritch Collection, Huntington Library, plus one Bancroft Library item. Taos materials listed in "Calendar of the microfilm edition of the Mexican archives of New Mexico" (1970). Filmed by the New Mexico State Archives, 1983, 4 fiches, FHL fiche #6331382.

"1793 & 1795 Census Surnames" [Printed Article], in *Herencia*, (Hispanic Genealogical Research Center, Albuquerque, NM), in Vol. 3, No. 4 (Oct 1995).

1793-1853. *New Mexico Baptisms (Tome, Valencia County): Nuestra Señora de la Inmaculada Concepción de Tomé* **[Printed Book]**, extracted by Margaret L. Buxton, et al.; compiled by Margaret Leonard Windham and Evelyn Lujan Baca, published by the New Mexico Genealogical Society, Albuquerque, NM, 1998. Includes index. Contents: vol. 1: 22 March 1793-8 May 1853. FHL book 978.992 K2b.

1801-1993. *New Mexico, Wills and Probate Records* **[Online Database]**, indexed at the Ancestry.com website. Source: Ancestry extractions from New Mexico County, District, and Probate Courts. This is an image only database, with probate records from Sandoval, Socorro, and Valencia counties only. Browse through the images, organized by county, record type, and date range. This database has 9,416 records. See http://search.ancestry.com/search/db.aspx?dbid=9075.

1803-1807. *Bernalillo and Las Huertas Census* **[Online Database]**, names listed at the USGenWeb site for Bernalillo Co NM. See http://files.usgwarchives.net/nm/bernalillo/census/1803/1803-bernalillo.txt.

1811-1849; 1861-1864, 1892 Records of the Sandia Mission: Located in the Vicinity of Albuquerque, New Mexico **[Printed Book]**, a typescript translated into English and typed by the Genealogical Society of Utah, 1963-1965, 302 pages. Includes marriage records from Sandia, Bernalillo, Los Corrales, Los Algodones, Albuquerque, Santa Fe and Cienaga, New Mexico for the years 1811-1849, 1861-1864, 1892; as well as a list of donors to the Sandia Mission. FHL book 978.9 K2 sp. Also on microfilm, filmed by the Genealogical Society of Utah, 1972, 1 roll, FHL film #874356.

1816. "Tax Revolt of 1816 (Taos)" [Printed Article], in *Ayer Y Hoy En Taos,* (Taos County Historical Society, Taos, NM), Vol. 26 (Spring 1999).

1818 Military Census, Santa Fe" [Printed Article], in *Herencia*, (Hispanic Genealogical Research Center, Albuquerque, NM), Vol. 4, No. 3 (Jul 1996).

1821. See *New Mexico Province, Santa Fe Parish, Census of 1821* **[Printed Book]**, compiled by Patricia Black Esterly, publ. New Mexico Genealogical Society, Albuquerque, NM, 1994, 165 pages. Includes index. Contains Santa Fe with barrios of San Francisco, Torreon, San Miguel and Nuestra Senora de Guadalupe and outlying districts with partidos of Rio Tesuque, Galisteo and Cienaga y Ranchos. FHL book 978.956 X2e.

"1821 Santa Fe Census" [Printed Article], in *Herencia*, (Hispanic Genealogical Research Center, Albuquerque, NM), in Vol. 2, No. 3 (Jul 1994).

1821. "Early Censuses for Middle Rio Grande" [Printed Article], in *Albuquerque Genealogical Society Quarterly*, Vol. 5, No. 2 (Aug 1980).

1821-1846. *New Mexico, Census, Military, and Other Records of Mexico* **[Online Database]**, digitized and indexed at Ancestry.com. Source: Mexican Archives, NM State Records Center & Archive, Santa Fe, NM. The materials in the collection vary but include records from the provincial administration, treasury, legislative, local government, judicial cases, military, Indian affairs, and some period newspapers. Lists in the hacienda, military, and miscellaneous record groups have been indexed; other record groups can be browsed by year and record group, see
www.ancestry.com/search/collections/8832.
- See also, *Calendar of the Microfilm Edition of the Mexican Archives of New Mexico, 1821-1846* **[Printed Book & Microfilm]**, by Myra Ellen Jenkins,

a microfilm project sponsored by the National Historical Publications Commission, published by the New Mexico Records Center, Santa Fe, 1970, 144 pages. The records identified are at the New Mexico State Archives in Santa Fe. FHL book 978.9 A3nn and FHL film #962164. To see if this microfilm was digitized yet, see the online FHL catalog: www.familysearch.org/search/catalog/156552.

1821-1853. San Miguel del Socorro, New Mexico Marriage Records [Printed Book], extracted by Joe Sanchez III; edited by Antoinette Duran Silva, published by J. Sanchez, Whittier, CA, 1999, 112 pages. Information was extracted from marriage books A & B. Includes index. FHL book 978.962/S1 K2s.

1821-1898. The Old Santa Fe Trail [Digitized Book], by Colonel Henry Inman, publ. 1898, the full text of this history of one of America's greatest wagon roads of all time. See http://genealogytrails.com/newmex/santafe/SantaFeTrail/SF_Trail.htm.

1821-1956 Socorro Church Records [Microfilm & Digital Capture], from the original records at the San Miguel Catholic Church, Socorro, New Mexico. Text partly in English and partly in Spanish. Includes indexes. Includes information from the San Marcial Mission and other nearby churches. Filmed by Golightly, El Paso, TX, 1957, 5 FHL rolls, as follows:
- Baptisms, 1821-1850, FHL film #16993.
- Baptisms, 1865-1931; Confirmations, 1877-1919; Baptisms 1894-1921 (San Marcial), FHL film #16994.
- Baptisms, 1921-1934 (San Marcial); Marriages, 1921-1931 (San Marcial); Deaths, 1921-1933 (San Marcial); Confirmations, 1926 (San Marcial); First communion, 1940-1944 (San Marcial), Baptisms, 1932-1956; Confirmations, 1900-1955, FHL film #16995.
- Marriages, 1821-1853; Deaths, 1821-1853, FHL film #16996.
- Marriages, 1882-1956; Marriages, 1883-1921 (San Marcial); Deaths, 1913-1956; Baptisms, 1869-1885 (San Marcial); Confirmations, 1869-1872 (San Marcial), FHL film #16997.

To access the digital images, see the online FHL catalog: www.familysearch.org/search/catalog/414524.

1826 Military Census – Families of the Presidio of Santa Fe Company [Online Database], names listed at the USGenWeb site for Santa Fe Co NM. See http://files.usgwarchives.net/nm/santafe/census/1826.

"1830 Santo Domingo Census" [Printed Article], in *New Mexico Genealogist,* (New Mexico Genealogical Society, Albuquerque, NM), Vol. 33, No. 1 (Mar 1994) through Vol. 33, No. 3 (Sep 1994).

1833-1845. New Mexico Censuses of 1833 and 1845: Socorro and Surrounding Communities of the Rio Abajo [Printed Book], by Teresa Ramírez Alief, Jose Gonzales, Patricia Black Esterly, published by the New Mexico Genealogical Society, Albuquerque, NM, 1994, 153 pages. Includes index. FHL book 978.962 X2a.

"1839 Census, Males Capable of Bearing Arms (Valencia)" [Printed Article], in *New Mexico Genealogist,* (New Mexico Genealogical Society, Albuquerque, NM), Vol. 20, No. 2 (Jun 1981).

1844-1973. New Mexico Newspaper Archives [Online Databases], digitized and indexed newspapers at the GenealogyBank website, for Albuquerque, Bernalillo, Bland, Carlsbad, Chloride, Columbus, Deming, Eddy, Elizabethtown, Espanola, Estancia, Farmington, Gallup, Hillsboro, Kingston, Las Cruces, Las Vegas, Lincoln, Lordsburg, Magdalena, Maldonado, Maxwell, Mesilla, Mora, Mountainair, Raton, Rincon, Roswell, San Acacio, San Marcial, Santa Fe, Santa Rosa, Silver City, Socorro, Springer, Taos, Wagon Mound, and White Oaks, New Mexico. See www.genealogybank.com/explore/newspapers/all/usa/new-mexico.

1846-1851. The History of the Military Occupation of the Territory of New Mexico from 1846-1851 by the Government of the United States: Together with Biographical Sketches of Men Prominent in the Conduct of the Government During that Period [Microfilm & Digital Capture], by Ralph E. Twitchell, publ. Rio Grande Press, Chicago, 1963, 394 pages, FHL film #1000222. To access the digital images, see the online FHL catalog: www.familysearch.org/search/catalog/202397.

1847-1907. A Genealogical Index of Early Doña Ana County, New Mexico, Deeds [Printed Book], compiled by Morton L. Ervin, published by Ervin Publishing, Albuquerque, NM, 2002, 2 vols. Contents: vol. 1: Grantor name; includes index to grants and patents; vol. 2. Grantee name. Arranged in alphabetical order by surname. FHL Library has bound vol. 1-2 together. FHL book 978.966 R22e vol. 1-2.

1850. *New Mexico Territory, 1850 Federal Census: Population Schedules* **[Microfilm & Digital Capture],** filmed by the National Archives, 1964, 4 rolls, beginning with FHL film #16603 (Bernalillo and Rio Ariba counties). To access the digital images, see the online FHL catalog:
www.familysearch.org/search/catalog/744491.

1850-2000. *Western States Marriage Index, 1809-2011* **[Online Database],** indexed at the Ancestry.com website. This database is also accessible at the BYU-Idaho website. The New Mexico counties, included years, and numbers of marriages:
- Bernalillo, 1850-1933, 2,028
- Colfax, 18896-1900, 29
- Curry, 1929, 1
- Eddy, 1887-2000, 9,596
- Grant, 1868-1912, 182
- Lea, 1909-2000, 61
- Luna, 1900-1912, 109
- McKinley, 1900-1935, 49
- Mora, 1857-1900, 311
- Rio Arriba, 1903-1904, 73
- San Juan, 1900-1941, 27
- Taos, 1900-1929, 11

Each index record includes: Name, Spouse, Marriage date, Marriage place, and a link to the BYU-Idaho website. This database has 12,478 NM records. See http://search.ancestry.com/search/db.aspx?dbid=70016.

1852-1869. *Church Records, Our Lady of Sorrows Church, Arroyo Hondo, New Mexico* **[Microfilm & Digital Capture],** from the original records at the Our Lady of Sorrows Church, Arroyo Hondo, Taos County, New Mexico. Text in Spanish. Contents: Baptisms, 1852-1869; Marriages, 1852-1869; Deaths, 1852-1869. There are confirmations with the baptisms. Filmed by Golightly, El Paso, TX, 1956. FHL film #16622. To access the digital images, see the online FHL catalog: www.familysearch.org/search/catalog/354944.

1852-1951. *New Mexico Naturalization Records* **[Microfilm],** from the original records at the New Mexico State Archives, Santa Fe, NM. Various Naturalization Records for Colfax and Valencia County, 1852-1951. Filmed by the Genealogical Society of Utah, 2004, 1 roll, FHL film #2392555. To see if this microfilm was digitized yet, see the online FHL catalog:
www.familysearch.org/search/catalog/1204409.

1853-1920. *Abstract of Title to the Entire Sangre de Cristo Grant* **[Typescript & Microfilm],** author-publisher-date not noted, 14 pages. Shows the chain of title to the entire Sangre de Cristo grant, from the original source of title to Morton C. Fisher, and the chain of title to the original Costilla Estate from Morton C. Fisher to the United States Freehold Land and Emigration Company. FHL book 978.9 A1 No. 5 and FHL film #962324. To see if this microfilm was digitized yet, see the online FHL catalog:
www.familysearch.org/search/catalog/156705.

1858-1956 *Church Records, Our Lady of Sorrows Catholic Church* **[Microfilm & Digital Capture],** from the original records at the Our Lady of Sorrow Church, Manzano, Torrance County, New Mexico. Text partly in English and partly in Spanish. Includes indexes. Filmed by Golightly, El Paso, TX, 1956, 2 FHL rolls, as follows:
- Baptisms, 1867-1956, FHL film #16845.
- Deaths, 1858-1946; Confirmations, 1868-1955; Marriages, 1876-1956; Deaths, 1946-1956, FHL film #16846.

To access the digital images, see the online FHL catalog: **www.familysearch.org/search/catalog/371657.**

1860. *New Mexico Territory, 1860 Federal Census: Population Schedules* **[Microfilm & Digital Capture],** filmed by the National Archives, 1967, 6 rolls, beginning with FHL film #803712 (Arizona, Bernalillo, Doña Ana, and Rio Ariba counties). To access the digital images, see the online FHL catalog: www.familysearch.org/search/catalog/705448.

1860, 1864 & 1870. See *Arizona and New Mexico Territories Census, Late 1800s* **[Online Database],** indexed at the Ancestry.com website. Originally printed as a Senate document, this database contains over 12,000 records, which are excerpts from the decennial census of 1860 for Arizona County in the Territory of New Mexico, excerpts from the decennial federal census of 1870 for the Territory of Arizona, and excerpts from the Special Territorial Census of 1864 taken in Arizona. Each record lists the name, age, sex and marital status of an individual, length of residence, occupation, place of birth, and the value of property. This database has 12,589 records. See http://search.ancestry.com/search/db.aspx?dbid=3085.

1861-1865. *New Mexico Civil War Service Records of Union Soldiers* **[Online Database],** indexed at the FamilySearch.org website. Source: National Archives microfilm series M427. Includes Union service records of soldiers who served in organizations from the Territory of New Mexico. The records include a jacket-envelope for each soldier, labeled with his name, his rank, and the unit in which he served. The jacket-envelope typically contains card abstracts of entries relating to the soldier as found in original muster rolls,

returns, rosters, payrolls, appointment books, hospital registers, prison registers and rolls, parole rolls, inspection reports; and the originals of any papers relating to the particular soldier. This database has 118,866 records. See
https://familysearch.org/search/collection/1932418.

1861-1865. *Index to Soldiers & Sailors of the Civil War* **[Online Database],** a searchable name index to 6.3 million Union and Confederate Civil War soldiers available online at the National Park Service website. A search can be done by surname, first name, state, or unit. New Mexico Territory supplied 12,970 men to the Union. (The Confederate Territory of Arizona supplied 271 Confederate troops. To search, go to the NPS website. See **www.civilwar.nps.gov/cwss**.

1862-1874 Internal Revenue Assessment Lists for the Territory of New Mexico **[Microfilm & Digital Capture],** from the originals at the National Archives, Washington, DC. Filmed by the National Archives, series M0782, 1988, 1 roll, FHL film #1578508. To access the digital images, see the online FHL catalog: **www.familysearch.org/search/catalog/578004.**

1862-1917. *Over 1,400 Naturalization Records for Various Courts of New Mexico* **[Printed Book],** extracts of original records at the National Archives, Denver Regional Branch. Compiled and published by the Foothills Genealogical Society of Colorado, 1998, 84 pages. Includes index. Includes name of individual, county applied in, date of application, book and page number, country of birth, and court where recorded. See FHL book 978.9 P48f.

1868-1908. *New Mexico, Doña Ana and Santa Fe Counties, Homestead Records* **[Digital Capture],** from microfilm at the National Archives, digitized by FamilySearch International, 2015. Included are Registers of Homesteads, Registers of Timber Culture Receipts, and Registers of Desert Land Entries. The Timber Culture Act was a follow-up act to the Homestead Act. The Timber Culture Act was passed by Congress in 1873. The act allowed homesteaders to get another 160 acres (0.65 km2) of land if they planted trees on one-fourth of the land. The Desert Land Act was passed by the United States Congress on March 3, 1877, to encourage and promote the economic development of the arid and semiarid public lands of the Western states. Through the Act, individuals may apply for a desert-land entry to reclaim, irrigate, and cultivate arid and semiarid public lands. This act amended the Homestead Act. To access the digital images, see the online FHL catalog:
www.familysearch.org/search/catalog/2526494.

1869. See *Some Early Death Records in Lincoln County, New Mexico: From File found in the Tucumcari Mortuary of Quay County, New Mexico* **[Printed Book],** copied by Charles Barnum, published 2000, 12 pages. FHL book 978.926/T1 V3b. Also on microfilm, filmed by the Genealogical Society of Utah, 2001, 1 roll, FHL film #1145773. To see if this microfilm was digitized yet, see the online FHL catalog: **www.familysearch.org/search/catalog/968922.**

1869-1893. *A Genealogical Index of Early Lincoln County, New Mexico, Deeds* **[Printed Book],** compiled by Morton L. Ervin and Doris Ann Ervin. Published by Ervin Publishing, Albuquerque, NM, 1999, 143 pages. Lists name of grantor and grantee, instrument type and date, recording date. Arranged in alphabetical order by surname. FHL book 978.964 R22e.

1870. *New Mexico Territory, 1870 Federal Census: Population Schedules* **[Microfilm & Digital Capture],** filmed by the National Archives, 1968, 7 rolls, beginning with FHL film #552392 (Bernalillo, Colfax, Doña Ana, and Grant counties). To access the digital images, see the online FHL catalog:
www.familysearch.org/search/catalog/698912.

1870-1895 Delayed Certificates of Birth **[Microfilm & Digital Capture],** from the original records at NM Dept of Health, Santa Fe, NM. Organized by county, then by date of birth. A delayed birth certificate was issued to those who visited the courthouse of residence, filed affidavits and documents attesting to the information, confirmed by witnesses. Many of these delayed birth certificates were issued after 1935 and were used by those near or over 65 years old who needed proof of birth to apply for Social Security benefits. The certificates are organized by the dates of birth, not the date of registration. Filmed by the Genealogical Society of Utah, 1995, 5 rolls, as follows:
- Bernalillo County, 1871-1895; Catron County, 1881-1895; Chaves County, 1897-1895; and Colfax County, 1873-1893, FHL film #1991905. Another filming of Bernalillo, Catron, Chaves, and Colfax, plus DeBaca, Eddy, and Dona Ana, FHL film #1991647.
- Colfax County (cont.), 1893-1895; Curry County, 1891; DeBaca County, 1882-1892; Eddy County, 1880-1895; Dona Ana County, 1868-1895; and Grant County (part), 1873-1895, FHL film #1992055.
- Grant County (cont.), 1895; Guadalupe County, 1870-1895; Harding County, 1882-1895; Hidalgo

County, 1883-1895; Lincoln County, 1876-1895; Luna County, 1882-1895; McKinley County, 1882-1895; Mora County, 1876-1895; Otero County, 1866-1895; Quay County, 1887-1895; and Rio Arriba County, 1871-1895; FHL film #1992056.
- Roosevelt County, 1891; Sandoval County, 1876-1895; San Miguel County, 1873-1895; San Juan County, 1877-1895; and Santa Fe County, 1869-1895; FHL film #1992057.
- Sierra County, 1867-1895; Socorro County. 1867-1895; Taos County, 1866-1895; Torrance County, 1877-1893; Union County, 1873-1895; and Valencia County, 1866-1895, FHL film #1992058.

To access the digital images, see the online FHL catalog: www.familysearch.org/search/catalog/749931.

1870-1918 Probate Records, Bernalillo County, New Mexico **[Microfilm]**, from the original records at the New Mexico State Archives, Santa Fe, NM. Some pages are light and may be difficult to read. Includes index in some volumes. Includes items covered during regular terms and special sessions of probate court. Filmed by the Genealogical Society of Utah, 2004, 3 rolls, as follows:
- Probate records, vol. 1-2 (p. 1-219, cont.), 1870-1893, FHL film #2203766.
- Probate records, vol. 2 (cont., p. 218-end) – vol. 4, 1893-1910, FHL film #2203767.
- Probate claim docket, vol. 1, 1894-1897; Estate docket, 1906-1918, FHL film #2203769.

To see if this microfilm was digitized yet, see the FHL catalog: **www.familysearch.org/search/catalog/1207350**.

1870-1970. *New Mexico and Texas, Select United Methodist Church Records* **[Online Database]**, digitized and indexed at Ancestry.com website. Source: United Methodist Church Conference Archives, Albuquerque, NM. This collection contains indexed images of United Methodist Church registers from parts of New Mexico and western Texas. The registers may contain baptisms, marriages, burials, memberships, and lists of clergy. Use the Browse to find a church, organized by state, county, and church name. Each index record includes: Name, Book title, Church name, Record place, and Record type. The image of the document/register may have much more information. This database has 14,413 records. See **http://search.ancestry.com/search/db.aspx?dbid=8974**.

1870-1987 Death Index, Grant County, New Mexico **[Microfiche]**, from original typescript compiled by Carl W. Scholl, publ. LDS Family History Center, Silver City, NM, 1993. Arranged in alphabetical order by name and gives Name of deceased, Cemetery name with notes, Location in cemetery (section, block, plot), state and city, Birth date and Death date. Information is sometimes incomplete. Contents: vol. 1: A-F; vol. 2. G-M; vol. 3; N-Z. From Intro: "This list of over 28,000 names consists of cemetery, sexton and funeral home records as well as New Mexico death certificates. As a result there is information on persons who died here but are buried elsewhere. The Lordsburg, NM cemetery is also included." Death dates cover ca. 1870-1987. Filmed by the Genealogical Society of Utah, 1993, 29 microfiches, FHL fiche #6075941 (vol. 1, 9 fiches); FHL fiche #6075942 (vol. 2, 10 fiches); FHL fiche #6075943 (vol. 3, 10 fiches).

1872-1956 Santa Clara Catholic Church Records, Wagon Mound, Mora County, New Mexico **[Microfilm & Digital Capture]**, from the original records at the Santa Clara Church, Wagon Mound, New Mexico. Text partly in English and partly in Spanish. Includes indexes. Includes information from surrounding missions of Cimarron, Ocate, Watrous (formerly La Junta), and others. Filmed by Golightly, El Paso, TX, 1956, 6 FHL rolls, as follows:
- Baptisms, 1872-1894 (Cimarron and Ocate); Baptisms, 1897-1901 (Ocate), FHL film #17035.
- Baptisms, 1873-1903 (Watrous); FHL film #17036.
- Baptisms, 1905-1920 (Watrous); FHL film #17037.
- Baptisms, 1920-1956 (Wagon Mound and missions), FHL film #17038.
- Confirmations, 1920-1955 (Wagon Mound and missions), FHL film #17039.
- Marriages, 1872-1889,1893-1894 (Cimarron and Ocate); Marriages, 1873-1908 (Watrous and Ocate); Marriages, 1908-1956 (Wagon Mound and missions); Deaths, 1873-1956 (Wagon Mound and missions), FHL film #17040.

To access the digital images, see the online FHL catalog: **www.familysearch.org/search/catalog/431592**.

1873-1964. See *Deed Records, 1873-1922, 1930-1964; Indexes, 1873-1925, Valencia County, New Mexico* **[Microfilm & Digital Capture]**, from the original records at the Valencia County Court House in Los Lunas, NM. Deeds may be recorded in English or Spanish. The County Clerk also acted as the County Recorder. Some pages are faded and light and may be hard and difficult to read. The Old Spanish Grants, Inc., was a corporation organized in California and had its main offices in Los Angeles, California. It sold property within the exterior boundaries of the Nicholas Duran de Chavez Grant or San Clemente Grant in Valencia County, New Mexico. The corporation also sold property within the town of Dalies, Valencia County, New Mexico. Some volumes also contain bonds and oaths of office, notary public, etc. Some volumes include separate indexes. Filmed by the Genealogical Society of Utah, 1988, 2004, 13 rolls,

beginning with FHL film #2388332 (Indirect index to real property, grantee, 1873-1926). To access the digital images, see the online FHL catalog:
www.familysearch.org/search/catalog/451543.

"1877 List of Special US Taxpayers, Bernalillo County, New Mexico Territory" [Printed Article], in *New Mexico Genealogist*, (New Mexico Genealogical Society, Albuquerque, NM), Vol. 28, No. 2 (Jun 1989).

"1877 Taxpayers, Valencia County, New Mexico Territory" [Printed Article], in *New Mexico Genealogist*, (New Mexico Genealogical Society, Albuquerque, NM), Vol. 34, No. 3 (Sep 1995).

1880. *New Mexico Territory, 1880 Federal Census: Soundex and Population Schedules* [Microfilm & Digital Capture], filmed by the National Archives, c1970, 9 rolls, beginning with FHL film #1254802 (Bernalillo, Colfax, Doña Ana, Grant, and Lincoln counties). To access the digital images, see the online FHL catalog:
www.familysearch.org/search/catalog/676497.

1880-1920. *Some Marriage Records of the State of New Mexico* [Microfilm], from a typescript compiled by members of the Daughters of the American Revolution (New Mexico), published by the DAR, 1971-1973, 2 vols. Includes index. Contents: vol. 1: Bernalillo Co.; vol. 2: Chaves Co., Eddy Co., San Juan Co., Otero Co., Quay Co., Roosevelt Co., and Curry Co. FHL book 978.9 V25d v. 1-2. Also on microfilm filmed by the Genealogical Society of Utah, 2 rolls, FHL film 908289 (vol. 1), and FHL film #928026 (vol. 2). To see if this microfilm was digitized yet, see the online FHL catalog:
www.familysearch.org/search/catalog/157315.

1881-1983. *New Mexico, Federal Naturalization Records* [Online Database], digitized and indexed at the Ancestry.com website. Source: National Archives, records of District Courts of the U.S. Includes Declarations of Intention to become a citizen, Petitions for naturalization, Oaths of Allegiance, and Naturalization certificates. Each index record includes: Name, Record type, Birth date, Spouse, and Relatives (list of names & relationships). The document images have much more information about a person. This database has 26,962 records. See
http://search.ancestry.com/search/db.aspx?dbid=61207.

"1882 Delinquent Taxpayers, Bernalillo County, New Mexico Territory" [Printed Article], in *New Mexico Genealogist*, (New Mexico Genealogical Society, Albuquerque, NM), Vol. 28, No. 2 (Jun 1989).

1882-1935. *New Mexico, Chaves County, Reverse Deed Index, Releases, Etc.* [Printed Book], compiled and published by the Roswell Chapter New Mexico, Daughters of the American Revolution, 11 vols., FHL book 978.943 R22n A-Z. Also on microfilm, filmed by the Genealogical Society of Utah, 1982-1983, 1989, 1992, 1998, 9 rolls, beginning with FHL film #1320810 (Al-Az). To see if this microfilm was digitized yet, see the online FHL catalog:
www.familysearch.org/search/catalog/626686.

1882-1983. *New Mexico Naturalization Records* [Online Database], digitized at the FamilySearch.org website. Source: National Archives, records of district courts of the U.S. This is an image only database, with naturalization papers from Bernalillo, Rio Arriba, San Miquel, and Santa Fe counties. Browse the images, organized by County, Record type (Declarations of Intentions, Petitions, Etc.), Year range, and Volume number. This database has 29,163 records. See
https://familysearch.org/search/collection/2187007.

1883. *Albuquerque and Las Vegas Business Directory for 1883* [Microfilm], from the original directory published by Armijo Brothers & Borradaile, 1883, 97 pages. Filmed by University Microfilms International, Ann Arbor, MI, 1970, FHL film #1303032 (Albuquerque and Las Vegas Business Directory for 1883).

1884-1905. *A Genealogical Index of Early Eddy County, New Mexico Deeds* [Printed Book], compiled by Morton L. Ervin, Doris Ann Ervin, Barbara Duckworth, published by Ervin Publishing, Albuquerque, NM, 1998, 204 pages. Includes index to grantees. May include name of grantor and grantee, type of instrument, date of instrument, and recording date. FHL 978.942 R22e.

1884-1948. *Sierra County, New Mexico, Marriage Records* [Printed Book], originally compiled by Iva Hartsell Weiss; expanded and augmented by Elinor Weiss Peacock; edited by Tillie Torres Candelaria, et al., published by the Sierra County Genealogical Society, Truth or Consequences, NM, 1990, 1998, 3 vols. Includes groom and bride indexes. Arranged in alphabetical order by groom's name and gives the Names of the groom and bride, their Birthdates, Birth places, Ages, Date and Place of marriage, Name and title of official, Book and page number, Filing date, and Remarks. Information is not always complete. Contents: vol. 1: 1884 to 1920; vol. 2: 1918-1938 (books 2-3); vol. 3: 19 Apr 1938-30 Oct 1948 (books 4-5). FHL book 978.967 V2w vol. 1-4.

1885 New Mexico Territory Census (Federal Copy) [Microfilm & Digital Capture], from the federal copy at the National Archives, Washington, DC, series T1175 6 rolls. Film may be viewed at many NARA affiliated facilities, including the New Mexico State Archives, but there is no film of the federal copy at the Family History Library in Salt Lake City, Utah. An 1885 census was taken with partial federal funding only in Colorado, Dakota Territory, Florida, Nebraska, and New Mexico Territory. The 1885 census included population schedules, agricultural schedules, industry & manufacturers schedules, and mortality schedules. Two complete sets of the census schedules were prepared, one which was sent to the Census Office in Washington, DC, the other retained at the state/territory. New Mexico Territory's federal set is complete for all counties in place in 1885, the originals now located at the National Archives. To access the digital images, see the online FHL catalog: www.familysearch.org/search/catalog/2110742.
- See also, **New Mexico, Territorial Census, 1885 [Online Database],** digitized and indexed at the Ancestry.com website. Source: National Archives microfilm series T1175, 6 rolls (Federal Copy). This is a database of the 1885 Territorial Census of New Mexico. The census included all counties in the territory and was partly paid for by the Federal Government. The census was taken for two months starting the first Monday in June of 1885, and contains schedules for population, agriculture, manufactures, and mortality. These records were transferred from the Census Bureau to the National Archives in 1944. Each index record includes: Name, Gender, Race, Age, Birth date, Birthplace, Enumeration district, Residence, Relation to head, Marital status, Father's birthplace, Mother's birthplace, Page number, and Household number. The census page image has more information. This database has 138,198 records. See http://search.ancestry.com/search/db.aspx?dbid=1976.
- See also, **New Mexico Territorial Census, 1885 [Online Database],** digitized and indexed at the FamilySearch.org website. Source: National Archives microfilm series T1175. Each index record includes: Name, Event type, Event year, Event place, Gender, Age, Relationship to head of household, Birth year, and Page number. The census image has much more information about a person. This database has 59,040 records. See https://familysearch.org/search/collection/2110742.

1885 New Mexico Territory Census (Territory's Copy) [Microfilm & Digital Capture], from the duplicate originals at the University of New Mexico, Special Collection Library, Albuquerque, NM. Missing population schedules: Bernalillo, Rio Arriba, Santa Fe, and San Miguel Counties. Filmed by Golightly-Payne-Coon Co., El Paso, TX, 1957. FHL has 2 rolls, as follows:
- Bernalillo, Colfax, Dona Ana, Santa Fe (mortality schedules only), Sierra, Socorro, Mora and Rio Arriba (mortality schedules only), FHL film #16610.
- Taos, Valencia, Grant and Lincoln counties, FHL film #16611.

To access the digital images, see the online FHL catalog: www.familysearch.org/search/catalog/179492.

1885 Census of Albuquerque, New Mexico [Microfilm Only], from the territory's duplicate originals at the New Mexico State Archives in Santa Fe, NM. Lists date, name, occupation, age, sex, and remarks. Filmed by the Genealogical Society of Utah, 2004, 1 roll, FHL film #2203769.
- See also, **Territorial Census and Surname Index of the City of Albuquerque, Territory of New Mexico: Books 1, 2, and 3 - Book 4 is not extant, April 1885 [Printed Book],** by Howard W. Henry, editor and compiler, published by the Genealogy Club of Albuquerque, 2000, 81 pages. Index lists Name, Page and Line number. Includes photocopy of census from microfilm. See FHL book 978.961/A1 X2h 1885.

1885-1954. New Mexico, County Marriages [Online Database], digitized at the FamilySearch.org website. This is an image only database for marriage records from county courthouses of Sandoval, Socorro, and Valencia counties, New Mexico. Browse the images, organized by County, Record type, Year range, and Volume number. This database has 21,708 records. See https://familysearch.org/search/collection/2110325.

1887-1912. Early Marriage Records, San Juan County, New Mexico [Printed Book], compiled and published by the Totah Tracers Genealogical Society, Farmington, New Mexico, no date, 57 pages. From Preface: "The early San Juan County marriage records were recorded in two books. These two books have been combined into one publication divided into two sections, with each section indexed separately. Our publication shows the date of marriage and the name of the bride and groom." Includes indexes. FHL book 978.9 A1 No. 112.

1888-1896. *Surname Index of the Daily Citizen, Albuquerque, New Mexico* **[Printed Book],** compiled by Laurel E. Drew, editor; Howard W. Henry, compiler; Eldon W. Pierce, technical director, published by the Genealogy Club of Albuquerque, New Mexico, 1994-2001. In September 1892, the masthead of the newspaper started carrying the name, *The Evening Citizen*, but the ownership block on the succeeding pages never changed from *The Daily Citizen*. The newspaper index books for New Mexico newspapers continued to carry the name of *The Daily Citizen* as the name of the newspaper. Contents: 1888, 1889.1890, 1891, 1892, 1893, 1894, 1895, 1896. Arranged alphabetically by surname for each year. FHL has 1888-1893, 1896, 1893 bound as one volume. 1896 bound as one volume. FHL book 978.961/A1 1888-1896.

1889-1945. *New Mexico Deaths* **[Online Database],** indexed at the FamilySearch.org website. Source: NM Dept of Health. Each index record includes: Name, Event date, Event place, Race, Age, Birth date, Birthplace, Marital status, Father's name, Mother's name, Mother's birthplace, Burial place, Burial Date, and Additional relatives. This database has 167,925 records. See
https://familysearch.org/search/collection/1546466.

1889-1942. *Certificate and Record of Death* **[Microfilm & Digital Capture],** from the original records at Bureau of Vital Records & Health, Santa Fe, NM. Each record may include deceased's Name, Sex, Color or race, Marital status, Date and place of birth, Age, Occupation, Date, Place and cause of death, Place of burial and undertaker, Length of residence where death occurred, Name and birthplace of father, Name and birthplace of mother, and Name of person providing information. Organized by county/city, in chronological order by date of death. Filmed by the Genealogical Society of Utah, 1996, 29 rolls, as follows:
- Albuquerque (city) 1889-1907, FHL film #2032734.
- Curry County, 1909-1919; De Baca County, 1917-1919; Doña Ana County, 1907-1913; and Chaves County 1907-1915, FHL film #2032740.
- Chaves County, 1916-1919; Colfax County, 1907-1913; Doña Ana County, 1914-1919; Eddy County, 1908-1919; and Grant County, 1907-1914, FHL film #2032741.
- Lincoln County, 1910-1919; Luna County, 1907-1919; McKinley County, 1904-1919; and Mora County, 1907-1919, FHL film #2032742.
- Otero, Quay counties; 1907-1919; and Albuquerque (city), 1907-1910, FHL film #2032743.
- Albuquerque (city), 1910-1913; and Colfax County, 1913-1914, FHL film #2032876.
- Sierra County, 1907-1919; Socorro County, 1907-1919; Taos County, 1908-1919; Torrance County, 1908-1919; Union County, 1910-1920; Valencia County, 1899-1919; and Albuquerque (city), 1914-1915, FHL film #2032877.
- Albuquerque (city), 1916-1917; Colfax County, 1915-1917; Rio Arriba County, 1906-1918; Roosevelt County, 1910-1919; Sandoval County, 1916-1919; San Juan County, 1907-1919; and Santa Fe County, 1907, FHL film #2032878.
- Colfax County, 1918-1919; Grant County, 1915-1917; Guadalupe County, 1914-1919; and Harding County, 1897-1918, FHL film #2032879.
- Santa Fe County, 1908-1919; Sierra County, 1901-1913; and Albuquerque (city), 1919, FHL film #2032880.
- Albuquerque (city), 1920; Bernalillo County, and Chaves-Grant counties, 1920, (De Baca County missing), FHL film #2032881.
- McKinley-Otero, Guadalupe, 1920; Hidalgo, Luna, Lincoln, Lea - Quay, and Valencia counties, (Harding County missing), FHL film #2032882.
- Bernalillo-Luna counties, 1921; FHL film #2032883.
- McKinley-Valencia counties, 1921; Bernalillo County, Jan-Jul 1922, FHL film #2032884.
- Bernalillo County, Aug-Dec 1922; Catron-Quay counties, 1922, FHL film #2032885.
- Rio Arriba-Valencia counties, 1922; Bernalillo, Jan-Jun 1923, FHL film #2032886.
- Bernalillo County, Jul-Dec 1923; Catron-Harding counties, 1923, FHL film #2032887.
- Hidalgo-Union counties, 1923, FHL film #2032888.
- Valencia County, 1923; Bernalillo-Guadalupe counties, 1924, FHL film #2032889.
- Harding-Valencia counties, 1924, FHL film #2032890.
- Bernalillo-Eddy counties, 1925; Grant County, Jan-Mar 1925, FHL film #2032891.
- Grant County, Apr-Dec 1925; Guadalupe-Sierra counties, 1925, FHL film #2032892.
- Socorro-Valencia counties, 1925; Bernalillo-DeBaca counties, 1926, FHL film #2032893.
- Doña Ana-Sandoval counties, 1926, FHL film #2032894.
- San Juan-Valencia counties, 1926, FHL film #2032895.
- Indian death certificates: Bernalillo, McKinley, Otero counties, 1920-1927, FHL film #2032896.
- Indian death certificates: Rio Arriba, Sandoval, San Juan, Santa Fe, Taos counties, 1919-1927; Taos County, 1937-1938; Valencia County, 1920; Bernalillo County, 1927; Chaves, Lincoln, Grant counties, 1926; Hidalgo, Otero counties, 1938, FHL film #2032897.

- Bernalillo County, 1939-1942; McKinley County, 1926-1933; Santa Fe County, 1926-1942; Socorro County, 1936-1942; Taos County, 1927-1942; Union County, 1933; Valencia County, 1922-1942, FHL film #2032898.
- McKinley County, 1934-1942; Otero County, 1928-1942; Rio Arriba County, 1927-1942; Sandoval, San Juan counties, 1927-1942, FHL film #2032899.

To access the digital images, see the online FHL catalog: www.familysearch.org/search/catalog/763917. - See also, *Index to New Mexico Death Certificates, ca. 1889-1940* [Microfilm & Digital Capture], from the records at the NM Dept. of Health, Santa Fe NM. filmed by the Genealogical Society of Utah, 1995, 2 rolls, FHL film #1991645-6. To access the digital images, see the online FHL catalog: www.familysearch.org/search/catalog/754503.

1889-1985. *Marriage Indexes for Eddy County, New Mexico, Bride and Groom Indexes* [Printed Book & Microfilm], from a computer-generated typescript, 6 vols. The Index was compiled and produced by the Eddy County Clerk's Office, Eddy County Courthouse, in Carlsbad, New Mexico. Contents: vol. 1: Grooms. A - Gonyea; vol. 2: Grooms. Gonzales-Orozco, Enrique; vol. 3: Grooms. Orozco, Florencio - Z; vol. 4: Brides. A-Goodman, Nancy; vol. 5: Brides. Goodman, Norma-Owens, Dorothy; vol. 6: Brides. Owens, Effie-Z. Dates refer to date license was purchased, not date of marriage. Indexes are arranged in alphabetical order by name and give the date of issue, the groom's and bride's names, book number, and page number. FHL book 978.942 V22e v.1-6. Also on microfilm, filmed by the Genealogical Society of Utah, 1990, 1 roll, FHL film #1697323. To see if this microfilm was digitized yet, see the online FHL catalog: www.familysearch.org/search/catalog/537930.

"**1890 Poll Tax List, Valencia County, New Mexico Territory**", in *New Mexico Genealogist*, (New Mexico Genealogical Society, Albuquerque, NM), Vol. 37, No. 3 (Sep 1998).

"**1891 Tax Assessment Roll, Chaves County, New Mexico Territory**" [Printed Article], in *New Mexico Genealogist,* (New Mexico Genealogical Society, Albuquerque, NM), Vol. 18, No. 3 (Sep 1979) and Vol. 18, No. 4 (Dec 1979).

1891 Assessment Roll for Colfax County, Territory of New Mexico: Names of Property Owners [Printed Book], transcribed by Nancy Robertson, published by Friends of Raton Anthropology, Raton, NM, 1980, 17 pages. Arranged alphabetically within precincts of Elizabethtown, Ute Park, Cimarron, Rayado, Elkins, Raton, Folsom, Madison, Chico, Pena Flor, Ponil Park, Springer, Cimilario, Clayton, Red Lake, Blossburg, Ponil, Maxwell City, Colmor, Buena Vista Raton, Gladstone, Black Lakes, Carrizo Frampton, Road Canon, Catskill, and Mesa. FHL book 978.9 A1 No. 103.

1891-1903. *Private Land Claims Adjudicated by the U.S. Court of Private Land Claims* [Microfilm & Digital Capture], from the Court of Private Claims for the adjudication of Spanish and Mexican Land Titles in Colorado, New Mexico, Arizona, Nevada, Utah, and Wyoming. Original records filmed by the Genealogical Society of Utah, 1957, 22 rolls, beginning with FHL film #1016975 (Appearance docket, 1891-1903). To access the digital images, see the online FHL catalog: www.familysearch.org/search/catalog/411458.

1891-1916. *A Genealogical Index of Early Guadalupe County, New Mexico Deeds* [Printed Book], compiled by Morton L. Ervin, published by Ervin Publishing, Albuquerque, NM, 1999, 159 pages. Includes separate index to grantor and index to grantee. Arranged in alphabetical order by surname. Grantor index for USA is located between grantor and grantee index. FHL book 978.925 R22e. Also on microfilm, filmed by the Genealogical Society of Utah, 2001, 1 roll, FHL film 1440328.

1892-1899 Presbyterian Church Records, Ocate, Mora County, New Mexico [Microfilm & Digital Capture& Digital Capture], from the original records at the Presbyterian Historical Society in Philadelphia, Pennsylvania. Text in Spanish. Filmed by the Genealogical Society of Utah, 1966, 1 roll, FHL film #504311 (Session minutes, 1892-1899). To access the digital images, see the online FHL catalog: www.familysearch.org/search/catalog/23178.

1893-1990. See *New Mexico Marriages, Union County* [Printed Book], extracted by June Lofgreen; edited by Margaret Leonard Windham, published by the New Mexico Genealogical Society, Albuquerque, NM, 1994, 1998, 3 vols. Includes index. Contents: vol. 1: 1893-1940; vol. 2: 1941-1955; vol. 3: 1956-1990. Arranged in alphabetical order by surname of groom. FHL has bound vols. 1-3 together, FHL book 978.923 V28L vol. 1-3.

1893-1995. *Union County, New Mexico Death Records* [Microfilm], from records compiled by June Lofgreen, information gathered from Union County newspaper death notices and obituaries, cemetery inscriptions, mortuary records, and some death certificates. Includes index. Includes Clayton, New

Mexico burials: Clayton Cemetery, IOOF Cemetery, Clayton Memorial Cemetery, and Old Clayton Cemetery; Miscellaneous burials: Burial place unknown, cremated, ranch burials, and war causalities; Union County burials out of Clayton; New Mexico burials out of Union County; Burials outside of New Mexico. Filmed by the Genealogical Society of Utah, 1995, 1 roll, FHL film #1750790. To see if this microfilm was digitized yet, see the online FHL catalog: www.familysearch.org/search/catalog/724928.

1894-1956 San Jose Catholic Church Records **[Microfilm & Digital Capture]**, from the original records at the San Jose Church, Mosquero, Harding County, New Mexico. Includes indexes. Filmed by Golightly, El Paso, TX, 1956, 4 rolls, as follows:
- Baptisms 1894-1914, FHL film #16833.
- Baptisms 1925-1956, FHL film #16834.
- Marriages 1894-1955, FHL film #16835.
- Deaths 1931-1956; Confirmations 1921-1954, FHL film #16836.

To access the digital images, see the online FHL catalog: www.familysearch.org/search/catalog/369608.

"1895 Silver City Tax Roll, Grant County, New Mexico Territory" [Printed Article], in *New Mexico Genealogist,* (New Mexico Genealogical Society, Albuquerque, NM), Vol. 17, No. 1 (Mar 1978) through Vol. 17, No. 3 (Sep 1978).

"1898 Silver City Tax Roll, Grant County, New Mexico Territory" [Printed Article], in *New Mexico Genealogist,* (New Mexico Genealogical Society, Albuquerque, NM), Vol. 17, No. 3 (Sep 1978).

1899-1920. *McKinley County, New Mexico Index of Probate Court Records and Wills* **[Printed Book],** compiled by Joyce V. Hawley Spiros, published by the author, Gallup, NM, 1980, 48 pages. FHL book 978.983 P2sp. Also on microfilm, filmed by the Genealogical Society of Utah, 1988, 1 roll, FHL film #1421875.

1900. *New Mexico Territory, 1900 Federal Census: Soundex and Population Schedules* **[Microfilm & Digital Capture],** filmed by the National Archives, c1970, 28 rolls, beginning with FHL film #1240999 (Bernalillo, Chaves, and Colfax Co). To access the digital images, see the online FHL catalog: www.familysearch.org/search/catalog/639111.

1900. See **"Taxpayers, June 1900, Eddy County, New Mexico Territory," [Printed Article],** in Pecos Trails, (Eddy County Genealogical Society, Carlsbad, NM), in Vol. 7, No. 1 (May 1987).

1900-1917. *A Genealogical Index of Early Lea County, New Mexico Deeds* **[Printed Book],** compiled by Morton L. Ervin; Doris Ann Ervin; Barbara Duckworth, published by Ervin Publishing, Albuquerque, NM, 1999, 93 pages. May include name of grantee and grantor, type of instrument, date of instrument, and filing date. Arranged in alphabetical order by surname. FHL book 978.933 R22e.

1900-1951 Marriage Records, Santa Fe County, New Mexico **[Microfilm],** from the original records at the Santa Fe County Courthouse in Santa Fe, New Mexico. The office of Probate Clerk and Recorder were held by the same person. Includes index in each volume. The marriage books change from page numbers to certificate numbers. Filmed by the Genealogical Society of Utah, 2004. 12 rolls, beginning with FHL film #2312279 (Marriages, 1900-1910). To see if this microfilm was digitized yet, see the online FHL catalog: www.familysearch.org/search/catalog/1176720.

"1903 Tax List, Roosevelt County, New Mexico Territory" [Printed Article], in *Roosevelt County Searchers Genealogical Society,* (Portales, NM), Vol. 1, No. 2 (Aug 1998) through Vol. 2, No. 2 (Apr 1999).

1903-1920. *A Genealogical Index of Early Torrance County, New Mexico, Deeds* **[Printed Book],** compiled by Morton L. Ervin; Doris Ann Ervin; Barbara Duckworth, published by Ervin Publishing, Albuquerque, NM, 1998, 241 pages. Includes index to grantors. May include name of grantor and grantee, date of instrument, type of instrument, and date of recording. Arranged in alphabetical order by surname of grantee. FHL book 978.963 R22e.

1903-1953. See *50 Years of Marriages in Roosevelt County, NM* **[Printed Book],** compiled by the Roosevelt County Searchers Genealogical Society, Portales, NM, 2001, 330 pages. Includes name of bride and groom, marriage date, book and page number. Arranged in alphabetical order in two sections by the last name of groom and by the last name of the bride. FHL book 978.932 V2f. Also on microfilm, filmed by the Genealogical Society of Utah, 2001, 1 roll, FHL film # 1440533.

"1904 Census, Weed, Pinon, Avis & McDonald Flats, Eddy County, New Mexico" [Printed Article], in *Pecos Trails*, (Eddy County Genealogical Society, Carlsbad, NM), in Vol. 3, No. 1 (May 1983) through Vol. 4, No. 1 (May 1984).

1905-1908. See *Marriages Performed in the Area of Curry County, New Mexico, 1905-1908, When it Was Still a Part of Roosevelt County, New Mexico Territory* **[Printed Book]**, copied by Sallie Foster and Louise Reithel, published by the Curry County Genealogical Society of New Mexico, 1985, 8 pages. Transcripts are in the Curry Courthouse located in Clovis, New Mexico. Includes groom's Name, Bride's name, Date, Book number, Page number, and Bride's index. FHL book 978.9 A1 No. 18.

***1905-1935 City Directories, Albuquerque, New Mexico* [Microfilm],** from the originals published by various publishers. Filmed by Research Publications, Woodbridge, CT, 1980-1984, 7 rolls, as follows:
- 1905-1906, 1907, 1908-1909, 1909-1910, 1910-1911, FHL film #1843249.
- 1912, 1913, 1914, 1915, 1916, FHL film #1843250.
- 1917, 1918, 1919, 1920, FHL film #1843251.
- 1921, 1922, 1923, 1924, FHL film #1843252.
- 1925, 1926, 1927, 1928, FHL film #1843253.
- 1929, 1930, 1931, 1932, FHL film #1843254.
- 1933, 1934, 1935, FHL film #1843255.

***1905-1950 Marriage Records, Valencia County, New Mexico* [Microfilm & Digital Capture],** from the original records at the Valencia County Courthouse in Los Lunas, New Mexico. Includes index in each volume. Filmed by the Genealogical Society of Utah, 2004, 7 rolls, as follows:
- Marriage records, vol. 1, 1905-1910, FHL film #2388039.
- Marriage records, vol. 2-4, 1910-1921, FHL film #2388189.
- Marriage records, vol. 5-7, 1921-1931, FHL film #2311199.
- Marriage records, vol. 8-10, 1931-1937, FHL film #2388190.
- Marriage records, vol. 11-13, 1937-1942, film #2388191.
- Marriage records, vol. 13-15, 1942-1947, film #2388192.
- Marriage records, vol. 16-17, 1947-1950, FHL film #2388330.

To access the digital images, see the online FHL catalog: www.familysearch.org/search/catalog/1155593.

1905-1958. *New Mexico, Prison and Correctional Records* **[Online Database],** digitized and indexed at the Ancestry.com website. Source: NM State Archives, records of Dept of Corrections. These records include inmate files, intake records, and work and misconduct reports for inmates in the custody of the New Mexico Department of Corrections for the years 1905–1958. Each index record includes: Name, Gender, Age, Birth year, Birth date, Received date, Received place, Crime, Prisoner number, and Box serial number. The document image usually has detailed descriptions and photographs. This database has 11,258 records. See http://search.ancestry.com/search/db.aspx?dbid=9171.

***1907-1928 Register of Deaths, Valencia County, New Mexico* [Microfilm & Digital Capture],** from the original records at the Valencia County Courthouse in Los Lunas, New Mexico. Includes index. Lists Name of deceased, Date of death, Place of death, Sex, Race, Occupation, Age, Cause of death, Place of burial, and Other information. Filmed by the Genealogical Society of Utah, 2004, 1 roll, FHL film #2388039. To access the digital images, see the online FHL catalog: www.familysearch.org/search/catalog/1155585.

1907-1935. *Index of Death Register for McKinley County, New Mexico* **[Printed Book & Microfilm],** compiled by Joyce V. Hawley Spiros, published by Verlene Publishing, Gallup, NM, 1982, 43 pages. This index does not include dates. It refers to page numbers in the original records. FHL book 978.983 V22s. Also on microfilm, filmed by the Genealogical Society of Utah, 1988, 1 roll, FHL film #1320699. To see if this microfilm was digitized yet, see the online FHL catalog: www.familysearch.org/search/catalog/273383.

1907-1952. *New Mexico, County Death Records* **[Online Database],** digitized at the FamilySearch.org website. This is an image only database for death records from county courthouses of Sandoval, Socorro, and Valencia counties, New Mexico. Browse the images, organized by County, Record type, Year range, and Volume number. This database has 5,479 records. See https://familysearch.org/search/collection/1966081.

***1907-1956 Catholic Church Records, Clayton, New Mexico* [Microfilm & Digital Capture],** from the original records at the St. Francis Xavier Church, Clayton, New Mexico. Text in Spanish and English. St. Francis Xavier was formerly Our Lady of Sorrows. Includes indexes. Includes baptisms of the St. Joseph of Nazareth Hospital, Clayton, Union, New Mexico. Also includes baptisms and confirmations of the St. Joseph Church, Folsom, Union, New Mexico. Filmed by Golightly, El Paso, TX, 1956, 2 rolls, as follows:
- Baptisms, 1907-1930 (St. Joseph); Baptisms, 1927-1955 (St. Francis Xavier); Baptisms, 1922-1938 (St. Joseph of Nazareth); Confirmations, 1921-1941 (St. Joseph); Confirmations, 1946-1956 (St. Francis Xavier), FHL film #16750.

- Marriages, 1907-1956 (St. Francis Xavier); Deaths, 1907-1956 (St. Francis Xavier); Confirmations, 1909 (St. Francis Xavier), FHL film #16751.

To access the digital images, see the online FHL catalog: www.familysearch.org/search/catalog/385942.

1909-1915 Marriage Records, Curry County Courthouse, Clovis, New Mexico **[Microfilm]**, from a book compiled by Louise E. and Robert J. Reithel, published under the auspices of the Curry County Genealogical Society of New Mexico, Clovis, NM. The book has alphabetized listings for groom and bride for each year. Each entry gives Groom's name, Bride's name, Date, Book number and Page number. Book filmed by the Genealogical Society of Utah, 1990, FHL film #1597655. To see if this microfilm was digitized yet, see the online FHL catalog: www.familysearch.org/search/catalog/522089.

1909-1920. See *Marriages in Curry County, New Mexico, Before 1921* **[Printed Book]**, by Walter Conner; assisted by Louise Smith and Wanda Dunn, published 1987, from the original records in the Curry County Court House, Clovis, New Mexico. Contents: vol. 1, pt. 1: Alphabetically by the groom; vol. 1, pt. 2: Alphabetically by the bride, FHL 978.927 V22c.

1910. *New Mexico Territory, 1910 Federal Census: Population Schedules* **[Microfilm & Digital Capture]**, filmed by the National Archives, c1970, 7 rolls, beginning with FHL film #1374926 (Bernalillo, Chaves, and Colfax Co). To access the digital images, see the online FHL catalog: www.familysearch.org/search/catalog/639058.

1912-1913. *Polk's Arizona and New Mexico Pictorial State Gazetteer and Business Directory* **[Online Database]**, digitized and OCR indexed at Ancestry.com, see
www.ancestry.com/search/collections/27490.

1912-1956 Church Records, St. Alice Mission Catholic Church **[Microfilm & Digital Capture]**, from the original records at the St. Alice Mission, Mountainair, Torrance County, New Mexico. Text partly in English and partly in Spanish. Includes indexes. Filmed by Golightly, El Paso, TX, 1956, 2 rolls, as follows:
- Baptisms, 1912-1956, FHL film #16847.
- Confirmations, 1917-1955; Marriages, 1915-1956; Deaths, 1929-1956, FHL film #16848.

To access the digital images, see the online FHL catalog: www.familysearch.org/search/catalog/371661.

1916-1956 St. Joseph's Catholic Church Records **[Microfilm & Digital Capture]**, from the original records at St. Joseph's Church, Lordsburg, Hidalgo County, New Mexico. Includes indexes. Contents: Baptisms, 1916-1956; Communions, 1921-1956; Confirmations, 1919-1955; Marriages, 1916-1956; Deaths, 1921-1956. Filmed by Golightly, El Paso, TX, 1956, 1 roll, FHL film #16801. To access the digital images, see the online FHL catalog: www.familysearch.org/search/catalog/388732.

1917. See *Curry County, New Mexico, Registration for the Draft for World War I: Published by the Clovis Journal, Thursday, July 26, 1917* **[Microfilm]**, from an edited copy by the Clovis Branch Family History Center, 1996. 17 leaves Includes registration list of young men between the ages of 21-31, and an alphabetical list which includes hometown. Filmed by the Genealogical Society of Utah, 1996, 1 roll, FHL film #1598430. To see if this microfilm was digitized yet, see the online FHL catalog: www.familysearch.org/search/catalog/776092.

1917-1918. *New Mexico, World War I Selective Service System Draft Registration Cards* **[Microfilm & Digital Capture]**, filmed by the National Archives, 1988, 16 rolls, beginning with FHL film #1711857 (Bernalillo County, A-Z). To access the digital images, see the online FHL catalog: www.familysearch.org/search/catalog/746989.

1917-1919. *New Mexico, World War I Records* **[Online Database]**, indexed at the Ancestry.com website. Source: NM State Archives, Santa Fe, NM, records of the Adjutant General. When the U.S. entered World War I, New Mexicans had recently been involved in hostilities closer to home. The Mexican Punitive Expedition, launched to capture Pancho Villa, formally ended in February 1917, just two months before the U.S. declared war on Germany. The New Mexico National Guard was once again called into service, along with troops from across the U.S. This collection from the Adjutant General of New Mexico contains a diverse array of records documenting the state's service in the "war to end all wars." Each index record includes: Name, Birth date, Age, Gender, Enlistment date, Residence, and Folder title. The document image may include Service records, Biographical materials, Letters, Casualty lists, Awards/commendations, or Photographs. This database has 110,254 records. See
http://search.ancestry.com/search/db.aspx?dbid=8803

1917-1919. *New Mexico, World War I American Expeditionary Forces, Deaths* **[Digital Capture],** digitized by FamilySearch International, 2018. To access the digital images, see the online FHL catalog: www.familysearch.org/search/catalog/3023941.

1917-1929. *A Genealogical Index of Early De Baca County, New Mexico, Deeds* **[Printed Book],** compiled by Morton L. Ervin; Mae Allen Form, published by Ervin Publishing, Albuquerque, NM, 2000, 2 vols. Lists name of grantor and grantee, type of instrument, and date recorded. Contents: vol. 1: Grantor index; vol. 2: Grantee index. Arranged in alphabetical order by surname. FHL book 978.944 R22e v. 1-2.

1917-1930. See *Lea County, New Mexico, Marriage Book 1, 07 August 1917-12 June 1930 With Groom's and Bride's Indexes* **[Printed Book],** copied by members of the Southeastern New Mexico Genealogical Society, published by the society, Hobbs, NM, 1991, 72 pages. Includes indexes. Arranged in order by date of marriage and gives the Names of groom and bride, Date and place of marriages, and Page number. FHL book 978.933 V2L.

1917-1954. *Border Crossings: From Mexico to U.S.* **[Online Database],** digitized and indexed at the Ancestry.com website. Source: National Archives microfilm of manifests, card indexes, etc. for various ports of entry from California to Texas. Included is an index of aliens and some citizens crossing into the U.S. from Mexico via the New Mexico port of entry at Columbus, NM, 1917-1954. Each index record includes: Name, Gender, Age at arrival, Birth date, Birthplace, Arrival date, Arrival place, accompanied by, Departure contact, Record has photo and Record type. The document or card image usually has more information. This database has 5,878,615 records. See http://search.ancestry.com/search/db.aspx?dbid=1082.

1918-1955 Index of the Vital Records in the Albuquerque Journal, Albuquerque, New Mexico **[Printed Book],** Laurel E. Drew, editor; Howard W. Henry, compiler; Eldon W. Pierce, technical director; John M. Puckett, compiler; et al., published by the Genealogy Club of Albuquerque, PAF Users Group, 1994. Title varies slightly as newspaper changed its name. Index compiled on an annual basis with some events carried over to the next year especially if it occurred toward to the latter months of the year. Names are alphabetical by surname with date of event and page where it appeared. Contents: 1918, 1920, 1921, 1922, 1923, 1924, 1925, 1926, 1936, 1937, 1939, 1940, 1942, 1943, 1944, 1947, 1948, 1949 & 1955. FHL Library has bound 1921-1922, 1924-1926, and 1939-1940 together. FHL book 978.961/A1 B32h 1918-1955. See also, *Index to Obituary Notices and Death Articles: In the Albuquerque Journal, Albuquerque, New Mexico* **[Printed Book],** compiled by Hugh M. Bivens, et al., published by the Genealogy Club of Albuquerque, 1997-2000, 2 vols. Listed in alphabetical order by surname for each year. Lists name, date and page number of the newspaper. Contents: vol. 1: 1960, 1961, and 1962; vol. 2: 1963, 1964, and 1965, 1951, 1999, 2000, 2001. FHL book 978.961/A1 V4b 1951-2001.

1918-1956 Holy Family Catholic Church Records **[Microfilm & Digital Capture],** from the original records at Holy Family Church, Roy, Harding County, New Mexico. Includes indexes. Contents: Baptisms, 1918-1956; Marriages, 1918-1956; First Communion, 1926-1949; Confirmations, 1920-1954; Deaths, 1918-1956. Filmed by Golightly, El Paso, TX, 1956, 1 roll, FHL film #16880. To access the digital images, see the online FHL catalog: www.familysearch.org/search/catalog/383048.

1920. *New Mexico, 1920 Federal Census: Soundex and Population Schedules* **[Microfilm & Digital Capture],** filmed by the National Archives, c1970, 38 rolls, beginning with FHL film #1821074 (Bernalillo, Chaves, and McKinley counties). To access the digital images, see the online FHL catalog: www.familysearch.org/search/catalog/577750.

1925-1952. *Death Records; Index to Births & Deaths (Sandoval County, New Mexico)* **[Microfilm & Digital Capture],** from records of the NM Bureau of Public Health, filmed by the Genealogical Society of Utah, 2003, 3 rolls, beginning with FHL film #2366363 (Index to births & deaths, Vol. 1). To access the digital images, see the online FHL catalog: www.familysearch.org/search/catalog/1140035.

1927-1945 New Mexico Death Certificates **[Microfilm & Digital Capture],** from the original records at the New Mexico Department of Health, Vital Records & Health Statistics, Santa Fe, NM. Arranged chronologically in each county by date of death. Filmed by the NM Dept. of Health, 1978, 46 rolls, cataloged by the FHL as follows:
- Bernalillo - Doña Ana counties, 1927, FHL film #1913277.
- Eddy - San Juan counties, 1927 San Miguel County, Jan-Jul 1927, FHL film #1913278.

- San Miguel County, 1927; Santa Fe - Valencia counties, 1927, FHL film #1913279.
- Bernalillo - Doña Ana counties, 1928, FHL film #1913280.
- Eddy - Sandoval counties, 1928, FHL film #1913281.
- San Juan - Valencia counties, 1928, FHL film #1913282.
- Bernalillo - Grant counties, 1929, FHL film #1913283.
- Guadalupe - Sandoval counties, 1929, FHL film #1913284.
- Rio Arriba - Valencia counties, 1929, FHL film #1913285.
- Bernalillo - De Baca counties, 1930, FHL film #1913286.
- Dona Ana - Rio Arriba counties, 1930, FHL film #1913287.
- Roosevelt - Valencia counties, 1930, FHL film #1913288.
- Bernalillo - Grant counties, 1931, FHL film #1913289.
- Guadalupe - Socorro counties, 1931, FHL film #1913290.
- Taos - Valencia counties 1931; Bernalillo - Dona Ana counties, 1932, FHL film #1913291.
- Eddy - San Miguel counties, 1932, FHL film #1913292.
- Santa Fe - Valencia counties, 1932; Bernalillo – Colfax counties, 1933, FHL film #1913293.
- Curry - San Juan counties, 1933, FHL film #1913294.
- San Miguel – Valencia, 1933; Bernalillo 1934, FHL film #1913295.
- Catron - Otero counties, 1934, FHL film #1913296.
- Quay - Valencia counties, 1934, FHL film #1913297.
- Bernalillo - Grant counties, 1935, FHL film #1913298.
- Guadalupe - Santa Fe counties, 1935, FHL film #1913299.
- Sierra - Valencia counties, 1935; Bernalillo - Colfax counties, 1936, FHL film #1913300.
- Curry - Roosevelt counties, 1936, FHL film #1913301.
- Sandoval - Valencia counties; 1936; Bernalillo County, 1937, FHL film #1913302.
- Bernalillo County, 1937; Catron - Harding counties, 1937, FHL film #1913303.
- Hidalgo - Santa Fe counties, 1937, FHL film #1913304.
- Sierra - Valencia 1937; Bernalillo, Curry, De Baca, and Dona Ana counties, 1938, FHL film #1913305.
- Catron - Colfax counties, 1938; Eddy - San Juan counties, 1938, FHL film #1913306.
- San Miguel - Valencia counties, 1938; Bernalillo County, 1939, FHL film #1913307.
- Catron - Quay counties, 1939, FHL film #1913308.
- Rio Arriba - Valencia counties, 1939, FHL film #1913309.
- Bernalillo - Grant counties, 1940, FHL film #1913310.
- Guadalupe - San Miguel counties, 1940, FHL film #1913311.
- Sierra - Valencia counties, 1940; Bernalillo - Colfax counties, 1941, FHL film #1913312.
- Curry - Sandoval counties, 1941, FHL film #1913313.
- San Juan - Valencia counties, 1941; Bernalillo County 1942, FHL film #1913314.
- Catron - Quay counties, 1942, FHL film #1913315.
- Rio Arriba - Valencia counties, 1942, FHL film #1913316.
- Bernalillo - Grant counties, 1943, FHL film #1913317.
- Guadalupe - Santa Fe counties, 1943, FHL film #1913318.
- Sierra - Valencia counties, 1943; Bernalillo - De Baca counties, 1944, FHL film #1913319.
- Doña Ana - San Juan counties, 1944, FHL film #1913320.
- San Miguel - Valencia counties, 1944; Bernalillo County, 1945, FHL film #1913321.
- Catron - Quay counties, 1945, FHL film #1913322.

To access the digital images, see the online FHL catalog: www.familysearch.org/search/catalog/749833.

1928-1935 Santa Fe (New Mexico) City Directories [Microfilm], from the original records located in various libraries and societies. Microfilm of original records by various publishers. Filmed by Research Publications, Woodbridge, CT, 1990, 1 roll, FHL film #2309618 (contains 1928-1929, 1930-1931, 1932-1933, and 1934-1935 directories).

1930. *New Mexico, 1930 Federal Census: Population Schedules* **[Microfilm & Digital Capture],** filmed by the National Archives, c1970, 9 rolls, beginning with FHL film #2341127 (Bernalillo Co). To access the digital images, see the online FHL catalog: www.familysearch.org/search/catalog/1037461.

1938-1956 St. Helena Catholic Church Records [Microfilm & Digital Capture], from the original records at the St. Helena Church, Hobbs, Lea County, New Mexico. Includes indexes. Contents: Communions, 1938-1941; Confirmations, 1943; Baptisms, 1939-1954; Mar-riages, 1940-1956; Deaths 1940-1956; Confirmations, 1940; Baptisms, 1951-

1956; Confirmations, 1951-1954; Communions, 1951-1956. Filmed by Golightly, El Paso, TX, 1956. FHL film #16778. To access the digital images, see the online FHL catalog:
www.familysearch.org/search/catalog/388671.

1940. *New Mexico, 1940 Federal Census: Population Schedules* **[Digital Capture],** digitized by the National Archives, 2012, from microfilm of the original records held by the Bureau of the Census in the 1940s. After microfilming, Congress allowed the Census Bureau to destroy the originals to free up space for WWII-related files. Digitized beginning with FHL Digital File Folder #546173 (Bernalillo Co). To access the digital images, see the online FHL catalog:
www.familysearch.org/search/catalog/2057774.

1940 Federal Census Finding Aids **[Online Database].** The National Archives prepared a special website online with a detailed description of the 1940 federal census. Included at the site are descriptions of location finding aids, such as Enumeration District maps, Geographic Descriptions of Census Enumeration Districts, and a list of 1940 City Directories available at the National Archives. The finding aids are all linked to other National Archives sites. The National Archives website also has a link to 1940 Search Engines using Stephen P. Morse's "One-Step" system for finding a 1940 E.D. or street address conversion. See www.archives.gov/research/census/1940/general-info.html#questions.

1940-1947. *New Mexico, World War II Draft Registration Cards* **[Digital Capture],** digitized by FamilySearch International, 2016, from records at the National Personnel Records Center, St. Louis, MO. To access the digital images, see the online FHL catalog: www.familysearch.org/search/catalog/2659400.

1941-1945. *New Mexico, World War II Records* **[Online Database],** digitized and indexed at the Ancestry.com website. Source: NM State Archives, Santa Fe, NM, records of the Adjutant General. This collection includes a variety of records related to New Mexicans' service during World War II. Included are enlistment records, military discharges, photographs, and service records. Each index record includes: Name, Race, Birth date, Enlistment place, and Record type. The image/document may give more information. This database has 118,976 records. See http://search.ancestry.com/search/db.aspx?dbid=8867.

1942. *Men in U.S. Military Service, WWII: As Listed in the Clovis News Journal, Curry County, New Mexico, July 15, 1942; Taken from the Wednesday, July 15, 1942, "Heroes Edition" (Section 2), Over 700 Curry County Men Are Now in the Armed Forces* **[Microfilm],** transcribed by Don McAlavy, microfilm of original and photocopies: [Clovis, New Mexico: D. McAlavy, 2000, 23 pages. Filmed by the Genealogical Society of Utah, FHL film #1573646. To see if this microfilm was digitized yet, see the online FHL catalog: www.familysearch.org/search/catalog/1176339.

1946-1956 Immaculate Heart of Mary Catholic Church Records **[Microfilm & Digital Capture],** from the original records at the Immaculate Heart of Mary Church, Los Alamos, Los Alamos County, New Mexico. Includes indexes. Contents: Baptisms, 1946-1956; Confirm-ations, 1950-1954; Marriages, 1946-1956; Deaths, 1946-1956. Filmed by Golightly, El Paso, TX, 1956. FHL film #16805. To access the digital images, see the online FHL catalog:
www.familysearch.org/search/catalog/388707.

1957-1988. See *Tucumcari (Quay County, New Mexico) City Directory* **[Printed Book],** R. L. Polk and Company, Dallas, TX, 1957-1988. FHL has directories for the years 1957, 1967, and 1988. FHL book 978.926 E4h 1957-1988.

1966, 1967, 1985 Greater Las Cruces (Dona Ana County, New Mexico) City Directory: Including Mesilla, Mesilla Park and University Park, Contains Buyers' Guide and a Complete Classified Business Directory **[Printed Book],** publ. R. L. Polk and Company, Dallas, TX. FHL has 1966, 1967, 1985 directories. FHL book 978.966 E4p 1966-1985.

1994-Current. See *New Mexico Recent Newspaper Obituaries* **[Online Database],** digitized and indexed newspaper obituaries at the GenealogyBank website, including newspapers for Alamogordo, Albuquerque, Carlsbad, Deming, Farmington, Gallup, Grants, Las Cruces, Las Vegas, Los Alamos, Roswell, Ruidoso, Santa Fe, Silver City, and Taos. See
www.genealogybank.com/explore/obituaries/all/usa/new-mexico.

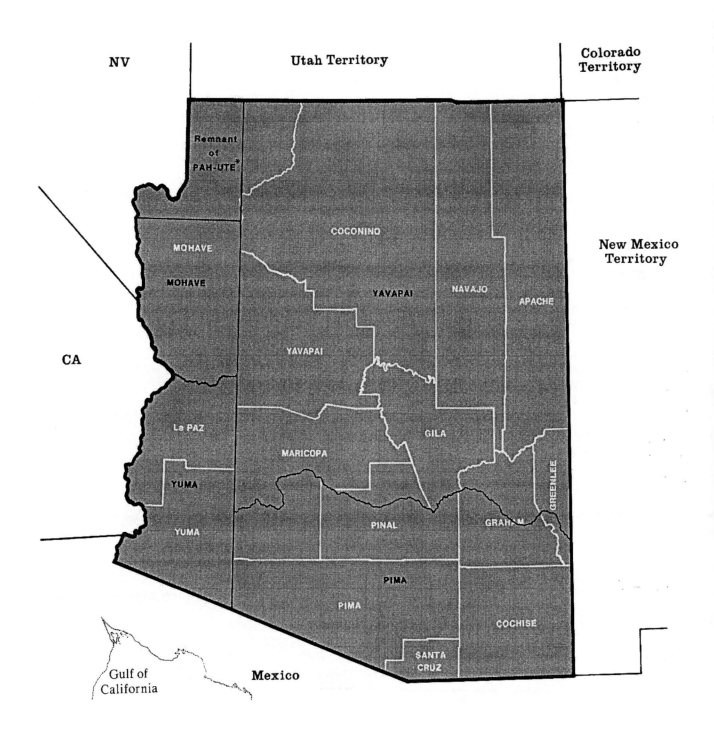

1870 Arizona Territory. The five counties of Arizona Territory at the time of the June 1870 federal census are shown in black. The fifteen current counties of the state of Arizona are shown in white. When Arizona Territory was created by Congress in 1863, its northern border extending west to the California line. The first four counties of the territory were created in 1864 (Mohave, Pima, Yavapai, and Yuma counties). *In 1865, Pay-Ute County was created from Mohave and spanned the Colorado River into the area of present Clark County, Nevada. In 1869, Arizona Territory's northwestern border was adjusted to the Colorado River, leaving only a remnant of old Pah-Ute County in Arizona. Apparently, the 1870 census taker for Pay-Ute county did not know about the boundary change and proceeded to identify every person he found from the California border to Pay-Ute's eastern boundary with Yavapai. That area included Mormon Fort, now the city of Las Vegas. The remnant area was returned to Mohave County in 1871.

Arizona
Censuses & Substitute Name Lists

Historical Timeline for Arizona, 1100 – 1912

Before 1100 AD. The Hopi village of Oraibi was founded. It may be the oldest continuously inhabited settlement within the United States. The Hopi Reservation is in Arizona's Navajo County, completely surrounded by the Navajo Reservation.

1536. Spanish explorer Cabeza de Vaca entered the area of present New Mexico via Texas. He was credited with initiating the story of the Seven Cities of Gold (or Seven Cities of Cibola). The local natives perpetuated the rumor, by continually telling the Spaniards that the cities of gold were just a little further away. This ploy worked for nearly 60 years, keeping the Spanish soldiers from staying very long in one place.

1539. Franciscan friar Marcos de Niza and his black slave Esteban de Dorantes explored Nuevo Mexico looking for the Seven Cities of Cibola. They reached the Zuni village of Hawikuh (near the present Arizona border with New Mexico), where Esteban was killed.

1540. Francisco Vasquez de Coronado of Spain came searching for the Seven Cities of Cibola. Coronado never found the cities of gold, but he did find the Gulf of California, the Colorado River, the Grand Canyon, parts of present southern Utah and Colorado, and a piece of southwest Kansas. He claimed the entire region as part of New Spain.

1590. The first attempt to colonize Nuevo Mexico was made by Spaniard Gaspar Castaño de Sosa. He led a party of 170 Spaniards and a large number of livestock into the Rio Grande Valley. Castaño was the first to give a name to the Rio Grande.

1598. Juan de Oñate founded the first permanent Spanish colony at San Juan de los Caballeros (near present-day Española, New Mexico). San Juan became the first capital of the Province of Nuevo Mexico.

1600. San Gabriel was founded at the confluence of the Rio Grande and Chama Rivers. San Gabriel became the second capital of Nuevo Mexico.

1609. Governor Pedro de Peralta founded Santa Fe as the new capital of the Spanish Province of Nuevo Mexico.

1680. The Pueblo Indians revolted and drove the Spanish out of northern New Mexico, who fled to El Paso del Norte.

1692. Diego de Vargas conquered New Mexico (again) for Spain. The same year, Jesuit priest Eusebio Francisco Kino founded the Guevavi mission near present Nogales, Arizona.

1700. Founding of the San Xavier del Bac mission (White Dove of the Desert), near present Tucson, Arizona.

1743. French trappers, following an Indian trail from the Missouri River, reached Santa Fe and began trade with the Spanish colonists.

1752. After many revolts from the Pima and Papago tribes, a Spanish settlement was established at Tubac Pueblo, about 45 miles south of present Tucson, Arizona.

1776. A Spanish presidio (fort) was built at Tucson. That same year, a pack mule route from Santa Fe to Los Angeles was explored, which later became known as the Old Spanish Trail.

1800. The Spanish population of Nuevo Mexico was at about 20,000.

1804. Hearing of an intrusion of Americans into their territory, Spanish troops were dispatched from Santa Fe to intercept the Lewis and Clark Expedition, but failed to find them.

1821. Mexico gained independence from Spain and exerted military control over Nuevo Mexico. That same year, trappers and traders from the United States come into the area via a new route which became known as the Santa Fe Trail.

1829. The first commercial caravan along The Old Spanish Trail from Santa Fe to Los Angeles was led by Mexican trader Antonio Armijo. Finding an artesian spring en route, he named it *Las Vegas*.

1836. The new Republic of Texas claimed all land to the Rio Grande, including the eastern half of present New Mexico, and a portion of southern Colorado.

1841. Texas soldiers invaded New Mexico but they were held at bay by Mexican troops under the command of Governor Manuel Armijo.

1845. Texas was annexed to the United States. The U.S. honored the Texas claim to the Rio Grande Valley, which led to a war with Mexico.

1846. April. **Mexican-American War.** U.S. Forces quickly took control of the Rio Grande Valley. The captured area from the Texas line at the Nueces River to the Rio Grande was annexed to the United States, based on the acquired Texas claim.
- Soon after, a **Provisional New Mexico Territory** was organized by General Stephen Watts Kearny. The provisional territory operated until replaced by the official New Mexico territorial government in 1850.

1848. Mexican Cession. As part of the Treaty of Guadalupe Hidalgo ending the war with Mexico, the United States gained ownership to the remainder of New Mexico west of the Rio Grande, including the present areas of Arizona (north of the Gila River), Colorado (west of the continental divide), a portion of southwestern Wyoming; and all of California, Nevada, and Utah. In compensation, the U.S. paid Mexico a sum of 18 million dollars for an area that was over half of the Republic of Mexico and was comparable in size to the Louisiana Purchase.

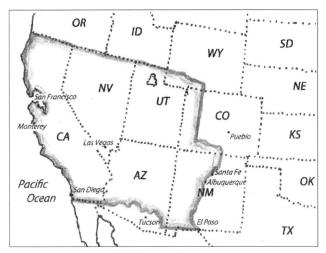
1848 Mexican Cession

1850. Jun 1. **Federal Census**. The Provisional Territory of New Mexico was included, with the original seven counties of Bernalillo, Rio Arriba, Santa Ana, Santa Fe, San Miguel, Taos, and Valencia counties. The area of present Arizona north of the Gila River was also part of New Mexico Territory, but no population was enumerated there.

1850. Sep 9. California was admitted to the Union as the 31st state; and on the same day, Congress established both Utah Territory and New Mexico Territory.

1852. Doña Ana County was established, stretching across the southern portion of New Mexico Territory, well into the area that later became Arizona.

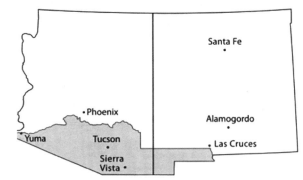

1853. Gadsden Purchase. Seeking access for a southern railroad route, the U.S. paid Mexico a sum of 10 million dollars to purchase a 45,000 square mile tract of land south of the Gila River. The purchase was negotiated by James Gadsden, minister to Mexico, who, along with Jefferson Davis, had earlier proposed a plan to build a transcontinental railroad that would link southern states from the Atlantic to the Pacific leading to a southern-confederate dominance of the region. The area of the Gadsden Purchase was added to New Mexico Territory, which immediately expanded Doña Ana County to include the entire area.

1859. New Mexico Territory created Arizona County from Doña Ana, the Gadsden Purchase area of present Arizona south of the Gila River.

1860. April. Proposed Territory of Arizona. The Territory of New Mexico had concerns about being able to govern the southern part of its territory, given the difficult desert separating the northern and southern areas. In 1858, New Mexico's territorial legislature had adopted a resolution in favor of the creation of Arizona Territory. The resolution went to the U.S. Congress, but in 1860, after two years of no action, New Mexico delegates met in Tucson and drafted a constitution for a U.S. Territory of Arizona, with a capital at Tucson. The impending Civil War caused Congress to table the matter indefinitely.

1860. Jun. Federal Census. New Mexico Territory's population of 93,516 people was enumerated in areas of present southern Colorado, and all of present Arizona and New Mexico. Arizona's enumeration was in Arizona County, New Mexico Territory, including the few settlements south and north of the Gila River; plus Fort Mojave on the Colorado River, technically in New Mexico's Valencia County, but enumerated with Arizona County.

1861. Feb. The U.S. Congress created **Colorado Territory**. In doing so, New Mexico Territory lost the northern-most parts of Taos and Mora counties to the new Colorado Territory.

1861. Feb. The **Provisional Territory of Arizona** was self-declared, matching the exact area proposed in 1860 by New Mexico Territory. This "Horizontal Territory of Arizona" immediately petitioned the Confederate Congress for recognition.

1861. Mar. The **Confederate Territory of Arizona**, with a capital at La Mesilla, was recognized by the Confederate Congress, incorporating the area of pre-war New Mexico Territory south of the 34th parallel.

1861. Apr. American Civil War. A Confederate force fired on Union troops occupying Fort Sumter, Charleston Harbor, South Carolina - the onset of the Civil War.

1862. Feb. Confederate troops from Texas entered the Confederate Territory of Arizona, mostly settlements along the Rio Grande Valley, but also as far west as Tucson.

1862. April. The Civil War battle of Glorietta Pass in Northern New Mexico Territory was fought to a stalemate. But U.S. troops had burned the Confederate supply trains, and killed or drove off their horses and mules, forcing their eventual retreat from New Mexico. - A few Confederate troops held on in the Tucson area, but after a force of some 2,000 Union troops from California marched on Tucson, the last of the Confederate troops retreated back to Texas in May 1862. Upon the U.S. capture of Tucson, the Confederate Territory of Arizona was returned to New Mexico Territory.

1862. April. Arizona County, New Mexico Territory, was abolished, the area returned to its parent, Doña Ana County.

1863. Feb. U.S. Arizona Territory. A year after the short-lived Confederate Territory of Arizona was overrun by Union Troops, the U.S. Congress decided to reassert Union influence in the area again by creating a U.S. Arizona Territory, with Prescott as the capital. No civil government was established in the new territory for over a year, and as a Civil War baby, Arizona Territory was first governed as a military district. The northern boundary of Arizona Territory extended west to the California line, and included all of present Clark County, Nevada. When Congress divided New Mexico Territory vertically on the same meridian as Colorado's western line, the resulting map created the "Four Corners" of Colorado, Utah, Arizona, and New Mexico, the only point in the U.S. where four states touch at a quadripoint.

1864. Feb. An Arizona Territorial census was conducted, mandated by the organic act under which the territory was formed, and enumerated within three judicial districts (before the first counties were created). The 1864 census was a federal census, financed and enumerated by the U.S. military government.

1864. Nov. One of the first actions of the newly elected Arizona Territorial legislature was the creation of four original counties. Mohave, Pina, Yavapai, and Yuma counties.

1865-1871. Pah-Ute County was created from Mohave in Dec 1865. It was the first county created after the four original counties created by Arizona Territory in late 1864. The original area of Pah-Ute spanned both sides of the Colorado River, east to the present Mohave line, and west to the original 1863 border with California. Until 1869, Pah-Ute covered most of present-day Clark County, Nevada, and included Mormon Fort, now the city of Las Vegas. No county records for Pah-Ute County exist, but at least one census was taken under the name Pah-Ute. (See the 1866 AZ territorial census). When the Nevada-Arizona boundary was adjusted in 1869 to the Colorado River, only a remnant of old Pah-Ute east of the river was left as part of Arizona Territory. That remnant was returned to Mohave County in 1871.

1866. Arizona Territorial Census. This was the only census authorized by the territorial legislature. (The 1864 territorial census was a federal enumeration). The census includes surviving schedules for all five counties in place in 1866: Mohave, Pah-Ute, Pima, Yavapai, and Yuma counties.

1867. The Arizona territorial capital was moved from Prescott to Tucson.

1869. John Wesley Powell and party explored and mapped the Grand Canyon, traveling exclusively by river boats.

1870. Jun. Federal Census. Arizona Territory's population was at 9,658. Refer to the AZ 1870 map on page 212.

✓ **1870 NOTE:** The 1870 Mortality Schedule for Tombstone, Arizona Territory listed the name, age, nativity, and cause of death of all persons who died between June 1, 1869 and May 31, 1870. Most of the deaths were caused by gunshots or knife wounds, with a couple of hangings, and one rattlesnake bite. At the end of the schedules, the census enumerator wrote a few words of explanation, saying ". . . many of our young men settle their differences of opinion in the middle of the street."

1880. In March, the Southern Pacific railroad reached Tucson, Arizona Territory, completing the route from Los Angeles. The Southern Pacific had purchased railroads running from the Atlantic Coast to Texas and was now starting the connection from Arizona Territory to Texas. In 1881, The Southern Pacific crossed Arizona and New Mexico territories, and with the completion of the leg to Sierra Blanca, Texas, the SP became the second transcontinental railroad. It was no coincidence that the same "big four" California investors of the first transcontinental railroad of 1869, were also the owners of the second. Stanford, Crocker, Huntington, and Hopkins bought the Southern Pacific in 1868, merged it into the Central Pacific in 1870, and completed the connection from San Francisco to Los Angeles in 1876. By 1877, the SP was well on its way to Arizona.

1880. Federal Census. Arizona Territory's population was at 40,440. After microfilming, the National Archives gave away the original 1880 census schedules for Arizona Territory, which was bound into one large volume. That bound volume ended up at the DAR Library in Washington, DC.

✓ **1881 NOTE:** On October 26, 1881, Wyatt Earp, Doc Holliday, and three more Earp brothers were involved in a gunfight at Tombstone's OK Corral. According to the last five movies depicting the event, the Earps were the good guys.

1886. After leaving his hideout in Arizona, the great Apache Chief Geronimo surrendered to soldiers on September 4th, marking the end of the Indian wars in the West.

1889. The Arizona territorial capital was moved from Tucson to Phoenix.

1890 Federal Census. The population of Arizona Territory was at 88,243.

1900 Federal Census. The population of Arizona Territory was at 122,931.

1910 Federal Census. The population of Arizona Territory rose to 334,162.

1912. Feb. 14th (Valentine's Day), Arizona became the 48th state, with Phoenix as the state capital.

Arizona State Library, Archives & Public Records, Phoenix, AZ

There are two divisions with major genealogical collections, each with online sites for finding much more information:

• **The State of Arizona Research Library.** Online tools include Digital Arizona Library, Research for State Employees, Research Library Catalog, and FAQs. See **https://azlibrary.gov/starl**.

• **Arizona State Archives.** There are many collections of original manuscripts here relating to Arizona history. The home page lists: Accessing Arizona Public Records, Maps at the Arizona State Archives, Arizona State Knowledge (ASK), and Genealogy Collection. See **https://azlibrary.gov/archives**.

Bibliography
Arizona Censuses & Substitutes

This chronological listing of censuses and substitutes is related to Arizona's Colonial, Territorial, and State Eras:

1536-1820. Spanish Era: An area of the old Sonora Province of Spanish Mexico extended into what is now Arizona. Called the Pimeria Alta (upper land of the Pimas), the main Spanish settlements in the region were at the Guevavi Mission, near Nogales; the Tubac Pueblo, south of Tucson; and the Presidio of Tucson. (All of the Pimeria Alta settlements were within the area of the Gadsden Purchase, transferred from Mexico to the U.S. in 1853). Extant censuses/substitutes include: 1) An online database for vital records (1684-1848) from three Pimeria Alta missions. 2) A Spanish census for Tucson taken in 1797 survives, and 3) a census for the Pimeria Alta region taken in 1801, which also survives.

1821-1852. Mexican Era. Extant censuses include: 1) A census survives for Tucson, Tubac, and Santa Cruz taken by the Mexicans in 1831. 2) The area of the Gadsden Purchase was still in Mexico in 1852, and a census taken there by the Mexican government in that year included parts of the Pimeria Alta region.

1848-1862. New Mexico Territory Era. No Arizona population was enumerated in the 1850 New Mexico federal census. In the 1860 New Mexico federal census, the Arizona population was mostly in Arizona County, south of the Gila River (the area acquired by the U.S. as part of the Gadsden Purchase in 1853). At that time, the U.S. citizens were mostly former Mexican citizens of the Pimeria Alta region. There were no known territory-wide census substitutes created during this period.

1863-1912. Arizona Territory Era. Territorial censuses were taken only in 1864 and 1866. Other years reported by some as "Territorial Censuses" were actually county censuses.

1912 – Current. The State of Arizona Era: After two censuses taken as Arizona Territory, the State of Arizona never took a state census. The statewide substitute name lists identified in the bibliography are enhanced by including several countywide name lists for Arizona. Putting the county lists together for the same time period may increase the number of name lists for the entire state, or at least large regions of the state.

Census Substitutes. In addition to the territorial and federal censuses, there are many census substitute name lists that fill out the bibliography. Name lists may include Local Census Records, County Court Records, Directories, County Histories, State Militia Lists, Tax Lists, Church & Vital Records, and Voter Lists. They begin below in chronological order:

◆ ◆ ◆ ◆ ◆

1684-1848. *Mission 2000* **[Online Database].** This is a searchable database of Spanish mission records of the Pimeria Alta (Southern Arizona and Northern Sonora, Mexico) containing baptisms, marriages, and burials from 1684 to 1848, the year of the Mexican Cession. The records from three Spanish missions were provided by the Tumacacori National Historic Park, National Park Service, U.S. Department of the Interior. See **www.NPS.gov/tuma/historyculture/mission-2000.htm**.

1752-1837. See *Early California and Nogales, Arizona Lists of Expeditionary Members, Soldiers and Residents, 1752, 1775, 1781-1837: Material Emphasizes Santa Barbara, California* [Microfilm], from the original manuscripts at the Santa Barbara Historical Society, Santa Barbara, California. Text in English and Spanish. Includes Santa Barbara censuses taken in 1834 and 1837. Includes lists of military personnel and other areas of California, plus Nogales, Arizona. Filmed by the Genealogical Society of Utah, 1988, 1 roll, FHL film #1548299.

"1797 Tucson Census" [Printed Article], name list published in *Revista*, a publication of the Instituto Genealógico e Histórico Latinoamericano, Highland, Utah, Vol. 1, No. 3 (July 1989).

1801. *Mexican Census Pre-territorial: Pimeria Alta* **[Printed Book],** transcribed by Eugene L. Sierras, published by the Arizona State Genealogical Society, Tucson, AZ, 1986, 61 pages, Pimeria Alta was an area of land now stretching from Sonora, Mexico to Pima, Cochise, and Santa Cruz Counties, Arizona. See FHL book 979.1 X2s 1801.

1831. *Mexican Census Pre-territorial: Tucson, Tubac & Santa Cruz* **[Printed Book],** transcribed by Eugene L. Sierras, published by the Arizona State Genealogical Society, Tucson, AZ, 1986, 30 pages. From page 7: The National Republican Congress at Mexico City in 1824 combined the provinces of Sonora and Sinaloa under the name Estado Interno de Occidente (Interior State of the West). In 1830, the Congress divided Occidente, Sonora, and southern Arizona was again independent. The following year, 1831, a census was taken. This is the only name-by-name census of the Sonoran Desert for 1831. The census includes Tucson, Tubac and Santa Cruz." FHL book 979.1 A1 no. 62.

1831. *Index to the 1831 Census of Arizona and Sonora* **[Printed Book],** compiled by Instituto Genealógico e Histórico Latinoamericano, published by the Institute, Highland, UT, 1983, 30 pages. Includes name (listed alphabetically by surname), biographical information (relationships), house no., and reference to census. FHL book 979.1 A1 no. 87. Also on microfilm, filmed by the Genealogical Society of Utah, 1990, 1 roll, FHL film #1697282.

"**1831 Tucson Census, Civilian Households**" **[Printed Article],** in *Copper State Bulletin*, Vol. 16, No. 1 (Spring 1981); and "**1831 Military Households,**" in Vol. 16, No. 2 (Summer 1981).

"**1831 Mexican Census, Civilian Households, (now Santa Cruz County, New Mexico)**" **[Printed Article],** in *Copper State Bulletin*, Vol. 17, No. 1 (Spring 1982) through Vol. 17, No. 4 (Winter 1982).

1831-1880. *Arizona, Compiled Census Index* **[Online Database],** indexed at the Ancestry.com website. Source: Accelerated Indexing Systems, 1999. This collection contains the following indexes: 1831 Mexican Census (Santa Cruz Co. only); 1864 Territorial Census Index; 1866 Territorial Census Index; 1867 Territorial Census Index (Pina Co only); 1870 Federal Census Index; 1880 Federal Census Index. This database has 32,716 records. See
https://search.ancestry.com/search/db.aspx?dbid=3533.

1844-1960 & 1855-1935. See *Arizona Genealogy Birth and Death Certificates* **[Online Database],** a free searchable database for non-certified (PDF) facsimile copies of AZ birth and death certificates. After a surname search, the results page is a valuable tool, giving the name of the subject, and often the name of the subject's spouse and/or parents. Many of the entries have multiple documents, all included in the image database as pictorial PDF files. The webpage is part of the Arizona Department of Health Services official website. The database includes only public documents and was extracted by volunteers from the Mesa Family History Center. Arizona public birth certificates are those that occurred at least 75 years ago; and Arizona public death certificates are those that occurred at least 50 years ago. See
http://genealogy.az.gov/.

✓ **1850 NOTE:** Areas of present-day Arizona north of the Gila River were part of the Provisional Territory of New Mexico in 1850, but the census enumerators found no population there. (Or, it may be more likely that the census taker simply refused to undertake the 500-mile horseback ride from Santa Fe through hostile Indian country to get there).

1852. *Mexican Census Pre-Territorial: Pimeria Alta* **[Printed Book],** transcribed by Eugene L. Sierras, published by the Arizona State Genealogical Society, Tucson, AZ, 1986, 104 pages. The areas of 1852 Pimeria Alta in present-day Arizona were below the Gila River, within the area of the Gadsden Purchase of 1853. See FHL book 979.1 X2se 1852.

1855-1926. *Arizona Birth Certificates* **[Microfilm & Digital Capture],** from original records at the Arizona State Archives, Phoenix, AZ. Birth certificates are listed by date of recording. Filmed by the Genealogical Society of Utah, 1998-1999, 2001, 63 rolls, beginning with FHL film #2135642 (Birth Certificates, Pima County, 1855-1893). To access the digital images, see the online FHL catalog:
www.familysearch.org/search/catalog/815536.

1860. *New Mexico Territory, 1860 Federal Census: Population Schedules* **[Microfilm & Digital Capture],** from the original records at the National Archives, Washington, DC. Arizona County was part of New Mexico Territory, within an area south of the Gila River. Filmed by the National Archives, 1st filming, 1950, second filming, 1967, 6 rolls total. For Arizona County, see FHL film #803712 (1st filming: Arizona, Dona Ana, and Rio Arriba Counties); and FHL film #16602 (2nd filming, Entire NM Terr.). To access the digital images, see the online FHL catalog: www.familysearch.org/search/catalog/705448.

1860. *Arizona 1860 Territorial Census Index* **[Printed Index],** compiled by Ronald Vern Jackson, et al, published by Accelerated Indexing Systems, 1978, 36 pages. The names come from the New Mexico Territory federal census, Arizona County. Arizona Territory was not created until 1863. See FHL book 979.1 X2.

1860. *Arizona 1860 Mortality Schedule* **[Printed Index],** compiled by Ronald Vern Jackson, et al, published by Accelerated Indexing Systems, 1984, 15 pages, FHL book 979.1 X22.

1860 Census, Pima Villages, Surname Index **[Printed Index],** compiled and published by the Mesa Family History Center, 2005, 6 pages, FHL book 979.1 X22m.

1860, 1864 & 1870. See *Federal Census – Territory of New Mexico and Territory of Arizona: Excerpts from the Decennial Federal Census, 1860, for Arizona County in the Territory of New Mexico, the Special Territorial Census of 1864 Taken in Arizona and Decennial Federal Census, 1870, for the Territory of Arizona* **[Printed Book & Online Database],** Government Printing Office, Washington, DC, 1965, 253 pages. Arranged in alphabetical order by surname. May list name, age, sex, occupation, value of property, and state or country of birth. FHL book 979.1 X2pa. This federal publication (already in alphabetical order) was digitized as *Arizona and New Mexico Territories Census, late 1800s* **[Online Database],** at Ancestry.com. See http://search.ancestry.com/search/db.aspx?dbid=3085.

1860-1993. *Arizona Obituary Card Index* **[Microfilm & Digital Capture],** from a large card index at the Mesa FamilySearch Library, Mesa, Arizona. The cards were organized in alphabetical order by the name of the deceased person. Filmed by the Genealogical Society of Utah, 1993, 39 rolls, as follows:

- Aarni, John C. - Andrews, William A, FHL film #1877927.
- Andreyka, Theodore E. - Ballard, William Henry, FHL film #1892217.
- Ballato, Thomas L. - Berridge, Sally, FHL film #1892218.
- Berringer, Ida M. - Branche, Louise, FHL film #1892219.
- Brand, Frank B. - Burnum, Fannie, FHL film #1892220.
- Buros, Arline - Casey, William, FHL film #1892221.
- Cash, Aubrey O. - Cole, William, FHL film #1892222.
- Coleman, J. J. - Crismon, William Alma, FHL film #1892400.
- Crisp, Arnold - Dennis, William, FHL film #1892401.
- Dennison, Annie Mae - Earp, Wyatt, FHL film #1892402.
- Earps - Ferguson, Willie Leon, FHL film #1892403.
- Fergusson, Erna - Fulton, William Shirley, FHL film #1892404.
- Fults, Lawrence A. - Goetz, William F., FHL film #1892476.
- Geoury, Perle - Gurley, William Donald, FHL film #1892477.
- Gurnee, Hazel - Hatton, William, FHL film #1892478.
- Hatz, Albert - Hirn Esther B., FHL film #1892479.
- Hirose, Elki - Huskey, Mark, FHL film #1892480.
- Huskinson, Della Eliza - Jones, Jerry William, FHL film #1892481.
- Jones, Jesse - Kirby, Wesley Daniel, FHL film #1892482.
- Kirchback, Myrtle Briner - Leibovitz, Minnie, FHL film #1892483.
- Leibsohn, Mayer - Lujan, Yrene, FHL film #1892787.
- Lujar, M. - Matlock, W. W., FHL film #1892788.
- Matlow, Lester - McNelly, William T., FHL film #1892789.
- McNelty, Frank H. - Monck, Fred L., FHL film #1892790.
- Moncrief, John - Nail, Pete, FHL film #1892791.
- Naile, Emma Elvira - O'Neal, W. J., FHL film #1892792.
- O'Neall, Elva - Pena, Virginia, FHL film #1892793.
- Penberthy, Ann Seely - Prescott, Thomas J., FHL film #1892794.

- Presley, Charles - Reynolds, June, FHL film #1893098.
- Reynolds, Kate - Roseveare, Joseph, FHL film #1893099.
- Rosin, Henry E. - Schneidewind, Naomi E., FHL film #1893100.
- Schneidmiller, Ann - Sims, Willis W., FHL film #1893101.
- Simser, Morris N. - Staff, Mabelle E., FHL film #1893102.
- Stafford, Annette - Swanson, William, FHL film #1893437.
- Swanty, Elva B. - Toth, Twyla, FHL film #1893438.
- Totress, Ferdinand - Vining, Edith R., FHL film #1893439.
- Vinnedge, Sadie H. - West, William D., FHL film #1893440.
- Westall, Daniel Edward - Wilson, Zula Jane, FHL film #1893441.
- Wilstach, Emma M. - Zynda, Keith R., FHL film #1893442.

To access the digital images for certain rolls, see the online FHL catalog:
www.familysearch.org/search/catalog/656141.

1860s-1980s. *Arizona Death Records: An Index Compiled from Mortuary, Cemetery, and Church Records* **[Printed Book]**, compiled and published by the Arizona State Genealogical Society, Tucson, AZ, 1976-1982, 3 vols., FHL book 979.1 V3a v.1-3.

1861-1862. *A Brief History of the Independent Arizona Territory Confederate States Battalions in Arizona Territory* **[Printed Booklet & Microfilm]**, compiled by Sherman Lee Pompey, published by Pacific Specialties, Kingsbury, CA, 1971, 7 pages, FHL book 979.1 A1 No. 3. Also on microfilm, FHL film #874332. To see if this microfilm was digitized yet, see the online FHL catalog:
www.familysearch.org/search/catalog/194833.

1861-1865. *Index to Compiled Service Records of Volunteer Union Soldiers Who Served in Organizations from the Territory of Arizona* **[Microfilm & Online Database]**, from the original records at the National Archives, Washington, DC, filmed by the National Archives, 1 roll, FHL film #881608. To access the National index, see the online FHL catalog:
www.familysearch.org/search/collection/1910717.

1861-1865. *Index to Compiled Service Records of Confederate Soldiers Who Served in Organizations from the Territory of Arizona* **[Microfilm & Digital Capture]**, from the original records at the National Archives, Washington, DC, filmed by the National Archives, series M375; 1 roll, FHL film #821837. To access the digital images, see the online FHL catalog:
www.familysearch.org/search/catalog/523155.

1861-1865. *Index to Soldiers & Sailors of the Civil War* **[Online Database]**. Both of the microfilm publications shown above are included in a searchable name index to 6.3 million Union and Confederate Civil War soldiers now available online at the National Park Service website. A search can be done by surname, first name, state, or unit. The U.S. Arizona Territory supplied 655 men to the war; the Confederate Territory of Arizona supplied 271 soldiers. See
www.nps.gov/civilwar/soldiers-and-sailors-database.htm.

1861-1865. *Compiled Service Records, Union & Confederate Soldiers* **[Online Database]**. This fully searchable database contains digitized images of the card abstracts of a soldier's Compiled Service Record, with information collected from original muster rolls, returns, rosters, payrolls, appointment books, hospital registers, prison registers and rolls, parole rolls, and inspection reports. Located at the Fold3.com site, both Union and Confederate records can be searched at one search screen. This database is the source of the Index to Soldiers and Sailors of the Civil War, online at the National Park Service and FamilySearch sites. That index found 6.3 million compiled service records. This database is the images and includes a whole new index that can be compared with the earlier S&SCW index. See www.fold3.com/category_19/.

1861-1865. *Arizona Civil War Service Records of Confederate Soldiers* **[Online Database]**, digitized and indexed at the FamilySearch.org website. The records include a jacket-envelope for each soldier, labeled with his name, his rank, and the unit in which he served. The jacket-envelope typically contains card abstracts of entries relating to the soldier as found in original muster rolls, returns, rosters, payrolls, appointment books, hospital registers, Union prison registers and rolls, parole rolls, inspection reports; and the originals of any papers relating solely to the particular soldier. For each military unit, the service records are arranged alphabetically by the soldier's surname. The Military Unit field may also display the surname range (A-G) as found on the microfilm. This collection is a part of RG 109, War Department Collection of Confederate Records and is National Archive Microfilm Publication M318. Index courtesy of Fold3. See
www.familysearch.org/search/collection/1854310.

1861-1865. *Genealogy Records of the First Arizona Volunteer Infantry Regiment* **[Printed Book]**, by Lonnie E. Underhill, published by Roan Horse Press, Pueblo, CO, 1980, 124 pages, FHL book 979.1 M2u.

1862-1912. *Some Early Arizona Marriages* **[Printed Book]**, edited by Blaine R. Bake. Includes records from counties and years with some gaps: Apache 1879-1900; Coconino 1891-1900; Gila 1881 (incomplete); Maricopa 1871-1900; Mohave 1866-1900; Navajo 1895-1900; Pima 1864-1900; Pinal 1874-1900; Santa Cruz 1899-1900; Yavapai 1864-1910; and Yuma 1864-1890. Published by the Upper Snake River Family History Center, Rexburg, ID, 1993, 191 pages, FHL book 979.1 V2s.

1864 Territorial (Federal) Census of Arizona **[Microfilm & Digital Capture]**, from the original records at the Arizona Department of Libraries, Archives & Public Records in Phoenix, Arizona. This census was provided for in the federal organic act establishing Arizona Territory, one of only three such censuses ever conducted by the federal government between decennial census years. (The other two were the 1857 Minnesota Territory and 1907 Oklahoma Territory/Indian Territory). The results of the enumeration were used in forming judicial districts and for the election of members to the territorial legislature and other offices. The census schedule questions include a person's name, age, sex, marital status, where born, how long a local resident, citizenship status, occupation, residence of all married individuals, and value of personal and real estates. Filmed by the Arizona Department of Libraries, Archives & Public Records, 1997. FHL has 1 roll, FHL film #2114989. To access the digital images, see the online FHL catalog: www.familysearch.org/search/catalog/815203.

- See also, *The 1864 Census of the Territory of Arizona* **[Printed Book]**, extracted by the Historical Records Survey, division of Women's and Professional Projects, Works Progress Administration, 1938, 210 pages, FHL book 979.1 X2p 1864. Also on microfilm, filmed by the Genealogical Society of Utah, 1973, 1 roll, FHL film #897437. (Digitized by Ancestry.com).

- See also, *Arizona Territory Census, 1864* **[Online Database]**. The Historical Records Survey project extracted by the WPA was digitized and indexed at the Ancestry.com site. See http://search.ancestry.com/search/db.aspx?dbid=3121.

1864-1882. *Arizona, Territorial Census Records* **[Online Database]**, digitized and indexed at the Ancestry.com website. Original data: Territorial Census Records. AZ History and Archives Division, Phoenix, AZ. Ancestry's description says that the census years included in this database are for 1864, 1866, 1867, 1869, 1874, and 1882. Complete censuses were taken in Arizona Territory for 1864 and 1866 only. All of the other years indicated were for county censuses. The database includes the 1867 and 1869 countywide censuses for Pina County only. A search of the database for a residence year of 1874 brought up a number of entries from Pina and Yavapai County. And, a search for a residence year of 1882 brought up entries from Cochise, Gila, Maricopa, and Pina counties. There may be more counties involved in both years. Each index record includes: Name, Gender, Marital status, Age, Birth year, Birthplace, Residence year, and Residence place. For place searching, one must use the Any Event/Location search to find an Arizona county, since all records give only "Arizona Territory, USA" as the residence place – click on the image View box to see the scanned image of the register pages, which gives the name of the district/county. This database has 85,038 records. See https://search.ancestry.com/search/db.aspx?dbid=61064.

1864-1912. See *Arizona Naturalizations, 1864-1911, 1882-1912; Index, 1864-1911* **[Microfilm & Digital Capture]**, from the original records at the National Archives, Pacific Southwest Region, Laguna Niguel, California. Volumes include indexes. The Second Judicial District court sat at Tucson, Pima County, and also at Tombstone, Cochise County. Filmed by the Genealogical Society of Utah, 1989, 4 rolls, as follows:
- Index of naturalizations, 1864-1911; Declarations of Intention, 1881-1906 FHL film #1638109.
- Record of naturalizations, 1882-1898, FHL film #1638403.
- Final record of naturalizations, 1903-1906; 1904-1906, FHL film #1638404.
- Petitions for naturalization, 1907-1910; 1909-1912, FHL film #1638405.

To access the digital images, see the online FHL catalog: www.familysearch.org/search/catalog/516961.

1864-1982. *Arizona Marriage Collection* **[Online Database]**, indexed at the Ancestry.com website. This database contains information on individuals who were married in Arizona between 1864 and 1982. It is comprised of information compiled by the Upper Snake River Family History Center and BYU-Idaho. The records compiled by this group include marriages from select counties of Arizona between 1864 and 1982. Not all counties are included and within the counties that

are included not all years may be covered. These records were extracted from marriage books located at county courthouses. No images are available for these records. In addition, more records came from the State of Arizona, including an index to marriages from Maricopa County (Phoenix area) and cover the years 1969-1978 (includes images of the index pages). Information available in this database includes: Name, Spouse's name, Marriage date, Marriage place, Residence, and Source info. This database has 265,633 records. See
https://search.ancestry.com/search/db.aspx?dbid=7847.
- See also, *Western States Marriage Index, 1809-2011* [Online Database], indexed at the Ancestry.com website. This database was published by BYU-Idaho for all states west of the Mississippi (Including Arizona). This database has 1,334,001 records, see www.ancestry.com/search/collections/70016.

1864-1995. *Arizona, Wills and Probate Records* [Online Database], digitized and indexed at the Ancestry.com website. Source: Arizona County, District and Probate Courts. Probate records include Wills, Letter of Administration, Inventories, Distributions and Accounting, Bonds, and Guardianships. Some of the case files may have 500 or more pages. Each index record includes: Name, Probate place, Inferred death place, Case number, and Item Description. A Table of Contents indicates the number of papers by category. Note: The inclusive dates in the title starts with 1803, which came from a probate in Maricopa Co dated 1893. The first courts in Arizona began in 1864. This database has 37,403 records. See
https://search.ancestry.com/search/db.aspx?dbid=9043.

1865-1949. *Arizona Marriages* [Online Database], indexed at the FamilySearch.org website. Source: FamilySearch extractions from microfilm at the Family History Library, Salt Lake City. Each index record includes: Name, Spouse's name, Event date, Event place, and FHL film number. This database has 75,010 records. See
www.familysearch.org/search/collection/1674679.

1865-1972. *Arizona, County Marriage Records* [Online Database], digitized and indexed at the Ancestry.com website. Original data: County Marriage Records. AZ History and Archives Division, Phoenix, AZ. This collection includes various types of marriage records from counties in Arizona, such as affidavits, applications, licenses, and certificates. Details may vary depending on the type of record, but typically include the following for both the bride and groom: Name, Age at marriage, Birth date, Marital status, Residence, Marriage date, and Marriage place. The document image may have more information. This database has 1,272,390 records. See
https://search.ancestry.com/search/db.aspx?dbid=60873.

1866 Arizona Territorial Census [Microfilm], from the original records at the Arizona Department of Libraries, Archives and Public Records, Phoenix, Arizona. This was the only census authorized by the territorial legislature. (The 1864 territorial census was a federal enumeration). Includes schedules for all five counties in place in 1866: Mohave, Pah-Ute, Pima, Yavapai, and Yuma counties. Filmed with An Index to the 1866 Census of Arizona Territory, by Jim Schreier. Filmed by the Genealogical Society of Utah, 1976, 1 roll, FHL film #928107. To see if this microfilm was digitized yet, see the online FHL catalog:
www.familysearch.org/search/catalog/199867.

1866. *Arizona 1866 Territorial (Census)* [Printed Index], edited by Ronald Vern Jackson, et al., published by Accelerated Indexing Systems, North Salt Lake, 1982, 64 pages, FHL book 979.1 X2j 1866.

1866-1882. See *Census for Pima County, Arizona, 1866, 1867, 1872, 1874, 1876, and 1882.* [Microfilm & Digital Capture], from the original records at the Pima County courthouse in Tucson, AZ. Each census year includes name, residence, whether head of family, number of single persons over 21, number between 10 and 21, number under 10, and remarks. 1882 lists name only. Filmed by the Genealogical Society of Utah, 1999, 1 roll, FHL film #2155710. To access the digital images, see the online FHL catalog:
www.familysearch.org/search/catalog/955205.

1866-1900. *Will Books 1 & 2, Pima County, Territory of Arizona* [Microfilm & Digital Capture], from a typescript by Mary Jessamine Bland James, ca1945, filmed by the Genealogical Society of Utah, 1970, 1 roll, FHL film #844408. To access the digital images, see the online FHL catalog:
www.familysearch.org/search/catalog/299214.

1866-1955. *Arizona, Voter Registrations* **[Online Database]**, digitized and indexed at the Ancestry.com website. Original data: Great Registers of Voters, at the AZ History and Archives Division, Phoenix, AZ. This database consists of Voting Registers compiled by county recorders for each county in Arizona, by district. They list the names of eligible voters who registered to vote within the state of Arizona. From the first Great Registers recorded in 1866, until statehood in 1912, eligible voters were males over 21 years of age. Women gained the right to vote in Arizona in 1912. Each index record includes: Name, Age, Registration date, and Residence place. The document image may have more extensive information, depending on the county and year, such as: Name, Occupation, Age, Height, Complexion, Color of eyes, Color of hair, Visible marks or scars, Country of nativity, Place of residence; Date, place, and court of naturalization; Date of voter registration, Post office address, Able to read Constitution, Able to write name, Able to mark ballot, Nature of disability, and Transferred from a different voting precinct. This database has 1,141,349 records:
https://search.ancestry.com/search/db.aspx?dbid=60875.

1866-1977. *Arizona Newspaper Archives* **[Online Database]**, digitized and indexed at the GenealogyBank.com website, historic newspapers are available for the following cities: Globe, Kingman, Nogales, Phoenix, Pinal City, Poston, Prescott, Rivers, Tombstone, Tubac, Tucson, and Yuma. See www.genealogybank.com/gbnk/newspapers/explore/USA/Arizona.

1867. *Arizona 1867 Census Index* **[Printed Index]**, by Ronald Vern Jackson, et al., published by Accelerated Indexing Systems, Salt Lake City, UT, 1983, 54 pages. This was taken from what appears to be a census of Pima County (Tucson) only. FHL book 979.1 X2j 1866.

1869. *An Index to the 1869 Census of Yavapai County, Territory of Arizona* **[Printed Index]**, by Jim and Mary Schreier, published by Arizona Territorial Censuses, 1976, 21 pages. Copy at the Arizona Department of Libraries, Archives and Public Records, Phoenix, Arizona.

1869. *Arizona 1869 Territorial Census Index* **[Printed Index]**, by Ronald Vern Jackson, et al., published by Accelerated Indexing Systems, Salt Lake City, UT, 1983, 100 pages. No territorial census was taken in Arizona in 1869. This appears to be a county census taken in Yavapai County only. FHL book 979.1 X22a.

1869-1993. *Arizona, State Court Naturalization Records* **[Online Database]**, digitized and indexed at the Ancestry.com website. Source: AZ History and Archives Division, Phoenix, AZ. Includes Petitions, Declarations, and Certificates. Each index record includes: Name, Gender, Record type, Birth date4, Birthplace, and Petition number. The document image may have more information. This database has 17,647 records. See
https://search.ancestry.com/search/db.aspx?dbid=60877.

1870. *Arizona Territory, 1870 Federal Census: Population Schedules* **[Microfilm & Digital Capture]**, from the original records at the National Archives, Washington, DC. 2nd filming by the National Archives, 1968, 1 roll, FHL film #545545 (Mohave, Pima, Yavapai, and Yuma Counties). To access the digital images, see the online FHL catalog: www.familysearch.org/search/catalog/698884.

1870. *Arizona 1870 Census Index, A–Z* **[Printed Index]**, edited by Raeone Christensen Steuart. Includes the name, age, sex, race, state or country of birthplace, county, and city of census, roll and page number. Published by Heritage Quest, 2000, 51 pages, FHL book 979.1 X22s.

1870. *Arizona 1870 Territorial Census Index* **[Printed Index]**, edited by Ronald Vern Jackson, et al, published by Accelerated Indexing Systems, Bountiful, UT, 1978, 111 pages, FHL book 97j9.1 X2j.

1870. See *Deaths in Arizona Territory, Year Ending May 31, 1870* **[Typescript]**, this is an apparent transcript of names from the 1870 Arizona Mortality Schedule. Author/publisher not noted, 1947, 25 pages, FHL book 979.1 V2d.

1870. *Arizona 1870 Mortality Schedule* **[Printed Index]**, compiled by Ronald Vern Jackson, et al, published by Accelerated Indexing Systems, Bountiful, UT, 1980, 4 pages, FHL book 979.1 X2.

1870 and 1880. See *Federal Mortality Census Schedules and Related Indexes: Arizona, 1870 (Mohave-Yuma Counties); 1880 Apache-Yuma Counties* **[Microfilm]**, from the original records in the custody of the Daughters of the American Revolution, Washington, DC. Filmed by the National Archives, Series T0655, 1962, 1 roll, FHL film #422410. To see if this microfilm was digitized yet, see the online FHL catalog: www.familysearch.org/search/catalog/783024.

1870-1910. *Northern Arizona Territorial Death and Burial Records* **[Printed Book],** compiled by Dora M. Whiteside. Information was obtained from cemetery, mortuary, hospital records, coroner's inquests, and mortality schedules. Published by the author, 1988, 30 pages, FHL book 979.1 V2w.

1870-1930. *Arizona, Maricopa County Probate Records* **[Online Database],** digitized at the FamilySearch.org website. Images of the probate case files from the Maricopa County Superior Court, Phoenix, AZ. This database has 612,719 images. Browse through the images, organized by Year and Case Number. See
www.familysearch.org/search/collection/1987651.

1870-1959. See *Death Certificates (Arizona)* **[Microfilm & Digital Capture],** from the original records at the Arizona State Archives. The certificates are arranged in chronological order within each Arizona county. Filmed by the Genealogical Society of Utah, 1998-1999, 2001, 129 rolls, beginning with FHL film #2114396. For a complete list of roll numbers and contents of each roll, see the online FHL catalog page: www.familysearch.org/search/catalog/734295.

1870-1951. *Arizona Deaths* **[Online Database],** digitized and indexed at the FamilySearch.org website. This database has published images from the FHL microfilm, and an added index to Arizona Death Certificates, arranged in chronological order within each Arizona county. This database has 265,726 records. See
www.familysearch.org/search/collection1534450.

1871-1964. *Arizona, County Marriages* **[Online Database],** digitized and indexed at the FamilySearch.org website. Source: Various courthouse records at the AZ State Archives. Includes marriage licenses and returns. Each index record includes: Name, Even type, Event date, Event place, Gender, Marital status, Spouse's name, and Spouse's gender. This database has 372,732 records. See
www.familysearch.org/search/collection/2185173.

1872, 1882 *Census, Mohave County, Arizona* **[Microfilm & Digital Capture],** from the original records at the Mohave County Courthouse in Kingman, Arizona. Arranged by first letter of surname. These censuses were conducted by Mohave County, separate from any territorial or federal censuses. Filmed by the Genealogical Society of Utah, 2002, 1 roll, FHL film #2295145 (Mohave County census, 1872, and Mohave County census, 1882). To access the digital images, see the online FHL catalog:
www.familysearch.org/search/catalog/1149150.

1872-1951. See *Marriage Records, 1872-1951; Indexes, 1877-1951, Pima County, Arizona* **[Microfilm & Digital Capture},** filmed by the Genealogical Society of Utah, 2002, 15 rolls, beginning with FHL film #2210640 (Index to Marriages, 1877-1901). To access the digital images, see the online FHL catalog: www.familysearch.org/search/catalog/994444.

"1873 Territorial Poll Tax Records, Yavapai County, Arizona Territory" [Printed Article], name list in *Family Connections*, a publication of the Family History Society of Arizona, Phoenix, AZ, Vol. 3, No. 1 (Winter 1986).

1873-1876. *Arizona Territorial Poll Tax Records, Yavapai County, Prescott, Arizona* **[Printed Book],** compiled by Dora M. Whiteside, published 1984, 40 pages. Includes surname index. From preface: "The book from which these records were extracted is located in the Sharlot Hall Museum and Archives in Prescott." FHL book 979.1 A1 no. 21, and FHL film #1698293.

1873-1927. *Teacher's Monthly Reports and School Census Marshal's Report, Yavapai County, Arizona* **[Microfilm & Digital Capture],** from the original records at the Arizona Department of Libraries, Archives and Public Records, Phoenix, Arizona. Includes name and age of student and names of parents. Filmed by the Genealogical Society of Utah, 2002, 4 rolls, beginning with FHL film #2293497 (1873-1874, 1877-1885 teacher's monthly report). To access the digital images, see the FHL catalog:
www.familysearch.org/search/catalog/1135726.

1875-1905. *Surname Index for the Arizona Sentinel (Yuma, Arizona)* **[Printed Book],** compiled and published by the Genealogical Society of Yuma, Arizona, 1997, 244 pages. Arranged in alphabetical order by surname. Lists name, description, subject, page number, and date. FHL book 979.171 B32g.

1875-1929. *Arizona, Prison Records* **[Online Database],** digitized and indexed at the Ancestry.com website. Source: AZ History and Archives Division, Phoenix, AZ. This collection includes a variety of records from Arizona state prisons, including convict registers, description records, lists of commutations, and prison diaries (conduct records). The description records often contain photographs of the prisoners. Each record can include the following: Name, Age, Nativity, Race, Religion, Physical description, Occupation, Education, Crime, Sentence date and term, Date arrived/received (at prison), County received from, Discharge date, and Prison number. This database has 9,660 records. See https://search.ancestry.com/search/db.aspx?dbid=61065.

1875-1932 Official Electors Registers, Yavapai County, Arizona **[Microfilm & Digital Capture],** from the original records at the Yavapai County Recorder's Office, Prescott, Arizona. Records sometimes titled "Great Register" or "Precinct Register." Filmed by the Genealogical Society of Utah, 1995, 13 rolls, as follows:
- 1875, 1884, 1881, 1875-1899 election registers, FHL film #1299283.
- 1916 election register, FHL film #1299282.
- 1920 election register, FHL film #1299279.
- 1920 & 1922 election register (Ashfork to Date Creek), FHL film #1299280.
- 1922 election register, FHL film #1299281.
- 1900-1902, 1904-1908, 1910-1913 great registers, FHL film #1299284.
- 1914, 1916, 1918 great registers, FHL film #1299285.
- 1924, 1926 election registers, FHL film #1299286.
- 1920, 1922, 1924 election registers, FHL film #1299287.
- 1924 election register, FHL film #1299288.
- 1930, 1932, 1876, 1882, 1884, 1886, 1886 supplement, 1890, 1892, 1894, 1896, 1898, 1900, 1902, 1904, 1906 great registers, FHL film #1299289.
- 1924 election register, FHL film #1299290.
- 1930, 1932 register, FHL film #2028173.

To access the digital images, see the online FHL catalog: www.familysearch.org/search/catalog/274965.

1876. *Arizona Territorial Great Register of 1876, Yavapai County, Arizona* **[Printed Book],** by Dora M. Whiteside, published 1987, 28 pages. From Intro: "In 1876 Yavapai County included what was later to be Coconino, Apache, Navajo, a portion of the northern parts of Gila, Maricopa, Graham, and Greenlee Counties." FHL book 979.1 A1 no. 68, and FHL film #2055163.

1876-1881 Great Registers for Pima County, Arizona **[Microfilm & Digital Capture],** from the original records at the Arizona Department of Libraries, Archives and Public Records in Phoenix, Arizona. Filmed by State Library and Archives, 1984, 1 FHL roll, FHL film #1405047. To access the digital images, see the online FHL catalog: www.familysearch.org/search/catalog/366875.

1876-1899 Tax Rolls and Property Sold for Taxes, Mohave County, Arizona **[Microfilm & Digital Capture],** from the original records located in the Mohave County Courthouse in Kingman, Arizona. Lists name, description of property, value, amount of tax and if paid. Filmed by the Genealogical Society of Utah, 2002, 3 rolls, as follows:
- 1876-1886 tax assessment rolls, FHL film #2295146.
- 1887-1895 tax assessment rolls; 1876-1880 delinquent tax rolls, FHL film #2295358.
- 1888-1895 delinquent tax rolls; 1881-1899 record of property sold, delinquent taxes, FHL film #2295147.

To access the digital images, see the online FHL catalog: www.familysearch.org/search/catalog/960916.

1876-1920 Great Registers, Pinal County, Arizona **[Microfilm & Digital Capture],** from the original records in the Pinal County Courthouse in Florence, Arizona. Lists name, age, country of nativity, local residence, date, place and court of naturalization, date of registration to vote and remarks. Filmed by the Genealogical Society of Utah, 2003, 3 rolls, as follows:
- 1876-1894 great registers, FHL film #2321650.
- 1882-1894, 1890, 1892, 1894, 1896-1911, 1912, 1916 great registers, FHL film #2321651.
- 1916 duplicate, 1918, 1920 great registers, FHL film #2321652.

To access the digital images, see the online FHL catalog: www.familysearch.org/search/catalog/1151413.

1876-1920 Great Registers of Mohave County, Arizona **[Microfilm & Digital Capture],** from the original records at the Mohave County Courthouse in Kingman, Arizona. Some pages are dark and may be hard to read. Lists name, age, country or state of birth, local residence, date, and place of naturalization if listed, and date of registration. Filmed by the Genealogical Society of Utah, 2002, 4 rolls, as follows:
- 1876-1890 great registers, FHL film #2295022.
- 1892-1914 great registers, FHL film #2295141.
- 1914 great registers, cont.: 1918 great registers, precincts A-F, FHL film #2295142.
- 1918 great registers, cont., precincts F-Z; 1920 great registers, FHL film #2295143.

To access the digital images, see the online FHL catalog: www.familysearch.org/search/catalog/1148386.

1876-1932. *Official Registers of Electors for Maricopa County* **[Microfilm & Digital Capture],** from the original records at the Department of Libraries, Archives and Public Records, Phoenix, Arizona. Usually filed chronologically, arranged somewhat alphabetically in registration years. Some rolls include missed records or retakes in an appendix at the end. Filmed by the State Library & Archives, 1984, 33 FHL rolls: Great Registers, Maricopa County, Arizona:
- 1876-1890, 1894-1895, FHL film #1405007.
- 1894-1895, 1904-1906, FHL film #1405008.
- 1904-1906 (cont.), 1906-1908, 1902, 1909-1911 Electors: 1910-1911, 1912 (A-B), FHL film #1405009.
- 1912-1913 (C-Z), FHL film #1405010.
- 1913, 1914, FHL film #1405011.
- 1914, FHL film #1405012.
- 1914, FHL film #1405013.
- 1914, 1916, FHL film #1405014.
- 1916, FHL film #1405015.
- 1916, 1918, FHL film #1405016.
- 1918, FHL film #1405017.
- 1918, FHL film #1405018.
- 1918, FHL film #1405019.
- 1918, 1920, FHL film #1405020.
- 1920, FHL film #1405021.
- 1920, FHL film #1405022.
- 1920, FHL film #1405023.
- 1920, 1922, FHL film #1405024.
- 1922, FHL film #1405025.
- 1922, FHL film #1405026.
- 1922, FHL film #1405027.
- 1922, 1924, FHL film #1405028.
- 1924, FHL film #1405029.
- 1924, FHL film #1405030.
- 1924, FHL film #1405031.
- 1924, FHL film #1405032.
- 1924, 1926, FHL film #1405033.
- 1926, FHL film #1405034.
- 1926, FHL film #1405035.
- 1926, FHL film #1405036.
- 1926, FHL film #1405037.
- 1926, 1928, 1930, FHL film #1405038.
- 1930, 1932, FHL film #1405039.

To access the digital images, see the online FHL catalog: **www.familysearch.org/search/catalog/319562**.

1878-1895 *Tax Assessment and Delinquent Tax Rolls, Yavapai County, Arizona* **[Microfilm & Digital Capture],** from the original records at the Arizona Department of Libraries, Archives and Public Records, Phoenix, Arizona. A couple of volumes include indexes. Filmed by the Genealogical Society of Utah, 2002, 7 rolls, as follows:
- 1878-1881 tax rolls, A-K, FHL #2293306.
- 1881 tax rolls, K-Z; 1885, A-S, FHL film #2293307.
- 1885 tax, S-Z; 1889 tax rolls, A-P, FHL film #2293308.
- 1889 tax rolls, P-Z; 1893 tax rolls, A-M, FHL film #2293309.
- 1893 tax rolls, M-Z; 1895 tax rolls; 1878-1881 delinquent tax rolls, FHL film #2293495.
- 1882-1891 delinquent tax rolls, FHL film #2293496.
- 1892-1895 delinquent tax rolls, FHL film #2293497.

To access the digital images, see the online FHL catalog: **www.familysearch.org/search/catalog/1135371**.

1879-1894 *Assessment Rolls; 1898 Assessment and Tax Roll, Pima County, Arizona* **[Microfilm & Digital Capture],** from the original records at the Arizona Department of Libraries, Archives and Public Records in Phoenix, Arizona. Includes name of taxpayer, description of property, value of land and improvements and personal property, poll tax, and total volume. The assessment roll information is repeated in the tax roll books with the indication whether the tax has been paid or not paid. The county sheriff was also the county assessor. Some records are light and may be hard to read. Filmed by the Genealogical Society of Utah, 1999, 5 rolls, as follows:
- 1879-1883 assessment and tax rolls, A-S, FHL film #2148738.
- 1883 assessment and tax rolls, T-Z, FHL film #2148739.
- 1886-1890 assessment and tax rolls, FHL film #2148740.
- 1890-1892 assessment rolls, FHL film #2171017.
- 1893-1894 assessment rolls, and 1898 assessment and tax roll of the city of Tucson, FHL film #2171018.

To access the digital images, see the online FHL catalog: **www.familysearch.org/search/catalog/839745**.

1880. *Arizona, 1880 Federal Census: Soundex and Population Schedules* **[Microfilm & Digital Capture],** from the originals at the National Archives, Washington, DC (in 1970), now located at the DAR Library, Washington, DC. Filmed by the National Archives, 1970, 4 rolls, as follows:
- Soundex: A000 thru G560, FHL film #445404.
- Soundex: G610 thru Institutions, FHL film #44405.
- Population schedules: Apache, Maricopa, Mohave, Pima, and Pinal Co., FHL film 1254037 (Digitized).
- Population schedules: Pinal Co, Yavapai, and Yuma Co., FHL film 1254037 (Digitized).

To access the digital images, see the online FHL catalog: **www.familysearch.org/search/catalog/670360**.
- See also, *10th Census, 1880; Arizona Territory* **[Microfilm],** an alphabetical index compiled by the Southern Arizona Genealogical Society, Filmed by the

National Archives, Central Plains Region, 4 rolls, as follows:
- Index, A-F, FHL film #882917. Another filming: FHL film #882932. Another filming: FHL film #132378.
- Index, G-M, FHL film #882918. Another filming: FHL film #882933. Another filming: FHL film #1323379.
- Index, N-S, FHL film #882919. Another filming: FHL film #882934. Another filming: FHL film #1323380.
- Index, T-Z, FHL film #882920. Another filming: FHL film #882935. Another filming: FHL film #1323381.

To see if this microfilm was digitized yet, see the FHL catalog: www.familysearch.org/search/catalog/304076.
- See also, *Arizona 1880 Census Index* [Printed Index], edited by Ronald Vern Jackson, published by Accelerated Indexing Systems, Bountiful, UT, 1980, 507 pages, FHL book 979.1 X2.

1880-1935. *Arizona, Birth Records* [Online Database], indexed at the Ancestry.com website. The Arizona Department of Health Services compiled this collection of Arizona birth records. When available, each record contains the full name of the individual, the full names of their parents, birth date, death date, county of birth, as well as an image of the original birth certificate. This database has 528,126 records. See https://search.ancestry.com/search/db.aspx?dbid=8703.

1881. See *Directory of the City of Tucson for the Year 1881: Containing a Comprehensive List of Inhabitants With Their Occupations and Places of Residence* [Microfilm & Digital Capture], from the original directory compiled by G. W. Barter, published by H. S. Crocker & Co., San Francisco, 1881, 114 pages. Filmed by Xerox University Microfilms, Ann Arbor, MI, ca1975. FHL has 1 roll, FHL film #1299604. To access the digital images, see the FHL catalog: www.familysearch.org/search/catalog/214373.

1881, 1888-1902 *Tax Assessment Records, Yuma County, Arizona Territory* [Microfilm & Digital Capture], from the original records located at the Arizona Department of libraries, Archives and Public Records, Phoenix, Arizona. Includes name of taxpayer, description of property, value of property and personal property, total value, year, and remarks. Filmed by the Genealogical Society of Utah, 2002, 1 roll, FHL film #2293272. To access the digital images, see the FHL catalog: www.familysearch.org/search/catalog/1134744.

1881-1900 *Assessment and Tax Rolls, Graham County, Arizona* [Microfilm & Digital Capture], from the original records at the Graham County Courthouse in Safford, Arizona. May include name of taxpayer, description of property, and total tax amount. Filmed by the Genealogical Society of Utah, 1999, 3 rolls, as follows:
- 1881-1891 assessment & tax rolls, FHL film #2133939.
- 1892-1898 assessment and tax rolls, FHL film #2133940.
- 1899-1900 assessment and tax rolls, FHL film #2134263.

To access the digital images, see the online FHL catalog: www.familysearch.org/search/catalog/825662.

1881-1895 *Duplicate and Original Assessment and Delinquent Tax Records, Gila County, Arizona* [Microfilm & Digital Capture], from the original records at the Arizona Department of Libraries, Archives & Public Records located in Phoenix, Arizona. Includes name of taxpayer, description of property, value of personal and real property, amount of tax, total value, and remarks. Filmed by the Genealogical Society of Utah, 2002, 3 rolls, as follows:
- 1881-1890 duplicate and original assessment rolls, (A-K), FHL film #2293846.
- 1890 duplicate and original assessment rolls (cont., K-Z); 1895 duplicate and original assessment rolls; 1887-1892 tax collector's record of property sold for delinquent taxes, FHL film #2293847.
- 1893-1895 tax collector's record of property sold for delinquent taxes, FHL film #2293848.

To access the digital images, see the online FHL catalog: www.familysearch.org/search/catalog/1135660.

1881-1910 & 1912-1926 *Great Registers, and 1922-1932 Index to Great Registers, Cochise County, Arizona* [Microfilm & Digital Capture], from the originals and photocopy of typescript at the Cochise County Courthouse in Bisbee, Arizona. The Great Register for 1898 is missing and was not filmed. Lists name, age, country of nativity, occupation, local residence, date and court of naturalization, date of voter registration, date of cancellation, if any; height, weight, color of eyes and hair, race, and political party. Some precincts are not listed in alphabetical order. Filmed by the Genealogical Society of Utah, 1997, 18 rolls, as follows:
- 1881, 1882, 1884, 1886, 1888, 1890, 1892, 1894, 1896, 1900, 1902 great registers, FHL film #2079898.
- 1902, 1904, 1906, 1908, 1909, 1910 great registers, FHL film #2079899.
- 1910, 1912 great registers, FHL film #2079900.
- 1913 supplement & 1914 ledger, FHL film #2080412.
- 1914 county register, FHL film #2080413.
- 1915 county registers, FHL film #2080414.

- 1916 & 1918 great registers, FHL film #2080415.
- 1918 great registers, FHL film #2080416.
- 1918 great register, Douglas, FHL film #2080417.
- 1920 great register, FHL film #2080418.
- 1920 & 1922 great registers, FHL film #2080450.
- 1922 great register, FHL film #2080451.
- 1922 & 1924 great registers, FHL film #2080452.
- 1924 & 1926 great registers, FHL film #2080453.
- 1926 great register, FHL film #2080454.
- 1926 great register; 1922 & 1924 Index to great registers, FHL film #2080455.
- 1924, 1926, 1928, 1930 Index to great registers, FHL #2080456.

To access the digital images, see the online FHL catalog: **www.familysearch.org/search/catalog/680042**.

1881-1920 Great Registers and Census of Gila County, Arizona [Microfilm & Digital Capture], from the original records at the Arizona Department of Libraries, Archives & Public Records located in Phoenix, Arizona. Includes the Gila County census of 1882, the great register for 1888 which also is listed as the jury list for 1890, and the great registers for 1894, 1896, 1898, 1900, 1902, 1904, 1906, 1908, and 1910. Lists name of voter, age, country of birth, local city of residence, date-place-court of naturalization, and date of registration to vote. Filmed by the Genealogical Society of Utah, 1998, 2002, 6 rolls, as follows:
- 1881, 1888, 1894-1910 great registers, 1882 census, 1890 jury list, FHL film #2321349.
- 1890, 1892, 1894, 1896, 1898, 1900, 1902, 1904, 1905, 1906, 1908, 1910, 1912 great registers, FHL film #2321350.
- 1912, 1914, 1916 county registers, FHL film #2321404.
- 1916, 1918 general registers, FHL film #2321405.
- 1918, 1920 general registers, FHL film #2321406.
- 1920 register of electors, FHL #2321407.

To access the digital images, see the online FHL catalog: **www.familysearch.org/search/catalog/815322**.

1881-1948. *Arizona, Birth Records* **[Online Database],** digitized and indexed at the Ancestry.com website. Original data: County Birth Records. AZ History and Archives Division, Phoenix, AZ. Each index record includes: Name, Gender, Birth date, Birthplace, and Name of father. The document image may have more information. This database has 68,285 records. See
https://search.ancestry.com/search/db.aspx?dbid=60886.

1881-1971. *Arizona, County Coroner and Death Records* **[Online Database],** indexed at the Ancestry.com website. Source: AZ History & Archives, Phoenix, AZ. This collection includes a variety of death and coroner's records from counties in Arizona. Details will vary depending on the type of record, but can include the following: Date of death, Place of death, Age at the time of death, Cause of death, Occupation, Dates and locations of obituaries, Date and place of birth, Location of interment, Marital status, and parents' names and birthplaces. This database has 67,153 records. See
https://search.ancestry.com/search/db.aspx?dbid=60874.

1882-1895 Tax Assessment Rolls, Apache County, Arizona [Microfilm & Digital Capture], from the original records located at the Arizona Department of Libraries, Archives & Public Records, Phoenix, Arizona. Arranged in alphabetical order by surname Includes name of taxpayer, description of property, value of property, amount of tax, and when paid. Filmed by the Genealogical Society of Utah, 2002, 3 rolls, as follows:
- 1882-1889 tax assessment rolls, A-C, FHL film #2293303.
- 1889 tax assessment rolls, C-Z; 1894 tax assessment rolls, A-U, FHL film #2293304.
- 1894 tax assessment rolls, U-Z; 1895 tax assessment rolls, FHL film #2293305.

To access the digital images, see the online FHL catalog: **www.familysearch.org/search/catalog/1135355**.

1882-1912. *Naturalizations (Federal)* **[Microfilm & Digital Capture],** from the original records at the National Archives, Pacific Southwest Region, Laguna Niguel, CA. Volumes include indexes. Naturalization records from the Third Judicial District Court of Phoenix, AZ, including declarations of intentions, records of naturalizations, final record of naturalization, and petitions. Filmed by the Genealogical Society of Utah, 1989, 4 rolls, as follows:
- Declarations of Intention, 1882-1906, FHL film #1638109.
- Record of Naturalizations, 1899-1903, FHL film #1638403.
- Final Record of Naturalizations, 1903-1906; Petitions for Naturalizations, 1906-1911, FHL film #1638404.
- Petitions for Naturalizations, 1910-1912, FHL film #1638405.

To access the digital images, see the online FHL catalog: **www.familysearch.org/search/catalog/516961**.

1882-1926 Great Registers for Pima County, Arizona [Microfilm & Digital Capture], from the original records at the Arizona Department of Libraries, Archives and Public Records in Phoenix, Arizona. May include name, age, country of birth, precinct, occupation, political party, naturalization information,

address, height and weight, signature, and date of registration. Filmed by the Genealogical Society of Utah, 1999, 2002, 9 rolls, as follows:
- 1882-1901 great register, FHL film #2169803.
- 1901 great register, FHL film #2148436.
- 1912 great register, 1914 great register, FHL film #2148437.
- 1914 great register, 1920 (Tucson precincts 1-5), FHL film #2148438.
- 1916 general register, Pima County, FHL film #2293854.
- 1920 great register, Tucson precincts 6-10; 1920 Outside precincts: Ajo 1, Ajo 2, Arivaca, Condon, Continental, Cottonwood, Ft. Lowell, Greaterville, Helvetia, Indian Oasis, Langhorn, Olive Camp, Pantano, Quijotoa, Reddington, Sahuarita, San Xavier, Silverbell, Tanque Verde, Twin Buttes, Vail; 1922 great register, Tucson, precincts 1-5; 1922 Outside precincts: Pastime Park, Ajo, Continental, Langhorn, FHL film #2148439.
- 1922 outside precincts: Fort Lowell, Greaterville, Twin, Buttes, Silverbell, Pantano, Cottonwood Helvetia, Arivaca, Sahuarita, Olive Camp, San Xavier, Condon, Tanque Verde, Reddington, Quijotoa, Indian Oasis, Vail, FHL film #2148628.
- 1924 great register, Tucson precincts 1-11, FHL film #2148628
- 1924 great register, outside precincts; 1926 great register, Tucson precincts, 1-6; FHL film #2148629.
- 1926 great register, outside precincts; 1926 great register, Tucson precincts 7-11, FHL film #148630.

To access the digital images, see the online FHL catalog: **www.familysearch.org/search/catalog/839595**.

***1882-1920 Great Registers and 1882 Census of Graham County, Arizona* [Microfilm & Digital Capture],** from the original records at the Arizona Department of Libraries, Archives & Public Records located in Phoenix, Arizona, and at the Graham County Recorder's Office in Safford, Arizona. Lists information for the 1882 census. May list the following information on the great register: name, age, place of birth, and residence, date and place of naturalization, and date of registration; and lists statistics of Graham County for acres of land cultivated, acres of wheat-barley-corn-or potatoes raised, number of horses, mules, cattle, calves, hogs, and sheep. Filmed by the Arizona Dept. of Libraries, Archives & Public Records, 1998-1999, and by the Genealogical Society of Utah, 6 rolls, as follows:
- 1882 great register, FHL film #2111296.
- 1882-1888, 1890-1898 great registers, FHL film #2134224.
- 1892-1898, 1890-1898, 1904 great registers, FHL film #2134264.
- 1882 census, 1894, 1902, 1906-1908, 1910, 1912, 1914 great registers, FHL film #2134422.
- 1916, 1918 general registers, FHL film #2134265.
- 1920 great register, FHL film #2134266.

To access the digital images, see the online FHL catalog: **www.familysearch.org/search/catalog/815257**.

***1882-1920 Great Registers, Apache County, Arizona* [Microfilm & Digital Capture],** from the original records at the Apache County Courthouse in St. Johns, Arizona. Each voter register lists name, place of birth, date of naturalization, and date of registration. Filmed by the Genealogical Society of Utah, 2002, 3 rolls, as follows:
- 1882-1884 great register, FHL film #2297313.
- 1884 great register; 1916 great register, Adamana precinct – Vernon precinct, A-Mc, FHL film #2297314.
- 1916 great register, Vernon precinct, Mc-Z thru Concho precinct; 1920 great register; 1888-1898 great registers, duplicate typed and published copy, FHL film #2320534.

To access the digital images, see the online FHL catalog: **www.familysearch.org/search/catalog/1141303**.

"1882 Delinquent Tax List, Maricopa County, Arizona Territory" [Printed Article], name list in *Desert Tracker*, a publication of the West Valley Genealogical Society, Sun City, AZ, Vol. 14, No. 2 (Summer 1993).

***1883 Pensioners List (Arizona Territory)* [Online Database],** extracted from List of Pensioners on the Roll (US Pension Bureau, 1883). See **www.kinyon.com/military/pensionlist1883/arizona/arizcounties.htm**.

1884-1909. *Birth and Death Records of Tucson, Pima County, Arizona* **[Microfilm & Digital Capture],** from the original records at the Arizona State Archives in Phoenix, AZ. Includes birth records, 1899-1900 and death records, 1884-1909. Filmed by the Genealogical Society of Utah, 1998, 1 roll, FHL film #2132125. To access the digital images, see the online FHL catalog: **www.familysearch.org/search/catalog/821790**.

1884-1917. *Register of Marriages of the City of Tucson, Arizona* **[Microfilm & Digital Capture],** from the original records, filmed by the Genealogical Society of Utah, 2000, 1 roll, FHL film #2210640. To access the digital images, see the online FHL catalog: **www.familysearch.org/search/catalog/994445**.

1884-1910. *Records of Yuma Territorial Prison* **[Microfilm & Digital Capture],** from the original records, filmed by Reproductions, Inc., Tucson, AZ, 1967, 3 rolls, beginning with FHL film #956170. To access the digital images, see the online FHL catalog: www.familysearch.org/search/catalog/82620.

1884-2007. *Bisbee, Arizona, Evergreen Cemetery Index* **[Online Database],** indexed at the Ancestry.com website. Original data: The Evergreen Cemetery Project. Bisbee Mining & Historical Museum. Each index record includes: Name, Burial place, Cemetery, and a link to the Bisbee Museum website for more searching options. This database has 13,821 records. See
https://search.ancestry.com/search/db.aspx?dbid=70728.

1885-1960. *Arizona, Maricopa, Mesa City Cemetery Records* **[Online Database],** digitized and indexed at the FamilySearch.org website. Includes images of cemetery and other records from the Mesa City Cemetery. The collection includes permits for graves, tax roll, block book, sexton ledgers, burial, and funeral records. This database has 12,192 records. See
https://familysearch.org/search/collection/1929533.

1885-1962. *Arizona Statewide Births (1885-1937) and Arizona Statewide Deaths (1861-1962)* **[Online Database],** a searchable database sponsored by the Arizona Department of Health Services. See http://genealogy.az.gov.

1887-1900s. *Pinal County Cemeteries, Newspapers, Obituaries, Tombstone Photos, Vitals, and More* **[Online Database],** indexed at the AZGenWeb site. See http://usgwarchives.net/az/pinal/pinal.html.

1887-1912. *Birth and Death Records for Various Arizona Counties* **[Microfilm & Digital Capture],** from original records at the Arizona State Archives, Phoenix, AZ. Filmed by the Genealogical Society of Utah, 1998, 1 roll, FHL film #2132129. To access the digital images, see the online FHL catalog: www.familysearch.org/search/catalog/822039.

1887-1960. *Arizona, Death Records* **[Online Database],** digitized and indexed at the Ancestry.com website. The Arizona Department of Health Services compiled this collection of Arizona death records. When available, each record contains the full name of the individual, the full names of their parents, birth date, death date, county of death, as well as an image of the original death certificate. This database has 681,344 records. See
https://search.ancestry.com/search/db.aspx?dbid=8704.

1888-1908. *Arizona, Select Marriages* **[Online Database],** indexed at the FamilySearch.org website. Source: FamilySearch extractions from microfilm at the FHL in Salt Lake City. Each index record includes: Name, Gender, Age, Birth date, Marriage date, Marriage place, Father, Mother, Spouse, and FHL film number. This database has 152,897 See
https://search.ancestry.com/search/db.aspx?dbid=60236.

1889-1909. *Register of Births and Deaths for Phoenix, Maricopa County, Arizona; and Pima County, Arizona* **[Microfilm & Digital Capture],** from the original records at the Arizona State Archives, Phoenix, AZ Filmed by the Genealogical Society of Utah, 1998, 2 rolls, as follows:
- Register of deaths, Pima Co, v.1, 1903-30 May 1909; Register of births, Pima Co. v.1, 1903-1909; Register of births, Phoenix, Maricopa Co, AZ, 1903-1907; Register of births, Pima Co, 1889, 1897, 1908, FHL film #2132124.
- Certificates of birth, Pima Co, 1909, FHL film #2132125.

To access the digital images, see the online FHL catalog: www.familysearch.org/search/catalog/821784.

"1890 Great Register Census, Gila County, Arizona Territory" **[Printed Article],** in *Gila Heritage,* a publication of the Northern Gila County Genealogical Society, Payson, AZ, Vol. 14, No. 4 (Nov 1996).

1890 Territorial Great Register, Cochise County, Arizona, A to E, **[Online Database].** The list gives the Surname, Given name, Age, Nativity, Occupation, Local Address, Naturalized Date and Place, and Voter Registration date. Originally indexed at the MyCochise website.
- For an archived database, see
https://web.archive.org/web/20140916103148/www.mycochise.com/1890greatrega2e.php.
- For F to K, see
https://web.archive.org/web/20140914194120/www.mycochise.com/1890greatregf2k.php.
- For L to R, see
https://web.archive.org/web/20140914194125/www.mycochise.com/1890greatregl2r.php.
- 1890 Great Register, Cochise Co AZ. For S to Z, see
https://web.archive.org/web/20140914202132/www.mycochise.com/1890greatregs2z.php.

1890 Great Register of Mohave County, Arizona Territory **[Digital Capture],** from the original publ. 1890, Mohave Co Miner Print, Kingman, AZ, 14 pages. To access the digital images, see the online FHL catalog: www.familysearch.org/search/catalog/2215883.

1892 City Directory of Phoenix, Mesa, and Tempe, Arizona **[Online Database],** scanned images indexed by first letter of surname. Originally indexed for alpha groups at the DistantCousin.com website. For an archived database, see https://web.archive.org/web/20140704231526/http://distantcousin.com/Directories/AZ/Phoenix/1892.

1892-1960. See *Arizona Cities in U.S. City Directories, 1822-1995* **[Online Database],** digitized and indexed at the Ancestry.com website. This collection is one of the largest single databases on the Internet, with a total of 1.56 billion names, all indexed from full scanned images of the city directory book pages. All states are represented except Alaska and included are directories for the following cities in Arizona: **Bisbee,** 1914-1959; **Chandler,** 1929; **Douglas,** 1915-1959; **Globe,** 1916-1928; **Phoenix,** 1892-1960; **Prescott,** 1916-1929; **Safford,** 1973; **Scottsdale,** 1956, 1958; and **Tucson,** 1881, 1897-1960). Use Ancestry's Browse this Collection feature to choose a state, choose a city, and choose a directory year available for that city. See https://search.ancestry.com/search/db.aspx?dbid=2469.

1893-1915. See *Record of Deaths, Phoenix, Arizona, 1893-1915* **[Microfilm & Digital Capture],** from the original records at the Arizona State Archives in Phoenix, AZ. Includes records of deaths and statistics of how many deaths per illness or disease. Filmed by the Genealogical Society of Utah, 1998, 1 roll FHL film #2132123. To access the digital images, see the FHL catalog: www.familysearch.org/search/catalog/821507.

1894-1911 Great Registers, Coconino County, Arizona **[Microfilm & Digital Capture],** from the original records at the Arizona Department of Libraries, Archives & Public Records, Phoenix, Arizona. Includes Great Registers for 1894, 1902, 1906, 1908, 1910, and 1911 supplement. Lists name, age, country of birth, place of residence, naturalized (date, place, court), date of registration and number, and voter number. Filmed by the Arizona Dept. of Libraries, Archives & Public Records, 1998. FHL has 1 roll, FHL film #2111296. To access the digital images, see the online FHL catalog: www.familysearch.org/search/catalog/815236.

1895-1932 Great Registers and Registration of Electors, Navajo County, Arizona **[Microfilm & Digital Capture],** from the original manuscripts at the Arizona Department of Libraries, Archives & Public Records, Phoenix, Arizona. Filmed by the state archives, 1984, 8 FHL rolls, as follows:
- 1895-1898 great registers, FHL film #1405040.
- 1900-1904, 1906, 1908, 1910, 1912-1914, 1916 great registers, FHL film #1405041.
- 1918, 1920, registration of electors, FHL film #1405042.
- 1906-1911 registers & supplemental records, FHL film #1405043.
- 1922, 1924 registers, FHL film #1405044.
- 1924, 1926, 1928, 1930, FHL film #1405045.
- 1932 registers, FHL film #1405046.

To access the digital images, see the online FHL catalog: www.familysearch.org/search/catalog/42545.

1896. See *A Historical and Biographical Record of the Territory of Arizona* **[Printed Book & Digital Version],** compiled and published by McFarland & Poole, Chicago, IL, 1896, 612 pages, FHL book 979.1 H2. Also on microfilm, FHL film #1033949. To access the digital version, see the online FHL catalog: www.familysearch.org/search/catalog/124387.

- See also, *A Historical and Biographical Record of the Territory of Arizona* **[Online Database],** digitized and OCR indexed at the Ancestry.com site. See https://search.ancestry.com/search/db.aspx?dbid=27509.

1896-1902. *Tax Sale Certificate, Navajo County, Arizona* **[Microfilm & Digital Capture],** from the original records at the Navajo County Courthouse in Holbrook, Arizona. Lists description of property, date of sale, name of person who owed assessed tax, name of purchaser, assessed value, amount paid, date to which taxes have been paid, and remarks. Filmed by the Genealogical Society of Utah, 2002, 1 roll, FHL film #2296955 (Tax sale certificates, 1896-1902). To access the digital images, see the online FHL catalog: www.familysearch.org/search/catalog/1150314.

1899-1935 City Directories, Tucson, Arizona **[Microfilm],** from the originals published by various publishers. Filmed by Research Publications, Woodbridge, CT, 1980-1984. FHL has 5 rolls, containing directories for 1899-1901, 1902, 1912, 1913, 1914, 1917-1922, 1924, 1926-1935. See the FHL catalog: www.familysearch.org/search/catalog/619064.

1900. *Arizona, 1900 Federal Census: Soundex and Population Schedules* **[Microfilm & Digital Capture],** from the original records at the National Archives, Washington, DC, filmed by the National Archives, ca1970, 26 rolls (Soundex and schedules), beginning with FHL film #1242047 (Soundex Codes A00-A534); followed by FHL film #1240045 (1900 population schedules, Apache, Cochise, Coconino, Gila, Graham and Maricopa Counties). To access the digital images, see the online FHL catalog: www.familysearch.org/search/catalog/647003.

1900-1920 Great Registers, Santa Cruz County, Arizona **[Microfilm & Digital Capture],** from the original records at the Arizona Department of Libraries, Archives & Public Records, Phoenix, Arizona. Includes name, age, country of birth, local residence, date, place and court of naturalization, and date of registration to vote. Beginning in 1912 at statehood, the occupation and signature of elector was added. Filmed by the Genealogical Society of Utah, 2002, 3 rolls, as follows:
- 1900-1914 great registers, FHL film #2317753.
- 1914 great registers (cont'd); 1918 great register, FHL film #2317754.
- 1920 great registers, FHL film #2317755.

To access the digital images, see the online FHL catalog: **www.familysearch.org/search/catalog/1122510.**

1902-1918 Great Registers of Yuma County, Arizona **[Microfilm & Digital Capture],** from the original records located at the Arizona Department of Libraries, Archives and Public Records, Phoenix, Arizona. Lists name, age, country of birth, local residence, date, place, and court of naturalization, and date of registration. After statehood in 1912, the occupation and signature were added. Filmed by the Genealogical Society of Utah, 2002, 3 rolls, as follows:
- 1902-1914 great registers, FHL film #2318335.
- 1914 & 1918 great registers, FHL film #2318336.
- 1918 great registers, FHL film #2318337.

To access the digital images, see the online FHL catalog: **www.familysearch.org/search/catalog/1122550.**

1903-1910. *Texas and Arizona Arrivals* **[Online Database],** indexed at the FamilySearch.org website. Source: National Archives microfilm A3365. This collection contains Lists of Aliens Arriving at Brownsville, Del Rio, Eagle Pass, El Paso, Laredo, Presidio, Rio Grande City and Roma, Texas, May 1903-June 1909, and at Aros Ranch, Douglas, Lochiel, Naco and Nogales, Arizona, July 1906-December 1910. The records are arranged in order by the port city then by date and usually contain the date of arrival, full name, age, gender, marital status, occupation, ability to read and write, nationality, race, town and country of last residence, birthplace, and final destination. Other forms might also include a physical description of the person. This database has 2,923 records. See www.familysearch.org/search/collection/2423050.

1903-1912. See *Naturalizations (Federal)* **[Microfilm & Digital Capture],** from original records of the US District Court, 4th Judicial District, Prescott, AZ, now located at the National Archives, Pacific Southwest Region, Laguna Niguel, CA. Filmed by the Genealogical Society of Utah, 1989, 2 rolls, FHL film #1638404 and #1638405. To access the digital images, see the online FHL catalog: To access the digital images, see the online FHL catalog: www.familysearch.org/search/catalog/518076.

1903-1931. *Naturalizations (Federal)* **[Microfilm & Digital Capture],** from original records of the US District Court, Tucson, AZ, now located at the National Archives, Pacific Southwest Region, Laguna Niguel, CA. Filmed by the Genealogical Society of Utah, 1989, 4 rolls, FHL film #1638406-1638409. To access the digital images, see the online FHL catalog: www.familysearch.org/search/catalog/518129.

1903-1935 City Directories, Phoenix & Maricopa County, Arizona **[Microfilm],** from the originals published by various publishers. Includes directories for 1903, 1912, 1913, 1915, 1916-1920, 1923, 1925, 1928-1931, 1932, & 1935. Filmed by Research Publications, Woodbridge, CT, 1984, 6 FHL rolls, see the FHL catalog: www.familysearch.org/search/catalog/620794.

1904 Great Register of Santa Cruz County, Arizona, Territory of Arizona **[Microfilm & Digital Version],** published by authority; made and done pursuant to the Revised Statutes of Arizona, from the original great register of Santa Cruz County, Territory of Arizona, 1904, 11 pages. Filmed by the Genealogical Society of Utah, 1994, 1 roll, FHL film #1750769. To access the digital version, see the online FHL catalog: www.familysearch.org/search/catalog/697250.

1904-1906. *Naturalizations (Federal)* **[Microfilm & Digital Capture],** from original records of the US District Court, 5th Judicial District, Globe, AZ, now located at the National Archives, Pacific Southwest Region, Laguna Niguel, CA. Filmed by the Genealogical Society of Utah, 1989, 1 roll, FHL film #1638403. To access the digital images, see the FHL catalog: www.familysearch.org/search/catalog/517589.

1905-1952. *Border Crossing: From Mexico to U.S.* **[Online Database],** digitized and indexed at the Ancestry.com website. This database contains an index of aliens and some citizens crossing into the U.S. from Mexico via various ports of entry along the U.S.-Mexican border between 1895 and 1964. This database includes the following Arizona ports, and years: **Ajo, Lukeville,** and **Sonoyta** (Jan. 1919-Dec. 1952); **Douglas** (Jul. 1908–Dec. 1952); **Naco** (1908-1952); **Nogales** (Jul. 1905-1952); **San Luis** (Jul. 24, 1929-Dec. 1952); and **Sasabe/San Fernando** (1919-1952). The entire database has 5,878,615 records. See https://search.ancestry.com/search/db.aspx?dbid=1082.

- See also, *Arizona, Nogales, Index and Manifests of Alien Arrivals, 1905-1952* **[Online Database].** This collection contains over 455,000 manifests and related index cards of permanent and temporary alien arrivals at Nogales, Arizona, 1905-1952. The cards are arranged alphabetically by surname and include such information as name, age, gender, marital status, occupation, citizenship, race, last permanent residence, birthplace, etc., see www.familysearch.org/search/collection/3041280.

1906-1955. See *Manifests of Alien Arrivals at Douglas, Arizona* **[Microfilm & Digital Capture],** from the original records at the National Archives, College Park, MD. Includes over 65,000 manifests of permanent, temporary, statistical, and non-statistical alien arrivals at Douglas, Arizona, September 1906 - October 1955. Some U.S. citizen arrivals are also included, as well as some records of aliens excluded from admission. Filmed by the National Archives, 2000, 13 rolls, series M1760, beginning with FHL film #2241356. To access the digital images, see the online FHL catalog: www.familysearch.org/search/catalog/1125728.

- See also, *Arizona, Douglas, Arrival Manifests, 1906-1955* **[Online Database],** digitized and indexed at the FamilySearch.org website. Source: National Archives microfilm M1760. This database includes manifests (names of persons crossing into the U.S.) for the Douglas, Arizona check point. Each index record includes: Name, Event type, Event date, Event place, Gender, Age, Birth year, and Birth country. The document image may have more information. This database has 20,852 images. See www.familysearch.org/search/collection/2299376.

1908-1910. *Great Register of Gila County, Territory of Arizona* **[Microfilm],** from the original printed volume published by Silver Belt Print, Globe, AZ, 1910, 76 pages. Certified by E.T. Stewart, County Recorder. Includes naturalization information. Filmed by the Genealogical Society of Utah, 1987, 1 roll, FHL film #1421818. To see if this microfilm was digitized yet, see the online FHL catalog: www.familysearch.org/search/catalog/182267.

1909-1915. *Index to Cochise County School Censuses* **[Online Database],** from the microfilm of originals at the Arizona State Library & Archives, Phoenix, AZ. This searchable index covers all school districts. The census was conducted by the school districts by visiting each house in the district and recording the names of children under 21 along with the parents' or guardians' names. Originally indexed at the MyCochise.com website. For an archived database, see https://web.archive.org/web/20140914201853/www.mycochise.com/schools.php.

1909-1917. *Arizona Births and Christenings* **[Online Database],** indexed at the FamilySearch.org website. Source: FamilySearch extractions from microfilm at the FHL in Salt lake City. This is a name index to birth, baptism, and christening records from the state of Arizona. Each index record includes: Name, Gender, Birth date, Birthplace, Father's name, Mother's name, and FHL film number. This database has 25,794 records. See www.familysearch.org/search/collection/1674580.
- This database is also available at the Ancestry.com website. See https://search.ancestry.com/search/db.aspx?dbid=60001.

1909-1991. *Arizona, Naturalization Records* **[Online Database],** digitized and indexed at the Ancestry.com website. Source: Records of District Courts of the U.S. at the National Archives, Riverside, CA. The records include Petitions, Declarations, and Certificates. Each index record includes: Name, Gender, Petition age, Record type, Birth date, Birthplace, Petition date, Petition place, Spouse, and Petition number. The document image may have more information. This database has 81,136 records. See https://search.ancestry.com/search/db.aspx?dbid=60614.

1910. *Arizona, 1910 Federal Census: Population Schedules* **[Microfilm & Digital Capture],** from the original records at the National Archives, Washington, DC, filmed by the National Archives, ca1970, 5 rolls, beginning with FHL film #1374051 (1910 population schedules: Apache and Cochise Co.). To access the digital images, see the online FHL catalog: **www.familysearch.org/search/catalog/652076.**

1910. *The 1910 Arizona Territory Census Index: Over 88,000 Key Names From all 14 Counties of the Territory in 1910 and the Townships and Counties in which they are listed* **[Printed Book],** compiled and published by the Family History Society of Arizona, Phoenix, AX, 2000, 590 pages. FHL book 99.1 X22

1910. *Navajo County, Arizona Census, 1910* **[Online Database],** indexed at the Ancestry.com website. This database is an index to the federal census of the county in that year and was taken from microfilm copies of the original records. It covers all areas of the county except the Navajo Reservation and parts of the Hopi Reservation. It contains information concerning the resident's first and last names, relationship to the head of household, approximate age, birthplace, and occupation. This database has 5,235 records. See **https://search.ancestry.com/search/db.aspx?dbid=4180.**

1910 Great Register of Greenlee County, Arizona **[Microfilm & Digital Capture],** from the original records at the Arizona Department of Libraries, Archives & Public Records, Phoenix, Arizona. Lists information for the 1910 great register of Greenlee County, Arizona. Lists name, age, place of residence, naturalized, register and voter number. Filmed by the Arizona Dept. of Libraries, Archives & Public Records, 1998, 1 roll, FHL film #2111296. To access the digital images, see the online FHL catalog: **www.familysearch.org/search/catalog/815299.**

1910-1974. *Arizona, School Census Records* **[Online Database],** digitized and indexed at Ancestry.com. This collection consists of school census records for school districts in the Arizona counties of Cochise, Coconino, Gila, Maricopa, Navaho, Pinal, and Yavapai. Arizona began recording school census records as early as the 1870s. In 1891, Arizona School Law required that, in each school district, a Census Marshall should record annually the names of all district children between the ages of six and eighteen years. The information recorded in each school census report varies, depending on the year of the report, but the following information was typically recorded for each child: Name, Age, Sex, Color, Names of parents or guardians. This database has 323,105 records, see **www.ancestry.com/search/collections/60876.**

1910-1994. See *Arizona Deaths and Burials, 1910-1911; 1933-1994* **[Online Database],** indexed at the FamilySearch.org website. Source: FamilySearch extractions from microfilm at the FHL in Salt Lake City. This is a name index to death and burial records from the state of Arizona. Each index record includes: Name, Gender, Death date, Death place, Marital Status, and FHL film number. See **www.familysearch.org/search/collection/1674678.**
- This database is also available at the Ancestry.com website. See **https://search.ancestry.com/search/db.aspx?dbid=60002.**

1911-2000. *Arizona Pioneers' Home Resident Index* **(Online Database],** this is an index to the Arizona Pioneers' Home records. The Home was established by the Territory of Arizona in 1911 in order to take care of aged and infirm Arizonans. Initially, a "men only" institution (principally miners), a woman's wing was added in 1916. Today the Pioneers' Home admits "pioneers" who are at least 70 years of age and have been an Arizona resident for at least 50 years. Indexed at the Sharlot Hall Museum, Prescott, AZ. See **www.sharlot.org/archives/gene/aph/index.html.**

1912-1926 General County Register, Greenlee County, Arizona **[Microfilm & Digital Capture],** from the original records at the Arizona Department of Library, Archives and Public Records, Phoenix, Arizona. May include date of registration, name, occupation, age, country of birth, declaration of naturalization, city of residence, signature of elector and recorder, and remarks. Arranged in the register by the first letter of A surname. Filmed by the Genealogical Society of Utah, 1999, 4 rolls, beginning with FHL film #2166322 (1912, 1913, 1914, 1916 General County Register). To access the digital images, see the online FHL catalog: **www.familysearch.org/search/catalog/830321.**

1917-1918 World War I Selective Service System Draft Registration Cards, Arizona **[Microfilm & Digital Capture],** from the original records at the National Archives branch in East Point, Georgia. The draft cards are arranged alphabetically by state, then alphabetically by county or city, and then by surname

of the registrants. Filmed by the National Archives, Series M1509, 20 rolls, Beginning with FHL film #1473300 (Apache County; Cochise County, A - Escalnate). To access the digital images, see the online FHL catalog: www.familysearch.org/search/catalog/746966.
- See also, *Arizona, World War I, Deaths, 1917-1919* **[Digital Capture]**, digitized by FamilySearch International, 2018. To access the digital images, see the online FHL catalog: www.familysearch.org/search/catalog/3023913.

1918 *Official Military Register of Electors, Navajo County, Arizona* **[Microfilm & Digital Capture]**, from the original records at the Navajo County Courthouse in Holbrook, Arizona. Lists name, military command, post office address, and legal residence. Filmed by the Genealogical Society of Utah, 2002, 1 roll, FHL film #2297104 (Official military register of electors, 1918). To access the digital images, see the online FHL catalog: www.familysearch.org/search/catalog/1149956.

1918. *Naturalizations (Federal)* **[Microfilm & Digital Capture]**, from original records of the US District Court, 2nd District, Douglas, AZ, now located at the National Archives, Pacific Southwest Region, Laguna Niguel, CA. Filmed by the Genealogical Society of Utah, 1989, 2 rolls, FHL film #1638409 and #1638410. To access the digital images, see the online FHL catalog: www.familysearch.org/search/catalog/518157.

1918-1926. *Naturalizations (Federal)* **[Microfilm & Digital Capture]**, from original records at various US District Court in Arizona, now located at the National Archives, Pacific Southwest Region, Laguna Niguel, CA. Filmed by the Genealogical Society of Utah, 1989, 2 rolls, FHL film #1638410 and #1638411. To access the digital images, see the online FHL catalog: www.familysearch.org/search/catalog/518172.

1920. *Arizona, 1820 Federal Census: Soundex and Population Schedules* **[Microfilm & Digital Capture]**, from the original records at the National Archives, Washington, DC, filmed by the National Archives, ca1970, 37 rolls (Soundex and schedules), beginning with FHL film #1823235 (Soundex Codes A00-A524); followed by FHL film #1820046 (1920 population schedules, Apache, Coconino, and Cochise Counties). To access the digital images, see the online FHL catalog: www.familysearch.org/search/catalog/534275.

1927-1994. *Arizona, Gila County, Cemetery Records* **[Online Database].** Cemetery records from the Dudleyville, Ft. Grant, Mammoth, Superior, Ray, and Hayden cemeteries in Gila County, Arizona for the years 1927-1994. Digital images of originals held by the Gila County Historical Museum in Globe, Arizona. This database has 4,511 records, see www.familysearch.org/search/collection/2816842.

1929-1955. *Naturalization and Citizenship Petitions Granted, Continued, or Denied, Nov. 25, 1929 – Dec. 30, 1955* **[Microfilm & Digital Capture]**, from original records at the US District Court of Arizona in Tucson, now located at the National Archives, Pacific Southwest Region, Laguna Niguel, CA. Filmed by the Genealogical Society of Utah, 1989, 2 rolls, FHL film #1638411 (1929-1949) and FHL film #1638527 (1949-1955). To access the digital images, see the online FHL catalog: www.familysearch.org/search/catalog/518198.

1930. *Arizona, 1930 Federal Census: Population Schedules* **[Microfilm & Digital Capture]**, from the original records at the National Archives, Washington, DC, filmed by the National Archives, ca1970, 9 rolls, beginning with FHL film #2339790 (Apache, Mohave, and Cochise Counties). To access the digital images, see the online FHL catalog: www.familysearch.org/search/catalog/1034456.

1936-1969. *Northern Arizona Death and Burial Records* **[Printed Book]**, compiled by Dora M. Whiteside. From preface: Births, deaths, and burial sites of 3,000 people who lived in northern Arizona during 1936-1969... entries are in alphabetical order by surname of the deceased and include a name, birth date and place, death date and place, and a code indicating the burial site. Published by the author, 1990, 59 pages, FHL book 979.1 A1No. 60.

1940. *Arizona, 1940 Federal Census: Population Schedules* **[Digital Capture]**, digitized images from the microfilm of original records held by the Bureau of the Census in the 1940s. After microfilming, Congress allowed the Census Bureau to destroy the originals to free up space for WWII-related files. Digitizing of the 1940 census schedules microfilm images was done for the National Archives and made public in 2012. To access the digital images, see the online FHL catalog: www.familysearch.org/search/catalog/2057740.

1940 Federal Census Finding Aids **[Online Database].** The National Archives has prepared a special website online with a detailed description of the 1940 federal census. Included at the site are descriptions of location finding aids, such as Enumeration District Maps, Geographic Descriptions of Census Enumeration Districts, and a list of 1940 City Directories available at the National Archives The finding aids are all linked to other National Archives sites. The National Archives website also has a link to 1940 Search Engines using Stephen P. Morse's "One-Step" system for finding a 1940 E.D. or street address conversion. See **www.archives.gov/research/census/1940/general-info.html#questions.**

1940-1947. *Arizona, World War II, Draft Registration Cards* **[Digital Capture],** digital images of originals held by the National Personnel Records Center, St. Louis, MO. To access the digital images, see the FHL catalog: **www.familysearch.org/search/catalog/2659396.** - See Also, *Arizona, Military Records: World War II 4th Draft Registration Cards, 1942* **[Digital Capture].** These cards represent older men, ages 45 to 65 in April 1942, that were registered for the draft. They had birth dates between 28 Apr 1877 and 16 Feb 1892. Includes name of individual, date and place of birth, address, age, telephone number, employer's name and address, name and address of person who would know where the individual can be located, signature, and physical description. To access the digital images, see the online FHL catalog: **www.familysearch.org/search/catalog/2487363.**

1941. See *Guide to Public Vital Statistics Records in Arizona* **[Microfilm & Digital Version],** from the original 62-page typescript prepared by the Arizona Statewide Archival and Records Project, Division of Community Service Programs, Work Projects Administration (WPA). This is a rare original copy of one of the few statewide Historical Records Survey projects of the depression era WPA. The project included a survey of available records of birth, deaths, marriages, and divorces at the state vital statistics office, and for every county of Arizona, as of August 1941. If such a book existed for every U.S. State, genealogy would get easier - this book is the authority for what records were actually in an Arizona courthouse in 1941, despite what a clerk working there today may or may not know. Filmed by the Genealogical Society of Utah, 1972, 1 roll, FHL film #908046. To access the digital version, see the online FHL catalog: **www.familysearch.org/search/catalog/195058.**

1948-2008. See *Arizona, Payson, Obituaries* **[Online Database],** digitized and indexed at the FamilySearch.org website. Source: Newspaper clippings from Phoenix and Payson, AZ, many located at the Northern Gila County Genealogical Society Library, Payson. Each index record includes: Name, Event type, Event date, Event place, Gender, Age, Relationship to deceased, Birth year, Death date, and Death place. The newspaper obituary image may have much more information. This database has 213,416 records. See **www.familysearch.org/search/collection/2351020.**

1950-1957. *U.S. Military Personnel Who Died from Hostile Action (Including Missing and Captured Declared Dead) in the Korean War: Arizona* **[Digital Capture],** from the original pub. 1957, National Archives. This is a two-page computer printout listing names alphabetically. To access the digital images, see the online FHL catalog: **www.familysearch.org/search/catalog/2560131.**

1958-1962. *Arizona, Passenger and Crew Manifest of Airplanes* **[Online Database],** digitized and indexed at the Ancestry.com website. National Archives microfilm A3540, A3729, and A3916. Details requested on the forms varied, but they typically include the name of the vessel and arrival date, ports of departure and arrival (as well as future destinations on a ship's itinerary), dates of departure and arrival, shipmaster, full name, age, gender, physical description, military rank (if any), occupation, birthplace, citizen of what country, and residence. For military transports, you may find the next of kin, relationships, and address listed as well. Later manifests may include visa or passport numbers. This database has 8,164 records. See **https://search.ancestry.com/search/db.aspx?dbid=9271.**

1959-2014. *Arizona, Mesa LDS Family History Center, Obituary Index* **[Online Database].** Gift Index of Arizona obituaries that were previously hosted on the Mesa LDS Family History Center's website which has now been decommissioned. Fields include given name, surname, the name of the newspaper, and date obituary was published. This database has 852,445 records, see **www.familysearch.org/search/collection/3159286.**

1979-2003. *Gallup Independent Newspaper, Gallup, New Mexico: Clippings of Births, Marriages and Obituaries* **[Microfilm],** from clippings recording events which took place in New Mexico and Arizona. There are many for Navajo Indians. Filmed by the Genealogical Society of Utah, 1991-2003, 4 rolls, beginning with FHL film #1597900. For a complete list of roll numbers and contents of each roll, see the FHL online catalog page:
www.familysearch.org/search/catalog/473381.

1991-Current. See *Arizona Recent Newspaper Obituaries* **[Online Database],** digitized and indexed at the GenealogyBank.com website, newspaper obituaries are available for the following cities: Apache Junction, Arizona City, Benson, Bullhead City, Casa Grande, Cave Creek, Clifton, Coolidge, Douglas, Eloy, Flagstaff, Gilbert, Glendale, Green Valley, Kearny, Marana, Maricopa, Nogales, Phoenix, Queen Creek, Safford, San Manuel, Sierra Vista, Sonoita, Sun City, Superior, Tucson, Vail, Wickenburg, Willcox, Window Rock, and Yuma. See www.genealogybank.com/gbnk/obituaries/explore/USA/Arizona.

1993-1994. See *Obituary Card Index to Arizona Newspapers* **[Microfilm & Digital Capture],** from index cards and newspaper clippings from Arizona Daily Star (Tucson), Arizona Daily Sun (Flagstaff), Arizona Republic (Phoenix), Daily News Sun (Sun City), Independent (White Mountain, Show Low),and Mesa Tribune (Mesa) located at the Mesa FamilySearch Library. Filmed by the Genealogical Society of Utah, 1993, 9 rolls, beginning with FHL film #1992915 (Aaby, Pearl – Branningan, Daniel). To access the digital images, see the online FHL catalog: www.familysearch.org/search/catalog/747426.

- See also, *Arizona Obituary Index to Arizona Newspapers, 1993-1994* **[Online Database],** digitized and indexed at the FamilySearch.org website. The cards usually contain a newspaper clipping of the obituary, as well as typed vital statistics for the deceased. The index record includes: Name, Event type, Event date, Event place, Gender, Age, Relationship to deceased, Birth year, Birthplace, and Name of newspaper. This database has 50,880 records. See www.familysearch.org/search/collection/2289078.

1997 Surname Project, Family History Society of Arizona (Phoenix, AZ) and Arizona Genealogical Computer Interest Group **[Printed Book].** Lists names being researched in 1996-1997. Lists name, event, year, county or city, state, and country. Published by the society, Phoenix, AZ, 1997, 303 pages, FHL book 979.1 D21.

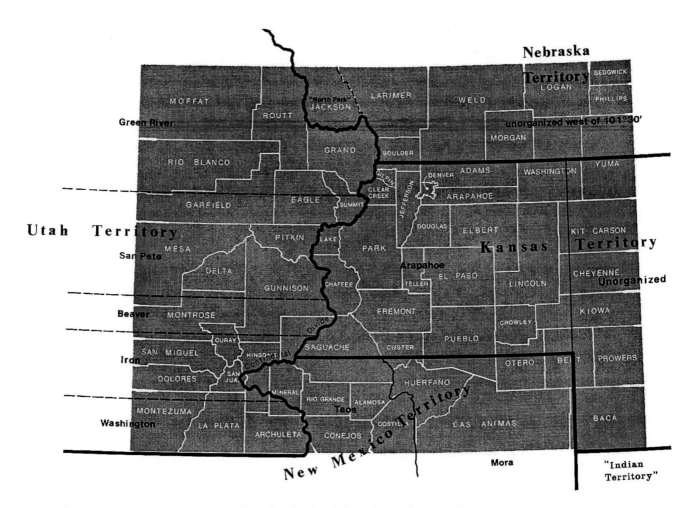

Pre-Territorial Colorado • June 1860. The map above shows in black, the jurisdictions at the time of the 1860 federal census. Underlying, the current state of Colorado and its 64 counties are shown in white. Colorado Territory was created in February 1861 and became a state in 1876. Censuses were taken in 1860 in three of the four territorial jurisdictions: **Kansas Territory:** Denver City, and other mining camps in the part of Colorado then Kansas Territory were enumerated in Arapahoe County. Five paper counties created by Kansas Territory from Arapahoe were never organized and are omitted from the map. Also not shown are the ephemeral counties legislated by the *Territory of Jefferson*, the local government not recognized by Congress. **Nebraska Territory:** Boulder, Altoona, and other northeastern Colorado towns were enumerated at the end of the Nebraska Territory census as the *Unorganized area west of 101°30'*. A legal ruling concerning "North Park" in present-day Jackson County is mentioned in the Historical Timeline, 1870-1886. **New Mexico Territory:** The Rio Grande Valley (known as the San Luis Valley in Colorado) was enumerated in Taos County, NM Territory. **Utah Territory:** The dashed lines on the map show the statutory eastern limits of five Utah counties, but this Colorado area was not settled in 1860 and not enumerated. **Map Source:** Page 52, **Map Guide to the U.S. Federal Censuses, 1790-1920,** by William Thorndale and William Dollarhide.

Colorado
Censuses & Substitute Name Lists

Historical Timeline for Colorado, 1541 – 1900

1541. After months of searching for the Seven Cities of Gold from the Gulf of California and the Grand Canyon, and as far north as the Arkansas River of present Colorado and Kansas, Spanish Conquistador Vasquez de Coronado finally gave up, and headed back to Mexico via the southeastern corner of present Colorado. The route Coronado followed would later be called the Santa Fe trail.

1682. French explorer René-Robert Cavelier (Sieur de la Salle) erected a cross near the mouth of the Mississippi River, claiming the entire Mississippi Basin for France, and naming the region Louisiana after King Louis XIV. The mostly unexplored Louisiana claim included all of present Colorado east of the Continental Divide.

1720. After several Spanish expeditions noted the existence of the river, the name Rio Colorado first appeared on a Spanish map in 1720. Colorado is Spanish for "colored red," the color of the river water derived from the red sandstone for much of its length.

1763. The Seven Years War / French and Indian War ended with the 1763 Treaty of Paris. France lost virtually all of its North American claims: the western side of the Mississippi went to Spain; the eastern side of the Mississippi and all of Quebec went to Britain.

1765. Spanish explorer Juan Maria Rivera led an expedition into the San Juan and Sangre de Cristo Mountains in search of gold and silver.

1776. Fathers Silvestre Velez de Escalante and Francisco Atanasio Dominguez searched for a new route from New Mexico to California, and in doing so, they explored parts of present southern Colorado and Utah. The route they followed would become known as the Old Spanish Trail.

1800. Louisiana. Napoleon acquired title of Louisiana from Spain. At the Third Treaty of San Ildefonso, the Spanish acknowledged that it was too costly to explore the country and could not see the rewards being worth the investment. Spain retroceded Louisiana to France in exchange for the Grand Duchy of Tuscany. (Essentially, Napoleon got Louisiana, and Spain got the Leaning Tower of Pisa).

1803 Louisiana Purchase. The United States acquired Louisiana from France, a vast area which had as a legal description, "the drainage of the Mississippi and Missouri rivers," including all of Colorado east of the Rocky Mountains. However, Spain disagreed with that description and still claimed much of the Louisiana tract, including the entire length of the Arkansas River. From their base in Santa Fe, the Spanish vowed to vigorously defend the area from any American intruders.

1804. Lewis and Clark's Corps of Discovery left St. Louis via the Missouri River in search of a passage to the Pacific Ocean. Soon after, Spanish troops were dispatched from Santa Fe into present Colorado to intercept and arrest them. But Lewis and Clark were well into present South Dakota by the time the Spanish troops finally gave up looking for them.

1806-1807. Captain Zebulon Pike and a party of about 20 U.S. soldiers were sent to explore routes across the southern area of the Louisiana Purchase to the Rocky Mountains. Capt. Pike's expedition was credited as the first Americans to follow what would become known as the Santa Fe Trail, as well as the first Americans to follow the Arkansas River into the Rocky Mountains. Pike crossed the Sangre de Cristo Mountains to the Conejos River in the San Luis Valley, where he built Pike's Stockade. The party documented the discovery of Pikes Peak, and spent time trying to find the headwaters of both the Red and Arkansas Rivers.

Pike and his entire party were arrested by Spanish soldiers near the Arkansas River on their return trip. These were the same soldiers who had been sent north from Santa Fe to arrest the Lewis & Clark party, but were unable to find them. Pike and his party were taken to Santa Fe de Nuevo Mexico, where they were treated fairly well, and soon after were escorted back to U.S Territory. In 1810, Pike's published narrative of his expedition was the first English language description of Spanish culture in North America. It was a best seller in America and Europe and became the primary source of information to a new breed of would-be trappers and Mountain Men curious about routes to the Rocky Mountains.

1819 The **Adams-Onís Treaty** set the boundary between American and Spanish territory, which included the Red River as the boundary between Spanish Texas and U.S., then north to the Arkansas River as the division between the Spanish Province of Nuevo Mexico and U.S. Missouri Territory, and then north along the Continental Divide to the 42nd Parallel, and finally, west to the Pacific Ocean. Before the treaty, the Spanish claims were loosely defined as everything west of the Mississippi River to the Pacific Ocean and north to at least the 42nd Parallel. As a result of the treaty, the northeastern section of present Colorado was first recognized by Spain as part of the United States (the area east of the Continental Divide and north of the Arkansas River).

1820. Major Stephen H. Long was sent by President Monroe to explore the present Colorado region of the Louisiana Purchase. Long's party came by way of the Platte and South Platte Rivers. Long's Peak was named for him. Dr. Edwin James, historian of Long's expedition, led the first recorded ascent of Pike's Peak. James Peak, west of Denver, was named for him. Before entering present Colorado, Long and James established the main route to the Rocky Mountains via the Platte River through present Nebraska, on what would become known as the Oregon Trail.

1821. Mexico gained independence from Spain and soon after, Mexico reaffirmed the 1819 Spanish-U.S. treaty line as the Mexican-American boundary. Mexican lands were from the Louisiana line at the Sabine River, including all of present Texas, New Mexico, Arizona, and California; all of present Utah and Nevada; and present Colorado west of the Continental Divide and south of the Arkansas River. Also in 1821, the first traders from the United States came into the Mexican Province of Nuevo Mexico via southeastern Colorado on what would become known as the Mountain Route of the Santa Fe Trail.

1825. Fur-traders, trappers and Mountain Men began operations in present Colorado, including the Bent brothers, Ceran St. Vrain, Louis Vasquez, Kit Carson, Jim Baker, James Bridger, Thomas Fitzpatrick, "Uncle Dick" Wooten, and Jim Beckworth. The first trading posts they established were located in either the Arkansas River Valley or the South Platte Valley.

1832. Bent's Fort was built by the Bent brothers and St. Vrain near the present city of La Junta, Colorado. For anyone following the Arkansas River from Fort Dodge, Bent's Fort became a mandatory stop on the Santa Fe Trail.

1836. The new Republic of Texas asserted a claim to all land east of the Rio Grande through present New Mexico and a narrow strip of mountain territory extending into present Colorado as far north as the 42nd parallel.

1841. Texas soldiers invaded present New Mexico, seeking to possess their claim to the region. But Texas was never successful in taking political control away from Mexico.

1842. Lieutenant John C. Fremont undertook the first of his five exploration trips into the Rocky Mountains and beyond.

1845. After the annexation of Texas, the Texas Claim to parts of New Mexico and Colorado was taken over by the United States. A war with Mexico resulted from this action.

1846. General Stephen W. Kearney led troops along the Santa Fe Trail through southeastern Colorado en route to his conquest of Nuevo Mexico during the Mexican War. Kearney established the Provisional New Mexico Territory, which included a portion of present Colorado south of the Arkansas River.

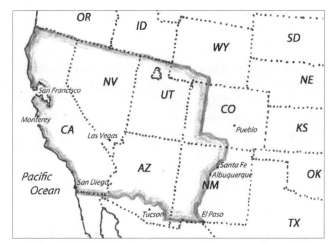

1848 Mexican Cession. At the Treaty of Guadalupe Hidalgo ending the war with Mexico, the United States annexed the area of present California, Nevada, Utah, Arizona (north of the Gila River), New Mexico, and a part of Colorado west of the Continental Divide. The U.S. paid Mexico a sum of eighteen million dollars for an area that was over half of the Republic of Mexico and comparable in size to the Louisiana Purchase.

1850. June. The 1850 Federal Census was taken in New Mexico Territory (Jun 1850) and Utah Territory (Apr 1851). New Mexico Territory included present Colorado south of the Arkansas River; Utah Territory included present western Colorado; and eastern Colorado was in the "Unorganized Territory" of the great plains. No population was returned from the Colorado areas.

1851. The first permanent white settlement in present Colorado was founded at Conejos in the San Luis Valley; irrigation was begun; and Fort Massachusetts was established. The settlement was in New Mexico Territory at its founding.

1853. In May, Captain John W. Gunnison led an exploring party across southern and western Colorado to survey a feasible route for a railroad through the Rocky Mountains. He was successful in mapping much of the area between the 38th and 39th parallels but was killed in an Indian attack in October 1853. Much of Gunnison's survey work was the completion of surveys begun by John C. Fremont's 1847 expedition.

1854. Kansas and Nebraska Territories were established. Both extended from the Missouri River to the Continental Divide. The area of present Colorado was now within four U.S. Territories: Utah, New Mexico, Kansas, and Nebraska Territories.

1858. July. **Birth of Colorado.** Green Russell's discovery of placer gold deposits near the confluence of the South Platte River and Cherry Creek, precipitated a gold rush from the East. The "Pikes Peak or Bust" slogan began. Montana City, St. Charles, Auraria, and Denver City were founded. Pueblo was founded as Fountain City. Arapahoe County, Kansas Territory was established (but not organized).

1859. In October, **Jefferson Territory** was organized to govern the first mining camps and towns of present Colorado. Officers were elected, several counties were established, and in 1860, the territorial capital was established at Golden, where it would return in 1862 after Colorado City was named the first capital of Colorado Territory in 1861. Although the territorial government was never sanctioned by the U.S. Congress, Jefferson Territory operated with the consent of the local population. Also in this year, prospectors spread throughout the mountains and established camps at Boulder, Colorado City, Gold Hill, Hamilton, Tarryall, and Pueblo. Gold was found by George A. Jackson along Chicago Creek on the present site of Idaho Springs. John Gregory made his famous gold-lode strike on North Clear Creek, stimulating a rush of prospectors, who established camps of Black Hawk, Central City and Nevadaville.

1860. June. For the 1860 federal census, the U.S. Census Office ignored Jefferson Territory, but included an enumeration of any inhabitants of present Colorado as part of four U.S. territories: New Mexico, Nebraska, Kansas, and Utah Territories. Also in 1860, rich placer discoveries caused a stampede of miners to California Gulch at the present site of Leadville. The Colorado region continued to be administered by Jefferson Territory officials, Miners' Courts, and People's Courts. See the 1860 Colorado Maps on page 238.

1861. After a successful invasion of the Rio Grande Valley by Confederate troops, the Confederate Territory of Arizona was declared with the capital at La Mesilla. The territory included the southern half of present New Mexico and Arizona.

1861. In February, **Colorado Territory** was established by the U.S. Congress with the same boundaries as the present state, ending the ephemeral reign of Jefferson Territory. The first Colorado Territorial Assembly met, created 17 counties, authorized a university, and selected Colorado City as the capital. The wild west town of Colorado City was a bit too wild for even early Colorado, where saloons outnumbered churches 20 to 1. After a year, the capital was moved to Golden, about 15 miles from Denver. As part of the organic act creating Colorado Territory, a territory-wide census was required. In late 1861, the territory conducted a census as part of an election poll taken by each of the county assessors, the combined county name lists at the state archives now called the *1861 Poll Book for Colorado*.

1862. Colorado troops led by Col. John M. Chivington were instrumental in holding off Confederate General Henry H. Sibley's Army at La Glorietta Pass. Soon after, the confederate control of New Mexico/Arizona ended, and the U.S. Territory of Mexico was restored to its pre-war condition.

1863. Arizona Territory was created by the U.S. Congress. The northern boundary of Arizona Territory extended west to the California line, and included all of present Clark County, Nevada. When Congress divided New Mexico Territory on the same meridian as Colorado Territory's western line, the resulting map created the "Four Corners" of Colorado, Utah, Arizona, and New Mexico, the only point in the U.S. where four states touch at a quadripoint.

1866. A Colorado Territorial Census/Poll List was taken by county assessors. The lists included the names of all males over 21. Only two county lists survive.

1867. The Colorado Territorial capital was moved from Golden to Denver.

1870. Federal Census. The Population of Colorado Territory was at 39,864. Also in 1870, the Denver and Pacific Railroad was constructed to connect Denver with the Union Pacific at Cheyenne, Wyoming Territory.

1870-1886. The valley called North Park, which is present-day Jackson County, Colorado, lies east of the Continental Divide, as shown on the 1860 map on page 238. The valley was not settled by whites in 1860, but in 1870 was assumed by local officials to be part of Summit County. North Park in the 1880 and 1885 censuses was enumerated as part of Grand County, despite being claimed by Larimer. In 1886, the Colorado Supreme Court ruled that statutorily North Park had been in Larimer County since 1861.

1876. Colorado was admitted to the Union as the 38th State, one hundred years after the Declaration of Independence of the United States, hence, Colorado's nickname became "The Centennial State." The territorial capital of Denver became the state capital.

1880. Federal Census. The Population of Colorado was at 194,327.

1885. Colorado State Census was taken with federal assistance. This was the only state census taken by Colorado.

1900. Federal Census. The Population of Colorado was at 539,700. In 1900, Gold production reached a peak of more than $20,000,000 annually at Cripple Creek, the second richest gold camp in the world.

Historical Records Index Search at the Colorado State Archives Website

Archives Search. This is a database that is searchable by name, record type, and time span. For the search screen, see
www.colorado.gov/pacific/archives/archives-search.
This webpage has several useful sections: Request a Record, View our Associated Fees, and Find Something You're Interested In? Click on **List of Records** included in the Archives Search to see what is searchable online, which may have updates to the incredible list of 160 databases included:

Records By County
Adams County Divorces 1904-1913
Adams County Inheritance Tax 1929-1943
Adams County Old Age Pension 1933-1936
Adams County Teachers 1913-1935
Adams County Wills 1903-1938
Arapahoe County Civil Docket Book 1867-1869
Arapahoe County Old Age Pension 1933-1936
Arapahoe County Hospital 1891-1899
Arapahoe County Poor Hospital 1895-1899
Arapahoe County Probate Cases 1902-1937
Arapahoe County Teachers Cards Dist 1 & 6 1953
Arapahoe County Voter Registrations 1893-1905
Bent County Divorce 1907-1921
Boulder County Birth Index 1892-1906
Boulder County Divorce 1904-1918
Boulder County Mothers Compensations 1914-1934
Boulder County Inheritance Tax Records 1941-19
Conejos County Probate Cases 1894-1918
Costilla County Poor Record 1890-1932
Costilla County Probate Record 1876-1914
Custer County Inheritance Tax 1907-1946
Custer County Probates 1879-1989
Custer County Teachers Registers of Students 1880-1896
Custer County Wills 1887-1966

Colorado • 243

Dearfield and surrounding area School Census 1909-1946
Denver Birth Index 1875-1909
Denver Death Index 1870-1909
Denver Inheritance Tax 1909-1912
Denver Lot and Block Index 1862-1917
Denver Old Age Pension 1933-1936
Denver War Risk Insurance Applications 1914-1917
Dolores County Court Cases 1881-1953
Douglas County Inheritance Tax 1911-1944
Douglas County Justice of the Peace Docket 1871-1892
Douglas County Old Age Pension 1933-1936
Douglas County Probate Cases 1865-1962
Douglas County Wills 1886-1961
Eagle County Probate 1884-1935
Elbert County Birth Index 1869-1906
Elbert County Divorce 1870-1910
Elbert County Inheritance Proceedings 1922-1941
Elbert County Judges Docket 1928-1938
Elbert County Old Age Pension 1933-1936
Elbert County 8th Grade Promotions 1918-1930
Elbert County Wills 1887-1966
El Paso County Civil District Court 1946-1961
El Paso County Divorce 1903-1941
El Paso County Old Age Pension 1933-1936
El Paso Co Placer Mine Location Certificates 1892-1942
El Paso County Probates 1880-1969)
El Paso County School Census Dist. 3 1911
El Paso Co School Census Dist.11 (Colo. Spgs.) 1910, 1920
Fremont County Inheritance Tax 1913-1943
Fremont County Old Age Pensions 1933-1936
Garfield County Divorce Record 1906-1916
Garfield County Inheritance Tax 1909-1919, 1926-1942
Gilpin County Bankruptcy Docket 1867-1876
Gilpin County Chancery Cases 1862-1878
Gilpin County District Court Filings 1861-1882
Gilpin County Probate Court Civil Case Filings 1874-1892
Gilpin County Inheritance Tax 1910-1922
Gilpin County Marriages 1864-1944
Huerfano County Inheritance Tax 1910-1946
Huerfano County Poor Records 1916-1923
Huerfano County School Census 1913-1915, 1919
Huerfano County Tax List 1873
Jefferson County Coroner Reports (1868-1930)
Jefferson County Inheritance Tax 1913-1945
Jefferson County Civil Cases 1864-1886
Jefferson County Probates 1862-1977
Kit Carson County Birth Report Register 1892-1907
Kit Carson County Death Register 1893-1907
Kit Carson County Land Registration Receipts 1913-1939
Kit Carson County Old Age Pension 1933-1936
Lake County Births to 1909
Lake County Justice of the Peace Cases 1883-1884
Lake County School District #6 1880-1903
Lake County School District #12 1893-1900
Lake County School District #15 1952-1958
La Plata County WPA Enrollments 1935-1942
Larimer County Mothers Compensations 1920-1933
Larimer County Naturalization Index 1885-1958
Larimer County Old Age Pensions 1933-1936
Larimer County Water Cases 1899-1926
Las Animas County Naturalizations 1878-1906
Las Animas County Old Age Pensions 1933-1936
Leadville School Census 1883-1910
Lincoln County Old Age Pension 1933-1936
Lincoln County Probate Cases 1890-1981
Logan County Inheritance Tax 1913-1942
Logan County School Census 1915-1920
Mesa County CCC Enrollments 1934-1942
Mesa County Divorce Cases 1950-1970
Mesa County Inheritance Tax 1920-1934
Mesa County Motor Vehicle Licenses 1913-1917
Mesa County Persons Subject to Military 1885-1887
Mesa County Persons Exempt from Military 1887
Mesa County Probate 1883-1910
Mineral County Old Age Pension 1935-1936
Mineral County Probate 1894-1970
Moffat County Inheritance Tax 1920-1943
Montrose County Probate Cases (1883 – 1939)
Morgan County Mothers Compensation 1935
Morgan County Old Age Pension 1933-1936
Morgan County Probates 1890-1964
Ouray County Births 1891-1902
Ouray County Probate Cases 1878-1919
Park County Divorce Record 1957-1974
Park County School Board Oaths 1918-1959
Park County Will Record 1895-1926 & 1959-1976
Pitkin County Divorce Record 1931-1964
Pitkin County Inheritance Tax 1938-1956
Pitkin County Probate 1881-1953
Pitkin County Quit Claim Deeds (1881-1883)
Pitkin County School Census #16 1896, 1898
Prowers County Old Age Pensions 1933-1936
Pueblo County Probate Cases 1862-1961
Rio Blanco Burial Permits & Removals 1917-1951
Rio Grande Co Teacher Certificate Applications 1874-1893
Rio Grande School Census #22 1917-1918
Rio Grande Probate Cases (1874 – 1921)
Rocky Ford School Census 1877-1892
Routt County Ditch Claim Statements 1902-1903
Routt County Inheritance Tax 1918-1923
Routt County School Census 1910
Routt County School Census 1920
Routt County Will Record 1888-1905
Saguache County Burial Records 1923-1925
Saguache County Poor Records 1915-1926
Saguache County Teacher Certificate Registers, 1894-1914
San Miguel County Old Age Pension 1934
San Miguel Teacher Exams 1885-1906
Summit County Probate Cases/Record 1877-1916
Teller County Inheritance Tax 1917-1936
Teller County Wills 1894-1971
Washington County Pauper Record 1896-1897
Weld County Old Age Pensions 1931
Weld County Poor Record 1902-1913
Weld County Probate Cases (1876 – 1981)
Weld County WW1 Vets

Miscellaneous records
1870 Federal Census (State Copy)
Amache Japanese Internment Camp Teachers List 1942-1945

Bar Admission Files 1899-1950
Civilian Conservation Corps Enrollments
  (Statewide) 1936-1942
Civil War Casualties
Court of Appeals Case Files 1891-1911
Divorce Index (Statewide) 1880-1939
Governor's Appointments 1861-1981
Horse (Docked) Register 1899-1907
Horseshoers 1897-1920
Horticulture Awards 1894-1899
Incorporation Index 1861-1914
Indian Industrial Schools Census 1900
Land Commissioners Patents 1878-1970
Mine Accidents, Non-fatal 1883-1900
Mine Location Certificates 1905-1910
Prohibition Arrests 1918-1926
Spanish-American War Volunteers 1898-1899

Bibliography
Colorado Censuses & Substitutes

Available Censuses and Substitutes can be related to Colorado's historical eras:

1850-1859. Pre-Territorial. The 1850 Federal Census was taken in New Mexico Territory which included present Colorado south of the Arkansas River; and in Utah Territory, which included present western Colorado; while most of eastern Colorado was in the "Unorganized Territory" of the great plains. No population was recorded in any of the present Colorado areas.

1859-1860. Jefferson Territory Era. Established in 1859, Jefferson Territory was recognized by the local population (but not the U.S. Congress). In 1860, the U.S. Census Office included an enumeration of any inhabitants of Jefferson Territory/Colorado area as part of four U.S. territories: 1) Utah Territory: no Colorado population; 2) New Mexico Territory: the settlements in the San Luis Valley of Taos County; 3) Kansas Territory: Denver City and the other mining camps and towns in Arapahoe County; and 4) Nebraska Territory: Boulder, Altoona, and other northwestern towns at the end of the Nebraska census schedules labeled as Unorganized Area West of 101°30'. See the 1860 Map on page 238.

1861-1876. Colorado Territory Era. Colorado Territory was created by Congress in February 1861, two months before the onset of the Civil War. The Territory of Colorado conducted censuses in 1861 and 1866. The 1861 name lists survive (as poll lists) and were extracted and indexed as the *1861 Colorado Poll Book*. Although there is evidence that the statistics of the 1866 census were in fact reported by the Governor to the territorial legislature, there is no record of the 1866 name lists ever being collected at the territory level. The 1866 census was similar to the 1861, in that it was a list of males over 21, taken as a poll list. Only two counties with 1866 name lists survive.

1876-Current. State of Colorado Era. The State of Colorado took only one statewide census, that of 1885. This census was suggested by the United States Census Office, and federal funds were used to pay for half of the costs in conducting the census. The same forms used for the 1880 federal census were printed and provided by the Census Office for the 1885 Colorado State Census, and the Census Office asked for a duplicate copy of the statewide schedules. The state's microfilmed copy has numerous missing counties but using both the federal and state copies together allows for a complete set for all but one missing county (Garfield).

Census Substitutes. In addition to the territorial and federal censuses, there are many census substitute name lists that fill out the bibliography. Name lists may include Local Census Records, County Court Records, Directories, County Histories, State Militia Lists, Tax Lists, Church & Vital Records, and Voter Lists. They begin below in chronological order:

♦ ♦ ♦ ♦ ♦

1858-1939 Colorado Marriages **[CD-ROM],** an index to over 456,000 names of both brides and grooms, listing the date and place of marriage, and the license number. Published by the Denver Public Library. The work to index the marriages came from a WPA project during the late 1930s, when the typed index cards were first produced. There have been many corrections and upgrades to the original index. See FHL CD No. 2425.

- See also, ***Colorado Statewide Marriage Index, 1853-2006* [Online Database],** digitized and indexed at FamilySearch.org. Source: CO Dept. of Health records at the CO State Archives. No record could be found with an 1853 date, but there were a few with an 1858 date, see
www.familysearch.org/search/collection/1932434.

1858-1985. See ***Colorado, Divorce Index* [Online Database],** indexed at the Ancestry.com website. Source: "Various public records" (some of which are untrustworthy, e.g., an Otero Co divorce in 1851 - the county was not formed until 1889). When available, each record contains the full names of both individuals, their date and location of divorce, as well as the certificate number. This database has 711,716 records: https://search.ancestry.com/search/db.aspx?dbid=60927.

1858-1908. See *Burial Records of Calvary Cemetery, Denver, Colorado* **[Microfilm & Digital Capture]**, from a 167-page manuscript prepared by Sallie L. George in 1945. Includes name and date of burial, arranged alphabetically by the first letter of the surname of the decedent. The cemetery was started around 1858 and used until 1908. It was known as City Cemetery, Prospect Hill, or Mt. Prospect Cemetery before being named Calvary Cemetery. The area may originally have been known as Jack O'Neill's Ranch. 2nd filming: Denver, American Micro-Photo, 1970, 1 roll, FHL film #833164. For access to the digital images of this roll, see the online FHL catalog page for this title: www.familysearch.org/search/catalog/197840.

1858-1985. Colorado Cemetery Directory [Printed Book & Digital Capture], by Kay R. Merrill, publ. Colorado Council of Genealogical Societies, 1985, 623 pages, FHL book 978.8 V34. To access the digital images, see the online FHL catalog: www.familysearch.org/search/catalog/340869.
- See also, *Complete List of Colorado Cemeteries and Graves* **[Digital Capture]**, from a 33-page typescript at the Family History Library, Salt Lake City, UT. Author, publisher not stated. This is a list of names of cemeteries only, organized by county. To access the digital images, see the online FHL catalog: www.familysearch.org/search/catalog/192058.

1858-2006. *Colorado Statewide Marriage Index* **[Online Database]**, indexed at the FamilySearch.org website. Source: Dept of Health records at the CO State Archives. Name index and images of card index created by the Division of Vital Statistics, Department of Health in Colorado. The index is arranged alphabetically by groom's name providing county, names of husband and wife, age, race, date and place of marriage, certificate number. This database has 452,357 records. See www.familysearch.org/search/collection/1932434.

1858-2010. *Colorado USGenWeb Archives* **[Online Database]**, includes databases for all 64 counties of Colorado, plus defunct counties. **Projects:** The Tombstone Project, The Census Project, Obits Project, and Colorado Maps. **Record categories:** Birth Records, Biographies, Cemeteries, Census and Tax Lists, Church Records, City Directories, Court Records, Death Records, Deeds and Real Estate Records, Divorce Records, Historical Records, Marriage Records, Military Records, Newspaper Articles, Obituaries, Photographs, Publications, and Schools. See *http://usgwarchives.net/co/cofiles.htm*.

1858-2010. *Linkpendium – Colorado: Family History & Genealogy, Census, Birth, Marriage, Death Vital Records & More* **[Online Database]**. Linkpendium is a portal to website with genealogical information. The Colorado section is organized by Location (Number of Sites), as follows: Statewide Resources Selected sites (306), Independent Cities, Renamed Counties, Discontinued Counties (6), Adams County (147), Alamosa County (94), Arapahoe County (230), Archuleta County (96), Baca County (94), Bent County (139), Boulder County (293), Broomfield County (49), Chaffee County (163), Cheyenne County (109), Clear Creek County (169), Conejos County (111), Costilla County (108), Crowley County (89), Custer County (115), Delta County (175), Denver City and County (1,301), Dolores County (83), Douglas County (142), Eagle County (179), El Paso County (461), Elbert County (113), Fremont County (175), Garfield County (221), Gilpin County (151), Grand County (106), Gunnison County (149), Hinsdale County (94), Huerfano County (122), Jackson County (65), Jefferson County (228), Kiowa County (96), Kit Carson County (157), La Plata County (159), Lake County (207), Larimer County (285), Las Animas County (190), Lincoln County (113), Logan County (144), Mesa County (215), Mineral County (94), Moffat County (141), Montezuma County (114), Montrose County (164), Morgan County (136), Otero County (150), Ouray County (121), Park County (126), Phillips County (101), Pitkin County (203), Prowers County (120), Pueblo County (421), Rio Blanco County (142), Rio Grande County (121), Routt County (252), Saguache County (116), San Juan County (116), San Miguel County (133), Sedgwick County (103), Summit County (123), Teller County (146), Washington County (106), Weld County (370), and Yuma County (121). See www.linkpendium.com/co-genealogy.

1859-1900. *Colorado, Compiled Marriages from Mesa, Arapaho, and Boulder Counties* **[Online Database]**, indexed at the Ancestry.com website. Original data: Dodd, Jordan, Liahona Research, Colorado Marriages, 1859-1900. This database is a collection of marriage records from three counties in

Colorado. Taken from microfilm copies of original county documents, each record provides spouses' names, marriage date, and county of residence. The database lists the names of more than 37,000 men and women. See
http://search.ancestry.com/search/db.aspx?dbid=4364.

1859-1986. *Colorado Newspaper Archives* **[Online Database],** digitized and indexed at the GenealogyBank.com website. One search screen for names and keywords in the following city newspapers: Amache, Antonito, Bellevue, Black Hawk, Boulder, Canon City, Central City, Colorado Springs, Crested Butte, Denver, Eastonville, Elbert, Fruita, Fulford, Grand Junction, Greeley, Gunnison, Julesburg, Lake City, Maysville, Ouray, Pitkin, Pueblo, Saguache, Saint Elmo, San Luis, Tincup, Trinidad, and White Pine. See www.genealogybank.com/gbnk/newspapers/explore/USA/Colorado.

1860. *Index to Gilpin County, Colorado 1860 U.S. Census, Extracted From the 1860 U.S. Census of Arapahoe County, Kansas Territory* **[Printed Index],** by Alan Granruth, published by the Foothills Genealogical Society, Lakewood, CO, 1995, 134 pages. For the areas of old Arapahoe County that included present Gilpin County, Colorado, this is an alphabetized extract of the census households including dwelling, name, age, sex, color, occupation, personal property, & birthplace. FHL book 978.862 X28g. Also on microfilm, FHL film #2055223.

1860-1880. *Alphabetized Listing of Census Returns and Mortality Schedules for Boulder County, Colorado* **[Microfilm],** by Sanford Charles Gladden, published by the University of Colorado Libraries, Boulder, CO, 1978. Includes 1860, 1870 and 1880 federal censuses and 1885 state censuses. FHL purchased microfilm from the author in 1981, 1 roll, FHL film #1294357. To see if this microfilm was digitized yet, see the online FHL catalog: www.familysearch.org/search/catalog/11585.

1861. *Colorado Voters in the 1861 Territorial Election for a Delegate to the 37th Congress* **[Printed Book & Microfilm],** an extraction of the original name lists at the Colorado State Archives by the Computer Interest Group of the Colorado Genealogical Society, Denver, CO, 1996, 156 pages. Includes index. This series of original countywide name lists is titled, *1861 Poll Book for Colorado at the Colorado State Archives.* In satisfaction of the requirement for a territorial census to be taken by the organic act of 1861 in which the Territory of Colorado was created, the territory incorporated the names of males over 21 as part of the assessor's polls for the first territorial election. See FHL book 978.8 N4c. Also on microfilm, FHL film #1750820. To see if this microfilm was digitized yet, see the online FHL catalog:
www.familysearch.org/search/catalog/766436.

1861 Territorial Election, Huerfano County, Colorado **[Online Database],** list of elected officials and all voters, indexed at the kmitch.com site. See www.kmitch.com/Huerfano/voter1861.htm.

1861-1865. *Civil War Index Cards* **[Microfilm & Digital Capture],** from the original records at the Colorado State Archives, Denver, CO. Each card gives a name, rank, age, organization, when and where enrolled, by whom enrolled, when and where mustered, by whom mustered, book and page numbers, and other information. Filmed by the Genealogical Society of Utah, 1992, 4 rolls, as follows:
- Civil War index cards: A – Franklin, Ashley M., FHL film #1862946.
- Civil War index cards: Franklin, Ashley M. – McFadden, Owen, FHL film #1862947.
- Civil War index cards: McFadden, Owen – Shock, Adam L., FHL film #1862948.
- Civil War index cards: Shock, Adam L. – Z, FHL film #1862949.

To access the digital images, see the online FHL catalog: www.familysearch.org/search/catalog/647671.

1861-2004. *Colorado Collection Catalog at MyHeritage.com* **[Online Database],** digitized and indexed at the MyHeritage website. This is a subscription site, but an index search of the records is free. The records for Colorado include vital records, censuses, histories, and directories, see
www.myheritage.com/research/catalog?q=colorado.

1861-1865. *Index to Compiled Service Records of Volunteer Union Soldiers Who Served in Organizations From the Territory of Colorado* **[Microfilm & Digital Capture],** from the original records at the National Archives, Washington, DC, filmed by the National Archives, Series M0534, 1964, 3 rolls, as follows:
- Index, A-Hap, 1861-1865, NARA M534 roll 1, FHL film #821998.
- Index, Har-O, 1861-1865, M534 roll 2, FHL film #821999.
- Index, P-Z, 1861-1865, M534 roll 3, FHL film #822000.

To access the digital images, see the online FHL catalog: www.familysearch.org/search/catalog/317046.

1861-1865. *Index to Soldiers & Sailors of the Civil War* **[Online Database],** a searchable name index to 6.3 million Union and Confederate Civil War soldiers available online at the National Park Service Website. A search can be done by surname, first name, state, or unit. Colorado Territory supplied 8,461 men to the war (all Union). See
www.nps.gov/civilwar/soldiers-and-sailors-database.htm.

1861-1880s. *Index to Book 1, Huerfano County, Colorado* **[Online Database].** Present Huerfano County was originally part of Mexico until 1848, and New Mexico until Colorado became a territory in 1861. Most of the earliest records begin in 1861, but the earliest land record on file here was a copy of a Mexican Land Grant to Ceran St. Vrain in 1845. St. Vrain and the Bent Brothers were the first non-Indian settlers in southern Colorado. The court records from the Clerk's Book 1 were indexed at the kmitch.com site. See **www.kmitch.com/Huerfano/book1.html.**

1862. *Index to Colorado Volunteers in the Civil War: The New Mexico Campaign* **[Printed Index],** an index of names from a book by William Clarke Whitman, index compiled by Jane Verhasselt, published by the Foothills Genealogical Society of Colorado, Lakewood, CO, 1986, 6 pages, FHL book 978.8 A1 No. 110.

1862-1866. *Internal Revenue Lists for the Territory of Colorado* **[Microfilm & Digital Capture],** from the originals at the National Archives, Washington, DC. Filmed by the National Archives, 1968, Series M0757, 3 rolls, as follows:
- Revenue name lists, divisions 1-14 Annual, monthly, special 1862-1863 (NARA M757 roll 1), FHL film #1578500.
- Revenue name lists, divisions 1-14 Annual, monthly, special 1864 (NARA M757 roll 2), FHL film #1578501.
- Revenue name lists, divisions 1-14 Annual, monthly, special 1865-1866 (NARA M757, roll 3), FHL film #1578502.

To access the digital images, see the online FHL catalog: www.familysearch.org/search/catalog/577976.

1862-1908. *Denver Land Office Records* **[Online Database],** indexed at the Ancestry.com website. Source: Robinson, Doreen and Alan Campbell, *Denver Land Office Records, 1862-1908.* This database contains claim records for persons who applied for land ownership between 1862 and 1908 and includes the location of their claim. Each index record includes: Name, Township, Range, Book, Type, BLM No., and Application Number. This database has 68,165 records: https://search.ancestry.com/search/db.aspx?dbid=3313.

1862-1949 Veterans' Grave Registration, Saguache County, Colorado **[Online Database],** indexed at the USGenWeb site for Saguache Co CO:
http://files.usgwarchives.net/co/saguache/military/vetgrave.txt.

1862-2006. *Colorado, County Marriage Records and State Index* **[Online Database],** digitized and indexed at the Ancestry.com website. Original data: Colorado Marriages, State Index, Denver, CO. This collection consists of county marriage records from various counties in Colorado. Marriages were recorded by the clerk of the district court for each county from the time the county was formed. Details vary, but may include the following information for both the bride and groom: Name, Age at marriage, Marriage date, Marriage place, and Parents' names. This database has 1,142,276 records. See
https://search.ancestry.com/search/db.aspx?dbid=61366.

1864-1995. *Colorado, County Marriages* **[Online Database],** digitized and indexed at the FamilySearch.org website. Source: CO State Archives. Includes marriages from Clear Creek, Fremont, Kit Carson, Logan, Moffat, Phillips, Saguache, Sedgwick, Washington, and Yuma counties. This database has 118,783 records. See
www.familysearch.org/search/collection/1942851.

"1865-1867 Taxpayers, Clear Creek County, Colorado Territory" [Printed Article], name list published in *Foothills Inquirer* (Foothills Genealogical Society of Colorado, Lakewood, CO), Vol. 16, No. 1 (Spring 1996) through Vol. 16, No. 3 (Fall 1996).

"1866 Heads of Families, Jefferson County, Colorado Territory" [Printed Article], name list published in *Foothills Inquirer* (Foothills Genealogical Society of Colorado, Lakewood, CO), Vol. 17, No. 3 (Fall 1997) and Vol. 18, No. 4 (Winter 1998).

1866-1903. *Index to Colorado Mining Claims* **[Printed Book],** author/publisher not noted. Contents: Alamosa, Archuleta, Boulder, Chaffee, Clear Creek, Conejos, Costilla, Custer, Dolores, Eagle, El Paso, Fremont, Garfield, Gilpin, and Grand Counties, FHL book 978.8 R22i.

1866-1994 Colorado City/County Directories, as part of *U.S. City Directories, 1822-1995* **[Online Database],** digitized and indexed at the Ancestry.com website. See each directory title page image for the full title and publication information. This collection is one of the largest single databases on the Internet, with a total of 1.56 billion names, all indexed from scanned images of the city directory book pages. All states are represented except Alaska. Directories are included for a **Colorado Place** (No. of years), and Date Range: **Alamosa** (1) 1911, **Boulder** (27) 1896-1975, **Casper** (1) 1952, **Colorado Springs** (52) 1897-1988, **Colorado Statewide** (1) 1935, **Cripple Creek** (3 1900-1905, **Delta** (1) 1912, **Denver** (96) 1866-1953, **Durango** (1) 1911, **Florence** (1) 1905, **Fort Collins** (10) 1906-1995, **Grand Junction** (43) 1902-1994, **Greeley** (5) 1906-1946, **Jefferson County** (2) 1932-1933, **Larimer County** (1) 1976, **Leadville** (30) 1880-1913, **Longmont** (5) 1912-1943, **Loveland** (3) 1973-1975, **Montrose** (1) 1912, **Pueblo** (61) 1879-1991, **Salida** (5) 1903-1913), **Sterling** (1) 1911, and **Trinidad** (17 1892-1935. Use Ancestry's *Browse this Collection* feature to choose a state, choose a city, and choose a directory year available for that city. This U.S. database has 1,560,284,702 records. See
https://search.ancestry.com/search/db.aspx?dbid=2469.

1868-1990. *Colorado, State and Federal Naturalization Records* **[Online Database],** digitized and indexed at the Ancestry.com website. Source: Naturalization records at the National Archives, Denver, CO. Includes Declarations, Petitions, and Certificates. Each index record includes: Name, Naturalization age, Relation to head, Record type, Birth date, Birthplace, Naturalization date, Naturalization place, and Names of any relatives. The document image has more information. This database has 220,846 records. See
https://search.ancestry.com/search/db.aspx?dbid=61194.

1869-1917. *Early Denver Marriages* **[Microfilm & Digital Capture],** from a 225-page typescript by the Daughters of the Founders and Patriots of America, Vol. 11, the majority of the marriages took place in the City of Denver, but a number took place elsewhere in Colorado and in Wyoming, and some out of state. FHL film #165997. To access the digital images, see the online FHL catalog:
www.familysearch.org/search/catalog/290484.

1870. See *Colorado Territory, 1870 Federal Census: Population Schedules (Federal Copy)* **[Microfilm & Digital Capture],** from the original schedules at the National Archives, Washington, DC, filmed twice by the National Archives, 1962, 1968. The 2nd filming (on 2 rolls) is listed first and is usually easier to read. However, since some of the records were faded or lost between filming, search the 1st filming (on 1 roll) whenever the material on the 2nd is too light to read:
- 1870, 2nd filming, Arapahoe, Bent, Boulder, Clear Creek, Summit County (part) Includes Breckenridge, folio 146 only, Conejos, Costilla, Douglas, and El Paso, FHL film #545593.
- 1870, 2nd filming, Fremont, Gilpin, Greenwood, Huerfano, Jefferson, Lake, Larimer, Las Animas, Park, Pueblo, Saquache, Summit (part), and Weld Counties, FHL film #545594.
- 1870, 1st filming, Arapahoe, Bent, Boulder, Clear Creek, Conejos, Costilla, Douglas, El Paso, Summit, Fremont, Gilpin, Greenwood, Huerfano, Jefferson, Lake, Larimer, Las Animas, Park, Pueblo, Saquache, and Weld Counties, FHL #2686.

To access the digital images, see the online FHL catalog:www.familysearch.org/search/catalog/698887.

1870 Colorado Territory Federal Census (State Copy) **[Microfilm & Online Database],** from the Colorado Secretary of State's original schedules at the Colorado State Archives, filmed by the State Archives. An 1870 searchable database is accessible as part of the **Archives Search** (all databases listed on pages 243-4): www.colorado.gov/pacific/archives/archives-search.

1870. *Colorado Territory Census Index* **[Printed Index],** compiled and published by the Weld County Genealogical Society, Greeley, CO, 1977, FHL book 978.8 X2w 1870 index.

1870. *Colorado 1870 Census Index* **[Printed Index],** edited by Ronald Vern Jackson, published by Accelerated Indexing Systems, North Salt Lake, UT, 1981, 55 pages. FHL book 978.8 X22j 1870.

1870. *Colorado 1870 Census Index, A-Z* **[Printed Index],** edited by Raeone Christensen Steuart, published by Heritage Quest, Bountiful, UT, 2000, 131 pages. FHL book 978.8 X22c 1870.

1870-1880. *Federal Mortality Census Schedules and Related Indexes: Colorado* **[Microfilm],** from the original records at the DAR Library, Washington, DC. Each year includes an index prepared by the DAR. Filmed by the National Archives, 1962, 1 roll, Series T0655. FHL film #422411. To see if this microfilm was digitized yet, see the online FHL catalog:
www.familysearch.org/search/catalog/783096.

Colorado • 249

1870. *Colorado 1870 Mortality Schedule* **[Printed Index],** edited by Ronald Vern Jackson, et al, published by Accelerated Indexing Systems, Bountiful, UT, 1981, 20 pages. FHL book 978.8 X28j 1870.

1870. *Index to Gilpin County, Colorado 1870 U.S. Census* **[Printed Index],** by Alan Granruth, published by the Foothills Genealogical Society, Lakewood, CO, 1995, 146 pages. The alphabetical listings include house and family numbers, name, age, sex, color, occupation, real estate, personal property, and birthplace. FHL book 978.862 X28g. Also on microfilm, FHL film #2055223.

1870-1890 Pioneer Listing, Yuma County, Colorado **[Online Database],** indexed at the USGenWeb site for Yuma Co CO. See http://files.usgwarchives.net/co/yuma/history/ycpioneers.txt.

1870-1893 Court Records Index, El Paso County, Colorado **[Online Database],** indexed at the HomeTownChronicles.com website. See http://hometownchronicles.com/co/elpaso/epcourt7093.txt.

1870-1900 Federal Censuses, and 1885 Census, included in Archuleta County Records **[Printed Book],** transcribed by the Archuleta County Genealogical Society, Pagosa Springs, CO, ca1985-ca1995, 3 vols., Contents: vol. 1. Maps (1850 Iron County, Utah; 1860 Iron and Washington Counties, Utah; 1870, 1883 Conejos County, Colorado) and census records (1880 Conejo County, Colorado; 1885 Archuleta County, Colorado); vol. 2: Deaths (cemetery records, 1885 mortality schedule, misc. obituaries); vol. 3. 1900 census. Vol. 1 and 2 bound together by library. Includes indexes. FHL book 978.832 H2a v. 1-3. Also on microfiche, FHL fiche #6104872.

1871. *The Rocky Mountain Directory and Colorado Gazetteer for 1871: comprising a brief history of Colorado ... together with a complete and accurate directory of Denver, Golden City, Black Hawk, Central City, Nevada, Idaho, Georgetown, Boulder, Greeley, Colorado City, Pueblo, Trinidad, etc.* **[Microfilm & Digital Capture],** from the original publ. S. S. Wallihan & Co, Denver, 1870, 442 pages. Filmed by W.C. Cox & Co., 1974, 1 roll, FHL film #1000143. To access the digital images, see the online FHL catalog: www.familysearch.org/search/catalog/239943.

1871-1973. *Colorado State Penitentiary: Prisoner Index: Index A-Z* **[Printed Book],** compiled by Joy L. Snow, published by the author, c2000, 205 pages, FHL book 976.8 J62s.

1876 City Directory, Denver, Colorado **[Online Database],** includes Arapahoe County listings. Indexed in eight alpha sections at the USGenWeb site for Arapahoe Co CO, beginning with names A-B. See http://files.usgwarchives.net/co/denver/directories/den76ab.txt.

1873-1967. *Colorado, Roman Catholic Diocese of Colorado Springs Sacramental Records* **[Online Database],** indexed at the Ancestry.com website. This collection contains indexes for baptisms, confirmations, marriages, and burials. The starting date is based on the history of Colorado Springs's first catholic church. This database has 118,472 records. See https://search.ancestry.com/search/db.aspx?dbid=61562.

1875-1974. *Colorado, Wills and Probate Records* **[Online Database],** digitized and indexed at the Ancestry.com website. Probate records include Wills, Letters of Administration, Inventories, Distributions and Accounting, Bonds, and Guardianships. Each index record includes: Name, Probate date, Probate place, Inferred death year, Inferred death place, and Item description. A Table of Contents indicates the number of images and type of papers. The document images may have much more information. This database has 33,204 records. See https://search.ancestry.com/search/db.aspx?dbid=8665.

1876-1990. *Colorado, Naturalization Records* **[Online Database],** digitized and indexed at the FamilySearch.org website. Source: National Archives, Denver, eight collections, including declarations of intention, court orders granting petitions, and case files. Browse through the images, organized by these record types: Amended petitions, applications for oaths and court orders; Declarations index; Declarations of intention; Examiner's docket list; Naturalization cards; Naturalization case files; Naturalization reports; Oath of allegiance applications; Orders of the court; Petition evidence; Petitions for naturalization; Petitions for naturalization, petition evidence and special naturalizations; Petitions index; Transfer petitions; and Transfer petitions and petition evidence. This database has 259,357 images. See www.familysearch.org/search/collection/2285702.

- See also, *Colorado Naturalization Records, 1876-1990* [Microfilm & Digital Capture], this microfilm series has the digital images accessible for each of the 322 rolls of film, the first 17 rolls are for the Card File Index, organized in alpha order by the name of the petitioner, see the FHL catalog page:
www.familysearch.org/search/catalog/2285702.

1877-1952. *Naturalization Records Created by U.S. District Courts in Colorado* [Microfilm & Digital Capture], filmed by the National Archives, series M1192, 79 rolls. Most volumes are individually indexed. This series was digitized, and the digital images for each roll are accessible at the online FHL catalog page for this title:
www.familysearch.org/search/catalog/362325.
- See also, *Naturalization Records: Index to U.S. District Court – Denver, Colorado* [Printed Book], compiled and alphabetized by Patricia Crayne-Tudell and Joan Thomas, publ. Foothills Genealogical Society, Lakewood, CO, 1997, 245 pages. See FHL book 978.883 P42, Also on microfilm, FHL film #1425184.

1878-1882 Early Residents, Eagle County, Colorado [Online Database], names extracted from an article in the Eagle Valley Enterprise, April 1912, listing names of persons who settled in the county before it was organized in 1883. Indexed at the USGenWeb site for Eagle Co CO. See
http://files.usgwarchives.net/co/eagle/pioneers/pre1883.txt.

1879 Tax Roll, Colorado Springs, El Paso County, Colorado [Online Database], extracted from the Colorado Springs Gazette newspaper, Jan 4, 1880. Indexed at the USGenWeb site for El Paso Co CO:
http://files.usgwarchives.net/co/elpaso/taxes/1879tax.txt

1879-1880 City Directory, Manitou and Colorado City, El Paso County, Colorado [Online Database], indexed at the USGenWeb site for El Paso Co CO:
http://files.usgwarchives.net/co/elpaso/directories/1879mdr.txt.

1880. *Colorado, 1880 Federal Census: Soundex and Population Schedules* [Microfilm & Digital Capture], from the original records at the National Archives, Washington, DC (in 1970), now located at Colorado State Archives, Denver, CO. Filmed by the National Archives, 1970, 14 rolls, beginning with FHL film #377999 (1880 Soundex A160 – C415); and FHL film #1254087 (1880 Population Schedules, Arapahoe Co.). To access the digital images, see the online FHL catalog:www.familysearch.org/search/catalog/670371.

1880. *Colorado, 1880, Census Index, An Every-Name Index to Colorado's Population of 39,864 People* [Printed Book], edited by Ronald Vern Jackson, published by Accelerated Indexing Systems, Bountiful, UT, 1981, 470 pages. FHL book 978.8 X22j 1880.

1880. *Clear Creek County, Colorado Census of 1880* [Printed Extract & Index], a transcript of the original "1880 Short Form" records at the Clear Creek County Courthouse, compiled by Dorothy Kyler and Fae Tarrant, published by the Foothills Genealogical Society of Colorado, Lakewood, CO, 1987, 305 pages. Features an every-name index, arranged in alphabetical order by first letter of surname, age, color, and sex. From introduction: "On the completion of the 1880 Federal Census, some Colorado counties prepared lists of persons residing in the individual counties from the census schedule. Clear Creek County was one of the counties to prepare such a list." (Editor's comment: Actually, every county in the United States compiled the 1880 Short Forms, but few of them still survive). See FHL book 978.861 X2k. Also on microfilm, 1 roll, FHL film #1425410.

1880. See *Colorado 1880 Mortality Schedule* [Printed Index], edited by Ronald Vern Jackson, et al, published by Accelerated Indexing Systems, Bountiful, UT, 1981, 34 pages. FHL book 978.8 X28j 1880.

1880-1910 Federal Censuses and 1885 State Census, Gunnison County. See *Census Records, Gunnison County, Colorado, Present Precinct 2* [Printed Book], copied by Oscar D. McCollum, Jr., for Marble Historical Society, Marble, CO, 1983, 50 pages. Includes index. Includes 1880 census, Rockland Dainage; 1885 census, Crystal City and Scofield; 1900 census, Marble Village and Crystal; 1910 census, several localities in and near Crystal and Marble. Portions of Precinct 2 were formerly in Precincts 10, 22, and 24. FHL book 978.841 X2c

1880s-1920s. *Naturalization Index Cards, Archuleta County, Colorado* [Online Database], indexed at the USGenWeb site for Archuleta Co CO:
http://files.usgwarchives.net/co/archuleta/court/immigration/indxcard.txt.

1882 City Directory, Manitou and Colorado City, El Paso County, Colorado [Online Database], indexed at the USGenWeb site for El Paso Co, see http://files.usgwarchives.net/co/elpaso/directories/1882mccd.txt.

1882-1942. *Colorado, Church Records* [Online Database], digitized and indexed at FamilySearch.org. The records are from these film collections: *Baptisms, marriages, deaths, 1882-1906, Twenty-third Avenue Presbyterian Church* (Denver, Colorado); *Church records, 1882-1901, Methodist Church, Florence Circuit* (Florence, Colorado); *Church records, 1882-1943, Frazer Methodist Church* (Florence, Colorado); *Church records, 1891-1910, Rockvale Methodist Church* (Rockvale, Colorado); and *Church records, 1908-1935, Rockvale Methodist Church* (Rockvale, Colorado). See www.familysearch.org/search/collection/2353034.

1883 Tax List, Montrose County, Colorado [Online Database], indexed at the RootsWeb site for Montrose County, CO, see www.rootsweb.ancestry.com/~comontro/taxRoll1883.htm.

1883-1900 Death Records, Eagle County, Colorado [Online Database], indexed at the USGenWeb site for Eagle Co CO. See http://files.usgwarchives.net/co/eagle/vitals/deaths/deaths.txt.

1883-2010. *Mesa County, Colorado, Marriage Index* [Online Database], indexed at the Ancestry.com website. Original data: Mesa County Marriage Records. Mesa County Clerk and Recorder, Grand Junction, Colorado. Information that may be found in this database includes: Full Name, Spouse's Full Name, and Marriage Date. This database has 123,804 records: https://search.ancestry.com/search/db.aspx?dbid=61050.

✓ **1885 NOTE:** In 1885, the US Census Office offered federal assistance (half the cost) to any state or territory wanting to take a census in 1885. Only five states or territories took up the government's offer: Colorado, Dakota Territory, Florida, Nebraska, and New Mexico Territory. Each state/territory was to supply the federal government with a duplicate original (federal) copy of the census schedules for all counties and retain a duplicate (state) copy. For Colorado, both the federal copy and the state copy were microfilmed, but the federal set was much more complete. The federal set microfilmed by the National Archives is missing Fremont and Garfield counties, while the state copy filmed by the Colorado State Archives has Fremont but is missing Garfield and eighteen other counties. Although territorial censuses were taken in 1861 and 1866, the 1885 census was the only state census taken in Colorado.

1885 Colorado State Census- State Copies [Microfilm & Digital Capture], from the state's duplicate originals at the Colorado State Archives, Denver, CO. Filmed by the Colorado State Archives Microfilm Department, ca1957, 4 rolls, as follows:
- 1885 State Census (state copy), Arapahoe County, FHL film #929067.
- 1885 State Census (state copy), Chaffee, Conejos, Custer, Delta, Dolores, Douglas, Eagle, El Paso, Fremont, Gilpin, Gunnison, Huerfano, Jefferson Counties, FHL film #929068.
- 1885 State Census (state copy), Lake, Las Animas, Mesa, Park, Rio Grande, Weld counties, FHL film #929069.
- Another filming of Fremont County original at the Local History Center, Canon City Public Library in Canon City Colorado, filmed 1998, FHL film #2109433.

To access the digital images, see the online FHL catalog:www.familysearch.org/search/catalog/60816.

- See also, *1885 Colorado State Census-Federal Copies* [Microfilm & Digital Capture], from the duplicate originals at the National Archives, Central Plains Region, Kansas City, MO, filmed by the National Archives, 1949, Series M0158, 8 rolls, as follows:
- 1885 State Census (federal Copy), Arapahoe, vol. 1, FHL film #498503.
- 1885 State Census (federal copy), Archuleta – Clear Creek vol. 2, FHL film #498504.
- 1885 State Census (federal copy), Conejos – Elbert, vol. 3, FHL film #498505.
- 1885 State Census (federal copy), El Paso – Huerfano, vol. 4, FHL film #498506.
- 1885 State Census (federal copy), Jefferson – La Plata, vol. 5, FHL film #498507.
- 1885 State Census (federal copy), Larimer – Ouray, vol. 6, FHL film #498508.
- 1885 State Census (federal copy), Park – Routt, vol. 7, FHL film #498509.
- 1885 State Census (federal copy), Saguache – Weld, vol. 8, FHL film #498510.

To access the digital images, see the online FHL catalog:www.familysearch.org/search/catalog/173172.

- See also, *1885 Colorado State Census – Federal Copies* [Online Database], digitized and indexed at the FamilySearch.org website, taken from the 8 rolls of FHL microfilm, the federal set was missing Fremont and Garfield counties. The microfilmed state set includes Fremont but not Garfield. See www.familysearch.org/search/collection/1807096.

- See also, *1885 Colorado State Census – Federal Copies* [Online Database], digitized and indexed at the Ancestry.com website, This database has 195,979 records. See
http://search.ancestry.com/search/db.aspx?dbid=6837.

1885 Colorado State Census, Arapahoe County: Including the City of Denver and Portions of Present-day Adams and Arapahoe Counties [CD-ROM], a database compiled and published by the Colorado Genealogical Society, Denver, CO, 2002, FHL CD-ROM No. 1442.

1885. See *Bent County, Colorado, 1885 State Census* [Printed Extract & Index], compiled and published by the Southeastern Colorado Genealogical Society, Pueblo, CO, 51 pages. Includes index. FHL book 978.897 X2b.

1885. *Clear Creek County, Colorado Census Index, 1885* [Printed Extract], copied by Dorothy Kyler & Fae Tarrant, a photocopy of the original census book at the Clear Creek County Courthouse in Georgetown, CO, published by the Foothills Genealogical Society of Colorado, Lakewood, CO, 1988, 162 pages. FHL book 978.861 X2k.

1885. *Combined 1885 Clear Creek County, Colorado State Census: Being a Comparison of the Clear Creek County, Colorado Census Book and the State Census on Microfilm* [Printed Extract & Index], compiled and published by the Foothills Genealogical Society of Colorado, Lakewood, CO, 1994, 213 pages. Includes index. The comparison is between the county's original census book and the federal copy on microfilm. The county's copy was not microfilmed as part of "1885 Colorado State Census - State Copies," cited above. FHL book 978.861 X2c. Also on microfilm, 1 roll, FHL film #1698163.

The 1885 Census of Delta County, Colorado (Delta County's First Census) [Printed Extract & Index], transcribed by John W. Lynn, published by Lynn Research, Grand Junction, CO, 1987, 40 pages. FHL book 978.8 A1 No. 46.

1885 Census of Dolores County, Colorado (Dolores County's First Census) {Printed Extract & Index], transcribed by John W. Lynn, published by Lynn Research, 1987, 22 pages. FHL book 978.8 A1 No. 47.

1885 Census Index, Names A – L, Eagle County, Colorado [Online Database], indexed at the USGenWeb site for Eagle County, CO. See
http://files.usgwarchives.net/co/eagle/census/1885/1885ndxa.txt.

1885 Census Index, Names M – Z, Eagle County, Colorado [Online Database], indexed at the USGenWeb site for Eagle County, CO. See
http://files.usgwarchives.net/co/eagle/census/1885/1885ndxm.txt.

1885. *Index for the Colorado, El Paso County 1885 Census* [Printed Index], indexed by members of the Pikes Peak Genealogical Society, published by the society, Colorado Springs, CO, 1992, 176 pages. FHL book 978.856 X2i. Also on microfilm, FHL film #1425410.

1885. *Gilpin County, Colorado 1885 State Census* [Printed Extract & Index], computerized by Julie McKeown, published by the Foothills Genealogical Society, Lakewood, CO, 1992, 332 pages. Includes family/dwelling no., name, color, age sex, relationship, marital status, occupation, birth place of individual and parents. FHL book 978.862 X28m. Also on microfilm, FHL film #2055223.

1885 Census, Huerfano County, Colorado [Printed Abstract & Index], abstracted by Noreen I. Riffe, published by the Southeastern Colorado Genealogy Society, Pueblo, CO, 1994, 135 pages. Contains a list from Colorado postal history. The Post Offices, by William H. Bauer, James L. Ozment, and John H. Willard, 1885 mortality schedule and 1885 census listings for Huerfano County, Colorado. Includes index. Map on cover. FHL book 978.851 X2.

1885 Colorado State Census, Jefferson County [Printed Extract & Index], compiled and published by the Foothills Genealogical Society of Colorado, Lakewood, CO, 1998, 214 pages. Includes index. FHL book 978.884 X2c. Also on microfilm, FHL film #1425184.

1885. *Larimer County, Colorado 1885 State Census* [Printed Extract & Index], compiled and published by the Larimer County Genealogical Society, Ft. Collins, CO, 2000, 215 pages, FHL book 978.868 X2L.

1885 Census of Mesa County, Colorado (Mesa County's First Census) [Printed Extract & Index], transcribed by John W. Lynn, published by Lynn Research, Grand Junction, CO, 1987, 52 pages. FHL 978.8 A1 No. 48.

Colorado • 253

1885. *Park County, Colorado: 1885 state Census* **[Printed Extract & Index],** computerized by Opal Kendall Langino, published by the Foothills Genealogical Society of Colorado, 1995, FHL book 978.859 X28L. Also on microfilm, FHL film #2055223.

1885 Census, Pueblo County, Colorado **[Printed Abstract & Index],** abstracted by Noreen Riffe and Betty Polunci, published by the Southeastern Colorado Genealogical Society, Pueblo, CO, 1995, 397 pages. FHL book 978.855 X28r.

1885 Colorado State Census, Saguache County, Colorado **[Online Database],** indexed at the USGenWeb site for Saguache Co CO. See http://files.usgwarchives.net/co/saguache/census/1885ndxa.txt.

1885 State Census of Weld County, Colorado: With Index **[Printed Extract & Index],** copied and compiled by Jacquelyn Gee Glavinick, published by the Weld County Genealogical Society, Greeley, CO, 1984, 408 pages. FHL book 978.872 X28g.

1885-1910. See *Custer County, Colorado, Census Index: 1885 State Census, 1900 & 1910 Federal Census* **[Printed Extract & Index],** extracted by members of the Southeastern Colorado Genealogy Society, Inc., published by the society, 1987, 106 pages. Includes excerpts of births, marriages and deaths from several newspapers and lists of towns still in existence and extinct. Maps on covers. The 1885 state census is printed in full, with an index and followed by indexes to the 1900 and 1910 federal census records. FHL book 978.852 X2c. Also on microfiche, FHL fiche #6087804.

1885-1925 Court Case Index, Archuleta County, Colorado **[Online Database],** indexed at the USGenWeb site for Archuleta Co CO. See http://files.usgwarchives.net/co/archuleta/court/indx1885.txt.

1876-1923. See *Colorado State Business Directories* **[Online Databases],** digitized and OCR indexed at the Ancestry.com website. The following years are available, one database per year:
- *1876 Colorado State Business Directory.* See https://search.ancestry.com/search/db.aspx?dbid=27599.
- *1878 Colorado State Business Directory.* See https://search.ancestry.com/search/db.aspx?dbid=27600.
- *1879 Colorado State Business Directory.* See https://search.ancestry.com/search/db.aspx?dbid=27601.
- *1880 Colorado State Business Directory.* See https://search.ancestry.com/search/db.aspx?dbid=27602.
- *1881 Colorado State Business Directory.* See https://search.ancestry.com/search/db.aspx?dbid=27536.
- *1882 Colorado State Business Directory.* See https://search.ancestry.com/search/db.aspx?dbid=27533.
- *1883 Colorado State Business Directory.* See https://search.ancestry.com/search/db.aspx?dbid=27603.
- *1884 Colorado State Business Directory.* See https://search.ancestry.com/search/db.aspx?dbid=27604.
- *1885 Colorado State Business Directory.* See https://search.ancestry.com/search/db.aspx?dbid=27605.
- *1886 Colorado State Business Directory.* See https://search.ancestry.com/search/db.aspx?dbid=27606.
- *1887 Colorado State Business Directory.* See https://search.ancestry.com/search/db.aspx?dbid=27598.
- *1889 Colorado State Business Directory.* See https://search.ancestry.com/search/db.aspx?dbid=27543.
- *1890 Colorado State Business Directory.* See https://search.ancestry.com/search/db.aspx?dbid=27544.
- *1894 Colorado State Business Directory.* See https://search.ancestry.com/search/db.aspx?dbid=27607.
- *1896 Colorado State Business Directory.* See https://search.ancestry.com/search/db.aspx?dbid=27608.
- *1899 Colorado State Business Directory.* See https://search.ancestry.com/search/db.aspx?dbid=27609.
- *1900 Colorado State Business Directory.* See https://search.ancestry.com/search/db.aspx?dbid=27610.
- *1901 Colorado State Business Directory.* See https://search.ancestry.com/search/db.aspx?dbid=27611.
- **1903** *Colorado state business directory* https://search.ancestry.com/search/db.aspx?dbid=27612.
- *1906 Colorado State Business Directory.* See https://search.ancestry.com/search/db.aspx?dbid=27613.
- *1909 Colorado State Business Directory.* See https://search.ancestry.com/search/db.aspx?dbid=27614.
- *1910 Colorado State Business Directory.* See https://search.ancestry.com/search/db.aspx?dbid=27615.
- *1911 Colorado State Business Directory.* See https://search.ancestry.com/search/db.aspx?dbid=27616.
- *1920 Colorado State Business Directory.* See https://search.ancestry.com/search/db.aspx?dbid=27617.
- *1921 Colorado State Business Directory.* See https://search.ancestry.com/search/db.aspx?dbid=27618.
- *1923 Colorado State Business Directory.* See https://search.ancestry.com/search/db.aspx?dbid=27619.

1887-1939. See *Colorado State Reformatory Prisoner Records, 1887 through 1939* **[Printed Book],** by Gerald E. Sherard. Contains historical notes about the reformatory and an alphabetical list of inmates (usually 16-25 years of age), inmate number and volume or source. The Colorado State Reformatory is Buena Vista, CO. Published by the author, Lakewood, CO, 1995, 305 pages, FHL book 978.847/B1 J6s.

1887-1979. *Colorado, Steelworks Employment Records* **[Online Database]**, digitized and indexed at the Ancestry.com website. Source: Steelworks Center of the West. These employment applications and records contain a variety of information, including: Name of employee, Gender, Occupation, Birth date, Birthplace, Spouse of employee, and Parents of employee. The document image has more information. This database has 350,223 records. See
https://search.ancestry.com/search/db.aspx?dbid=61411.

1889 Tax Roll, Phillips County, Colorado **[Online Database]**, indexed at the USGenWeb site for Phillips Co CO. See
http://files.usgwarchives.net/co/phillips/taxes/1891taxroll.txt.

1890 Tax Roll, Archuleta County, Colorado **[Online Database]**, indexed at the USGenWeb site for Archuleta County, CO. See
http://files.usgwarchives.net/co/archuleta/taxes/tax1890.txt.

1891 Tax Roll, Archuleta County, Colorado **[Online Database]**, indexed at the USGenWeb site for Archuleta County, CO. See
http://files.usgwarchives.net/co/archuleta/taxes/tax1891.txt.

1892 Tax Roll, Archuleta County, Colorado **[Online Database]**, indexed at the USGenWeb site for Archuleta County, CO. See
http://files.usgwarchives.net/co/archuleta/taxes/tax1892.txt.

1892 City Directory, Denver, Colorado **[Online Database]**, indexed at the OldDirectorySearch site:
http://olddirectorysearch.com/Denver__Colorado_1892/index.html.

1893 Tax Roll, Archuleta County, Colorado **[Online Database]**, indexed at the USGenWeb site for Archuleta County, CO. See
http://files.usgwarchives.net/co/archuleta/taxes/tax1893.txt.

1894 Tax Roll, Archuleta County, Colorado **[Online Database]**, indexed at the USGenWeb site for Archuleta County, CO. See
http://files.usgwarchives.net/co/archuleta/taxes/tax1894.txt.

1895 Tax Roll, Archuleta County, Colorado **[Online Database]**, indexed at the USGenWeb site for Archuleta County, CO. See
http://files.usgwarchives.net/co/archuleta/taxes/tax1895.txt.

1896 Tax Roll, Archuleta County, Colorado **[Online Database]**, indexed at the USGenWeb site for Archuleta County, CO. See
http://files.usgwarchives.net/co/archuleta/taxes/tax1896.txt.

1897 Tax Roll, Archuleta County, Colorado **[Online Database]**, indexed at the USGenWeb site for Archuleta County, CO. See
http://files.usgwarchives.net/co/archuleta/taxes/tax1897.txt.

1897-2000. *Western States Marriage Index* **[Online Database]**, indexed at the Ancestry.com website. This is a project of the Special Collections & Family History department of BYU-Idaho, Rexburg, ID. The Colorado portion of the index has a small number of marriages for most counties, with a larger number for a few counties. To access the list, do a search at the Ancestry.com website database, and go to the link to the BYU-Idaho website, where more details about the county list and number of marriages is available. This database has 5,719 Colorado records. See
https://search.ancestry.com/search/db.aspx?dbid=70016.

1900. *Colorado, 1900 Federal Census: Soundex and Population Schedules* **[Microfilm & Digital Capture]**, from the original records at the National Archives, Washington, DC, filmed by the National Archives, 83 FHL rolls, beginning with FHL film #1242399 (1900 Soundex A000 – A450); and FHL film #1240117 (Population schedules: Arapahoe Co., City of Denver (ED's 1-37). To access the digital images, see the online FHL catalog:
www.familysearch.org/search/catalog/647801.

1900. *Boulder County, Colorado, 1900 Census Index* **[Printed Index]**, prepared under the direction of Lois Wescott and Mary McRoberts for the Boulder Genealogical Society, Boulder, CO, 1986, 187 pages, FHL book 978.863 X22b.

1900. *Index to Twelfth Census of the United States: 1900, Weld County, Colorado* **[Printed Index]**, copied compiled by Jacquelyn Gee Glavinick, published by the Weld County Genealogical Society, Greeley, CO, 1992, 163 pages. FHL book 978.872 X22g. Also on microfilm, FHL film #2055249.

1900-1925. *Colorado, Denver County Probate Case File* **[Online Database]**, digitized at the FamilySearch.org website. Includes probate case files acquired from the Colorado State Archives in Denver.

Files regarding insanity records and adoption material were restricted by the state when the records were acquired and are missing from this collection. This database has 1,544,153 images. Browse through the images, organized by Case File, and Date Range. See www.familysearch.org/search/collection/2015591.

1900-1939, 1975-1992 Statewide Marriage index **[Microfilm & Digital Capture],** from the original records of the Colorado Department of Health now at the Colorado State Archives, Denver, CO, filmed by the archives, 1975-1992. The card index images are arranged alphabetically by groom's name and gives county, names of husband and wife, their ages, race, date and place of marriage, certificate number, and other information. The computer print-out gives the names of the groom and bride, the county, and date of ceremony. These films are the best copies available. Original cards have been destroyed. The index for 1900-1939 has omitted many names, has poor alphabetizations and many cards are out-of-order. FHL has 106 microfilm rolls, beginning with FHL film #1690047 (Colorado Statewide Marriage Index, 1900-1939 Aab, Alexandra - Allen, Edgar J.). To access the digital images, see the online FHL catalog:
www.familysearch.org/search/catalog/565974.

1900-1992. *Statewide Divorce Index* **[Microfilm & Digital Capture],** from the original records of the Colorado Health Department now at the Colorado State Archives, Denver, CO, filmed by the archives, 1975-1992. A card index gives names of plaintiff and defendant, county, date and place of marriage, names and ages of minor children, date of decree, name of court, and docket number. A computer print-out index gives the names, decree date and type, and docket number. These films are the best copies available. Original cards have been destroyed. The index is in two formats: 1900-1939 is a card index and 1975-1992 is a computer print-out index. The index for 1900-1939 has omitted many names, has poor alphabetizations and many cards are out-of-order. FHL has 14 rolls, beginning with FHL film #1690153 (Colorado Divorce Records Index, 1900-1939 Aaby, Catherine - Bechwith, Maggie). For a complete list of roll numbers, roll contents, and the digital images of each roll, see the online FHL catalog page for this title:
www.familysearch.org/search/catalog/566255.
- See also, *Colorado Statewide Divorce Index, 1900-1939* **[Online Database],** digitized and indexed at FamilySearch.org with 89,708 records, see www.familysearch.org/search/collection/2043439.

1900-1939. *Colorado, Statewide Marriage Index* [Online Database], digitized at the Ancestry.com website. This database has 454,881 images. See https://search.ancestry.com/search/db.aspx?dbid=60251.

1900-1950. *Colorado, Jefferson County, Wheat Ridge, Crown Hill Cemetery Records* **[Online Database].** This database has 27,583 records, see www.familysearch.org/search/collection/3235393.

1901. *Ballenger & Richards Twenty-Ninth Annual Denver City Directory for 1901; Containing a Complete List of Inhabitants...* **[Online Database],** digitized and OCR indexed at the Ancestry.com website. This database has 1,737 pages. See https://search.ancestry.com/search/db.aspx?dbid=27994.

1902. *Ballenger & Richards Thirtieth Annual Denver City Directory for 1902; Containing a Complete List of Inhabitants...* **[Online Database],** digitized and OCR indexed at the Ancestry.com website. This database has 1,445 pages. See https://search.ancestry.com/search/db.aspx?dbid=28139.

1903. *Ballenger & Richards Thirty-First Annual Denver City Directory for 1903; Containing a Complete List of Inhabitants...* **[Online Database],** digitized and OCR indexed at the Ancestry.com website. This database has 1,503 pages. See https://search.ancestry.com/search/db.aspx?dbid=28140.

1904-1905. *R.L. Polk & Co.'s Colorado Springs, Colorado City, and Manitou City Directory, 1904-1905: Containing Complete Alphabetical ...* **[Online Database],** digitized and OCR indexed at the Ancestry.com website. This database has 638 pages: https://search.ancestry.com/search/db.aspx?dbid=27887.

1904-1905. *R.L. Polk & Co.'s Pueblo City Directory, 1904-1905; Containing an Alphabetically Arranged List of Businesses and Private ...* **[Online Database],** digitized and OCR indexed at the Ancestry.com website. This database has 638 pages: https://search.ancestry.com/search/db.aspx?dbid=27887.

1905 Tax Roll, Archuleta County, Colorado **[Online Database],** indexed at the USGenWeb site for Archuleta Co CO. See
http://files.usgwarchives.net/co/archuleta/taxes/tax1905.txt.

1906 County Directory, Larimer County, Colorado **[Online Database],** indexed at the USGenWeb site for Jackson Co CO. See
http://files.usgwarchives.net/co/larimer/misc/directories/1906drv3.txt.

1906-1921. See *Naturalization Records: Index to U.S. District Court – Denver, Colorado* **[Printed Index],** compiled and alphabetized by Patricia Crayne-Trudell and Joan Thomas. Indexed from the original volumes, entry 51, record group 21, located at the National Archives, Rocky Mountain Region, Denver, CO. Published by Foothills Genealogical Society of Colorado, 1997, 245 pages, FHL book 978.88s P42c.

1907 County Directory, Larimer County, Colorado **[Online Database],** indexed at the USGenWeb site for Jackson Co CO. See
http://files.usgwarchives.net/co/larimer/misc/directories/1907dir4.txt.

1907 Telephone Directory, Yuma County, Colorado **[Online Database],** indexed at the USGenWeb site for Yuma Co CO. See
www.cogenweb.com/yuma/data/teldir/yuma1907.htm.

1907-1928 Naturalization Petitions, Eagle County, Colorado **[Online Database],** indexed at the USGenWeb site for Eagle Co CO. See
http://files.usgwarchives.net/co/eagle/vitals/naturalization/natural.txt.

1910. *Ballenger & Richards Thirty-Eighth Annual Denver City Directory for 1910; Containing a Complete List of Inhabitants…* [Online Database], digitized and OCR indexed at the Ancestry.com website. This database has 2,043 records. See https://search.ancestry.com/search/db.aspx?dbid=27620.

1910. *Colorado, 1910 Federal Census: Population Schedules* **[Microfilm & Digital Capture],** from the original records at the National Archives, Washington, DC, filmed by the National Archives, 15 FHL rolls, beginning with FHL film #1374125 (1910 population schedules, Adams, Arapahoe, Archuleta, Baca, Bent, Chaffee, Cheyenne, and Clear Creek Co. (National Archives Series T624 roll 112). To access the digital images, see the online FHL catalog:
www.familysearch.org/search/catalog/648322.

1910. *Colorado 1910 Census Index* **[Printed Index],** compiled and published by Heritage Quest, division of ProQuest Information and Learning Company, North Salt Lake, UT, 2002, 3 vols. From introduction: "Only Heads-of-Household are extracted with the following exceptions: 1) Someone residing within the home who has a different surname, regardless of age. 2) All individuals living in an institution such as an orphanage, hospital, or poorhouse." Contents: vol. 1: A – Got; vol. 2: Gou – Oku; vol. 3: Ola – Z. FHL book 978.8 X22cc 1910.

1910. *Colorado, Montana, and Wyoming 1910 U.S. Federal Census Index* **[CD-ROM],** a publication compiled and published by Heritage Quest, North Salt Lake, UT, 2002. The Colorado name list is the same database as the published book shown above. See FHL CD-ROM No. 1164.

1910 Roster of Civil War Veterans, GAR Post, Grand Junction, Colorado **[Online Database],** indexed at the USGenWeb site for Alamosa Co CO:
http://files.usgwarchives.net/co/alamosa/military/civilwar/rosters/gargrand25nmt.txt.

1910 Roster of Civil War Veterans, GAR Post, Idaho Springs, Clear Creek County Colorado **[Online Database],** indexed at the USGenWeb site for Clear Creek Co CO:
http://files.usgwarchives.net/co/clearcreek/military/civilwar/rosters/garedbak22nmt.txt.

1910 United States Population Census, 1910 Index, Baca County, Colorado and 1890 Tax Assessment Roll, Baca County, Colorado **[Printed Index],** compiled by Valorie Millican, published by V. Millican, Campo, CO, 1998, 45 pages. Names are listed alphabetically; 1890 listing is alphabetical by location. 1910 listing includes names, age, sex, etc.; 1890 listing is name only. FHL book 978.899 X22m.

1910. *Boulder County, Colorado, 1910 Census Index* **[Printed Index],** by Mary McRoberts, published by the Boulder Genealogical Society, Boulder, CO, 1989, 150 pages. Index is alphabetical arranged by name and includes name, age, enumeration district, sheet, and line number. FHL book 978.863 X22m.

1910. *Weld County, Colorado, Index to Thirteenth Census of the United States, 1910* **[Printed Index],** compiled by Jacquelyn Glavinick, published by the

Weld County Genealogical Society, Greeley, CO, 1993, 358 pages. FHL book 978.872 X22w. Also on microfilm, FHL film #1750772.

1912-1913. *The Longmont City Directory, 1912-13: With the Longmont Rural Routes, the Towns of Mead, Lyons, Hygiene, Niwot, and Highland…* **[Online Database],** digitized and OCR indexed at the Ancestry.com website. See https://search.ancestry.com/search/db.aspx?dbid=27884.

1912-1941 Naturalization Records, Moffat County, Colorado **[Online Database],** indexed at the USGenWeb site for Moffat Co CO. See http://files.usgwarchives.net/co/moffat/vitals/natural.txt.

1913. *The R.L. Polk Directory Co.'s Pueblo City Directory, 1913* **[Online Database],** digitized and OCR indexed at the Ancestry.com website. This database has 360 pages. See https://search.ancestry.com/search/db.aspx?dbid=27888.

1913-1926. *Naturalization Records: Index to U.S. District Court – Pueblo, Colorado* **[Printed Index],** compiled and alphabetized by Patricia Crayne-Trudell and Joan Thomas. Indexed from the original volumes, entry 93, record group 21, located at the National Archives, Rocky Mountain Region, Denver, CO. Published by Foothills Genealogical Society of Colorado, 1997, 43 pages, FHL book 978.855/P1 P42c.

1914. R.L. Polk's Pueblo City Directory **[Online Database],** digitized and OCR indexed at the Ancestry.com website. This database has 528 records: https://search.ancestry.com/search/db.aspx?dbid=27889.

1917-1918. *Colorado Soldiers in WWI* **[Online Database],** indexed at the Ancestry.com website, from the book published by the Adjutant General, Colorado National Guard, 1941. This book lists more than 43,000 Colorado men and women who served in the military during World War I. The names are listed alphabetically and separated into sections by county, with the post office listed for the place where the person lived. The database gives each person's name, rank, and Armed Forces organization. See http://search.ancestry.com/search/db.aspx?dbid=5442.
- See also, *Colorado, World War I American Expeditionary Forces, Deaths, 1917-1919* **[Digital Capture],** To access the digital images, see the online FHL catalog: www.familysearch.org/search/catalog/3023916.

1917-1918. *Colorado, World War I Selective Service System Draft Registration Cards* **[Microfilm & Digital Capture],** from the original records at the National Archives, Washington, DC. The draft cards are arranged alphabetically by state, then alphabetically by county or city, and then alphabetically by surname of the registrants. Filmed by the National Archives, series M1509, 41 rolls, beginning with FHL film #1544462 (Adams County, A-Z). To access the digital images, see the online FHL catalog: www.familysearch.org/search/catalog/746969.

1917-1918 Information from Draft Registration Cards **[Online Database],** indexed at the USGenWeb sites for several Colorado counties. At the main directory list, select a county, then review the list of genealogical databases available online for each. See the Military category to find the 1917-1918 database. See the CO index at http://files.usgwarchives.net/co.

1917-1918 Servicemen, Washington County, Colorado **[Online Database],** extracted from the Roster of Men and Women Who Served in the World War from Colorado, 1917-1918, published by the Adjutant General, Colorado National Guard. Indexed at the USGenWeb site for Washington Co CO. See http://files.usgwarchives.net/co/washington/military/ww1/wcww1.txt.

1917-1945 Military Rosters, Cheyenne County, Colorado **[Online Database],** indexed at the USGenWeb site for Cheyenne Co CO. See www.cogenweb.com/cheyenne/honor.htm.

1919. *R.L. Polk Directory Co.'s Pueblo City Directory, 1919: Containing an Alphabetically Arranged List of Business Firms and Private…* **[Online Database],** digitized and OCR indexed at the Ancestry.com website. This database has 616 pages: https://search.ancestry.com/search/db.aspx?dbid=27890.

1920. *Colorado, 1920 Federal Census: Soundex and Population Schedules* **[Microfilm & Digital Capture],** from the original records at the National Archives, Washington, DC, filmed by the National Archives, Series 99 rolls, beginning with FHL film #1823723 (Soundex, A000 Frank thru A424), and National Archives Series T625, roll 155, FHL film #1820155 (Population schedules: Adams Co., Bent Co., Alamosa Co., Arapahoe Co., and Boulder Co.). To access the digital images, see the online FHL catalog: www.familysearch.org/search/catalog/557226.

1920. *Beeler's Official Map of the City and County of Denver: Approved by the City Engineers* **{Printed Map],** original published 1921 by the Beeler Map Co., Denver. This is a photocopy of the original map annotated by the Census Bureau, located at the National Archives, Central Plains Region, Kansas City, MO to show 1920 U.S census enumeration districts for the city of Denver in four parts. FHL map 978.883 E7b part 1-4 (Map Case). Also on microfiche, FHL fiche #6117550.

1923. *The R.L. Polk Directory Co.'s Pueblo City Directory, 1923* **[Online Database],** digitized and OCR indexed at the Ancestry.com website. This database has 541 pages. See
https://search.ancestry.com/search/db.aspx?dbid=27892.

1923-1952. *Colorado Air National Guard Service Records* **[Printed Index],** by Gerald E. Sherard. Listing includes name, box (container) no., unit, and birth date. Includes names of service personnel with service record at the Colorado State Archives in Denver. Includes historical sketches of the 120th Observation Squadron and 120th Photo Section (45th Division Aviation) unit and Buckley Air National Guard Base, FHL book 978.8 M22s.

1930. *Polk's Pueblo (Colorado) City Directory, 1930…***[Online Database],** digitized and OCR indexed at the Ancestry.com website. This database has 610 pages, see
https://search.ancestry.com/search/db.aspx?dbid=27893.

1930. *Colorado, 1930 Federal Census: Population Schedules* **[Microfilm & Digital Capture],** from the original records at the National Archives, Washington, DC, 24 rolls, beginning with National Archives Series T626, roll 2291, FHL film #2339964 (Population schedules: Adams, Archuleta, Alamosa, Baca, Cheyenne, and Clear Creek counties). To access the digital images, see the online FHL catalog:
www.familysearch.org/search/catalog/1034481.

1938-1939 *Telephone Directory, Delta County, Colorado* **[Online Database],** indexed at the USGenWeb site for Delta Co CO. See
http://files.usgwarchives.net/co/delta/misc/directory1938.txt.

1940. *Colorado Federal Census: Population Schedules* **[Digital Capture],** digitized images from microfilm of the original records held by the Bureau of the Census in the 1940s. After microfilming, Congress allowed the Census Bureau to destroy the originals to free up space for WWII-related files. Digitizing of the 1940 census schedules microfilm images was done for the National Archives and made public on April 2, 2012. To access the digital images, see the online FHL catalog: **www.familysearch.org/search/catalog/2057744.**

1940 Federal Census Finding Aids **[Online Database].** The National Archives prepared a special website online with a detailed description of the 1940 federal census. Included at the site are descriptions of location finding aids, such as Enumeration District Maps, Geographic Descriptions of Census Enumeration Districts, and a list of 1940 City Directories available at the National Archives. The finding aids are all linked to other National Archives sites. The National Archives website also has a link to 1940 Search Engines using Stephen P. Morse's "One-Step" system for finding a 1940 E.D. or street address conversion. See
www.archives.gov/research/census/1940/general-info.html#questions.

1940-1947. *Colorado, World War II Draft Registration Cards* **[Microfilm & Digital Capture],** from the originals at the National Personnel Records Center, St. Louis, MO. Filmed by the Genealogical Society of Utah, 270 rolls, digitized 2016. To access the digital images, see the online FHL catalog:
www.familysearch.org/search/catalog/2659397.
- See also, *Colorado, World War II Draft Registration Cards, 1942* **[Digital Capture],** Digital images of original records housed at the National Personnel Records Center in St. Louis, Missouri. These cards represent older men, ages 45 to 65 in April 1942, that were registered for the draft. They had birth dates between 28 Apr 1877 and 16 Feb 1892. Each card includes name of individual, date and place of birth, address, age, telephone number, employer's name and address, name and address of person who would know where the individual can be located, signature, and physical description. To access the digital images, see the online FHL catalog:
www.familysearch.org/search/catalog/2487364.

1941-1945 *WWII Veterans, Washington County, Colorado* **[Online Database],** indexed at the USGenWeb site for Washington Co CO. See
http://files.usgwarchives.net/co/washington/military/ww2/wcww2vet.txt.

1942. See *Colorado, Military Records: World War II 4th Draft Registration Cards, 1942* **[Microfilm & Digital Capture],** from the originals at the National Personnel Records Center, St. Louis, MO. Filmed by

the Genealogical Society of Utah, 153 rolls, digitized 2015. To access the digital images, see the online FHL catalog:
www.familysearch.org/search/catalog/2487364.

1943-1956. *Colorado Land Records* **[Digital Capture],** digitized by Family Search International, 2015, from originals held by the National Archives branch, Denver, CO. Include are serial registers of land transactions. To access the digital images, see the online FHL catalog:
www.familysearch.org/search/catalog/2526504.

1959-1960. *Colorado, Passenger and Crew Manifests* **[Online Database],** indexed at the Ancestry.com website. Original data: *Selected Passenger and Crew Lists and Manifests,* National Archives, Washington, DC. Each index record includes: Name, Birth date, Birth place, Arrival date, Port of arrival, and Nationality. The document (card) image may have more information. This database has 310 records. See
https://search.ancestry.com/search/db.aspx?dbid=9120.

1963. Colorado City Directories (Colorado Springs) [Online Database], digitized and OCR indexed at the Ancestry.com website. This database has 1,174 records: See
https://search.ancestry.com/search/db.aspx?dbid=8984.

1988-Current. *Colorado Newspaper Obituaries* **[Online Database],** digitized and indexed at the GenealogyBank.com website. includes obituaries from the following city newspapers: Akron, Arvada, Aspen, Bayfield, Boulder, Brighton, Broomfield, Brush, Burlington, Cañon City, Centennial, Colorado Springs, Conifer, Cortez, Dolores, Mancos, Craig, Denver, Dolores, Durango, Englewood, Estes Park, Evergreen, Fort Collins, Fort Morgan, Fowler, Frisco, Glenwood Springs, Golden, Granby, Grand Junction, Greeley, Gypsum, Highlands Ranch, Idaho Springs, Julesburg, La Junta, Lakewood, Lamar, Las Animas, Littleton, Lone Tree, Longmont, Loveland, Mancos, Meeker, Montrose, Parker, Rifle, Snowmass Village, Steamboat Springs, Sterling, Thornton, Vail, Westminster, Wheat Ridge, and Woodland Park. See
www.genealogybank.com/gbnk/obituaries/explore/USA/Colorado.

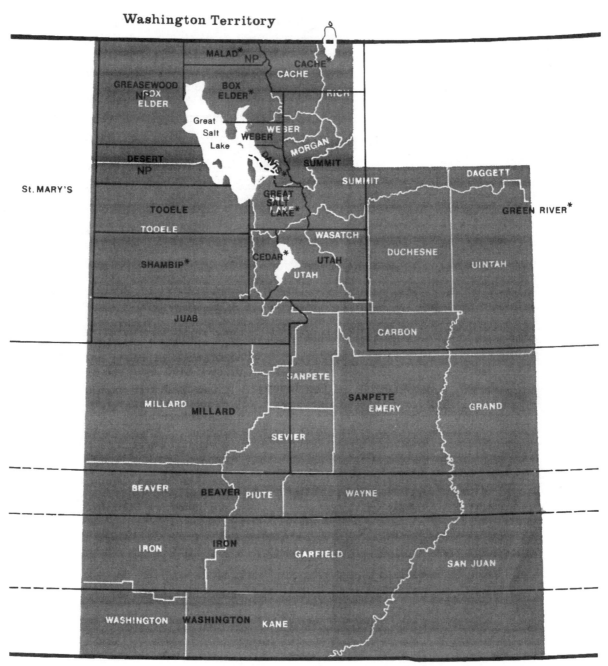

Utah Territory • June 1860. 21 of the 23 counties of Utah Territory at the time of the 1860 Federal Census are shown in black. The current 29 counties of the state of Utah are shown in white. The 1860 population was at 40,273 people. Beaver, Iron and Washington all extended west into present-day Nevada and east into present-day Colorado (no population recorded outside of present Utah). St. Mary's County had a few ranches enumerated, and Humboldt and Carson counties (not shown) both had populations recorded. About 90% (4,500 miners) of Carson's population was near the Comstock Lode/Virginia City area (now Nevada). *** Notes:** Desert, Greasewood, and Malad counties are shown as NP (no population). They were never organized. Cache County included a few Cache Valley families in present-day Idaho (they thought they were in Utah). Great Salt Lake County was renamed Salt Lake County in 1868. Cedar and Shambip counties were abolished in 1868. The settled part of Green River County was in the present-day Wyoming area. **Map Source:** Page 343, *Map Guide to the U.S. Federal Censuses, 1790-1920*, by William Thorndale and William Dollarhide.

Utah
Censuses & Substitute Name Lists

Historical Timeline for Utah, 1776-1896

1776. Fathers Silvestre Velez de Escalante and Francisco Atanasio Dominguez searched for a new route from Santa Fe to the missions in California. They were the first Europeans to explore present Utah.

1819. A Spanish-American treaty set the boundary between the Western U.S. region and Spanish region, which placed present Utah entirely within New Spain.

1821. Mexico won independence from Spain and reaffirmed the Spanish-American treaty boundaries of 1819 which included all of Utah, now part of Alta California, Mexico.

1824. General William Ashley's American Fur Company sent fur traders to northern Utah. One of them, Jim Bridger, discovered the Great Salt Lake.

1826. Jedediah Smith led the first overland expedition to California via present northern Utah.

1832. Antoine Robidoux established a trading post in the Uintah region of present Utah.

1841. Capt. John Bartleson led the first wagon train of settlers from Missouri to California. The route they followed became the northern Utah section of the California Trail.

1843. John C. Fremont and Kit Carson explored the basin of the Great Salt Lake.

1846. Near the beginning of their great migration from their winter camp at Council Bluffs, Iowa to the Salt Lake Valley, Brigham Young agreed to provide the U.S. Army with a battalion of 500 men, with orders to march on San Diego and secure it for the United States. Wages for the Mormon soldiers were paid in advance in gold and helped finance the main party's trip west. This act of support for the United States with the Mormon Battalion and their involvement in the Mexican-American war, was what obligated the Mormons to remain in the U.S. thereafter.

1847. The first parties of Mormon pioneers arrived in the Salt Lake Valley. It was the single largest migration group in American history. Over the next twenty years, as many as 50,000 followed the Mormon Trail to Utah. For their first year in the Salt Lake area, the Mormons laid claim to lands in the name of the United States, but the area was still part of Mexico.

1848. The Treaty of Guadalupe Hidalgo ended the war with Mexico. In the Mexican Cession of 1848, the Utah region was annexed to the United States, with an area that included Utah, Nevada, and parts of present Colorado and Wyoming.

1849. The first Constitutional Convention in Salt Lake proposed the State of Deseret which would encompass the region from the Continental Divide to California between Oregon Territory and New Mexico Territory.

1850. In September, the U.S. Congress rejected Statehood for Deseret, but established Utah Territory, encompassing the same region as earlier proposed for Deseret. Also in 1850, the University of Deseret (later University of Utah) was chartered. The *Deseret News* started in June.

1851. April. The 1850 Federal Census for Utah Territory was taken with a census day of April 1, 1851. The population was 11,380. Hundreds of the original pioneers had already left Utah to establish Mormon communities in present Idaho, Nevada, Arizona, and California.

1851. October. Governor Brigham Young picked a site at the geographic center of Utah for the first territorial capital. The town of Fillmore was built at the site. The first territorial capitol building was built in 1852, and still stands today.

1852. The LDS Church authorities publicly acknowledged the doctrine of plural marriage.

1853. The LDS Church began construction of the Salt Lake Temple.

1854. A grasshopper plague endangered crops. Thousands of seagulls converged to feed on the grasshoppers, saving the harvest. The Mormons saw it as an act of God, and the seagull remains a venerated symbol in Utah today – the California Seagull is the official state bird of Utah.

1856. The second Utah Statehood petition to Congress was rejected. Utah had reached the minimum population required for statehood, but Congress would deny Utah's petitions for statehood a total of six times over the next forty years. Also in 1856:
- Handcarts were first used exclusively by the pioneers traveling to Utah. For the next four years, over 3,000 people traversed the Mormon Trail with only the means of human power to pull their possessions.
- A territorial census was taken in this year.
- The territorial capital was moved from Fillmore to Salt Lake City.

1857. Brigham Young was removed as governor by President James Buchanan, who sent a 2,500-man military force to accompany the new governor, Alfred Cumming, to the territory.

1860. Federal Census taken in Utah Territory. Population at 40,273. Refer to the 1860 map on page 260.
- Also in early 1860, the Pony Express was extended from Salt Lake City to Sacramento.

1861. The final link of the first transcontinental telegraph line came together near present Wendover, Utah. The telegraph essentially ended the need for the Pony Express, which discontinued after less than two years of operation.

1862. The third petition for Utah Statehood was rejected by Congress.

1869. The Union Pacific and Central Pacific railroads met on May 10 at Promontory Summit in Utah Territory.
- The First non-Mormon church building in Utah (Church of the Good Samaritan-Episcopal) in Corinne was constructed.

1870. Federal Census taken in Utah Territory. Population at 86,336.

1871. Dedication of the first Catholic Church in Utah (St. Mary Madeleine).

1872. The fourth Utah Statehood petition was rejected by Congress.

1873. The Poland Act was passed in Congress making it legal to prosecute Mormons for practicing polygamy by defining the practice as bigamy, already covered by law as a felony. As a result, the Mormons began making their marriage records secret with no civil recording. Without proof of marriage, the federal law was essential unenforceable.

1879. The first telephone service was established in Ogden.

1880. Federal Census taken in Utah Territory. Population at 143,963.

1882. The Edmunds Act was passed in Congress, making "unlawful cohabitation" illegal. Unlike earlier laws, The Edmunds Act removed the need for prosecutors to prove that actual marriages had occurred. More than 1,300 Utah men were imprisoned under the terms of this measure.

1887. The sixth Statehood petition was rejected by Congress.

1890. LDS Church President Wilford Woodruff issued a Manifesto ending church-sanctioned polygamy.

1890 Federal Census showed a growth in Utah Territory to 210,779 inhabitants.

1896. January 4th. Utah became the 45th state in the Union. Salt Lake City was the state capital.

Utah State Archives

Over 70 separate databases are available online at the Utah State Archives website. Each database has a searchable list of names. The indexes are grouped within the categories of State and Territory, Counties and Cities, Courts, and Special Districts. The databases may include statewide military death certificates, birth certificates, and death certificates; countywide birth registers, incorporation case files, and divorce registers; and court records with naturalizations, case files, and much more. To review the complete list of databases, see the **List of Indexes** page at the UT State Archives website. See
http://archives.utah.gov/research/indexes/index.html#indexlist.

Bibliography
Utah Censuses & Substitutes

Available Censuses and Substitutes can be related to Utah's historical eras:

Utah Territory, 1847-1895. There were authorized territorial censuses in 1856 and 1895 but only the 1856 name lists survive. The Utah Bureau of Statistics reported to the first state legislative session that a "house-to-house canvas" was taken for Utah Territory in February and March 1895, but no name lists can be found.

Utah Federal Censuses, 1850-1940. Federal censuses are complete for all counties, with the exception of the 1890, lost in a fire for all states. The 1950 opens to the public in April 2022.

State of Utah, 1896-Present. The State Constitution of Utah was ratified soon after statehood in 1896 and authorized state censuses to be taken every ten years, beginning in 1905, but no record of an actual state census has been found.

Census Substitutes, 1847-Present. There are church censuses of members (head of households) of The Church of Jesus Christ of Latter-day Saints made public and filmed by the Genealogical Society of Utah. In addition to the territorial and federal censuses, there are many census substitute name lists that fill out the bibliography. Name lists may include Local Census Records, County Court Records, Directories, County Histories, State Militia Lists, Tax Lists, Church & Vital Records, and Voter Lists. They begin below in chronological order:

◆ ◆ ◆ ◆ ◆

1830-1900. Utah, FamilySearch, Early Church Information File [Online Database], digitized at the FamilySearch.org website. This is an image only database with index cards in alphabetical order for early members of the LDS Church. The names on the cards come primarily from sources from 1830 to the mid-1900s. The Early Church Information File (ECIF) was created using various sources including LDS church records, journals, biographies, cemetery records, immigration records and published books. Browse the images, organized by First and Last names. This database has 1,091,919 records. See
https://familysearch.org/search/collection/2078505.

- See also, *Mormons and Their Neighbors: An Index to Over 75,000 Biographical Sketches from 1820 to Present* [Printed Book & Digital Version], compiled by Marvin E. Wiggins, publ. Harold B. Lee Library, BYU, 1984, 2 vols., FHL book 974 D32. To access the digital version, see the online FHL catalog:
www.familysearch.org/search/catalog/212999.

- See also, *Cemetery Records and Index of Utah* [Printed Book & Digital Capture}, copied by members of the Church of Jesus Christ of Latter-day Saints, publ. Genealogical Society of Utah, 1953-1955, 17 vols. There are cemeteries in virtually all Utah counties. To review the contents of each volume and to access the digital images, see the online FHL catalog:
www.familysearch.org/search/catalog/289471.

- See also, *Utah, Cemetery Abstracts* [Online Database], records compiled by the Genealogical Society of Utah, 2020, see
www.familysearch.org/search/collection/2576051.

1840-1932. *Mormon Migration Database* [Online Database], indexed at the FamilySearch.org website. Source: BYU, Provo, UT. Index of pioneer immigrants with image links to journals, autobiographies, letters, and other narratives. The immigrants were from the British, Scandinavian, Swedish, and Netherlands

Missions. Images of the materials are found on the Brigham Young University website. This database has 143,658 records. See
https://familysearch.org/search/collection/2365248.

1846-1848. *We'll Find the Place: The Mormon Exodus* **[Printed Book],** by Richard E. Bennett, published by Deseret Book, Salt Lake City, UT, 1997, 428 pages. History of the Mormon pioneers from Nauvoo, Illinois to Salt Lake City, Utah. Includes a list of the original 1847 pioneers with birth and death dates and places. Includes index. FHL book 978 H2b.

1847. *Utah Pioneers of 1847* **[Online Database],** a complete list of the Pioneers of 1847, alphabetically arranged. It gives place and time of birth and death of most of the members, and also the present whereabouts of surviving pioneers. Indexed at the GenealogyTrails site for Utah. See
http://genealogytrails.com/utah/1847pioneers.html.

1847. *Index of the 1847 Pioneers* **[Printed Book],** photocopy of newspaper column originally publ. Salt Lake City: Salt Lake Tribune, 1934. Consists of abstracts of biographical sketches arranged alphabetically, with date of publication in the newspaper series, Day by day with the Utah pioneers, 1847, by Andrew Jenson. FHL book 979.2 H2saa.

1847-1850. *Sons of Utah Pioneers Card Index* **[Online Database],** indexed at the Ancestry.com website. Source: Sons of the Utah Pioneers, Salt Lake City, UT. This database is an index of people who came to Utah between 1847 and 1850. Information found within this database includes the pioneer's name, birth date, birthplace, death date, death place, and name of the pioneer company he or she traveled with. This database has 1,778 records. See
http://search.ancestry.com/search/db.aspx?dbid=6465.

1847-1859. *Pioneer Immigrants to Utah Territory* **[Online Database],** indexed at the Ancestry.com website. Source: Sons of the Utah Pioneers, Salt Lake City, UT. This database is an index to questionnaires completed by members of the National Society of the Sons of the Utah Pioneers (SUP). The forms contain 32 questions that provide vital information and other data of interest about individuals. This database has 2,548 records. See
http://search.ancestry.com/search/db.aspx?dbid=5423.

1847-1868. *Utah Mormon Pioneer Overland Travel Database* **[Online Database],** indexed at the FamilySearch.org website. Database from the LDS Church History Library containing a compilation of names obtained from rosters and other reliable sources of individuals who immigrated to Utah during this two-decade period. Many company pages include a list of diaries, journals, letters, and reminiscences written by company members, as well as contemporary reports about the company. The content of several thousand of those narratives has been transcribed and is included in the database. This database has 59,257 records. See
https://familysearch.org/search/collection/2517340.

1847-1868. *Mormon Pioneer Overland Trail* **[Online Database],** a website sponsored by the LDS Church History Department. The Home page has a great map of the Mormon trail through the states of Illinois, Iowa, Nebraska, Wyoming, and Utah. There are lists of the names of pioneers within the many companies organized. See
https://history.lds.org/overlandtravel/?lang=eng.

1847-1868. *Pioneers and Prominent Men of Utah* **[Online Database],** digitized and indexed at the FamilySearch.org website. Source: Book, same title, by Frank Esshorn, publ. 1913. Each index record includes: Name, Titles and terms, Event type, Birthplace, Father's name, and Mother's name. The images may include photographs and text, with more information about a person. This database has 5,897 records. See
https://familysearch.org/search/collection/2202712.
- See also, *Pioneer and Prominent Men of Utah Index* **[Microfilm & Digital Capture],** from a card index publ. Western Epics, Salt Lake City, 1966, 1,319 pages. Filmed by the Genealogical Society of Utah, 1979, 24 rolls, beginning with FHL film #1206309 (A-Ayton, James Edward). To access the digital images, see the online FHL catalog:
www.familysearch.org/search/catalog/595715.

1847-1948. *Utah, Juab County Records* **[Online Database],** digitized at the FamilySearch.org website. Source: FamilySearch extractions from Juab county courthouse records, Nephi, UT. This is an image only database with images of land and probate records. Browse the images, organized by Record Category, Record Type, and Record Description. This database has 62,885 records. See
https://familysearch.org/search/collection/2111252.

1847-1966. *Utah, Veterans with Federal Service Buried in Utah, Territorial to 1966* **[Online Database],** digitized and indexed at the FamilySearch.org website. This project was indexed in partnership with the Utah Genealogical Association. Name index and images of cemetery cards of veteran burials in the state of Utah to 1966. This database has 18,924 records. See
https://familysearch.org/search/collection/1542862.

1847-1966. *Utah Death Registers* **[Online Database],** digitized and indexed at the Ancestry.com website. Source: UT Dept of Health, Vital Records. Each index record includes: Name, Age, Birth date, Death date, Death city, Death county, Father, and Mother. The register image page may have more information. This database has 307,098 records. See
http://search.ancestry.com/search/db.aspx?dbid=6967.

1847-2000. *Utah Cemetery Inventory* **[Online Database],** indexed at the Ancestry.com website. Source: UT State Historical Society. Each index record includes: Name, Gender, Birth date, Death date, Death place, Burial date, Cemetery, Source, and Grave location. This database has 350,016 records. See
http://search.ancestry.com/search/db.aspx?dbid=5232.

1847-2000s. *Utah GenWeb Archives* **[Online Database].** The UTGenWeb site offers free genealogical databases with searchable statewide name lists and for all Utah counties. Databases may include Bibles, Biographies, Cemeteries, Censuses, Court Records, Deaths, Deeds, Directories, Histories, Marriages, Military, Newspapers, Obituaries, Photos, Schools, Tax Lists, Wills, and more. See
http://usgwarchives.net/ut/utfiles.htm.

1847-2000s. *Linkpendium – Utah: Family History & Genealogy, Census, Birth, Marriage, Death, Vital Records & More* **[Online Databases].** Linkpendium is a genealogical portal site with links to state, county, town, and local databases. Currently listed are selected sites for Utah statewide resources (401), Renamed Counties, Discontinued Counties (10), Beaver County (161), Box Elder County (263), Cache County (293), Carbon County (177), Daggett County (78), Davis County (267), Duchesne County (97), Emery County (148), Garfield County (117), Grand County (127), Iron County (146), Juab County (143), Kane County (115), Millard County (143), Morgan County (119), Piute County (97), Rich County (108), Salt Lake County (918), San Juan County (115), Sanpete County (202), Sevier County (137), Summit County (181), Tooele County (210), Uintah County (134), Utah County (478), Wasatch County (130), Washington County (199), Wayne County (88), and Weber County (346). See www.linkpendium.com/ut-genealogy.

1848-1992. *Salt Lake City, Utah, Cemetery Records* **[Online Database],** indexed at the Ancestry.com website. Source: Index from cemetery inscription and records from the Salt Lake City cemetery. Each index record includes: Name, Birth date, Death date, Plot, and Burial date. This database has 100,756 records. See
http://search.ancestry.com/search/db.aspx?dbid=7829.

1848-2001. *Utah, State Archives Records* **[Online Database],** digitized at the FamilySearch.org website. Source: UT State Archives. This is an image only database with images of various record types held by the Utah State Archives. Record types include civil and criminal case files, divorce records, probate case files and naturalization records for Beaver, Box Elder, Carbon, Davis, Emery, Garfield, Grand, Iron, Juab, Kane, Piute, Salt Lake, San Juan, Sanpete, Sevier, Summit, Tooele, Wasatch, and Weber counties. Coverage of record type and date range varies by county. This collection also include cemetery records for Beaver, Charleston, Fillmore, Garland, Glenwood, Grantsville, Hyrum, Junction, Kaysville, Marysville, Midvale, Murray, Paragonah, Salt Lake City, Scipio, and Spring City. This database has 433,665 records:
https://familysearch.org/search/collection/2001084.

1849-1877. *Utah, Territorial Militia Records* **[Online Database],** indexed at the FamilySearch.org website. Source: UT State Archives. This database includes records of the territorial militia (Nauvoo Legion) from Utah Territory. Papers include muster rolls, correspondence, payrolls, morning reports, receipts, returns, and journals. The collection is arranged by document number. The muster rolls, pay rolls, rosters, and officer lists have been indexed. This database has 63,053 records. See
https://familysearch.org/search/collection/1462415.

1849-1925. *European Emigration Card Index* **[Microfilm & Digital Capture],** from the originals at the Church Historian's Office. Also known as: *Crossing the Ocean Index, 1849-1925.* This is an alphabetical card index of names of many LDS Church members who emigrated from European countries to the United States. Contains names, age, nationality of emigrant; number of persons in group; name of ship;

date and place of departure and arrival; and source of information. The index is incomplete. To access the digital images, see the online FHL catalog: www.familysearch.org/search/catalog/331055.

1849-1949. *Utah, Salt Lake County Death Records* **[Online Database],** indexed at the FamilySearch.org website. This project was indexed in partnership with the Utah Genealogical Association. Name index and images for Salt Lake County death records from 1908-1949. The volumes are arranged chronologically. The entries are arranged numerically. Deaths from 1908-1949 were recorded on certificates. They are arranged numerically by registered number then by date of death (i.e. month & year). Some records in this collection may be for deaths occurring before 1908 where the remains were re-interred between 1908 and 1949. This database has 118,620 records. See https://familysearch.org/search/collection/1459704.

1849-1972. *Miscellaneous Marriage Index* **[Microfilm & Digital Capture],** compiled from civil records by various wards and branches and organized by the Genealogical Society of The Church of Jesus Christ of Latter-day Saints. From intro: "The Marriage License Card Index (also referred to as the Miscellaneous Marriage Index) contains names of persons compiled from marriage license records in the following county court houses: 1. Utah (Box Elder, Millard, Morgan, Salt Lake, Sanpete, Sevier, Summit, Utah, Wayne and Weber) 2. Idaho (Franklin and Lemhi) 3. Wyoming (Lincoln)." Card index arranged alphabetically by the surnames of both bride and groom. Filmed by the Genealogical Society of Utah, 1972. 190 rolls, beginning with FHL film #820155 (A – Anderson). To access the digital images, see the online FHL catalog: www.familysearch.org/search/catalog/282764.

1849-1985. See *Utah, Wills and Probate Records, 1800-1985* **[Online Database],** digitized and indexed at Ancestry.com. This collection was gathered from Utah State, County, District, and Probate courts. The inclusive date of 1800 was for a probate in Weber County dd 1890. The earliest county courts began in 1849. The collection includes wills, estates, letters of administration, inventories, and more. This database has 41,786 records, see www.ancestry.com/search/collections/9082.

1850. *Utah, Pioneer Index* **[Online Database],** indexed at the Ancestry.com website. Source: Sons of the Utah Pioneers, Salt Lake City, UT. Each index record includes: Name, Birth date, Birthplace, Departure age, Departure, date, and Company. This database has 3,020 records. See http://search.ancestry.com/search/db.aspx?dbid=5477.

1850 *Utah Territory, 1850 Federal Census: Population Schedules* **[Microfilm & Digital Capture],** from the original records at the National Archives, Washington, DC. The Utah Territory enumeration was conducted with a census day of April 1, 1851, revealing a population of 11,380 inhabitants. Filmed by the National Archives, 1964, 1 roll, FHL film #25540. To access the digital images, see the online FHL catalog: www.familysearch.org/search/catalog/744501.

- See also, *First families of Utah as Taken From the 1850 census of Utah* **[Printed Book & Digital Version],** a photocopy of the original census schedules, compiled and published by Annie Walker Burns; edited with an historical introduction by J. Emerson Miller, 1949, 115 pages. Includes index. FHL book 979.2 X2ba. Also on microfilm, FHL film #432616. To access the digital version, see the online FHL catalog: www.familysearch.org/search/catalog/183451.

- See also, *Index to Utah 1851 [i.e., 1850] Census* **[Printed Book],** typed by the Genealogical Society of Utah, 1950, 125 pages. FHL book 979.2 X22i.

- See also, *Utah 1850 Census Index* **[Printed Book],** edited by Ronald Vern Jackson, et al, published by Accelerated Indexing Systems, Bountiful, UT, 1978, 53 pages. FHL book 979.2 X22u.

- See also, *1851 Census of Utah* **[Printed Book & Digital Version],** transcribed by William Bowen, published 1972, 228 pages, a computer listing of all names in surname order. FHL book 979.2 X2b oversize. Also on microfilm, FHL film #924039. To access the digital images, see the online FHL catalog: www.familysearch.org/search/catalog/186877.

1850. *U.S. Census 1850, Davis County Utah* **[Printed Book],** copied by George Olin Zabriskie and Dorothy Louise Robinson, published 1937. Lists name of individuals, occupation of head of family, age, sex, and state or county of birth from the 1850/51 census of Utah Territory. FHL book 979.227 X2p. Also on microfilm, FHL film #824060.

1850. *U. S. Census 1850, Iron County, Utah* **[Printed Book],** copied by George Olin Zabriskie and Dorothy Louise Robinson, published 1937. 979.2 A1 No. 115.

***1850 Utah Mortality Schedule* [Printed Book],** edited by Ronald Vern Jackson, et al, published by Accelerated Indexing Systems, Bountiful, UT, 1980, 3 pages. FHL book 979.2 X2jm.

1850. ***Utah Supplemental Census Schedules, 1850*** **[Microfilm],** from the original records at the Utah Historical Society, Salt Lake City. Includes agricultural schedules, social statistics schedules; and mortality schedules for persons who died during the year ending June 1, 1850. Filmed by the Office of the Church Historian of the LDS Church, 1969, 1 roll, FHL film #1550328. To see if this microfilm was digitized yet, see the online FHL catalog:
www.familysearch.org/search/catalog/564540.

1850. ***Tooele County, Utah, 1850 Census*** **[Printed Book],** copied from the original 1850 federal census records (taken in April 1851) by George Zabriskie, typescript donated to the Family History Library, 1945. FHL book 979.2 A1 No. 128. See also The 1851 Census Records of Tooele County, Utah, copied by Sherman Lee Pompey, published by Historical and Genealogical Publishing Co., Independence, CA, 1965, 5 pages. Filmed by W.C. Cox, Tucson, AZ, 1974, FHL film #10000618, item 9.

1850. ***Utah County, Utah, 1850 Census*** **[Printed Book],** copied from the original 1850 federal census (taken in April 1851) by George Zabriskie, FHL book 979.224 X2p. Also on microfiche, FHL fiche #6105059.

1850. ***Sanpete County, Utah, 1851 Census*** **[Printed Book],** copied from the original 1850 Federal Census schedules (taken in April 1851) with an added index, by George Zabriskie, published 1945, FHL book 979.2 A1 No. 174.

1850. ***Census, 1851, Great Salt Lake County, Utah*** **[Printed Book],** a photocopy of the original 1850 federal census schedules (taken in April 1851) with an added name index. Published by the Genealogical Society of Utah, 216 pages. FHL book 979.225 X2p. Also on microfilm, FHL film #1307594.

1850. ***Census of Weber County, Excluding Green River Precinct: Provisional State of Deseret 1850*** **[Printed Book],** typescript prepared by the Historical Records Survey, Division of Women's and Professional Projects, Works Progress Administration. Includes index. FHL book 979.228 X2c.

1850-1870. ***Index to the 1850, 1860 & 1870 Censuses of Utah: Heads of Households*** **[Printed Book],** compiled by J. R. Kearl, Clayne L. Pope and Larry T. Wimmer, published by Genealogical Publishing Co., Inc., Baltimore, 1981, 402 pages. FHL book 979.2 X2k. Also on 5 microfiche, FHL fiche #6051336.

1850-1886 ***Deeds, Salt Lake County, Utah,*** **[Microfilm & Digital Capture],** from the handwritten copies of originals in the Utah State Archives, Salt Lake City, Utah. Some records have indexes. Records include deeds, land certificates, transfers of city lots, and records of bounty land grants for military service. Filmed by Holton, Jacobsen, Roach, Salt Lake City, 1955-1983, 63 rolls, beginning with FHL film #929288 (Deeds, Vol. A-B, 1850-1862). To access the digital images, see the online FHL catalog:
www.familysearch.org/search/catalog/208585.

1850-1890. ***Utah, Compiled Census and Census Substitutes Index*** **[Online Database],** indexed at the Ancestry.com website. Source: Accelerated Indexing Systems, Salt Lake City, UT, 1999. This collection contains the following indexes: 1850 Federal Census Index; 1856 Statehood Census Index; 1859 Tax List; 1860 Federal Census Index; 1870 Federal Census Index; 1880 Federal Census Index; 1890 Veterans Schedule. Each index record includes: Name, State, County, Township, Year, Page number, and Database. This database has 77,086 records. See
http://search.ancestry.com/search/db.aspx?dbid=3576.

1850-1962. ***Utah, Utah County Records*** **[Online Database],** digitized at the FamilySearch.org website. Source: FamilySearch extractions from the Utah County courthouse records. This is an image only database with images of naturalizations, land, and vital records. Browse the images, organized by Record Category, Record Type, Record Description, and Year Range. This database has 105,474 records. See
https://familysearch.org/search/collection/2257542.

1850-2005. ***Utah, Obituaries from Utah Newspapers*** **[Online Database],** indexed at the FamilySearch.org website. Source: J. Willard Marriott Library, University of Utah, Salt Lake City, UT. Each index record includes: Name, Titles and Terms, Event type, Event date, Event place, Gender, Age, Relationship to deceased, Birth year, Death year, and Newspaper name. This database has 109,185 records. See
https://familysearch.org/search/collection/2302011.

1851-1945. ***Utah Newspaper Archives*** **[Online Databases],** digitized and indexed newspapers at the GenealogyBank website, for Fillmore, Ogden, Salt Lake City, and Topaz. See
www.genealogybank.com/explore/newspapers/all/usa/utah

1851-1961. *Utah Probate Records* **[Online Database],** digitized at the FamilySearch.org website. This is an image only database with probate records, including case files and other documents created by the Probate Courts of various Utah counties. Probates were generally recorded in the county of residence. This collection covers probate records created 1851-1961, but the content and time period of the records will vary by county. Browse the images, organized by County, Record Type, and Record Description. This database has 427,179 records. See
https://familysearch.org/search/collection/1916182.

1852-1881. *Salt Lake County, Index to Probate Case Files* **[Online Database],** indexed at the Ancestry.com website. Source: UT State Archives, records of the Utah district court. Most probate cases that are included in this index involve either settling the estate of a deceased person or the guardianship of minors and the inept. However, adoption files may also be found in this index. Each index record includes: Given name, Middle name, Surname, Case number, and Subject. This database has 3,331 records. See
http://search.ancestry.com/search/db.aspx?dbid=6907.

1852-1887. See *Salt Lake County, Utah Civil and Criminal Case Files* **[Online Database],** indexed at the Ancestry.com website. Source: UT State Archives. During this time period, civil and criminal court cases were under the jurisdiction of the Probate Court. In addition to the civil and criminal cases, the index includes some probate case files, such as divorces, or debts. Each index record includes: Names, Plaintiff or Defendant, Case type, Filing date, Opposing party, Case, Reel, and Box/Folder number. This database has 7,751 records. See
http://search.ancestry.com/search/db.aspx?dbid=7074.

1853-1878 Salt Lake County Assessment Rolls **[Microfilm & Digital Capture],** from the original records at the Salt Lake County Clerk's Office, filmed by the Genealogical Society of Utah, 1966, 7 rolls, as follows:
- Assessment rolls, 1853, 1858-1861, FHL film #485541.
- Assessment rolls, 1862-1866, FHL film #485542.
- Assessment rolls, 1867-1868, FHL film #485543.
- Assessment rolls, 1868-1869, FHL film #485544.
- Assessment rolls, 1870-1874, FHL film #485545.
- Assessment rolls, 1875-1876, FHL film #485546.
- Assessment rolls, 1877-1878, FHL film #485547.

To access the digital images, see the online FHL catalog: www.familysearch.org/search/catalog/15108.

1855-1956. *Utah, Tooele County Records* **[Online Database],** digitized at the FamilySearch.org website. Source: FamilySearch extractions from Tooele county courthouse records, Tooele, UT. This is an image only database with marriage affidavits, grantor and grantee indexes, deeds, land abstract, discharges, naturalization records, will index and other land indexes. Browse the images, organized by Record Category, Record Type, Volume, and Year Range. This database has 114,486 records, see
https://familysearch.org/search/collection/1992424.

1856 Utah Census Returns **[Microfilm],** from the original records at the LDS Historical Dept. This is the only surviving territorial or state census conducted by Utah. Filmed by the Genealogical Society of Utah, 1981, 1 roll, FHL film #505913. To see if this microfilm was digitized yet, see the online FHL catalog: **www.familysearch.org/search/catalog/12915.**
- See also, *1856 Utah Census Index: An Every-name Index* **[Printed Book]** compiled by Bryan Lee Dilts, published by Index Publishing, Salt Lake City, 1983, 292 pages. FHL book 979.2 X22d. Also on microfiche, 3 microfiche, FHL fiche #6331392.
- See also, **Utah 1856 Territorial Census Index [Printed Book],** edited by Ronald Vern Jackson, et al, published by Accelerated Indexing Systems, Bountiful, UT, 1983. An every-name index. FHL book 979.2 X22u.

1856-1860. *Handcarts to Zion: The Story of a Unique Western Migration 1856-1860, With Contemporary Journals, Accounts, Reports, and Rosters of Members of the Ten Handcart Companies* **[Printed Book],** by LeRoy R. Hafen and Ann W. Hafen, published by Arthur H. Clark, Glendale, CA, 1960, 1976, 328 pages. Includes index. FHL book 973 W2hL. Also on microfilm, FHL film #1059487. Also on microfiche, FHL fiche #6031590. To see if this microfilm was digitized yet, see the online FHL catalog: **www.familysearch.org/search/catalog/54974.**

1856-1912. See *Church Records, 1856-1912* **[Microfilm],** from the original records at the LDS Church Archives, Salt Lake City, UT. The records are from the Utah Stake: Lake View, Mapleton, Pleasant Valley, Provo 1st-6th, Scofield, Springville 1st-4th, Thistle, Timpanogos, and Vineyard Wards. Filmed by the Genealogical Society of Utah, 1956-1962, 3 rolls, as follows:
- Priesthood quorum minutes 1856-1905 (some years missing), FHL film #26361.

- Annual genealogical report, Form E, 1907, FHL film #781501
- Record of children blessed and priesthood ordinations, 1912, FHL film #889347.

To see if this microfilm was digitized yet, see the online FHL catalog:
www.familysearch.org/search/catalog/100002.

1856-1960. *Utah, Box Elder County Records* **[Online Database]**, digitized at the FamilySearch.org website. Source: FamilySearch extractions from Box Elder county courthouse records, Brigham City, UT. This is an image only database with county records, marriages, naturalizations, military, probate, and land and property. Browse the images, organized by Record Type, Volume, and Year Range. This database has 68,348 records. See
https://familysearch.org/search/collection/1935517.

1858-1959. Utah, *Naturalization and Citizenship Records, 1858-1959* **[Online Database]**, digitized and indexed at the Ancestry.com website. Source: UT State Archives, records of Utah courts. Each index record includes: Name, Age, Birth date, Death date, and County. The document image has more information about a person. This database has 34,636 records. See
http://search.ancestry.com/search/db.aspx?dbid=2235.

1860. *Utah Territory, 1860 Federal Census: Population Schedules* **[Microfilm & Digital Capture]**, from the original records at the National Archives, Washington, DC. Filmed by the National Archives, 1950, 1967. The 1860 census was filmed twice. The second filming (2nd) is listed first and is usually easier to read. However, since some of the records were faded or lost between the first and second filming, search the first filming (1st) whenever the material on the second filming (2nd) is too light or missing. FHL has 3 rolls, as following:
- 1860 Utah: (2nd) Salt Lake, Great Salt Lake, Tooele, Green River, Summit, Davis, Weber, and Box Elder Counties, FHL film #805313.
- 1860 Utah: (2nd) Cache, Sanpete, Millard, Beaver, Iron, Juab, Utah, Washington, Shambip, Cedar, St. Mary's, Humboldt (Humboldt), and Carson, Davis, and Great Salt Lake and Slave Schedules, FHL film #805314.
- 1860 Utah: (1st) Entire territory, FHL film #25541.

To access the digital images, see the online FHL catalog: www.familysearch.org/search/catalog/707067.

1860 Utah Territorial Census Index **[Printed Book]**, edited by Ronald Vern Jackson, et al, publ. Accelerated Indexing Systems, Salt Lake City, UT, 1979, 576 pages. FHL book 979.2 X2j.

1860 Utah Supplemental Census Schedules **[Microfilm]**, from the original records at the Utah Historical Society, Salt Lake City, UT. Includes mortality schedules for persons who died during the year ending June 1st, 1860. Also includes agricultural, industrial, and social statistics schedules. Filmed by the Office of the Church Historian, LDS Church, 1969, 1 roll, FHL film #1550328. To see if this microfilm was digitized yet, see the online FHL catalog:
www.familysearch.org/search/catalog/276583.

1860 Utah Mortality Schedule **[Printed Book]**, edited by Ronald Vern Jackson, et al, published by Accelerated Indexing Systems, 1980, 5 pages. FHL book 979.2 X2jm.

1860-1937. *Utah, Early Mormon Missionary Database* **[Online Database]**, indexed at the FamilySearch.org website. Index and images of registers recording the departure and return of missionaries of The Church of Jesus Christ of Latter-day Saints. Images are from the Church History Department. This database has 42,039 records. See
https://familysearch.org/search/collection/2517343.

1860-1989. *Naturalization Index (District Court, 4th District)* **[Microfilm & Digital Capture]**, from records of the U.S. District Court, Salt lake City. Includes naturalization information for many residents in several Utah counties. Filmed by the Genealogical Society of Utah, 1989, 2 rolls, FHL film #1643939 (Aagaard, Hans G – Gourley, Robert); and FHL film #1643989 (Grace, Elizabeth – Zollinger, Jacob). To access the digital images, see the online FHL catalog:
www.familysearch.org/search/catalog/584307.

1861-1865. *Utah, Civil War Service Records of Union Soldiers* **[Online Database]**, indexed at the FamilySearch.org website. Source: National Archives microfilm series M692. Union service records of soldiers who served in Captain Lott Smith's Company, Utah Cavalry. The records include a jacket-envelope for each soldier, labeled with his name, his rank, and the unit in which he served. The jacket-envelope typically contains card abstracts of entries relating to the soldier as found in original muster rolls, returns, rosters, payrolls, appointment books, hospital registers, prison registers and rolls, parole rolls, inspection reports; and the originals of any papers relating solely to the particular soldier. Each index record includes: Name, Event type, Event Year, and Military unit note.

Each record also has a link to the images at the Fold3 subscription site. This database has 231 records. See **https://familysearch.org/search/collection/1932426**.

1861-1865 Index to Compiled Service Records of Volunteer Union Soldiers Who Served in Organizations From the Territory of Utah **[Microfilm],** from the original records at the National Archives, Washington, DC. Includes records from Captain Smith's Co., Utah Cavalry. Each index card gives name, rank, and unit in which the soldier served. Cross references are given for names that appear in the records under different spellings. Filmed by the National Archives, Series M556, 1 roll. FHL film #1292645.

1861-1865. Index to Soldiers & Sailors of the Civil War **[Online Database],** a searchable name index to 6.3 million Union and Confederate Civil War soldiers now available online at the National Park Service Web site. A search can be done by surname, first name, state, or unit. Utah Territory supplied 96 men to the war (all Union). To search the NPS Web site, see **www.nps.gov/civilwar/soldiers-and-sailors-database.htm**.

1861-1955. Utah, Cache County Records **[Online Database],** digitized at the FamilySearch.org website. This is an image only database with deeds and soldier discharges acquired from the Cache County courthouse in Logan. Browse the images, organized by Record Type, Volume, and Year Range. This database has 89,197 records. See **https://familysearch.org/search/collection/1951443**.

1861-1970. See *Utah, Military Records* **[Online Database],** digitized and indexed at the Ancestry.com website. Source: UT State Archives. This database contains military records on Utah servicemen and women created or collected by various state government agencies. They include questionnaires, index cards, photographs, and newspaper clippings going back to the days of Utah's territorial militia. The specific records groups include: 1) World War I Service Questionnaires, 1914-1918; 2) Military Service Cards, ca. 1878-1975; 3) Governor Wells Spanish-American War Scrapbook, 1898-1899; 4) Spanish-American War, Philippine Insurrection Service Cards, 1898-1902; and 5) Utah Indian Wars, Territorial Militia Service Cards, 1850-1880. Each index record includes: Name, and birthdate. The document image has more information about a person. This database has 217,181 records. See **http://search.ancestry.com/search/db.aspx?dbid=2228**.

1862-1867. Assessment Book, Division No. 1, for the Territory of Utah **[Microfilm],** from the original manuscripts at the Utah State Archives. Includes a name list of taxpayers and assessment details in alphabetical order. Filmed by the Genealogical Society of Utah, 1956, 1 roll, FHL film #25780. To see if this microfilm was digitized yet, see the online FHL catalog: **www.familysearch.org/search/catalog/21405**.

1863-1911. Utah, Select Marriage Index **[Online Database],** indexed at the Ancestry.com website. Source: UT Dept of Health, Vital Records, and UT County Clerks. Each index record includes: Name, Gender, Marriage date, Marriage place, Spouse, Spouse gender, and Certificate number. This database has 28,395 records: **http://search.ancestry.com/search/db.aspx?dbid=60978**.

1865-1915 Assessment Rolls **[Microfilm & Digital Capture],** from the original records at the Utah State Historical Society. May include the following records either within the record or as a separate part of the record: sheep tax, businesses, corporations, school tax records, mine proceeds and beginning in 1907 copies of the published delinquency notices. Filmed by the Genealogical Society of Utah, 1958-1965, 91 rolls, beginning with FHL film #164645 (1865-1866, 1870-1872, 1876-1877). To access the digital images, see the online FHL catalog: **www.familysearch.org/search/catalog/161530**.

1868-1869. Certificates of Citizenship, Box Elder County, Utah **[Online Database],** list of names extracted from the Box Elder County Probate Court. Gives a Name, Date, Country, and Page number. Indexed at the GenealogyTrails website for Box Elder Co UT. See **http://genealogytrails.com/utah/boxelder/immigration_certificates.html**.

1869-1953. Utah, Davis County Records **[Online Database],** digitized at the FamilySearch.org website. This is an image only database with images of naturalization, birth, deaths, land, and cemetery records from the county courthouse in Farmington, UT. Browse the images, organized by Category, Record Type, Volume, and Year Range. This database has 40,381 records. See **https://familysearch.org/search/collection/1922448**.

1870. Utah, 1870 Federal Census: Population Schedules **[Microfilm & Digital Capture],** from the original records at the National Archives, Washington,

DC. Filmed by the National Archives, 1962, 1968. The 1870 census was filmed twice. The second filming (2nd) is listed first and is usually easier to read. However, since some of the records were faded or lost between the first and second filming, search the first filming (1st) whenever the material on the second filming (2nd) is too light to read. FHL has 5 rolls, as following:
- 1870 Utah: (2nd) Beaver, Box Elder, Cache, Davis, Iron, and Juab Counties, FHL film #553109.
- 1870 Utah: (2nd) Kane, Millard, Morgan, Piute, Rich, Rio Virgin, and Salt Lake Counties, FHL film #553110.
- 1870 Utah: (2nd) Sanpete, Sevier, Summit, Tooele, and Utah Counties, FHL #553111.
- 1870 Utah: (2nd) Wasatch, Washington, and Weber Counties, FHL film #553112.
- 1870 Utah: (1st) Beaver, Box Elder, Cache, Davis, Iron, Juab, Kane, Millard, Morgan, Piute, Rich, Rio Virgin, Salt Lake, Sanpete, Sevier, Summit, Tooele, Utah, Wasatch, Washington, and Weber Counties, FHL #25542.

To access the digital images, see the online FHL catalog: www.familysearch.org/search/catalog/698922.

1870 Utah Census Index, A – Z **[Printed Book]**, edited by Raeone Christensen Steuart, published by Heritage Quest, Bountiful, UT, 2000, 154 pages. Includes name, age, sex, race, birthplace, county, and locale of census, roll and page number. Arranged in alphabetical order by surname. FHL book 979.2 X22s. See also, *Utah, 1870,* (Index), edited by Ronald Vern Jackson, et al, published by Accelerated Indexing Systems, North Salt Lake, UT, 1987, 273 pages. FHL book 979.2 X22u.

1870 Utah Mortality Schedule **[Printed Book],** edited by Ronald Vern Jackson, published by Accelerated Indexing Systems, Bountiful, UT, 1980, 12 pages. FHL book 979.2 X2jm.

1870. *Utah Supplemental Census Schedules, 1870,* **[Microfilm]** from the original manuscripts in the possession of the Utah Historical Society. Includes agricultural, industrial, and social statistics schedules. Filmed by the Office of the Church Historian, LDS Church, 1969, 1 roll, FHL film #1550328. To see if this microfilm was digitized yet, see the online FHL catalog: www.familysearch.org/search/catalog/274817.

1870-1896. *Utah Territorial Case Files of the U.S. District Courts* **[Online Database],** indexed at the FamilySearch.org website. Source: National Archives microfilm series M1401. This database includes 2,593 territorial case files of the U.S. district courts of Utah, 1870-1896. The district courts were located in Salt Lake City, Ogden, Provo, and Beaver. Most of the cases involve polygamy, but other issues were dealt with as well, including robbing of the mails, illegal voting, violations of liquor and tobacco tariff laws, possession of counterfeit coins, and embezzlement. Records were arranged by the surname of the defendant and numbered. This database has 39,040 records. See https://familysearch.org/search/collection/1854318.

1870-1937. See *Salt Lake County, Utah Coroners' Inquest Case Files, 1870-1871, 1886-1937* **[Online Database],** indexed at the Ancestry.com website. Source: UT State Archives, records of the district court. Inquests were held on individuals who died by unlawful means and on individuals whose cause of death was not certain. The case file of an inquest contains the result of the inquiry. This database is an index to the inquest case files of Salt Lake County from 1870 to 1871 and 1886 to 1937. Information provided in this index includes the name of the deceased, the date of inquest, and a reference to the location of the original record. This database has 508 pages. See http://search.ancestry.com/search/db.aspx?dbid=7345.

1873. *Salt Lake City Directory: Embracing a General List of Residents, and a Business Directory...* **[Microfilm & Digital Version],** from the original publ. Hannahs, Salt Lake City, 1873. To access the digital version, see the online FHL catalog: www.familysearch.org/search/catalog/311694.

1874-1920. *Utah County, Utah, Obituary Index* **[Online Database],** indexed at the Ancestry.com website. This database is also accessible at the BYU website. Each index record includes: Name, Publication date, Publication place, Death date, and a link to the BYU website. This database has 192,671 records. See http://search.ancestry.com/search/db.aspx?dbid=70483.

1875-1886. *Davis County, Utah Divorce Case Files* **[Online Database],** indexed at the Ancestry.com website. Source: UT State Archives, Probate Court, Divorce Case Files. Each index record includes: Plaintiff, Defendant, Box, Folder, Filing date, Case number, and Series number. This database has 178 records. See http://search.ancestry.com/search/db.aspx?dbid=7155.

1877-1880. *Davis County, Utah Divorce Registers of Actions* **[Online Database],** indexed at the Ancestry.com website. Source: Utah State Archives.

Each index record includes: Plaintiff, Defendant, Box, Folder, Filing date, Case number, and Series number. This database has 169 records. See
http://search.ancestry.com/search/db.aspx?dbid=7154.

1877-1918. *Utah, LDS Mission Calls and Recommendations* **[Online Database],** indexed at the FamilySearch.org website. Source: LDS Church History Department. This collection contains the letters to and from prospective missionaries as they received and accepted mission calls. Each index record includes: Name, Event type, Event Date, and Event place. This database has 39,590 records. See
https://familysearch.org/search/collection/2553860.

1879-1934. *Utah Grand Army of the Republic Membership Records* **[Online Database],** indexed at the FamilySearch.org website. UT State Archives. The collection consists of registers, lists and descriptive books of local post (chapters). Each index record includes: Name, Event type, Event date, Event place, and Birthplace. The document images may include town of residence, military unit, date of enlistment, date of discharge, age, and birthplace. This database has 5,612 records. See
https://familysearch.org/search/collection/2203361

1880. *Utah Territory, 1880 Federal Census: Soundex and Population Schedules* **[Microfilm & Digital Capture],** from the original records at the National Archives, Washington, DC. Filmed by the National Archives, 12 rolls, beginning with FHL film #378011 (Soundex, A000 – C400); and FHL film #1255335 (Population schedules, Beaver, Box Elder, and Cache counties). To access the digital images, see the online FHL catalog:
www.familysearch.org/search/catalog/676527.

1880 Utah Federal Census Index **[Printed Book],** edited by Ronald Vern Jackson, et al., published by Accelerated Indexing Systems, 1989, 380 pages. FHL book 979.2 X22u. See also Index to the 1880 Census of Utah, compiled by the BYU Research Center, Provo, UT, transcription filmed by the Genealogical Society of Utah, 1970, 7 rolls, as follows:
- Chinese and Indians; all others, A – B, FHL film #538587.
- C – Fe, FHL film #538588.
- Fi – I, FHL film #538589.
- J – Ma, FHL film #538590.
- Me – Q, FHL film #538591.
- R – S, FHL film #538592.
- T – Z, FHL film #538593.

1880 Utah Mortality Schedules **[Microfilm],** from the original records at the Historian's Office of The Church of Jesus Christ of Latter-Day Saints. Lists persons who died during the year ending May 31, 1880. Also includes supplemental schedules for the defective, dependent, and delinquent classes and special manufacturing schedules. Filmed by Office by the Church Historian of L.D.S. Church, 1969, 1 roll, FHL film #1550325. To see if this microfilm was digitized yet, see the online FHL catalog:
www.familysearch.org/search/catalog/564546.
- See also, *Utah 1880 Mortality Schedule* **[Printed Book],** edited by Ronald Vern Jackson, published by Accelerated Indexing Systems, Bountiful, UT 1981, 31 pages. FHL book 979.2 X2jm.

1880 Agriculture Section of the 10th Census for the State of Utah **[Microfilm & Digital Capture].** from the manuscripts at the Church Historian's Office, Salt Lake City and National Archives, Washington, DC, filmed by the Genealogical Society of Utah, 1959, 2 rolls, FHL #205643 (all counties except Cache); and FHL film #1255336 (Cache County agricultural schedules filmed after the Cache County population schedules). To access the digital images, see the online FHL catalog:
www.familysearch.org/search/catalog/178040.

1883-1889 Salt Lake City Directories. See *The (1883) Utah Directory Containing the Name and Occupation of Every Resident of Salt Lake City, and a Complete Business Directory of Every City and Town in Utah, Together With a Compendium of General Information* **[Microfilm & Digital Capture],** from the original published by J.C. Graham, Salt Lake City, 1883. Filmed by Utah State Archives and Records Service, 1975. 1 roll, FHL film #1004515. To access the digital images, see the online FHL catalog:
www.familysearch.org/search/catalog/312934.
- See also, *1885-1886 SLC Directories* **[Microfilm & Digital Capture],** FHL film #1004518. To access the digital images, see the online FHL catalog:
www.familysearch.org/search/catalog/810581.
- See also, *Utah Gazetteer and Directory of Salt Lake, Ogden, Provo, and Logan Cities for 1888, and a Complete Business Directory of the Territory* **[Microfilm & Digital Capture],** from original published by Lorenzo Stenhouse, 1988, FHL film #1004522. Another filming, FHL film #1670794. To access the digital images, see the online FHL catalog:
www.familysearch.org/search/catalog/313626.

- See also, *(1889) Salt Lake City Directory: Containing a Description of the City and its Attractions, Public Buildings, Churches, Schools, Libraries, Banks, Resorts, Amusements, etc., etc.* **[Microfilm & Digital Capture],** from the original by Kelly & Co., 1889, 264 pages, filmed by the Utah State Archives, 1975, 1 roll, FHL film #1004522. Another filming: FHL film #1670794. To access the digital images, see the online FHL catalog:
www.familysearch.org/search/catalog/311745.

1887-1914. *Utah, Select Marriage Records* **[Online Database],** indexed at the Ancestry.com website. UT State Archives. In this database are Utah marriage licenses, applications and certificate record books dating from the counties of Box Elder, Carbon, Davis, Iron, Juab, Kane, Utah, and Weber. The regulatory legislation for marriage ceremonies and records in Utah was defined by the Edmunds-Tucker Act of 1887. Each index record includes: Name, Gender, Birth date, Age, Spouse's name, Spouse's birth date, Spouse's age, Marriage date, and Marriage place. The document image has more information about the persons involved. This database has 33,402 records. See
http://search.ancestry.com/search/db.aspx?dbid=1971.

1887-1935. *Utah Marriages* **[Online Database],** indexed at the FamilySearch.org website. Source: FamilySearch extractions from records on microfilm at the Family History Library. Each index record includes: Name, Birth date, Age, Spouse's name, Spouse's Birth date, Spouse's, Event date, and Event place. This database has 245,379 records. See
https://familysearch.org/search/collection/1675546.

1887-1937. *Utah, Select County Marriages* **[Online Database],** indexed at the Ancestry.com website. Source: FamilySearch extractions from records on microfilm at the Family History Library, Salt Lake City, UT. Each index record includes: Name, Gender, Marriage date, Marriage place, Father, Mother, Spouse, and FHL film number. This database has 1,122,817 records. See
http://search.ancestry.com/search/db.aspx?dbid=60198.

1887-1939. *Utah, Weber County Marriages* **[Online Database],** indexed at the FamilySearch.org website. Source: Weber Co Courthouse, Ogden, UT. Each index record includes: Name, Titles and terms, Event type, Event date, Event place, Age, Birth year, Spouse's name, Spouse's birth year. The document images have much more information. This database has 94,859 records. See
https://familysearch.org/search/collection/2291514.

1887-1940. *Utah, County Marriages* **[Online Database],** indexed at the FamilySearch.org website. FamilySearch extractions from county marriage records on microfilm at the Family History Library. Each index record includes: Name, Titles and Terms, Event type, Event date, Event place, Gender, Age, Birth year, Spouse's name, Spouse's gender, Spouse's age, Spouse's birth year, and Page. This database has 448,984 records. See
https://familysearch.org/search/collection/1803977.

1887-1966. *Utah, Select Marriages* **[Online Database],** indexed at the Ancestry.com website. Source: FamilySearch extractions from records on microfilm at the Family History Library, Salt Lake City, UT. Each index record includes: Name, Gender, Marriage date, Marriage place, Father, Mother, Spouse, and FHL film number. This database has 698,243 records. See
http://search.ancestry.com/search/db.aspx?dbid=60201.

1887-1985. *Utah, Select Marriage Index* **[Online Database],** indexed at the Ancestry.com website. Source: UT Vital Records Office and UT County Clerks Offices. Each index record includes: Name, Gender, Marriage date, Marriage place, Spouse, Spouse gender, and Certificate number. This database has 883,216 records. See
http://search.ancestry.com/search/db.aspx?dbid=60965.

1888-1929. *Utah, Uintah County Naturalization and Citizenship Records* **[Online Database],** digitized at the FamilySearch.org website. Source: FamilySearch extractions from Uintah county courthouse records, Vernal, UT. This is an image only database with images of naturalization records, including declarations of intent, certificates of naturalization, orders of admission and petitions. Browse the images, organized by Record Type, Volume, and Year Range. This database has 409 records. See
https://familysearch.org/search/collection/2479767.

1888-1937. *Utah, Uintah County Marriage Records* **[Online Database],** digitized at the FamilySearch.org website. This is an image only database with images of marriage applications and certificates located in the county courthouse in Vernal, UT. Browse the images, organized by Record Type, Volume, and Year Range. This database has 8,687 records. See
https://familysearch.org/search/collection/2479768.

1888-1946. *Utah Deaths and Burials* **[Online Database],** indexed at the FamilySearch.org website. Source: Family Search extractions from records on

microfilm at the Family History Library. Each index record includes: Name, Gender, Burial date, Death date, Age, Birth date, Birthplace, Occupation, Race, Marital Status, Father's name, Father's birthplace, Mother's name, and Mother's birthplace. This database has 144,303 records. See
https://familysearch.org/search/collection/1675547.

1888-2004. Utah, Uintah County Land and Property Records [Online Database], digitized at the FamilySearch.org website. Source: FamilySearch extractions from Uinta Courthouse records. This is an image only database with images of deeds, deed indexes, and mining claims. Browse the images, organized by Record Category, Record Type, Volume, and Year Range. This database has 195,963 records. See https://familysearch.org/search/collection/2479771

1890. Utah Directory, 1890: Salt Lake City, Logan, and Provo [Online Database], indexed at the Ancestry.com website. Source: R. L. Polk Co, Excelsior Address Book Co, and Utah Gazetteer and Directory. This combined index is a good substitute for the lost 1890 federal census. Each index record includes: Name, Location, City, State, Occupation, and Year. This database has 41,516 records. See http://search.ancestry.com/search/db.aspx?dbid=4421.

1889-1908. Index to Mormons Incarcerated in the Utah Territorial/State Prison [Printed Book & Digital Version], by Melvin L. Bashore, publ. SLC, UT, 1987, 21 pages, FHL book 289.3 A1. To access the digital images, see the online FHL catalog: www.familysearch.org/search/catalog/568140.

1890 Utah Census Index: Special Schedule of the Eleventh Census (1890) Enumerating Union Veterans and of Union Veterans of the Civil War [Printed Book], edited by Ronald Vern Jackson, published by Accelerated Indexing Systems, 1983, 15 pages. FHL book 979.2 X22jv.

1890-1908. Utah, Salt Lake County Birth Records [Online Database], indexed at the Ancestry.com website. Source: Salt Lake County Clerk. This collection consists of a name index and images of Salt Lake County Birth records from 1890. Each index record includes: Name, Gender, Spouse's name, and Child name. This database has 99,292 records. See http://search.ancestry.com/search/db.aspx?dbid=60202.

1890-1915. Utah, Salt Lake County Birth Records [Online Database], digitized and indexed at the FamilySearch.org website. Source: UT State Archives, Salt Lake County birth records. Each index record includes: Name, Event type, Event date, Event place, Gender, Race, Father's name, Mother's name, and Source reference. This database has 33,262 records. See https://familysearch.org/search/collection/1464677.

1890, 1915, 1935 Salt Lake County Assessment Rolls [Microfilm & Digital Capture], from a typescript at the State Capitol Building, Salt Lake City, Utah. Includes 1915 index. Filmed by the Genealogical Society of Utah, 1966, 1969, assessment rolls beginning with FHL film #1654546 (1890); FHL film #497721 (1915); and FHL film #497720 (1935). There are indexes to the 1915 assessment rolls on 4 rolls. To access the digital images, see the online FHL catalog: www.familysearch.org/search/catalog/514900.

1892-1944. Utah, Birth Registers [Online Database], indexed at the Ancestry.com website. Source: UT State Archives, County Birth Registers. Each index record includes: Name, Gender, Birth date, Birthplace, Residence, and Father's name. The register image may have more information. This database has 35,934 records. See
http://search.ancestry.com/search/db.aspx?dbid=1908.

1892-1941. Utah Births and Christenings [Online Database], indexed at the FamilySearch.org website. Source: FamilySearch extractions from records on microfilm at the Family History Library, Salt Lake City, UT. Each index record includes: Name, Gender, Birth date, Birthplace, Race, Father's name, and Mother's name. This database has 34,079 records. https://familysearch.org/search/collection/1675542.

1895. Utah, Salt Lake County, Enrolled Militia [Online Database], digitized and indexed at FamilySearch.org. Rolls give name, age, address, and whether foreign or native born. Names are in alphabetical order by the first letter of the last name. This database has 8,901 records, see www.familysearch.org/search/collection/3031546.

1898-1905 Utah Death Index [Printed Book], compiled by Professional Chapter of Utah Genealogical Association; edited by Judith W. Hansen, published by Utah Genealogical Association, 1995,

1998, 2 vols. Statewide registration of births and deaths began in September 1905, but most counties began in 1898 with a few earlier. Includes Name, Sex, Age, Death date, County page number and entry or registration number. Listed in alphabetical order by surname. Contents: vol. 1: All counties, excluding Salt Lake County; vol. 2: Salt Lake County. FHL book 979.2 V42u.

1900. *Utah, 1900 Federal Census: Soundex and Population Schedules* **[Microfilm & Digital Capture],** from the original records at the National Archives, Washington, DC, filmed by the National Archives, 36 rolls, beginning with FHL film #1249012 (Soundex, B140 – B164); and FHL film #1241683 (Population schedules, Davis, Emery, Garfield, Grand, Iron, Juab, Kane, Millard, Morgan, Piute, and Rich Counties). To access the digital images, see the FHL catalog: **www.familysearch.org/search/catalog/653815**.

1901-1936. *Utah, Latter-Day Saint Biographical Encyclopedia* **[Online Database],** digitized and indexed at FamilySearch.org. This is the index and images to Andrew Jensen's compilation of biographical sketches, 4 vols., (1901-11936), see **www.familysearch.org/search/collection/2243396**.

1903-1914. *Utah, Birth Certificates* **[Online Database],** indexed at the FamilySearch.org website. Index and images of birth certificates acquired at the Utah State Archives. The records are organized by county, birth year, birth month and date. Some years are not currently available. This database has 66,432 records. See **https://familysearch.org/search/collection/1390750**.

1903-1911. *Utah, Birth Certificates* **[Online Database],** digitized and indexed at the Ancestry.com website. Source: UT Dept of Health, Vital Records. Each index record includes: Name, Gender, Birth date, Birthplace, Father, Mother, and State file number. The certificate image has more information. This database has 74,374 records. See **http://search.ancestry.com/search/db.aspx?dbid=9172**.

1904-1951 Utah Death Certificates **[Microfilm & Digital Capture],** from the original records at the Utah State Department of Health, Bureau of Vital Records & Statistics, Salt Lake City, UT. Arranged in chronological order by county of death. Some records may be filmed out of chronological order. Filmed by the Genealogical Society of Utah 2001, 157 rolls, beginning with FHL film #2230661 (Death Certificates, 1904, Beaver County – Salt Lake County). To access the digital images, see the online FHL catalog: **www.familysearch.org/search/catalog/1004924**.

1904-1961. *Utah, Death and Military Death Certificates* **[Online Database],** indexed at the Ancestry.com website. Source: UT State Archives, and UT Dept of Health, Vital Records. In Utah, statewide registration of births and deaths began in 1904. Death records are closed by Utah law for 50 years. In addition to records of those who died in Utah between 1904 and 1961, this collection includes military death certificates for soldiers who died in World War II and the Korean War. Although they died overseas, when the remains of soldiers were sent home for reburial, a death certificate was required by law for burial. Each index record includes: Name, Birth date, Age, Gender, Death date, and Death or Registration place. The certificate image has more information. This database has 295,282 records. See **http://search.ancestry.com/search/db.aspx?dbid=9174**.

1904-1964. *Utah Death Certificates* **[Online Database],** digitized and indexed at the FamilySearch.org website. Index and images of state death certificates acquired from the Utah State Archives. The records are arranged by year, county, box, and folder number. This database has 322,898 images. See **https://familysearch.org/search/collection/1747615**.

1905-1912. *Utah Applications Indian War Service Medals* **[Online Database],** indexed at the FamilySearch.org website. Source: UT State Archives. Index and images of applications for Indian war service medals. In 1905 the Utah legislature awarded service medals to veterans who served between 1850 and 1872 in conflicts with Native Americans. The collection is located at the Utah State Archives and is Series 2220. The applications are arranged alphabetically by veteran's name and include age, birthplace, residence, war served, date enrolled, rank, commanding officer, places served, years served, and type of service. This database has 8,017 records. See **https://familysearch.org/search/collection/2485051**.

1906-1930. *Utah Naturalization Records* **[Online Database],** digitized and indexed at FamilySearch.org. Source: National Archives, records of the U.S. District

Courts. This is a database with records filed at the U.S. District Court for the District of Utah. Browse the images, organized by Record Type, Year Range, and Volume Number. This database has 2,553 records. See https://familysearch.org/search/collection/2174938.

1906-1930. See *Utah, Federal Naturalization Records* **[Online Database],** digitized and indexed at the Ancestry.com website. Source: National Archives, records of district courts. Each index record includes: Name, Age, Birth date, Naturalization date, Naturalization place, Spouse, and Household members, listed by name and relationship. The document image has more information about a person. This database has 2,599 records. See
http://search.ancestry.com/search/db.aspx?dbid=61210.

1908-1949. *Salt Lake County, Utah, Death Records* **[Online Database],** indexed at the Ancestry.com website. Source: FamilySearch database of records obtained from Archives and Management, Salt Lake County, Salt Lake City, UT. Each index record includes: Name, Death date, Gender, Age, Marital Status, Race, Birth date, Birthplace, Father's name, Mother's name, and Document type. This database has 354,047 records. See
http://search.ancestry.com/search/db.aspx?dbid=60203.

1909-1917. *Utah, Indian War Service Affidavits* **[Online Database],** digitized at the FamilySearch.org website. Source: UT State Archives. This is an image only database with service affidavits of veterans who served in the militia during the Indian Wars. Original records located at the Utah State Archives. The collection is arranged alphabetically by surname within box and folder number. The affidavits were created to assist in validating pension claims. There are three types of forms: affidavit of soldier, affidavit of widow or child, and affidavit of witness. In most cases there will be two images per affidavit. Browse the images, organized by Surname Range, Box Number, and Folder Number. This database has 13,038 records. See
https://familysearch.org/search/collection/1392781.

1909-1919. *Utah, Index to Indian War Service Affidavits* **[Online Database],** indexed at the Ancestry.com website. Source: UT State Archives. Beginning in 1909 in Utah veterans of the Indian wars, under the direction of the Board of Commissioners of Indian War Records, completed affidavits of their service. The affidavits provide information such as the veteran's name, residence, age, date of enrollment in the military, type of company, captain's name, length of service, etc. If a veteran was deceased his wife or children could fill out an affidavit in his place. Affidavits were filled out mainly to authenticate pension claims. This database is an index to the affidavits. Each index record includes: Name, Reel number, and Note (with names of widow, signatures, and more). This database has 2,839 records:
http://search.ancestry.com/search/db.aspx?dbid=6887.

1910. *Utah, 1910 Federal Census: Population Schedules* **[Microfilm & Digital Capture],** from the original records at the National Archives, Washington, DC, filmed by the National Archives, 10 rolls, beginning with FHL film #1375615 (Population schedules, Beaver, Box Elder, and Cache Counties). To access the digital images, see the online FHL catalog: www.familysearch.org/search/catalog/646867.

1910 Census Index **[Printed Book],** by Heritage Quest, North Salt Lake, UT, 2001, 750 pages. Arranged in alphabetical order by surname. FHL book 979.2 X22h. See also *Arizona, Nevada, New Mexico and Utah 1910 U.S. Federal Census Index,* CD-ROM publication by Heritage Quest, North Salt Lake, UT, 2001. FHL CD-ROM No. 1191.

1914-1960 Church Census Records **[Microfilm & Digital Capture],** from the original records in the LDS Church Historian's Office. Church census records include name lists arranged alphabetically by head of household for the years 1914, 1920, 1925, 1930, 1935, 1940, 1950, 1955, and 1960. Included with the 1914-1935 census are some delayed birth certificates which originated in the Church Historian's Office and a few Salt Lake Granite Stake genealogical survey cards. Filmed by the Genealogical Society of Utah, 1962, 651 rolls, beginning with FHL film #25708 (1914-1935: Aabo – Alex). To access the digital images, see the online FHL catalog:
www.familysearch.org/search/catalog/126146.

- See also, **LDS Church Census, 1930-1935, Peterson Miscellaneous [Microfilm],** filmed by the Genealogical Society of Utah, 1966, 1 roll, FHL film #423837. To see if this microfilm was digitized yet, see the online FHL catalog:
www.familysearch.org/search/catalog/257765.

1917-1918. *Utah, World War I County Draft Board Registers, Name Index* **[Online Database],** digitized and indexed at FamilySearch.org. Source: UT State Archives. See
www.familysearch.org/search/collection/3019074.

- See also, *Utah, World War I Selective Service System Draft Registration Cards, 1917-1918* [Microfilm & Digital Capture], The draft cards are arranged alphabetically by state, then alphabetically by county or city, and then alphabetically by surname of registrants. filmed by the National Archives, 1988, 20 rolls, beginning with FHL film #1983881 (Beaver, Box Elder, and Cache counties). To access the digital images, see the online FHL catalog:
www.familysearch.org/search/catalog/754898.

- See also, *Utah, World War I American Expeditionary Forces, Deaths* [Digital Capture], from the originals at the National Archives, digitized by FamilySearch International, 2018. To access the digital images, see the online FHL catalog:
www.familysearch.org/search/catalog/3023954.

- See also, *Utah, World War I Service Questionnaires, 1914-1918* [Online Database], digitized and indexed at FamilySearch.org. Source: UT State Archives. This database has 6,496 records, see
www.familysearch.org/search/collection/3028759.

- See also, *Utah, World War I Militia Lists, 1917-1918* [Online Database], digitized and indexed at FamilySearch.org. Source: UT State Archives. Lists of Utah militia men ages 18-45 in Salt Lake County who served in WWI during the years 1917-1918. These lists contain the name, address, age, and occupation of each person on the list. This database has 26,019 records, see
www.familysearch.org/search/collection/3031545.

1920. *Utah, 1920 Federal Census: Soundex and Population Schedules* [Microfilm & Digital Capture], of original records at the National Archives, Washington, DC, filmed by the National Archives, 42 rolls, beginning with FHL film #1830770 (Soundex, A000-A126); and FHL film #1821861 (Population schedules, Beaver, Box Elder, and Cache Counties). To access the digital images (Population Schedules), see the online FHL catalog:
www.familysearch.org/search/catalog/534285.

1920 Utah Census [CD-ROM], containing all census sheet images from the population schedules, with an added index to the entire population. Compiled and published by the Utah Valley Regional Family History Center at Brigham Young University's Harold B. Lee Library; index by Deanne Roberts; Clinton Ashworth, coordinator. FHL CD-ROM No. 756.

1920. *Extracted Soundex Index, Utah, 1920 U.S. Census: From Microfilm 1830770 to 1830802* [Printed Book], by Deanne Roberts, et al., published by Brigham University Library, Provo, UT, 2 vols., 2001. From intro: "Names in this index are extracted from card images on 33 Soundex microfilms for the Utah 1920 U.S. Census (LDS numbers 1830770-1830802). Generally only heads of households and occupants with different surnames are included." Contents: vol. 1. A123 - L200 (Evan); vol. 2: L200 (Mable) - Z612. Arranged in alphabetical order by Soundex code, with some mixed codes. FHL book 979.2 X22r 1920 v. 1-2.

1923-1977. *The Salt Lake Tribune, Salt Lake City, Utah* [Online Database], indexed at the Ancestry.com website. This database is a fully searchable text version of the newspaper. With an OCR index to Names, Dates, Locations, and Keywords. This database has 206,884 records. See
http://search.ancestry.com/search/db.aspx?dbid=6872.

1930. *Utah, 1930 Federal Census: Population Schedules* [Microfilm & Digital Capture], from the original records at the National Archives in Washington, DC. Filmed by the National Archives as microfilm publication T626, 12 rolls, beginning with FHL film #2342148 (Population schedules: Beaver, Box Elder, and Cache Counties). To access the digital images, see the online FHL catalog:
www.familysearch.org/search/catalog/1037525.

1933-1939. *Daughters of Utah Pioneers Obituary Scrapbook* [Online Database], indexed at the Ancestry.com website. Source: Daughters of Utah Pioneers, Salt Lake City, UT. This database, extracted from newspaper clippings faithfully extracted from Utah publications by the Daughters of the Utah Pioneers, lists vital events from 1933 to 1939. Hundreds of individuals and their families are listed in connection with obituaries, marriage notices, etc. Search by keyword, Title, or Comment. This database has 5,887 records. See
http://search.ancestry.com/search/db.aspx?dbid=3238.

1940. *Utah, 1940 Federal Census: Population Schedules* [Digital Capture]. After microfilming, Congress allowed the Census Bureau to destroy the originals to free up space for WWII-related files. Microfilm for the 1940 federal census was acquired by the Family History Library, but the film is in storage

at the Granite Mountain Vault and not available for library viewing. Digitizing of the 1940 census schedules microfilm images was made public on April 2, 2012. To access the digital images, see the online FHL catalog:
www.familysearch.org/search/catalog/2057793.

1940 Federal Census Finding Aids [Online Database]. The National Archives prepared a special website online with a detailed description of the 1940 federal census. Included at the site are descriptions of location finding aids, such as Enumeration District Maps, Geographic Descriptions of Census Enumeration Districts, and a list of 1940 City Directories available at the National Archives. The finding aids are all linked to other National Archives sites. The National Archives website also has a link to 1940 Search Engines using Stephen P. Morse's "One-Step" system for finding a 1940 E.D. or street address conversion. See
www.archives.gov/research/census/1940/general-info.html#questions.

1940-1947. *Utah, World War II Draft Registration Cards* [Digital Capture], from the originals at the National Personnel Records Center, St. Louis, MO. Draft registration cards of men who registered during World War II, with the exception of the fourth registration. Images courtesy of Ancestry. The event place is the residence of the registrant. To access the digital images, see the online FHL catalog:
www.familysearch.org/search/catalog/2659402.

- See also, *Utah, Military Records: World War II Draft Registration Cards, 1942* [Digital Capture], from the originals at the National Personnel Records Center, St. Louis, MO. These cards represent older men, ages 45 to 65 in April 1942, that were registered for the draft. They had birth dates between 28 Apr 1877 and 16 Feb 1892. Includes name of individual, date and place of birth, address, age, telephone number, employer's name and address, name and address of person who would know where the individual can be located, signature, and physical description. To access the digital images, see the online FHL catalog:
www.familysearch.org/search/catalog/2624864.

1941-1945. *Index to Military Records of World War II, Veterans From Utah* [Microfilm & Digital Capture], from the original records at the Utah State Archives, Salt Lake City. An alphabetical index to veterans, with separate lists for army, navy, coast guard, marines, and maritime service veterans. Filmed by the Genealogical Society of Utah, 1966, 11 rolls, as follows:
- Army vets, A-Comstock, FHL film #536228.
- Army vets, Conant-Hjortsberg, FHL film #536229.
- Army vets, Hoadley-Mortensen, FHL film #536230.
- Army vets, Mortensen, E.-Shytles, FHL film #536231.
- Army vets, Sibert-Zwillman, FHL film #536232.
- Navy vets, Aagard-Gyll, FHL film #536233.
- Navy vets, Haacke-Smyth, FHL film #536234.
- Navy vets, Snarr – Zwaharn, FHL film #536235.
- Coast Guard vets, A – Z, FHL film #536236.
- Marine vets, A – Z, FHL film #536237.
- Maritime service vet, A – Z, FHL film #536238.

To access the digital images, see the online FHL catalog: www.familysearch.org/search/catalog/172752.

1947-1976. *Utah, Salt Lake City Cemetery Records* [Online Database], digitized at the FamilySearch.org website. Source: US State Archives. This is an image only database with city cemetery records acquired from the UT State Archives. The collection includes a general index, plat books, interment records, deed registers, record of the dead and grave opening orders. Browse the images, organized by Record Type. This database has 70,504 records. See
https://familysearch.org/search/collection/2094273.

1959-2013. *Utah, Tremonton, and Garland Obituaries* [Online Database], digitized and indexed at the FamilySearch.org website. Index and images of obituaries collected by the LDS family history center in Tremonton and Garland. The images are mostly the newspaper clipping of the obituary. This database has 18,360 records. See
https://familysearch.org/search/collection/2427925.

1969-1953. *Utah, Davis County Records* [Online Database], indexed at the Ancestry.com website. Source: FamilySearch database. This database is for images only of these records from the county courthouse in Farmington: Births (1898-1905); Deaths (1898-1953, dates vary by registration district); Marriages (1887-1907); Land records (1869-1946); Land record indexes (various years); Naturalization and citizenship papers (1932-1938); Cemetery records (Lakewood Cemetery, no dates); Wills (1877-1968); and Mining claims (1871-1918). Many of the record types have indexes which are included in this collection. Browse the images, organized by Record Type, Volume, and Year Range. This database has 40,381 records. See
http://search.ancestry.com/search/db.aspx?dbid=60199.

1988-Current. *Utah Recent Newspaper Obituaries* **[Online Database],** digitized and indexed newspaper obituaries at the GenealogyBank website, including newspapers for Bountiful, Castle Dale, Logan, Ogden, Park City, Price, Provo, Richfield, Roosevelt, Salt Lake City, and Vernal. See **www.genealogybank.com/explore/obituaries/all/usa/utah.**

2010-2014. *ObitsUtah Obituary Index* **[Online Database],** indexed at the FamilySearch.org website. Every name index to obituaries listed on ObitsUtah.com, a statewide obituary listing developed in association with the Utah Funeral Directors Association and its member mortuaries. ObitsUtah began publishing obituaries online in 2010. This database has 22,113 records. See **https://familysearch.org/search/collection/2285847.**